Australia

a travel survival kit

Immigration & Ethnic Affairs
30 SEP 1977
DEPARTED
AUSTRALIA
MELBOURNE 20

TO REMAIN IN AUSTRALIA
SYDNEY 2

DEPARTMENT OF IMMIGRATION
PERMITTED ON
24 SEP 1976
TO ENTER AUSTRALIA
PERTH AIRPORT

DEPARTMENT OF IMMIGRATION
PERMITTED ON
23 OCT 1977
TO ENTER AUSTRALIA
MELBOURNE AIRPORT 59

IMMIGRATION AUSTRALIA
PERMITTED TO REMAIN AND REMAIN
FOR RESIDENCE REMAIN
ON -6 DEC 1982
THIS PERMIT HAS NO FORCE OR EFFECT AFTER THE HOLDER LEAVES AUSTRALIA
Melbourne Airport

& ETHNIC AFFAIRS
Person
AN 1977
ARTED
RALIA
Y 33

D0126533

DEPARTMENT OF IMMIGRATION
PERMITTED TO ENTER
AUSTRALIA
QA -7 DEC 1972
TWEZVC (12)
For stay of MONTHS
EXMOUTH 32

Front Cover: One of Australia's best known symbols — the Sydney Opera House.
Back Cover: Another national symbol — the kangaroo — in a state symbol — the magnificent spring wildflowers of Western Australia.

Australia — a travel survival kit

Published by
Lonely Planet Publications
PO Box 88, South Yarra
Victoria 3141, Australia

Printed by
Colorcraft
Hong Kong

Photographs by
NSW Government Tourist Bureau 64AB, 96ABC, 97BC; Northern Territory Governmen
Tourist Bureau 192ABC, 193AC; South Australian Government Travel Centre 352BC
353BC; Tasmanian Government Tourist Bureau 384AB, 385AB; Western Australia Depart
ment of Tourism back cover, 512ABC, 513AB; Tony Wheeler front cover, 64C, 65ABC
97A, 193B, 224 ABC, 225 ABC, 352A, 353A, 384C, 480ABC, 481 AB, 513C

Cartoons & Illustrations by
Tony Jenkins 13, 114, 163, 173, 228, 313; Ernie Althoff (from *Australian Underground
Comix*, Wild & Wooley, Sydney) 15; Elizabeth Honey 27; Michael Leunig (from *The Bea
time Leunig*, Angus & Robertson, Sydney) 50, 433; John Stanton 94

First Published
February 1977

This Edition
May 1983

National Library of Australia
Cataloguing in Publication Data

Wheeler, Tony
    Australia, a travel survival kit.

    3rd ed.
    Previous ed. : South Yarra, Vic. : Lonely
    Planet, 1979.
    Includes index.
    ISBN 0 908086 39 3.

    1. Australia — Description and travel — 1976—
    — Guide-books. I. Title.

919.4'0463

© Tony Wheeler, 1983

THIS EDITION

This new edition of *Australia — a travel survival kit* has been long delayed, principally by other projects pushing it to one side (our India guide turned out to be a much bigger book than planned) but also because this guide has grown considerably. In fact this new edition is three times as large as the previous one! Researching this new edition was a four part operation. First there was the on-going updating that all our books go through — letters and suggestions from travellers, general research, my own travels which since the last edition have included an island by island jaunt up the Barrier Reef coast.

Secondly I did a whirlwind updating trip right round Australia. Using an around-Australia airline ticket I made 22 flights in aircraft ranging from DC-3s to 737s. Along the way I also rented six cars, drove over 4000 km, picked up one speeding ticket, hired bicycles in five locations and a motorcycle in one. I also made a number of bus trips, several ferry and boat trips, one longish train trip, walked more distance than I care to remember and even hitched a few rides. I stayed in everything from country hotels to modern motels, YMCAs to a number of youth hostels. And I had a terrifically good time!

Meanwhile two other researchers were also checking out parts of Australia for me. Simon Hayman, who has also worked on *New Zealand — a travel survival kit*, covered Tasmania, Canberra, Wollongong, Sydney and Newcastle. Alan Samagalski, who has subsequently updated *Hong Kong, Macau & Canton* and is now working on our forthcoming China guide, did his first LP stint in Ballarat, Bendigo and Geelong. All the Lonely Planet staff chipped in with advice and suggestions, particularly on places to eat and entertainment — funny how we all like to research restaurants!

In the production stages thanks must go to Isabel (who typeset it), Joy (who drew almost all the new maps, something like 100 of them in all!), Evelyn (who pasted it up) and Mary (who proofread and indexed). Life was made much easier by our fancy new word processor which not only made writing it a lot easier but also turned that damned index from an impossible to a merely terrible task.

Outside Lonely Planet thanks to the tourism departments of South Australia, Western Australia, Northern Territory, New South Wales and Tasmania for providing colour transparencies. To Tony Jenkins, Elizabeth Honey, Wild & Wooley and Angus & Robertson for cartoons and illustrations (credits on the imprint page). As usual, however, this book is all paid for — there were no free flights, no free meals, no free nothings. And the opinions are totally our own! On my way round the country thanks go as usual to all the pleasant people I met, particularly at youth hostels. Thanks to Geoff Schaefer in Port Hedland and to Liesme and Alison at Cape Tribulation. Finally, but far from least important, a big thank you to all 'our' travellers. Because the last edition has been so long out of print the letters have dropped off but we're always pleased to hear from those of you out on the road. Thanks to Angus Kingon, John King, Tony Noakes, Alan Bonsteel, Marina & David Irwin, Mary Wiseman, Ted van Geldermalsen, Bruce Barret, Arthur Tope, Anne & Eric Wallbank and Brent Mander.

AND THE NEXT EDITION

Things change — prices go up, good places go bad, bad places go bankrupt. So if you find things better, worse, cheaper (unlikely), more expensive, recently opened or long ago closed please don't blame us but please do write and tell us. We love letters from out on the road and the best ones score a free copy of the next edition (or any other LP title if you prefer). And note our BIG offer on page 224.

Tony Wheeler

Born in England, Tony spent most of his younger days overseas due to his father's airline occupation. Those years included a lengthy spell in Pakistan, a shorter period in the West Indies and all his high school years in the US. He returned to England to do a university degree in engineering, worked for a short time as an automotive design engineer, returned to university again and did an MBA, then dropped out on the Asia overland trail with his wife Maureen. Since they set up Lonely Planet in the mid-70s they've been travelling, writing and publishing ever since. Travel for Tony and Maureen is now considerably enlivened by their two year old daughter Tashi, although she did not come along on the final solo updating trip for this book.

Simon Hayman

Arriving in New Zealand in 1957, age four, Simon has subsequently tramped, hitched, worked and skiied all around that country, picking up a university degree on the way. After a year on the Asia overland trail Simon was dragged back from the depths of a Scottish winter to work on the second edition of our New Zealand guide and followed that up with travels in Australia for this guide.

Alan Samagalski

The world's most unemployed 'Atomic Folk Musician' and never-to-be-employed geneticist was saved from a life of dole-bludging by LP who couldn't find anyone else who'd go to Ballarat, Bendigo and Geelong. Alan admits to living in trendy Fitzroy but claims not to know what 'trendy' means. He does ride a bicycle to work and can claim to have visited a few countries!

Contents

Introduction

Where Australia is, south of South-East Asia, at the western end of the Pacific.

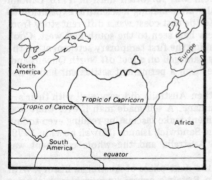

Where Australia isn't, but where its antipodes (geographically opposite position) would be — in the Atlantic Ocean stretching from North Africa/Central America in the south to North America/southern Europe in the north.

Australians have a well earned reputation for being great travellers but I've met Australians on top of the Khyber Pass who haven't been on top of Ayer's Rock. It's kind of boring to say Australia is a big country but there are few places on earth with as much variety as Australia has to offer. And not just variety in things to see — in things to do, places to eat, entertainment, activities and just general good times.

What to see and do while tripping around our island continent is an open ended question. There are cities big and small, some of them amazingly beautiful. Flying in over its magnificent harbour, for example, Sydney is a city which can simply take your breath away but to really get to grips with the country you have to get away from the cities. Australia is a country of cities, not the outback that provides the Australian myth, but it's in the outback where you really find Australia — the endless skies, the endless red dirt, the laconic Aussie characters. That still leaves you mountains and coast, superb bushwalks and big surf, the Great Barrier Reef and the Northern Territory's 'top end'.

Best of all Australia can be far from the rough and ready country its image might indicate. In the big cities you'll find some of the prettiest Victorian architecture going; Australian restaurants serve up an astounding variety of national cuisines with the freshest ingredients you could ask for (it's all grown here) and it's no problem at all to fall in love with Australian wines; plus Australia is one of those lucky countries where you can walk down almost any street at any time of day or night without worrying about your safety. It's not just exciting and invigorating, it's also very civilised. There's some fantastic travelling waiting for you out around Australia, get into it.

Facts about the Country

HISTORY

Australia was the last great area to be discovered during the European period of exploration — if we accept the belief that a place simply doesn't exist until a European 'discovered' it. Although Captain Cook is the name commonly connected with Australia's discovery it was probably a Portuguese who first sighted the country and to Dutchmen must go the credit for its early coastal exploration.

Portuguese navigators had come within sight of the coast in the first half of the 16th century and in 1606 the Spaniard Torres sailed through the strait which still bears his name between Cape York and New Guinea. Dutch explorers then proceeded to chart much of the north and west coast right round to the Great Australian Bight but what they found was a dry, harsh, unpleasant country and they rapidly scuttled back to the kinder climes of the Dutch East Indies. In 1642 Abel Tasman set out from Batavia, that is Jakarta in Indonesia today, to find out just what was down there. He would have entirely bypassed the south coast had he not arrived in Tasmania which he gratefully named Van Dieman's Land after the Governor General of the East Indies.

The prize for being Australia's original pom goes back to the enterprising pirate William Dampier who made the first investigations ashore nearly a hundred years before Cook. He would also have walked off with the award for being the first whinging pom as he came back with sensational, but accurate reports of the wildlife and the general conclusion that it was a lousy place with the 'miserablest people on earth' as its only inhabitants.

For a long period this dismal continent was forgotten until in 1770 Captain Cook arrived at the east coast of Australia after making a scientific expedition to Tahiti to observe the planet Venus. The fertile east coast was a different story from the inhospitable land the earlier explorers had seen to the south and west. Cook sailed north all the way to Cape York making the first temporary settlement on the way, when his ship *Endeavour* was badly damaged on a reef off North Queensland. With no support ship it could well have been a permanent settlement had it not been possible to repair it.

If a country needs a founding figure then Australia did very well with their's — Cook was resourceful, intelligent and humane. A self-made man if ever there was one, his incisive reports of the new continent make fascinating reading even today. By the time he met his untimely end in the Sandwich Islands (Hawaii now) in 1779, he had led two further expeditions to Australia and the whole continent was roughly mapped.

The American revolution then led to the next phase of Australian history. With America cut off as a good place to ship Britain's excess undesirables, a convict colony was sent out to Sydney in 1788 and the period of colonisation began. Australia was a harsh and horrible place to be sent and the reasons for 'transportation' were often relatively minor. At first the convicts were dependent upon supplies from Europe until farming could be developed and a late, or even worse shipwrecked, supply ship could be disastrous.

By 1792 the first difficult years had been completed but the cruel power of the military convict guards continued to make Australia a prison hell. Gradually as free settlers started to supplement the original convicts Australia became a more hospitable land and a new period of discovery started as the vast inland area was explored.

The Blue Mountains at first proved an impenetrable barrier, fencing in Sydney to the sea, but in 1813 a path was finally forced through and the western plains were reached.

Australia never enjoyed the systematic push westward that characterised the European settlement of America. Here colonial expansion often took place for one of two reasons — to find yet another place to keep convicts (particularly the real nasties) or to occupy another patch of land before anyone else (particularly the French) arrived — a false alarm as no other European power ever tried.

Thus in 1803 the first settlement in Tasmania was founded close to the present site of Hobart before the French could arrive and by the 1820s Hobart was actually a rival town to Sydney. Port Phillip Bay in Victoria was considered as a site for the second settlement in Australia at the same time but was rejected, so it was not until 1835 that settlers from Tasmania, in search of more land, arrived at the present site of Melbourne.

For similar, 'keep anybody else out', reasons, Perth was first settled in 1829 but, isolated from the rest of the country, growth here was very slow. The first settlement in the Brisbane area was a convict party sent north from NSW because the (by now) good citizens of Sydney were getting fed up with having all those crims about the place. By the time the Brisbane penal colony was abandoned in 1839 free settlers had moved in in force. Adelaide was initially set up in 1837 as an interesting experiment in free enterprise colonisation — it failed due to bad management and the British government had to take over from the bankrupt organisers.

Australia then progressed steadily for a period but it was gold that next lit the fuse. In 1851 gold was discovered in Victoria and in little more than a year the population had doubled. Similar discoveries in other states, in particular the WA gold rush of the 1890s, boosted the populations and levels of economic activity, for although few people made fortunes many settled in the country and became farmers and workers. At the site time the industrial revolution in England started to produce a strong demand for the agricultural and grazing potential of the vast country and Australia's economic base was secure.

During the 19th century development of Australia also had a darker side. The Aboriginals were looked upon as little more than animals and were thoughtlessly pushed off their tribal lands. In some places, Tasmania in particular, they were hunted down and destroyed like vermin. Today the Aboriginals are a dispossessed, lost people and belated efforts (generally unsuccessful) are being made to find them a place in modern society. Equally belatedly the strength of much of their culture is being discovered and the realisation of the close harmony in which they lived with their rugged environment.

The gold rushes brought floods of diligent Chinese miners onto the Australian gold fields and violent white opposition led to a series of unpleasant race riots and a morbid fear of Asian immigration which has persisted right into this century. The shipping of large numbers of convicts to Australia naturally provided it with a ready made criminal class and escaped convict 'bushrangers' preyed upon unwary settlers. Later bushrangers, not always escapees, became the nearest thing Australia was to develop to cowboy style folk heroes.

Although Australia became increasingly self-sufficient and independent from the 'mother country' of England it followed the British lead on most matters of foreign policy and duly marched off to the Boer War in South Africa and then to WW I. Australia, as a political entity, actually came into existence in 1901 when the separate states were federated and the decision to find a national capital was made.

Despite Australia's strong basis for self sufficiency it was far from economically independent of the rest of the western world and the depression of the '30s had an enormous effect on Australia. In WW II Australia once more marched off dutifully beside England but with the entry of Japan into the war, soon found the fighting right on the doorstep. When Singapore abruptly collapsed and the Japanese swept down through Indonesia Australia not only found itself being bombed from Japanese bases on the island of Timor but also involved in a bitter hand to hand struggle along the terrible Kokoda trail in Papua New Guinea. It was in Papua New Guinea, only a short flight from the north of Queensland, and in the Coral Sea off the Queensland coast, that the tide of the Pacific war turned against Japan.

The war had two immediately obvious effects on the country — a realisation of its dependence upon the US on the other side of the Pacific and a clearer understanding that while Australia might be a European type of country it was actually in Asia. With the prosperity and growth of the '50s and '60s, Australia appeared to once again slip into a period of sleepy inactivity. The conservative Liberal-Country Party coalition lethargically dominated the political arena; intellectuals and artists felt they had to escape to prove themselves and the whole place more or less went into mothballs. The only change was a retrograde one when England was replaced as the parent figure with America and Australia slavishly marched off to Vietnam, just as it had followed Britain into various imperial wars.

The Vietnam fiasco did its bit to wake Australia up and the real upheaval came with the election of a Labor government in 1972. Unfortunately Gough Whitlam's government was long on great ideas but short on practical experience of governing and the oil crisis certainly didn't help them. In 1975 the Labor government was overturned by the Liberal-Country coalition in an underhanded manner that still rankles today. With the conservative forces back at the helm Prime Minister Malcolm Fraser has been searching for a new status quo ever since. That's really Australia's position today — a country still unsure of what it is doing and where it is going. It's certainly no longer just a chunk of Europe displaced into the Pacific but if not then just what is it? A farm and a mine for the Japanese industrial juggernaut? Should it co-operate with its rapidly growing Asian neighbours or should it try and shut itself off from them? Will it prosper by taking on the world at what it can do best or should it try and protect inefficient industries by shutting out potential competition through high import duties and fierce quota restrictions?

This confusion even extends to Australia's idea of itself. It's certainly not the wide empty land of the outback legend for most of the population lives in large cities. It's certainly not the independent spirited place some people would like to believe either for much of the country's employment and industries are propped up by grants, aids, bounties, protection and other forms of governemnt support and intervention. Meanwhile the unemployed are indignantly labelled as 'dole bludgers'. Any answers?

Explorers

At the start of the last century, by which time 'unknowns' were becoming pretty few and far between, most of Australia was still one big blank. It was even suspected that it might be two large, separate islands and until the middle of the century it was hoped that there might be a vast inland sea in the centre. Some of the early explorers, particularly the men who braved the hostile centre, suffered great hardships and on more than one occasion lost their lives. Some of those early explorers:

Bass & Flinders George Bass charted the coast south of Sydney almost down to the present location of Melbourne in 1797-98. In 1798-99, in company with Matthew Flinders, he sailed right round Tasmania (Van Diemen's Land) thus establishing that it was an island and not joined to the rest of Australia. Flinders went on, in 1802-03, to sail right round Australia.

Eyre Edward John Eyre left Adelaide in 1840 to try to reach the centre of Australia, he gave up at Mt Hopeless and then decided to attempt a crossing to Albany in Western Australia. The formidable task nearly proved too much as both food and water were virtually unobtainable and his companion, Baxter, was killed by two of their Aboriginal guides. Eyre struggled on and by a stroke of luck came across a French whaling ship in Rossiter Bay. Reprovisioned, Eyre managed to reach Albany. The road across the Nullarbor Plains from South Australia to Western Australia is named the Eyre Highway.

Leichardt A German scientist, Leichardt travelled up through North Queensland and skirted round the Gulf of Carpenteria to Port Essington, near modern Darwin, during 1844-45. He turned back during an 1846-47 attempt to cross Australia from east to west, but soon started out once more and was never seen again.

Burke & Wills Leaving Melbourne in 1860, the Burke & Wills expedition's attempt to cross the continent from the south to north was destined to be one of the most tragic. Leaving a depot at Cooper's Creek in Queensland, they intended to make a dash north to the Gulf of Carpenteria with a small party of four. Their camels proved far slower than anticipated in the swampy land

close to the gulf and on their way back one of the party died of exhaustion.

Burke, Wills and the third survivor, King, eventually struggled back to Cooper's Creek virtually at the end of their strength and nearly two months behind schedule, only to find the depot group had given up hope and left for Melbourne. Not realising that the group's departure had been hours earlier, they remained at Cooper's Creek and Burke and Wills both died of starvation before a relief party arrived.

Stuart Departing Adelaide in 1860, chasing a £2000 reward for the first south-north crossing. John Stuart reached the geographical centre of Australia, Central Mt Stuart, but shortly after was forced to turn back. A second attempt in 1861 got much closer to the top before again having to return. Finally in 1862 he managed to reach the north coast near Darwin. The overland telegraph line, completed in 1872, and the modern Stuart Highway follow a very similar route.

Kennedy In 1848 Edmund Kennedy set out to travel by land up Cape York Peninsula while the ship *HMS Rattlesnake* explored the coast and islands. Starting from Rockingham Bay, south of Cairns, the expedition almost immediately struck trouble when their heavy supply carts could not be dragged through the swampy ground around Tully. The rugged land, harsh climate, lack of supplies, hostile Aboriginals and missed supply drops all took their toll and in all nine of the 13 man advance party died. Kennedy himself was speared to death in an attack by Aborigines when only 30 km from the end of their fearsome trek. His faithful Aboriginal servant Jacky Jacky was the only expedition member to finally reach the supply ship.

FACTS & FIGURES
Population

Australia's population is approaching 15 million. The most populous states are New South Wales and Victoria, each with capital cities (Sydney and Melbourne) where the population is in the 2½ to three million range. The population is principally found along the east coast strip from Adelaide to Cairns and in the similar but smaller coastal region in Western Australia. The centre of the country is very sparsely populated. About 150,000 of the population are Aboriginals.

Area

Australia's area is 7,686,884 square km, about the same as the mainland 48 states of the USA and half again as large as Europe excluding the USSR. Australia is about 4000 km from east to west and 3200 km from north to south and has a coastline 36,735 km long.

Government

Australia has a parliamentary system of government based upon that of the UK with a prime minister leading the party holding the greatest number of lower house seats. The lower house is the House of Representatives, the upper house the Senate. Voting in Australian elections is compulsory and also somewhat complicated as a preferential voting system is used where each candidate has to be ranked in order of preference. This can result in Senate elections with 50 or more candidates to be ranked. The federal parliament is based in Canberra, the capital of the nation. Like Washington DC in the USA, Canberra is in its own separate area of land, the ACT or Australian Capital Territory, not in one of the states. The ACT is, however, completely surrounded by NSW. Each state also has its own state government led by the state premier. The two main political groups are the Australian Labor Party (ALP) and the coalition of the Liberal Party and the National Party. The latter was, until recently, known as the National Country Party since it mainly represents country seats.

Economy

Australia is an affluent industrialised nation but much of the country's wealth comes from the land either from agriculture or mining. The small population base means that most Australian industries are comparatively weak and require protection from imports in order to survive. The last few years have not been happy ones for Australia's economy with local industries being further squeezed by imports from more efficient producers, Japan in particular, while mining exports have fallen due to the worldwide recession.

GEOGRAPHY

Australia is an old, worn down country — much of it uncompromisingly bleak and inhospitable. Much of the interest Australia's 'red centre' holds is its sheer emptiness — come to the centre of Australia and see great expanses of nothing! Almost the entire population is crowded into a narrow strip along the east coast and an even smaller section around the south-west corner of the continent.

From the east coast a narrow fertile strip merges into the almost continent long 'Great Dividing Range'. The mountains are mere reminders of the mighty range that stood here millions of years ago and only in the Snowy Mountains section, straddling the NSW/Victoria border, and in Tasmania, do they have winter snow. West of the range the country becomes increasingly flat and dry until virtually all habitation ceases and the endless flatness is broken only by salt lakes, occasional mysterious protuberances, like Ayers Rock and the Olgas, and some starkly beautiful mountains, like the MacDonnell Range near Alice Springs. In places the scanty vegetation is sufficient to allow some grazing, so long as each animal has a seemingly enormous area of land, but much of the Australian outback is an eternally barren land — harsh stone deserts and dry lakes with evocative names like Lake Disappointment.

In the far west a repeat of the mountain range, coastal strip heralds the Indian Ocean, but this is only in the far south. In the north central part of Western Australia the dry country runs right to the sea. The extreme north of Australia, the 'top end', is a tropical area within the monsoon belt. Although the annual rainfall here looks very adequate on paper it comes in more or less one short, sharp burst. This has prevented the top end from ever becoming seriously productive.

One in three in Australia works for the government. One in ten is unemployed. At times it is difficult to tell which is which. 'Road works' is a bit of wishfull thinking that occupies a good few Suntanned gladeators in an arena full of potholes Never in the history of man have so many taken so long to do so little

Tea boy 'Boiling the billy'

Some of the varied ways of announcing 'Not finished yet mate maybe next year.'

Road 'work' crew, Queensland Australia

Wildlife

Australia's got a normal enough collection of zoos, but of more interest for visitors from abroad will probably be the reserves and wildlife parks for Australia's own exotic collection of animals. Actually they're of equal interest to most Australians as many of them are quiet, reclusive creatures not readily seen in the wild. It's quite surprising how many Australians have never seen a roo in the bush — but they're very common if you just look in the right place (and at the right time). Some favourites:

Kangaroos There are actually more of Australia's national animal now than when Europeans first arrived, due to the greater availability of water and other necessities of kangaroo life. The danger to kangaroos is to certain species. There are many different types of roo; wallabies are part of the kangaroo family — they're smaller editions of the big bounders. Odd examples include the quokka, a cat-sized wallaby found only on two islands off the west coast, and the even smaller rat kangaroos.

Possums Another species that has managed to get on well with man — far too well for many Australians as they delight in getting into attics and creating havoc. Possums can become very tame, a whole family came down from the trees to demand their share of our meal in a campsite in the Barossa Valley once. They'll live almost in the city centre — I've seen them right beside the Yarra River in the very heart of Melbourne. Like roos they come in a variety of types from the tiny pygmy possum to the common brush-tailed possum.

Wombats With a name like that it'd be hard to dislike a wombat — imagine a cross between a very small bear and a very large guinea pig and you've got one. Wombats are solid, powerfully built creatures, prodigious diggers and, like possums, can become quite tame.

Koalas They may look cuddly but the teddy bear-like koala actually has a rather short temper and a very uncooperative nature. They'd rather be flaked out in a handy eucalyptus tree.

Tasmanian Devil Unlike other marsupials (animals which carry their young in a pouch) the devil is carnivorous. It's an ugly, fierce looking little monster, about the size of a small dog and is found only in Tasmania. When Europeans arrived Tasmania also had an awkward dog-like creature known as the Tasmanian Tiger but it was gradually exterminated and in 1933 the last known tiger died in Hobart Zoo. Despite frequent 'sightings' there has been no positive evidence of a Tasmanian Tiger since that time.

Platypus Undoubtedly Australia's weirdest animal the platypus is a sort of stepping stone between reptiles and mammals. It has a duck-like bill, webbed feet, lays egg but suckles its young and the male has a poisonous spur on its hind feet! The platypus is amphibious and very graceful when cruising around underwater. The only other monotreme, or egg-laying mamal, is the echidna, or spiny ant-eater, which is also found in Australia.

Snakes We've got a few of these too, although fears of the poisonous types are largely unfounded. They're generally shy creatures only too ready to avoid trouble. The deadliest varieties are the taipan and the tiger snake although death adders, copperheads, brown snakes and red-bellied black snakes are also worth keeping away from.

Emus The only larger bird than the emu is the equally flightless African ostrich. They're a shaggy, scruffy looking bird and often rather curious — only too happy to wander over and have a look at you. The emu is unusual in that after the female lays the eggs she plays no further part — the male hatches it and raises the young. Cassowaries are slightly smaller and much more colourful. They're found in the rainforests of north Queensland.

THE BEAR FACTS

HAVE YOU EVER SEEN A KOALA ON THE GROUND? NOTICE HOW STUPIDLY HELPLESS HE IS; HOW HE SHUFFLES AND STUMBLES.

© WORDS + PICTURES - ERNIE ALTHOFF.
THEORY - PETER ANDREW.

EVEN IN THEIR EUCALYPTUS HABITAT, THEY ARE VERY INACTIVE AND DROWZY, STARING SLEEPILY DOWN AT YOU THROUGH THEIR **TINY** EYES AS THEY MUNCH THEIR LEAVES.

AT LAST THE FACTS CAN BE REVEALED. OUR TEAM OF SCIENTISTS HAS FOUND THAT A CHEMICAL EXISTS IN GUM LEAVES THAT AFFECTS KOALAS THE SAME WAY THAT THE KILLER WEED **MARIJUANA** AFFECTS HUMAN BEINGS.

THERE THEY SIT ALL DAY, PERMANENTLY EATING, PERMANENTLY STONED; HIGH IN THE TREES, HIGH IN THEIR MINDS; NEVER COMING DOWN AND PASSING THE HABIT FROM GENERATION TO GENERATION.

IMAGINE IF WE LIVED THE WAY THEY DO!

IT'S A GOOD THING THAT AUSTRALIA HAS A FINE HEALTHY UPSTANDINGLY NOBLE ANIMAL LIKE THE KANGAROO FOR ITS NATIONAL CREATURE, INSTEAD OF THIS GROTTY LITTLE DOPE FIEND.

Parrots & Cockatoos There are an amazing variety of these often colourful birds scattered throughout Australia. The noisy galahs are amongst the most common — they certainly make their presence known. Rosellas have one of the most brilliant colour-schemes and in some parks they're not at all backward about hopping down for a free feed from the visitors. Budgerigars are found mainly towards the centre, they often fly in enormous flocks numbering 10,000 or more brightly coloured birds.

Crocodiles There are a number of types of crocodiles found in northern Australia, ranging from the potentially dangerous saltwater crocodiles to smaller, shyer, harmless varieties.

Kookaburra A member of the kingfisher family, the kookaburra is heard as much as it is seen — you can't miss its loud, raucous guffaw. Kookaburras can become quite tame and pay regular visits to friendly households; but only if the food is excellent. You can't fob a kookaburra off with anything but top class steak.

Spiders Two to keep away from are the redback, a relative of the American black widow, and the Sydney funnel web. The latter are found almost solely in Sydney while the former are more widespread and have a legendary liking for dunny seats. Both are extremely poisonous and have been lethal. There is a well tried antivenene for the redback but a funnel web bite is a nastier thing altogether.

Bower Birds The bower bird has a quite unique mating practice. The male builds a bower which he decorates with blue and green objects to attract females. In the wild, flowers or stones are used but if man made objects (clothes pegs, plastic pens, bottle tops, anything blue or green) are available they'll certainly use it. The females are impressed by the males' neatly built bower and attractively displayed treasures but once they've mated all the hard work is left up to her. He goes back to refurbishing the bower and attracting another female while she hops off to build a nest.

Other That's only a small selection of the creatures you may get a glance at. Others include penguins, particularly the delightful fairy penguins which perform a nightly parade on Philip Island in Victoria. There are a number of beaches in Queensland frequented by turtles. Seals of various types can be seen in a number of places in the south. Until Australia's black swans were first seen it was thought all swans were white. Frogs are common, particularly in Queensland. In the dry areas you can see an amazing variety of lizards, some grow to a very hefty size. And I've not mentioned the undersea life you may come across, especially on the Barrier Reef.

OCCASIONS & HOLIDAYS

As noted in climate the Australian seasons are inverted compared to the northern hemisphere and the summer holiday season also coincides with Christmas. At that time of year things are likely to be rather crowded in the holiday areas, rather quiet in the cities. There are happenings and holidays in Australia year round — the following is just a brief overview. Some of the most enjoyable Australian festivals are the ones which are most typically Australian. Like the surf lifesaving competitions on beaches around Australia during the summer months. Or the outback race meets when tiny stations come alive once a year and eccentric characters from the bush appear out of nowhere.

January	This is the busiest summer month with lots of beach events, pop festivals and like. Australia day is a national holiday, falling on the first Monday after 26 January.

February	In Hobart there's Regatta Day with boat races and other water activities. The Snowy Mountains Festival takes place in Cooma, NSW.
March	On even numbered years the Festival of the Arts takes place in Adelaide. It's Australia's biggest arts festival with music, drama and light entertainment. Wine enthusiasts flock to the Hunter Valley north of Sydney for the Hunter Valley Vintage Festival with wine tasting, grape picking and treading contests. Moomba takes place in Melbourne, a week-long festival when sometimes staid Melbourne actually shines a little.
March-April	The Festival of the Rocks takes place the week before Easter in Sydney. There's a street procession, a Rocks pub crawl and a mock court on the green. Over Easter, Sydney also has the Royal Agricultural Show with livestock contests and exhibits, ring events and rodeos.
April	Anzac Day, the national war memorial day, is another public holiday on 25 April. On odd numbered years the Barossa Vintage Festival takes place in South Australia with all the usual wine activities and entertainment.
May	As the southern states drift into winter the emphasis moves north and particularly to the Northern Territory where there are all sorts of colourful events like the Bangtail Muster in Alice Springs with a colourful float parade and other events. There are also a whole series of country race meets at remote Northern Territory stations in the coming months.
June	In Darwin the Beer Can Regatta features boat races for boats constructed entirely out of beer cans — there are plenty of those in the world's beer drinking capital. In Sydney there's a bathtub race across the heads.
July	Scuba divers head to Heron Island in Queensland for the Divers' Rally.
August	In the Northern Territory there's something on almost every weekend in Alice Springs. The Camel Cup features camel racing while the Apex Rodeo is one of the biggest rodeos in Australia -- the town fills up with swaggering Territorian cowboys. Big event is the Henley on Todd Regatta on the last Saturday in the month when boats race down the Todd River -- even though the Todd River hardly every has any water in it! Meanwhile in Sydney, Australia's biggest race takes place with up to 25,000 competitors pounding the 14 km from Hyde Park to Bondi Beach in the City to Surf. I've survived it three times. At the Whitsundays in Queensland it's time for another aquatic festival with yacht races and a 'Miss Figurehead' contest while near Yeppoon, also in Queensland, it's time for the national 'cooeeing' contest.

September	Sporting attention turns to Melbourne with the Grand Final for Australian rules football and the MCG fills up beyond its 100,000 capacity. It's the biggest sporting event in Australia. Also in Melbourne the Sun Superrun is another big-crowd fun run with the competitors running across the huge Westgate Bridge. The Royal Melbourne Show attracts agricultural folk and lots of children in the same month and the Royal Perth Show also takes place in Perth. Up on the Sunshine Coast in Queensland it's time for the Sunshine Coast Spring Festival.
October	Motor racing enthusiasts flock to Bathurst in NSW where the annual 1000 km touring car race on the superb Mt Panorama circuit is Australia's best known car race. More wine fun with the Bushing Festival in McLaren Vale, South Australia while in Swan Hill, on the Murray River in Victoria, it's time for the annual Pioneer Festival. Cairns in the far north of Queensland has Fun in the Sun.
November	The Melbourne Cup on the first Tuesday in November is Australia's premier horse race. It's a public holiday in Victoria but the whole country shuts down for the three minutes or so which the race takes. Also near Melbourne the Australian Grand Prix takes place at Calder Motor Racing Circuit. In beautiful Paddington, Sydney the Queen Street Festival features a street fair and arts activities.
December	The Sydney-Hobart Yacht Race starts on 26 December, a fantastic sight as the yachts stream out of the harbour and head south. In Hobart there's a Mardi Gras to celebrate the finish of the race. This is the busiest holiday season of the year in Australia when accommodation is most likely to be full and the big cities will be quietest.

ACTIVITIES

In each state section there is some information on a number of locally popular participant sports and activities. Around the country you'll also find plenty of opportunities for gold, squash, tennis, trail riding (horse and motorcycle), fishing and so on. Surfing is almost a religion for many Australians who follow the waves around the country and there are a number of important surfing contests. Australia is also a great place for bushwalking, it's unfortunate that some of the superb walks are not better known as walking enthusiasts rate walks like Cradle Mountain-Lake St Clair the equal of the better known walks in New Zealand. If you can't find what you want from the telephone yellow pages then contact the state tourist info offices. If you want your sport as a spectator rather than a participant there is also plenty of scope. You'll find football of assorted types including the unique Australian rules football (related to Gaelic football) which is played most avidly in Melbourne and there's motor and motorcycle racing, horse racing, yacht racing, cricket matches and lots more.

LANGUAGE

Any visitor from abroad who thinks Australian (that's 'strine') is simply a weird variant of English/American will soon have a few surprises. For a start half of Australia doesn't even speak Australian — they speak Italian, Lebanese, Turkish or Greek (Melbourne is said to be the third largest Greek city in the world). Then those who do speak the native tongue are liable to lose you in a strange collection of totally unique Australian words, words with completely different meanings to English speaking countries north of the equator and commonly used words which are shortened almost beyond recongnition.

There is no real regional variation in the Australian accent and the city/country difference is mainly a matter of speed of talking. Of course some of the most famed Aussie words are hardly ever heard at all — I don't think I've every heard anyone called 'cobber', plenty of 'mates' though. If you want to pass for a native try speaking slightly nasally, shortening any word of more than two syllables and then adding a vowel to the end of it, making anything possible into a diminutive (even the Hell's Angels can become more 'bikies') and peppering your speech with as many insults as possible. The brief list that follows may help:

abo — aboriginal

amber fluid — beer

am I ever — not half

apples (she'll be) — it'll be all right

arvo — afternoon

ASIO — Aussie CIA

avagoyermug — traditional rallying call, especially at cricket matches

award — minimum pay rate

back of Bourke — back of beyond

bail up — hold up, rob

banana bender — Queenslander

barbie — barbecue

barrack — cheer on team at sporting event

beaut, beauty, bewdie — great, fantastic

beef road — outback road for transporting cattle

beg yours — I beg your pardon

bell (give someone a) — phone someone up

bible basher — religious fanatic

billabong — water hole in dried up riverbed, more correctly an ox bow bend which has been cut off
bed, more correctly an ox bow bend which has been cut off

billy — tin container used to boil up tea in the bush

bikies — motorcyclists

bitumen — sealed road

black stump — where the 'back of Bourke' begins

blowies — blow flies

bludger — lazy person, one who won't work

blue (to have a) — to have an argument

bluey — swag

boomer — big, particularly large kangaroo

boong — Aborigine

bonzer — ripper

bottle shop — liquor shop

bug (Moreton Bay Bug) — a small yabby

bull dust — fine dust on outback roads, also bull shit

bunyip — Australia's yeti or Loch Ness monster

bush — country, anywhere away from the city

bush (go) — go back to the land

BYO — Bring Your Own (booze) to a restaurant

Chiko roll — vile Australian junk food

chook — chicken, as 'chook'n chips'

chunder — vomit

cobber — mate

cockie — small farmer

cooee — bush call, signal

come across — will she?
come good — turn out all right
compo — compensation, as unemployment compensation
cow cockie — small cattle-farmer
crook (to be) — to be ill
cut lunch — sandwiches

dag, daggy — dirty lump of wool at back end of a sheep, also term of abuse
daks — trousers
damper — bush loaf made from flour and water
deli — delicatessen, milk bar
didgeridoo — long, tube-like aboriginal musical instrument which emits a low, mournful note
dill — idiot
dingo — native Australian wild dog

dingo — native Australian wild dog
dinkum, fair dinkum — honest, genuine, really?
dinky-di — the real thing
don't come the raw prawn — don't try and fool me
drongo — worthless person
duco — car paint
dunny — outhouse

fair go! — give us a break
fair crack of the whip! — fair go!
fall pregnant — become pregnant
financial (to be) — to be OK for $$
fire plug — fire hydrant
FJ — most revered Holden car
flake — shark meat, used in fish & chips
floater — meat pie floating in pea soup, yuk
fossicking — hunting for gems or semi-precious stones

galah — noisy parrots, thus noisy idiots
garbo — person who collects your garbage
gibber — stony desert
give it away — give up
g'day — good day, traditional Australian greeting

good on yer — well done
grazier — large-scale sheep or cattle farmer

hump — to root, also to carry as in 'hump your bluey'
humpy — aboriginal's shack

interstate — to be in another state

joey — baby kangaroo

king hit — hit from behind, stab in the back
knock — criticise, deride
knocker — one who knocks

lair — layabout, ruffian
lairising — acting like a lair
lamington — square cake covered in chocolate icing & coconut
larrikin — a bit like a lair
lay-by — put a deposit on an article so the shop will hold it for you
lollies — sweets, candy
lolly water — soft drinks
lurk — a scheme

Manchester — household linen, sheets
mate — friend, partner
middy — medium beer glass
milkbar — corner shop
milko — milkman
mozzies — mosquitoes

new Australian — recent immigrant
no hoper — hopeless case, ne'er do well
northern summer — summer in the northern hemisphere
no worries — she'll be right

ocker — basic, down to earth Aussie
off-sider — assistant
OS — overseas, as 'he's gone OS'
outback — remote part of the bush, back of Bourke
OYO — own your own (flat or apartment)
Oz — Australia

pastoralist — large-scale grazier

pavlova — traditional Australian meringue & cream dessert

pineapple (rough end of) — stick (sharp end of)

piss turn — boozy party

pom — English person

poofter, poof — member of the gay persuasion

poser — one who poses, as driving in a flash car

postie — mailman

pot — large mug of beer

push — gang of larrikins

ratbag — friendly term of abuse

ratshit — lousy

rapt — delighted, enraptured in

rego — registration, as car rego

ripper — good (also 'little ripper')

road train — semi-trailer-trailer-trailer

root — euphemism for sexual intercourse

rubbish (to) — deride, tease

salvo — member of the Sally Army

school — group of drinkers

schooner — large beer glass

scuse I — excuse me

sea wasp — very dangerous jelly fish

sealed (road) — surfaced road

semi-trailer — articulated truck

she'll be right — no worries

shoot through — leave in a hurry (particularly 'shoot through like a Bondi tram')

shout — buy round of drinks (as 'it's your shout')

sickie — day off work, ill

sly grogger — after hours drinking place

smoke-o — tea-break

squatter — pioneer farmer who didn't bother about buying or leasing his land from the government

squattocracy — Australian 'old money' folk, who made it by being first on the scene and grabbing the land

station — large farm

strides — daks

strine — Australian language

stubby — small bottle of beer

sunbake (to) — to sunbathe (well the sun's hot in Australia)

surfies — members of the surf persuasion

swag — gear, possessions

tall poppies — achievers, what knockers like to cut down

thingo — thing, whatchamacallit

tinny — can of beer

too right! — absolutely!

true blue — dinkum

tube — can of beer

tucker — food

two pot screamer — person unable to hold their drink

two-up — traditional heads/tails gambling game

uni — where you go for an education

ute — utility, pickup truck

wag (to) — to skip school

walkabout — lengthy walk away from it all

wet — rainy season in the north

wharfie — docker

whinge — complain, moan

whinging pom — the very worst sort of pom

wog — an illness

woolgrower — sheep farmer

wowser — spoilsport, puritan

yabby — small freshwater crayfish

yous — plural of you

Facts for the Visitor

VISAS & IMMIGRATION

Once upon a time Australia was fairly free and easy about who was allowed to visit the country, particularly if you were from Britain or Canada. These days only New Zealanders get any sort of preferential treatment, almost everybody else has to have a visa to visit Australia. Even New Zealanders have to have at least a passport these days. Visas are issued by Australian consular offices abroad, they are free and valid for a stay of up to six months. Applications for visa extensions can be made at Department of Labor & Immigration offices in Australia.

On top of the visa visitors are also required to have an onward or return ticket and 'sufficient funds' — the latter is obviously open to interpretation. Like any country Australian visas seem to have their hassles. We've heard from Japanese and other young Asian travellers from time to time about the difficulties of obtaining Australian visas. One young Japanese even recommended applying for an Australian visa in a country where there was no Australian embassy, since in that case the application would be handled by the British embassy and 'British do not care who goes to Australia!' If you do hit visa problems, while trekking around Asia for example, the best advice is to try somewhere else. Extending your six month stay can also be fraught mainly because the office is notoriously slow at renewing visas. We've actually heard of people still waiting for an extension after they'd been in Australia for a year! Apply for an extension and then don't worry about it is probably the best advice, you shouldn't have to be responsible for the snail's pace of Australian bureaucracy.

Young visitors from some countries — including Britain, Ireland, Canada and Japan — may be eligible for a 'working holiday' visa. Young is fairly loosely interpreted as around 18 to 30 and working holiday means up to three years but the emphasis is supposed to be on casual employment rather than a full time job. This visa can only be applied for in your home country. Officially working in Australia is completely verboten on a regular tourist visa but in actual fact it's relatively simple to get away with working — so long as you can find a job that is. There are no social security cards, national insurance cards or the like in Australia and generally not too many questions are asked. Travellers kicking around Australia often seem to pick up odd jobs as they go although like anywhere in the western world times are tough and jobs are no longer there for the asking.

Although Australia doesn't have any borders with other countries we still manage to get plenty of illegal immigrants. Twice in the past 10 years the government has held an amnesty for illegal immigrants, if they had been in the country for at least six months and were otherwise acceptable they could stay. On both occasions the number of illegal immigrants who stepped forward was highly surprising.

A few of the more useful Australian consular offices overseas include:

Canada	Australian High Commission, The National Building, 130 Slater St, Ottawa K1P 5H6 (tel 613 236-0841)
	also in Toronto & Vancouver
Denmark	Australian Embassy, Kristianagade 21, 2100 Copenhagen (tel 262244)
Germany, West	Australian Embassy, Godesberger Allee 107, 5300 Bonn 2 (tel 02221 376941-7)

Greece	Australian Embassy, 15 Messogeion St, Ambelokipi, Athens (tel 360 4611/15)
Hong Kong	Australian Commission, Connaught Centre, Connaught Rd, Hong Kong (tel 5 227171/8)
India	Australian High Commission, Australian Compound, No 1/50-G Shantipath, Chanakyapuri, New Delhi (tel 69 0336) also in Bombay
Indonesia	Australian Embassy, Jalan Thamrin 15, Jakarta (tel 323109)
Ireland	Australian Embassy, Fitzwilton House, Wilton Terrace, Dublin 2 (tel 76 1517/9)
Italy	Australian Embassy, Via Alessandria 215, Rome 00198 (tel 84 1241) also Milan & Messina
Japan	Australian Embassy, No 1-14 Mita 2 Chome, Minato-ku, Tokyo (tel 453 0251/9)
Malaysia	Australian High Commission, 6 Jalan Yap Kwan Seng, Kuala Lumpur (tel 42 3122)
Netherlands	Australian Embassy, Koninginnegracht 23, 2514 AB The Hague (tel 070 63 0983)
New Zealand	Australian High Commission, 72-78 Hobson St, Thorndon, Wellington (tel 73 6411/2) also Auckland
Papua New Guinea	Australian High Commission, Waigani, Hohola (tel 25 9333) Also Lae
Singapore	Australian High Commission, 25 Napier Rd, Singapore 10 (tel 737 9311)
Sweden	Australian Embassy, Sergels Torg 12, Stockholm C, S-101 86 Stockholm (tel 24-46-60)
Thailand	Australian Embassy, 37 South Sathorn Rd, Bangkok 12 (tel 286 0411)
UK	Australian High Commission, Australia House, The Strand, London WC2B 4LA (tel 01 438 8000) also Edinburg & Manchester
USA	Australian Embassy, 1601 Massachusetts Avenue NW, Washington DC 20036 (tel 202 797 3000) also Los Angeles, Chicago, Honolulu, New York, San Francisco

CONSULATES & EMBASSIES

The principal diplomatic representations to Australia are in Canberra and you'll find a list of the addresses of relevant offices in the Canberra section. There are also representatives in various other major cities, particularly from countries with major connections with Australia like the USA, UK or New Zealand, or in cities with important connections, like Darwin to Indonesia. Big cities like Sydney and Melbourne have nearly as many consular offices as Canberra. Look up addresses in the telephone yellow pages under 'Consulates & Legations'.

CUSTOMS

For visitors from abroad the usual sort of 200 cigarettes, bottle of whisky regulations apply to Australia, but there are two areas you should be very careful about. Number one is, of course, dope — Australian customs have a positive mania about the stuff and can be extremely efficient when it comes to finding it. Unless you want to make first hand investigations of conditions in Australian jails (not very good), don't bring any with you. This particularly applies if you are arriving from Indonesia or South-East Aisa. You will be a subject of suspicion!

Problem two is animal and plant quarantine, they are naturally keen not to allow weeds, pests or diseases into the country — with all the sheep in Australia, that scruffy Afghani sheepskin coat over your arm is not going to be popular. Fresh food is also unpopular — particularly meat, sausages, fruit, vegetables and flowers. There are also various restrictions on taking fruit or vegetables between states.

When it comes time to split there are duty free stores at the international airports and their associated cities. Treat them with healthy suspicion, though. 'Duty Free' is one of the world's most over-worked catch phrases — just an excuse to sell things at prices you can easily beat by a little shopping around.

MONEY

Australia's currency is good, old-fashioned dollars and cents. When they were changing over from pounds, shillings and pence some years back there was consideration of calling the new unit the 'Royal' — that foolish idea soon got the chop. Over the past year Australia's dollar has weakened against many other country's currencies, most particularly against the US dollar. For Americans, in fact, Australia has become a real bargain. Note that travellers' cheques generally enjoy a better exchange rate than cash in Australia. Current exchange rates are:

A$1	=	US$0.97	US dollars	US$1	=	A$1.03
A$1	=	NZ$1.35	New Zealand dollars	NZ$1	=	A$0.74
A$1	=	£0.63	pounds sterling	£1	=	A$1.59
A$1	=	S$2.02	Singapore dollars	S$1	=	A$0.50
A$1	=	HK$6.40	Hong Kong dollars	HK$1	=	A$0.16
A$1	=	y230	Japanese yen	y100	=	A$0.43
A$1	=	DM2.35	Deutsche marks	DM1	=	A$0.43
A$1	=	fl2.60	Dutch guilders	fl1	=	A$0.38
A$1	=	C$1.18	Canadian dollars	C$1	=	A$0.85

There are a whole variety of ways to carry your money round Australia with you. If your stay is limited then travellers' cheques are the most straightforward but if you're planning to stay longer than just a month or so it's worth considering some other possibilities which give you more flexibility and are more economical. With travellers' cheques it is obviously easiest to travel with Australian dollar travellers' cheques as these can be exchanged immediately at the bank cashier's window without having to have them converted from a foreign currency. Changing travellers' cheques denominated in other currencies — yen, Deutsche Marks, pounds, US dollars or whatever — is certainly no problem though. It's done quickly and efficiently and never involves the sort of headaches and grand production that changing foreign currency in the US can entail. American Express, Thomas Cook and other well-known international brands of travellers' cheques are all widely used in Australia.

If your stay in Australia is for longer than a month or so, and this applies equally to Australians setting off to travel around the country, then it's worth considering an alternative to travellers' cheques. One of the neatest solutions is to open a passbook savings acount. All the banks operate these systems and with your passbook you can withdraw money from any branch of the bank in question in the country. There are limitations to how much you can pull out in one hit but it's quite reasonable. This way instead of paying to buy travellers' cheques you actually get paid for having your money on deposit. Probably the best bank for the traveller to be with is the Commonwealth Savings Bank. This is a government-owned bank with branches all around the country but also in almost every post office. So finding a place to withdraw money is no problem at all and the hours are also longer than normal banking hours. If the branch has 'black light' signature identification facilities you can draw out up to $800 every seven days. Otherwise you can withdraw $200 with suitable identification. In London you can simply walk into the Commonwealth Bank branch there and ask them to transfer whatever you require to Australia and open an account for you.

Credit cards are widely accepted in Australia and this is another alternative, for the better heeled, to carrying large numbers of travellers' cheques. The most common credit card, however, is the purely Australian Bankcard system. For awhile Visa and Mastercharge tied in with Bankcard but that affiliation has now been dropped and Visa is no longer anywhere near so widely accepted. Diners Club and American Express are widely accepted but mainly in the ritzier sort of places. If you're planning on renting cars while travelling around Australia a credit card makes life much simpler, they're looked upon with much greater favour by rent-a-car agencies than nasty old cash.

Another cash possibility for those with an Australian account is a cash card which you can use in the automatic banking machines now found all over Australia. You just put your card in the machine, key in your number and can then withdraw what you like from your account. Bankcard can also be used to draw out cash but in that case you are charged interest until you pay it back.

On departure day from Australia you're allowed to take out what you brought in if you stayed for less than six months. Otherwise you're allowed A$250 in local, A$250 in foreign currency and the balance (whatever it might be) in travellers' cheques.

COSTS

In comparison to the USA and European countries Australia is cheaper in some respects, more expensive in others. Manufactured goods tend to be more expensive because they're either imported and have all the additional costs of transport and duties or if they're locally manufactured they suffer from the extra costs entailed in making things in comparatively small quantities. Thus you pay more for clothes, cars and other manufactured items. On the other hand food is both high qualiity and low in cost. Restaurants and hotels tend to have their prices jacked up by the high labour costs in Australian service industries — as soon as 5 pm rolls around everything goes on to overtime rates. On the plus side what you see is what you get — there are no service charges, no add-on sales or value added taxes, even tipping doesn't feature in the picture. If something costs $x (including a hotel room or a restaurant meal) then that's what it costs, not $x plus 10% plus 12% plus whatever else you can load on

CLIMATE

Australian seasons are opposite to those in Europe and North America. Christmas falls in the middle of summer while August is mid-winter. The seasons start summer in December, autumn in March, winter in June and spring in September. The climatic extremes in Australia are relatively mild and even in Melbourne, the furthest south capital city on the mainland, it's a rare occasion when the mercury hits freezing point. Of course the poor Tasmanians, hung off to the south, have a better idea of what cold is.

As you head north the seasonal variations become smaller and smaller until in the far north — around Darwin — you are in the monsoon belt where there are just two seasons: hot and wet or hot and dry. When the wet hits Darwin around November or December it really does get wet. In the Snowy Mountains in the south of NSW and the north of Victoria there's a snow season with good skiing. The climate in the centre is desert like, hot and dry during the daytime but often bitterly cold at night.

Australia is such a big country that there is a main 'season' for some places almost year round. Down in the south, for example, Victoria and Tasmania are probably at their best at the height of the summer although spring and autumn are pretty good too. You might head south for the skiing but otherwise Melbourne can be rather cold, grey and miserable in the July-August winter months when it's best to avoid it! By contrast in the far north the real season is mid-winter. Darwin in July-August is just right whereas in mid-summer (December-January) it's often unbearably hot and humid, plus the sea is full of sea wasps, plus if there are cyclones about this is when they'll appear. Similarly in Alice Springs the mid-summer temperatures can be far too high for comfort while in mid-winter the nights may be chilly but the days are delightful.

Apart from climatic seasons to travel around Australia it's worth bearing the holiday seasons in mind too. Christmas is not only the regular holiday season associated with Christmas it's also the middle of the long summer school vacations. This is the most likely time of year to find accommodation booked out and long queues everywhere. School holidays also take place in May and August and these too can be more difficult times to travel. The school holidays often vary by a week or two from state to state.

A climatic synopsis of average daily maximum and minimum temperatures and rainfall for the month follows. Note that these are average maximums — even Melbourne gets a fair number of summer days topping 40°C (100°F).

Adelaide — maximum temperatures from 25 to 30°C from November to March, minimums drop below 10°C between June and September. Rainfall is heaviest, 50 to 70 mm per month, from May to September.

Alice Springs — daily maximums of 30°C and above from October to April, minimums drop to 10°C and below from May to September. Rainfall is low year round, December to February gets an average of 30 mm plus.

Brisbane — daily maximums are rarely below 20°C year round peaking towards 30°C from November to February, rainfall is fairly heavy year round with December to March getting over 130 mm per month.

Canberra — mid to high 20°Cs in the summer and daily minimums often close to freezing between May and October, rainfall is usually between 40 and 70 mm a month year round.

Cairns — average maximums are around 25 to 33°C a year round with minimums rarely dropping below 20°C, rainfall is below 100 mm a month from May to October (lowest in July and August) but peaks from January to March with around 400 to 450 mm.

Darwin — even temperatures year round with average maximums around 30 to 34°C and minimums around 20 to 25°C, rainfall is minimal from May to September but December to March gets 250 to 400 mm a month.

Hobart — only from December to March do averages top 20°C but from April to November average minimums are below 10°C, rainfall is about 40 to 60 mm a month year round.

Melbourne — Melbourne hits 20°C and above from October to April and drops

below 10°C from May to October, rainfall is even year round at 50 to 60 mm almost every month.

Perth — average maximums get to around 30°C from December through March but minimums rarely drop below 10°C, rainfall is lightest from November through March (20 mm and below) and heaviest in May thorugh August (120 to 200 mm).

Sydney — only in the middle of winter do average minimums drop below 10°C with summer maximums around 25°C from November through March, rainfall is in the 75 to 130 mm range year round.

BOOKS & BOOKSHOPS

Australians have a fascination with Australia.........and with Australians. In almost any bookshop you'll find a section devoted to Australiana. There are books on every Australian subject you care to mention. If you want a souvenir of Australia, something to take back home, one of the numerous coffee table photographic books, like *A Day in the Life of Australia*, can't be beat. There are numerous other

Australian books to enjoy — look for children's books with very Australian illustrations or cartoon books by some of Australia's excellent cartoonists. We've also got a
ot of bookshops and some of the better bookshops are mentioned in the various
city sections.

MEDIA

Australia has a wide range of media although a few big companies (Rupert Murdoch
being one of the best known internationally) tend to dominate. There's a national
advertising-free television and radio network, the Australian equivalent of the BBC
which is known as the ABC. In Sydney and Melbourne there are also three commercial television stations and a government sponsored multi-cultural station.
Around the country the number of stations varies from place to place, in some
remote areas the ABC may be all you can receive. Radio also has the ABC, usually
a couple of ABC stations, plus a whole host of commercial stations both AM and
FM featuring the whole gamut of radio possibilities from pop to 'beautiful music'.

Each major city tends to have at least one important daily, often backed up by a
tabloid paper and also by evening papers. They include the *Sydney Morning Herald*
and the Melbourne *Age*, two of the most important dailies. Plus there's *The Australian*, a nationwide daily paper. Weekly newspapers and magazines include *The
Bulletin* (a Time-Newsweek clone) and the *National Times*. Pacific editions of *Time*
and *Newsweek* are also readily available throughout Australia.

FILM & PHOTOGRAPHY

If you come to Australia via Hong Kong or Singapore it's worth buying film there
but otherwise Australian film prices are no longer too far out of line with the rest
of the western world. Including developing 36 exposure Kodachrome 64 slide film
is readily available for $8 a reel or less, particularly if you buy in quantity. There
are plenty of camera shops in all the big cities and standards of camera service are
high. Developing standards are also high with many places now offering instant
developing of print film. Australia is the main centre for developing slide film in the
South-East Asian region as well as for Australia.

Photography is no problem but in the outback you have to allow for the exceptional intensity of the light. Best results in the outback regions are only obtained
early in the morning and late in the afternoon. As the sun gets higher colours all get
washed out. In the outback, especially in summer, you must also allow for temperature extremes and do your best to keep film as cool as possible, particularly after
exposure. Other film hazards are dust in the outback and humidity in the tropical
regions of the far north.

HEALTH

So long as you have not visited an infected country in the past 14 days (aircraft
refuelling stops do not count) smallpox vaccination is not required for entry.
Cholera vaccination is not required and yellow fever only if you come from an
endemic area. Naturally if you're going to be travelling around in outlandish places
apart from Australia, a good collection of immunisations is highly advisable.

Medical care in Australia is first class and expensive. Health insurance cover is
available in Australia but there is usually a waiting period after you sign up before
any claims can be made. A health and accident insurance policy is a wise investment.

POST

Australia's postal services are relatively efficient but not too cheap. The main postal rates are:

standard letter in Australia	27c
aerogram to anywhere in the world	36c
air letter - up to 20 gm (postcard)	
New Zealand	40c (30c)
Singapore, Malaysia	50c (35c)
Hong Kong, India	55c (40c)
USA, Canada	65c (40c)
UK, Europe	75c (45c)

Post offices are open 9 am to 5 pm Monday to Friday but you can often get stamps from local post offices operated from newsagencies or shops on Saturday mornings. All post offices will hold mail for visitors and some city GPOs will have very busy poste restantes — Cairns, for example, can get quite hectic. You can also have mail sent to you at the American Express offices in big cities — if you have an Amex card or carry American Express travellers' cheques.

TELEPHONES

The Australian phone system is really remarkably efficient and, equally important, easy to use. Local phone calls all cost 20c for an unlimited amount of time. You can make local calls from red phones — often found in shops, hotels, bars, etc — and from STD phones. If you want to make a long distance (trunk) call from a public phone, look for a grey-green STD (Standard Trunk Dialling) phone which allows you to dial direct and only pay for the time actually used — no three minute minimum as on operator-connected calls. The trick is to have plenty of 20c and 50c coins to hand and be prepared to feed them through at a fair old rate. You can insert a handful of coins at the beginning and they just drop down as they're used up. When you're about to be cut off a red light flashes faster and faster and you can either hurriedly insert more coins or simply speak quicker! If you complete your call before the money is used up the change is returned. STD calls are cheaper after 6 pm and before 8 am, cheaper still if you wait until 9 pm. There's also a slightly cheaper rate between 12.30 and 1.30 pm Monday to Saturday and from 8 am to 6 pm on Sunday.

From some STD phones you can also make ISD (International Subscriber Dialling) calls just like making STD Calls. ISD phones are not yet very widespread but you will often find them at airports and at city GPOs or other central city Telecom centres. Dialling ISD you can get through overseas almost as quickly as locally and if your call is brief it needn't cost very much — 'hi, I'll be on the flight to London next Tuesday' can cost half the price of a postcard. All you do is dial 0011 for overseas, the country code (44 for Britain, 1 for the USA or Canada, 64 for New Zealand), the city code (1 for London, 212 for New York), and then your number. And have plenty of coins to hand. The USA or Britain costs $1.90 a minute, New Zealand is $1.20 a minute.

FACTS
Emergencies
for police, fire or ambulance dial 000.

Electricity

Voltage is 220-240 volts and the plugs are three pin but not the same as British three pin plugs. Men who shave electrically should note that apart from in fancy hotels it's very difficult to find converters to take either American flat two pin plugs or the European round two pin plugs. You can easily bend the American plugs to a slight angle to make them fit, however.

Measurements

Australia went metric in the early '70s. We buy petrol and milk by the litre, apples and potatoes by the kilogram, measure distance by the metre or km, our speed limits are in km per hour. But there's still a degree of confusion, it's hard to think of a six foot guy as being 183 cm.

Consulates & Embassies

Most diplomatic representations to Australia will be in Canberra and are listed in the ACT section. Some larger countries or with particular connections to Australia, the USA and UK in particular, will also have consular representation in Sydney, Melbourne and possibly other state capitals.

Opening Hours

Although Australians aren't great believers in long opening hours they are a long way ahead of the kiwis thank you! Most shops close at 5 or 5.30 pm daily and noon on Saturdays. They are closed all day on Sundays. There is usually a late night shopping night when the doors stay open until 9 or 9.30 pm — it's Thursday night in Sydney, Friday nights in Melbourne.

Banks are open from 9.30 am to 4 pm, Monday to Thursday, and until 5 pm on Friday. Of course there are some exceptions to Australia's unremarkable opening hours and all sorts of places stay open till late hours and all weekend — particularly milk bars, delis and city bookshops.

Tipping

Australians have a world wide reputation as lousy tippers because in Australia tipping isn't done much and it isn't a habit the way it is in the US or Europe. Perhaps it is part of the great Australian egalitarian 'I'm as good as you are, mate' feeling. So taxi drivers don't expect tips (of course they don't hurl it back at you if you decide to leave the change, but just try getting out of a New York cab, or even a London one, without leaving your 10%). Nor do any but the flashiest restaurants require tipping; there isn't even the service charge that gets added to the bottom of the bill in many countries. So if you are going to tip, make it for what tipping was supposed to be for in the first place — especially good service.

INFORMATION

There are a number of information sources for visitors to Australia and, in common with a number of other tourist conscious western countries, you can easily drown yourself in brochures and booklets, maps and leaflets. Forests fall to inform you about what Australia has to offer.

Australian Tourist Commission

The Australian Tourist Commission is the government body intended to inform potential visitors about the country. There's a very definite split between promotion outside Australia and inside it. The ATC is strictly an external operator, they do no promotion at all within the country and have no contact with visitors to Australia. Within the country tourist promotion is handled by state or local tourist offices. The ATC have a number of items of interest for potential visitors. First there's *Australia — Your Travel Planner*, a glossy magazine-style introduction to the country, its geography, flora, fauna, states, transport, accommodation, food and so on. They also have a good map of the country and an excellent guide to the Great Barrier Reef. Note, however, that this literature is intended for distribution overseas only, if you want copies get it before you come to Australia.

Addresses of the ATC offices for literature requests are:

Australia	414 St Kilda Rd, Melbourne 3000 (GPO Box 73B, Melbourne 3001)
Asia	Distribution Centre, PO Box 453, Singapore 9155
Canada	Kirks Mailing House, 1067 Granville St, Vancouver, BC V6Z ILA
Europe	Presse-U Touristikdienst, Heribert Nentwich, Sporthallenstr 7, D-6117 Schaafheim
Japan	Sankaido Building 7F, 9-13, Akasaka 1-Chome, Minato-ku Tokyo 107
New Zealand	PO Box 166, Auckland 1
UK	Distribution Department, Park Farm Industrial Estate, Park Farm Rd, Folkestone, Kent
USA	Western Folder Distributors, PO Box A-1, Addison, II 60101

State & Local Offices

Within Australia tourist information is handled by the various state and local offices. Each state and the ACT and Northern Territory have a tourist office of some form and you will find information about these centres in the various state sections. Apart from a main office in the capital cities they often have regional offices in main tourist centres and also in other states. As well as supplying brochures, price lists, maps and other information the state offices will often book transport, tours and accommodation for you. Unfortunately very few of the state tourist offices maintain information desks at the airports and furthermore the opening hours of the city offices are very much of the 9 to 5, weekdays only and Saturday morning varieties.

Addresses of the state tourist offices are:

Australian Capital Territory	ACT Government Tourist Bureau, London Circuit & West Row, Canberra City 2601
New South Wales	NSW Government Travel Centre, 16 Spring St, Sydney 2000
Northern Territory	Northern Territory Government Tourist Bureau, 9 Parsons St, Alice Springs 5750
Queensland	Queensland Government Tourist Bureau, Adelaide & Edward Sts, Brisbane 4000
South Australia	South Australian Government Tourist Bureau, 18 King William St, Adelaide 5000
Tasmania	Tasmanian Government Tourist Bureau, 80 Elizabeth St, Hobart 7000
Victoria	Victorian Government Travel Centre, 272 Collins St, Melbourne 3000
Western Australia	Western Australian Government Travel Centre, 772 Hay St, Perth 6000

A step down from the state tourist offices are the local or regional tourist offices. Almost every town in Australia seems to maintain a tourist office or centre of some

type or other and in many cases these are really excellent with much local information not readily available from the larger state offices. In Cairns, Queensland, for
example, there's an office of the Queensland Government Tourist Bureau and also
of the Far North Queensland Promotion Bureau. There are similar situations in a
number of other places around the country, particularly where there is a strong
local tourist activity.

Automobile Associations

Australia has a national automobile association, the Australian Automobile Association, but this exists mainly as an umbrella organisation for the various state associations and to maintain international links. The day to day operations are all
handled by the state organisations who provide free emergency breakdown service,
literature, excellent maps and detailed guides to accommodation and camp-sites.
The state organisations have reciprocal arrangements between the various states in
Australia and to the equivalent organisations overseas. So if you're a member of the
NRMA in NSW you can use RACV facilities in Victoria. Similarly if you're a
member of the AAA in the US or the RAC or AA in the UK you can use any of the
state organisations' facilities. But bring proof of membership with you. More details
about the state automobile organisations can be found in the relevant state sections.
Some of the material they produce is of very high standard, in particular the superb
set of regional maps to Queensland produced by the RACQ. The state offices are:

New South Wales	National Roads & Motorists Association (NRMA), 151 Clarence St, Sydney 2000
Northern Territory	Automobile Association of the Northern Territory, 79-81 Smith St, Darwin 5790
Queensland	Royal Automobile Club of Queensland (RACQ), 190-194 Elizabeth St, Brisbane 4000
South Australia	Royal Automobile Association of South Australia (RAA), 41 Hind-marsh Square, Adelaide 5000
Tasmania	Royal Automobile Club of Tasmania (RACT), Patrick & Murray Sts, Hobart 7000
Victoria	Royal Automobile Club of Victoria (RACV), 123 Queen St, Mel-bourne 3000
Western Australia	Royal Automobile Club of Western Australia (RAC), 228 Adelaide Terrace, Perth 6000

National Park Organisations

Australia has an extensive collection of national parks, in fact the Royal National
Park just outside Sydney is the second oldest national park in the world. Only
Yellowstone Park in the USA pre-dates it. The National Park organisations in each
state are state operated, however, not nationally. They tend to be a little hidden
away in their capital city locations although if you search them out they often have
excellent literature on the state parks. They are much more up front in the actual
parks where in many cases they have very good guides and leaflets to bushwalking,
nature trails and other activities. The state offices are:

New South Wales	National Parks & Wildlife Service, 189-193 Kent St, Sydney 2000
Northern Territory	Conservation Commission of the Northern Territory, Gap Rd, Alice Springs 5750
Queensland	National Parks & Wildlife Service, 138 Albert St, Brisbane 4000
South Australia	National Parks & Wildlife Service, 129 Greenhill Rd, Unley 5061

Tasmania	National Parks & Wildlife Service, 16 Magnet Court, Sandy Bay 7005
Victoria	National Parks Service, 240 Victoria Parade, East Melbourne 3002
Western Australia	National Parks Authority, Hackett Drive, Crawley 6009

National Trust

The National Trust is dedicated to preserving historic buildings in all parts of Australia. They actually own a number of buildings throughout the country which are open to the public and many other buildings are 'classified' by the National Trust to ensure their preservation. The National Trust also produces some excellent literature including a fine series of walking tour guides to many cities around the country, large and small. These guides are often available from local tourist offices or from National Trust Offices and are usually free whether you're a member of the National Trust or not. Membership of the trust is well worth considering, however, because it entitles you to free entry to any National Trust property for your year of membership. If you're going to be doing much travelling around Australia this could soon pay for itself. Annual membership costs $16 for individuals, $24 for families and includes the monthly or quarterly magazine put out by the state organisation which you join. Addresses of the various National Trust state offices are:

Australian Capital Territory	42 Franklin St, Manuka 2603
New South Wales	Observatory Hill, Sydney 2000
Northern Territory	74 Esplanade, Darwin 5790 (GPO Box 3520)
Queensland	Old Government House, George St, Brisbane 4000 (GPO Box 1494)
South Australia	Ayers House, 288 North Terrace, Adelaide 5000
Tasmania	81 St Johns St, Launceston 7250
Victoria	Tasma Terrace, Parliament Place, Melbourne 3000
Western Australia	Old Perth Boys School, 139 St Georges Terrace, Perth 6000

TIME ZONES

Australia is divided into three time zones — Western Time is +8 hours from Greenwich Mean Time (WA), Central Time is +9½ hours (NT, SA), and Eastern Time is +10 (Tas, Vic, NSW, Qld). During the summer things get slightly screwed up as daylight saving time does not operate in Western Australia or Queensland (of course) so those two states are an hour behind.

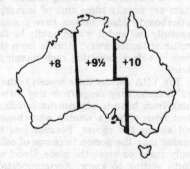

ACCOMMODATION

Finding a cheap place to stay can be a major stumbling block to seeing Australia at a reasonable price. It's not impossible, however, and these days Australia certainly offers as good value as you'll find in most western countries. We're actually very well equipped with youth hostels and campsites, the cheapest shelter you can find. Furthermore there are plenty of motels around the country and in the holiday regions like the Queensland coast intense competition tends to keep the prices down.

Hostels

The number one accommodation choice for backpackers has to be the youth hostel chain. Australia has a very active youth hostel association and you'll find hostels all over the country with more popping up all the time. It's indicative of the growing popularity of hostelling not only that the official hostel association is opening more hostels but also that more and more 'unofficial' hostels are springing up.

Basically youth hostels are places providing basic accommodation usually in small dormitories or bunkrooms. The nightly charges are rock bottom — usually just \$4 to 5 a night — but in return there are a number of rules and regulations you have to observe. Most important to stay at a youth hostel you must be a YHA (Youth Hostel Association) member. In Australia this costs \$12 a year plus a \$6 joining fee. Youth Hostels are an international organisation so if you're already a member of the YHA in your own country your membership entitles you to use of the Australian hostels. Hostels are great places for meeting people, great travellers' centres, and in many busier hostels the visitors will outnumber the Australians.

The rules and regulations for use of the hostels are all fairly simple and are outlined in the *Australian Youth Hostels Handbook* which is available from any YHA office in Australia. This booklet also lists all the hostels around Australia with useful little maps showing how to find them so it's quite invaluable. YHA members are eligible for various discounts at various places and these facilities are also listed in the handbook. The first rule is that you must have a sheet sleeping bag — a regular sleeping bag or sheets will not do. If you've not got one they can be rented at many hostels (usually for 50c) but it's cheaper, after a few nights' stay, to have your own. YHA offices and some larger hostels sell the official YHA sheet bag. Secondly the hostels are generally not available during the day time. You've got to get up and out in the morning and generally can't get back in until 5 pm. Other rules are mainly of the no alcohol, don't disturb people at night variety.

Most hostels have cooking facilities and some place where you can sit and talk. There are usually some sort of laundry facilities and hostels often have excellent noticeboards. Many hostels have a maximum stay period — some hostels are permanently full and it would hardly be fair for people to stay too long when others are being turned away. Hostels keep their costs down by getting you to do the work — before departing each morning there will be some chore you must complete.

The YHA defines their hostels as the simpler 'shelter' style and the larger 'standard' hostels. They range from tiny little places to modern big buildings with everything from historic old convict buildings to a disused railway station in between. Most hostels have a warden who checks you in when you arrive, keeps the peace and assigns the chores. Because you have so much more contact with a hostel warden than the person in charge of other styles of accommodation he (or she) can really make or break the place. Good wardens are often great characters and well worth getting to know. Accommodation can usually be booked ahead with the warden or, in some cases, with the state head office. The YHA handbook tells all.

The national head office of the Australian YHA is at Eagle House, 1st floor, Suite 2, 118 Alfred St, Milsons Point, NSW 2061 (tel 929 3407). The state membership offices of the YHA are:

New South Wales	355 Kent St, Sydney 2000 (tel 29 5068)
Northern Territory	PO Box 39900, Winnellie 5789
	or enquire at the Darwin youth hostel

Queensland	462 Queen St, Brisbane 4000 (tel 221 2022)
South Australia	72 South Terrace, Adelaide 5000 (tel 51 5583)
Tasmania	133A Elizabeth St, Hobart 7000 (tel 34 9617)
Victoria	122 Flinders St, Melbourne 3000 (tel 63 5421)
Western Australia	257 Adelaide Terrace, Perth 6000 (tel 325 5844)

Not all of the approximately 110 hostels listed in the handbook are actually owned by the YHA. Some are 'associate hostels' which provide all the usual hostel facilities and abide by the all the hostel regulations but are owned by other organisations or individuals. Others are 'alternative accommodation' which do not totally fit the hostel blueprint. They might be a motel which keeps some hostel style accommodation available for YHA members or a campsite with an on-site van or two kept aside, or even a place just like a hostel but where the operator doesn't want to abide by all the hostel regulations.

In addition there are quite a few unofficial hostels, a lot more of these have sprung up in the past few years. In some cases they're in competition with the official YHA places. In others they enjoy good relations with the YHA but are simply not up to the YHA's standards or simply don't want to be a part of the association. Youth hostelling is very popular in Australia and city hostels are often packed right out. When this happens they're generally only too happy to recommend other hostel style possibilities you could turn to.

The Y's

In a number of places in Australia there are accommodation places run by the YMCA or YWCA. They vary from place to place — some are mainly intended for permanent accommodation, some are run like normal commercial guest houses. They're generally excellent value and usually conveniently located. You don't have to be a YMCA or YWCA member to stay at them although sometimes you get a discount if you do. Accommodation in the Y's is usually in fairly straightforward rooms — usually with share bathroom facilities. Some Y's also have dormitory-style accommodation. Note, however, that not all YMCA or YWCA organisations around the country offer accommodation — it's mainly in the big cities. Another organisation which sometimes offers accommodation is the CWA (Country Women's Association) but this is mainly in the country and mainly for women only.

Colleges

Although it is students who get first bite at these, non-students can also stay at many university colleges during the uni vacations. These can be relatively cheap and comfortable plus there is the opportunity to meet other people. Costs can go as low as $5 a day or less for room only (if you're a student) although around $10 is more normal. With meals it can go up to around $20. There's usually a student and a higher non-student rate. A problem with this type of accommodation is that it is usually available only during the vacations (summer is November through February, the others are in May and August). Additionally it must almost always be booked ahead, you can't just turn up. Many of Australia's new universities are way out in the suburbs (we call them 'bush unis') and inconvenient to get to unless you have wheels. The Australian Tourist Commission puts out a comprehensive booklet listing all the college accommodation possibilities — ask for *Campus Accommodation*.

Hotels

For the budget traveller hotels in Australia are generally older places — new accommodation will usually be motels. To understand why Australia's hotels are the way they are requires delving back into the history books a little. At the same time as the powers that be decided that Australia's drinking should only be at the most inconvenient hours, they also decided that drinking places should also be hotels. So every place which in Britain would be a 'pub' in Australia is a 'hotel', but often in name only. The original idea of forcing them to provide accommodation for weary travellers has long faded into history; many of them have just a handful of rooms which are always 'occupied'. This ludicrous law is gradually being rolled back as 'tavern' licences are issued which allow alcohol to be provided without the required sideline of having rooms. A 'private hotel', as opposed to a 'licensed hotel', really is a hotel and does not serve alcohol. A 'guest house' is much the same as a 'private hotel'.

New hotels being built today are mainly of the Hilton variety — smaller establishments will usually be motels. So if you're staying in a hotel it will normally mean an older place, usually with rooms without private facilities. Unfortunately many of them are definitely on the drab, grey and drear side. You get a strong feeling that they've got the rooms there so they might as well try to turn a dollar on them. Fortunately some are also colourful places with some real character. They're also often very centrally located. Although the words 'hotel' doesn't always mean they'll have rooms the places that do have rooms usually make it pretty plain that they are available. If a hotel is listed in an accommodation directory you can be pretty sure it really will offer you a bed. If there's nothing that looks like a reception desk or counter just ask in the bar.

You'll find hotels all around the town centres in smaller towns while in larger towns the hotels that offer accommodation are often to be found close to the railway stations. In some older towns or in historic centres like the gold mining towns the old hotels can be really magnificent. The rooms themselves may be pretty old-fashioned and unexciting but the hotel facade and entrance area will often be quite exotic. In the outback the old hotels are often places of real character. Here they are often the real 'town centre' and you'll meet all the local eccentrics there. While researching this edition I stayed in one little outback town with a population of about 10, seven of whom were in the bar that night!

A bright word about hotels (guest houses and private hotels too) is that the breakfasts are usually A1. A substantial breakfast is what this country was built on and if your hotel is still into serving a real breakfast you'll probably feel it could last you until breakfast rolls around next morning. In these places B&B stands for 'bed & breakfast'. Generally hotels cost about $12 to 17 for a single, around $22 to 28 for a double. When comparing prices remember to check if it includes breakfast or not.

The state auto clubs produce accommodation directories listing hotels and motels in almost every little town in the country. They're updated every year so the prices will generally be fairly current and are available from the clubs for a nominal charge if you're a member or a member of an affiliated club enjoying reciprocal rights. Alternatively the state tourist offices also put out frequently updated guides to local accommodation. In airports, bus and railway stations there are often information boards with direct dial phones to book accommodation. Sometimes these places offer a discount if you book through the direct phone. Some hotels around the bus and railway stations also offer discounts to bus-pass travellers. The staff at he bus stations are good local sources of information on cheap and convenient accommodation.

Motels, Serviced Apartments & Holiday Flats

If you've got wheels and want a more modern place with your own bathroom and other facilities then you're moving into the motel bracket. Motels cover the earth in Australia, just like in the US, but they're usually located away from the city centres. Prices vary and with motels, unlike hotels, singles are often not much cheaper than doubles. Sometimes there is no difference at all between a single and a double. The reason why is quite simple — in the old hotels many of the rooms really are singles, they're relics from the days of single men heading off somewhere to find work or whatever. In motels the rooms are almost always doubles. You'll sometimes find motel rooms as low as $20 and in most places will have no trouble finding something at $30 or less. You can take $25 to 28 as a reasonable average for an economically priced motel room.

Holiday flats and serviced apartments are much the same thing and bear some relationship to motels. Basically holiday flats are found in holiday areas, serviced apartments in cities. A holiday flat is much like a motel room but usually has a kitchen or kitchen facilities so you can fix your own food. Usually holiday flats are not serviced like motels — you don't get your bed made up every morning and he cups washed out. In some holiday flats you actually have to provide your own sheets and bedding but others are operated just like motels but with a kitchen. Note that most motels in Australia will provide at least tea and coffee making facilities but a holiday flat will also have cooking utensils, dishes, cutlery and so on. Basically a holiday flat is a bit like having your own small flat or apartment but on a short term basis.

Holiday flats are often rented on a weekly basis but even in these cases it's worth asking if a daily rate is available. Remember also that paying for a week even if you only stay for a few days can still be cheaper than having those days at a higher daily rate. If there's more than just two of you another advantage of holiday flats is that you can often find them with two or more bedrooms. A two bedroom holiday flat is typically priced at about 1½ times the cost of a comparable single bedroom unit.

In holiday areas like on the Queensland coast motels and holiday flats will often be virtually interchangeable terms — there's nothing to really tell one from another. In big cities, on the other hand, the serviced apartments are often a little more obscure although they are often advertised in the newspaper small ads. As with hotels you'll find motels and other similar accommodation listed in car club accommodation directories, tourist office lists and at airports and other arrival points.

Camping & Caravanning

The camping story in Australia is partly excellent and partly rather annoying! The excellent side is that there are a great number of campsites and you'll almost always find space available. If you want to get around Australia on the cheap then camping is the cheapest way of all with nightly costs for two people of around $4 or 5. The drawbacks are that first of all campsites are often intended more for caravanners house trailers for any Americans out there) than for campers — the tent campers get little thought in these places. The New Zealanders could certainly show Australian campsite operators how it's done. Over there campsites often have a kitchen room and a dining area where you can eat. If it's raining you're not stuck with huddling in your car or, even worse, tent. Even the fact that most of the sites are called

'caravan parks' indicates who gets the most attention. Equally bad in cities mos
sites are well away from the centre. Things are not so bad in smaller towns but i
in general if you're planning to camp around Australia you really need your ow
transport. In this respect European countries can show how it's done with man
cities having sites right in the middle of town — ever camped in Florence, fo
example, where the site is beautifully situated overlooking the river and tow
centre. Brisbane is the worst city in Australia in this respect because counci
regulations actually forbid tents within a 22 km radius of the centre. Althougl
there are some sites in Brisbane within that radius they're strictly for caravans
no campers allowed.

Still it's not all gloom — in general Australian campsites are well kept, con
veniently located and excellent value. Many sites also have 'on-site vans' whicl
you can rent for the night and enjoy the comforts of caravanning without th
necessity of towing a caravan around with you. An on-site van typically cost
around $12 to 16 a night. A variance of this are cabins, much the same facilities as
caravan but without the pretence that it might be towed away somewhere. As wit
hotels and motels the state car clubs put out camping directories and informatio
sheets are also available from state and local tourist offices.

I've made trips around Australia using every sort of accommodation goin
from youth hostels to motels but one of the most successful was a trip Mauree
and I made on a motorcycle. We had a little tent strapped across the handlebar
and managed to camp almost everywhere we went from Canberra to Cooktow
Airlie Beach to Ayers Rock. On the few occasions when sitting in a tent listenin
to the rain beat down (one of those times being in Alice Springs believe it or not!
we managed to find an on-site van to shelter in. In the Alice Springs site they let u
use a vacant on-site van free during the daytime.

Other Possibilities

That covers the usual conventional accommodation possibilities but there are lot
of less conventional ones. You don't have to camp in camp sites, for example
There are plenty of parks where you can camp for free, or roadside shelters wher
short time camping is permitted. Australia has lots of bush where nobody is goin
to complain about you putting up a tent.

In the cities if you want to stay longer the first place to look for a flat or
room is the classified ad section of the daily paper. Wednesdays and Saturdays ar
the usual days for these ads. Noticeboards in universities, youth hostel offices
certain popular bookshops and other contact centres are good places to look fo
flats to share or people with rooms in houses to rent out.

Australia is a land of farms (sorry, stations) and one of the best way to get t
grips with Australian life is to spend a week on a farm. Many farms offer accom
modation where you can just sit back and watch how it's done or have a go your
self. The state tourist offices can advise you on what's available, the costs ar
pretty reasonable. Or how about life on a houseboat (see South Australia).

FOOD & DRINK

The culinary delights can be one of the real delights of Australia. Time was, like 2
years ago or even less, when Australia's food (mighty steaks apart) had a reputatio
for being like England's, only worse. Well perhaps not quite that bad, but getting o
that way. Miracles happen and Australia's miracle was immigration. The Greeks
Yugoslavs, Italians, Lebanese and many others who flooded in to Australia in th

'50s and '60s brought, thank God, their food with them.

So in Australia today you can have excellent Greek moussaka (and a good, cheap bottle of retsina to wash it down with), delicious Italian saltimboccas and pastas, good heavy German dumplings, you can perfume the air with garlic after stumbling out of a French bistro, try all sorts of Middle Eastern and Arab treats and, of course, the Chinese have been sweet & souring since the gold rush days. In the last few years there has even been an amazing influx of Indian restaurants so you can now find good tandoori food in most big cities!

Australian Food

Although there is no real Australian cuisine there is certainly some excellent Australian food to try. And I don't mean witchetty grubs, the giant sized maggots that are an Aboriginal delicacy — eat 'em live! Any mention of Australian food has to give the nod to a couple of firm favourites that are not going to win any competitions. For a start there's the great Australian meat pie — every bit as sacred an institution as the hot dog is to a New Yorker. And just as frequently slandered as tasteless, unhealthy and not nearly as good as it used to be. The meat pie is an awful concoction of anonymous meat, dark gravy and a soggy pastry container. You'll have to try one though, the number consumed in Australia each year is phenomenal and they're a real part of Australian culture. See the Port Douglas section in Queensland for the place to find a meat pie that really is worth eating.

Even more central to Australian eating habits is Vegemite. This strange dark coloured yeast spread is something only an Australian could love. You have to be born here to appreciate it. Australians spread Vegemite on bread and become so addicted to it that anywhere in the world you find an Aussie the jar of Vegemite is bound to be close to hand. Australian embassies the world over have the location of the nearest Vegemite retailer as one of their most asked for pieces of information. Another Australian staple is beetroot, the purple vegetable which manages to show up in almost any salad. It's hard to imagine a real Aussie hamburger without the obligatory slice of beetroot.

The good news about Australian food is the fine ingredients. Leave the fancy cooking to the French, simple food and simple preparation is what works best in Australia. Nearly everything is grown right here in Australia so you're not eating food which has been shipped half way around the world. Everybody knows about good Australian steaks ('this is cattle country so eat beef you bastards', announce the farmers' bumper stickers) but there are lots of other things to try. Like Australia's superb range of seafood. Fish like John Dory or the esteemed barramundi or superb lobsters and other crustaceans like the engagingly named yabbies or Moreton Bay bugs! Even vegetarians get a fair go in Australia, there are some excellent vegetarian restaurants and once again the vegetables are as fresh as you could ask for.

Where to Eat

If you want to feel right at home there are McDonalds, Kentucky Frieds, Pizza Huts and all the other familiar names looking no different than they do anywhere from New York to Amsterdam. There are also Chinese restaurants where the script is all in Chinese, little Lebanese places where you'd imagine the local PLO getting together for a meal and every other national restaurant type you could imagine. For real value for money there are a couple of dinky-die Aussie eating places you should certainly try though. For a start Australian delis are terrific and they'll put together a superb sandwich. Hunt out the authentic looking ones in any big city and you'll get a sandwich any New York deli would have trouble matching and I'm willing to bet it'll be half the price.

That covers your lunch time appetite and in the evening the number one value is to be found in the pubs. Look for 'counter meals', so called because they used to be eaten at the bar counter. Some places still are just like that while others are fancier, almost restaurant like. Good counter meals are hard to beat for value for money and although the food is usually of the simple steak-salad-french fries variety the quality if often excellent and prices commendably low. The best counter meal places usually have serve yourself salad tables where you can add as much salad, French bread and so on as you wish. Counter meals are usually served as counter lunches or counter teas, the latter a hang over from the old northern English terminology where 'tea' meant the evening meal. One catch with counter meals is that they usually operate fairly strict hours. The evening meal time may be just 6 to 7.30 or 8 pm. At the appointed hour the gates are slammed shut! Pubs doing counter meals often have a blackboard menu outside but some of the best places are quite anonymous — you simply have to know that this is the pub that does great food and furthermore that it's in the bar hidden away at the back. Counter meals vary enormously in price with the establishment but in general the better class places with good serve-yourself salad tables will cost in the $4 to 6 range for all the traditional steak, veal, chicken and so on dishes.

For rock bottom prices the real shoestringers can also check out university and college cafeterias, the big department store (Woolworths and Coles for example) cafeterias, or even try sneaking in to public service office cafeterias. Australians love their fish & chips just as much as the English and, just like in England, they can be enormously variable — all the way from stodgy and horrible to really superb. We've also got the full range of take-aways from pizzas to Mexican, Chinese to Lebanese.

Drinks

In the non-alcoholic department Australians knock back coke and flavoured milk like there's no tomorrow and also have some excellent mineral water brands. Coffee enthusiasts will be relieved to find good Italian cafes serving cappuccino and other coffees and often to the wee small hours and beyond. Beer and wine need their own explanations.

Beer

Australia's beer has to be considered along with the country's drinking habits. Way back in WW I the government of the day decided that all pubs should shut at 6 pm as a war time austerity measure. Unfortunately when the war ended this wartime emergency move didn't. On one side the wowsers didn't want anybody to drink and if Australia couldn't have prohibition like America stopping drinking at 6 pm was at least a step in the right direction in their view. The other supporters of this terrible arrangement were, believe it or not, the breweries and pub owners. They discovered that shutting the pubs at 6 pm didn't really cut sales at all and it certainly cut costs. You didn't have to pay staff until late in the evening and you certainly didn't have to worry about making your pub a pleasant place for a drink. People left work, rushed around to the pub and packed as much beer away as they could before 6 pm. They certainly didn't have time to admire the decor.

. This unhappy story didn't end after WW I or even after WW II. In fact it carried right on into the '50s before commonsense finally came into play and the 'six o'clock swill' was consigned to the bin where it belonged. Since that time the idea of the Australian pub as a bare and cheerless beer barn has gradually faded and there are now many pleasant pubs where an evening drink is a real pleasure. More recently drinking hours have been further liberalised and in the last few years pubs have been able to open later in the evening and even, finally, on Sundays. As usual Melbourne and Victoria is at the tail end of all this liberalisation!

Enough of the history and around to the beer — to most partakers it's superb. Fosters is, of course, the best known international brand with a firm following in England and even some supporters in the USA. Each state has it's own beer brand and there'll be someone to sing the praises of everything from Fourex (Queensland) to Swan (Western Australia) and even some fine local brands like Coopers (Adelaide). A word of warning to visitors — Australian beer has a higher alocohol content than British or American beers, Australian beer sold in the US has to be watered down to meet US regulations. And another warning, drinking drivers lose their licences but unhappily drunk driving is a real problem in Australia. Take care.

Beer Consumption

Australians are not the world's greatest consumers of beer — that achievement goes to the West Germans who knock back nearly 150 litres per capita per year. But Darwin is reckoned to be the number one city for beer drinking. Its peak year was 230 litres per man, woman and child; with so much beer disappearing down Darwinians' throats it's no surprise that they can run a boating regatta solely for boats made out of beer cans. When a party of Darwinians sailed to Singapore in a beer can boat it was locally mooted that they inspired boat loads of Vietnamese refugees to take their chances in the opposite direction. Australians are, incidentally, reckoned to be about the third biggest beer consumers in the world, about five to 10 litres behind the Germans, a litre or so less than the Belgians and neck and neck with the equally thirsty Czechs. The poms are about 25 litres back in 10th place, Americans don't even rate.

Wine

If you're not a beer fancier then turn to wines. Australia has a great climate for wine producing and some superb wine areas. Best known are the Hunter Valley of New South Wales and the Barossa Valley of South Australia but there are a great number of other wine producing areas, each with their own enthusiastic promoters. The Australian wineries have often been compared with their Californian counterparts since the climate and soil are similar and the history of wine making in both areas has been alike. Recent blind tastings in Europe have given some established European areas a shock so Australian wines can certainly mix it with the best. Best of all, though, Australia's wines are cheap and readily available. We pay less for our wine than the Californians do and the price of a decent bottle in England, Common Market or not, is positively horrifying.

It takes a little while to become familiar with Australian wineries and their styles but it's an effort worth making! All over Australia, but particularly in Melbourne, you'll find restaurants advertising that they're BYO. The initials stand for 'bring your own' and it means that they're not licensed to serve alcohol but you are permitted to bring your own with you. This is a real boon to the wine-loving but budget-minded traveller because you can bring your own bottle of wine from the local bottle shop or from that winery you visited last week and not pay any fancy restaurant mark ups. In fact most restaurants make no charge at all for you bringing your own booze with you even though it's conceivable that without it they might sell you a bottle of mineral water or something. An even more economical way of drinking Australian wine is to do it free at the wineries. In all the wine growing areas most wineries have free tastings, you just zip straight in and say what you'd like to try.

THINGS TO BUY

Australia is not a great place for buying amazing things — there's nothing in particular which you simply 'have' to buy while you're here. There are, however, lots of things definitely not to buy — like plastic boomerangs, Aboriginal ashtrays and all the other terrible souvenirs which tacky tourist shops in the big cities are stuffed full with. Most of it comes from Taiwan anyway. Top of the list for any real Australian purchase, however, would have to be Aboriginal art. It's an amazingly direct and down to earth art which has only recently begun to gain wide appreciation. If you're willing to put in a little effort you can see superb examples of the Aboriginals' art in its original form, carved or painted on rocks and caves in many remote parts of Australia. Now, and really just in time, skilled Aboriginal artists are also working on their art in a more portable form. There are Aboriginal art galleries in most big cities but the best displays are probably in the Northern Territory. Nobody captures the essence of outback Australia better than the Aboriginals so if you want a real souvenir of Australia this is what to buy.

Otherwise there are some alternative interesting possibilities. Like the sturdy farming gear as worn by those bronzed Aussie he-men on outback stations — boots, jeans and shirts, all made to last. Or there are all sorts of sheepskin products from car seats covers to Ugg boots. Surfing equipment, of course, is a major industry in Australia. You can find some terrific Australian books of the coffee table variety and Australian children's books are equally attractive. Recently some amusing Australiana shops have popped up selling delightfully silly examples of Australian kitsch — like lamingtons-in-perspex paperweights or a vegemite jar in an 'in case of emergency break glass' box. Australia's national gemstone is the opal, found particularly in South Australia. They're very beautiful but buy wisely, as with all precious and semi-precious stones there are many tall tales and expert 'salesmen' around.

Aboriginal Art

A real appreciation of Aboriginal art is a comparatively recent development possibly because it was not a widely observed art. Much of it was a temporary creation like the amazingly intricate sand paintings which were destroyed after their ceremonial use. Or it was very permanent but also very remote, like the superb rock carvings and paintings still being discovered in places like the wild Kakadu National Park in the Northern Territory. Today, however, you can find excellent examples of all forms of their art in the Aboriginal craft shops in most state capitals but particularly in Darwin and Alice Springs.

A useful introduction to these crafts can be found in the *Aboriginal Art* series of pamphlets available at the various craft shops. They include a general introduction and a number of separate brochures on rock art, baskets, carvings, sculptures, paintings and weapons. One of the best known of these crafts is the bark paintings from Arnhem Land. These traditionally show Australian native animals in a style known as x-ray paintings because some of the internal organs are shown. From the central Australian deserts the sand paintings are a more recent addition. Sand paintings were traditionally made for ceremonial occasions and were often of great size. They used an intricate pattern of dots, whorls, circles and lines, brightly coloured to symbolise events and stories. Recently artists have started to reproduce these dramatic patterns more permanently with paint on hardboard. Interestingly they can still only be reproduced by certain initiated men and considerable planning is required before a painting can be produced.

Carvings are found in many regions but some of the best known are the large carvings of the Tiwi people from Bathurst and Melville Islands. Their ceremonial grave poles are particularly interesting. In the Kimberley region of Western Australia the large nuts of the boab tree are carved with intricate patterns. Boomerangs, woomeras (spear throwers) and didgeridoos (a long, tube-like musical instrument) are other wooden objects. Baskets are woven from bark fibres or pandanus palm in a number of Aboriginal communities.

Getting There

Basically getting to Australia means flying. Once upon a time the traditional route between Europe and Australia was to go by ship but those days have ended. Infrequent and expensive cruise ships apart the only regular shipping service to Australia runs between Singapore and Fremantle, the port for Perth on the west coast. Fares on this service vary with the cabin class and the cheaper cabins are often booked out some time ahead. There's no real saving on this ship compared to air travel.

The basic problem with getting to Australia is that it's a long way from anywhere. In recent years there have been lots of cheaper fares introduced and there is certainly a lot more competition than there used to be — Qantas no longer has it absolutely all its own way — but there's no way you can get around those great distances, and hence high costs.

Australia has a large number of international gateways. Sydney and Melbourne are the two busiest international airports with flights from Asia, the Pacific, Europe, New Zealand and North America. Hobart in Tasmania has flights from New Zealand. Adelaide has just started to take international flights. Perth is a major international arrival point for flights from Asia and Europe. Port Hedland, believe it or not, has a flight to and from Bali in Indonesia. Then there's Darwin with flights from Europe and Asia while in north Queensland you can fly to Cairns from Papua New Guinea, the absolutely cheapest place to fly to or from Australia. Townsville has flights to and from New Zealand and USA and Brisbane is another major international arrival point from Europe, Asia, New Zealand and the USA. One place you can't arrive in Australia at is Canberra, the national capital.

From Europe

Official discount fares to Australia are Apex advance purchase fares and excursion fares. Stopovers are not permitted on Apex fares and are limited on the excursion fares. A return Apex London-Sydney runs from around £700 to £1000 depending on when you go out and back. One-way Apex fares range from £450 to £550. There are also excursion fares which are somewhat more expensive than Apex fares ranging from around £800 to £1300 again depending on the season. They do not require advance purchase and firm advance reservations but do have restrictions on minimum and maximum period of stay and there are restrictions on stop-overs or extra charges. The one-way excursion fare, which does not permit stopovers, is £730. The regular economy one-way fare is £910.

You can generally find tickets through London bucket shops at fares pleasantly lower than the Apex prices and with stopovers permitted. These do not involve any of the Apex cancellation penalties but you have to shop around and the prices tend to vary from week to week and airline to airline. The last time I flew back from London to Australia I went Air Lanka London-Sri Lanka-Singapore then Thai International Singapore-Australia, comfortably undercut the regular Apex fare and had stopovers in Sri Lanka and Singapore. Currently one-ways to Australia are available from London bucket shops from around £350. From Germany you can find return tickets for around DM2600.

For up-to-date information on what's available scan the travel ads in the giveaway paper *Australasian Express* or get a copy of the wekly what's-on-guide *Time Out*. Although most bucket shops (the label usually applied to discount travel

44

agents) are pretty straight up and down there are always some sharp operators around. *Time Out* gives some useful advice on precautions to take. A couple of the major London operators who are usually OK are Trail Finders at 46 Earls Court Rd, London W8 and STA Travel 74 Old Brompton Rd, London W7.

On to New Zealand There are no official cheap fares from London to New Zealand which include a stop-over in Australia. The cheapest way of doing it is either to get a discounted ticket to Australia and then get a cheap Australia-New Zealand fare, which requires advance purchase, or shop around for a cheap ticket from the bucket shops such as one using UTA through Australia.

From the USA
From America you can fly to Australia with Pan Am, Continental and Qantas on direct special fares. Other airlines that fly between North America and Australia include Canadian Pacific, UTA and Air New Zealand. America is not a good place for unofficial cheap tickets although there ae plenty of official cheap deals around.

The regular economy fare is US$1089 Los Angeles-Sydney on a single carrier. Stopovers are permitted but you must fly all sectors with the same airline. For US$1268 you can get essentially the same ticket but with the option of flying other trans-Pacific carriers along the way.

Special economy fares also permit stopovers but the fares are variable with season and there is a cancellation penalty once you have booked and paid for your ticket. The fares are US$990 in the low season, US$1023 in the shoulder, US$1056 in the high season. Basically the low season for flights to Australia covers the April to August winter months, the high season covers the November to February summer months.

Finally there are Apex fares requiring that the ticket be booked and paid for 30 days prior to departure and with heavier cancellation penalties although again stopovers are permitted. One-way fares are US$536 in the low season, US$728 in the shoulder, US$816 in the high.

Via New Zealand Many travellers from the US will want to visit New Zealand and Australia. The cheapest way to do this is to buy an Epic return fare USA-New Zealand and then a cheap return ticket New Zealand-Australia. But the fare saving varies with the season and at some times of year the difference between this ticketing combination and straightforward economy return to Australia, which permits stopovers in New Zealand, is minimal. In that case it's hardly worth the cancellation penalty possibility and other restrictions which the cheap tickets entail. Note that Auckland is the usual entry point from the USA but that there are flights between most Australian state capitals and the major New Zealand cities. Extensions beyond Auckland for a regular economy ticket bring the fare up to the same level as a ticket through to Australia. In fact a USA-Auckland-Christchurch ticket is actually more expensive than a USA-Auckland-Christchurch-Australia ticket! For more information on flying to New Zealand in combination with Australia see *New Zealand — a travel survival kit.*

From New Zealand
Air New Zealand and Qantas operate a network of trans-Tasman flights linking Auckland, Wellington and Christchurch in New Zealand with Brisbane, Sydney and Melbourne on the east coast of Australia. More recently direct flights have started

from Townsville, Adelaide and Perth to New Zealand. TAA also fly between Christchurch and Hobart in Tasmania. So basically you can fly between a lot of places in New Zealand and a lot of places in Australia.

Fares vary depending which cities you fly between but the economy one-way range is from NZ$334 to $386 while Apex returns, which also vary with season range between NZ$364 to $520. The TAA Apex return between Christchurch and Hobart ranges from NZ$390 to $558 depending on the season.

From Asia

Ticket discounting is widespread in Asia, particularly in Singapore, Hong Kong (currently the discounting capital), Bangkok and Penang. There are a lot of fly by nights in the Asian ticketing scene so a little care is required. For much more information on South-East Asian travel and on to Australia see *South-East Asia on a Shoestring*.

From Hong Kong Apex fares to Australia range from HK$3081 to $3919 one-way or HK$4752 to $6150 return. Discounted one-way tickets go down to HK$2000 or less one-way, from about HK$4100 return. Bangkok is in the B12,275 to B15,665 bracket for an Apex one-way ticket or B18,460 to B25,325 return. Singapore Apex costs S$903 to S$1150 one way, S$1294 to S$1768 return. Discounted tickets go down to about S$800 one-way or S$1250 return, depending on the season. These fares are all to the east coast capitals. Brisbane is sometimes a bit cheaper than Sydney or Melbourne. From Singapore it's cheaper to Perth or Darwin.

You can also pick up some interesting tickets in Asia to include Australia on the way across the Pacific. UTA were first in this market but Qantas and Air New Zealand are also offering discounted trans-Pacific tickets. On the UTA ticket you can stop-over in Jakarta, Sydney, Noumea, Auckland, Tahiti or Hawaii en route to Los Angeles for around US$750 or less.

Round the World

Round the world tickets have become very popular in the last few years and many of these will take you through Australia. The official airline RTW (Round the World) tickets are much cheaper than the regular fares and you can also get interesting unofficial RTW packages in ticket discounting centres in Asia and Europe.

The official tickets are put together usually by a combination of two airlines and permit you to fly anywhere you want so long as you do not backtrack. Other restrictions are that you (usually) must book the first sector in advance and cancellation penalties then apply. There may be restrictions on how many stops you are permitted and usually the tickets are valid for from 90 days up to a year. A typical RTW package that includes Australia is the Continental-KLM combination which costs US$2095. Qantas and TWA offer a similar deal. A variation of these airline round the world packages is a round the Pacific combination. Qantas and Singapore Airlines have one, so do Continental and Thai International, Japan Air Lines or Philippine Airlines.

A do-it-yourself RTW package might be London-Singapore with a London bucket shop ticket, then Singapore-Los Angeles via Australia and New Zealand with one of the discounted trans-Pacific tickets like UTA's and then a stand-by ticket from LA back to London.

Arriving in Australia

For information about how to get to the city from the airport when you first arrive in Australia check the Airport section under the relevant city. In most cities there is an airport bus service and there are always taxis available. There is currently a little confusion over airport bus services because TAA and Ansett, the two domestic airlines, dropped their airport bus services in late '82. In some cases there were already competing private bus services, in others new services have sprung up, in still others new services are talked of but not yet actually working. Hence the confusion over just what transport is and is not available and what it costs.

Leaving Australia

Australia is much better than it used to be for cheap ticket deals but still relatively 'straight'. At present some discounting is going on for tickets to Europe, nothing much at all to Asia. Apex tickets are available to all the usual destinations. The big catch about leaving Australia, however, is the terrible departure tax. It's A$20, one of the worst in the world and a very definite discouragement to visitors to the country.

Getting Around

FLYING

Australia is so vast (and at times so empty) that unless your time is unlimited you're quite possibly going to have to take to the wing sometime. It has been calculated that something like 80% of long distance trips by public transport are made by air — against only 12% by rail and a mere 4% by bus. Unfortunately the two major domestic airlines are far from the cheapest per km in the world, although they are amongst the safest.

The two airlines are TAA (Trans Australian Airlines), which is government owned, and Ansett, which is privately owned, newspaper magnate Rupert Murdoch being one of the principal owners. The difference in ownership makes almost no discernable difference to the traveller because they are quite remarkably similar. In fact their sameness is one of the most interesting things about them. They offer near identical service, absolutely identical prices and until recently identical aircraft. This follow the leader tradition was quite amazing just a few years back. If Ansett wanted to buy two new Boeing 727 series 200s then TAA would also buy two new Boeing 727 series 200s. If one should arrive before the other then it would be held back until both aircraft could enter service on exactly the same day. And then as the ultimate absurdity TAA and Ansett usually operated services at virtually exactly the same time. If TAA flew from A to B daily at 9 am and 3 pm then Ansett would fly from A to B daily at 9.05 am and 3.05 pm (or perhaps even 8.55 am and 2.55 pm). If they were going to have just one flight a week then they would both probably go on the same day of the week too!

Fortunately these things have changed a bit. TAA now operates Airbuses, 727s and DC-9s while the Ansett fleet will soon consist of 767s, 727s and 737s. Nor do they operate to quite so slavishly similar schedules although there is still a certain degree of similarity on many routes. Unfortunately the fares are still identical and what's worse they're also a lot higher than they used to be. In the last three years the general level of air fares has doubled in Australia and the continuous escalation shows no signs of slowing down. Price rises several times a year are the norm these days and just before this edition was completed there were two rises, both of around 10% in the space of about two months.

There are a number of reasons for the high cost of Australian air travel although compared to prices in Europe it's not really all that bad. One is the government policy of loading the cost of air operations in Australia disproportionately onto the domestic carriers -- thus only the domestic airlines pay fuel tax, none of the international airlines flying into Australia do. This tax goes to cover the costs of air traffic control, airport upkeep and so on. The domestic airlines also have to cover Australia's high airport landing charges.

Another reason is the poor utilisation of the aircraft since very few flights are made at night. Except for flights between Perth and the east coast, only a couple a night for each airline, most of the fleet sits on the tarmac every night. Stringent regulations about night operations at Sydney and Brisbane airports (no arrivals after 10 pm) are a major reason for this poor utilisation.

Again it's government policy which accounts for another continuing absurdity of Australian air travel. The government has ruled that only Qantas shall fly abroad, only Ansett and TAA within Australia. So since Qantas has no suitable aircraft to fly, for example, Cairns-Port Moresby or Darwin-Bali there are no Australian airlines on these sectors. At the same time Sydney-Perth and Melbourne-Perth are domestic sectors so Qantas 747s fly these long sectors often half empty and domestic passengers aren't allowed to use them. There's a toe in the door on these regulations in that TAA now flies Hobart to New Zealand and Ansett has some Pacific connections on behalf of the Pacific island nations but there's a long way to go.

Of course the biggest reason for the lack of competition is that the two domestic airlines simply don't have to. They've got a perfect little duopoly going and nobody else is allowed into the game. It's only when people simply stop flying on their aircraft or public complaints become overwhelming that some attempt is made to come to grips with reality. In the last few years that has resulted in some cheaper fare possibilities and improved service — you actually get meals on longer sectors these days. Once upon a time they'd fly you from one end of Australia to the other with little more than a cup of tea and biscuit. In the fare field there are now Apex round trip fares available and standby fares on some sectors.

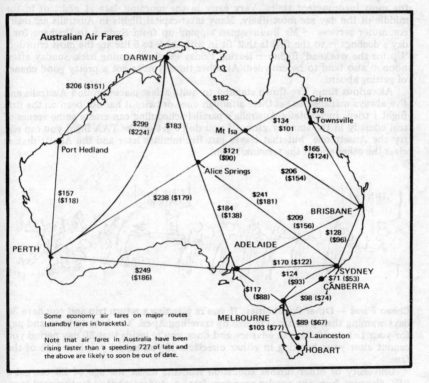

Australian Air Fares

DARWIN

$206 ($151)

$182

$299 ($224) $183

$157 ($118)

Port Hedland

$238 ($179)

$184 ($138)

PERTH

$249 ($186)

Cairns

$78

$134

Townsville

$101

Mt Isa

$121 ($90)

$165 ($124)

Alice Springs

$206 ($154)

$241 ($181)

$209 ($156)

BRISBANE

$128 ($96)

ADELAIDE

$170 ($122)

$124 ($93)

SYDNEY

$71 ($53)

CANBERRA

$117 ($88)

$98 ($74)

$89 ($67)

MELBOURNE

$103 ($77)

Launceston

HOBART

Some economy air fares on major routes (standby fares in brackets).

Note that air fares in Australia have been rising faster than a speeding 727 of late and the above are likely to soon be out of date.

Cheap Fares — Standby For travellers the best story on the cheap fares side is the availability of standby fares on some main routes. The air fares chart shows the regular fares and the standby fares in brackets. Basically standby fares save you around 25% of the regular economy fare — Melbourne-Sydney, for example, is

$124, only $93 standby. You have no guarantee of a seat when travelling standby. You buy your ticket at the airport, register at the standby desk and then wait for the flight to board. If at that time there is sufficient room for the standby passengers, on you go. If there's room for 10 additional passengers and 20 are on standby then the first 10 to have registered get on. If you miss the flight you can standby for the next one (you'll be that much further up the line if some standby passengers have got on) or you can go try the other airline.

A catch with standby fares is that they only work on a sector basis. If you want to fly Melbourne-Perth and the flight goes via Adelaide you have to standby on the Melbourne-Adelaide section and then for the Adelaide-Perth sector. Furthermore the fares will be a combination of the two sectors, not a reduction from the direct Melbourne-Perth fare. Fortunately there are a lot more direct flights these days.

If you intend to standby the most likely flights will be, of course, the ones at the most inconvenient times. Very early in the morning, late at night or in the middle of the day are most likely. Many inter-capital flights in Australia are really commuter services — Mr Businessman zipping up from Sydney to Brisbane for a day's dealings — so the flights that fit in with the 9 to 5 life are the most crowded. 'Up for the weekend' flights — leaving Friday evening, coming back Sunday afternoon — also tend to be crowded. At other times you've got a pretty good chance of getting aboard.

At various times I've flown standby to quite a few places around Australia and I've always managed to get there although once or twice it has not been on the first flight I tried. Incidentally Australia's parallel scheduling can create some scenes of real comedy in the standby game. If you don't get on the TAA flight you can still try the Ansett one, but that leaves just five minutes later and the Ansett desk is clear the other end of the terminal! Run!

Cheap Fares — Other Possibilities If you're planning a return trip and you have 30 days warning then you can save 35% by travelling Apex. You have to book and pay for your tickets 30 days in advance and once you're inside that 30 day period you cannot alter your booking in either direction. If you cancel you lose 50% of the fare.

University or other further education students under the age of 26 can get a 25% discount from the regular economy fare. A student photo identity card is required for Australian students. Overseas students can use their International Student Identity Card, a New Zealand student card or an overseas airline ticket issued at the 25% student reduction. The latter sounds a good bet!!

International visitors to Australia can get a 30% discount on internal fares so long as the total distance to be travelled exceeds 1000 km and so long as they flew to Australia on other than regular full fare tickets. The idea behind this latter ruling is that business travellers are excluded, it's only for real tourist visitors travelling on an Apex or similar ticket. Unfortunately budget travellers who come to Australia on a bucket shop ticket will find that their ticket, discounted though it may be, is officially a 'full fare ticket'. Some offices may be flexible on this ruling so ask around.

Other cheap deals include night coach fares which operate on certain long-haul sectors overnight and save 20%. These sectors are Perth-Adelaide, Perth-Melbourne, Perth-Sydney, Darwin-Adelaide and Darwin-Brisbane. There are also some worthwhile cheap deals with other regional airlines such as East West's Club 25 deal. Keep your eyes open too for special deals at certain times of year. When the Melbourne Cup horse race is on and the football grand final (also in Melbourne) lots of extra flights are put on. These flights would normally be going in the opposite direction nearly empty so special fares are often offered to people wanting to leave Melbourne when everybody else wants to go there.

Round Australia Fares Ansett and TAA both have special round the country fares — TAA's is called *Discover Australia*. Ansett's is *Explore Exciting Australia*. These fares ticket you right around the country on routes some of which are shown below:

$989
Melbourne-Adelaide-Perth-Geraldton-Carnarvon-Learmonth-Karratha-Port Hedland-Broome-Derby-Kununurra-Darwin-Gove-Cairns-Townsville-Mackay-Rockhampton-Brisbane-Gold Coast*-Sydney-Canberra-Melbourne

$756
Melbourne-Adelaide-Alice Springs-Darwin-Mt Isa-Cairns-Townsville-Mackay-Rockhampton-Brisbane-Gold Coast*-Sydney-Canberra-Melbourne

$760
Melbourne-Adelaide-Alice Springs-Darwin-Gove-Cairns-Townsville-Mackay-Rockhampton-Brisbane-Gold Coast*-Sydney-Canberra-Melbourne

$570
Adelaide-Perth-Alice Springs-Adelaide

*under your own steam
dotted lines indicate alternative routes

$1148

Melbourne-Adelaide-Perth-Geraldton-
Carnarvon-Learmonth-Karratha-Port Hedland-
Broome-Derby-Kununurra-Darwin-Alice
Springs-Mt Isa-Carins-Townsville-Mackay-
Rockhampton-Brisbane-Gold Coast*-Sydney-
Canberra-Melbourne

$615

Melbourne-Adelaide-Alice Springs-Mt Isa-
Cairns-Townsville-Mackay-Rockhampton-
Brisbane-Gold Coast*-Sydney-Canberra-
Melbourne

*under your own steam
dotted lines indicate alternative routes

If you want to see a lot of Australia but haven't got much time these fares are excellent value as they are much cheaper than the addition of all the separate fares. They're not even bad value compared to the bus pass tickets since on a bus pass quite a lot of your travel time is spent actually travelling. You can make the loop in either direction so long as you keep moving in that direction and complete the loop within 90 days. You can also miss out sectors if you wish and travel by land, although there is no refund if you choose to do this. On sectors where the flight frequencies are limited you can switch from TAA to Ansett or vice versa if the carrier you are ticketed with has no flight on that day.

Certain other changes from the two regular airlines are also possible. Through Western Australia, between Perth and Darwin, you can fly Airlines of Western Australia. They have a much more comprehensive route network along the WA coast than either Ansett or TAA. Between Alice Springs and Darwin you can opt to fly Airlines of Northern Australia and stop at Katherine and Tennant Creek for an extra $45. Between Mackay and Townsville it's possible to fly Air Queensland in order to stop at Proserpine for the Whitsunday Islands, for an additional $120. Alternatively you can fly from Mackay direct to the Whitsunday airstrip at the regular fare of $38. Neither Ansett or TAA fly between Brisbane and the Gold Coast but if you wish you can be ticketed into one airport and out of the other, travelling between the two by bus, which only takes two hours. You can also tack on Tasmania from Melbourne at about a 10% discount from the regular fare, 30% if you're a student. Certain discounts are also available on local tours, accommodation and rent-a-cars if you present your round Australia ticket.

Note that neither TAA or Ansett seem to be totally informed about these tickets themselves. You get varying responses from varying people. During the researching of this new edition I used a round Australia ticket issued by Ansett and had a number of interesting minor problems. For a start the Melbourne office issued it to include Townsville-Proserpine-Mackay on Ansett flights when Ansett don't fly to Proserpine. Half way round I discovered about the discounts on rent-a-cars, etc. Later when I tried to rent a car and asked for the discount the agency denied it applied! Finally an annoyingly disinterested individual in the Cairns office announced I could not fly through Proserpine under any condition short of throwing the ticket away and buying another on Air Queensland — I eventually went by land. Fortunately some of this confusion went very much in my direction when I managed to get on a delightful Air Queensland flight between Mt Isa and Cairns — see the Queensland section for the best flight I've ever made in Australia.

Other Airlines

There are a number of secondary airlines apart from the two major domestic carriers. In WA there's Airlines of Western Australia with an extensive network of flights to the mining towns of the north-west and to Darwin in the Northern Territory. Airlines of WA is associated with Ansett as is Airlines of Northern Australia who operate from Darwin down to Alice Springs and Ayers Rock and across through Gove to Cairns. Air Queensland is one of Australia's most colourful regional airlines with an extensive network to some of the most out of the way places in northern Australia. They operate a varied fleet which includes everything from modern mini-airliners to elderly DC-3s. In NSW there's Ansett Airlines of NSW and also East-West Airlines who operate mainly to northern NSW but also to the Gold Coast and Sunshine Coast in Queensland, down to Melbourne in Victoria, across to Tasmania and also to Norfolk Island. If you're between 15 and 25 you can join East-West's Club 25 (it's free) and get a 20% discount on almost all of their flights. In South Australia there's Airlines of South Australia who fly around the state including to Kangaroo Island and up to Broken Hill in NSW. There are many other smaller regional and local airlines around Australia.

Airport Transfers

You'll find some uncertainty and confusion in some parts of this guide about airport bus transport. Until late '82 Ansett and TAA both operated bus services to connect with all their departures and arrivals throughout Australia. Since both carriers had flights departing at the same time it was a little wasteful having two buses also departing from their often adjacent locations at the same time. So they got together and decided to operate just one bus between them. *No, No, No,* of course they didn't, that's not the way Australia's airline system operates at all. No they got together and both stopped their bus service on the same day.

In some cases there were already private airport bus services operating. In some cases private bus service have started up since or are currently at the planning stage. In some cases there is no longer any airport bus service. In WA, Airlines of WA still operate airport services. In almost all cases it's not 100% certain just what is going to happen!

RAIL

Australia's railway system has never really recovered from the colonial bungling which accompanied its early days over a century ago. Before Australia became an independent country it was governed as six separate colonies, all administered from London. And when the colony of Victoria, for example, wanted to build a railway line it checked not only with adjoining colony of New South Wales but with the colonial office in London. When the colonies were federated in 1901 and Australia came into existence by what must rate as a sheer masterpiece of planning not one state had railway lines of the same gauge as a neighbouring state!

The immense misfortune of this inept planning has dogged the railway system every since. The situation betwen Victoria and New South Wales is a typical example. When NSW started to lay a line from Sydney to Parramatta in 1850 their railway engineer was Irish and convinced the authorities it should be built to wide gauge — five foot three inches. Victoria also started to build this gauge in order to

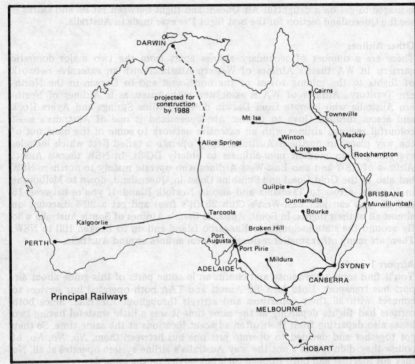

Principal Railways

tie in with the NSW system if, at some time in the future, a Melbourne-Sydney rail link was completed. Unfortunately NSW then switched railway engineers and their new man was not Irish and not enamoured of wide gauge. NSW railways accordingly switched to standard gauge — four foot eight inches — but Victoria decided their railway construction had gone too far to change now. Thus when the NSW and Victoria railway lines met in Albury in 1883 they, er, didn't meet. The Victorian railway lines were seven inches wider apart than the NSW ones. For the next 79 years a rail journey between Melbourne and Sydney involved getting up in the middle of the night at the border and changing trains!

In 1962 a standard gauge line was opened between Albury and Melbourne and standard gauge lines have also been built between the NSW-Queensland border and Brisbane. In 1970 the standard gauge rail link was completed between Sydney and Perth and the famous, and very popular, Indian-Pacific run was brought into operation. There are also, however, narrow gauge railways in Australia. They came about because it was felt to be cheaper but the old ghan line between Adelaide and and Alice Springs was only replaced by a new standard gauge line a couple of years ago. Apart from different gauges there's also the problem of different operators. In the early '70s Whitlam era Australian National Railways (ANR) was set up to try and bring the railways under one national umbrella but due to non-Labor governed states not wanting to co-operate the ANR only operates railways in South Australia, the Melbourne-Adelaide service plus the two really well known services, the Adelaide-Alice Springs ghan and the Sydney-Perth Indian Pacific. Other services are operated by the state railways or a combination of them for interstate services.

So rail travel in Australia today is basically something you do because you really want to — not because it's cheaper (it isn't) and certainly not because it's fast. Rail travel is generally the slowest way to get from anywhere to anywhere in Australia. On the other hand the trains are comfortable and you certainly see Australia at ground level in a way no other means of travel permits. Australia is one of the few places in the world today where new lines are still being laid or under consideration. The new line from Tarcoola to Alice Springs, to replace the rickety old ghan line, was an amazing piece of work and its success has inspired thoughts of finally building a railway line between Alice Springs and Darwin.

Although not all important services are operated by ANR there is cooperation under the Railways of Australia banner. You can write to them at 325 Collins St, Melbourne, Victoria 3000 for a copy of their handy and concise timetable of all the major Australian railway services. State booking office phone numbers are NSW 217 8812, Queensland 225 0211, South Australia 212 6699, Tasmania 34 6911, Victoria 62 0771 and Western Australia 326 2811.

Main Routes

Sydney-Melbourne	day and overnight services every day of the week, 13 or 14 hours
Sydney-Murwillumbah	daily overnight service for the Gold Coast, 17 hours
Sydney-Canberra	six days a week, five hours
Sydney-Brisbane	daily overnight, 16 hours
Brisbane-Rockhampton	six days a week, 11 hours
Brisbane-Cairns	six days a week, 37 hours
Townsville-Mt Isa	twice weekly, 21 hours
Melbourne-Adelaide	daily overnight, 12 hours
Melbourne-Mildura	six days a week, overnight, 11 hours
Sydney-Adelaide	four days a week via Broken Hill, 26 hours
Sydney-Perth	four days a week, 2½ days
Sydney-Alice Springs	starting 1983
Adelaide-Perth	three days a week, 1½ days
Adelaide-Alice Springs	once weekly, 24 hours
Perth-Kalgoorlie	six days a week, eight hours

Austrail passes allowing unlimited travel on all Australian rail systems are available but only for purchase overseas and only for foreign passport holders. Costs are the local currency equivalent of A$260 for 14 days, A$330 for 21 days, A$420 for one month, A$590 for two months and A$680 for three months. These passes are for first class travel but do not cover meals or berth charges where these are charged as additional costs. The agent for Austrail passes in the UK is Thomas Cook, in the US it is Tour Pacific.

BUS

Australia has two major nationwide bus operators and a string of more localised firms. Bus travel is generally the cheapest way from A to B, apart from hitching of course. Note, however, that the bus companies do not operate identical routes and

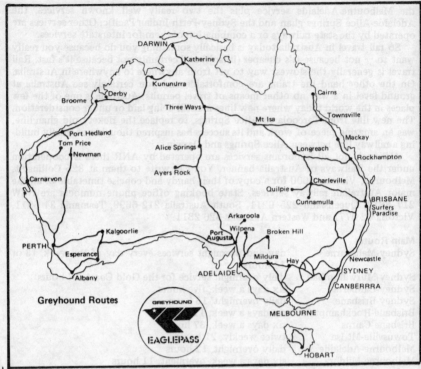

their ticket prices are not always identical either. The various bus companies also operate a number of package tours to places of touristic interest. A large variety of public and private bus companies operate local services and country routes around the various states.

The big two are Ansett Pioneer and Greyhound. Ansett Pioneer are connected with Ansett Airlines and in most cases operate from the Ansett city terminals. Greyhound, despite their similar logo, are not related to Greyhound buses in the USA. Both, however, are very much like the big US bus companies — the buses look similar, they're similarly equipped with air-conditioning and toilets, and, since the distances are just as great, Australian bus travel has many similarities to bussing it in the US.

A great many travellers see Australia by bus because it's one of the best ways to come to grips with the country's size and variety of terrain and because the bus companies have such comprehensive route networks — far more comprehensive than the railway system. Most important, however, the big two have unlimited travel passes which can be excellent value. A brief run down on the passes:

Greyhound Eaglepass The Eaglepass allows unlimited travel on Greyhound routes for either 30 days for $430 or 60 days for $640. Shorter period Eaglepasses are

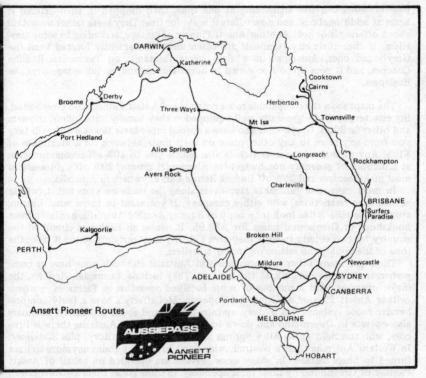

Ansett Pioneer Routes

AUSSIEPASS

ANSETT PIONEER

available overseas. The pass also gives you 25% off Budget Rent-a-Cars and 10 to 20% off local sightseeing tours. Although both companies go to all the major centres Greyhound does have a more extensive network and, more important, more frequent services. One place where services are infrequent, along the north-west coast of WA, the Greyhound and Ansett Pioneer passes are interchangeable, however. Both companies now extend to Tasmania since their passes can be used on Tasmanian Redline Coaches' services. In Western Australia the Eaglepass can be used on Westrail bus services from Perth to Albany, making a loop of the south and south-west of the state possible. Your Eaglepass will also take you up into the Flinders Ranges of South Australia, another advantage over Ansett Pioneer.

Ansett Pioneer Aussiepass The Aussiepass is available in three permutations — 15 days for $240, 30 days for $340 and 60 days for $640. A major plus point for the Aussiepass is that it covers free sightseeing in Adelaide, Canberra/Cooma, Melbourne, Perth and Sydney. In Alice Springs, Brisbane, Cairns, Darwin, Surfers Paradise and Townsville you get a 50% discount on sightseeing tours. There are lots of places where this can be very useful — where attractions are too far from the centre to get to easily by yourself or on public transport. The Phillip Island fairy penguins outside Melbourne are a good example. Note, however, that the Aussiepass included this free sightseeing at one time, then dropped it, then offered it again at additional cost and now offers it again for free. They seem rather uncertain about offering it or not! Another Ansett Pioneer advantage, according to some travellers, is that their city terminals are often more conveniently located than the Greyhound ones. Aussiepass now also covers Tasmania, on Tasmanian Redline Coaches, and it goes up to Cooktown in north Queensland, an advantage over the Eaglepass.

The maps show the comparable route networks of Ansett Pioneer and Greyhound. Big city terminals are generally well equipped — they usually have toilets, showers and other facilities. Greyhound also have a special super-saver ticket which will take you from any place to any other place on their route network for a maximum of $195. Any of their super-saver tickets also entitle you to 10% off accommodation at a number of generally non-budget-traveller motel groups, 20% off sightseeing in most major centres and 25% off Budget Rent-a-Cars anywhere in Australia.

In most cases you can make stop-overs along the route on your ticket, within certain time restrictions, with either company. If you want to know what bussing around Australia is like look for a copy of *Bussing Around Australia*, available from bookshops or Greyhound buses for A$9.95. It relates an Eaglepass circuit of the country by two elderly (well if they aren't elderly they certainly sound it from the tone of the book!) and rather 'organised' travellers.

There are many other bus companies in Australia although none have as comprehensive a route network as the big two. They include Tasmanian Redline, the major operator, plus a number of more localised operators in Tasmania — where neither Ansett Pioneer or Greyhound operate. McCafferty's have a fairly comprehensive route system from Sydney up into Queensland as far as Mackay. Skennars also operate in Queensland and down to Sydney. In South Australia there is Briscoes, who run right up to Alice Springs in the Northern Territory, plus Stateliner. In Western Australia there's Westrail, who don't have many trains anymore so have turned to buses instead. In many cases services are operated on behalf of Ansett Pioneer or Greyhound by these local operators. In some states there are restrictions on using interstate buses for intrastate travel — these rules particularly affect travel in NSW. It means you can't, for example, use a Sydney-Melbourne bus to get somewhere in NSW only.

DRIVING

Australia is a big, sprawling country with large cities where public transport is not always very comprehensive or convenient. Like America the car is the accepted means of getting from A to B and many visitors will consider getting wheels to explore the country — either buying a car or renting one.

Driving in Australia holds few real surprises. We drive on the left hand side of the road just like in England, Japan and most countries in south and east Asia and the Pacific. There are a few local variations from the rules of the road as applied elsewhere in the west. The main one is the 'give way to the right' rule. This means that if you're driving along a main road and somebody appears in a minor road on your right you must give way to them — unless they have a stop sign or give way sign against them. This rule caused such confusion over the years — with cars zooming out of tiny tracks onto main highways and expecting everything to screech to a stop for them — that more and more intersections are now being signposted to indicate which is the priority road. It's wise to be careful because while almost every intersection will be signposted in southern capitals when you get up to towns in the north of Queensland stop signs will still be few and far between and the old give way rules will apply.

The give way ruling has a special and very confusing interpretation in Victoria where if two cars travelling in opposite directions both turn into the same street the vehicle turning across the other lane has priority — see diagram. This causes no end of headaches and confusion and only seems to apply in Victoria. There's another special hazard in Melbourne — trams. You can only overtake trams on the inside and must stop behind them when they stop to pick up or drop off passengers. In central Melbourne there are also a number of intersections where a special technique, mastered only by native Melbournians, must be employed when making right hand turns. You must turn from the left hand side of the road. Be careful of trams, they weigh about as much as the Queen Mary and do not swerve to miss foolish drivers.

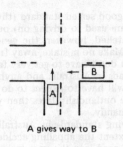

A gives way to B

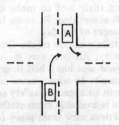

In Victoria A must give way to B

The general speed limit in built up areas in Australia is 60 kph (about 38 mph) and out on the open highway it's usually 100 or 110 kph (60 to 70 mph) depending on the state. The police have radar speed traps and are very fond of using them in carefully hidden location in order to raise easy revenue — don't exceed the speed limits in inviting areas where the gentlemen in blue may be waiting for you. On the other hand when you get very far from the cities and traffic is light you'll see a lot of vehicles moving a lot faster than 100 kph.

NEXT 5 km

On the Road

Australia is not criss-crossed by multi-lane highways with cars in profusion. There simply isn't enough traffic and the distances are too great to justify it. You'll certainly find stretches of divided road, particularly on busy routes like the Sydney-Melbourne Hume Highway or close to the state capitals — the last stretch into Adelaide from Melbourne, the Pacific Highway from Sydney to Newcastle, the Surfers Paradise-Brisbane road, for example. In general, however, Australian roads are of good sealed standard (though a long way from the billiard table surfaces the poms are used to driving on) on all the main routes. Many roads are rather bumpy and patched, however, the generally light traffic makes it hard to justify perfect roads. Make no mistake, away from the cities traffic is generally light.

You don't have to get very far off the beaten track, however, to find yourself on dirt roads in Australia and anybody who sets out to see the country in reasonable detail will have to expect to do some dirt road travelling. And if you really want to explore outlandish places then you'd better plan on four-wheel drive and having a winch handy.

Driving standards in Australia aren't exactly the highest in the world but to a large extent the appalling accident rate is due to the habit of country drivers flying off the road into the gum trees. Suitably boozed. Drive carefully, especially on the weekend evenings when the drinking drivers are about. Note also that the police are doing their best to make drinking and driving a foolish practice even if you don't hit something. Random breath tests and goodbye licence if you exceed '.05' are the order of the day.

Australia was one of the first countries in the world to make wearing seat belts compulsory. All new cars in Australia are required to have belts back and front and if your seat has a belt then you're required to wear it. You're liable to be fined if you don't. In some states small children are only allowed in the front seats if belted into an approved safety seat.

Petrol is available from stations sporting all the well-known international brand names. Prices vary from place to place and price war to price war but generally it's in the 40 to 45c a litre range (say around $1.80 to $2 an imperial gallon). In the outback the price can soar and some outback garages are not above exploiting their monopoly position. Distances between fill ups can be long in the outback and in some remote areas deliveries can be haphazard — it's not unknown to finally arrive at that 'nearest station x hundred km' only to find there's no fuel until next week's delivery!

Although overseas driving licences are acceptable in Australia for genuine overseas visitors an International Driving Permit is even more acceptable. Between cities signposting on the main roads is generally quite OK but around cities it's usually absymal. You can spend a lot of time trying to find street name signs and as for signs indicating which way to go to leave the city — you're half way to Sydney from Melbourne before you see the first sign telling you you're travelling in the right direction.

Buying a Car

If you want to explore Australia by car and you haven't got one or can't borrow one then you've either got to buy one or rent one. Australian cars are not cheap — it's a factor of the small population once again. Locally manufactured cars are made in uneconomically small quantities and imported cars are heavily taxed so they won't undercut the local products. If you're buying a second hand vehicle reliability is all important. Mechanical breakdowns way out in the outback can be very inconvenient — the nearest mechanic can be a hell of a long way down the road.

Shopping around for a used car involves much the same rules as anywhere in the western world but with a few local variations. First of all used car dealers in Australia are just like used car dealers anywhere in the world from Los Angeles to London — they'd sell their mother into slavery if it turned a dollar. For any given car you'll probably get it cheaper buying privately through newspaper small ads rather than through a car dealer. Buying through a dealer does give you the advantage of locally legislated guarantees but a guarantee is not much use if you're buying a car in Sydney and intending to set off from Perth next week. Used car guarantee requirements vary from state to state, check with the local automotive organisation.

There's much discussion amongst travellers about where is the best place to buy used cars. Popular theories exist that you can buy a car in Sydney or Melbourne, drive it to Darwin and sell it there for a profit. Or was it vice versa? It's quite possible that car values do vary from place to place but don't count on turning it to your advantage. What is rather more certain is that the further you get from civilisation the better it is to be in a Holden. New cars can be a whole different ball game, of course, but if you're in an older vehicle, something that's likely to have the odd hiccup from time to time, then life is much simpler if it's a Holden. When your fancy Japanese car goes kaput somewhere back of Bourke it's likely to be a two week wait while the new bit arrives fresh from Fukuoka. On the other hand when your rusty old Holden goes bang there's probably another old Holden sitting in the ditch by the roadside with a perfectly good widget waiting to be removed. Every scrap yard in Australia is full of good ole Holdens.

Note that in Australia third party personal injury insurance is always included in the vehicle registration cost. This ensures that every vehicle (so long as it's currently registered) carries at least minimum insurance. You're wise to extend that minimum to at least third party property insurance as well — minor collisions with Rolls-Royces can be surprisingly expensive. When you come to buy or sell a car there are usually some local regulations to be complied with. In Victoria, for example, a car has to have a compulsory safety check (roadworthiness certificate) before it can be registered in the new owner's name — usually the seller will indicate that the car already has a 'RWC'. In NSW, on the other hand, safety checks are compulsory every year when you come to renew the registration. Stamp duty has to be paid when you buy a car and since this is based on the purchase price it's fairly common for sellers and buyers to agree privately to understate the price! It's much easier to sell a car in the same state it's registered in. Otherwise it has to be re-registered in the new state.

Finally make use of the automotive organisations — see the Information section for more details about them. They can advise you on any local regulations or restrictions you should be aware of, can advise you in general about buying a car and, most important, for a fee will check a used car over and report on its condition before you agree to purchase it.

Renting a Car

If you've got the cash there are plenty of car rental companies ready and willing to put you behind the wheel. Competition in the Australian car rental business is pretty fierce so rates tend to be very variable and lots of special deals pop up and disappear again. Whatever your mode of travel on the long stretches it can be very useful to have a car for some local travel. Between a group it can even be reasonably economical and there are some places — like around Alice Springs — where if you haven't got your own wheels you really have to choose between a tour and a rented vehicle since there is no public transport and the distances are too great for walking or even bicycles.

The three major companies are Budget, Hertz and Avis with offices in almost every town bigger than one pub and a general store. The second string companies which are also represented almost everywhere in the country are Thrifty and National. Then there are a vast number of local firms or firms with outlets in a limited number of locations. You can take it as read that the big operators will generally have higher rates than the local firms but it ain't necessarily so, so don't jump to conclusions. The big firms have a number of big advantages, however. First of all they're the ones at the airports — three car rental companies are allowed to be represented at each airport and those three are almost always Budget and Hertz with Thrifty usually the third company although in some places Avis take the third desk. If you want to pick up a car or leave a car at an airport then they're the best ones to deal with. In some, but not all, airports other companies can also arrange to pick up or leave their cars there. It tends to depend on how convenient the airport is.

The second advantage of the big companies is if you want to do a one-way rental — pick it up in Adelaide, leave it in Sydney. There are, however, a variety of restrictions on these. Usually it's a minimum hire period rather than repositioning charges. If you want to go from A to B you're better off with Budget who require a minimum hire of two days for less than 400 km, three days for more than 400 km. Hertz require a minimum of three days. Avis and Thrifty are so expensive you might as well forget it. One-way rentals are only available on the civilised east coast — you can't hire in Sydney and leave in Perth, Darwin or Alice Springs.

The major companies all offer unlimited km rates in the city but in country and 'remote' areas it's flat charge plus so many cents per km. The big companies all go on about how economical they are and what great cars they've got. You can take most of it with the usual pinch of scepticism, during the course of researching this book I even rented a clunker from Hertz with over 100,000 km on the clock which would have been rejected by rent-a-wreck. If you just want a straightforward city rental Thrifty are usually the cheapest but they're not very keen on you renting a car in downtown Melbourne and driving it to the black stump and back. Nor do they like their cars starting in A and going to B. In those cases you're better with Budget. Hertz try and charge similar prices to Budget. Avis are generally the most expensive in every way.

The chart below shows you typical rates for smaller cars.

		Avis	Budget	Hertz	Thrifty
small car	city	$29-38	$26-33	$26-33	$22
	country	$41-44	$31-38	$38	$30
	remote	$45-48	$43	$43	$31
medium car	city	$42	$39	$39	$24-26
	country	$48	$44	$44	$32-34
	remote	$52	$49	$49	$33-36

city rates	unlimited km
country rates	Avis includes 200 km, excess at 22c a km all others 250 km, excess at 18c a km
remote rates	includes 100 km, excess Avis 22c a km, all others 18c a km

Small cars are typically Geminis, Colts or Lasers. Geminis are the same as a Chevrolet Chevette, Vauxhall Chevette or the old Opel Kadett. Colts are the smaller Mitsubishi car (Mitsubishi is known in some markets as Colt and Colts are known in some markets as Mirages). Lasers are the same as a Mazda 323, known in the US as a Mazda GLC.

Medium cars are typically Sigmas, Bluebirds or Camiras. Sigmas are the larger Mitsubishi car. Bluebirds are Datsun 200s. Camiras are the same as a Vauxhall Cavalier, Opel Ascona, Chevrolet Cavalier or Pontiac J-2000.

There are a whole collection of other thoughts about this rent-a-car business. For a start if you're going to want it for a week, a month or longer then they all have lower rates. If you're in Tasmania, where competition is very fierce, there are often lower rates especially in the low-season. If you're in the really remote outback (some places like Darwin and Alice Springs are only vaguely remote) then the choice of cars is likely to be limited to the larger, more expensive ones. Daily insurance is usually an extra $6. You usually must be at least 21 to hire an Avis or Hertz car, 23 for Budget, 25 for Thrifty.

Finally, with the big companies, look for special deals. In the big cities, where most cars are hired to businessmen from Monday to Friday, there are often special weekend rates. Budget even offers a 'standby' rate. Keep your eyes open and there may be special one-way hires available — while researching this edition I even saw cars offered free in Townsville, so long as you got them to Cairns within 24 hours!

OK, that's the big hire companies, what about all the rest of them? Well some of them are still pretty big in terms of numbers of shiny new cars. In Tasmania, for example, the car hire business is really big since many people don't bring their cars with them. There's a plethora of hire companies and lots of competition. In many cases local companies are markedly cheaper than the big boys but in others what looks like a cheaper rate can end up quite the opposite if you're not careful. Quick, what's cheaper $30 a day or $12 a day plus 12c a km in excess 100 km — if you do 200 km? And if you do 300? A recent upheaval in the local rental business is the proliferation of 'rent-a-wreck' companies. They specialise in renting older cars — at first they really were old and a flat figure like $10 a day and forget the insurance was the usual story. Now many of them have a variety of cars from not too old, through reasonably old to very old and a variety of rates to go with them. If you just want to travel around the city or not too far out they can be worth considering.

Mokes

In lots of popular holiday areas — like on the Gold Coast, around Cairns, on Magnetic Island, around Alice Springs, in Darwin — right at the bottom of the rent-a-car rates will be the ubiquitous Moke. To those not in the know a Moke is a totally open vehicle looking rather like a miniature Jeep. They're based on the Mini so they're front-wheel drive not four-wheel drive and are not suitably for getting way the hell off the beaten track. But for general good fun in places with a sunny climate they simply can't be beat. No vehicle has more air-conditioning than a Moke. And as the stickers say 'Moking is not a wealth hazard', they cover lots of km on a litre of petrol. If you do hire a Moke a few points to watch — don't have an accident in one, they offer little more protection than a motor-

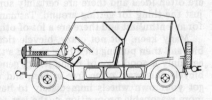

cycle. There is absolutely no place to lock things up so don't leave your valuables inside. And the fuel tanks are equally accessible so if you're leaving it somewhere at night beware of petrol thieves — not that there are a great number in Australia but it does happen.

Renting Other Vehicles

There are lots of other vehicles you can rent apart from cars. In remote outback areas you can often rent four-wheel drive vehicles. In many places you can rent campervans, they're particularly popular in Tasmania. Motorcycles are also available in a number of locations — they're particularly popular on Magnetic Island for example. Hertz also rent the whole range of Yamaha motorcycles from selected outlets but they're fairly pricey. Best of all in many places you can rent bicycles — many Australian cities now have special bike tracks and often a bicycle will be the ideal way of getting around. Much easier than walking, no hassles with parking, altogether an ideal way of seeing a city so long as the hills aren't too steep or the traffic too horrendous. In the course of researching this edition I rented bicycles in half a dozen places as widely scattered as Surfers Paradise, Darwin and Broome.

BIKING

Motorcycles are a very popular way of getting around although the accident rate is also rather frightening — due to the practice of letting novice riders start learning on multi-cylinder super-bikes? The climate is just about ideal for biking most of the year and the long open roads are really made for large capacity highway cruisers. Maureen and I have ridden two-up from Melbourne all the way to Darwin (via Sydney-Brisbane-Cairns-Cooktown-Mt Isa-The Alice-Ayers Rock) on a 250 cc trail bike so doing it on a small bike is not impossible, just more boring.

Doing it on a pushbike is closer to being impossible — or at least impossible to any normal reasonably sane human being! Yes, plenty of people have ridden push-bikes around Australia but you have to have a large helping of masochism and a fair share of nuttiness in your character to attempt it. Round cities, however, bicycles are often ideal and there are certainly some places where the old pushbike can be just the thing for getting around. Tasmania, for example, is certainly bikeable size for an enthusiast and there are a lot of other compact areas worth considering.

Many keen, but not crazy, bicycle riders see Australia by riding the interesting bits and then putting their bike aboard a train, bus or plane for the dull bits. That is certainly a good way of doing it. It's generally not too expensive to transport your bicycle this way, often free in fact, and when you get to your destination you've got your own wheels immediately to hand. Bike rental has also become a much more reasonable proposition in the last few years — you can now hire bikes by the hour, day or longer period in a great number of locations around the country.

Travelling around Australia is city and country, old and new.

a. The classic view of Sydney, looking from North Sydney across to Sydney city centre with the Harbour Bridge and the Opera House.

b. In complete contrast rolling green fields near Byron Bay in the north of New South Wales.

c. Old meets new in the centre of Perth, Western Australia.

HITCHING

Travel by thumb may be frowned upon by the boys in blue in some places but it can be a good way of getting around and it is certainly interesting. Sometimes it can even be fast but usually it is foolish to try and set yourself deadlines when travelling this way — you are depending on luck. Successful hitching depends on several factors, all of them just plain good sense.

Most important is your numbers — two people is really the ideal, any more makes things very difficult. Those two should be one male and one female — two guys hitching together can expect long waits. Women's lib or not I do not recommend ladies hitching unaccompanied and a girl should never ever hitch solo.

Factor two is position and appearance — look for a place where vehicles will be going slowly and where they can stop easily. A junction or freeway slip road are good places if there is stopping room. Position goes beyond just where you stand, the ideal location is on the outskirts of a town — hitching from way out in the country is as hopeless as from the centre of a city. Take a bus out to the edge of town. The ideal appearance for hitching is a sort of genteel poverty — threadbare but clean. Looking too good can be as much of a bummer as too bad! And don't carry too much gear — if it looks like it's going to take half an hour to pack your bags aboard you'll be left on the roadside.

Factor three is knowing when to say no. Saying no to a car load of drunks or your friendly rapist is pretty obvious but it can be time saving to say no to a short ride that might take you from a good hitching point to a lousy one. Wait for the right, long ride to come along.

Hitching in Australia is really very easy, we are supposed to be friendly remember, and if you can take care with your rides is reasonably safe. Of course people do get stuck in outlandish places but that is the name of the game. If you're visiting from abroad a nice prominent flag on your pack will help, a sign announcing your destination can also be useful. Uni and youth hostel noticeboards are good places to look for hitching partners. The main law against hitching is 'thou shalt not stand in the road' — so when you see the law coming, step back.

SHIPPING

Not really. Once upon a time there was quite a busy coastal shipping service but now it only applies to freight and apart from specialised bulk carriers even that is declining rapidly. The only regular shipping service is between Victoria and Tasmania and unless you are taking a vehicle with you the very cheapest ticket on that often choppy route is not all that much cheaper than the air-fare. You can occasionally travel between Australian ports on a line bound for somewhere but very few people do that.

ACT

A
B | C

a. Gar's Mahal, the sumptuous High Court building on the shores of Lake Burley Griffin in Canberra.

b. Beside the War Memorial in Canberra stands the twisted remains of a Japanese miniature submarine, sunk in Sydney Harbour during WW II.

c. Looking from the front of the War Memorial a wide avenue looks directly towards Parliament House, across the lake.

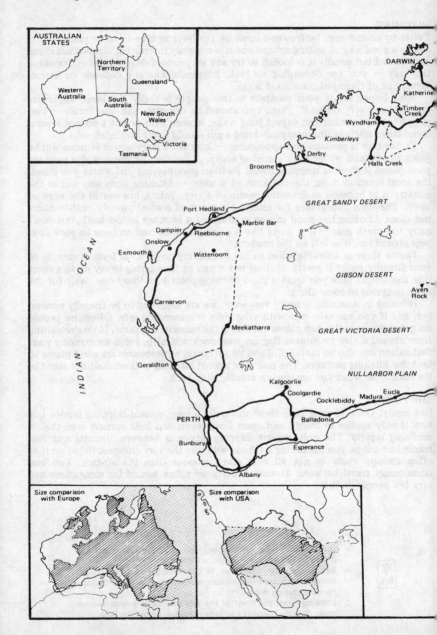

AUSTRALIAN STATES

Western Australia

Northern Territory

Queensland

South Australia

New South Wales

Victoria

Tasmania

DARWIN

Katherine

Timber Creek

Wyndham

Kimberleys

Derby

Halls Creek

Broome

Port Hedland

GREAT SANDY DESERT

Dampier   Marble Bar

Onslow   Roebourne

Exmouth

Wittenoom

INDIAN OCEAN

GIBSON DESERT

Carnarvon

Ayers Rock

GREAT VICTORIA DESERT

Meekatharra

Geraldton

NULLARBOR PLAIN

Kalgoorlie

Coolgardie   Madura

Cocklebiddy   Eucla

PERTH

Balladonia

Bunbury   Esperance

Albany

Size comparison with Europe

Size comparison with USA

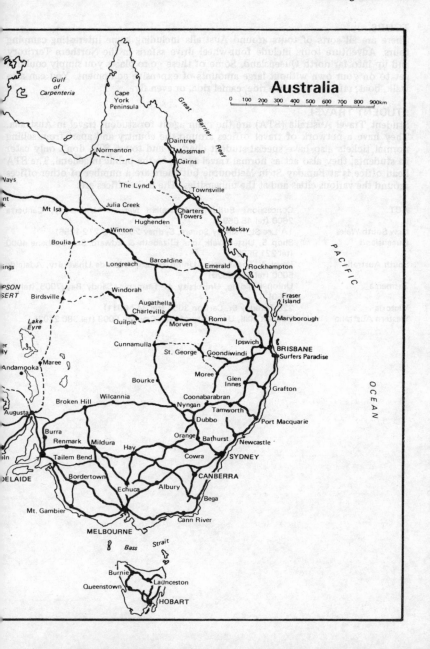

TOURS

There are all sorts of tours around Australia including some interesting camping tours. Adventure tours include four-wheel drive safaris in the Northern Territory and up into far north Queensland. Some of these go to places you simply couldn't get to on your own without large amounts of expensive equipment. You can also walk, boat, raft, canoe, horse ride, camel ride, or even fly.

STUDENT TRAVEL

Student Travel Australia (STA) are the main agent for student travel in Australia. They have a network of travel offices around the country and apart from selling normal tickets also have special student charters and tours. STA don't only cater to students, they also act as normal travel agents to the public in general. The STA head office is at Faraday St in Melbourne but there are a number of other offices around the various cities and at the universities. The main offices are:

ACT	Concessions Building, Australian National University, Canberra 2600 (tel 48 6591)
New South Wales	1A Lee St, Railway Square, Sydney 2000 (tel 212 1255)
Queensland	Shop 5, Ulster Walk, cnr Elizabeth & Edward Sts, Brisbane 4000 (tel 221 9629)
South Australia	Level 4, The Arcade, Union House, Adelaide University, Adelaide 5000 (tel 223 6620)
Tasmania	Union Building, University of Tasmania, Sandy Bay 7005 (tel 34 1850)
Victoria	220 Faraday St, Carlton 3053 (tel 347 6911)
Western Australia	Hackett Hall, University of WA, Crawley 6009 (tel 380 2302)

Australian Capital Territory

Area 2366 square km
Population 230,000

Don't miss: the national capital, a beautiful planned city with monuments, museums, a brand new art gallery and Australia's parliament house.

Like many other world capitals, Canberra is a planned city. When the separate colonies of Australia were federated in 1901 and became states the decision to build a national capital was part of the constitution. Not until 1908 was the site selected, diplomatically situated between arch rivals Sydney and Melbourne, and an international competition to design the capital was won by the American architect Walter Burley Griffin. In 1911 the commonwealth government bought up the land of the ACT, Australian Capital Territory, and in 1913 decided to call the capital Canberra, believed to be an Aboriginal term for 'meeting place'.

Early development of the site was painfully slow due to WW I. Not until 1927 did parliament first convene in the capital, in the interim Melbourne acted as the national capital. Then the depression again virtually halted development and it was not until after WW II that things really got underway. In the '50s, '60s and '70s progress was incredible and for some time Canberra was Australia's fastest growing city. Satellite cities sprang up at Belconnen and Woden and in 1960 the population topped 50,000, sprinted to 100,000 by 1967 and today is around the 200,000 mark.

The city is unlike other large Australian metropolises both for its amazingly orderly neatness and because it is inland — not a coastal city. Canberra is still principally a place of government and public services, there are few local industries. The population is fairly young and you are no distance at all from good bushwalking country in the NSW winter snowfields.

INFORMATION

The Canberra Tourist Bureau only has a couple of offices, unlike the other state tourist offices which seem to have scattered all over. In Melbourne you can also get information on Canberra from the NSW Government Travel Centre, however.

ACT	Canberra Tourist Bureau, cnr London Circuit & West Row, Canberra City, ACT 2601 (tel 49 7555)
NSW	Canberra Tourist Bureau, 9 Elizabeth St, Sydney, NSW 2000 (tel 233 3180)
Victoria	c/- NSW Government Travel Centre, 345 Little Collins St, Melbourne, Vic 3000 (tel 60 1378)

ACTIVITIES

Bushwalking The Canberra Bushwalking Club's address is PO Box 160, Canberra. A book called *25 Family Bushwalks in & around Canberra* by Graeme Barrow can be found in most city bookshops for about $4. Several of the parks and reserves in the south of the ACT have good bushwalks. Tidbinbilla Fauna Reserve has marked trails, other good

69

areas include Mt Kelly-Gudgenby, around Cotter Reserve and Mt Franklin.

Boating Canoes, paddleboats and sailing boats can be rented by the hour or longer periods from Dobell's Boat Hire, Ferry Wharf, Acton, so you can get out on Lake Burley Griffin. They're only open on weekends, though, except during school holidays. The Canberra Rowing Club (tel 88 7782) and the YMCA Canoe Club (tel 49 8733) both welcome visitors. The YMCA Sailing Club (tel 81 1396) will tell you about YMCA organised races. A brochure on safety procedure and weather conditions on the lake is available — no powerboats are permitted on the lake.

Bicycling Canberra has a series of bicycle tracks — they are probably the best and most extensive bike riding facilities in Australia. A map of the Canberra Cycle Ways is available, as is a brochure called *Canberra: on a Bike Tour*. You can rent bikes from the youth hostel or from Mr Spokes Bike Hire (tel

81 3250) near the Acton Ferry Terminal.

Skiing The NSW Snowy Mountain snowfields are within four hours easy drive of Canberra so check the NSW section for info. The ACTTB can supply the latest news on conditions, as can the YMCA (tel 49 8733) who also have lodges at Guthega and Thredbo. A number of local garages, as well as the conventional ski shops, hire out equipment.

Swimming & Diving It's a 150 km drive to the nearest surf beaches at Bateman's Bay in NSW — there's a daily bus service. There are a number of swimming pools around the city plus river or lake swimming at Kambah Pool (21 km), Pine Island (27 km on the Murrumbidgee River) and Casuarina Sands (19 km near Cotter Dam). There's even one nude bathing stretch along the Murrumbidgee. Swimming in Lake Burley Griffin is not recommended. There are some good skindiving areas around Bateman's Bay.

CANBERRA CITY
The capital is an amazingly orderly and planned looking place. There's no gradual disintegration into a jumble of used car lots as you get further from the centre. In fact it's so squeaky clean and artificial looking that the city has a very mixed reputation in Australia. Its popular image is of a soul-less string of suburbs, a playground for politicians and public servants who, if they're far enough up the scale, jet away to somewhere more interesting come the weekend. There's probably still a fair bit of truth in that image but Canberra today is becoming more and more a real city yet it's still as basically attractive as ever.

Information
The Canberra Tourist Bureau (tel 49 7555) is in the Jolimont Centre on Northbourne Avenue. It's open Monday to Friday 8.30 am to 5.15 pm, Saturday 9 to 11.30 am and has a good collection of brochures and information leaflets. By the time this is in print the Jolimont Centre should be complete. It will also house TAA, the Canberra City Post Office and will be the departure point for Greyhound and most other bus services, but not Ansett Pioneer. The Jolimont Centre is the block bounded by Northbourne Avenue, Alinga St, Moore St and Rudd St.

There's another information centre at Northbourne Avenue, Dickson, which you pass as you drive into the city. The NRMA (tel 49 6666) has an office at 92 Northbourne Avenue where you can get a copy of their excellent map of Canberra.

The YHA has a useful walking tour leaflet. There is a university information centre at Balmain Crescent, Acton with an info noteboard. The Petrie Plaza and Monaro Mall shopping complexes both have community notice boards. Check the interesting notice board in the Alternative Bookshop too. As a capital should be Canberra is well stocked with overseas information centres and libraries — good places to keep up with foreign magazines, papers and films. For detailed information on Canberra it may be worth purchasing *The Canberra Handbook*, published by ANU and retailing for $2.75. Canberra has a number of good bookshops, Dalton's in Garema Place is probably the best.

If you're getting mail sent to you in Canberra have it addressed to poste restante at the Canberra City post office rather than the GPO Canberra, which is inconveniently situated behind the parliament building.

Orientation

Canberra is neatly divided into two parts by the very natural looking Lake Burley Griffin — which in actual fact is artificial. The north side of the lake can be thought of as the living part and the south side as the working part. Today, as Canberra expands in all directions, that's a haphazard description but it will do since for the short-term visitor most accommodation is to the north while the major government attractions are principally to the south.

The huge circle north of the lake, Vernon Circle, is the centre point for the north side. Close to this circle you will find the tourist office, post office, airline and bus terminals, and the shops and restaurants of the Civic Centre, Canberra's oldest and most established

shopping centre. The fine old merry-go-round is in the centre.

From Vernon Circle, Commonwealth Avenue runs arrow straight across the lake to Capital Circle, the future site of the new parliament building. Capital Circle is the apex of Walter Burley Griffin's parliamentary triangle — bordered by Commonwealth Avenue, King's Avenue and the lake. Most of the government buildings are concentrated within this triangle including the National Library, the High Court, the National Gallery and the old Parliament building. King's Avenue also runs across the lake to the north side.

Lookouts

The hills that range around the city provide fine views of the artificial lake that more or less divides the government working area from the public living area as well as across the city itself. Try 825 metre Black Mountain topped by the controversial 195 metre Telecom Telecommunications Tower. It's even got a, wait for it, revolving restaurant on the top. According to reports the food is the revolving restaurant norm — expensive and far inferior to the views. The view alone costs $1 and is available from 9 am to 10 pm.

There are good bushwalks around the mountain. Apart from the 9 am Canberra Explorer bus there is no public transport up the hill. Between a group a taxi to the top wouldn't be too expensive or you can walk up there — quite a pleasant stroll apart from the mad traffic.

Other mountain viewpoints, all with roads running up to the top, are 722 metre Red Hill, 840 metre Mount Ainslie and 665 metre Mount Pleasant. Mount Ainslie is close to the city on the north-east side and has particularly fine views across the city and out over the airport — you can see the Ansett and TAA aircraft lining up behind each other. From up top you'll also appreciate what a green and park-like city Canberra is.

Lake Burley Griffin
The artificial lake around which the city is built was named after Canberra's original designer but the lake was not finally created, by damming the Molonglo River which flows through Canberra, until 1963. Although the lake is not recommended for swimming you can go boating on the lake (hire boats from beside the Acton Ferry Terminal) or bike ride around it (bikes available from the same place), plus there are a number of places of interest around the lake. The shoreline of the lake extends for 35 km.

Most visible is the **Captain Cook Memorial Water Jet** which flings six tonnes of water 140 metres into the air and will give you a free shower if the wind is in the right direction — despite an automatic switch-off device if the wind speed gets too high. The huge water jet usually operates from 10 am to 12 noon and 2 to 4 pm daily and was built in 1970 to commemorate the bicentenary of Cook's visit to Australia. On the shoreline at Regatta Point is a skeleton globe, three metres in diameter, with Cook's three great voyages of discovery traced out.

The **Regatta Point Development Display** is open daily from 9 am to 5 pm and has models, illustrations and audiovisual displays of the growth of the capital. Further round the lake is **Blundell's Cottage** which dates from 1858, long before the selection of the area as the capital site and even longer before a lake suddenly appeared beside it. The simple stone and slab cottage is a reminder of the city's early history as a farming area. It's now maintained as a small museum and is open 2 to 4 pm daily and 10 am to 12 noon on Wednesdays.

A little further around the lake is the **Carillon** on Aspen Island. The 53-bell

Canberra

200 0 200 600m

🚉 Central Station

✉ GPO

1 Botanic Gardens
2 Institute of Anatomy
3 Ferry Terminal, Bike & Boat Hire
4 Parliament Building
5 Site of New Parliament

tower was a gift from Britain on Canberra's 50th anniversary in 1963. Completed in 1970 the bells weigh from seven kg all the way to over six tonnes. There is a carillon recital on Sundays from 2.45 to 3.30 pm and guided tours of the tower are available on Sundays from 9 am to 2 pm, Saturdays and public holidays from 1 to 4 pm.

The lake is bordered on the northeast side, from Regatta Point to the Carillon, by Commonwealth Park while to the north-west Black Mountain Peninsula juts out into the lake. The parliamentary triangle fronts on to the lake on the south-east side and several of the most impressive new government buildings are sited along the lakeside here.

Old Parliament House
It's another indicator of Canberra's initial slow development that the Parliament building is just a 'temporary' one. Walter Burley Griffin's original plan included a parliamentary triangle which would include all the major government offices. Only in the last 20 years have they all started to appear in this triangle and the 'permanent' parliament will eventually stand at the apex of the triangle. The present building was the result of a 1923 competition and was opened in 1927.

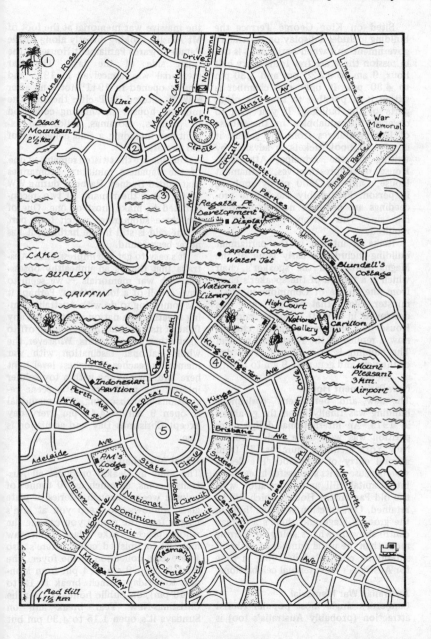

Sited on King George Terrace the building includes a display on Australia's government and when parliament is not in session there are free tours every half hour, 9 am to 12.30 pm and 1.30 pm to 4.30 pm. If only one chamber is sitting it is possible to tour the other parts of the building. If you wish to observe the squabbles in the House of Representatives from the gallery it is wise to book tickets in advance by writing to the Principal Attendant, House of Representatives, Parliament House, Canberra 2600 or by applying in person. Presumably the Senate proceedings are nowhere near as interesting since no advance ticketing is required.

Items of interest in the parliament building include an early issue of the Magna Carta and the speaker's chair which is a replica of the speaker's chair from the House of Commons in Westminster. Since that original chair was destroyed in WW II in an air raid the House of Commons' speaker's chair is now a replica of the Australian replica! The building is open almost every day of the year and generally 9 am to 5 pm.

New Parliament House

The new, and 'permanent', parliament building was finally given the go-ahead in 1979. An international design competition was won by a design from a New York architect, number 177 from a total entry of over 300. The design won because of its successful integration into Capital Hill and its relation with the old Parliament House, which will be retained. Construction is at the 'hole in the ground' stage and there's a display centre showing what's going on. Barring more than the usual number of strikes it should be completed in 1988, in time for Australia's bicentennial celebrations.

Australian War Memorial

Canberra's single most popular tourist attraction (probably Australia's too) is the massive war memorial at the foot of Mt Ainslie, looking directly along Anzac Parade towards Parliament House on the other side of the lake. The war memorial was conceived in 1925 and finally opened in 1941; not long after WW II entered its Pacific theatre. The museum houses an amazing collection of pictures, dioramas, relics and exhibitions including a fine collection of old aircraft.

Outside are the twisted remains of one of the Japanese miniature submarines that raided Sydney Harbour during WW II. Or rather the remains of two, reconstructed to make most of one. One of the three submarines which took part in the raid is still in the harbour, it has never been found.

It's easy to get the impression in Australia that there's an unhealthy obsession with war memorials — we seem to have a hell of a lot of them. Perhaps it has something to do with Australia coming together as a nation not through any fight of its own but through going off to fight other peoples' wars. Whatever, the whole national fascination with war memorials reaches its highest level right here and for anyone with a toy soldier interest the miniature battle scene recreations are absorbing. The memorial is open 9 am to 4.45 pm every day except Christmas Day and admission is free.

Royal Australian Mint

The mint in Deakin produces all Australia's coins, as much as 70 tonnes of coins a week. Through a series of plate glass windows (to keep you at arm's length from the ready) you can see the whole process take place from raw material to finished coins. There's also a rare coin collection in the foyer. The mint is open 9 am to 4 pm from Monday to Friday (lunch break is 12 to 12.40 pm), on public holidays, over the Christmas-New Year break and on Sundays it's open 1.15 to 4.30 pm but no coins are produced.

National Library

On Parkes Place beside Lake Burley Griffin the National Library is probably the most elegant building in Canberra. The library has a number of displays including rare books, paintings, early manuscripts and maps plus a cannon from Cook's ship the *Endeavour* and a fine model of the ship. The foyer is dominated by three huge tapestries. The library's exhibition area is open 9 am to 10 pm Monday to Friday, 9 am to 4.15 pm Saturdays, Sundays and public holidays. There are guided tours Monday to Friday at 11.15 am and 2.15 pm.

Embassies

With Canberra's slow development as the capital it was hardly surprising that embassies were slow to show up here, preferring to stay in the established cities, particularly Sydney and Melbourne, until Canberra was really there. The British High Commission was the first diplomatic office in Canberra in 1936, followed by the US Embassy in 1940. Today there are about 60 High Commissions (what Commonwealth countries have instead of embassies) and embassies in Canberra.

Enthusiasts for embassy-spotting can pick up the tourist office's *Embassies in Canberra* folder or buy *Canberra's Embassies* by Graeme Barrow (Australian National University Press) which is a useful little guidebook to the city's diplomatic offices. A few of them are worth looking at although many of Canberra's embassies operate from nondescript suburban houses. The US Embassy, however, is a splendid facsimile of a Williamsburg, Virginia mansion — a style of architecture which in turn owes much to English Georgian.

Although, as you might expect, the South African Embassy gets its fair share of protests the building is an im-

posing structure on State Circle. The Thai Embassy, with its pointed, orange-tiled roof, is in a style similar to the typical Thai temples of Bangkok. The Indonesian Embassy is no architectural jewel but beside the dull embassy building there's a small display centre exhibiting Indonesia's colourful cultural activities. It's open 10 am to 12 noon and 2 to 4 pm; if you're lucky you might catch an impromptu shadow puppet play put on for a visiting school group. The steps up to the centre are flanked by Balinese stone temple guardian statues.

Papua New Guinea's High Commission looks like a 'haus tambaran' cult house from the Sepik River region of PNG. There's a display room with colour photos and artefacts, open weekdays from 10 am to 12 noon and from 2 to 4 pm. As for the British High Commission — that first diplomatic office in Canberra — the present building dates from 1953 but it's strictly dullsville.

Addresses of the embassies above plus some of the other embassies in Canberra which might be useful for a visitor include:

Austria	107 Endeavour St, Red Hill
Canada	Commonwealth Avenue, Yarralumla
Germany (W)	119 Empire Circuit, Yarralumla
Indonesia	8 Darwin Avenue, Yarralumla
Ireland	2nd floor, Bank House, Civic Square, Canberra City
Japan	112 Empire Circuit, Yarralumla
Malaysia	71 State Circle, Yarralumla
Netherlands	120 Empire Circuit, Yarralumla
New Zealand	Commonwealth Avenue, Yarralumla
Norway	3 Zeehan St, Red Hill
PNG	Forster Crescent, Yarralumla
Singapore	81 Mugga Way, Red Hill
South Africa	cnr State Circle & Rhodes Place, Yarralumla
Sweden	Turrana St, Yarralumla

Switzerland	7 Melbourne Avenue, Forrest
Thailand	111 Empire Circuit, Yarralumla
UK	Commonwealth Avenue, Yarralumla
USA	State Circle, Yarralumla

High Court

The High Court building on the lake side is open from 10 am to 4 pm daily. Opened in 1980 it's a structure of such grandiose magnificence that it has been dubbed 'Gar's Mahal' — a reference to Sir Garfield Barwick, the chief justice of the Australian High Court, who was primarily responsible for much of the grandeur over-kill. Truth to tell there is a touch of the Indian Moghul palace about the ornamental water streams burbling down beside the entrance path.

Australian National Gallery

On Parkes Place, beside the High Court and Lake Burley Griffin, the art gallery opened in 1982 after many years of build up. It started way back in the '70s when the gallery, which didn't even have a gallery at that time, paid a 'truly fabulous' sum for Blue Poles. More geewhiz purchases from time to time since that first big buy kept the gallery firmly in the public eye. It was worth it because the gallery is a fine building with a really superb collection of Australian art and collections from the rest of the world which are particularly strong post-1950 but form a good basis for further expansion prior to that time. Admission to the $50 million collection is $2 and, believe it or not, Burley Griffin had a gallery in his original plan. In fact not just one gallery, two of them!

Institute of Anatomy

On McCoy Circuit in Acton the Institute of Anatomy is opposite the Academy of Sciences and has exhibitions on, as the name suggests, anatomy plus another exhibition on the culture of Aboriginals and of the Melanesian people of Papua New Guinea. It's open from Monday to Saturday from 9 am to 5 pm, Sundays from 2 to 5 pm and holidays from 10 am to 4.30 pm.

Old Buildings

The Church of St John the Baptist was built between 1841 and 1845 and thus predates the city of Canberra. The stained glass windows in the church show pioneering families of the region. There is an adjoining school house with some early relics. Now the Royal Military College, Duntroon was once an early homestead, parts of it dating from the 1830s. On Denman St, Yarralumla, the old Canberra Brickworks is the site of the brickworks used for Canberra's early construction. You can see the brick kilns plus some old cars and steam engines. It's open daily.

Other Buildings

You can do no more than drive by and peek in the gates of the Prime Minister's Lodge — Australia's Number 10 Downing St or White House. Ditto for Government House at Yarralumla although there's a lookout beside Scrivener Dam at the end of the lake which gives a good view of the building, the Governor General's residence. Worth driving by is the building locally known as 'the Martian Embassy' — situated on McCoy Circuit in Acton the Australian Academy of Sciences does indeed look like a misplaced flying saucer. On Parkes Way the Australian-American Memorial is a 79-metre high shaft topped by an eagle, it's a memorial to US support for Australia during WW II. You can get a guide-yourself leaflet for the Australian National University from the Information Office opposite Union House. The university was founded in 1946. The Serbian Orthodox Church in Forrest has its walls and ceiling painted with a series of Biblical murals. Canberra also has a mosque, for the diplomatic staff from Islamic countries, on the corner of

Hunter St and Empire Circuit.

Botanic Gardens

Yes, a botanic garden was part of Walter Burley Griffin's grand plan too — a botanic garden dedicated to Australian native flora. Like so much of Canberra it took a long time for his vision to become a reality and planting only started in 1950 and the garden was finally officially opened in 1970. Situated on the lower slopes of Black Mountain the beautiful gardens have a couple of arrowed educational walks. One of the walks indicates plants used by Aboriginals and the uses they made of them. A highlight of the garden is the rainforest zone, achieved in Canberra's dry climate by a 'misting' system which creates a suitably damp environment in a gully. The gardens are reached from Clunies Ross St and are open 9 am to 5 pm daily. There are guided tours at 10 am and 2 pm on Sunday.

Places to Stay

Hostels The *Canberra Youth Hostel* (tel 48 9759) is at Dryanda St, O'Connor — about six km from the city centre. Nightly charges are $6 and there is a bus service to the city about every half hour (see Getting Around for details). Or you can hire bicycles at the hostel. It's a nice hostel, but the warden takes effort.

The *YWCA* is very central at 2 Mort St in the city (tel 47 3033). The hostel takes males and females, but it's essentially for solo travellers since there's only one mixed bedroom. Otherwise it's guys on one floor, girls on another. Charges are $11.50 per night in a shared double, $13.50 in a single, including breakfast, dinner costs $5. Sleeping bag accommodation in the recreation room is $4.50, a dorm bed is $9.50, and a flat, $26. If you are a permanent visitor, which means a stay of at least eight weeks, the rates are much lower.

Ainslie Village at the end of Quick St, Ainslie (tel 48 6931) is cheap (especially by the week), but a bit rough. It costs $18 per week or $9 per day — in either case there's an $8 linen charge, but if you have a sleeping bag you can avoid this. Breakfast is $1 and dinner $2.

The *Gowrie Private Hotel* (see Guest Houses & Private Hotels) has bunk rooms for $27.10 for two people.

Guest Houses & Private Hotels Just as you enter Canberra from Sydney or Melbourne on Northbourne Avenue, there are three prominently signposted guest houses. They are all much of a muchness in standards and prices. The *Chelsea Lodge* at 526 (tel 48 0655) costs $12 a night for bed & breakfast single, doubles from $18, cheaper rates by the week.

The *Blue & White Lodge* (which actually includes another guest house in the same building) at 524 (tel 48 0498) has a wide range of prices all including cooked breakfast. If you don't mind not having the room to yourself it's $8 Monday to Thursday, and $10 weekends, a double is $16 and $20 respectively, and for a room on your own for one person $10 and $12 respectively. At 522 *Platon Lodge* (tel 47 9139) costs are $12 single and $16 double, both bed & breakfast.

All three are plain and straightforward but clean, quite comfortable and in true Australian fashion the breakfast is very filling.

Closer to the city centre and north of Northbourne Avenue at 21 Stephen St, Ainslie (tel 47 9200) is *Tall Trees* where singles/doubles cost $16/19 without breakfast. Continental breakfast is $3, cooked breakfast $5. It's a little more expensive but then it's also a little bit nicer — a modern single floor building, centrally heated and situated in pleasant grounds.

Within easy walking distance of the

city centre, *Gowrie Private Hotel* is a large tower block at 210 Northbourne Ave, Braddon (tel 49 6033). It's an ex-government place with no less than 568 rooms. A single is $16.90 including breakfast and a bunkroom with two bunks $27.10 for two. There's a choice of dinner for around $3. You have to wander down the corridor to a bathroom but the place is very well equipped with cafeteria, recreation facilities, TV lounges, laundries and so on. *Macquarie Private Hotel*, across the lake at 18 National Circuit, Barton (tel 732325) has 500 rooms and the same setup and prices as Gowrie. There are a number of other guest houses around Canberra, but they're mostly not so conveniently situated or their prices are a lot higher.

Hotels There are a couple of hotels that aren't too expensive. *Hotel Civic* is right in town on Northbourne Ave (tel 48 7622) with singles/doubles at $15/26 room only. About 4.5 km out on the corner of Canberra Ave and Giles St in Kingston is the *Hotel Kingston* (tel 95 0481) with singles/doubles at $17/22.

Motels Most motels in Canberra are quite expensive. *Acacia Motor Lodge* at 65 Ainslie Ave has bed and light breakfast for $17 for one, $23 for two, and it's only 500 metres from the Civic Centre (tel 49 6955). *Motel 7* in Jerrabomberra Ave, Narrabundah (tel 95 1111) is about eight km out from the centre and excellent value. It's got most mod-cons, a swimming pool, 63 units and costs just $19 for a single, $22 for a double, room only. The rooms are small but the prices are lower. You can get there on a 323 bus.

Next up the price range would be a couple more motels in Canberra South: *Regency Motel* at McMillan Crescent, Griffith (tel 95 0074) where singles/doubles are $22/27; and *Good Motel* in Jerrabomberra Avenue again (tel 95 0174) where singles/doubles are $25/30.

Both are room only. Prices of other motels range upwards to the sky.

Colleges The Australian National University has quite a selection of residential places which may well have some room during May, August or the November to February uni vacations. Charges are $12 for students, $16 for non-students for a room and food. In fact they can't get enough people these days, so you may even get in in term time if you stay for a week or so. The Canberra College of Advanced Education also has a hostel, which takes students only and usually in groups of five or more. To find out what the story is check with:

Australian National University
   Ursula College (tel 48 0770)
   Bruce Hall (tel 49 2784)
   Burgmann College (tel 47 9811)
   Toad Hall* (tel 49 4722)
   Burton & Garran Halls* (tel 49 3082, 49 3137)

College of Advanced Education*
   Accommodation Officer (tel 52 2121)

* students only

Camping There are a couple of camping sites close to Canberra catering for people with tents. The *Canberra Lakes Carotel* (tel 41 1377) is 6½ km north of the city on the Sydney road. Tent sites here cost $6 for two people. There are also on-site vans from $20 for four people and a variety of chalets, flats and cabins from as little as $8 per person. The *South Side Motor Park* is eight km south of the city on the road to Queanbeyan and charges from $6 for two people with a tent. More rural camping (and cheaper too) can be found 22 km out at the Cotter Reserve.

Places to Eat
Canberra has a reasonable selection of

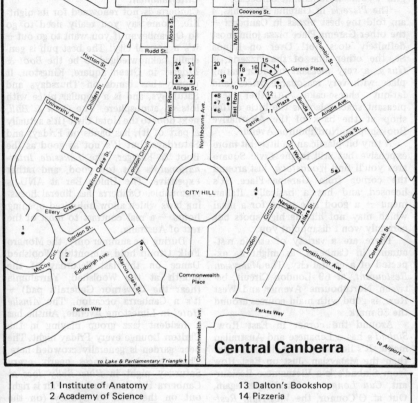

Central Canberra

1 Institute of Anatomy
2 Academy of Science
3 Lakeside International Hotel
4 Canberra Theatre Centre
5 Bushgear
6 Malaysian Restaurant
7 Alternative Bookshop
8 Private Bin Bistro
9 Sinbad's Restaurant
10 Action Info Centre (local buses)
11 Merry-go-Round
12 Woodstock Restaurant

13 Dalton's Bookshop
14 Pizzeria
15 Gus's
16 Angus & Robertson
17 YWCA
18 Civic Theatre
19 Hotel Civic
20 Ansett & Ansett Pioneer
21 Tourist Office
22 TAA
23 Post Office
24 Greyhound & Other Buses

eating places in and around Civic Square. The *Cock & Bull* by the Civic Hotel is good for lunch (noon to 2 pm) and pretty cheap. A notch expensive but absolutely enormous helpings at the *Private Bin* at 50 Northbourne Avenue.

Two other pub-food style places are the *Civic Hotel* on Northbourne Avenue and the *Ainslie Hotel* at the corner of Ainslie Avenue and Limestone Avenue — quite close to the War Memorial. The latter operates a 'choose your steak and grill it yourself' lunchtime barbecue.

The *Pizzeria* in Garema Place has, I am told the best pizzas in Canberra — the other Garema Place pizza joint most definitely does not! Over on Bunda St, the other side of the Pizzeria, is *Gus's*, a very pleasant outdoor eating place with very reasonable prices (and far-out cheese-cake). Another very pleasant snack place is the little coffee shop at the back of the Alternative Bookshop on Northbourne Avenue.

A tiny bit plastic and a little bit more expensive but still in the Civic Square area you'll find *Woodstock*, just around the corner from Garema Place. It's licensed and has a basically Italian menu — a good safe place for a meal which may not hit the high spots but certainly won't disappoint you.

There are a variety of ethnic restaurants in Canberra, as might be expected of a capital city. The *Malaysian Restaurant*, at 69 London Circuit, between Northbourne Avenue and West Row, is good with main courses around the $6 mark.

Around the corner in East Row, *Sinbad's* has a Lebanese and Australian menu. It's licensed, and a little cheaper than the Malaysian. Just up East Row from Sinbad's is a Vietnamese Restaurant, *Cuu Long* — a bit cheaper again. Out at O'Connor, the *Viet Nam Restaurant* at 1 Sargood St is good value and very popular. *Dalat* in Yarralumla is another Vietnamese place offering excellent value for money.

Cheap food can be found, as usual, at the union refectory in the university. Late night appetites are catered to by the *Tuckerbuses* (known as 'Dog Houses') which appear nightly at strategic spots like Belconnen Way before the Macquarie turn-off. They're open till very very late. *Dolly's*, at the corner of Marcus Clark St and Barry Drive is the best of the Tuckerbuses.

Entertainment

Canberra is not renowned for its nightlife. Some say you really need to go to Queanbeyan if you want to go out — it's a normal city! The best pub is generally acknowledged to be the *Boot & Flogger* in Green Square, Kingston. It usually has bands on Thursdays and Saturdays, and is a popular place with lots of atmosphere. The *Cock & Bull*, next door to the Hotel Civic (it's actually a part of it), has bands on Fridays and Saturdays, but it's not as good as the Boot & Flogger. The *Lakeside International* is not too good, and rather expensive. The Union Bar at ANU is reasonable. Canberra has liberal licensing laws which allow unlimited opening hours — a real contrast to most of the rest of Australia.

During the summer only, the Monaro Folk Group hold a monthly Woolshed Dance on the last Saturday of the month at the Woolshed, Yarralumla (near the Governor General's pad) — it's a Canberra occasion. The *Ainslie Hotel* in Limestone Avenue, Ainslie has a resident jazz group playing in the Carlton Lounge every Friday night. The beer garden is generally crowded here. There are barn dances nearly every Saturday night in *Blue Belly Joes* at Canberra Fair, but Canberra Fair is right out on the road to Sydney (on the corner of Federal Highway and Antill St, Watson).

Not surprisingly, Canberra has quite a lot of film showings. Check with the various cultural centres — Maison de France, Goethe Centre — to find out what's on — also the ANU film group. Lots of regular cinemas around the Civic Square area too. The Canberra Theatre Centre comprises a complex of stages where you can see anything and everything.

Getting There

Air Most flights to Canberra are from Sydney or Melbourne although there are now some direct flights from Brisbane and Adelaide. Although Canberra is Australia's capital it is not an international airport. Air fares to Canberra are rumoured to be inflated as the airlines know that most flights are being paid for by the government anyway!

From Sydney it's just half an hour to Canberra, fare is $71 or $53 standby. Melbourne is about an hour's flight for $98 or $74 standby. You can also standby on the direct flight to Adelaide for $113 or Brisbane for $112.

Rail The Monaro Express runs daily between Sydney and Canberra, departing Sydney at 7.30 am and arriving Canberra at 12.19 pm. Canberra-Sydney departs at 5.25 pm and arrives at 10.15 pm. The fare is $15.80. There is no direct train between Melbourne and Canberra, you take a regular Sydney train as far as Yass ($31.70) and then a bus ($5) for the one hour ride into Canberra. Although all the Melbourne-Sydney trains go through Yass only the Intercapital Daylight connects directly with the bus. Otherwise you might have to kill five hours or so in Yass. Leaving Melbourne at 9 am you arrive at Yass 5.15 pm and Canberra at 6.15 pm. In the other direction leaving Canberra on the bus at 10.45 am you arrive at Melbourne 8.20 pm. There is no service on Sunday. Phone 95 1555 for railways information in Canberra.

Road Ansett Pioneer and Greyhound operate between Sydney and Canberra but only Ansett Pioneer have traffic rights unless you're on an interstate ticket. Sydney-Canberra takes about five hours and costs $25, rather more than the train.

Ansett Pioneer, Greyhound and Deluxe operate Melbourne-Canberra. The trip takes about 11 hours and costs $28. Deluxe are now only marginally cheaper than the big companies and

their services are not nearly as frequent.

You can book on these buses and also on the bus to Yass and other regional centres at the Tourist Bureau. Four times a week there's a Canberra-Orange bus which costs $22.30. A bus runs Canberra-Wollongong five times weekly for $16.10. A bus also runs to Bateman's Bay on the coast and continues from there to Moruya.

Getting Around

Bus Apart from cruises on Lake Burley Griffin, road is about the only way there is to get around the ACT. Canberra is a very sprawling place, a perfect suburb in fact, and even crossing the street is a long walk at some of the wider boulevards.

Around Canberra there are quite frequent bus services on modern buses. The bus information kiosk is on the corner of Alinga St and East Row and is open Monday to Saturday 6 am to 11 pm and Sunday from 9 am to 6 pm. Phone 47 6185 or 47 7052 for bus info; they're answered during the same hours. A free map of the whole bus system is available, as well as individual timetables for each route. There's a flat fare of 60c per journey or you can get a day pass for $2.30.

You can also buy a Canberra Explorer ticket for $5 a day or $10 a week. The Canberra Explorer plies a route connecting points of interest to visitors. You get a printed guide and can get on and off the bus wherever you like. The $10 week ticket includes use of the ordinary Action local buses. The main advantage of the Explorer bus over the cheaper Action day pass is that it goes up Black Mountain; but only once a day at 9 am. Otherwise the ordinary $2.30 pass will get you everywhere except Black Mountain if you don't mind the odd walk occasionally and having to sort out the bus routes.

For the youth hostel catch a 380 bus to the Scrivener St stop in Miller St on weekdays and Saturday mornings. On Saturday afternoons and Sundays you have to take a 360. Route 380 is half-hourly, route 360 hourly. There's a free inner city bus service but it just goes around London Circuit, and only during the middle of the day.

Car Rental The cheapest car rental outfit is Discount Rent-a-Car (tel 49 6551) at 16 Mort St, where unlimited km rates range from $12 a day to $20 depending on the size of car. Next cheapest is old faithful Thrifty (tel 47 0174) at 13 Lonsdale St. Budget, Thrifty and Hertz can be found at Canberra airport.

Bicycles Canberra is a cyclists paradise with its network of cycleways making it possible to ride around the city hardly touching a road. Get a copy of the invaluable *Canberra Cycleways* map from the tourist office. You can hire bikes from Mr Spokes Bike Hire near the Acton Ferry Terminal from $2 an hour, $8 daily, $15 weekly. Bikes are also hired

out by the youth hostel.

Airport Canberra's airport is just seven km from the city centre, it's a compact little airport, mainly notable for the government cars lined up outside waiting to pick up returning pollies. Hertz, Budget and Thrifty have airport desks. There's a city-airport bus service run by AAT for $2.75 but a taxi is only about $3.50. TAA (tel 68 3333) is in the Alinga Place Civic Centre, Ansett (tel 45 1111) is at 62 Northbourne Avenue.

Tours Try the Canberra Tourist Bureau, who have all the latest info on ACT tours. They can tell you about half-day city tours or half-day or longer tours to the surrounding countryside and sheep stations. A variety of other day trips visit the Mt Kosciusko Alpine area, the Snowy Mountains hydroelectric scheme or caves, nature reserves, satellite tracking stations, horse studs and fossicking areas around the ACT. They can also tell you about boat cruises on Lake Burley Griffin.

AROUND CANBERRA
New Towns

Canberra, once 'seven suburbs in search of a city', now has a collection of satellite new towns dotted around it. These new towns of Woden, Belconnen and Tuggeranong are separate, self-sufficient communities.

Picnic & Barbecue Spots

There are a whole series of popular picnic and barbecue spots in and around Canberra. Many of them have coin-operated gas barbecue facilities and at places along the Cotter River and Murrumbidgee River there are good swimming spots. Black Mountain, of course, is virtually in the city itself, but

others include Casuarina Sands (19 km on the Cotter River), Kambah Pool (21 km on the Murrumbidgee), Cotter Dam (23 km on the Cotter), Uriarra Crossing (24 km near the junction of the Murrumbidgee and Molonglo Rivers), Point Hut Crossing (26 km on the Murrumbidgee), Pine Island (27 km on the Murrumbidgee) and Gibraltar Falls (48 km on the Gibraltar Creek). The spectacular Lower Ginninderra Falls are in Parkwood, out along Parkwood Rd to the north-west of Canberra. They're open 10 am to 5 pm daily and reached by a fine nature trail to Ginnindera Gorge. There's an admission charge. The Tidbinbilla Nature Reserve, 40 km out near the space tracking station, has a

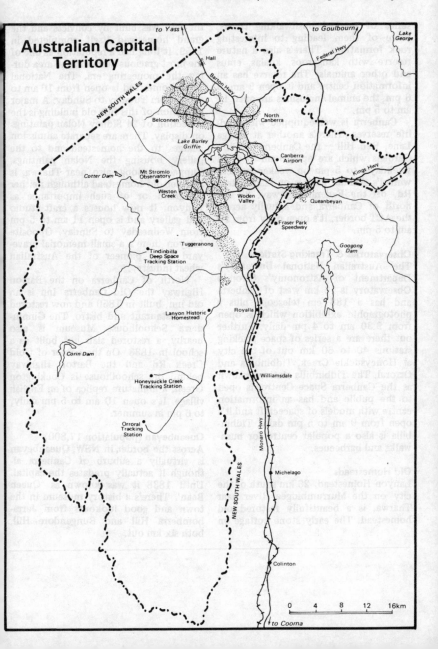

Australian Capital Territory

to Yass

to Goulbourn

Lake George

NEW SOUTH WALES

Federal Hwy

Hall

Barton Hwy

North Canberra

Belconnen

Lake Burley Griffin

Canberra Airport

Mt Stromlo Observatory

Cotter Dam

Weston Creek

Woden Valley

Kings Hwy

Queanbeyan

Fraser Park Speedway

Tuggeranong

Tindinbilla Deep Space Tracking Station

Googong Dam

Lanyon Historic Homestead

Corin Dam

Royalla

Honeysuckle Creek Tracking Station

Williamsdale

Orroral Tracking Station

NEW SOUTH WALES

Monaro Hwy

Michelago

NEW SOUTH WALES

Colinton

0   4   8   12   16km

to Cooma

series of marked bushwalking tracks, some of them leading to interesting rock formations. There's also a nature reserve with kangaroos, koalas, emus and other animals. The reserve has an information centre and is open 9 am to 6 pm, the animal enclosures are open 11 am to 5 pm.

Canberra is well-equipped with wildlife reserves. There's another at Mugga Lane, Red Hill — the Canberra Wildlife Gardens which are open 9 am to 4 pm weekdays, to 5 pm on weekends. Rehwinkel's Animal Park is on Macks Reef Rd, off the Federal Highway, 20 km north of Canberra and actually across the ACT border. It's open daily from 10 am to 5 pm.

Observatories & Tracking Stations

The Australian National University's Department of Astronomy's Stromlo Observatory is 16 km west of Canberra and has a 188 cm telescope plus a photographic exhibition which is open from 9.30 am to 4 pm daily. Further out there are a series of space tracking stations 40 to 60 km out of the city at Honeysuckle Creek, Tidbinbilla and Orroral. The Tidbinbilla station, known as the Canberra Space Centre, is open to the public and has an information centre with models of spacecraft and it's open from 9 am to 5 pm daily. Tidbinbilla is also a popular centre for bushwalks and barbecues.

Old Homesteads

Lanyon Homestead, 26 km south of the city on the Murrumbidgee River near Tharwa, is a beautifully restored old homestead. The early stone cottage on the site was built by convicts and the grand homestead itself completed in 1859. It long had a reputation as one of the most gracious homes in the area during the pioneering era. The National Trust homestead is open from 10 am to 4 pm from Tuesday to Sunday. A major attraction of this fine old building is the collection of 24 Sidney Nolan paintings on display. There are separate admission charges to the homestead and to the gallery housing the Nolan paintings. Cuppacumbalong, also near Tharwa, is another old homestead although neither so grand or of such importance as Lanyon. It now houses a craft studio and gallery and is open 11 am to 5 pm from Wednesday to Sunday. Opposite Lanyon there's a small memorial graveyard to a pioneer of the Australian wheat industry.

North of Canberra on the Barton Highway the Old Canberra Inn is an old inn, built in 1850 and now restored as a restaurant and bistro. The Ginninderra Schoolhouse Museum is also nearby, a restored slab hut built as a school in 1833. On the corner of Gold Creek Rd and the Barton Highway behind the schoolhouse is Cockington Green, a miniature replica of an English village. It's open 10 am to 5 pm daily, to 6 pm in summer.

Queanbeyan (population 17,800)

Across the border in NSW, Queanbeyan is virtually a suburb of Canberra although it actually predates the capital. Until 1838 it was known as 'Queen Bean'. There's a history museum in the town and good lookouts from Jerrabomberra Hill and Bungendore Hill, both six km out.

New South Wales

Area 802,000 square km
Population 5,000,000

Don't miss: Sydney, Australia's oldest, largest and most dramatic city with its beautiful harbour and well known Opera House.

New South Wales is the site of Captain Cook's original landing in Australia, the place where the first permanent settlement was established and today it is both the most populous state and has the country's largest city — Sydney. Of course NSW is much more than Sydney with its glistening Opera House and equally well known (if far less attractive) harbour bridge — but Sydney is certainly a good place to start.

It was down at Sydney Cove, where the ferries run from today, that the first settlement was made in 1788 so it is not surprising that Sydney has an air of age and history about certain parts of it which is quite missing from most Australian cities. That doesn't stop Sydney from being a far brasher and outwardly more lively looking city than its younger rival Melbourne. With a setting like Port Jackson (the harbour) to build around it would be hard for Sydney to be unattractive and from almost any angle it is an incredible looking city.

Sydney has much more than just the central city going for it; Paddington is without question one of the most attractive inner-city residential areas in the world and the whole Pacific shoreline of the city is dotted with good beaches sporting famous names like Bondi or Manly. Furthermore there are two particularly pleasant national parks marking the southern and northern boundaries of the city — Royal National Park and Ku-ring-gai Chase. Inland it is only a short drive to the Blue Mountains with some of the most spectacular scenery in Australia.

Nevertheless Sydney is far from everything in NSW, the Pacific Highway runs north and south from the capital and good beaches and surf are waiting for you all along the coast. A short trip north is the Hunter Valley, one of Australia's premier wine producing areas with a popular annual wine festival. Newcastle is the second city of NSW, a major industrial centre. Further north is the high plateau of the New England region and the long, sweeping, often deserted beaches of the north coast up to the Queensland border.

South of Sydney are the Southern Highlands with beautiful scenery and good bushwalks. There is more great coastline on the way down to Victoria too, plus Wollongong, the third city of NSW, another major industrial centre. The Great Dividing Range rises in the south of the state into the highest mountains in Australia with summer bushwalking and excellent winter skiing.

Finally there are the vast inland plains, sweeping expanses of agricultural and grazing land which finally dwindle into the harsh NSW outback. Out there you can find the town of Broken Hill, almost a small independent state, run by its powerful unions.

INFORMATION
There are NSW Government Travel Centres in Sydney, Melbourne and Brisbane and also information centres at Albury on the Victorian border and Tweed Heads on the Queensland border. The most useful items produced by the tourist department are a series of mag-

azine size regional guides with comprehensive information on tourist attractions, accommodation and transport. The NSW motoring association, the NRMA or National Roads and Motorists Association, also has some useful information including some excellent maps. Addresses of the government tourist offices are.

NSW	corner Pitt & Spring Sts, Sydney 2000 (tel 231 4444)
	Hume Highway, Albury 2640 (tel 21 2655)
	Pacific Highway, Tweed Heads 2485 (tel 36 2634)
Queensland	corner Queen & Edward Sts, Brisbane 4000 (tel 31 1838)
Victoria	345 Little Collins St, Melbourne 3000 (tel 60 1378)

GEOGRAPHY

es, parks, inlets and coastal lakes. The Great Dividing Range also runs from one end of the state to the other and includes the cool and pleasant New England section north of Sydney, the spectacular Blue Mountains directly inland from Sydney and in the south of the state the Snowy Mountains, famed for hydro-power developments and for winter skiing. Behind the Great Dividing Range the fertile farming country of the western slopes gradually fades into the plains which cover two thirds of the state. This far western region is NSW's stretch of the great Australian outback, often dry and barren, particularly towards the South Australian border, and with very little of the state's population. The south of the state has the Murray River as a natural border with Victoria.

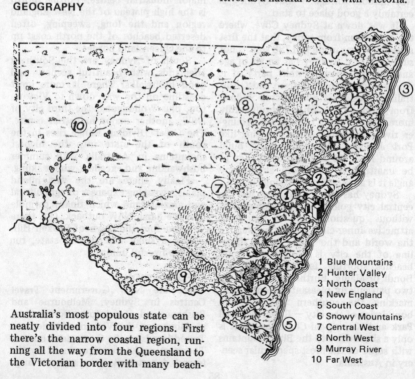

Australia's most populous state can be neatly divided into four regions. First there's the narrow coastal region, running all the way from the Queensland to the Victorian border with many beach-

1 Blue Mountains
2 Hunter Valley
3 North Coast
4 New England
5 South Coast
6 Snowy Mountains
7 Central West
8 North West
9 Murray River
10 Far West

GETTING AROUND

Rail The State Rail Authority of NSW has probably the most comprehensive rail service in Australia, see the bus section below for one of the reasons why. There are a variety of day tour fares and you can also get a 14 day Nurail Pass which gives you unlimited 1st class travel throughout the NSW rail system. Apart from trains of the usual Australian speed the NSW railways also boasts Australia's fastest train, the recently introduced XPT (Express Passenger Train) service which operates Sydney-Dubbo and can top (just) 160 kph (100 mph). XPT services are all 1st class, 40% more than economy, plus a $6 to $8 XPT zone fare. Some relevant economy fares and distances from Sydney include:

Albury	643 km	$26.40
Bourke	831	$30.00
Coffs Harbour	608	$26.40
Dubbo	462	$22.30
Goulburn	222	$10.30
Lightning Ridge	811	$30.00
Mudgee	308	$13.90
Murwillumbah	935	$31.90
Newcastle	168	$ 7.60
Nowra	153	$ 7.60
Orange	323	$14.90
Tamworth	455	$22.30
Wagga Wagga	518	$23.50
Yass Junction	315	$14.90

Bus Ansett Pioneer, Greyhound and various other carriers operate services through NSW but in order to protect the railways they are extremely limited in the services they can operate. Many interstate services cannot carry passengers on services within the state — thus there are lots of buses going up the Pacific coast from Sydney to Brisbane but you can't take those buses to Newcastle or other intermediate stops. Travellers on bus passes can, however, get on and off at will. Ansett Pioneer and Greyhound both have interstate

services that cross the state in various directions.

Air Sydney is connected to Canberra and to other state capitals by TAA and Ansett. Within the state Air New South Wales and East-West Airlines operate a comprehensive network. The chart below details some of the routes and the fare costs.

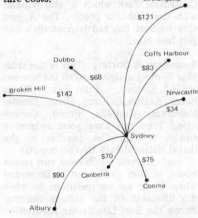

ACTIVITIES

Bushwalking The NSW Federation of Bushwalking Clubs or the National Parks & Wildlife Service are both good for information on bushwalking. A useful book on walks in the state is *100 Walks in NSW* by Tyrone Thomas which retails at around $6. There are a number of bushwalking shops in Sydney which have this and other titles on sale.

Closest to the city are walks like the fine cliff top paths in the Royal National Park or the walks in Ku-Ring-Gai Chase National Park where you can find some gigantic Aboriginal rock carvings. Inland the Blue Mountains have a whole series of fine walks and some spectacular scenery. The Southern Highlands are also within easy reach of the city.

Further afield the Kosciusko National Park in the south of the state has excellent longer walks, camping facilities and vivid wildflowers in late summer.

It's best to let the snow have plenty of time to thaw and dry up after the winter. Barrington Tops is north of Sydney, near to the New England tableland and Warrumbungle National Park.

Running & Biking There are tracks and facilities at Narrabeen Lakes north of Sydney. Sydney joggers do their stuff at Centennial Park which is also popular with the pushbike people. The August City to Surf fun run is Australis's biggest foot race.

Swimming & Surfing This is the true-blue Sydney activity and all the beaches around Sydney — Palm Beach, Whale Beach, Avalon, Collaroy, Manly, Bronte, Maroubra, Cronulla, Bondi, Coogee (need I go on) have good swimming and/or surfing. The beaches in the Royal National Park are also popular.

Surf carnivals — lifesavers, surf rescue boats, all that stuff, start in December when there are competitions between the lifesavers of the various beaches. Phone the Surf Life Saving Association to find out what's on and where, or contact the NSW Travel Centre.

Officially Sydney has 34 surf beaches and there are plenty more along the NSW coast. The north coast is more popular duing the winter months (warmer of course) at places like Seal Rocks (325 km), Crescent Head (497 km), Scott's Head (538 km), Angourie (744 km) and Lennox Heads (823 km). Byron Bay has a been a surfing mecca

for almost as long as Australia has had surfies. South of Sydney there is Stanwell Park (56 km), Wollongong (82 km), Huskisson (187 km) and Mollymook (222 km).

Skin Diving Excellent scuba diving and snorkelling can be found at a number of sites along the coast. North of Sydney popular spots include Terrigal (96 km), Port Stephens (235 km), Seal Rocks (325 km) or Byron Bay (850 km). Head south to Jervis Bay in the Royal National Park, to Wattamolia (198 km) or Eden (488 km).

Canoeing With dams, rivers, lakes and coastal lakes there are plenty of opportunities to go canoeing in NSW. If you are after white water then the Richmond and Murray Rivers are where you should be heading. The NSW Canoe Association (tel 241 3866) has info. Equipment can be hired from the NSW Sport & Recreation Service or from B-line Canoe Hire (tel 727 9402) at Lansvale.

Sailing Sydney Harbour and the Pittwater are both excellent areas for sailing so it is hardly surprising that the sport is so popular. Check with the Australian Yachting Federation about clubs and sailing instruction.

Skiing See the Snowy Mountains section for information about skiing in NSW.

SYDNEY (population 3,200,000)
As Australia's oldest and largest city it's not surprising that Sydney (Sinney to the locals) has plenty to offer. The harbour, around which the city is built, was noted by Captain Cook in 1770 and named by him Port Jackson. He actually anchored in Botany Bay, a few km to the south, and only passed

by the narrow entrance to the harbour, not entering the magnificent stretch of water that lay within the heads. In 1788 when the convict 'First Fleet' arrived in Sydney it too went first to Botany Bay but after a few days moved north to Port Jackson. These first settlers established themselves at Sydney Cove, still the centre of harbour shipping to this day.

As Sydney grew, it stretched back from that original landing spot but down near the waterfront in the area known as the Rocks you can still find some of the earliest buildings in Australia. Because Sydney grew in a somewhat piecemeal fashion, unlike other later Australian cities which were planned from the start, it's a tighter, more congested centre with narrower streets than the wide boulevards you find in other cities, Melbourne in particular. Despite that it's also a dazzlingly modern city, the place with the most energy and style in Australia. In Sydney the buildings soar higher, the colours are brighter, the consumption is more conspicuous! It all comes back to that stupendous harbour though. It's more than just the centrepiece for the city, everything in Sydney revolves around the harbour. Would the Opera House, for example, be anything like the place it is were it not perched right beside the harbour?

Information

The NSW Government Travel Centre (tel 231 4444) is at 16 Spring St on the corner with Pitt St. It's open Monday to Friday 9 am to 5 pm and has the usual range of brochures, leaflets and accommodation details. The Sydney Visitors' Bureau (tel 29 5311) at 95-99 York Sts is open the same hours. The privately-run Tourist Information Service is a telephone info service operating seven days a week from 8 am to 6 pm, phone 669 5111.

The National Roads & Motorists Association (NRMA) is the NSW auto club and it has its head office at 151 Clarence St (tel 236 9211) and a branch office at 324 Pitt St (tel 236 9781). There's a YHA shop at the Sydney YHA office at 355 Kent St. The national head office of the YHA is also in Sydney. As usual the universities are good info

sources and there are university newspapers at Sydney University and the University of NSW. The Wayside Chapel (tel 358 1010), up at 29 Hughes St, Kings Cross, is a crisis centre and good for all sorts of local information and problem solving.

Sydney — the Harbour City Handbook by Robyn Stone is a comprehensive handbook on sightseeing, accommodation, restaurants and entertainment in Sydney, including both low and high price places. It's published by George Allen & Unwin, 1981, and retails at $6.95. Another guide is *Out & About in Sydney* by Taffy Davies & Jill Wran. Although it also contains some info on cheaper places it is really more of a guide to the top end. Sydney has lots of good bookshops including a large Angus & Robertson and three Grahames on Pitt St, Dymocks on George St and the anarchic Gould's Book Arcade also on George St.

You can find Aboriginal art in several places in Sydney. The Argyle Primitive Art Gallery, in the Argyle Art Centre in the Rocks, has craft work from the Pacific region as well as Australia. Only a few steps away is the Collectors' Gallery of Aboriginal Art at 40 Harrington St. Both are operated by Aboriginal Arts & Crafts. New Guinea Primitive Arts on the 6th floor at 428 George St also has Aboriginal art along with an amazing collection of artefacts from PNG. The Boomerang School at 40 Darlinghurst Rd, Kings Cross not only sells boomerangs but will also teach you how to throw them at Sunday morning classes at Yarranabbe Reserve, Rushcutters Bay. Back in the Rocks you can find a variety of original Australian designs at the Australian Design Centre at 70 George St, open daily, and lots of interesting goodies at the Environment Centre, 399 Pitt St. The Village Bazaar on Oxford St in Passington is a superb arts, crafts and general odds and ends session on Saturdays. It's quite a scene.

Sydney

0   100   200   300 m.

🚆 Central station
✉ G.P.O.
✳ NSWGTB
1 YHA Office
2 TAA
3 Ansett & Ansett Pioneer
4 Greyhound
5 NRMA
6 Mitchell Library
7 Town Hall

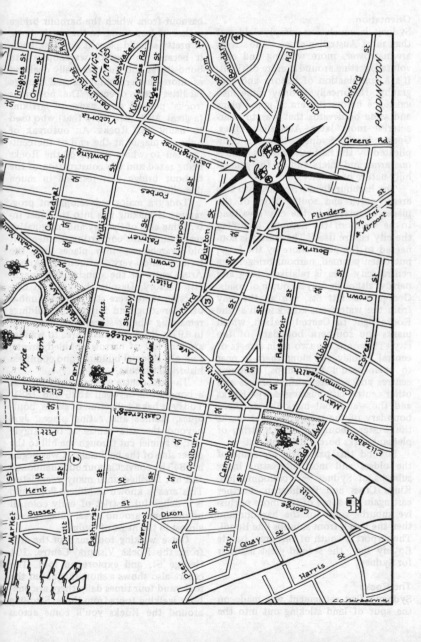

Orientation

Sydney is much less simply laid out than most Australian cities — the streets are narrower, more winding and convoluted, getting around is more difficult. It's a combination of history and geography. Historically Sydney came into existence before the era of grand plans and wide boulevards that was to characterise most later Australian cities. Geographically Sydney's layout is complicated by the harbour with its numerous arms and inlets and by the general hilly nature of the city.

The harbour divides Sydney into two areas, north and south. Most of the places of interest in the city area tend to be south of the harbour, including the city centre itself. The centre is connected to the north shore by the huge, but often jammed, harbour bridge. The central city area is relatively long and narrow although only a couple of roads, George and Pitt Sts, run all the way from the waterfront area known as the Rocks right to Central Station, which marks the southern boundary of the city. These are the two main streets of central Sydney and along them or near to them you'll find shops, shopping centres and arcades, airline offices and other central city businesses. The Rocks and the waterfront mark the northern boundary of the centre, an inlet marks the western boundary and a string of pleasant parks border it to the east.

Beyond this park strip are some of the oldest and most interesting inner suburbs of Sydney — Woolloomooloo, Kings Cross and Paddington. Further east again are some of the more exclusive suburbs south of the harbour and then the beach front suburbs like Bondi. The airport is south of this area, beside Botany Bay, the second great harbour for Sydney.

The Rocks

Sydney's first settlement was made on the spur of land sticking out into the harbour from which the harbour bridge makes its leap across to the north shore. A pretty squalid place it was too. Later it became an area of warehouses and bond stores and then gradually declined as more modern shipping and storage facilities were opened. The notorious 'rocks' pushes' were gangs of larrikins (a great Australian word that) who used to haunt the Rocks. An outbreak of bubonic plague at the end of the century led to whole streets of the Rocks being razed and the construction of the harbour bridge also resulted in much demolition.

Today a major redevelopment programme is making this into the most interesting area of Sydney and imaginative restorations are converting the decrepit old warehouses into places like the trendy and very interesting Argyle Arts Centre or the amusing Old Spaghetti Factory. Despite the years of destruction there were still a great number of interesting and important buildings remaining when restoration commenced in 1970. It's a delightful area to wander around, full of narrow cobbled streets, fine old colonial buildings and countless historical touches.

The arts centre was originally built as a bond store between 1826 and 1881. Today it has a collection of shops, boutiques, studios and eating places. Just beyond the arts centre is the Argyle Cut, a tunnel cut through the hill to the other side of the peninsula. It was begun in 1843 by convict labour but abandoned and not finished until many years later. This area is known as Millers Point and is a delightful district of early colonial homes some around a real village green, almost in the heart of Sydney.

Get a walking tour map of the area from the Rocks Visitors' Centre, 104 George St, and explore on foot. The centre also shows a short film about the rocks and four times daily there are one-hour walking tours from there. Strolling around the Rocks you'll come across

Camden Cottage (1816), the oldest house in Sydney. When it was built this was where the waterfront came to and the arches to the south of the cottage once housed longboats. You can also find the site of the public gallows, a colonial museum, an old observatory in the pleasant park on Flagstaff Hill (open by arrangement only) and much more. The Rocks also has several historic old pubs including the Hero of Waterloo and the Lord Nelson. There are also guided walking tours of the Rocks from the Argyle Arts Centre four times a day for $2.

Sydney Harbour Bridge

Down at the end of the Rocks the harbour bridge rises up on its path to the north shore. It's known affectionately as the 'old coathanger' and was a far from elegant, but very functional, symbol for the city until the Opera House came along. it was completed in 1932 at a cost of $20 million, quite a bargain today. Crossing the bridge costs just 20c, southbound only, there is no toll in the other direction. Trivia fans may be interested to know the bridge has only been repainted a handful of times since it was completed but that repainting is a continuous process — they start at one end, work to the other and by the time they get there it's time to start again. You can also walk across the bridge, there are stairs up to it from the Rocks. At rush hours the bridge gets very crowded and the possibility of a second harbour bridge or, more likely, a harbour tunnel is a subject for on-going discussion.

On the north shore, neatly framed beneath the bridge, is the grinning mouthpiece of another Sydney symbol — Luna Park. This long-running funfair was closed recently after a disastrous fire led to several deaths but it has now been re-opened, in a somewhat sanitised version. North Sydney has become a smaller replica of the Sydney centre in the past 20 years. Spiralling office rents and central congestion prompted the construction of this second city centre.

The Sydney Opera House

From the past symbol to the present one is a short walk around Circular Quay to the controversial Sydney Opera House. After countless delays and technical difficulties and with cost escalations like a land-bound Concorde, the Opera House finally opened in 1973, 14 years after work began. And I was there! During a cheap Sunday afternoon concert or sitting in the open air restaurant with a carafe of red, watching the harbour life, it's a truly memorable place.

There are tours of the building and although the inside is nowhere near as spectacular as the outside, they are worth taking. The tours cost $2 and operate every day of the year (except Christmas Day and Good Friday) every half hour from 9 am to 4 pm. There are also more expensive tours of the backstage area on Sundays only.

Popular performances at the Opera House tend to sell out quickly — there aren't a great number of seats in any of the halls but there are a limited number of 'restricted view' and standing room only tickets which go on sale just before the performances. On Sunday afternoons there are free performances on the outer walk of the building. You can also often catch a free lunchtime film or organ recital in the concert hall. One free thing to avoid at the opera house is the notorious band of free-loading seagulls who are expert at collecting free meals from outdoor diners at the Harbour Restaurant — guard your meal carefully.

Best show I've seen at the Opera House? — a Fairport Convention concert recorded live for an LP. The designer, Dane Jorn Utzon, won an international contest with his design but at the height of the cost overruns

THE OPERA HOUSE

and construction difficulties hassles he quit in disgust and the building was completed by a consortium of Australian architects. How were the enormous additional costs covered — not by the tax payer but in true-blue Aussie fashion by a series of Opera House lotteries. The Opera House looks fine from any angle but the view from a ferry, coming in to Circular Quay, is one of the best.

Circular Quay
There's nothing circular about Circular Quay, the departure point for the harbour ferries. Ferries may be plying a slowly dying trade but there is still no finer means of transport than the creaky old ships — take a lunchtime cruise to get the feel or zip to Manly on the high speed hydro-foils. Circular Quay was the original landing point for the First Fleet and at that time the Tank Stream ran down onto the harbour here.

Later this was the shipping centre for Sydney and early photographs show a veritable forest of sailing ship masts crowding the skyline here. Across Circular Quay from the Opera House, beside the Rocks, is the overseas passenger terminal where cruise ships and visiting liners moor. Some of the streets leading back from the Circular Quay are slightly seedy and run down but this is an interesting area with some colourful early morning opening pubs. There's a pleasant little park on the Rocks side of the quay.

City Views
Sydney is becoming a mini-Manhattan with highest-building stakes changing from year to year but from up top you can see the convoluted streets that are a relic of the unplanned convict past. George St is the main shopping street, once known as High St, while Pitt St was famous for its brothels way back then. Bridge St was so-named because it was the site of the first bridge in Australia across the Tank Stream, which is now funnelled underground.

The Australia Square Building was the highest building for awhile but has yielded that honour and is now several buildings from the top. It's very definitely circular, not square at all, but the views from the lookout deck are magnificent and cost $2.50. Highest, not only in Sydney but also Australia, is the Sydney Tower on top of the Centrepoint Complex. This is a tower built purely for the sake of being high — it's nothing more than a gigantic column with a circular viewing gallery and revolving restaurant on the summit. The construction of the tower was very interesting. First the column was constructed, in 46 prefabricated sections stacked one on top of another, then the top 'drum' was assembled at the bottom of the column and slowly jacked up to its position at the top, it's 305 metres above street level. The tower is open 9.30 am to 9.30 pm except Sundays and public holidays when it's open 10.30 am to 6.30 pm, admission is $3.50.

City Parks

Sydney has plenty of parks including a string of them which border the city centre on its eastern side. Stretching back from the harbour front, beside the Opera House, is Sydney's Royal Botanic Garden with a magnificent collection of South Pacific plant life. The gardens were originally established in 1816 and in one corner of the gardens you can find a stone wall marking the site of the convict colony's first vegetable patch.

The harbour bridge freeway separates the botanic gardens from the Domain, behind Macquarie St. Here on Sunday afternoon after 2 pm impassioned soap-box speakers entertain their listeners. Continue down beyond the Domain and the art gallery and you'll find Mrs Macquarie's Chair cut into the rock of Mrs Macquarie's Point. Here the wife of that early governor is said to have sat to watch how hubby's construction projects were coming along, just across Farm Cove. It's a popular place to photograph the Opera House from.

Third of this group of city parks is Hyde Park with its delightful fountains and the Anzac Memorial. This is a popular place for a city sandwich lunch on the grass since it's only a few steps from the centre. Sydney's biggest park, with running, bicycling and horse tracks, duck ponds, barbecue sites and lots more is Centennial Park, just beyond Paddington. You can hire bikes from Centennial Park Cycles, 50 Clovelly Rd, Randwick, open 9 am to 5 pm weekdays, 8.30 am to dusk on weekends.

Macquarie Place

Narrow lanes lead back from Circular Quay at the waterfront towards the real centre of the city. Find the pleasant little triangular open space of Macquarie Place where under the shady Moreton Bay figs you'll find a cannon and anchor from Phillip's First Fleet flagship HMS *Sirius*. There are a number of other places of colonial memorabilia in this interesting little square including gas lamps, a drinking fountain dating from 1857, a National Trust classified gentlemen's convenience and an obelisk indicating distances to various points in the colony of NSW.

Early Buildings

After the founding governor Phillip left in 1792 the colony was run by officials more intent on making a quick fortune through the rum monopoly than anything else and it was not until Macquarie took over in 1810 that order was restored. The narrow streets of parts of downtown Sydney are a reminder of that chaotic period. Some of the finest early buildings in Sydney were the work of convict architect Francis Greenway and there are examples of his buildings scattered around the city. St James Church and the Hyde Park Barracks are two of his early masterpieces on Queens Square at the northern end of Hyde Park.

Next to the barracks on Queen St is the Mint Building, originally built as a hospital in 1814 and known as the Rum Hospital because the builders constructed it in return for the lucrative monopoly on the rum trade. It became the mint in 1853 and the northern wing of the hospital is now the Parliament House. The Mint with its collection of historic decorative arts is open 10 am to 5 pm daily except Wednesday when it opens at 12 noon. In the same area the State Conservatorium of Music on Macquarie St was originally built, by Greenway again, as a stables and servants' quarters for government house.

City Centre

Sydney has some of the most attractive and imaginative shopping complexes in Australia including the delightful old Strand Arcade between Pitt and George Sts. The MLC Centre, Centrepoint and the Royal Arcade are just three of the many modern centres you will find off George and Pitt Sts in the centre. In the basement of the Hilton Hotel, under the Royal Arcade, you can find the Marble Bar, a Victorian extravaganza built by George Adams, the fellow with the prescience to foresee Australia's gambling lust and found 'Tatts' lotteries. When the old Adams Hotel (originally O'Brien's Pub) was torn down to build the Hilton, the bar was carefully dismantled and reassembled like some archaeological wonder.

Sydney's real centre is Martin Place, a pedestrian mall extending from Elizabeth St down to George St beside the massive GPO. It's a popular lunchtime entertainment spot with buskers and more organised entertainment. The Cenotaph war memorial is also here and in December a Christmas tree appears here in the summer heat.

Continuing along George St you'll come to the 1874 Town Hall and then the centre begins to fade, becoming rather grotty before you reach Central Station and the inner suburb of Glebe. Just off George St and before the station is the colourful Chinatown around Dixon St, packed with Chinese shops and restaurants.

Art Gallery of NSW

Situated on the Domain, only a short walk from the centre, the Art Gallery has an excellent permanent display and from time to time shows some really inspired temporary exhibits. The gallery also has a very good cafeteria, ideal for a genteel cup of tea. It's open 10 am to 5 pm Monday to Saturday, noon to 5 pm Sunday. There's no charge to the gallery itself but entrance fees may apply at certain times for major exhibitions. Free guided tours of the gallery are available. Sydney is packed with other galleries, particularly in Paddo and Woollahra.

Museums

The Australian Museum at the corner of College and William Sts, right by Hyde Park, is a natural history museum with an excellent collection of Australian wildlife, a very well laid out Aboriginal exhibit and an intriguing 'arid Australia' section. See the latter before you head off into the centre. This is Australia's largest museum, it's open Tuesday to Saturday 10 am to 5 pm, Sunday and Monday from 12 noon to 5 pm and admission is free. Taped guided tours are available.

The Museum of Applied Art & Science on Harris St, Ultimo has recently been refurbished and renamed the Power House Museum. It's also open daily and admission is free. Outside stands a life size lunar module model. There is also a Rail Transport Museum at Chullora and a Mining Museum at the top end of George St in the Rocks. Near Sutherland and the Royal National Park on the Princes Highway there's a Tramway Museum open on weekends — Sydney's last tram rumbled into the history books back in 1961. There's a 600-metre long tram track here.

At Birkenhead Point, just across the

NSW

a. At the start of the annual City to Surf race 25,000 runners launch themselves down Williams St from the centre of Sydney, bound for Kings Cross and........eventually........ Bondi Beach.

b. And what do you find at Bondi Beach?

c. Australia isn't all sun, surf and sand, as a lone skier at Thredbo demonstrates.

Iron Cove Bridge in Drummoyne, the Sydney Maritime Museum has ships and museum displays. It's open daily from 10 am to 5 pm except Mondays when it opens at 1 pm. There's an admission charge and you can get there on a 500 bus from Circular Quay or by ferry from number 2 wharf, Circular Quay. There's also a fishing museum here. Other Sydney museums include Macleay Museum and Nicholson Museum at Sydney University, natural history at the former, Greek antiquities at the latter. At 157 Gloucester St in the Rocks there's the Hall of Champions Sports Museum. Kings Cross has a waxworks in the Village Centre.

The State Library of New South Wales has one of the best collections of early works on Australia in the country. It includes maps, documents, pictures and many other items which can be seen in the library galleries. The galleries are open 10 am to 5 pm Monday to Saturday, 2 to 6 pm on Sunday.

Paddington

The trendy inner suburb of Paddington has to be one of the most attractive inner city residential areas in the world. 'Paddo' is a tightly packed mass of terrace houses, built for aspiring artisans in the later years of the Victorian era. During the lemming-like rush to the dreary outer suburbs after WW II the area became a run-down slum. Then a renewed interest in Victorian architecture (of which Australia has some gems) combined with the sudden recollection of the pleasures of inner city life led to

a quite incredible restoration of Paddo during the '60s.

Today it's a fascinating jumble of often beautifully restored terraces, tumbling up and down the steeply sloping streets. Surprisingly there was an older Paddington of fine gentlemen's residences, a few of which still stand although the once spacious gardens are now encroached upon by lesser buildings. Paddington is one of the finest examples of totally unplanned urban restoration in the world and is full of trendy shops and restaurants, some fine art galleries and interesting people. The best time to visit Paddo is Saturdays when you can catch the 'Paddo Fair' with all sorts of eccentric market stalls selling everything from Indian kaftans to pop art. I always manage to see something I just have to have.

While you're in Paddington visit the old Victoria Barracks where you can see the impressive changing of the guards at 10.30 am on Tuesdays except in December and January. The barracks were built between 1841 and 1848, at that time the area was sand dunes and swamps! Get a free copy of The Paddington Book (available from shops in the area) to find your way around with.

You can get to Paddo on a 380 bus.

Kings Cross

'The Cross', Sydney's sin centre, is rather a pale shadow of similar places abroad but it's the only place in Oz that gives it a try. Apart from the seedy strip joints it has some good restaurants, lots of late night eateries, plenty of hookers, the

NSW

a. The El Alamein fountain in Kings Cross, Sydney.
b. Terrace rooftops zig zag up the hill in the trendy inner-Sydney suburb of Paddington.
c. Painted doors in the 'hippy' centre of Nimbin, north New South Wales.

pleasant Kings Cross Village Centre and lots of travellers since the Cross has a string of popular hostels and is an excellent place to stay, lots of activity and very close to the centre. The attractive (when it's working) thistle-like El Alamein Fountain, down at the end of Darlinghurst Rd, is known locally as the 'elephant douche'! You can walk up to the cross, straight up William St, grab one of a multitude of buses which run there or take the very quick Eastern Suburbs train service which takes you right to the centre of the cross. Between the city and the Cross is Woolloomooloo, the 'loo', one of Sydney's older areas with many narrow streets.

Beyond the Cross

At the harbour front from the Cross is Elizabeth Bay where you'll find Elizabeth Bay House at 7 Onslow St, a fine old home, built in 1832 and overlooking the harbour. It's open Tuesday to Friday from 10 am to 4 pm, Saturday from 10 am to 5 pm and Sunday from 12 noon to 5 pm, admission is 50c.

Continuing through Kings Cross you come to Rushcutters Bay, trendy Darling Point and then even trendier Double Bay — swish shops and lots of badly parked Porsches and Benzes. Next up in this direction is Rose Bay then Vaucluse where Vaucluse House (admission $1) is an imposing example of 19th century Australiana. It was built in 1828 for William Wentworth and you can get there on a bus 325. Towards the end of the harbour is Watsons Bay with trendy Doyles restaurant, a couple of Sydney most 'to be seen there' harbour beaches and the magnificent view across the Heads. All along this side of the harbour there are superb views back down the harbour towards the city.

Other Suburbs

On the other side of the centre from Paddo and the Cross is Balmain, the arty centre of Sydney and in some ways a competitor for Paddo in Victorian era trendiness. Glebe, closer to the centre, is another area which has been going up the social scale in recent years. While the eastern suburbs (the harbour to the ocean area beyond the Cross) and the north shore (across the harbour) are the wealthy areas of Sydney, the western suburbs are the real suburbs. Heading west you come first to Redfern, parts of it quite interesting but other parts Australia's closest approach to a real slum. Further out it's the red-tile roofed, triple-front area of the slurbs, the dull Bankstowns of Sydney.

The Harbour

Sydney's harbour is best viewed from the ferries, it's extravagantly colourful and always interesting. People have often wondered out loud just which great city has the most magnificent harbour — Hong Kong, Rio, San Francisco or Sydney? I've still got to get to Rio but between the others I'd have to give Sydney first place. Out in the harbour Fort Denison, or Pinchgut as it was uncomfortably named, is an interesting relic of convict days which was fortified when Australians were having a bout of Russian-fears back in the Czar's days. There are tours there from jetty 6, Circular Quay at 10.15 am, 12.45 and 2.15 pm from Tuesday to Saturday. The trip takes 1½ hours and costs $2 return. It's best to book, phone 2 0545 (ext 29).

The Gap, the entrance to the harbour, is a popular spot for catching the sunrise and sunset. You can hire boats (rowboats, canoes, small sailboats and motorboats) from Walton's Hireboats, 2 The Esplanade, Balmoral. There are several other harbour boat hire places. There's a fine four km walking track along the harbourside at Ashton Park, below Taronga Park Zoo. Another harbourside walk takes you for three km around Cremorne Point. A favourite harbour activity is following the 18-

footer yacht races on Saturdays. Ferries, complete with on board bookies so you can bet on the outcome, follow the exciting races.

Taronga Park Zoo

A short ferry ride across the harbour will deposit you near Taronga Park Zoo which has one of the most attractive settings of any zoo in the world. Gradually the animal enclosures are being brought up to the same standard. The ferry goes from jetty 5, Circular Quay and the zoo is open daily 9.30 am to 5 pm, admission is $4.

Manly

It's a longer ferry ride, or a fast hydrofoil one, to Manly at the ocean end of the harbour. This is one of Sydney's oldest beach suburbs and here you can see the sharks, which are supposedly waiting for you if you fall off a ferry, at Marineland where there are daily feedings of the hungry monsters. It's open 10 am to 5 pm daily and admission is $3.50. The Manly Waterworks is one of the waterslides things which have appeared all over Australia in the last couple of years. A string of ocean front suburbs stretch north up the coast from Manly, finally ending in beautiful, and wealthy, Palm Beach and the spectacular Barrenjoey Heads.

Beaches

One of Sydney's greatest plus points is its beaches — they're very accessible and they're really very good. In fact for city beaches it's hard to imagine better. There are basically two sorts of beaches in Sydney — harbour beaches and ocean beaches. The harbour beaches are sheltered and calm and generally smaller. The ocean beaches often have quite good surf and they're usually smaller. Although they'll get crowded on hot summer weekends Sydney's beaches are never really shoulder to shoulder. Swimming is pretty safe at all these beaches —

at the ocean beaches you're only allowed to swim within the 'flagged' areas patrolled by the famed voluntary lifeguards. Efforts are made to keep the surfers separate from the swimmers. Shark patrols are operated through the summer months and the ocean beaches are generally netted — Sydney has only had one fatal shark attack since 1937. The shark-proof nets do not, incidentally, enclose the beaches — they're installed perpendicular to the beaches, not parallel to them. This dissuades sharks from patrolling along the beaches. A high point of Sydney's beach-life is the surf-lifesaving competitions with races, rescues and surfboat competitions at various beaches throughout the summer months. Many of Sydney's beaches are 'topless' but on other beaches it is not approved of so women observe what other people are doing before forgetting their bikini tops. There are also a couple of nude beaches. A brief resume of some of the beaches:

Harbour Beaches On the south side one of the most popular harbour beaches is trendy Camp Cove, a small but pleasant sliver of sand popular with families and also topless. This was the place where Governor Phillip first landed in Sydney. Back towards the city is Watson's Bay with the delightful outdoor seafood restaurant Doyle's, where you can dine in the open and gaze back along the harbour towards the city. In the opposite direction, just inside the heads (the harbour entrance), the tiny Lady Bay Beach achieved some notoriety in the process of becoming a nude beach. It's mainly a gay scene. There's another nude beach on the north shore of the harbour, Reef Beach, but it's quite a long walk to get to it. Two other popular harbour beaches are Balmoral with its little 'island' on the north side of the harbour and Nielson Park on the south side at Vaucluse.

South Ocean Beaches South of the heads there are a string of ocean beaches all the way to the entry to Botany Bay. They include Bondi; with its crowds, surfies and even fibreglass mermaids in pathetic imitation of Copenhagen it's probably the best known beach in Australia. Bondi's beachfront is backed by slightly seedy Victorian buildings which give it an air of a slightly seedy antipodean Brighton but that makes Bondi sound a lot worse than it is. It's really quite an enjoyable place and Maureen and I often stay at Bondi when we're in Sydney. The south end of the beach is topless. Rather like Earls Court is (or was) to young Australians in London so is Bondi to New Zealanders and other young visitors to Sydney. It's a popular gathering place.

Tamarama, a little south of Bondi, is another beautiful sweep of sand with strong surf and it's also topless. Then there's Bronte, a wide beach popular with families, and Coogee, another wide, sweeping beach where you'll also find the popular Coogee Bay Hotel with its beer garden overlooking the beach. Other beaches towards Botany Bay, which is more for sailing than swimming due to the sharks, include Maroubra.

Places to Stay

There's a wide variety of accommodation in Sydney including an excellent selection of rock-bottom priced hostels. Finding a place to stay in Sydney requires deciding where you want to stay first of all. The information that follows is subdivided by location as well as type. If you want a hotel or motel room booked the Public Transport Commission performs this service as well as the Government Travel Centre. There are cheap places in the rooms to let ads in the *Sydney Morning Herald* every day, but particularly on Wednesdays and Saturdays. Finding a room, even on a short term basis, is no problem from the ads.

When Maureen and I first set up Lonely Planet we lived in the basement of a Paddington terrace in Sydney and since then we've made lots of trips and visits to the harbour city and tried out all sorts of areas around the city either staying with friends or in a variety of cheap places to stay, more than a few of which feature below. The Cross is great fun, a bit noisy and seedy but if you like a little raucous squalor it's not at all a bad place to stay. Bondi is another very popular accommodation centre and also probably Sydney's best known beach. Like the Cross there's lots of activity and also lots of places to eat. If you'd like something quieter I can also recommend Manly and the distance is no big deal because you ride back and forth on the best transport Sydney has to offer — a harbour ferry.

Hostels From having no YHA hostel at all only a few years ago, Sydney now has two hostels plus a number of unofficial hostel-style places. The closest *YHA hostel* to the city centre is at 28 Ross St, just across the Parramatta Rd from Sydney Uni — phone number is 692 0747. This hostel, at Forest Lodge, has only 30 beds. The other *youth hostel* (tel 569 0272) is at 407 Marrickville Rd, Dulwich Hill. It's seven km from town but only four km from the airport, and has 120 beds. Both hostels charge $6 per night and are closed between 9.30 am and 5 pm. You can arrange to get in after 10 pm if they have already booked in.

The *YMCA* (tel 264 1011) at 325 Pitt St has accommodation for men only. Bed & breakfast rates are $12 single or $10 each in a share double. It's very central and close to the Town Hall Station but it's also very plain and spartan. At the time of writing there is no YWCA hostel but one is due to open in early 1984. You can phone the YWCA office on 264 2451 to find out what the story is.

The private hostels in Sydney are mainly around the Kings Cross area. At

1 Backpackers' Accommodation
2 Young Travellers' Hostel
3 Montpelier
4 El Alamein Fountain
5 Kings Cross Library
6 Clay's Bookshop
7 Wayside Chapel
8 Cross Country Travellers' Hostel
9 Gala Private Hotel
10 Macquarie Hotel
11 Cactus Cafe
12 Atoa Guest House
13 Springfields Lodge
14 Benly Guest House
15 Canberra Oriental Hotel
16 McCafferty's Bus Depot
17 Balkan Restaurant

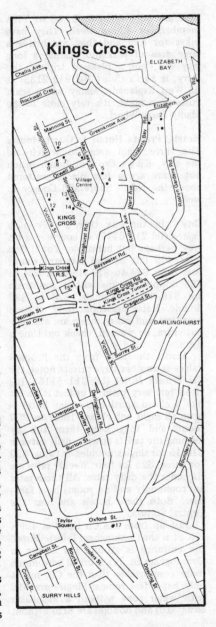

162 Victoria St the *Kings Cross Backpackers Hostel* (tel 356 3232) is quite a new one with 78 beds and a kitchen. It's open all day and you can get a key so you can get out at night. Close by at 25 Hughes St is the *Young Cross Country Travellers Centre* (tel 358 1143). It sleeps two to four people in a room, linen is supplied but if you don't have your own sleeping bag you must pay a deposit on blankets. There's also a key deposit.

Also at Kings Cross is the *Young Travellers Hostel* (tel 357 3509) at 15 Rosyln Gardens. There's a kitchen here and again no curfew but it may cease to exist soon because a wealthy Labor politician has bought the building and intends to renovate it for fun and PROFIT. For this hostel catch a 316 bus from Hunter St to the end of the run in Elizabeth Bay. For the other two hostels get a train to Kings Cross Station or, if your gear isn't too heavy, you can walk it from town. All these private hostels in the Cross cost $5 a night. Next door to the Kings Cross Backpackers Hostel, *Atoa House* (see guest houses) has some hostel style accommodation for $6 a day or $42 a week.

Beethoven Lodge (tel 698 4203) is at 663 South Dowling St, Surry Hills, not quite as central but still within walking distance of the city. Charges here are $5 a night or $4.50 to YHA members or $26 a week. They have bikes for hire and they are beside a large area of parkland. Rather a long way out, but a pleasant trip on the ferry, is *Earl's Court* (tel 949 2133) at 95 West Esplanade, Manly which again costs $5 a night. It's very close to the Manly Ferry Wharf.

Hotels, Private Hotels & Guest Houses
The three main areas to search are the city, King's Cross or Bondi Beach but there are a few places scattered about the North Shore and Coogee as well.

City In the city there's a *People's Palace* (tel 211 5777) of course — a bit grey perhaps but habitable. You'll find it at 400 Pitt St and standard rooms cost from $14 to $16 single or $24 to $28 double. Rooms with a washbasin are $16 to $18 single, $28 to $32 double. Rates are room only, a good breakfast and other meals are available but extra. Be warned, check out time is 9 am.

Across the road from the People's Palace is another large private hotel, the *CB Private Hotel* (tel 211 5115). It's clean but very plain — in fact it's a lot like a cheap South-East Asian hotel — open all night and cheap! There are 200 rooms and they keep them full by keeping the tariffs down — daily rates re $10/15 for singles/doubles or twins, $20 for three, $25 for four. Weekly rates are six times the daily rates. All these rates are room-only and no rooms have facilities. Both these hotels are near the Central Station.

Just up from the CB Hotel at 429A Pitt St is the *Cunningham Private Hotel*, the entrance is around the corner in Cunningham St. It's a brand new, much more comfortable than the CB, but it only has a few rooms. Singles are $12 with water (one without a washbasin costs $10) and doubles are $15, without

washbasin. Cheaper rates by the week. The Cozy Hotel across the road does not take travellers. Neither the CB nor the Cunningham have food available but there are eating places along the street.

Opposite Central Station at 356-358 Elizabeth St is the *Central Private Hotel* (tel 212 1068) where all rooms have hot and cold water and a refrigerator. Singles are $16, doubles $22, twins $24 and extra people $8. Weekly rates are cheaper and breakfast is $2. The office is open 8 am to 7 pm. In the same area the *Aranui* (tel 212 1005) at 75 Wentworth Avenue charges $12 single and $17 to $25 for two. Nearer downtown the *Ritz Private Hotel* (tel 264 5957) at 223 Elizabeth St has tea making facilities and charges $14/20 for singles/doubles.

There are a couple of pubs worth mentioning in the city. The *Red Lion Inn* (tel 264 3120) at 344 Pitt St has basic rooms for $15 single, $25 twin (four of each) and although there is no breakfast available there's a coffee shop next door. The *North British Hotel* (tel 27 2975) at 4 Loftus St near Circular Quay has 10 rooms with rates at $15/24 or $50/70 by the week. Again no meals are available but there are communal tea making facilities and plenty of eating places close by.

Kings Cross There are lots of places around the Cross. *Atoa House* (tel 358 3693) has cooking facilities and a free laundry and rates are $16 for a small room ($91 a week) and $21 for a double ($126 a week) — see the hostel section also. You can store luggage there for $1 a week per bag.

The *Gala Private Hotel* (tel 356 3406) is next door to the Young Cross Country Travellers' Centre at 23 Hughes St. Room rates are $15 single (share bathroom), $18 single with private bath (some of the bathrooms are next door but they are private) or $25 twin.

Weekly rates are times six. There are no cooking facilities except for one room which is equipped for 'light' cooking but there are tea and coffee making facilities. Across the road on the corner of Hughes and Tusculum Sts is the *Macquarie Private Hotel* (tel 358 4415) which has singles from $10 a night, doubles from $15 and flats from $60 a week.

The *Plaza Hotel* (tel 358 6455) is right in the heart of noisy Kings Cross. Per night it's $12/20 or per week $55/70 for singles/doubles. *Springfield Lodge* (tel 358 3222) at 9 Springfield Avenue is worth mentioning because they supply fridge, electric-jug, toasters, crockery and cutlery and deep fry pans. Rates are $18/24 or $84/126 per week if paid in advance.

There are some upper class budget hotels around Kings Cross, the best known of which is probably the *Canberra Oriental* (tel 358 3155) (don't know how it came up with that odd name). It's at 223 Victoria St, right in the middle of things, a strange location for a Temperance Union hotel in fact! There are a wide variety of rooms and all rates include a very good breakfast. Cheapest singles are $18.50 (with washbasin) and they go up through $23, $25 right up to $45 for the newest rooms with bathroom and colour TV. Equivalent doubles (there are no rock-bottom doubles) cost $54 and $55. The restaurant also does lunch and dinner.

East Sydney The *Park Hotel* (tel 357 5537) is at 20 Yurong St, East Sydney, right behind the museum and just across Hyde Park from the city. East Sydney is between the city and Kings Cross so it's very convenient. This is a very straightforward place but clean and some of the recently done up rooms are quite pleasant. A catch is that you can check in only between 9 am and 7 pm on weekdays, 9 am and noon on Saturdays — any other time you're out of

luck. Cost is $10 a night per person, but by the week it's only $38 for one, $70 for two.

Bondi Beach You can get to Bondi from the city by bus but it's far quicker to get the Eastern Suburbs train to Bondi Junction and change to a bus (buy a rail/bus ticket). There are quite a few places around Bondi, the most popular is probably at 11A Consett Avenue where *Thelellen Lodge* (tel 30 1521) has room-only rates from $11.50/19 plus $2 for a light breakfast. The pleasant rooms have fridges and tea-making equipment. The *Thelellen Beach Inn* (tel 30 5333) at 2 Campbell Parade used to be the Tarleton Hotel and is under the same management and has the same prices.

Bondi Beach Guest House (tel 371 0202) has some rooms at 124 Curlewis St and some at 11 Consett Avenue. Again there are fridges and tea-making equipment and also limited communal cooking facilities. Room only rates are from $10/16 for singles/doubles. *Bondi Lodge* (tel 30 5863) at 63 Fletcher St costs $12/20 including a cooked breakfast — all meals are available. There are cheaper weekly rates. Still in Bondi the *Sharon Private Hotel* (tel 30 1495) at 264 Bondi Rd is very simple, none of the rooms have washbasins and it's a bit noisy. Rooms are $15/24, an extra $3 for breakfast and there are cooking facilities at this popular place.

The *Hotel Astra* (tel 30 1201), at 34 Campbell Parade overlooking the beach, is a big, old-fashioned looking place with all sorts of rooms. The Astra's bars are a popular local gathering place, good food available too. Rooms are $10/20 or with attached bathroom they're $20/35. All the rooms have TVs and some (cheapies as well as the better ones) have a fine view over the beach — if you're staying there you might as well see it. At the corner of Campbell Parade and Curlewis St the *Hotel Bondi* (tel 30 3271) is another big, old rambling place and the rates here range from $13.50 to $22 for singles, $27 to $40 for twins and doubles.

Coogee Coogee is down the coast a bit from Bondi. There are a couple of places worth mentioning here. The *Grand Pacific Private Hotel* (tel 665 6301) at the corner of Carr and Beach Sts costs from $10 to $18 single or $20 to $35 double. There's a shared kitchen and it's pleasantly close to the beach. At the corner of Carr and Arden Sts the *Oceanic Hotel* (tel 665 5221) charges $12/20-25 for singles/doubles and twins in the more spartan rooms or $24/32 in the more luxurious ones. The cheaper rooms are usually permanently full. This is a hotel with other attractions — popular bars and music on weekends.

North Shore There are a number of private hotels on the north shore but they tend to be up a notch in price. The *Elite Private Hotel* (tel 922 2060) is just across the bridge at 133 Carabella St, Kirribilli and has rooms from $15 to $20 for singles, $25 to $30 doubles, 20% discount by the week. Tea and coffee are provided but a light breakfast is an extra $3. At 3 Milson Rd, Cremorne Point the *Waldorf Private Hotel* (tel 90 2621) is very handy to the ferry. Bed & breakfast is $18 to $25 single, $28 to $35 twin, 10% discount by the week. Like the Elite there's a guest kitchen.

If you don't mind being as far out as Manly (a nice trip to the city on the Manly ferry) then the following places all charge $15/25 for singles/doubles: *Manly Lodge* (tel 977 8514) at 22 Victoria Parade, *Sun Surf* (tel 977 3779) at 96 Ocean Beach and the *People's Palace* (another one) (tel 977 6177) at 61 Pittwater Rd. The Palace rate includes a light breakfast.

Motels The most central motel with a reasonable tariff is *Cron-Lodge Motel* (tel 331 2433) at 289 Crown St, Surry Hills. Rooms cost $25/30, extra people at $5 and they have a fridge, tea and coffee making facilities, toaster, crockery and cutlery.

At Bondi the *Alice Motel* (tel 30 5231) at 30 Fletcher St is excellent value, particularly if you want weekly or longer rates. Rooms are the usual motel standard (although the TVs are only black & white) and there's even a pool. Costs are $28 single, $32 to $40 for doubles and twins. In the off-season there are cheaper weekly rates.

Another fairly convenient low-priced place is the *Esron Motel* (tel 398 7022) at 96 St Pauls St, Ranwick (between Coogee and the city) where fully equipped singles/doubles cost from $25/29 and again there's a swimming pool.

If you don't mind being out a bit the *Bombora Motel* (tel 977 5461) at 46 Malvern Avenue, Manly has all the usual facilities including a light breakfast in its price of $20/28-30. It's only one block from the beach.

Colleges The usual rules apply — vacs only, students for preference. Best bets are the two 'International Houses'. The following colleges are at the University of NSW, Kensington. New College (tel 662 6066) costs $13 for students, $21 for non-students with full board. They also have weekly rates and bed & breakfast only rates. Werrane College (tel 662 6199) is a Catholic college which takes men only — $12 for students, $16 for non-students. Kensington College takes conference groups only. At International House (tel 663 0418) full board is $16 a day for students, $20 for non-students.

A lot of the colleges at the University of Sydney, Camperdown, tend to be booked out with conferences. Ones to try are Wesley College (tel 51 2024), Women's College (tel 51 1195), St John's College (tel 51 1240) which is closed December and January, Sancta

Sophia College (tel 51 2467) which usually has conferences and otherwise prefers students, St Andrew's College (tel 51 1449) and International House (tel 660 5364). These all charge around $15 a night.

Camping Unfortunately Sydney's campsites tend to be rather a long way out of town and many of the closer in places are for caravans only. You can expect to pay about $6 to 10 for two for a campsite or $16 to 22 for an on-site van (up to $30 for a de-luxe van). The sites listed below are within a 30 km radius of the centre.

If you want a break from the city without going too far afield you can camp at The Basin in Ku-ring-gai Chase National Park for $4 per tent per night. There are only cold showers and there's a scarcity of wood so it may pay to bring wood or a cooker in. Take all your food too although you can buy bread and milk off the ferry at 9.20 am. It's a one-hour walk from the road or a $1 ferry trip from Palm Beach (get to Palm Beach from Wynyard Station on a number 190 bus for $1.50, it takes one hour 50 minutes.

Woronora Caravan Park (tel 521 2291), Menai Rd, Woronora, 30 km south, camping $8 to 10, on-site vans $20 to 25 per day.
Sheralee Tourist Caravan Park (tel 599 7161), Bryant St, Rockdale, 13 km south, no tents, on-site vans $20 to 26 per day.
Bass Hill Tourist Park (tel 72 9670), 713 Hume Highway, Bass Hill, 23 km south, camping $6, on-site vans $16 to 20 per day.
Sundowner Ryde (tel 88 1933), Lane Cove Rd, North Ryde, 14 km north, camping $6, on-site vans $18 to 22 or de-luxe $22 to 26 per day.
Van Village Caravan Park (tel 88 3649), Plassey Rd, North Ryde, 14 km north, camping $6 to 8, on-site vans $18 to 20

per day.
Lakeside Caravan Park (tel 913 7845), Ocean Parade, Narrabeen, 26 km north, camping $3.
Ramsgate Beach Caravan Park (tel 529 7329), 289 The Grand Parade, Ramsgate, 18 km south, no camping, on-site vans.

Places to Eat
Melbourne's food snobs like to look down their sensitive noses at Sydney eateries but actually there's probably little difference. If you're going to eat out in Sydney very often a good book is *Cheap Eats in Sydney* by John Thackara & Vere Kenny. It costs $3.95, 'The same price', the cover notes, 'as a glass of water at one of those really expensive, overrated, poncy restaurants'. Sydney doesn't have the same distinct food areas the way Melbourne does — you'll find interesting restaurants all over Sydney: in the centre of course (particularly near Central Station and Circular Quay) but also in Paddo, Balmain, Glebe, Newtown, Redfern and most of the beach suburbs.

Greek A long standing favourite in Sydney is the *New Hellas* upstairs at 287 George St. Unlike a lot of Greek places this is very much white tablecloth, not bare formica, but you don't appear to pay too much more for the ambience. If you reserve a table in advance then ask for one by the window so you can enjoy the view over Hyde Park. The *Illiad*, just round the corner at 126 Liverpool St is probably a little more expensive but also popular.

Away from the centre in the basement at 336 Pitt St, *Diethnes* is Greek in the more spartan tradition. Open Monday to Saturday, it has low prices and lots of good food. If you're still in the souvlakia and moussaka mood, *Dilina* is at 158 Redfern St in beautiful inner-city Redfern and does excellent value set meals. You'll probably escape for $20 or less for a couple for a three-course meal without wine. They have Greek wines and are closed on Sundays.

Italian The humble pizzeria is everywhere in Sydney. If a very late night pizza is needed they try *Pinnochio's Pizzeria* at 87 Darlinghurst St, Kings Cross — they range from $4 to $8.

If you follow the crowds around 12.30 into a dull looking little house in Chapel Lane, East Sydney (close to the Crown and Stanely Sts junction) you will find yourself upstairs in *No Names*. So called because it has no name, no sign, no nothing but dirt cheap and very filling spaghetti and one or two other daily dishes. This is definitely a Sydney lunch time experience not to miss but it has become so 'in' of late that you may have to queue to get in (and no longer does the bottle of Fanta arrive with a plonk on your table at meal time, although Fantas is still about all there is on offer to drink). It's open 12 noon to 2 pm and 6 to 9 pm every day.

Another very popular Italian specialist is the *Italo-Australian Club* upstairs at 727 George St, down towards the Central Railway Station. The restaurant is open to the public and serves up really first class, highly authentic food at rock-bottom prices and in very plain surroundings. Or at least it did last time I was there, recent reports indicate that it may be in a period of decline.

Another place which has had some variable reports of late is *Tre Venezie* at 8 Liberty St, Stanmore. The decor here is not plain at all — garish would be a better description — but the food, particularly the pasta dishes, will take your mind off it. There's a string of authentic Italian eateries along the Parramatta Rd in Leichhardt if you want to explore but unfortunately Italian food has suffered excessively from price inflation in Sydney of late.

Italian in name only, the *Old Spaghetti Factory* at 80 George St in the Rocks is good, cheap fun and the range of spaghettis (with recommendations on the wall to avoid spaghetti with chocolate sauce) are mass market but not at all bad. The factory is full of Victoriana and odd bits and pieces — everything from confessional booths in the bar to a Bondi tram shooting through the middle of the dining area. It's a Sydney showpiece not to be missed.

Middle East In Surry Hills, where Cleveland and Elizabeth Sts meet, are a host of Lebanese places most of which are good or even better than good. Try *Abdul's*, right on the corner, for an excellent value square meal in unpretentious surroundings, or for good takeaways. *Emad's* at 298 Cleveland St, just up from the corner, has good food in slightly posher (but only very slightly) surroundings. A couple of doors down at 302 *Salinda's* is also excellent value with a $7 fixed price meal. At 423 Cleveland St you can shift across to Turkey at *Girne Pide* to try 'pide', a sort of Turkish pizza; cheap and very good.

The *Ya-Habibi* at 100 Campbell Parade, Bondi Beach, is Middle East by the seashore — very good food at good prices. It used to be known as the Sheik's Tent.

Chinese Dixon St, Haymarket — just a short walk up George St from the city — is Sydney's Chinatown with a whole flock of Chinese restaurants. The *Eastern* at 52 and the *Lean Sun Low* at 54 are two of the more basic cheapies. They share a kitchen so the food is very similar. Round the corner at 110 Hay St, and then up the stairs, will find you at *Tai Yuen* which is a little more expensive but not much flashier. This is a long running place with an excellent reputation.

The Chinese places spread along George and Hay Sts in this area too. The *Malaya* at 787 George St is a long standing favourite with local uni students for its reasonably cheap Malay-Chinese food. The prices haven't altered too much despite additions of more carpet and fancy decorations. It's licensed.

For a really good Chinese smorgasbord visit the *York St Lantern* at 131 York St near the town hall. For $3.30 you get all you can eat and that includes tea, coffee, soup and bread although desserts are extra. It's open Monday to Saturday from 11.30 am to 3 pm and 5 to 9 pm and is very popular. There are a couple of other Chinese smorgasbords, one in Oxford St close to Hyde Park for $3.50 and the other, the *Bamboo Kitchen* at 147 King St in the city for $3.80 which even includes a glass of wine.

Out at Bondi Junction the *Yung Sang* is a good restaurant and take-away on the corner of Bronte Rd and Ebley St. Or obscurely located at 80 The Corso, Manly, you can get excellent value Singaporean-Chinese food at the *Manly Asian Kitchen.*

Other Ethnics There are a couple of Indonesian places along Pitt St in the city. The *Garuda Indonesian Restaurant* at 382B is the more expensive of the two with gado gado, nasi goreng or sate for around $6. The emphasis here is on Sumatran food, for $16 you can have often fiery nasi padang for two. The *Java Indonesian Restaurant* at 435 is plainer and main courses are $4 to 5.

Sydney also has lots of Vietnamese restaurants, many of them excellent value like *Tien* at 95-97 Glebe Point Rd, Glebe. A real Sydney favourite of mine is *Salama* at 37 Cameron St, Birchgrove (that's really Balmain). It's North African and the food is delicious; you can sit up or lounge back on cushions on the floor, and it's reasonably priced. It's open Tuesday to Saturday.

Finally two popular and good value Europeans — close together on Oxford St, Darlinghurst. The *Balkan* at 209 specialises in those two basic Yugoslav-

ian dishes raznjici and cevapcici. Ask for a pola pola and you'll get half of each. It's basic and straightforward food, filling and very cheap but definitely for real meat eaters only. The Balkan is closed on Tuesdays. At 255 the *Stuttgarter Hof* offers hearty eating German style, although it is rather more expensive.

Vegetarian The *Whole Meal* is a natural health food restaurant on the first floor of Angel Arcade, 121 Pitt St, just down from Martin Place. Everything is really fresh and the prices are quite reasonable. The *Hare Krishnas* put on a free meal in Darlinghurst Rd, just south of Kings Cross, between 5 and 7 pm. It may, of course, include some 'spiritual' food.

In the city centre there are a couple of *Sanitarium* health food places. They are basically take-aways, very popular for city lunchtime sandwiches. One is on King St, the other on Hunter St, both between Pitt and George.

Basic Odds & Ends Up at Kings Cross the *Astoria* on Darlinghurst Rd, round the corner from the fountain, is famous for its good value, basic, home-cooked, Australian-style food. You can get a big meal for around $3.20. Still in the Cross, *New York* at 23 Bayswater Rd is another basic place offering straight forward food at very low prices. Another old-fashioned place which is great value is *Johnnie's Fish Cafe* at 57A Fitzroy St, Surry Hills, where there's takeaway fish & chips and also eat there facilities.

Meals with a View If you're visiting the opera house and want to eat consider the *Harbour Restaurant* — it's overpriced and the food is nothing to get excited about but the view is not to be missed. Just make sure it's a sunny day so you can sit outside. The expensive Bennelong Restaurant is to be avoided unless you're in the Lear Jet class.

At Watsons Bay on Marine Parade, *Doyle's on the Beach* has good but expensive seafood but more important a view and atmosphere which is unsurpassed. It's BYO, very popular and doesn't take bookings so you've just got to get there early. And again make sure the sun is shining, you got to Doyle's in order to eat outside, the food is really just upper class fish & chips. There was another Doyle's at Rose Bay but it has now closed.

Another place to consider for the setting as much as the food is the *Sydney Tower Level 2*, atop the Centrepoint Tower. Yes it is a revolving restaurant (just over an hour for the complete revolution) where the views are usually more important than the food but the food really isn't bad and the views are indeed superb. Eat before 7.45 pm and it'll cost you a mere $14 ($16 on Saturdays). Wine is from $3.50 for a small carafe. After 7.45 the prices start to soar. The glossy *Pier One* centre in the Rocks also has meals with a view.

Chains & Pub Food The *McDonald* plague started its march around Australia in Sydney so there are plenty of them. There's one up on George St all done up in art nouveau style — worth a hamburger just to look at. There are also plenty of *Pizza Huts* and *Kentucky Fried*s.

A bit plastic and also a good notch up market, good quality food can be found at the *Cahill's Brass Rail Taverns*. There are more than a dozen of them scattered all over town with serve-yourself food at lunchtime or in the early evening. One is under Goldfields House on the corner of Alfred and George Sts near Circular Quay, another is downstairs in Angel Arcade on Pitt St, another in the Ansett terminal building on Oxford St. The *Cahill's Dutch Village* under the Park Regis Hotel at 27 Park St in the city is a good and conveniently

central place for breakfast.

The huge *Centrepoint Tavern*, under the central Centrepoint shopping complex, is popular for its large assortment of quite reasonably priced meals and lower priced children's dishes. There are also lots of regular counter meal pubs — try the one across from the mining museum in the Rocks.

Locations Since Sydney's restaurants are not found in specific national quarters to anything like the same extent as Melbourne a location guide follows:

City *Bamboo Kitchen* (Chinese), *Centrepoint Tavern* (general), *Diethnes* (Greek), *Eastern* (Chinese), *Garuda Indonesian Restaurant* (Indonesian), *Harbour Restaurant* (general), *Illiad* (Greek), *Italo-Australian Club* (Italian), *Java Indonesian Restaurant* (Indonesian), *Lean Sun Low* (Chinese), *Malaya* (Chinese), *New Hellas* (Greek), *No Names* (Italian), *Old Spaghetti Factory* (Italian), *Pier One* (general), *Sanitarium* (vegetarian), *Sydney Tower Level 2* (general & views), *Tai Yuen* (Chinese), *Whole Meal* (vegetarian), *York St Lantern* (Chinese).

Inner City *Abdul's* (Lebanese, Surry Hills), *Astoria* (plain & simple, Kings Cross), *Balkan* (Yugoslav, Darlinghurst), *Dilina* (Greek, Redfern), *Emad's* (Lebanese, Surry Hills), *Girne Pide* (Turkish, Surry Hills), *Hare Krishnas* (vegetarian, Kings Cross), *Johnnie's Fish Cafe* (fish & chips, Surry Hills), *New York* (plain & simple, Kings Cross), *Pinnochio's Pizzeria* (Italian, Kings Cross), *Salama* (North African, Birchgrove), *Salinda's* (Lebanese, Surry Hills), *Stuttgarter Hof* (German, Darlinghurst), *Tien* (Vietnamese, Glebe), *Tre Venezie* (Italian, Stanmore), *Yung Sang* (Chinese, Bondi Junction).

Beaches *Doyles on the Beach* (fish & chips, Watsons Bay & Rose Bay), *Manly Asian Kitchen* (Chinese, Manly), *Ya-Habibi* (Lebanese, Bondi Beach).

All Over *Cahills* (mainly in the city area), *Kentucky Frieds, Pizza Huts, McDonalds.*

Entertainment

Check the *Sydney City Express*, a free weekly paper, for what's on or listen to the What's On service at 6.30 pm on radio 2JJJ. A lot of Sydney evening entertainment takes place in the Leagues Clubs or other 'private' clubs where the profits from the assembled ranks of one-armed bandits (you're in gambling country) finance big name acts at low, low prices. They may be 'members only' for the locals but as an interstate or, even better, international visitor you're generally welcome to drop in. Simply ring ahead and ask, wave your interstate driving licence or your passport at the door. They're a Sydney institution so if you get a chance visit one, the most glittering and lavish of the lot is the St Georges Leagues Club.

Music Sydney doesn't have the same pub music scene that you get in Melbourne although there are a fair few places where you can count on something going on most nights of the week. What Sydney does have in this category is a whole stack of pleasant wine bars/bistros where for a low (even free) entry charge you can catch the music and even get a meal if you want. Some wine bars, pubs and discos which are worth a look include:

The Basement (tel 27 9727), 29 Reiby Place, Circular Quay — Monday to Wednesday till 12.30 am, Thursday to Saturday till 3 am — free admission except after 10 pm on Friday and Saturday when it's $2 — excellent modern jazz.
The Old Push (tel 27 2588), 109 George St, Sydney — Monday to Saturday nights — trad and other jazz.
The Cock 'n Bull Tavern, corner Bronte & Ebley Sts, Bondi Junction — live music Tuesday, Wednesday, Sunday — disco Thursday to Saturday.
Royal Antler Hotel (tel 913 7301), Narrabeen — Thursday to Saturday and Sunday afternoons — rock.

Salina's (in the Coogee Bay Hotel) (tel 665 0000), Coogee Bay Rd, Coogee Bay — Friday and Saturday — cover charge varies — rock.
Jenny's Wine Bar, Pitt St, City, opposite the People's Palace — Tuesday to Saturday till midnight, Tuesdays free, other nights variable — jazz — a nice little place with meals at reasonable prices and happy hour from 5 to 6 pm when all drinks are 50c.
Grand National (tel 32 3096), 161 Underwood St, Paddington — Friday and Saturday — no cover — live rock.
French's Wine Bar (tel 331 2824), Oxford St, just north of Taylor Square — every night 5 pm to 3 am — free admission — rock.
Astra (tel 30 1201), Bondi Beach — Thursday to Sunday — sometimes a cover charge — rock — can get a bit rough.
Paradise Club, basement on Darlinghurst Rd, between the fountain and Kings Cross station, near McDonalds — every night 10 pm to 4 or 5 am — no cover — jazz — good, not crowded but food rather pricey.
Benson's Wine Bar, 103 Oxford St, Bondi Junction — Tuesday to Sunday till 4 am — cover up to $3, Thursday to Saturday — rock — meals available.
Musician's Club, 94 Chalmers St, Surry Hills — Wednesday or Thursday to Saturday or Sunday — acoustic concert on Thursdays.

There are many, many other places including for rock the *Kings Cross Rex*, next to the El Alamein Fountain in the Cross or the *Windsor Castle Hotel* in Paddo. For jazz you could try the *Booth St Dispensary* wine bar in Annandale, the *Soup Plus Restaurant* in George St or the *And Now for Something Completely Different Restaurant* in Chatswood.

Theatre Sydney has the usual selection of theatres and more adventurous new theatre places. The *Nimrod* (tel 69 5003) at 500 Elizabeth St, Surry Hills has both a downstairs and upstairs stage and often simultaneous programmes. Or there's the *New Theatre* (tel 519 3404), 542 King St, Newtown, which isn't really so new at all since it's been going for years, and many others.

Film You'll find interesting films at the *Trak*, 150 Elizabeth St, between Liverpool and Goulburn Sts, where Australian and experimental films are regular features. The *Sydney University Union Theatre* can always be counted on for something good and at low prices. The *National Film Theatre of Australia* shows classic films at the Opera House and at the Paddington Town Hall Cinema. Other non-commercial (or less-commercial?) cinemas worth trying are the *Double Bay Village Twin*, the *Rose Bay Wintergarden* and the *Academy Twin* in Paddington.

Odds & Ends In the summer there are free music and rock performances in parks on the weekends. There's music at lunchtime in Martin Place between Pitt and Castlereagh Sts. You can always sit and listen to the buskers around the Cross and a wander through the Cross at night is always an education! Try and see something at the Opera House — they have film shows, live theatre, classical music, opera and even rock concerts.

Getting There

Air Sydney's Kingsford Smith Airport, better known as Mascot because that's where it's situated, is Australia's busiest both for domestic and international flights. It's fairly central which makes getting to or from it a breeze but also means that flights have to stop at 10 pm due to noise regulations. The main runway stretches out into Botany Bay and these problems of space restrictions and noise hassles have prompted lots of discussion, but no action, on building a new airport.

You can fly into Sydney from all the usual international points and from all over Australia. Between Melbourne and Sydney, for example, there are flights every hour for $124 ($93 standby). Other costs include Adelaide $170 ($128), Alice Springs $241 ($181), Brisbane $128 ($96), Canberra $71 ($53), Perth $322 ($242).

Rail All the interstate and principal regional services operate to and from the Central Railway Station. Between Melbourne and Sydney there are two overnight services daily (the Southern Aurora and the Spirit of Progress) plus the Intercapital Daylight Express from Monday to Saturday. The trip takes 12½ to 14 hours and the fares are $53 in economy, $75 in 1st. Sleeping berths are an extra $20 in 1st, there are no sleeping berths in economy. You can take a car on the Southern Aurora for $70.

Monday to Saturday the Canberra-Monaro Express departs Sydney at 7.30 am and arrives Canberra at 12.19 pm. The fare is $16 in economy. To continue to Melbourne by rail from Canberra you have to take a bus to Yass to connect with the Sydney-Melbourne services.

Travelling north there's a daily overnight service to Brisbane, the Brisbane Limited Express, which takes 16 hours and costs $53 conomy, $75 1st, exactly the same as to Melbourne. You can also train to Murwillumbah, just south of the Queensland border, from where a connecting bus runs into the Gold Coast. This trip takes 16½ hours and the fare is $31.90 in economy, $44.70 in 1st. A sleeping berth is an extra $30 on top of the 1st class fare. This is a much cheaper way of getting to Queensland, especially if you want to start your Queensland travels on the Gold Coast. Cars can be taken on this train for $84.

Direct Sydney-Adelaide train connections are made four days a week by taking the Sydney-Perth Indian Pacific between Sydney and Peterborough via Broken Hill and the connecting service between Peterborough and Adelaide. The trip takes about 29 hours and the fares are $118 in economy or $154 in 1st, plus $16 or $20 respectively for sleepers. The Indian-Pacific fare includes meals. You can also travel between the two cities via Melbourne and in that case the fares are a straight combination of the Melbourne-Sydney and Adelaide-Melbourne fares — this is cheaper than the direct route via Broken Hill.

Sydney-Perth is on the four times weekly Indian-Pacific service, see the Perth section for more details on this service. From early '83 there will also be a direct service from Sydney via Broken Hill and Tarcoola to Alice Springs on the new ghan line.

Services within the state include Sydney-Newcastle $7.60, Sydney-Albury $26.40, Sydney-Griffith $26.40, Sydney - Wollongong $2.85, Sydney - Orange $14.40. All these fares are economy. There's a 14-day Nurail Pass allowing unlimited use of railway services within the state. It's available in 1st class only and costs $90, no reductions for students. See the NSW introductory travel section for more details on rail travel.

Bus There are lots of bus services to and from Sydney with the big two operators and a host of others. Greyhound and Ansett Pioneer both have services to and from Canberra ($25, 5½ hours), Melbourne ($42, 14½ hours), Adelaide ($75, 24 hours) and Brisbane ($48, 17 hours). Often there are alternative routes between the cities — you can, for example, travel Brisbane-Sydney via the coast or via New England, Melbourne-Sydney via the Hume and Canberra or via the coast. Ansett Pioneer (tel 268 1881) operate from the Ansett terminal at Oxford Square, Oxford St, Darling-

hurst. Greyhound (tel 331 6611) are at 49 MacLachlan Avenue, Kings Cross.

Two other companies operating regularly scheduled services, principally north to northern NSW and Queensland, are Skennars and McCaffertys.

There are quite a few independent bus operators with interstate services to and from Sydney. Across Australia Coachlines is at Suite 44, 48 George St, Parramatta (tel 689 1000) and at Vikings of London, Shop 8, Sydney Square Arcade, near the Town Hall (tel 29 2201) and other agents. They operate air-conditioned, non-smoking coaches between Perth and Sydney twice a week. Fares to or from Sydney include Melbourne $25, Adelaide $40, Perth $99, there are no concession fares.

VIP Express (tel 521 2969 or 6402) have their Sydney booking office at 34 Toronto Parade, Sutherland. They operate daily to and from Brisbane with departures at each end at 7 pm, arriving at 10.30 am the next morning. The fare is $25. Continental Trailways (tel 264 3685 or 7855) are at Mike Eden Travel, Wesley Arcade, Pitt St. They have air-con buses with toilets and operate to Melbourne daily for $31, Brisbane daily for $34 and Perth three times weekly in conjunction with Ansett Pioneer for $110.

In the introductory NSW travel section note the bus travel restrictions in NSW where on many routes you are not allowed to use the interstate bus services for intrastate stops, unless you're on a bus pass tickets. Thus, for example, you cannot take a Sydney-Brisbane bus to Newcastle or other intermediate stops.

Getting Around

Rail If you can get to your destination in Sydney by rail it's generally far quicker than by bus. Quite a lot of Sydney is covered by the suburban rail service, which has frequent trains. Take ear muffs on the underground sections or you'll be deafened by the roar!

Bus There are extensive bus services in Sydney but they are very slow in comparison to the rail services. Most are run by the Urban Transit Authority, but some suburban services are run by private operators. Circular Quay, Wynyard Square and Central Railway Station are the main bus stops. There's a free 777 city bus service which goes from York St down King St, along Pitt St, into Park St, around the Domain, down Market St and Clarence St and back to its starting point. The 666 free service operates from Hunter St near Wynyard Station on a loop out to the Art Gallery and back.

The Sydney Explorer is a tourist bus service which operates a continuous loop around the tourist sights of the city at roughly 15 minute intervals from 9.30 am to 5 pm daily. It costs $8 for the day and you can then hop on and off wherever you like. It would be much cheaper to get around these places by the ordinary bus (in fact it's possible to walk around the places visited by the bus), the Explorer just makes it easier as you don't have to work out the bus routes. It goes from Circular Quay via the Opera House, Mrs Macquarie's Chair, the Art Gallery, Kings Cross, Woolloomooloo, Central Station and back through the Rocks to Circular Quay. The Explorer ticket also gets you a guidebook to the central sights, concessions on the Manly and Taronga Park ferries for that day and various other concessions.

Ferries Sydney's ferries are one of the nicest ways of getting around in Australia. Apart from the harbour itself there are also services at the Royal National Park to the south and on the Pittwater to the north. Not only are there the fine old harbour ferries (Manly 70c, other places generally 50c) but also newfangled hydrofoils to Manly ($1.30). A pleasant intro to harbour ferries is the short 50c hop across to Taronga Park Zoo (you can also get a return ticket that includes admission to the zoo).

All the harbour ferries depart from Circular Quay, close to where the original settlement in Sydney was made. The Urban Transit Authority put out a free ferry and hydrofoil timetable available for the Sydney Harbour services. Ferry services on the Pittwater operate from Church Point and Palm Beach. There's also a service from Palm Beach to Patonga, which is actually the first leg of a cruise up Cowan Waters. From Patonga it's possible to bus (changing once on the way) to Gosford. This service is $2, anywhere on the Pittwater costs $1.

There are a variety of more comprehensive harbour cruises as well as lunchtime and supper cruises. Generally the cruises run by public bodies are far cheaper than the private ones. The 2½ hour Urban Transit Authority Harbour Ferry Cruises for $3.50 are the best value; they depart on Wednesday, Saturday, Sunday and everyday on school holidays at 1.30 pm, or at 2.30 pm on Sundays and public holidays. At 2 pm on Sundays and public holidays you can cruise upriver for the same economy price of $3.50.

Special Deals The Public Transport Commission has several special deals. For $3.30 you can get a Dayrover which covers a day's travel on any suburban bus, train or ferry except the hydrofoils, after 9 am on weekdays or all day on weekends. You can even use them on the Harbour Cruises or Upriver Cruises. There is also a Weekly Rover available for $16.50 with the same conditions as the Dayrover. 'Mini Fares' are available during the same hours as the Dayrover tickets on return rail journeys over four km within the outer Sydney metropolitan and Sydney suburban areas — they give up to a third off normal fares.

If you use the Eastern Suburbs rail line you can get a combination bus-rail ticket so you can change to a bus to a destinations such as Bondi or Bondi Junction station, this works out cheaper than buying the tickets separately. Remember also on the trains that even if you known you'll have to change trains, buy a ticket to your ultimate destination when you board the first train, it's cheaper.

General Public Transport Gregory's produce *Sydney by Public Transport*, widely available from newsagents and bookshops for about $4. You can get info on all forms of public transport in Sydney from the Urban Transit Authority Travel & Tours Centre (tel 29 7614) at 11-31 York St, Sydney. There's a public transport map available for a small charge. It's not too helpful but does give you some idea of the services available and tells you where to enquire for further info on the particular services you require.

Car Rental There are a large number of rent-a-car operators in Sydney including all the big boys. You'll find Avis, Budget, Thrifty and Hertz all on William St up from the city to Kings Cross, together with a number of the local operators. In the telephone yellow pages there's a long list of agencies under 'Motor Car Rentals (Drive Yourself)'. Most of the cheap outfits won't let you take their cars very far afield, so worth mentioning because they do is Bargain Car Rentals (tel 648 1096) on the corner of Parramatta Rd and Alban St in Lidcombe. Their whole fleet is HQ Holdens, most automatics but some manuals, and you can use them anywhere in NSW (except the far west), in lower Queensland and in Victoria. Cost is $19.50 per day including insurance and 160 km. Their weekly rate is $117 including insurance and 1000 km. Excess km cost 9c each. These rates aren't bad for around the city but if you're going to do any sort of distance it soon begins to compare badly with big operators and their unlimited km rates.

Rent-a-Bug (tel 428 2098 or 747 3770) has a fleet of '70 to '74 VW beetles at $15.50 per day or $97.50 per week including insurance and unlimited km but only for use in Sydney. Rent-a-Wreck (tel 808 2888) have cars from $17 to 24 a day including insurance and unlimited km but again only for city use.

Bicycle Rental The bike hire places tend to be out in the suburbs. Centennial Park Hire (tel 398 5027) is at 50 Clovelly Rd, Randwick and charges $2.40 an hour, $15 a day or $25 a Monday to Friday week. The Bike Shop (tel 958 1465) at 195 High St, Willoughby charges $12 a day, $20 a weekend, $35 a week. Fit & Free (tel 547 1812) at 617 Princes Highway, Blakehurst charges $10 a day but they are a very long way out.

Airport The international and domestic terminals at Mascot Airport are some distance apart — a bus between the two costs $1.20. The private Kingsford Smith Airport Bus Service operates every hour between 6 am and 6 pm and costs $2.20. It picks up around the city and Kings Cross area but you must phone 677 3221-2-3 at least an hour beforehand to book.

If you're willing to walk half an hour to the Arncliff Station you can get into the city by train for just 75c. There are some public bus services from the domestic terminals to the city (302 and

385 to Circular Quay) or Bondi Junction (064) but they operate mainly for airport workers and principally on weekdays. A taxi between the airport and city will cost you about $6 or 7 depending on where you're going, possibly more if the traffic is heavy. Hertz, Budget and Avis have desks at the airport. Luggage lockers at the airport cost 40c.

In the city TAA's main office is centrally located at 16 Elizabeth St (tel 693 3333) while Ansett's is just beyond Hyde Park at Oxford Square on the corner of Oxford and Riley Sts (tel 268 1111).

Tours City tours cost around $10 to 14. Longer day tours include Katoomba in the Blue Mountains (around $20), the Hawkesbury River ($30), Old Sydney Town ($27), Jenolan Caves ($26), around Sydney ($32), Canberra ($44).

Cricket fan arriving at the Sydney Cricket Ground for a test match.

AROUND SYDNEY
One of the major attractions of life in Sydney is the superb national parks to the north and south of the city. There is much more also within easy reach, however. In the early days of European settlement small towns were soon established around the major centre and although some of these, like Parramatta, have been engulfed by Sydney's urban sprawl, they're still of great interest today.

Royal National Park
Only 30 km south of the city this is the second oldest national park in the world, only Yellowstone National Park in the USA predates it. The park offers some superb bushwalks including spectacular walks along the cliff tops. There are also good surfing beaches, a number of pleasant rocky swimming holes in the park and the Hacking River runs right through the park. You can hire rowboats on the river at Audley and the park also has camping sites for longer

stays. The park is carpeted with wildflowers in late winter and early spring. When I lived in Sydney this was a favourite getaway.

Ku-ring-gai Chase National Park
As the Royal Park is to the south so Ku-ring-gai is to the north. Just 24 km from the centre you can get to the park by public transport. There are many bushwalks again and the park also has some magnificent Aboriginal rock carvings which are quite easy to find. High points in the park offer magnificent views across the wide expanse of the Pittwater while from the northern tip of the park there's another fantastic view across to the hammerhead-like rock of Barrenjoey Point at the end of Palm Beach. Ku-ring-gai also has an excellent wildlife sanctuary and a camping area.

You can get to the park by public transport — take a bus from Wynyard to Church Point (1½ hours) then ferry or take a bus from Wynyard to Palm

Beach (nearly two hours) and ferry from there. There's a camping area at the Basin, a ferry runs from Palm Beach. Entry to the park costs $2 per car. On Namba Rd in Terrey Hills, close to the park, is the popular Waratah Park wildlife reserve. It's open Tuesdays to Sundays and on school holidays on Mondays too.

Botany Bay

It's a common misconception amongst first time visitors to Sydney that the city is built around Botany Bay. Actually Sydney Harbour is Port Jackson and Botany Bay is several km to the south, although the city has expanded today to encompass Botany Bay too. Botany Bay, named by Joseph Banks for the many botanical specimens he found here, was Cook's first entry point and the First Fleet also moored here at first, but quickly decided that Port Jackson was a better site for the first settlement. At Kurnell, on the south side of the bay, Captain Cook's landing place is marked with various monuments and a very interesting Captain Cook Museum with many exhibits and displays relating to the good captain's life and exploration. The centre is open 7 am to 7 pm daily. On the sea side of the landing point there's a stretch of spectacular rocky coast.

Across the bay entrance, beyond the oil tankers which bring crude oil to the Kurnell refinery, is La Perouse where the French explorer of that name turned up in 1788, just two days after the arrival of the first convict fleet. He gave the poms a good scare, they were hardly expecting the French to turn up at another place where the sun never set quite so soon. La Perouse sailed off into the Pacific and totally disappeared, it was not until many years later that the wreck of his ship was discovered on a Pacific island and revealed his unfortunate end. At La Perouse there's a fort on small Bare Island, open daily.

It was built in 1885 in order to repel or discourage a feared Russian (yes Russian) invasion of Australia. The fort is open daily from 8 am to 5 pm and admission is free.

Parramatta (population 128,000)

Sydney has sprawled out to encompass Parramatta, 24 km from the centre, today but in the early days of European settlement this was the second settlement in Australia. Sydney soon proved to be a poor area for farming and in 1788 Parramatta was selected as the first farm settlement. Parramatta Park is the oldest area of the city. Elizabeth Farm House, built in 1793 by John Macarthur, is one of the oldest homes in the country. The Experiment Farm Cottage at 9 Ruse St was built for James Ruse in the early 1800s, open Tuesday, Wednesday, Thursday and Sunday, admission is 60c. Roseneath is a fine example of colonial architecture of the 1830s. The Old Government House is another important early building in the Parramatta Park where there is also a Tramway Museum. You can also find St Johns Cemetery in Parramatta, the oldest in Australia. The interesting pioneer headstones include one dating from 1791, again the oldest in Australia.

There's a Parramatta Information Bureau at Prince Alfred Park on Market St. They have maps and brochures and a walking tour guide. Near Parramatta in Auburn is the Auburn Botanic Gardens which includes an ornamental Japanese garden.

Penrith (population 78,000)

Also on the edge of the capital's urban sprawl, Penrith is on the way to the Blue Mountains. From here you can visit the lion park at Warragamba Dam or Bullen's Animal World at Wallacia. At Doonside there's a large collection of native birds and other wildlife at the Featherdale Wildlife Park.

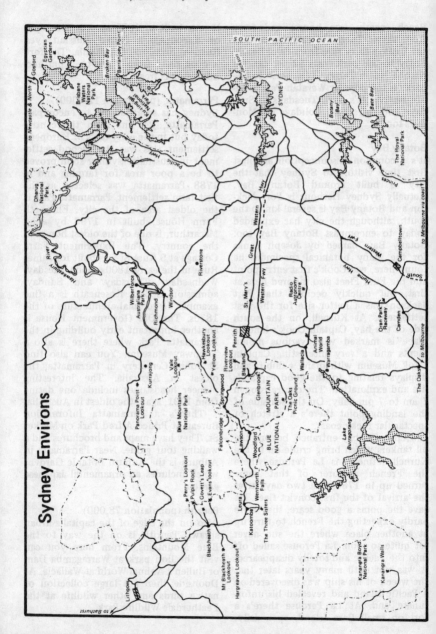

Windsor (population 4500)

One of Australia's earliest towns, Windsor has a number of important early buildings including the convict built St Matthew's Church from 1817. It was designed, like the court-house, by the convict architect Francis Greenway. George St and Thompson Square have a number of other historic buildings. On Thompson St the Tourist Information Centre and the Hawkesbury Museum are located in the old Daniel O'Connell Inn, dating from the 1840s.

The Australiana Village at Wilberforce is six km from Windsor — it has early buildings and a coal mine while on Sundays and public holidays sheepsheering demonstrations, bush-ranger holdups and other pioneering activities take place. At nearby Ebenezer the Presbyterian church was built in 1809 and is said to be the oldest in Australia still in regular use.

Richmond (population 3100)

Just eight km from Windsor, Richmond dates from 1810. Hobartville is an early mansion which is open Sunday to Thursday from 10.30 am to 5 pm. St Peter's Church dates from 1841 and a number of notable pioneers are buried in its cemetery.

Cambelltown (population 37,000)

South of Sydney this is another town which has been swallowed up by Sydney's outward expansion. Buildings in the town date right back to the 1820s including the 1824 St Peter's Church. Queen St in particular has some early houses. On the way south to Cambelltown is Liverpool (population 90,000), now completely swallowed up by Sydney but still with some fine

examples of colonial architecture from the 1820s.

Hawkesbury River

North of Sydney the Hawkesbury River enters the sea at Broken Bay, between Ku-ring-gai Chase and the Bouddi and Brisbane Waters National Park. This is one of the most attractive rivers in Australia and a very popular centre for boating of all types. At Bobbin Head you can hire boats from rowing dinghies to large houseboats and the river is dotted with coves, beaches, picnic spots and some fine riverside restaurants. An excellent way to get a feel for the river is to take the river mailboat run which operates up the river every weekday, departing Brooklyn at 9.30 am and completing its run at 12.30 pm. Passengers can come along for $7, enquire at the NSW Government Tourist Bureau. On Wednesdays the Public Transport Commission in Sydney has a connecting train from Central Station in Sydney at 8.10 am and from Gosford at 8.53 am. The same boat also operates a variety of other cruises on the Hawkesbury and out to Broken Bay.

The tiny settlement of Wisemans Ferry is a popular spot up the river. There are still vehicular ferries operating across the river today and the Wisemans Ferry Inn is named after the original ferry operator. Across the river the Dharug National Park is noted for its many Aboriginal rock carvings which are thought to date back nearly 10,000 years. The Great Northern road which continues north from Wisemans Ferry is a particularly interesting example of early convict road building because it has scarcely changed since its original construction.

THE BLUE MOUNTAINS

The Blue Mountains were once an impenetrable barrier to expansion inland

from Sydney. Despite many attempts to find a route through the mountains, and a bizarre belief amongst many convicts that China, and freedom, was just on the other side, it was not until 1813 that a crossing was finally made and the western plains were opened up. The Blue Mountains National Park has some fantastic scenery, excellent bushwalks and all the gorges, gum trees and cliffs you could ask for.

The hills rise up just 65 km inland from Sydney and even a century ago this was already a popular getaway for affluent Sydney-siders who came up here to escape the summer heat on the coast. The mountains rise as high as 1100 metres and despite the intensive tourist development much of the area is so precipitous that it's still only open for bushwalkers. The blue haze, which gave the mountains their name, is a result of the fine mist of oil given off by eucalyptus trees. The droplets refract the light and intensify the blue.

Places to Stay
There are plenty of hotels, motels and campsites in the Blue Mountains and also youth hostels in Katoomba and Springwood.

Getting There
There are no bus services from Sydney to the Blue Mountains although buses do operate around the various towns of the Blue Mountains. Katoomba is now virtually an outer suburb of Sydney, 109 km from the centre, and trains operate there regularly. The fare is just $4.30 while to Lithgow the 155 km trip costs $7.

Sydney to Katoomba
At Glenbrook the 1833 Lennox Bridge is the oldest bridge still standing on the Australian mainland, there are older bridges in Tasmania. The famous artist Norman Lindsay lived in Springwood from 1912 until he died in 1969. His home at 128 Chapman Parade is now a gallery and museum with exhibits of his paintings, cartoons, illustrations and, in the garden, his sculptures. It's open from 11 am to 5 pm on Fridays, Saturdays and Sundays.

Katoomba (population 12,300)
With its adjacent centres of Wentworth Falls and Leura this is the tourist centre of the Blue Mountains. The Scenic Skyway is a horizontal cable car crossing the gorge over Cooks Crossing with views of Katoomba Falls, Orphan Rock and the Jamison Valley.

The Explorer's Tree, just west of Katoomba, was marked by the original explorers Blaxland, Lawson and Wentworth, who crossed the mountains in 1813. Nearby there's a large aviary and there's also a deer park in Wentworth Falls. Two lookouts provide fine views of the Wentworth Falls which plummet 300 metres into the Jamison Valley. In Leura the National Trust has a garden at Everglades on Denison St with more excellent views over the mountains.

There's a Tourist Information Centre on the corner of Katoomba St and Waratah St.

Walks & Scenery The Blue Mountains National Park is the second largest national park in NSW. The park has many superb bushwalks although there are also some equally good ones outside the park. There's a park visitors' centre at Glenbrook on the eastern edge of the park. Immediately south of Katoomba is one of the park's landmarks, the magnificent Three Sisters rock formation. It's floodlit at night when it makes an awesome sight from Echo Point lookout.

Awesome is also the word to describe the bad taste of the 'three sisters' sculpture outside the restaurant nearby — an excellent example of Australian kitsch. A funicular railway runs down to the base of the Jamison Valley from near the restaurant and you can make a variety of easy, medium and even hard bushwalks to sites in the area. The railway was originally built in the 1880s for transporting miners to a coal mine and its $45°$ incline is one of the steepest in the world. The stroll to the aptly named ruined castle rock formation is one of the best but watch out for leeches if it has been raining.

Beyond Katoomba

The road from Katoomba continues to Lithgow and from there you can follow an alternate route back to Sydney along the scenic old Bells Line of Road. At Mt Victoria Railway Station the small Mt Victoria Historical Museum is a worthwhile visit in this interesting little town. It's open 2 to 5 pm on weekends and public holidays. Off the road at Mt York there's a memorial to the three explorers who first found a way across the Blue Mountains. There is also a short stretch of the original road across the mountains here.

Midway between Katoomba and Lithgow is the tiny town of Hartley, at one time a colonial travellers' halt, there are still a number of very original buildings from the 1830s and '40s. The convict built Court House is now a museum and is open from 10 am to 1 pm and 2

to 5 pm every day except Wednesday.

Near Bell, off Bells Line of Road, is the Zig Zag Railway, an amazing Victorian engineering feat which brought trains down from the Blue Mountains to the western plains. Construction of this complex line was completed in 1869 but with new technology the line was superseded in 1910. In the 1960s, however, railway enthusiasts restored the line and on weekends and public holidays steam trains operate along the old line.

Jenolan Caves

South-west of Katoomba are the best known limestone caves in Australia. There are eight caves open for inspection, the first of which has been open to the public since 1867, but parts of the complex have still not been explored. The caves are open from 10 am to 4 pm daily and after 8 pm. There are a network of walking trails around the caves. The Kanangra Boyd National Park, south of the caves, has excellent facilities for all the normal bush activities. You can camp in the park and there are terrific views from Kanangra Tops.

NORTH TO NEWCASTLE

The spectacular curves of the Pacific Highway between Sydney and Newcastle take you along one of the most scenic routes in Australia. You cross the mouth of the Hawkesbury River and then run beside a couple of large coastal lakes before reaching Newcastle. There are also some interesting spots along the coast, off the highway.

Gosford (population 38,000)

Less than 100 km north of Sydney this is the centre for visiting the Brisbane Waters Park. Old Sydney Town, see below, is a major Sydney area attraction near here. Gosford also has Eric Worrell's Reptile Park for the snake enthusiasts,

Henry Kendall's cottage, built in 1838 as an inn and lived in by the poet in 1874-75, and the Somersby Falls near Old Sydney Town. Near Gosford, Woy Woy (population 12,200) is more or less a dormitory suburb.

Old Sydney Town Only a few km from Gosford and about 70 km north of Sydney, Old Sydney Town is a major reconstruction of early Sydney with replicas of early ships including the brig *Lady Nelson* and trader *Perseverance*, houses and other buildings plus non-stop street theatre retelling events from the colony's early history. Children love the whippings, duels, hangings and floggings. It's open 10 am to 5 pm Wednesday to Sunday and every day during NSW school holidays. Admission for adults is $7. There's a rail tour there from Sydney for $15, it takes all day.

Parks Gosford is the jumping off point for the parks of the area. The Bouddi National Park is a coastal park, 17 km from Gosford with excellent bushwalking, camping and swimming. The beautiful Brisbane Waters National Park offers similar attractions at the mouth of the Hawkesbury.

Gosford to Newcastle

At Gosford you have the option of continuing straight up the Princes Highway or taking a coastal route around the Tuggerah Lake. Wyong (population 3700) is on the Princes Highway while on the coastal route you can visit Terrigal (population 7500), a popular surfing centre. The Entrance (population 20,000) is a very popular resort at the

ocean entrance to Tuggerah Lake. North of the lake is another coastal lake, Lake Macquarie, although here the Princes Highway runs on the ocean side of the lake. This is the largest seaboard lake in Australia and popular for sailing, waterskiing and fishing. Swansea, Belmont and Toronto (total population 17,000) are the main resorts on the lake. In Wangi Wangi, south of Toronto, you can visit the home of artist William Dobell.

There are cruises on the lake on the *Wangi Queen* each Sunday and Wednesday at 12 noon from Toronto and 12.30 pm from Belmont. Usually it's a two-hour cruise for $4 but on the last Sunday of each month there's a four-hour southern cruise for $5. Phone 58 2311 for details. There are also cruises on the *Lake Macquarie Princess* (tel 58 2067) from Speers Point on Wednesdays, Sundays and public holidays, leaving at 12 noon. There are train services to Toronto, bus services to Belmont and Speers Point.

NEWCASTLE (population 255,000)

New South Wales' second largest city and one of the largest in Australia, Newcastle actually has a larger population than Canberra or Hobart. It's also Australia's second biggest port. Situated 167 km north of Sydney at the mouth of the Hunter River it's a major industrial and commercial centre dominated by the massive BHP steelworks. It's also the export port for the northern NSW coalfields and until the steelworks opened in 1915 coal was Newcastle's lifeblood. Originally named Coal River the city was founded in 1804 as a place for the worst of Sydney's convicts — it soon gained the dubious distinction of being the 'hell of NSW'. The breakwater out to Nobby's Head with its lighthouse was built by convicts and Bogey Hole at King Edward Park was built as a bathing place for the convicts and their guards.

Information & Orientation

There's a Visitor Information Centre (tel 26 2323) in the basement of City Hall in King St, opposite Civic Park. It's open Monday to Friday from 9 am to 5 pm. They have various brochures and a city walks leaflet. Just north of Newcastle there's another info centre at Hexham at the junction of the Pacific and New England Highways.

The NRMA is at 8 Auckland St and their Newcastle map is better than the tourist office one. Information on Forestry Commission areas (not national parks) in the Hunter area may be obtained from the Forestry Commission, 35 Brunker Rd, Broadmeadow.

There are left luggage lockers at Newcastle Railway Station — one day use only and they cost 20c. The Scout Outdoor Centre opposite the Civic Hotel in Hunter St is a good place for bush gear.

The centre of Newcastle is a peninsula bordered by the ocean on one side and the Hunter River on the other. It tapers down to the long sandspit leading to Nobby's Head.

Around the City

Hunter St is the three km long main street, there are bronze plaques at various historical points around the city. The Captain Cook Memorial Fountain is by the central Civic Park. There's a modern Newcastle Region Art Gallery, the War Memorial Cultural Centre and a couple of interesting old churches. Newcastle also has several museums including the Maritime Museum in Fort Scratchley (admission free), the Shell Museum at Caves Beach (also free) and the Local History Museum at the corner of The Terrace and Pitt St (1 to 5 Saturdays, Sundays and public holidays, small admission charge).

North of the city is the Stockton breakwater which ends at a sandbank known as Oyster Bar where many ships were once wrecked. The last to go aground here was a four-masted barque, the *Adolphe*, in 1904. The hull of the *Adolphe* and various other shipwrecks are now built into the breakwater. Fort Scratchley is at the north-east end of the city, on Nobby's Rd. Originally built in the 1840s the present construction dates from the 1870s and '80s. The Bare Island fort in Botany Bay in Sydney is from the same period. The fort was actually attacked by a Japanese submarine during WW II. It's open from 12 noon to 4 pm on Tuesdays, Thursdays, Saturdays, Sundays and public holidays and admission is free.

Beaches

Newcastle is exceptionally well endowed with beaches, many of which have good surf. The main beach, Newcastle Beach, is only a couple of hundred metres from the centre of town and usually has good surf as well as an ocean

pool which is open at night. Mereweather Beach, further south, also has a pool which is open at night. Bar Beach is floodlit at night and the beach is protected by a rocky bar. More secluded Nobby's Beach is north of the centre and at the end of the beach is the old 1857 lighthouse -- you can usually enter the grounds around the lighthouse between 10.30 am and 2 pm but the lighthouse itself is not open to visitors.

BHP Steelworks

Situated at Fort Waratah, six km west of the city, the steelworks were opened in 1915 and today employ about 10,000 people and have the capacity to produce nearly three million tonnes of steel a year. There are free tours at 10 am and 3 pm, Monday to Friday. Arrive at the Tours Centre at least 15 minutes early and you must be wearing suitable shoes.

Places to Stay

Hostels Newcastle has quite a vacuum in the budget accommodation field. The nearest YHA hostel is 32 away at Catherine Hill Bay and the *YWCA Hostel* (tel 24 031) at 82 Parkway is full with permanents. If you're lucky you may get in to sleep on a mattress on the common room or TV lounge floor for $4 a night. If they have a room free a double is $10 a night and you can do your own cooking. Ask for a key at night as the doors are locked at 10 pm.

Mayfield Residential (ex YMCA) (tel 68 3777) takes men only for $4 a night. You have your own room but in a hostel setup.

Hotels The *Grand* (tel 2 3489), on the corner of Bolton and Church Sts is now a quiet place since the police station is right across the road! Singles/doubles are $12/20. At 95 Scott St the *George* (tel 2 1534) has a lot of permanents, if available rooms are $14/25 and there are larger rooms and weekly rates. They

1 Visitors Information Centre	6 Bogey Hole
2 GPO	7 Newcastle Railway Station
3 Local History Museum	8 Civic Station
4 Bus Information Booth	9 Maritime & Military Museum
5 Christchurch Cathedral	

do counter lunches and teas here and you can get breakfast next door.

The *Crown & Anchor* (tel 2 1027) on the corner of Hunter and Perkins Sts charges $12/22 while the *Clarendon* (tel 2 4347) at 347 Hunter St has 16 rooms at $15/20.

A little further out on the corner of Hunter and Wood Sts is the *Cambridge Hotel* with rooms from $15. If you don't mind the rock bands on some nights the *Beach Hotel* (tel 63 1574) on Frederick St, Mereweather is just across from Mereweather Beach, a short bus ride from town, and charges $12/22. The same distance from the centre but away from the beach in Broadmeadow is the *Premier* (tel 61 3670) at 1 Brunker Rd where bed & breakfast is $15/26. There are frequent buses to Broadmeadow. There are other hotels scattered among the more distant suburbs.

Motels Newcastle doesn't tend to be too cheap, Belmont South is probably the best bet. Here the *Lake Lodge Motel* (tel 45 0288) at 690 Pacific Highway only has small rooms but there are all the facilities you could expect including a swimming pool and doubles are just $25. Breakfast in your room is $4 and other meals are available in the restaurant.

Pelican Palms Motor Inn (tel 45 4545) at 784 Pacific Highway is $24/30 and again there's a pool. Newcastle has nothing much in the way of self-contained apartments. *Centennial Terrace Apartments* (tel 26 3463) at 58 Barry St, Cooks Hill is expensive even for four people at $60 a night.

Colleges Edwards Hall has accommodation in the uni holidays but at $26 for a single with breakfast ($140 a week) it's expensive. The rooms are bare and there are no cooking facilities.

Camping *Walsh's* (tel 68 1394) at 293 Maitland Rd, Mayfield West is the closest site to town but doesn't take tents. On-site vans in this very small site are $16.

Stockton is very handy for Newcastle if the ferry is operating, at the time of writing it isn't. Otherwise it's 19 km by road (there is a bus). *Stockton Camp* (tel 28 1393) is right on the beach in Pitt St. Camping costs $5.50, on-site vans are $17 a night, $60 a week.

Ponderosa Caravan Park (tel 64 8066), 14 km north on the Pacific Highway just over Hexham Bridge, has camping at $7 or on-site vans from $15 to 20 ($75 a week).

There are three sites at Belmont. *Belmont South Caravan Park* (tel 45 4750) is on the lake in Ethel St and has tent sites for $3.30 to 4 or less by the week. It's cheaper because it's a council camp. A bit further north there's no camping at *Gaytime Caravan Park* (tel 45 3405) at 687 Pacific Highway. On-site vans are $20 for two ($15 in the off-season) plus $1 for each extra person. They hold up to six people. *Belmont North Caravan Park* (tel 45 2044) is further north again on the Pacific Highway and has camping and on-site vans. There's also a site in Redhead and several in Swansea.

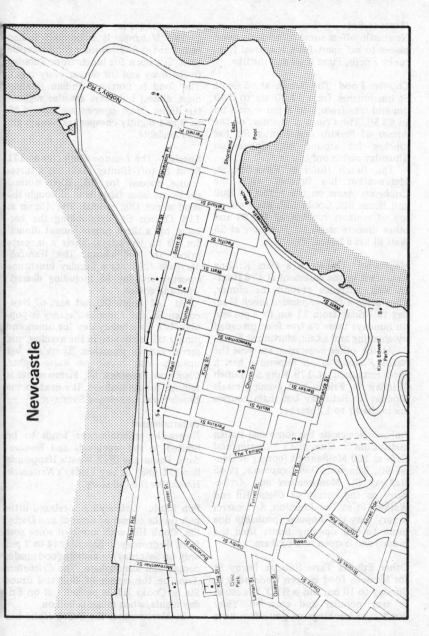

Newcastle

Places to Eat

Newcastle offers some surprisingly good places to eat apart from the usual Kentucky Frieds, Pizza Huts and the like.

Counter Food The *George* at 95 Scott St has lunches from 11.30 am to 2.30 pm and teas from 5 to 8 pm — cost up to $3.50. The *Crown & Anchor*, on the corner of Perkins and Hunter Sts has lunches for around $3, dinners on Thursday nights only.

The *Beach Hotel* in Frederick St, Mereweather has lunches while the *Cricketers Arms* on the corner of Bull and Bruce Sts, Cooks Hill, has a selection of counter lunches all for $3 and other dinners at $5.50. *Rumours* at 23 Watt St has a bistro.

Vegetarian *Gopala* is a Hare Krishna restaurant in the basement at 176 Hunter Mall, entrance around the corner. They serve a free vegetarian lunch Monday to Friday from 11 am to 3 pm and on Sundays there's a free feast preceded by chanting and a talk, starting at 5 pm.

At the other vegetarian extreme the *Earth Kitchen* is an expensive health food restaurant at 179 King St. Lunch Monday to Friday and evening meals Monday to Saturday but main courses are in the $7 to 11 bracket.

Italian Newcastle has some real Italian institutions: *Guiseppe's Continental Cafe* at 100 Maitland St (corner of Daniel St), Islington; *Don Beppino's* at 45 Railway St, Mereweather and *Arrivederci* on the corner of Glebe Rd and Watkins St at The Junction. *Arrivederci* is very busy and popular (probably due more to the opening hours than the pizzas) and is open to 2 or 3 am.

Other Ethnics *Taco Bills* on Darby St for Mexican food is open Wednesday to Sunday to 10 pm and is BYO. It's usually very popular and crowded. They don't take bookings so you often have to queue to get in.

The *Maharaja* is a licensed Indian restaurant at 653B Hunter St, Newcastle West. It's open for lunch from Tuesday to Saturday and for dinner every night. The food is northern Indian (mainly meat dishes) but there are also vegetarian dishes. Main courses are around $6 to 8 and slightly cheaper take-aways are also available.

Specials The *London Beefeater* at 171 Scott St (off Hunter Mall) has a three-course special for $6, their normal prices are also fairly low although the food is not that special. The *Alcron* at 116 Church St, overlooking the harbour, has a three course 'sunset dinner' for $8 on weekdays. Their a la carte prices are *not* cheap. The *Waratah-Mayfield RSL* has a Sunday lunchtime smorgasbord for $5 including dessert, wine and coffee.

At 141 Scott St, just east of Newcomen St, the *Pancake Factory* is popular. It's open every day for lunch and dinner till fairly late in the evening, and serves various pancakes. There's a bar upstairs with music on some nights. *Clams* on Frederick St, Mereweather is famous for its seafood. It's next to the Beach Hotel and closed Sundays.

Entertainment

Newcastle entertainment tends to be limited to the weekends and Wednesdays. Phone the 2NX What's Happening line (11 688) or buy Friday's *Newcastle Herald* for the full story.

Pub Music *Delaney's* is a relaxed little pub on the corner of Council and Darby Sts, Cook Hill with music of some sort from Wednesday to Saturday (4 to 7 pm only on Saturday) -- usually good music, people and atmosphere. The *Cricketers Arms* on the corner of Bull and Bruce Sts in Cooks Hill is packed out on Friday nights, when music is laid on.

In Mereweather the *Beach Hotel* has

good music (usually rock) on the usual nights - no dress hassles. The *Prince of Wales*, also in Mereweather, is very popular on Friday nights. In Newcastle West, the *Family*, at the corner of Hunter and Steel Sts is hardly a place to take the family! It's very crowded and raucous but good bands play on Wednesday and Friday nights till midnight and from 11.30 am to 3.30 pm on Saturday.

A bit further along the *Bellevue Hotel* on the corner off Hunter and Hannel Sts has music every night except Monday. Further along again, at the corner of Hunter and Wood Sts, the *Cambridge* has live music every night and Sunday afternoons, different music on different nights.

Other The *Newcastle Workers Club* in Union St has regular visiting bands. In the suburbs the *Cardiff Workers Club* also gets visiting bands. The clubs tend to be fussy about dress and can be quite expensive. Newcastle also has some nightclubs like the *Palais Royale* (loud rock), *Fannys* and the *Jolly Roger*. The *Pancake Factory* (see above) often has a guitarist upstairs.

Plays and concerts are held in the *Civic Theatre* behind the City Hall. You can also try the *Wood Street Theatre* in Newcastle West. The *Newcastle Workers Club* has a free film on Monday nights.

Getting There
You can fly between Sydney and Newcastle although the distance is so short you're unlikely to want to. Air fare from Sydney is $32 to 34, depending on the airline. Because Newcastle is on the railway line, and competition with railways is not allowed in NSW, you can only travel there by bus if you are travelling through interstate. Trains to and from Sydney operate about 15

times daily, the trip takes about three hours and costs $7.60. Three of the services are faster 'flyers' but you must book a seat on these.

Heading north the trains are far from regular. Most Brisbane buses stop in Newcastle. VIP is cheapest, a nightly overnight service for $25 — book with Newcastle Travel, opposite the main post office in Hunter St. Continental Trailways also operate nightly but cost $34 and McCafferty's are even more. Ansett Pioneer and Greyhound are both booked through Jayes Terminal at 204 King St, they costs $39 to Brisbane.

Getting Around
The Urban Transit Authority's buses cover all of Newcastle itself and the eastern side of Lake Macquarie. Their services are reasonably frequent but can be painfully slow. The Information Booth at the western end of the Mall has timetables but it's actual opening hours don't bear much relation to the posted ones. Buses are rather expensive.

Trains run to the western side of Lake Macquarie with connecting buses to the south-western shores. A private bus company operates to Stockton. A ferry used to operate there and may be restarted.

There's a bus to Nelson Bay, Maitland and a bus operates to Cessnock. To anywhere else in the Hunter region you have to go by train although there's a bus up to Forster. Newcastle has the same special local transport deals as in Sydney.

The Visitor Information Centre has a $1 Newcastle Bike Map. Bikes can be hired for local use only from Hadley Cycles (tel 52 5959) at 617 Glebe Rd, Adamstown. Out at Cessnock enquire at Batterham's Travel about bikes. There are no special car rental deals in Newcastle.

THE HUNTER VALLEY

The Hunter Valley has two curiously diverse products — coal and wine. In some places you can find both together. Singleton, 77 km inland from Newcastle, and Muswellbrook, a futher 47 km, are two wine producing/coal mining areas. The Pokolbin area is the centre of the Hunter Valley vineyards and some of the wineries date back to the 1860s. You'll find many of Australia's best known wine names — like Lindemans, Draytons, McWilliams, Tyrells and Tullochs — represented here. The first grapevines were actually planted in the Hunter in 1832 and the first winery was established in 1843 but depression in the 1930s, and a subsequent loss of interest in wine, contracted the wine industry to a shadow of its early 20th century peak. Then, in the mid-60s, the current wine boom started and today the Hunter Valley is one of Australia's premier wine producing areas.

Getting There

You cannot travel to the Hunter region by the main bus operators but there are a number of train services operating through the area. A variety of bus services operate around the Hunter Valley and between Sydney and Cessnock.

Wineries

There are about 20 vineyards in the valley where you can sample the wines or tour the winery. Generally the wineries are open for tasting from 9 am to 5 pm (some a little earlier, some a little later) from Monday to Saturday. Some are also open on Sunday afternoons. Many of the vineyards have picnic and barbecue facilities so you can enjoy your lunch while sipping on a bottle from their winery.

Starting from Cessnock a few of the more interesting wineries include Happy Valley (Saxonvale) with its rather expensive restaurant. Lindemans' Ben Ean

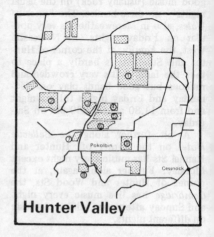

Hunter Valley

1 Rothbury Estate
2 Tyrell's
3 Hungerford Hill
4 Tamburlaine
5 Pokolbin Estate
6 Tulloch's
7 Lindeman's Ben Ean
8 McWilliam's Mt Pleasant
9 Saxonvale Happy Valley

is not, as you might expect, the home of Ben Ean moselle which is blended from a number of grape-growing regions. Tulloch's, Pokolbin Estate and Tamburlaine are all side-by-side. Hungerford Hill bills itself as a 'wine village', it has a restaurant, handicrafts shop, 'farmer's market' and wine tours as well as the usual tasting and wine sales facilities — commercial but interesting. Housed in a huge and splendid building the Rothbury Estate sells all its wines direct. Tyrell's is one of the longest established names in the Hunter. Finally the Wyndham Estate, again with a restaurant, is several km north of the main vineyard concentration, a little north of the New England Highway.

Cessnock (population 16,200)
Cessnock is the main town and accommodation centre for the vineyards, only a few km from Pokolbin, right in the centre of the wineries. Wollombi is a tiny town south of Cessnock with some interesting old buildings and there are some good lookouts around the valley. There's a Tourist Information Centre at 163 Vincent St.

Places to Stay Cessnock is the main town in the Hunter Valley and it has a variety of accommodation possibilities including several hotels and motels. The *Wentworth* (tel 90 1364) at 36 Vincent St is the cheapest hotel at $12 single, $18 to 20 for a double. The *United Services Hotel* (tel 90 1334) at 163 Vincent St is only $14 for a single including breakfast but $28 for a double. The *Cessnock Motel* (tel 90 2770) at 13 Allandale Rd has rooms from $28 to 35. There are also a couple of campsites in and around the town but there's no youth hostel near to hand.

Places to Eat For a good cheap meal in Cessnock try the *Cessnock Workers' Club* or the *RSL* (Chinese food). There are a number of restaurants around the vineyards — all of them rather expensive and some of them rather indifferent.

If you'd like to eat well while sampling Hunter wines they could make an interesting 'splash out' meal. It's wise to book ahead or, at the least, check if they're open since many of them open only on weekends or certain week nights.

Around Newcastle
There are a number of other places of interest around Newcastle apart from the Hunter Valley. Raymond Terrace (population 7000), just 23 km north of Newcastle, has a number of early buildings from the 1830s and '40s including a courthouse which is still in use and Irrawang, an 1830 homestead. There's also a lion safari park near the town.

Maitland (population 36,000) is the coal-mining centre only 30 km inland from Newcastle. It was settled by convicts way back in 1818 and the early buildings include Brough House, now used as an art gallery, and Grossman House. Both are run by the National Trust. There are a number of old homesteads in the area including the 1820 convict built Windermere Colonial Museum in nearby Lochinvar. Morpeth Town in particular has many reminders of its early history.

NORTH COAST
North of Newcastle a narrow band of country runs back from the coast and then rises into the Great Dividing Range area of New England. The coastal strip has some good resort towns and long, lonely beaches, some with notable surf. In places the Pacific Highway runs well inland from the coast and rougher coastal roads will take you along quite deserted stretches of beach.

Getting There
Airlines of NSW and East-West Airlines

operate to various centres in the north coast region, particularly Port Macquarie and Coffs Harbour. There are also services from Brisbane. By rail the train services between Sydney and Brisbane or Sydney and Murwillumbah (for the Gold Coast) both run up the coast. Ansett Pioneer, Greyhound, Skennars and various other bus operators have services along the coast between Sydney and Brisbane or more regionally.

Newcastle to Port Macquarie
It's about 250 km up the coast from

Newcastle to the popular resort town of Port Macquarie. North of Newcastle is Port Stephens where Nelson Bay (population 5400) is the main town. It's a popular fishing centre with many fine beaches and there are a variety of cruises from here. Bulahdelah (population 1000) is the jumping off point for the beautiful beaches and headlands of the coastal Myall Lakes National Park. You can drive from Bulahdelah to Bombah Point from where ferries cross to the park. The lakes and coastline with its sand dunes offer a variety of activities from swimming and boating to surfing and fishing plus you can bushwalk or camp at Seal Rocks, Mungo Brush and Bombah Point. There are some excellent bushwalks from Bulahdelah.

Between Bulahdelah and Taree you can take a loop off the Pacific Highway through the twin towns of Forster-Tuncurry. This road takes you closer to the coast and beside the Myall Lake Park. Forster-Tuncurry (population 3700) are connected by a bridge at the sea entrance to Wallis Lake. Places of interest in the towns include the Arts & Crafts Centre in Forster, the Vintage Car Museum a couple of km south and Talabah Park, amusing for children, 20 km north. Green Cathedral is an open air 'cathedral', created by the Mormons on the shores of Lake Wallis, 13 km south.

Another alternative to the Pacific Highway is to travel further inland along Bucketts Way on the eastern slopes of the Great Dividing Range. Dungog (population 2200) is a main access point to the Barrington Tops National Park, noted for its wildlife and some unusual local flora. The park boundary is at Barrington Guest House although an all-weather road proceeds higher up in the neighbouring state forest, giving access to the national park higher up. There are cabins in the neighbouring forestry area and camping on the Allyn River. Barrington Tops Forest Drive, linking

Gloucester and Scone (outside the main body of the national park), is a good drive if the weather is fine.

There are also some good walking trails along the Telegherry River in the Telegherry Forest Park. Chichester Dam on the Bandon Grove road is a popular spot for barbecues. About the same distance north of Newcastle as Dungog is Stroud (population 500) with a surprisingly large number of early buildings, most of them dating back to the 1830s. Gloucester (population 2300) is at the foot of the hills known as the Bucketts. There are some good lookouts in the hills, particularly at Copeland Tops and Kia-Ora.

Taree (population 13,400) is the main town in the Manning River District. Just inland from Taree is Wingham (population 3400) where the Brush is a park close to the town, inhabited by countless flying foxes between September and May each year. Places of interest around Taree include the Bulga Plateau where, 50 km north, you can see the 160 metre drop of the Ellenborough Falls. The varied attractions of the Crowdy Bay National Park are 40 km to the east. There is good surfing on beaches only 16 km east of Taree. Less than 50 km south of Port Macquarie and immediately north of the Crowdy Bay National Park are the fishing towns of Laurieton, North Haven and Dunbogan, collectively known as Camden Haven (population 2200). There's excellent fishing along the coast here and some fine bushwalks around the lakes close to the coast.

Port Macquarie (population 13,600)

A major resort centre, Port Macquarie makes a good stopping point on the trek up the coast from Sydney (430 km south) to Brisbane (602 km north). It has a very wide choice of accommodation and places to eat and the competition tends to keep prices down. Plus it has been blessed with a beautiful series of beaches starting right in the town — good for surfing, snorkelling or just collecting a suntan.

From the centre there's Town Beach (good swimming or surfing), Oxley Beach (an open sweep of sand), Rocky Beach (just that), Flynn's Beach (excellent surf), Nobby's Beach (interesting rock formations and a high headland at the north end), Shelly Beach (good swimming, interesting gem-like pebbles), Miner's Beach (secluded, good for sunbathing) and, finally, the endless stretch of Lighthouse (more good surfing).

Port Macquarie also has a selection of man-made attractions. On Wednesday and Saturday nights (Friday in the holiday season) you can observe the moon from the observatory near Town Beach for 45c. There's the Hastings Historical Museum on Clarence St (open daily, 50c). On Hay St you'll find the 1824-28 St Thomas Church which was built by convict labour and designed by the convict architect Francis Greenaway (see Sydney). It's the third oldest church in Australia. Close by on Gordon St is a historically interesting cemetery. Port Macquarie was founded in 1821 making it one of the oldest towns in NSW. It was a convict settlement until 1830. There's a marine and dolphin park called King Neptune Park by Town Beach, it's open daily. On Pacific Drive, five km south of Port Macquarie, there's a 30 hectare flora and fauna reserve, Sea Acres Sanctuary, also open daily. For the kids there's Fantasy Glades on Parklands Avenue, five km south and also open daily.

Finally there are a number of river cruises from Port Macquarie. The tourist office can advise you where and when. If you're heading north from Port Macquarie you can follow a dirt road (not too rough) north to Crescent Head where you turn inland to meet the Pacific Highway near Kempsey. You take a vehicle ferry across the Hastings River just out of Port Macquarie. The beach is virtually deserted — fine surf, good picnic spots, nice views.

There is an excellent information centre at the waterfront end of Horton St (the main street) and they can give you all the facts and figures on accommodation and things to do.

Places to Stay & Eat There are lots of hotels, motels (something like 40 of them), holiday flats and campsites in Port Macquarie so you've plenty of choice. The competition keeps the prices down so you can find motels for down towards $20 a double.

In the town centre the *Macquarie Hotel* (by the tourist office) and the *Innes Tavern* both have counter meals — probably more choice at the Macquarie Hotel which also has grill-it-yourself steaks. Or you can get a cheap meal at the *RSL* (visitors welcome). Otherwise there are plenty of take-aways, fast food joints and more expensive restaurants.

Port Macquarie to Coffs Harbour

Just inland from Port Macquarie is Wauchope (population 3500) with Timbertown, a working replica of a timber town of the 1880s. It's open 10 am to 5 pm daily. The Beranghi Folk Museum is in Kempsey (population 8900) but it's worth diverting off the Pacific Highway here to Trial Bay, 35 km north-east. Here the front section of the brig *The Trial* has been restored as a museum at the Trial Bay Gaol. The ship was stolen from Sydney by convicts in 1816 and wrecked here. The nearby Smoky Cape Lighthouse can be inspected on Tuesdays and Thursdays. South of Smoky Cape is the fine coastal region of the Hat Head National Park.

Macksville (population 2300) is on the Nambucca River and here you can visit the Mary Boulton Pioneer Cottage on River St or in nearby Bowraville there's yet another of Australia's many folk museums — the Joseph & Eliza Newman Folk Museum. Follow the road

27 km up-river to Taylors Arm and there you'll find the 1903 Cosmopolitan, the hostelry immortalised in that sad song *Pub with No Beer.*

Down at the mouth of the Nambucca River the popular resort of Nambucca Heads (population 3200) has a couple of museums — the Nambucca Historical Museum on the headlands and the Orama Mineral Museum. There are superb coastal views from the Yarrahappin Lookout here. A little inland is Bellingen (population 1400), a pleasant small town on the banks of the Bellingen River. Between here and Dorrigo (population 1200) is the rainforest of the Dorrigo National Park and the New England National Park, on the eastern side of the New England Plateau, is also in this region. The turn inland to Dorrigo is just beyond Uranga (population 1600), a popular fishing spot with a coastal lagoon.

Coffs Harbour (population 12,200)

With Port Macquarie, Coffs Harbour is the other major central north coast resort. It's got fine beaches and a Porpoise Pool on Orlando St (open daily) plus the Kumbaingeri Wildlife Sanctuary (14 km north, open daily) and the Bruxner Park Flora Reserve (nine km northwest in Korora) with fine views over the coast.

Coffs Harbour, capital of the NSW 'Banana Republic' is probably best known for its Big Banana — 10 metres long in reinforced concrete (you can walk through it) it's on the Pacific Highway three km north of town. The Big Banana, immortalised in thousands of visitors' photographs, is part of a banana complex. You can have a look around the banana plantation on the hill behind or sample banana cake, a banana split, a banana shake or even a chocolate covered banana. It's open daily from 8.30 am to 5.30 pm and it's free. Just eight km south of Coffs Harbour, Sawtell (population 3700) is another popular coastal

resort town.

Woolgoolga (population 1600)

Woolgoolga is a pleasant fishing port with a fine surf beach. The town has a sizeable Indian Sikh population who have a gurdwara, the Guru Nanak Temple, on River St. There are fine beaches with good swimming and excellent bushwalks and camping at the Red Rock National Park, 10 km north. Adventure Village and Sam's Place, five km north where you can see pottery making demonstrations, are other local attractions.

Grafton (population 16,500)

Grafton is noted for its beautiful flame of the forest and jacaranda trees; there's a Jacaranda Festival in November each year. The turn of the century Schaeffer House is now a local historical museum but ice cream fans might find the ice-cream factory on Fry St (inspections at 2 pm on weekdays) of more interest. There are walking tracks to the top of Glenugie Peak for fine views, south of the town. Fine view freaks can also try MacLean Lookout near the town. Canoeing and bushwalking enthusiasts might care to sample te Guy Fawkes River National Park to the west of Grafton but it's a difficult area to get to and there are zero facilities. The Gwydir Highway, running west from Grafton to Glen Innes in the New England region, runs through the Gibraltar Range National Park.

Grafton to Ballina

From Grafton the highway follows the Clarence River to MacLean (population 2500) close to the river mouth. This is one of the most important fishing ports in NSW. Attractions in the area include the Iluka rainforest, the Angourie surfing beach in the coastal Angourie National Park and the blue pool, a popular picnic spot at Angourie with a very deep pool only 50 metres back from the ocean. At the northern end of the park and right on the mouth of the Clarence River, Yamba (population 1600) is a prawning and fishing town and base for the park.

Further north is Evans Head (population1600), again off the main highway and a busy prawning centre which also boats an excellent seafood restaurant. You can make a loop off the highway through Evans Head and the Broadwater National Park just north of the town. There are good bushwalks here and Evans Head also has some magnificent surf beaches. You can see emus, koalas and wallabies in the Bundjulung Flora & Fauna Reserve, south of the Evans River. Woodburn (population 600) is the place where you turn off the highway for Evans Head, or turn inland for Casino and Lismore. Those with an interest in Papua New Guinea's history may want to see the monument and remains of New Italy, a settlement formed from the tattered remnants of the Marquis de Ray's plan to colonise the New Guinea island of New Ireland.

Ballina (population 7300)

This busy town, where the Richmond River meets the sea, has an interesting little Maritime Museum. It's situated at the information centre on Norton St by the riverside on the north-east side of town — open Monday to Friday, admission 50c. Here you'll find a balsa wood raft from the La Balsa expedition — group of three rafts, manned by a 12-person international crew, that drifted across the Pacific from Ecuador in South America to Ballina in 177 days in 1973. To prove whatever one does prove by crossing vast stretches of water in Heath Robinson creations!

Ballina also has the historic old Shaws Bay Hotel, a shell museum, a busy little shipbuilding yard and 11 km west is the Tropical Fruit Research Station which you can visit on Thursdays at 2 pm. The Tourist Information Centre is beside the Maritime Museum.

Lismore (population 22,000)

Inland from Ballina on the Bruxner Highway to Tenterfield in the New England district, Lismore is the centre of a productive rural district. There's a historical museum, an old Aboriginal ceremonial ground near the Tucki Koala Reserve and an open-air pioneer transport museum at Alstonville. Nightcap National Park has superb views and lots of wildlife, 25 km north of Lismore. Continuing inland from Lismore you reach Casino (population 9500) with many fine parks and a folk museum. On the road to Tenterfield, 20 km beyond Casino, there are some Aboriginal rock carvings.

Although Australia's 'back to the land movement' is past its heyday Nimbin, 30 km north of Lismore, is still a great alternative centre. In fact the back to the land folk, despite a few hassles from the cops, are almost establishment around these parts. No doubt Doug Anthony, their local parliamentary representative and leader of the right wing National Country Party, loves every one of them. Nimbin has a youth hostel.

A little west of Nimbin is Kyogle (population 3000), a good base for the mountains and forests in this area. Mt Warning is north-east, between Kyogle and Murwillumbah, while north on the Queensland border is Mt Lindesay with terrific views from its summit.

Ballina to Byron Bay

From Ballina the Pacific Highway again runs a little inland but you'll hardly add a km to your journey if you follow the coast road from Ballina, eventually rejoining the Pacific Highway just beyond Byron Bay. It's an excellent road with fine views over the sweeping beaches at Lennox Head, Broken Head and Byron Bay.

Byron Bay (population 2500) is a

surfing Mecca due to the superb waves at Watego's Beach on Cape Byron. The cape is the most easterly point in Australia and the picturesque little lighthouse that tops the headland was built in 1901 and is said to be the most powerful in the southern hemisphere and the second most powerful in the world. There are fine views of the beaches from the cape. The Everglades, five km south of Byron Bay, is a nature sanctuary with a notable collection of water lillies (open Tuesday to Sunday).

Byron Bay to Tweed Heads

Soon after Byron Bay the coastal road rejoins the Pacific Highway. Mullumbimby (population 2000) is in beautiful sub-tropical countryside and from here you can visit the Nightcap National Park or the Tuntable Falls. In the town Cedar House is a fine old restored house with a vintage car collection. Just after the Mullumbimby turn-off is Brunswick Heads (population 600), a busy fishing centre. The road continues through Burringbar (close to where one of Lonely Planet's busiest writers, Geoff Crowther, hides out on a banana plantation) to Murwillumbah (population 7300); this is a banana and sugar cane growing area. Murwillumbah has a very popular associate youth hostel on the Tweed River. They have canoes and bicycles available and also operate a variety of tours. There are many communes and 'back to the earth' centres in this area. The Kookendoon Wildlife Sanctuary is eight km north at Dungay.

Mt Warning, 1756 metres high, rises up behind Murwillumbah, a road leads up to the top. The mountain was named by Captain Cook, as a warning not to do what he nearly did, run aground at Point Danger off Tweed Heads. There are many good bushwalks around and on Mt Warning — allow about four hours to climb to the top and down again, although it has been done, in a competition, in 27 minutes!

It's just 32 km along the bank of the Tweed River from Murwillumbah to Tweed Heads and the Gold Coast. Alternatively you can take smaller roads inland through the hills and down to the coast. You can also take a coastal route by branching off the Pacific Highway between Mooball and Burringbar, then following the delightful stretch of coast known as the Tweed Coast, much less commercial than the Gold Coast to the north.

Tweed Heads (population 5200)

The last town on the coast in NSW, Tweed Heads marks the southern end of the Gold Coast strip (see Queensland) and is actually continuous with Coolangatta, the first town in Queensland. It's a quieter, less commercial place to stay than the resorts closer to Surfers. It's also a popular place for Queenslanders to hop across the state line and play the pokies (poker machines, banned in Queensland) or buy magazines banned in Queensland.

At Point Danger there's the towering Captain Cook Memorial which straddles the NSW-Queensland border. The 18 metre high monument was completed in 1970, the bi-centenary of Cook's visit, and is topped by a laser beam lighthouse visible 35 km out to sea. The replica of the *Endeavour's* capstan is made from ballast dumped by Cook after the *Endeavour* ran aground on the Great Barrier Reef further north. It was recovered, along with the ship's cannons, in 1968. Point Danger was named by Cook after he nearly ran aground here.

Tweed Heads also has Marineland on Coral St (open daily, $3) with aquarium, dolphins and sharks. The Tweed Head Waterworks is another (yes another, every town north of here seems to have one) of the waterslide centres. It costs $5 an hour but sometimes that hour can extend all day. Three km from Tweed Heads you can get a fine view over the Tweed Valley and the Gold Coast from the Razorback Lookout.

Information Tweed Heads has a NSW Government Tourist Information Centre on the Pacific Highway, open 9 am to 5 pm every day of the week. Like Albury this is treated as a major entry point to NSW for interstate visitors.

Places to Stay There's all sorts of accommodation in Tweed Heads, spilling over into Coolangatta and up the Gold Coast. See the Gold Coast section for more details. Cheaper motels include *Fisherman's Bend* (tel 36 1842) at 163 Pacific Highway with rooms from $22 to 35. The *Golden Wanderer* (tel 36 1838) at 153 Pacific Highway is a couple of dollars cheaper. They're both close to the busy main route through Tweed Heads so they can tend to be

noisy. Tweed Heads also has hotels and holiday flats like *Panorama* (tel 36 1620) at 16 Boundary St where flats by the week cost from $35 to 90.

Places to Eat In the eats department there's excellent seafood downstairs at *Markwell's Seafood Restaurant*, 64 Griffith St, including a good value fixed price 'catch of the day' which includes salad and tea or coffee. Or you can try their superb seafood platter with everything from calamari and Moreton Bay bugs to prawns and oysters. *Fisherman's Cove* on Coral St in Tweed Heads is another excellent and reasonably economical seafood specialist. Very ordinary counter food at the *Coolangatta Hotel* (Marine Parade) across the border, or the *Kirra Beach Hotel* which is cheap but bland.

NEW ENGLAND

The New England region is the area along the Great Dividing Range stretching north from around Newcastle to the Queensland border. The New England Highway is an alternative route to the coastal Pacific Highway which it runs parallel to. It's a vast plateau of valuable sheep and cattle country with many good bushwalking areas, good fishing, photogenic scenery and much to recommend it.

Getting There

East-West Airlines and other regional airlines operate a network of services to towns in the New England region. You can also travel to New England centres on the trains which operate from Sydney into the region. Although the NSW bus travel restrictions apply in New England there are many regional bus services and Ansett Pioneer and Greyhound both operate through New England on their Melbourne-Brisbane or

Sydney-Brisbane services.

Newcastle to Tamworth

Singleton (population 7900) is a coal mining town on the Hunter River and one of the oldest towns in NSW. In the 1841 jail at Burdekin Park there's a historic museum. Lake Liddell, northwest of the town, is a water sports centre. You're still in the coal-mining area at Muswellbrook (population 7800) and still on the Hunter River. Aberdeen (population 1100) overlooks the Liverpool Plains. Scone (population 3400) is located in beautiful country and has a Historical Society Museum. There's a coal seam at nearby Burning Mountain, Wingen, which has been burning for over a thousand years.

Murrurundi (population 900) is on the Pages River in lush, green countryside. Timor Limestone Caves are 43 km east and you can also reach Burning Mountain from here. Quirindi (population 3000) is high in the Liverpool

Ranges, slightly off the New England Highway which continues north to Tamworth.

Tamworth (population 27,500)

Spend much time riding the country roads of Australia and listening to a radio and you'll soon realise that country music has a big following. Tamworth, believe it or not, is the country music centre of the nation; an antipodean Nashville. Each Australia day weekend the country music awards are handed out here and at CWA Park there's the Country Music Hands of Fame memorial with the hand imprint of many Australian country and western singers. It makes the inevitable Historic Museum seem almost mundane. Tamworth also has Minamurra House, an old Victorian mansion, Old Mill Cottage, which now houses an art and crafts exhibit, the City Art Gallery and various other attractions. Nundle is an historic goldmining town, 63 km south-east.

Tamworth to Armidale

Walcha (population 1700) is off the New England Highway on the eastern slope of the Great Dividing Range. There's a Tiger Moth, the first aircraft used in Australia for crop-dusting, on display at the Pioneer Cottage. East of the town is Apsley Gorge National Park with magnificent waterfalls. Back on the highway Uralla (population 1900) is where the noted bushranger Captain Thunderbolt met the bullet with his name on it in 1870, his grave is in Uralla's cemetery. In the 1850s this was a goldrush area and some fossicking is still carried on today near the Rocky River diggings.

Armidale (population 20,000)

The main centre in the region and site of the New England University, Armidale is a popular halting point on the road to Brisbane. The 1000 metre altitude means Armidale is pleasantly cool in the summer. The university art collection is said to be the most important provincial collection in Australia. Armidale also has a Folk Museum, a number of other important early buildings and fine parks.

The Armidale area is noted for its magnificent waterfalls including the Wollomombi Falls, 39 km east, whose 457 metre drop makes them the highest falls in Australia. Other falls include the fine Chandler and Dangar Falls. You can also visit Hillgrove, a gold-mining ghost town.

Armidale to Tenterfield

Guyra (population 1900) is at an altitude of 1300 metres making it one of the highest towns in the state. There are fine views from Chandler's Peak and unusual 'balancing rocks' at Backwater. You're still at over 1000 metres at Glen Innes (population 5900) a good place to meet bushrangers a century ago. The town's old hospital now houses a huge folk museum with the unusual name of 'Land of the Beardies'. The road from Glen Innes to Grafton, near the coast, passes through the Gibraltar Range National Park — lots of lush rainforest and wildlife. There are a range of visitor facilities at the park centre at Dandahra Creek. Glen Innes is still a centre for sapphire mining and you can fossick at Dunvegan Sapphire Reserve on Reddeston Creek.

Tenterfield (population 3600) is the last town of any size before the Queensland border. In the town you can visit Centenary Cottage, dating from 1871, Hillview Doll Museum with more than 1000 dolls on display, or Stannum, a fine old home built in 1888. Historians will find the Sir Henry Parkes Memorial School of Arts interesting. Out of town Thunderbolt's Hideout, where bushranger Captain Thunderbolt did just that, is 11 km away. It's worth taking the rough road to the Boonoo Boonoo Falls, 32 km north. In Bald Rock

National Park the rock which gives the park its name can be climbed and from the top you'll enjoy superb views over Queensland and NSW.

WOLLONGONG (population 200,000)

Only 80 km south of Sydney this is NSW's third largest city, a heavily industrialised centre which includes the biggest steelworks in Australia at Port Kembla. Despite its industrial nature Wollongong is fronted by some fantastic surf beaches while the hills soar up behind it and from the lookout on the road you'll get fine views over the city and along the coast.

Information & Orientation

The Leisure Coast Tourist Association has an information centre (tel 28 7068) at 90 Crown St and is open Monday to Friday, 9 am to 5 pm. As well as the usual tourist info they organise tours, book buses (but not trains) and have a free accommodation booking service. They're also a YHA agent.

The Wollongong GPO is at 296-8 Crown St near the railway station but you might find the Wollongong East post office, lower down Crown St opposite the tourist centre, more convenient. The NRMA (tel 29 8133) are on the corner of Burelli and Kembla Sts and have a useful Wollongong and district map. Wollongong Saddlery & Bushcraft Equipment at 90 Burelli St (moving to 29 Stewart St during 1983) have bushwalking gear and there are also surplus shops on Crown St. A National Parks & Wildlife representative visits Wollongong every second Thursday. He's in Pig Alley opposite the Methodist Church on Crown St if you want information on the national parks.

Around Town

Enquire at the Visitors Centre, Port Kembla, about tours of the steelworks. Wollongong has an interesting harbour, fishing fleet and fish market and an his-toric old lighthouse open weekends and school holidays from 1 to 5 pm. Amongst the lookouts above the town is Bald Hill were pioneer aviator Lawrence Hargraves made his first attempts at flying early this century. Hang gliders hang out there today. At Mt Kembla village, where there was a mining disaster in 1902, there's a Historical Museum in Market Square, open Wednesday 10 am 1 pm, Saturday and Sunday 1.30 to 4.30 pm. The museum has reminders of the town's early days — including a reconstruction of the 1902 tragedy. The Sea Treasure Cave Museum in the tourist office has shells and sea animals — it's small but good and admission is 80c. On Burelli St there's an art gallery open 12 noon to 5 pm, Tuesday to Sunday. Australian wildlife roams free at the Symbio Animal Gardens, Helensburgh. There's a huge Moreton Bay Fig at Figtree.

Out of Town

The hills rise suddenly and dramatically behind Wollongong, you get spectacular views over the town and coast from the Bulli Pass which runs high above Wollongong. The country is equally spectacular heading inland (and up) through the Macquarie Pass National Park to Moss Vale or through the Kangaroo Valley. On the road to Moss Vale you can see a fine local example of Australian kitsch — a huge potato in the middle of town; also a motel called the Spud Motel. Yes, this is a potato growing area. South of the town Lake Illawarra is popular for watersports and there are also a number of reservoirs and dams in the vicinity. At Jamberon there's grass skiing and a twin waterslide.

1 Railway Station	6 Post Office (Wollongong East)
2 Post Office (Wollongong)	7 Tourist Centre
3 TAA	8 Ansett
4 Qantas	9 Wollongong Beach
5 NRMA	10 Wollongong Harbour

Places to Stay

The tourist office will make accommodation bookings free but there are no hostels or similar cheap accommodation in town.

Hotels *Tattersalls Hotel* (tel 29 1952) at 333 Crown St, up by the railway station, charges $12 per person room only, $4 more with breakfast. Reasonably priced snacks and meals are available at the bar. On Market St the *Hotel Illawarra* (tel 29 5421) charges $14 room only, $5 more with breakfast.

The *Grand Hotel* (tel 29 1911) on the corner of Keiri and Burelli Sts has motel type rooms for $15 per person, $12 for the standard rooms without attached bathroom. At 47 Crown St the *Oxford Hotel* (tel 29 2922) also has accommodation — sometimes.

Still within walking distance of the centre (but get off at the North Wollongong Station if you're travelling by rail) is the *Hotel North Wollongong* (tel 29 4177) on the corner of Flinders St (the Princes Highway) and Bourke St. Bed & breakfast here costs $16.50 per person. Four km south at Figtree, the *Figtree Hotel* (tel 28 4088) offers a bit more, with attached bathroom and tea-making facilities for $18/31 including breakfast.

Guest Houses Many of Wollongong's guest houses won't take casual visitors but the following are worth trying. *Breadalbane Guest House* (tel 29 1749) at 25 Kembla St is $12.50/15 including breakfast. They also have much cheaper weekly rates of $50/75. The *Excelsior Guest House* (tel 28 9320) at 5 Parkinson St is $12 per person bed & breakfast, again cheaper weekly rates are available. There's a rather obscure little

guest house at 117 Corrimal St which is very cheap, if you get in.

Motels Wollongong motels tend to be very expensive but the following might be worth trying. The *Piccadilly* (tel 29 6544) at 349 Crown St (between the post office and the railway) costs $20 to 24 single, $30 to 32 double. All rooms are fully equipped.

South at Figtree, *Sunsets Figtree Village* (tel 71 1122) on the Princes Highway has similar facilities at $24/30. At Fairy Meadow, 3.5 km north of Wollongong, the *Cabbage Tree Hotel-Motel* has units for $24/36 including a light breakfast.

Colleges *International House* on the Princes Highway in North Wollongong has accommodation during the vacations for about $12.

Camping As usual with Australian cities you have to go a little way out before you can camp. The Wollongong City Council have camping areas at Corrimal (at the beach), Bulli (in Farrell Rd, adjacent to the beach) and Windang (in Fern St with beach and lake frontage). Bulli is 11 km north, Corrimal about half way there and Windang is 15 km south, between Lake Illawarra and the sea. All charge $3.60 for two for camping. There's another camping ground in Windang — the *Oasis Caravan Park* (tel 95 1591) at 142 Windang Rd. It's much more expensive to camp ($6 for two) but it does have on-site vans ranging from $16 to 22.

Places to Eat

Wollongong's pubs offer the best value for money although there are also lots

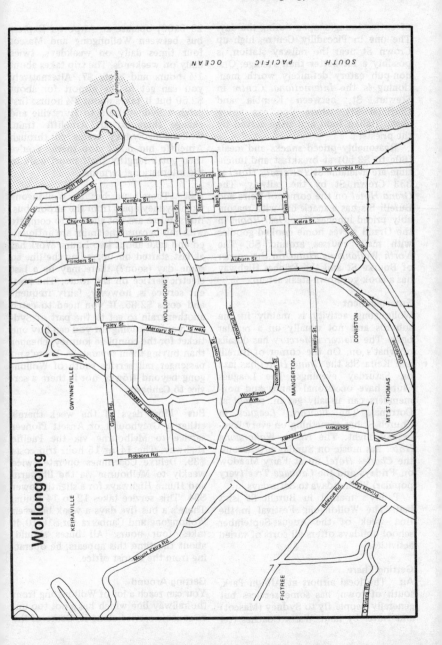

Wollongong

SOUTH PACIFIC OCEAN

Lighthouse

Cliff Rd

Harbour Dr

Corrimal St

Port Kembla Rd

Kembla St

Corrimal St

Church St

Campbell St

Crown St

Burelli St

Stewart St

Bank St

Beach St

Swan St

Keira St

Keira St

Flinders St

Auburn St

Foley St

Mercury St

New St

Crown St

Gipps St

WOLLONGONG

Rowland Ave

Heaslip St

CONISTON

Atchison St

Gladstone

Gipps Rd

Springhill Rd

Norman St

MANGERTON

Woodlawn Ave

MT ST THOMAS

GWYNNEVILLE

Bourke Crescent

Robsons Rd

Freeway

Southern

KEIRAVILLE

Mount Keira Rd

Gipps Rd

Princes Hwy

Bellevue Rd

O'Brien St

FIGTREE

of coffee lounges open during the day. The one in Piccadilly Centre, high up Crown St near the railway station, is possibly a bit better than average. One non-pub eatery definitely worth mentioning is the *International Centre* in Stewart St, between Kembla and Corrimal Sts, where you can enjoy cheap Italian food and wine served by the priests!

Reasonably priced snacks and meals (60c to $3.50) at breakfast and lunchtime are available at *Tattersalls Hotel* at 333 Crown St by the railway. The *Grand Hotel* on the corner of Keira and Burelli Sts has a snack bar with reasonably priced lunches. The *Oval Room* in the Grand serves home cooked goodies with main courses around $5. The *North Wollongong Hotel* on the corner of Bourke St and the Princes Highway has a cook-your-own-steak set up.

Entertainment

Wollongong activity is mainly in the suburbs and not usually on a regular basis. The *Illawarra Mercury* has details of what's on. On the corner of Burelli and Keira Sts the *Grand Hotel* has jazz on Saturday evenings. The Leagues Clubs have occasional bands and non-members can usually get in, except at Corrimal. The *Illawarra Leagues* in Church St has something on every Wednesday night. The *North Wollongong Hotel* has music on Sunday afternoons, the *Charles Hotel* up at Fairy Meadow on Fridays and the *Cabbage Tree* (very popular) Wednesdays to Saturdays.

Paddy's market in Burelli St isn't bad. The Wollongong Festival in the first week of the August-September school holidays offers all sorts of varied activities.

Getting There

Air The local airport at Albion Park, south of town, has some services but generally people fly to Sydney (Mascot) and travel by land. Watts Coaches (tel 29 5100) operate an Airporter Express bus between Wollongong and Mascot four times daily on weekdays, twice daily on weekends. The trip takes about 1½ hours and costs $7. Alternatively you can get to the airport for about $2.50 but it takes about 2½ hours: first catch a Sydney train to Hurstville and change there to an Arncliffe train. Wollongong-Sydney trains go through Arncliffe but don't stop there. You've then got a lengthy (half hour) walk to the international terminal.

Rail There's no bus to Wollongong from Sydney apart from the airport bus. Bus services are not allowed to compete with rail because the trains are antiquated and take about two hours. Work has at last started on upgrading the line so some day (soon?) there may be a fast electric service on the route. The present service is, however, fairly frequent and costs $2.85. If you need to catch another train to get to the part of Sydney you're heading for you can buy one ticket for the complete journey, cheaper than buying them separately. There's no passenger rail service south of Wollongong beyond Nowra, nor is there a service to Canberra.

Bus Most days of the week there's either a Greyhound or Ansett Pioneer service to Melbourne via the Pacific Highway. The 14 or 15 hour trip costs $39. Deluxe Coachlines operate twice weekly to Melbourne via the Illawarra and Hume Highways for a slightly lower $34. This service takes 12 to 14 hours. There's a bus five days a week between Wollongong and Canberra for $16.10, it takes four hours. All buses should, about the time this appears, be operating from the tourist office.

Getting Around

You can reach a lot of Wollongong from the railway line which has a not too unreasonable service along it. Some of the beaches are accessible by rail and there's a service to Kiama. Although the tourist office has a map of the local bus routes and timetables for each route there's nothing you can take away with you. There are no special deals like day passes on Wollongong buses.

You can hire bicycles from Arrow-smiths in Keira St or motorcycles from Frasers in Flinders St, North Wollongong. You can hire paddleboats, row boats, catamarans and power boats at Lake Illawarra and at Brighton Beach you can hire aqua-bikes.

Half day tours of Wollongong are available for $5.50.

SOUTH COAST
The Princes Highway runs right along the NSW south coast from Sydney through Wollongong and on to the Victorian border. Although this is a rather longer and slower route between Sydney and Melbourne than the quick Hume Highway it's infinitely more interesting. For much of the way the road runs right along the coast and there are lots of pleasant little towns, good surfing spots and other attractions. The northern part of this route is known as the Illawarra Coast and has fine views, good surf beaches and some busy prawning ports. The southern part is known as the Alpine Coast because it is only a short drive inland from the coast to the Snowy Mountains. There are many pleasant little fishing ports and beach resorts on this stretch of the coast from Bateman's Bay to the Victorian border.

Wollongong to Nowra
South of Lake Illawarra, Shellharbour (population 1800) is a popular holiday resort for Wollongong. It's one of the oldest towns along the coast and back in 1930 was a thriving port but it declined after the construction of railway lines. There are good beaches on the Windang Peninsula near the town.

Kiama (population 6000) is famous for its blowhole; illuminated at night it can spout up to 60 metres high. On Blowhole Point, Marineland displays blue-ringed octopus and other aquatic nasties. There is also a historical museum, good beaches and the scenic Cathedral Rock at Jones Beach. Just south of Kiama is Gerringong (population 1200) with fine beaches and surf. Pioneer aviator Charles Kingsford Smith took off from Seven Mile Beach to fly to New Zealand in 1933.

Berry (population 1100) was an early settlement and has a number of National Trust classified buildings and the almost inevitable historical museum. Nearby Coolangatta has a group of buildings now converted to use as a motel — they were constructed by convicts in 1822, the first buildings in the area.

Nowra & Around
On Shoalhaven River, Nowra (population 15,500) is popular for watersports. There are excellent views from Hanging Rock or you can visit the rain-forests in Riverside Animal Park. Nearby is Kangaroo Valley with old buildings which include the Friendly Inn, a pioneer farm museum and a reconstruction of an 1880 dairy farm. On the coast from Nowra is Culburra-Orient Port (population 1400), a quiet resort town with a busy prawning fleet. Jervis Bay has some beautiful holiday resorts around the bay. Ulladulla (population 4300) is an area of beautiful lakes, lagoons and beaches. There's good swimming and surfing at Bendalong or you can make the pleasant bushwalk to the top of Pigeon House Mountain in Moreton National Park.

Bateman's Bay (population 3500)
This popular resort is at the mouth of

the Clyde River — again there's good bushwalking and swimming. You can see penguins and other birds at Tollgate Island Wildlife Reserve, more birds are on view at Batehaven Birdland and there's a Shell Museum a km east. Like other towns along the coast Moruya (population 1900) is a dairy centre but oyster farming is also carried on here. The old Coomerang House is of interest but south-west is the beautifully situated old gold town of Nerrigundah and the Eurobodalla Historic Museum. About 80 km inland from Bateman's Bay on the route to Canberra is Braidwood (population 1000) with many old sandstone buildings classified by the National Trust and a historical museum.

Narooma & Around

Narooma (population 2000) is another oyster town. There are many inlets and lakes around Narooma while near Lake Corunna, Mystery Bay has coloured sand rock formations. Tilba, just 15 km south of town, is a well preserved little town which has undergone remarkably little change throughout this century. At the junction of the Princes and the Snowy Mountains Highways, Bermagui (population 600) is a fishing centre made famous 50 years ago by American cowboy-novelist Zane Grey. Inland and on the Princes Highway is Cobargo, another remarkably unspoilt old town. Bega (population 4300) is a useful access point to the snow country.

Mimosa Rocks National Park is immediately north of Bega while the town also has a couple of good lookout points and the Bega Historical Museum. Candelo, 39 km south-west, is a picturesque little village which, like Tilba, has had a Rip Van Winkle existence and seen few changes this century.

South to the Victorian Border

Continuing south you reach Merimbula (population 2000) another swim-fish-surf centre. On the main street the Old School Museum is just that — once an old stone school building, now used as a museum. Steamships used to dock at Merimbula's wharf.

At Eden (population 3000) the road bends away from the coast into Victoria. This old whaling town on Twofold Bay has a Whaling Museum with a fine killer whale skeleton. To the north and south of Eden is the Ben Boyd National Park, good for walking, camping and swimming.

Boydtown, south of Eden, was founded by a flamboyant early settler named Benjamin Boyd. His grandiose plans aimed at making Boydtown the capital of Australia but his fortune foundered and so did the town — later he did too, disappearing without trace somewhere in the Pacific. Some of his buildings still stand including a partially finished lighthouse and a ruined church. The Sea Horse Inn, built by convict labour, is still in use today.

THE SNOWY MOUNTAINS

Australia's snowfields straddle the NSW/ Victoria border but Mt Kosciusko is firmly in NSW and at 2238 metres its summit is the highest point in Australia. Much of the NSW snowies is within the boundaries of the Kosciusko National Park, an area of year round activity with skiing in the winter and bushwalking in the summer. The Snowy Mountains scheme is the best known hydro-electric power development in Australia and also irrigates extensive areas of the Murray region.

Cooma (population 7400)

Just 114 km south of Canberra, this is the gateway to the snowies and earlier was the centre for the Snowy Mountains scheme construction. You can walk down Lambi St and see 21 National

Trust classified buildings in this interesting town. A half km west of the town is the wreckage of the *Southern Cloud*, an aircraft which crashed in the snowies in 1931 and was only discovered in 1958. The Travellers' Rest Pioneer Museum is six km west, it dates from 1861 when it was built as a hotel and staging post for Cobb & Co. Other attractions include the Avenue of Flags in Centennial Park with flags of the 27 nationalities involved in the Snowy Mountains scheme. You can see wooden clogs made in Clogs Cabin while Raglan Gallery, dating from 1854, has paintings, pottery and rugs. Fairy Tale Park, three km out of town, is inteded for children.

The Cooma Visitors' Centre is on Sharp St, beside Centennial Park. Cooma is at the junction of the Monaro and the Snowy Mountains Highways. The Snowy Mountains Highway runs north-west to Tumut and then joins the Hume Highway a little south of Gundagai.

Kosciusko National Park

The 6000 square km of New South Wales' largest national park includes caves, glacial lakes, forest and all of the state's ski resorts as well as the highest mountain in Australia. You can drive most of the way towards the top of the mountain past Perisher and Charlotte Valley. The last eight km is on foot although there is a trail right to the top. The explorer who first discovered the peak and climbed to the top named it after Count Kosciusko from his native Poland. The park is also the source of the Snowy, the Murray and the Murrumbidgee Rivers. Although it is snow that the park is most famous for it is also very popular in summer when there are excellent bushwalks and marvellous alpine wildflowers.

Only eight km along the Snowy Mountains Highway from Cooma you can turn to the snowfields area and Mt Kosciusko. The Alpine Way runs

through Thredbo and can either be followed as a loop around the park, rejoining the Snowy Mountains Highway at Kiandra, or as a 'back roads' route into Victoria. Although part of the road is unsealed it's no problem unless there's deep snow.

Along the Snowy Mountains Highway, just before you enter the park, Adaminaby (population 400) is the jumping off point for Lake Eucumbene. Cruise boats go across the lake to the animal sanctuary at Grace Lea Island. Kiandra is actually in the park. It was the site of an 1859 gold rush and the crude ski races organised by miners probably predate the popularity of skiing as a sport in Europe. From here you can turn south to Cabramurra, Australia's highest town, and continue south to Khancoban in Victoria, although this road is often closed by snow. From here you follow the Alpine Way back into NSW, past the Murray 1 lookout on the Snowy hydro-power scheme. The road makes a loop south around Mt Kosciusko and through Thredbo to Lake Jindabyne.

On the shores of the lake is Jindabyne (population 1000), a popular fishing centre. There's a national park information centre at the entrance to the park, about midway between Jindabyne and Thredbo. A shuttle bus operates in winter from here to Smiggin Holes and Perisher Valley.

Skiing & Ski Resorts

Snow skiing in Australia can be a marginal activity — the benefits of pushing the mountains up 1000 metres higher or shoving the whole country 1000 km south (but only for the winter!) are frequently discussed topics on the slopes. The season is short (July, August, September is really all there is) and good snow is by no means a safe bet. Nor, despite claims that the Australian mountains offer more skiiable snow than the Swiss Alps, are the mountains ideal —

their gently rounded shapes means that most long runs are relatively easy and the hard, fast runs tend to be short and sharp. For a final bummer the short season means the operators have to get their returns quickly — costs can be high.

Having told you the bad, here's the good -- when the snow's there and the sun's shining the skiing can be just fine. So long as you re not some sort of antipodean Jean Claude Killy you will find all the fun (not to mention heart in the mouth fear) you could ask for. Plus, the long open slopes of the Australian Alps are a ski-tourers paradise -- nordic (cross-country or langlauf) skiing is becoming increasingly popular and many resorts now offer lessons and hire equipment.

For the budget-minded skier the cheapest (and by far the most fun) way to get out on the slopes is to gather a bunch of friends and rent a lodge for a week. You can all chip in for the food and booze and really enjoy yourselves. Costs vary enormously but if you can find a reasonably priced place it can be within the bounds of reason. Bring as much of your food and drink with you as you can, supplies in some resorts tend to be erratic and they're always expensive.

Other costs are tows, lessons and equipment hire if you do not have your own. Tows vary depending on the resort but count on $18 to 25 a day or $115 to 150 a week. Lessons average about $8 to 10 a session. Boots, skis and stocks can be hired for $18 to 25 a weekend or $40 for a week including both weekends. It's a trade off whether to hire in the city and risk damage and adjustment problems or at the resort and possibly pay more. Last time I skied I managed to break a ski and stock on my first run of the week! There are usually hire centres in towns close to the resorts and many garages also hire ski equipment as well as chains. Snow chains must be carried

in the mountains during winter even if there is no snow -- heavy penalties if you've not got them.

Australian ski resorts are short of the frenetic nightlife of many European resorts but compensate with lots of partying between the various lodges. Nor is there a great variety of no-skiing activities apart from toboggan runs. Australia also doesn't have the range of all-in skiing packages which are the cheapest way to get on the slopes in Europe. Weekends tend to get crowded because the resorts are so convenient, particularly from Canberra.

All the main resorts are connected by bus with Cooma which can be reached by road or air. Main resorts with distances in km from Sydney are:

Charlotte Pass (490 km) At the base of Mt Kosciusko this is the most isolated resort in Australia, you often have to snowcat the last eight km from Perisher. Good ski-touring country.

Thredbo (482 km) The best and most expensive skiing in Australia. Except in exceptional circumstances it is not possible to ski down to the village which is below the normal snow line. There's a youth hostel but it costs about $13 a night in the ski season. In the summer this is a popular bush-walking centre and the chairlift to the top of Mt Crackenback operates right through the summer.

Perisher Valley (510 km) Rated just one notch below Thredbo and on a par with the better Victorian resorts, Perisher has a wide variety of runs including the highest lifted point (2030 metres) in Australia. Perisher has 40 km of trails.

Smiggin Holes (514 km) The name comes from a Scottish word for a hole scraped by cattle. It's just down the road from Perisher and run by the same management so you can get a combined ski tow ticket for both resorts. A shuttle bus runs between the two resorts.

Guthega (480 km) Is small and still relatively new.

Tumut (population 5600)

On the other side of the park from Cooma this is an alternate entry point. Australia's largest commercial trout farm is at nearby Blowering Dam. The Tourist Information Centre here can tell you about visits to the various centres of the Snowy hydro scheme. Talbingo Dam and the Yarrangobilly limestone caves (60 km east, about mid-way between Tumut and Kiandra) are other points to visit. The caves are open for inspection at 11 am, 1 pm and 3 daily (more often in peak seasons). There's also a thermal pool here at a constant temperature of 27°C and some beautiful country in the reserve around the caves.

Batlow (population 1400) is south of Tumut in a fruit growing area, there's a 'Big Red Apple centre if you're collecting notable Australian 'big' tourist attractions. Near Batlow is Hume and Hovell's lookout where the two explorers did indeed pause for the view in 1824. Paddy's River Dam was built by Chinese gold miners back in the 1850s. Continuing south from Batlow you reach Tumbarumba (population 1500) a site for the early exploits of bushranger Mad Dog Morgan. There's great mountain scenery and good bushwalks in the area and the Paddy's River Falls are only 16 km from the town.

Beyond Tumut on the Snowy Mountains Highway, before it reaches the Hume Highway, is Adelong (population 800), an old gold-mining centre with a National Trust classified main street. There's a pleasant picnic area two km from the town on the Gundagai Rd at the cascade falls.

ALONG THE HUME HIGHWAY

The Hume Highway is the main road between Australia's two largest cities. It's the fastest and shortest road and although it's not necessarily the most interesting there are still a number of places worth pausing along that well worn route. You can also make some interesting diversions off the Hume. One of the simplest is right at the beginning — when you leave Sydney instead of taking the long, weary trek through the dull outer suburbs towards Camden and Campbelltown you can take the coastal Princes Highway past the Royal National Park to Wollongong. Then just after Wollongong you can cut inland on the Illawarra Highway through the superbly picturesque

Macquarie Pass and over beautiful rolling countryside to Moss Vale before rejoining the Hume. Further south you can make a diversion off the highway to visit Canberra or continue beyond Canberra to the Snowy Mountains, rejoining the Hume once again in Victoria.

A word of warning if you're driving along the Hume — this is Australia's broken windscreen centre. You've not travelled in Australia until you've smashed a windscreen on the Hume so beware of loose stones on the roadside. I've done one just outside Gundagai.

Getting There

There are flights to a number of the main towns along the Hume Highway.

The Melbourne-Sydney bus services run on the Hume and the train services run close to it.

Sydney to Goulburn

Only 60 km out of Sydney, Camden (population 7700) is virtually an outer suburb of the capital city today. This was one of Australia's first European settlements — John Macarthur arrived here in 1805 and his sheep breeding experiments formed the basis for Australia's sheep farming industry. The town has many early buildings with National Trust classification. Places of interest include Gledswood Cellars, a winery built in an 1810 coaching house — grape vines were first planted here in 1827 since Camden is also the first wine producing centre in Australia. Denbigh (1817-27), Camden Park (1834), Kirkham Stables (1816), the Church of St John (1840-49) and Hassall Cottage (1817) are other early buildings. At Camden Airport, south of Narellan, there's an aviation museum with 20 old RAF and RAN aircraft and others including a 1909 Bleriot. Green's Motorcade museum is in nearby Leppington and has more than 50 veteran and vintage cars plus a motorcycle section.

Continuing along the Hume, Picton (population 1700) is another early settlement with a Tollkeepers Cottage, an old railway viaduct and the early St Mark's Church of England. The Rail Transport Museum at Thirlmere has about 40 locomotives and other pieces including an 1864 engine from railway pioneer Robert Stephenson. Wirrimbirra fauna and flora sanctuary is 13 km south. Mittagong (population 3900) is a local agricultural centre and has a Doll Museum. West of Mittagong, Joadja is now a ghost town but it's on private property although visits can be made at certain times — check in Mittagong. Just south of Mittagong on the Hume is Berrima (population 700),

a tiny town which was founded in 1829 and has changed remarkably little in the last century. There are numerous interesting old buildings in the town including the old Surveyor-General Inn and a historical museum.

Bowral (population 6300) is another agricultural centre and from here you can visit the Mount Gibraltar wildlife reserve. Four km south of Mittagong a winding 65 km road leads to the Wombeyan Caves where five limestone caverns are open for inspection between 10 am and 4 pm daily. The drive to the caves is through superb mountain scenery and the caves themselves are in a very attractive bush setting.

Moss Vale (population 3600) is a pleasant town off the Hume. Throsby Park House, built between 1834 and 1837 is a fine old home built by the area's first settler. Near Moss Vale is the Morton National Park with excellent bushwalks for the more experienced walker. Bundanoon (population 800) is a pleasant little town near the entrance to the park.

Goulburn (population 22,000)

Another Hume centre with a long history, Goulburn was proclaimed a town way back in 1833. Old buildings of interest include the 1840 Riversdale coaching house with its beautiful gardens (open daily except Tuesdays). St Clair History House (about 1843) is a fine old restored mansion. You can visit the Pelican Sheep Station, 10 km south of the town, and see sheep shearing and sheepdog demonstrations — contact Eric Sykes at the station. Goulburn also has a Steam Museum on Crockwell Rd (daily except Monday and Tuesday) and an Applied Arts & Sciences Museum. Crookwell (population 2100) is north of Goulburn, this was once a gold-mining and bushranging region but today it's just quiet farming country.

Goulburn to Albury

At Yass (population 4300), 296 km south of Sydney, the Barton Highway branches off the Hume for Canberra. Yass is closely connected with the early explorer Hume, who gave the highway his name. He lived here for 40 years and on Comur St the Hamilton Hume Museum has some exhibits relating to him. Near Yass at Wee Jasper you can visit the limestone Cary's Cave on Sunday afternoons from 1 pm.

Gundagai (population 2100) is one of the most interesting small towns along the Hume. The highway now bypasses the town but it's worth the small extra distance to take the old road. It crosses a long wooden bridge over the flood plains of the Murrumbidgee River, a reminder that in 1852 Gundagai suffered Australia's worst ever flood disaster when 89 people were drowned. Gold rushes and bushrangers were also part of the town's colourful early history and the notorious Captain Moonlight was tried in Gundagai's National Trust classified 1859 court house. Other places of interest in town include the Gabriel Gallery on Sheridan St, the Historical Museum and the information centre, also on Sheridan St, with its 20,000 piece marble cathedral model.

Gundagai's most famous monument is eight km out of town for there, still sitting on his tuckerbox, is a sculpture of the dog who, in a well known early bush ballad, 'sat on the tuckerbox, five miles from Gundagai'. It's now a popular little tourist centre and roadside stop. Near here is the Five Mile Pub, an equally popular place to break your journey back in the pioneer days.

Holbrook (population 1200) was known as Germanton until WW 1, it was renamed after a local war hero and in Holbrook Park you can see a replica of the submarine in which he won a Victoria Cross. The local information centre is located in the interesting Woolpack Inn Museum, in an 1860 hotel.

Albury (population 30,000)

The NSW half of the Albury-Wodonga development centre is on the north side of the Murray River. It's a busy and expanding industrial centre and also an access point from Victoria to the NSW Snowy Mountains. Places of interest in Albury include the Folk Museum in the old Turk's Head Hotel, the tree marked by William Hovell where he crossed the Murray on his expedition from Sydney to Port Phillip (Melbourne wasn't there then) in 1824, and the Botanic Gardens. Outside the city there's the Ettamogah Wildlife Sanctuary, 11 km north, and the Jindera Pioneer Museum, 16 km north-west. The road across the state line between Albury and Wodonga runs across the Hume Weir dam, the lake behind the dam is a very popular water sport centre.

SOUTH-WEST & MURRAY RIVER

A number of roads run through the south-west area of the state — alternative inland routes to Melbourne from Sydney like the road from Cowra to Wagga Wagga and Albury or to West Wyalong and Narrandera. Or there are routes to Adelaide like the road through Hay and Wentworth. The Murray River forms the boundary between NSW and Victoria and although most of the most interesting towns are on the Victorian side NSW also has several interesting centres.

Wagga Wagga (population 33,000)

Wagga is a major inland city on the Murrumbidgee River. It's a busy farming centre with a Botanic Gardens and a zoo. Wallacetown Historical Arms Museum is 20 km south of Wagga. The name is pronounced 'wogga' not 'wagga' and usually abbreviated to just the one word. Just north of Wagga is Junee (population 4000) with some historic buildings including the lovely old homestead Monte Cristo.

West Wyalong (population 3500)

An old gold-mining town at the point where the Mid Western and Newell Highways meet, West Wyalong's District Museum includes a gold-mine model and also local fossils. When there's plenty of water available Lake Cowal, 48 km north-east, is the biggest lake in the state. When there isn't so much water it isn't. Lake Cargelligo (population 1200) is north-west of West Wyalong and has lots of bird life.

Narrandera (population 5000)

Near the junction of the Newell and Sturt Highways. Narrandera is in the Murrumbidgee Irrigation Area, there's an MIA information centre in the town. There's a koala reserve near the town and a group of swimming pools at Lake Talbot. Only 30 km away is Leeton (population 6600) with Australia's biggest fruit cannery. Between Narrandera and Deniliquin is Jerilderie (population 1000) immortalised by Ned Kelly who held up the whole town for two days back in 1879, locking the local force up in their own jail. Kelly relics can be seen in the Telegraph Office Museum on Powell St.

Griffith (population 12,000)

This busy farming centre was planned by Canberra's architect, Walter Burley Griffin. Apart from fruit, grain and grapes Griffith has also gained something of a reputation for local marijuana production and for the unpleasant events that have befallen people who found out too much about the local

marijuana growers activities. There's a Pioneer Park Museum just north of the town and bushwalking in the Cocoparra National Park, 19 km northeast. There's a Tourist Information Centre on the corner of Banna Avenue and Jondaryan Avenue.

Hay (population 2800)

At the junction of three highways Hay is a major sheep raising centre. There are some fine beaches along the Murrumbidgee in this area. The town has some interesting old buildings like the Hay Gaol Museum, a fine old 1883 fountain and a plaque in Lachlan St marking Charles Sturt's journey on the Murrumbidgee and Murray Rivers in 1828-30. There's a mini-zoo in South Hay.

Deniliquin (population 6900)

A sheep raising centre where much irrigated farming is also carried out, the town has the Denilakoon Exhibition Centre with Aboriginal artefacts and other displays. A footbridge from Cressy St runs to the Island Wildlife Sanctuary. There's good swimming at sandy McLeans Beach.

Along the Murray

Although the Murray River forms the boundary between NSW and Victoria from the Snowy Mountains right to the South Australian border, most of the important river towns are on the Victorian side. It's no problem to hop back and forth across the river as in many places roads run along both sides. Albury, see the Hume Highway section, is the main NSW town on the Murray and also the first big town on the river down from its source. The Murray was once an important means of communication with paddle steamers splashing up and down stream like on an antipodean Mississippi.

Corowa (population 3000) is a wine producing centre downstream from

Albury. The Lindeman winery here has been operating since 1860. On the second Sunday of each month and on public holidays there are train rides here on the miniature Bangerang Railway. Tocumwal (population 1100) is a quiet Murray town with a giant fibreglass codfish in the town square. The town has a sandy river beach and is a very popular gliding centre. The Rocks is a popular picnic spot 11 km from town.

Wentworth (population 1100)
Close to where the Darling and Murray

Rivers meet Wentworth is overshadowed by nearby Mildura, on the Victorian side of the Murray. The old paddle steamer *Ruby* is on display near the Darling River bridge in Fotherby Park. Wentworth has a Folk Museum & Arts Centre and the 1879-81 jail has a display of the sort of items the authorities used to be unpleasant to prisoners with. North of Wentworth on the Mungo Station is the Wall of China, a strange 30 km long natural wall. Tours operate there from Mildura in Victoria.

CENTRAL WEST

The central west region starts inland from the Blue Mountains and continues for about 400 km, gradually fading into the harsh environment of the far west of the state. This region, directly inland from Australia's first European settlement in Sydney, has some of the earliest inland towns in the country. Bathurst is the natural gateway to the region and from here you can turn north-east through Orange and Dubbo or south-west through Cowra and West Wyalong. The Western Highway, running from Bathurst through Cowra and Wagga Wagga to Albury, is an alternative Sydney-Melbourne route. Like the coastal Princes Highway it's longer than the direct Hume route but provides very different scenery and makes an interesting alternative for anyone suffering from that well known complaint 'Hume ennui'.

Getting There
Air Airlines of New South Wales fly from Sydney to a number of centres in the central west including Coonabarabran, Coonamble, Dubbo, Mudgee and Walgett. There are services from Dubbo to other locations in the central and far

west of the state.

Rail Trains operate from Sydney to Mudgee and Dubbo and from there connecting buses ooperate to Bourke, Brewarrina, Cobar, Coonamble, Walgett and other centres.

Bus The usual NSW bus travel complications apply to some extent in the central west region. Ansett Pioneer and Greyhound have services through the region on routes between Sydney and Broken Hill or Brisbane and Melbourne.

Lithgow (population 12,700)
On the western fringe of the Blue Mountains, Lithgow is noted for the famous Zig Zag railway line by which trains descended from the Blue Mountains until 1910. The line was quite an engineering wonder in its day. In the city Eskbank House on Bennet St is a gracious old home built in 1841. There are fine views from Hassan Wall's Lookout, five km south of town.

Bathurst (population 18,600)
Situated 208 km from Sydney, Bathurst is Australia's oldest inland city. It's a fine old town with many early

buildings reflecting its long, by Australian standards, history. They include the 1835 Holy Trinity Church and the remains of the Old Government House of 1817 which stands behind the Folk Museum. Apart from the usual pioneering exhibits the museum also displays Aboriginal artefacts. Bathurst also has an Art Gallery and a Museum of Applied Arts & Sciences. Eight km out of town is Abercrombie House, a huge mansion of the 1870s.

Close to the town is the Mt Panorama motor racing circuit, a true road circuit and the finest racing track in Australia. The country's premier car race, the Bathurst 1000 km for production cars takes place here each October and it's the annual event for which Bathurst is best known. The track is only used twice each year, the other occasion being the Easter motorcycle events which always seemed to be followed by an exciting bikie rampage. In fact mayhem during the races became such a monotonous feature that you almost had the feeling the newspapers had the *bikies cops clash* headlines all set up even before Easter rolled around. Part of the track is closed off and only open during the races but the rest of it is normal public road and you can drive round it any time. Apart from race time of course!

Mt Panorama also has a couple of more permanent attractions. The Sir Joseph Banks Nature Reserve at Mt Panorama has koalas, kangaroos and wallabies. The Bathurst Gold Diggings is a reconstruction of an early goldmining town. Bathurst has a Tourist Bureau in the Civic Centre.

Around Bathurst

The Abercrombie Caves are 72 km south of the city — the spectacular Arch Cave is a major feature of these limestone caverns. Between Bathurst and Cowra is Blayney (population 2500) close to Carcoar, an interesting little place very much like an English village.

North of Bathurst the old mining town of Hill End was the scene for a gold rush in 1871-74 and has many fine old buildings from that era. It's a particularly interesting and historic old town and well worth a visit. The Royal Hotel was opened at the height of the rush in 1872 and has been operating ever since. There's an information centre in the old Hill End Hospital. North-east of Bathurst is Rylstone (population 700) where some interesting Aboriginal rock paintings can be seen just outside the town (enquire at the shire council) while 16 km north there are fine tree ferns in Fern Tree Gully.

Mudgee (population 5700)

Further north, 126 km from Bathurst, Mudgee is a pleasant town with many fine old buildings and a Colonial Museum. Mudgee is becoming well known for the many enthusiastic small wineries that have sprung up here. People who find the Hunter Valley altogether too commercial report that Mudgee wineries are a delight to visit. And they make some nice wine too.

Only 30 km north-west is Gulgong (population 1600) an old gold town which features on the Australian $10 note. Although there are many fine restored old buildings here none of the ones that appear on the $10 note still remain! This was also the boyhood home of poet Henry Lawson who also appears on the note. Tours run from here to the Nagundie Aboriginal waterhole on Wednesdays, weekends and public holidays. Further east towards New England is Merriwa (population 900) at the western end of the Hunter with a number of historic buildings including an 1857 historical museum. Cassilis also has some historic old stone buildings and between there and Mudgee there are some Aboriginal cave paintings just off the road.

Orange (population 26,300)
This important fruit producing centre does not, curiously enough, grow oranges! It was considered as a site for the federal capital before Canberra was eventually selected. This was the pioneer poet Banjo Paterson's hometown and there is a memorial to him in the city. There's an art exhibition in the modern Civic Centre on Byng St while the Historical Museum on Sale St has exhibits including an Aboriginal carved tree about 300 years.

Australia's first real goldrush took place at Ophir, 27 km north of Orange. The area is now a wildlife reserve and it's still popular with fossickers. There are a number of other popular parks and centres around Orange. The Lake Canobalas Park is eight km south-west while a further six km brings you to the Mt Canobalas Park with a series of walking trails. You can hire bicycles to get around the Mini-Bike Tourist Park, 10 km north. Molong (population 1500) is north-west on the road to Wellington and four km south-east of the town is the grave of Yaranigh, the Aboriginal guide of explorer Sir Thomas Mitchell.

Cowra (population 7700)
On the alternative inland route to Melbourne the pleasant town of Cowra was the site of a Japanese prisoner of war camp during WW II. In 1944 an amazing mass prison break was made by the Japanese, which resulted in the death of nearly 250 prisoners, many of them by suicide. Four prison guards were also killed but all the escapees were soon rounded up. The strange tale of this impossible escape attempt was told in the book and film titled *Die Like the Carp*. There's a Japanese war cemetery five km south of the town and two km south-east of the cemetery a memorial marks the site of the escape attempt. A plaque tells the tale of the breakout.

The Wyangala dam and park is 40 km from Cowra and has good water sport facilities. North of Cowra is Canowindra (population 1700) is notable for its fine, curving main street and for the time in 1863 when bushranger Ben Hall bailed up the whole town!

Grenfell (population 2200)
This old gold-mining town is 56 km west from Cowra towards West Wyalong. It was the birthplace of Australia's famous poet and author, Henry Lawson. There are good walks in the Waddin Mountain National Park, 18 km southeast.

Young (population 6500)
South-west of Cowra towards Wagga Wagga, Young is a fruit growing centre with an earlier gold-mining history. This was the site of the anti-Chinese riots at Lambing Flats in 1861 and you can find out more about this unpleasant incident in the Lambing Flats Historic Museum. Between Young and Wagga is Cootamundra (population 6400).

Forbes (population 7800)
Another gold town Forbes has a Historical Museum and the notorious bushranger Ben Hall is buried in the town's cemetery. He was killed in a shootout in 1865. A km south of the town is the Lachlan Vintage Village which is open daily but does not have working demonstrations on Mondays or Tuesdays. Between Orange and Forbes is Eugowra (population 700) where one of early NSW's most spectacular goldescort robberies took place. The town has a small museum.

Parkes (population 8900)
On the Newell Highway Parkes has a Motor Museum, a Pioneer Park Museum and the pleasant Kelly Reserve on the north side of town. A huge radio telescope stands 23 km north of the town. It's open daily and there's a visitors' centre.

Wellington (population 5400)

Only 50 km from Dubbo, Wellington is noted for its limestone caves including the Wellington Cave, nine km from town. In the town there's a historical museum housed in a former bank. Walking trails lead to the lookout at Binjang in the Mt Arthur Reserve. Wellington also has several wineries.

Dubbo (population 20,000)

North of Parkes and Orange and 420 km from Sydney, Dubbo is another agricultural, sheep and cattle raising town with some old buildings and a pioneer museum on Macquarie St. The Old Dubbo Gaol, with the gallows on display, is another city attraction. There is a fair amount on the Governor family whose exploits are related in *The Chant of Jimmy Blacksmith*. Dubbo is a pleasant place, situated on the Macquarie River and Newell Highway, but its main interest is five km south-west of town. There the Western Plains Zoo is the largest open-range zoo in Australia with many animals in open enclosures. You can hire bicycles in the zoo and ride around the exhibits which are divided into their continent of origin.

NORTH-WEST

From Dubbo roads radiate out to the north-west of the state. The Newell Highway runs north-east right across the state, an excellent road which provides the quickest route between Melbourne and Brisbane. The Castlereagh Highway runs more or less directly north into the rugged opal country towards the Queensland's border, the sealed road ends just before Lightning Ridge. The Mitchell Highway heads off north-west to Bourke via Nyngan. At Nyngan the Barrier Highway forks off directly west to Broken Hill in New South Wales' far west.

Along the Newell

Gilgandra (population 2500) has the Gilgandra Observatory & Display Centre with an audio-visual of the moon landing and NASA Gemini flights plus a historical display. Gilgandra is a junction town where the Newell and Castlereagh divide and a road also cuts across to the Mitchell. At Coonabarabran (population 3000) you can visit Miniland, eight km west, where there are life-size prehistoric animal models and the almost inevitable historical museum. This is also the access point to the Warrumbungle National Park where there are excellent walks and rock climbing possibilities. You can get a walks' map from the park headquarters at Canyon Camp, the final 10 km of the road into the park is fairly rough. The largest optical telescope in the southern hemisphere is at Siding Springs, 24 km west at the edge of the park.

Narrabri (population 7000) is a cotton growing centre with a solar observatory and also a cosmic ray research centre. The town also has several agricultural research centres, one of them involved into research into cotton growing. The Mt Kaputar National Park is east of Narrabri while to the west is Wee Waa (population 1900) a wine and cotton growing centre. The huge dish of an OTC overseas communications antenna marks Moree (population 9400). The town is situated on the flood prone Gwydir River. From Moree the road is fairly dull until you finally reach Boggabilla and cross the border to Goondiwindi in Queensland.

Moree to New England

Between Moree and Glen Innes in the

New England area is Bingara (population 1300), a gemstone centre with an early gold mining history. The National Trust classified Historical Society Museum was probably the town's first hotel. Inverell (population 9400) is further east and is a popular fossicking centre, particularly for sapphires. The town has a National Trust classified courthouse and a Pioneer Village with buildings collected together which date from the 1830s. Warialda (population 1300) is another gemstone centre in the vicinity. A little south of Inverell is Tingha (population 900) with the excellent local Smith's museum of mining and natural history. Tingha is a tin-mining centre and a tin dredge still operates in Copes Creek.

South from here towards Tamworth is Barraba (population 400) in fine mountain country. The views from the top of Mt Kaputar, which can also be reached from Narrabri, are particularly fine. The Nandewar Mountains and the Horton River Falls are other scenic attractions. South again is Manilla (population 1800), noted for its production of honey and mead.

Along the Castlereagh

The Castlereagh Highway divides off from the Newall at Gilgandra and you can also reach the Warrumbungle Park from Gulargambone. Coonamble (population 3100) is at the edge of the Western Plains and from here you can travel west to the extensive Macquarie Marshes with their prolific birdlife. The road continues north to Walgett in harsh, dry country near the Grawin and Glengarry opal fields. This is a popular area for opal fossickers. Close to the Queensland border Lightning Ridge (population 800) is a huge opal field claimed to be the only site in the world for finding black opals. This remote centre is heavily into tourism with underground opal showrooms, an art gallery, bottle museum, opal mine which you can visit and much more. The town centres

around the Diggers Rest Hotel.

Along the Mitchell

From Dubbo the Mitchell Highway passes through the citrus growing centre of Narromine (population 2800). Warren, further north and off the Mitchell on the Macquarie Highway is another jumping off point to the Macquarie Marshes which are breeding grounds for ducks, water hens, swans, pelicans, ibis, herons and wild water fowl. Nyngan (population 2400) was the scene for fierce conflicts between Aboriginals and early pioneers.

The country up in the north-west, the western plains which stretch away on the inland side of the Great Dividing Range, is a vast, tree dotted plain eventually shelving off into the barren New South Wales outback — 'back of Bourke'. From Nyngan the highway and the railway both run arrow-straight for 206 km to Bourke and further west really is the 'back of beyond'.

Bourke (population 3500)

On the Darling River and the Mitchell Highway, nearly 800 km north-west of Sydney, Bourke is notable for nothing much apart from being the centre of a huge tract of outback. In fact 'back of Bourke' is synonymous with the outer-outback, the back of beyond. A glance at the map will show just how outback the area is — there's no town of any size for far around and the country is flat and featureless as far as the eye can see. Look for the Cobb & Co signs on the old Carrier Arms Hotel in Bourke. Fort Bourke Stockade was just south of Bourke and there's a memorial to the tangle an early explorer had with hostile Aboriginals here. Brewarinna (population 1400) is 100 km east of Bourke. The name is an Aboriginal word meaning 'good fishing' and there are Aboriginal stone fishing traps, known as the 'rocks' or the 'fisheries', just down from a weir they built in the Darling River.

THE FAR WEST

The far west of NSW is rough, rugged and sparsely populated but also produces a fair proportion of the state's wealth – particularly from the mines of Broken Hill. The Barrier Highway is the main access route into the region but Broken Hill is actually closer to Adelaide than Sydney and it's really more closely aligned to the South Australian capital. Although Broken Hill is so far from everywhere there are a number of places of great interest in the west of the state.

Mootwingee

In the Bynguano Range, 131 km north of Broken Hill, there is an aboriginal tribal ground with rock carvings and cave paintings — a national historic site which has, unfortunately, been badly defaced in the past by vandals. There is also much wildlife and birdlife in the area and this is a place of quite exceptional beauty. There is a very informative Visitors' Centre at the site and a ranger now protects the relics.

Menindee Lakes

This water storage development on the Darling River, 112 km south-east of Broken Hill, offers a variety of water sport facilities. Menindee (population 400) is the town for the area, Bourke and Wills stayed in the Maiden's Hotel on their unlucky trip north in 1860. The hotel was built in 1854 and has been with the same family for nearly one hundred years. The Kinchega National Park is close to the town and the lakes, overflowing from the Darling River, are a haven for birdlife.

The Barrier Highway

The Barrier Highway heads west from Nyngan, it's a 594 km from there to Broken Hill. This road is an alternative route between Sydney and Western Aus-

tralia. Cobar (population 3300) has a modern and highly productive copper mine but it also has an earlier history as evidenced by its old buildings, like the fine Great Western Hotel with its endless stretch of iron-lacework ornamented verandah. Enquire at the Tourist Information Centre in the main street about mine tours. Near Cobar you can see 'Towser's Huts', mud and stone huts rented out to miners in the 1890s. Weather balloons are released at 9 am and 3 pm daily from the met station near Cobar. The Mt Grenfell Aboriginal cave paintings are 40 km west of Cobar — you have to phone the homestead (Cobar 226) for permission to visit them.

Wilcannia (population 1000) is on the Darling River and in the days of paddle steamers was an important river port. It's a much quieter place today but you can still see old buildings from that era — including the Athenaeum Chambers where the Tourist Information Centre is located. About 100 km off the Barrier Highway is White Cliffs, an opal mining settlement where you can fossick for opals. There's a walk-in opal mine here and the skeleton of a plesiosaur, found in a mine, is also on display. You can also see various early buildings including Clancy's Hut, an old miner's home. As in Coober Pedy, in the outback of South Australia, there are many underground homes.

Back of Bourke

Back of Bourke really is just what the name says. There's no sealed road anywhere west of here in NSW and if you cared to drive from Bourke to Broken Hill via Wanaaring and Milparinka it's unsealed for the whole 713 km, apart from the final 10 km or so into Broken Hill. Milparinka, once a gold town, now consists of little more than a solitary hotel although some old sandstone buildings still remain. In 1845 Charles

Sturt's expedition from Adelaide, searching for a central Australian sea, were forced to camp near here for six months. The temperatures were high, the conditions terrible and their supplies inadequate. You can see the grave of James Poole, Sturt's second in command, about 14 km north-west of the settlement. Poole died of scurvy. There's a stone cairn built by the expedition members on Mt Pool, 20 km north-west.

Tibooburra (population 200) is right up in the north-west corner and has a number of local stone buildings from the 1880s and '90s, including two hotels. It used to be known as The Granite from the granite outcrops in the area. Tibooburra is an entry point to the Sturt National Park. At Cameron Corner,

right on the north-west corner of the state, there's a post to mark the place where Queensland, South Australia and NSW meet. It's a favourite goal for visitors to this area and four-wheel drive is not necessary to get there. It is recommended that you inform the park ranger before venturing into the park, however. This far-western corner of the state is a harsh, dry area of red plains, heat, dust and flies but also interesting physical features and prolific wildlife. The border between NSW and Queensland is marked by the dingo proof fence, partrolled every day by boundary riders who each look after a 40 km section. Always seek local advice before setting off to travel in this area, particularly on secondary roads.

BROKEN HILL (population 27,800)

Far out in the far west Broken Hill is a fascinating town, not only for its comfortable existence in an extremely unwelcoming environment but also for the fact that it was once a one company town which in turn brought about one equally strong union. The Barrier Industrial Council pretty well runs the place. The Broken Hill Company, after which the town was named, was formed after a silver lode was discovered near the present town. Miners were already working on other finds in the area and a false goldrush in 1867 had failed to notice the real wealth of the area. Today they are still working the richest silver-lead deposit in the world. Broken Hill is 1170 km west of Sydney but only 509 km from Adelaide so in many ways it is more aligned to South Australia than NSW. Even the clocks are set on Adelaide (central Australian) rather than Sydney (eastern Australian) time. It's really a hell of a long way from anywhere though, an oasis in the

wilderness.

Information & Orientation

Broken Hill has a very imposing tourist information centre on the corner of Bromide and Blende Sts. It's open every day of the week. The building is also the main bus station, houses rent-a-car agencies and has a snack bar. The RAA has its office on Argent St and provides reciprocal service to other auto club members. Broken Hill has a daily paper, the *Barrier Daily Truth.* The city is laid out in a straightforward grid pattern, the central area is quite compact and easy to get around on foot.

Mining

Four companies now operate the Broken Hill mines and you can take a free tour of the surface works of the North Mine on weekday afternoons at 2 pm. The tour takes two hours and you must wear sturdy footwear. Delprat's mine have an underground tour where you don miners' gear and descend 130 metres underground for a tour lasting nearly two hours. The cost is $10 and on weekdays the tours leave at 10.30 am, on Saturdays at 2 pm. Nobody under 12 years of age is allowed on the tours, phone 88 1604 for details. To get there go up Iodide St, across the railway tracks and follow the signs, about five minutes drive.

About 45 minutes drive south of Broken Hill is the Triple Chance Mine where you can fossick. The turn-off is 29 km south, then it's 14 km off the road. The mine is open Tuesday and Thursday from 9.30 am to 4.30 pm. The Gladstone Mining Museum in South Broken Hill has life size workings exhibits in an old hotel. It's open 2 to 5 pm daily and admission is 80c.

Other

Broken Hill has a Railway, Mineral & Train Museum housed in the old railway station. There are many old railway trains and other pieces of railway equipment here. It's open daily from 9 am to 5 pm but closed for lunch for an hour from 12.30 pm. Admission is $1. There's a relic of the Afghan camel trains of the last century in the Afghan Mosque, built in 1891. On the corner of William and Buck Sts is North Broken Hill, it's only open 2.30 to 4.30 pm on Sundays and admission is 10c.

Artists

Broken Hill seems to inspire artists and there is quite a plethora of galleries in the town. They include the Civic Centre Gallery and the Pro Hart Gallery on Wyman St. Pro Hart, a former miner, is Broken Hill's best known artist and quite a local personality. His gallery charges admission but many of the others don't and the artists are friendly local characters. I particularly liked Hugh Schultz's gallery at 51 Morgan St — I liked his naive art style and he's an interesting man to talk with. The Ant Hill Gallery at 110 Wyman St is a new

gallery featuring local and major Australian artists. In the Civic Centre is the 'Silver Tree', a sculpture commissioned by the man who first discovered the town's fabulous mineral wealth back in 1883. It was only acquired by the city council and put on public display in 1975.

Around Town

Eight km from the town you can visit the Royal Flying Doctor Service at 11.30 am and 4 pm each weekday, at 10 am on Saturday. You must ring 2341 and book in advance. If you want to sit in on a School of the Air, which broadcasts lessons to kids in isolated homesteads, you must check with the tourist centre first and all visitors must be seated by 8.45 am for the one hour session.

Silverton

Silverton, 25 km to the west, is an old silver-mining ghost town with historic buildings and a museum. This was the site of the original silver strike in 1883 and two years later it had a population of 3000 and solid public buildings designed to last for centuries. In 1889 the mines at Silverton were closed and the population shifted to Broken Hill. Today it's an interesting little ghost town, used as a setting in the film *Mad Max II (The Road Warrior* in the States) and *A Town Like Alice*. A number of buildings still standing include the old jail, now used as an interesting little historical museum (admission 30c) and the Silverton Hotel.

The road beyond Silverton becomes bleak and lonely almost immediately but the Umberumberka Reservoir, 10 km from Silverton, is a popular picnic spot and Penrose Park has animal and birdlife. In early '83 the reservoir was totally dry due to Australia's continuing drought conditions.

Places to Stay

Hotels, Motels & Guest Houses There is no youth hostel in Broken Hill but within a few steps of the information centre/bus station there are a couple of good possibilities. At 100 Argus St the *Tourist Lodge* (tel 88 2086) has dorm beds at $6 or at $5 for YHA members. There are also singles/doubles at $15/20 — spartan rooms with just a bed and a bedside table, no chair, no bedlight, no washbasin, no nothing! They are clean and well kept, however, and there's a lounge with TV and pool table and a room where you can fix yourself tea or coffee (supplied) and make yourself toast and cereal for breakfast. Compared to some other places in Broken Hill it's no special value though.

Across the road from the info centre at 34 Bromide, the *Black Lion Inn* (tel 4801) is excellent value at $9/15. The rooms are old fashioned but well kept with shower and toilet at the end of the corridor. Along Argent St there are a string of hotels, most of them very grand old places like *Mario's Palace Hotel* (tel 2385) at 227 with its reproduction of Botticelli's Venus on the ceiling over the stairs! Rooms are $12/22 with washbasins or $19/26 with your own bathroom, breakfast is an extra $3. Further down at 320 Argent St, on the corner of Chloride St, the *Royal Exchange* (tel 2308) is an equally grand old place with comfortable rooms at $15/20 or $20/28 with your own facilities. In between at 317 the *Grand Private Hotel* (tel 5305) is just $9 per person. There are lots more hotels around town.

Broken Hill also has plenty of motels

1 Tourist Lodge	7 Civic Centre
2 Tourist & Travel Centre	8 Post Office
3 Black Lion Inn	9 Grand Private Hotel
4 Mario's Motel	10 Royal Exchange Hotel
5 Railway Museum	11 RSL Club
6 Mario's Palace Hotel	

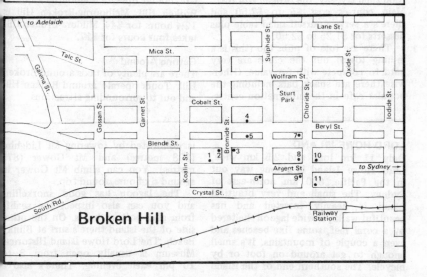

Broken Hill

although most of them are rather more expensive. *Mario's Hotel Motel* (tel 7134) at 172 Beryl St is one of the cheaper ones with rooms at $20/30. The others are almost all in the $30 to $40 bracket.

Camping The *Broken Hill Caravan Park* (tel 3841) is on Rakow St and has camping and on-site vans. The *Lake View Caravan Park* is at 1 Mann St, three km from the centre and is similarly equipped.

Places to Eat
Broken Hill is door to door with clubs, this is a NSW club town if ever there was one. They generally welcome visitors and in most cases you can sign yourself in — they'll even leave the visitors book at the door with the membership secretary's signature already down beside 40 blank spaces for the night's visitors! Background music consists of the continuous rattle of one-armed bandits but for reasonably priced, reasonably good, very filling food then try, say, the *Broken Hill RSL*. Main courses cost $5 to $7.50 and there's a serve yourself salad table plus desserts for $1.25 to $2.50.

There are lots of pubs too (this is a mining town) but the clubs are very hard to compete with for value. Otherwise there are snack bars including the popular cafe in the information centre,

pizzerias, or, if you really want to move up market, the pleasant *Black Lion Inn* with its blackboard menu offering dishes from steak to Mexican.

Getting There
Air Adelaide is the usual point to fly to Broken Hill from, it's $74 by Airlines of South Australia. From Sydney it's $135 with Air New South Wales.

Rail Broken Hill is on the Sydney-Perth railway line so it can be reached on the four times weekly Indian Pacific service and there are also regular services between Adelaide and Broken Hill connecting with the Indian Pacific trains. The train fare to Adelaide is about $22 in economy and the trip takes about eight hours.

Bus Stateliner-Greyhound, Murtons and Ansett Pioneer operate between Adelaide and Broken Hill at least once daily. The trip takes about seven hours and costs $18. Ansett Pioneer operate Sydney-Broken Hill (about 18 hours, $50) while Greyhound operate Melbourne-Mildura-Broken Hill. Melbourne-Broken Hill is 12½ hours for $44, Mildura-Broken Hill takes four hours for $17.

Getting Around
There are plenty of taxis around Broken Hill. Tours operate around Broken Hill and out to surrounding attractions.

LORD HOWE ISLAND
Only 11 km long and 2.5 km wide, Lord Howe Island is a long way out in the Pacific, 600 km north-east of Sydney. The small and very beautiful island is heavily forested and has beautiful walks, a wide lagoon sheltered by a coral reef, some fine beaches and even a couple of mountains. It's small enough to get around on foot or by bicycle. The southern end of the island

is dominated by towering Mt Lidgbird (808 metres) and Mt Gower (875 metres). You can climb Mt Gower in around six hours, round trip.

The lagoon has good snorkelling and you can also inspect the sealife from glass-bottom boats. On the other side of the island there's surf at Blinky Beach. The Lord Howe Island Historical Museum is usually open from 8 to 10 pm each evening. There's also a

Shell Museum, open Monday to Friday from 10 am to 4 pm and movies are shown in the Public Hall on Saturdays and Tuesdays.

Places to Stay

There's a variety of accommodation — hotel style, guest houses with meals and a lot of self-contained units. Lord Howe is really off the budget track, apart from the expense of getting there you won't find much by the way of cheap accommodation. Most visitors to Lord Howe are on package tours.

Getting There & Around

You used to get to Lord Howe by romantic old four-engined flying boats from Sydney. Today they've been retired and a small airport built on the island. You can fly there from Newcastle ($130 one-way) and Port Macquarie ($120 ditto) with Oxley Airlines. From Sydney Oxley are $135 and Avdev are $131.

Getting around the island you can hire bicycles from a number of locations. Mini-Mokes and motorcycles can also be hired. There is an overall 25 kph speed limit.

Country Race Meets

Some of the country race meetings are occasions in themselves — the most revered seems to be the annual meeting at Louth (that's in NSW about 100 km south-west of Bourke). The town's population is around 50 and in 1978 they recorded the number of planes 'flying in for the day' as 29!

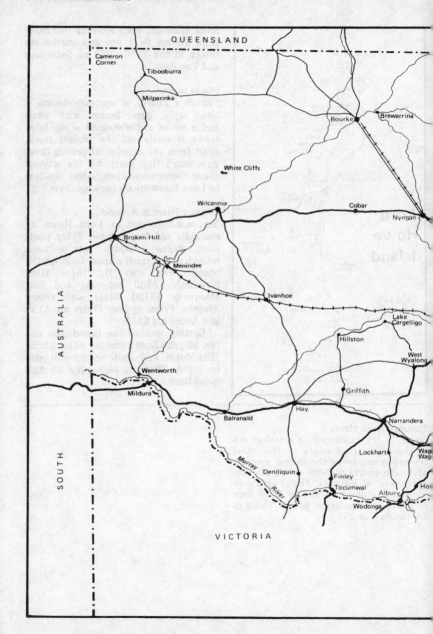

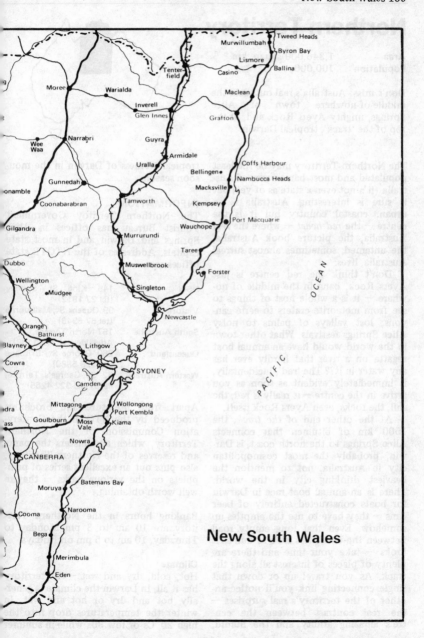

New South Wales

Northern Territory

Area   1,346,000 square km
Population   100,000

Don't miss: Australia's real outback, the middle-of-nowhere town of Alice Springs, mighty Ayers Rock and, at the top of the 'track', tropical Darwin.

The Northern Territory may be the least populated and most barren area of Australia (it's not even a state as of yet) but it sure is interesting. Australia is an urban, coastal country but it is the centre — the *red heart* — where the real Australia, the picture book Australia, the untamed, sometimes almost surreal Australia, lives.

Don't think the red centre is just Ayers Rock, bang in the middle of nowhere — it is a whole host of things to see from meteorite craters to eerie canyons, lost valleys of palms to noisy Alice Springs festivals. What other town in the world would have an annual boat regatta on a river that hardly ever has any water in it?? The 'red', incidentally, is immediately evident as soon as you arrive in the centre — it really is red, the soil, the rocks, even Ayers Rock itself.

At the other end of *the track*, the 1500 km of bitumen that connects Alice Springs to the north coast, is Darwin, probably the most cosmopolitan city in Australia, not to mention the heaviest drinking city in the world. There is an annual boat race in Darwin for boats constructed entirely of beer cans — they have to use the empties up somehow. Even that long empty road between the two cities isn't as dull as it looks — take your time and there are plenty of places of interest all along the track. As you travel up or down that single connecting link you'll notice another of the territory's real surprises — the real contrast between the centre's amazing aridity and the humid, tropical wetness of Darwin in the monsoon season.

INFORMATION

The Northern Territoy Government Tourist Bureau has offices in Alice Springs and Darwin and in most state capitals. Addresses of the NTGTB state offices are:

NSW	145 King St, Sydney (tel 27 1812)
Victoria	99 Queens St, Melbourne (tel 67 6948)
South Australia	157 North Terrace, Adelaide (tel 212 1133)
Queensland	260 George St, Brisbane (tel 229 5880)
Western Australia	62 St George's Terrace, Perth (tel 322 4255)

Apart from literature and brochures produced by the NTGTB the Conservation Commission of the Northern Territory, which administers the parks and reserves of the Northern Territory, also puts out an excellent series of pamphlets on the various parks — they're well worth obtaining.

Banking hours in the Northern Territory are 10 am to 3 pm Monday to Thursday, 10 am to 5 pm on Fridays.

Climate

Hot, cold, dry and wet — the territory has it all. In Darwin the climate is generally hot and dry or hot and wet. In winter the temperatures drop into the high 20°Cs or low 30s while in summer

40°C is the norm and it's sticky and humid to go with it. The May-October winter season is the dry when an average of just 25 mm of rain falls. Then from October round to May it's the summer wet when Darwin is deluged with 1500 mm!

In the centre the temperatures are much more variable — plummeting below freezing on winter nights (July-August), and soaring into the high 40°Cs on summer days (December-January). Come prepared for both extremes and the intensity of the sun at any time of year. Rainfall is light on an annual basis but it tends to come in short, sharp bursts at any time of the year. When it comes it comes hard and dirt roads often quickly become a sticky quagmire.

GETTING AROUND

See the Alice Springs and Darwin sections for details of getting to or from those centres or between them by bus, rail, road or air. The Northern Territory has its own scheduled airlines, Airlines of Northern Australia, which operates F27s and F28s. The chart below details their regular one way fares on the main routes. They also have advance purchase return fares (apex) on most of these routes. Note that where TAA or Ansett also fly the same route it will usually be cheaper — Darwin-Alice Springs is $183 by TAA or Ansett, rather more expensive by the territory airline which makes two stops along the way.

Driving in the Northern Territory

If you intend to get off the beaten track 'with care' is the thought to bear in mind. You can phone 52 3833 in Alice Springs for information on road conditions and the offices of the NTGTB will advise you on whether the roads you're planning to use require four-wheel drive. It's wise to carry a basic kit of spare parts in case of breakdown. It may not be a case of life-or-death but it can certainly save

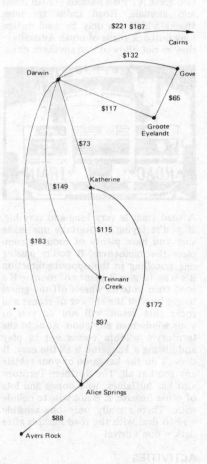

you a lot of time, trouble and expense. Carry spare water with you and if you do breakdown remain with the vehicle — you're more likely to be found there and you also have shade and protection from the heat.

Traffic may be fairly light in the

territory but a lot of people still manage to run into things so watch out for the two great NT road hazards — road trains and animals. Road trains are huge trucks which can only be used on the long outback roads of north Australia — they're not allowed into southern cities.

A road train is very long and very big. If you're trying to overtake one make sure you have plenty of room to complete the manoeuvre. If you're passing one travelling in the opposite direction it's wise to give it plenty of room — if a road train puts its wheels off the gravel to get by you the shower of stones and rocks that result will not do you or your windscreen any good. At night the territory's wildlife comes out to play and hitting a kangaroo is all too easy. It doesn't do the kangaroo or your vehicle any good at all. The Northern Territory also has buffaloes, wild horses and lots of other hazards it is not wise to collide with. There's really only one sensible way to deal with the road hazards after dark — don't drive!

ACTIVITIES
Bushwalking There are plenty of interesting bushwalking trails in the Northern Territory but care should be taken if you intend to venture off the beaten track. Around Alice Springs you can climb the surrounding ranges but wear stout shoes (the spinifex grass and burrs are quite amazingly sharp) and in summer you should wear a hat and carry water even for short walks. Walking in the top end is best in the dry although shorter walks are possible in the wet when the rain forests are at their best.

Rock Hounding There are plenty of worthwhile places in the territory for the avid fossicker. Check with the NTGTB about where to go and what permissions are required. Places to look include the Harts Range (72 km northeast of Alice Springs) for beryls, garnets and quartz; Eastern MacDonnell Ranges (east of Alice Springs) for beryls and garnets; Anthony Lagoon (215 km east of the Stuart Highway, north of Tennant Creek) for ribbonstone; Brock's Creek (37 km south-west of Adelaide, south of Darwin) for topaz, tourmaline, garnet and zircon.

Gliding Enormous thermals from the dry heat of the centre makes for fantastic gliding — there are gliding clubs in Darwin and Alice Springs. They operate from Batchelor, 88 km south of Darwin, and from Bond Springs, 25 km north of Alice Springs. Flying in to Alice Springs from Darwin once I saw a glider far below, bright white against the red.

Swimming Stay out of the water during the wet in Darwin — October/November to April/May. Sea wasp stings are not something you want to repeat. Darwin beaches are very popular, however, during the safe months. They include Casuarina Beach, claimed to be the longest 'free' beach in Australia. The sea is a long way from Alice Springs but the Speed St swimming pool is popular.

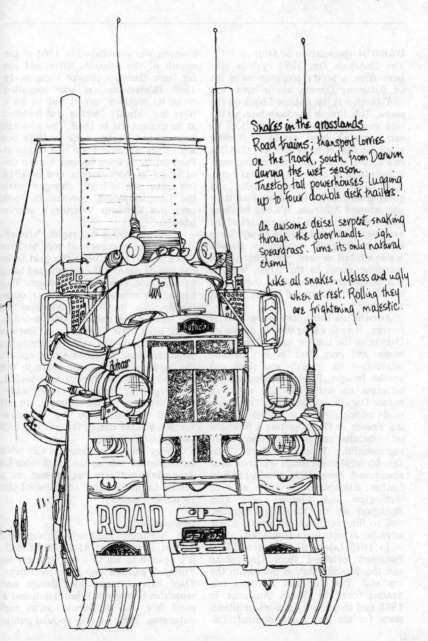

Snakes in the grasslands

Road trains; transport lorries on the Track, south from Darwin during the wet season. Treetop tall powerhouses lugging up to four double deck trailers.

An awsome deisel serpent, snaking through the doorhandle igh speargrass. Time its only natural enemy.

Like all snakes, Useless and ugly when at rest. Rolling they are frightening, majestic.

ROAD TRAIN

DARWIN (population 50,000)

The Christmas Day 1974 cyclone may have done a pretty comprehensive job of flattening Darwin but in true 'top end' fashion it has bounced back on the scene. This time it has been built so the odd gust of wind won't stand it on its ear. Darwin's hard drinking, frontier town reputation hides the fact that it is one of the most cosmopolitan and easy-going places in Australia. There is a constant flow of travellers coming and going from Asia or simply making their way around Australia. It's one of those places where backpacks seem part of the everyday scene and people always seem to be heading off somewhere. Darwin is also a bit of an oasis — whether you're travelling south to the Alice, west to WA or east into Queensland there are a lot of km to be covered before you get anywhere.

Darwin has had a stop-and-go sort of history. It took a long time to decide on Darwin as the site for the region's main centre and even after the city became established its growth was slow and trouble-fraught. There had been various attempts to settle the top end well before Darwin was founded. They were made principally due to British fears of the French or Dutch getting a foothold on Australia and were all remarkably unsuccessful. From 1824-29 Fort Dundas on Melville Island was tried then abandoned. From 1827-29 and 1838-49 further attempts were made at Fort Wellington and Victoria near Port Essington on the Cobourg Peninsula, well to the north-east of Darwin. These attempts at settlement also failed.

In 1845 Leichardt had reached Port Essington overland from Queensland and this aroused further interest in the top end. The Northern Territory was handed over to South Australia in 1863 and they drew up more ambitious plans for the area's development. Palmerston was established in 1864 at the mouth of the Adelaide River, not too far from Darwin's present location. In 1866 Palmerston too was forgotten when its location turned out to be a poor one. Finally Darwin was founded at its present site in 1869. The port had been named Darwin back in 1839 but at first the settlement was also known as Palmerston. It soon became known unofficially as Port Darwin and in 1911 the name was officially changed when the Commonwealth government took over the Northern Territory's administration.

Darwin's growth was rapidly accelerated by the discovery of gold at Pine Creek in 1871 but once the gold fever had run its course the city dropped back to slow and erratic development. The harsh and unpredictable climate combined with tenuous connections to the rest of the country held development back. WW II really put Darwin permanently on the map. It became an important base for allied action against the Japanese and the road south to the railhead at Alice Springs was sealed, finally putting the city in close contact with the rest of the country. In all Darwin was attacked by Japanese forces 64 times during the war and 243 people lost their lives.

Today Darwin is a modern city with an important role as the front door to Australia's northern region and as a centre for the mining activities of the Northern Territory.

Information

The Northern Territory Government Tourist Bureau is at 31 Smith St Mall. It's open 8.45 am to 5 pm, Monday to Friday, 9 am to 12 noon on Saturdays. They have a reasonable, though not astonishing, range of information and a good free map of Darwin centre and outer area. There's a very popular public noticeboard in the mall — a great place for buying and selling things or looking for rides. People often put notices up and then sit close by waiting for a result! Darwin has a daily newspaper, the *Darwin News*. The National Trust have their office on the corner of Knuckey and the Esplanade — pick up a copy of their Darwin walking tour leaflet. The GPO with its busy poste restante is on the corner of Smith and Knuckey Sts.

Remember they're very fussy about 'dress rules' up here — if you don't meet their 'standards' you don't get in. Don't swim in Darwin waters from October to May. You only get one sting from a sea wasp each lifetime.

Orientation

The centre of Darwin is a fairly compact area at the end of a peninsula. Smith St is the main shopping street of the centre and the main part of the street is an attractive pedestrian mall. The suburbs of Darwin sprawl away from the peninsula for some distance but the airport is conveniently central.

Darwin & Tracy

Everything in Darwin is still pre- and post-Tracy. The cyclone that tore the city apart on Christmas Day 1974 has had an enduring effect. For one thing it made the city, according to many people, a brighter, better place. You can hardly ask for a better urban renewal plan that starting with a clean slate and the pleasant, relaxed Smith St Mall makes an excellent comparison with its drab, pre-Tracy predecessor. Furthermore, say the pro-cyclone lobby, there's a strong Darwinian spirit since the cyclone. People are proud of the new, glossy Darwin and put more effort into making it an attractive, 'permanent' place.

The actual statistics of Tracy are frightening. The winds had been building up on Christmas Eve and by midnight were reaching their full fury. At 3.05 am the airport's anemometer cried

enough, just after recording a speed of 217 kph. It's thought the peak speeds were as much as 280 kph. Of Darwin's 11,200 houses 50 to 60% were either totally destroyed or so badly damaged that repair was impossible. Only 400 houses survived relatively intact and 66 lives were lost.

Much criticism was levelled at the design and construction of Darwin's houses but plenty of places a century or more old and built as solidly as you could ask for also toppled before the awesome winds. The new and rebuilt houses have been 'cyclone proofed' with strong steel reinforcements and roofs firmly pinned down. Cyclone proof or not some Darwin residents say that next time a cyclone is forecast they'll be jumping right into their cars and heading down the track. They'll come back afterwards to find out if they really were cyclone proof!

Around the Town

Despite its shaky beginnings and the destructions of WW II and cyclone Tracy Darwin still has a number of historic old buildings. The National Trust produce an interesting booklet titled *A Walk Through Historical Darwin*. Amongst the old buildings to look for there's the Victoria Hotel on Smith St Mall. Originally built in 1890 it was badly damaged by Tracy but has been restored. On the corner of the Mall and Bennett St the stone Commercial Bank dates from 1883. Built in the same year the old town hall was virtually destroyed by Tracy, despite its solid Victorian construction. It was used as a museum prior to the cyclone but only the walls remain. The Government Information Centre is beside it and here a locomotive from the old Darwin-Pine Creek railway line is on display. The line is no longer used but in the carriage behind the engine there's a small historic display and an interesting video clip about the line's history and the possibility of a line being constructed north from Alice Springs to Darwin. Ask in the information centre for the carriage to be opened. Across the road Browns Mart was also badly damaged by the cyclone but has been restored and now houses a theatre. There's a Chinese temple, glossy and new, on the corner of Woods and Bennett Sts.

Christ Church Cathedral, a short distance further towards the harbour, was destroyed by the cyclone. It was originally built in 1902 but all that remained after Tracy was the porch, which was a later addition from 1944. A new cathedral has been built and the old porch retained. Also badly damaged, the police station and old court house on the Esplanade have been restored and are used as government offices. Government House, built in stages from 1870, was known as The Residency until 1911 and has been damaged by just about every cyclone Darwin has been subject to. It is once again in fine condition, at the Esplanade corner. Continuing round the Esplanade you reach a memorial marking where the telegraph cable once ran from Darwin into the sea on its crossing to Banyuwangi in Java (just across from Bali). This for the first time put Australia into instant communication with England. Other buildings of interest along the Esplanade include the pleasantly tropical Hotel Darwin, Admiralty House and the old British and Australian Telegraph Company Residence (Lyons Cottage), now used by the National Trust.

Further out from the centre the National Trust also operates the old Fannie Bay Gaol which was in use for nearly 100 years up to 1979. You can visit it from 2 to 3.30 pm, Monday to Friday, admission is $1.50.

Aquascene

This is one of those 'tourist attractions' that's actually worth the cost of visiting. At Doctor's Gully fish have grown accustomed to coming in for a free feed every day at high tide. It has taken 20 years to convince them that this is the place for a daily meal but now half the stale bread in Darwin gets dispensed every day to a positive horde of milkfish, mullet, catfish and batfish. Some of them are quite big, the milkfish grow to over a metre and will demolish a whole slice bread in one go. It's a great scene and, of course, children positively love it — the fish will take bread right out of your hand. Feeding times depend on the high tides, admission is $1 for adults, the bread is free.

Botanic Gardens

The gardens' site was used to grow vegetables during the earliest days of Darwin but Tracy severely damaged the gardens, uprooting 75% of the plants in the garden. Fortunately vegetation grows fast in Darwin's climate and the botanic gardens, with their good collection of tropical flora, have been well restored. The gardens are now being extended down to Mindil Beach. It's an easy bicycle ride out to the gardens from the centre.

Museum of Arts & Sciences

Post-cyclone Darwin has acquired a really excellent museum. It's at Bullocky Point, Fannie Bay and houses a series of interesting exhibits within a fine new building. They include an Australian art collection, exhibits of Aboriginal art and archaeology, South-East Asian and Oceanic art exhibits, local historic items, natural science exhibits and also temporary exhibitions. A museum highlight is 'Sweetheart', a huge five-metre long saltwater crocodile which became quite a local personality before meeting its unfortunate end.

The museum is bright, spacious and yet not too big for museum over-kill to set in. Highly recommended. Admission is free and it's open Monday, Tuesday & Thursday from 9 am to 5 pm; Wednesday & Friday 9 am to 6 pm; Saturday & Sunday 10 am to 6 pm. You can get there on a bus 4 or 6.

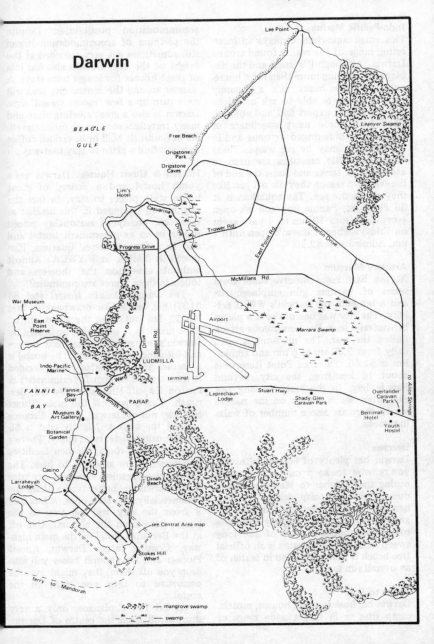

Indo-Pacific Marine

This small aquarium displays an interesting range of the sealife found around Darwin. Although it's small and the displays are nothing more than large home-aquarium-style tanks, it's a friendly place and you're able to ask questions and get a little expert fact and opinion. They have some nasty specimens of stonefish, a blue-ringed octopus and in season there may be sea wasps. These unpleasant little creatures are hard to keep alive in tanks and come the end of the sea wasp season they die off just like they do in the sea. The aquarium is at 36 Philip St, Fannie Bay and it's open every day from 10 am to 4 pm except on Fridays when it doesn't open until 1 pm. Admission is $2.50.

Artillery Museum

At the East Point Reserve there are a series of wartime gun emplacements and a museum on Darwin's WW II activity. The city was one of the few places in Australia to suffer continuous attack during the war. The museum is open daily from 9.30 am to 5 pm and admission is $1.50. The East Point Reserve is about 10 km from the city, beyond Fannie Bay. In the early evening you can often see wallabies on the reserve where there are also a number of walking tracks.

Beaches

Darwin has plenty of beaches although you're wise to keep out of the water during the October to May wet season due to the sea wasp danger. Popular beaches include Vestey's, Fannie Bay and Mandorah, across the bay from the town. The northern end of the long sweep of sand at Casuarina is an official free beach if you want to go in search of an overall sun tan.

Places to Stay

Darwin has hostels, guest houses, motels, camp sites — in fact a wide range of accommodation possibilities. Despite the plethora of accommodation it can still sometimes get very crowded at the height of the dry. Darwin also has lots of guest houses for longer term stays. A wander around the central city area will soon turn up a few 'rooms vacant' sign. Darwin is also a great meeting place and many travellers soon meet other travellers in Smith St Mall or in various coffee bars and find a place to stay that way.

Hostels & Guest Houses Darwin has a youth hostel and a variety of guest house style places to stay. In fact the city is well equipped in this bracket as there are plenty of reasonably priced rooms in an ex-government hostel and also in a former nurses' quarters. Plus there's a YMCA and YWCA. Almost without exception the showers and toilets in these places are communal.

The *Darwin Youth Hostel* (tel 84 3107) has one major drawback in that it's 12 km out from the town centre. That problem is somewhat mitigated by Darwin's remarkably cheap bus service and hitching is fairly easy. The hostel is a former remand centre (they decided it wasn't good enough for criminals!) at Beaton Rd, off Hidden Valley Rd, Berrimah. That's just off the main Stuart Highway out of Darwin, a short distance beyond the airport. Nightly cost is $5 and the usual hostel rules apply. There's a big common room, kitchen facilities and bicycles are available to hire. The warden also organises excellent day trips from Darwin — better value than the commercially operated ones. A bus 5 or 8 from the city will get you to the hostel (also from the airport). Get off at the Berrimah Hotel on the main highway. Coming in to Darwin, Ansett Pioneer and Greyhound buses will also drop you off there, they might even be persuaded to take you right to the hostel.

At 88 The Esplanade, only a very short stroll from the centre of Darwin, the *Lameroo Lodge* (tel 81 9733) is a big ex-government hostel with 200-plus rooms. Bed & breakfast costs $20/30 for singles/doubles. The rooms are pleasant — they have fans, sinks and fridges plus tea and coffee making facilities. Plus there's a TV room, a laundry and a swimming pool. For those on a tight budget, rooms are also available without the fridges and tea/coffee facilities on a room-only basis at $11/17. If you're staying longer they also have weekly and permanent rates. Lunch and dinner is also available. The lodge also operates the *Ross Smith Hostel* (tel 81 2162) at Parap and the *Bayview Lodge* (tel 81 6227) at Fannie Bay.

Larrakeyah Lodge (tel 81 2933) is another big building, this one used to be the nurses' quarters. It's at Kahlin Avenue, about 1.5 km from the centre and has fan cooled rooms in the annex at $12/18 or air-con rooms in the main building at $19/30. The more expensive rooms have fridges and tea/coffee facilities. There are also large family rooms at $42. The prices are on a room-only basis but meals are available — a continental breakfast is $3.50. The lodge has a pool and laundry facilities.

The YMCA and YWCA are both mid-distance between the Lameroo Lodge and the Larrakeyah Lodge relative to the city. At Doctor's Gully, at the end of The Esplanade, the *YMCA* (tel 81 8377) has dorms at $9, singles at $11.50 (50c more for a single with washbasin), doubles at $20 or $11 each on the share basis. Rooms have fans but you'll only find sinks in some of the single rooms (not in doubles). Again prices are room-only but meals are available — breakfast costs $2 or $3. There's a pool, games room and laundry. Like the YMCA the *YWCA* (tel 81 8644) also takes males or females. It's at 119 Mitchell St and here all prices are bed & breakfast. Dormitory accommodation costs $10.50, singles $15, doubles $24. There are also a handful of rooms with private facilities at $17/30. Rooms are all fan-cooled and there's a laundry.

Finally there's a *Salvation Army Hostel* (tel 81 8188) at 49 Mitchell St, right in the centre. The emphasis here is rather more on permanent accommodation than at the other places —although all the others (the youth hostel apart) offer weekly or longer rates. The Sally Army rates, however, are strictly weekly at $40 for a single, $38 per person for a share twin, $5 less if you're unemployed.

Hotels & Motels There's not much in the way of hotels in Darwin, most of the older hotel-style places must have been swept away by the cyclone. Right in the centre of town at 35 Cavenagh St the *Windsor Tourist Lodge* (tel 81 9214) has air-con rooms — all with shower & toilet, fridges and tea/coffee making facilities — at $25/30 room-only. There are also triples at $35 but the rooms are a bit small and boxy. Round the corner at 37 Knuckey St the *Central City Lodge* (tel 81 2931) has rooms at $25/35 including a proper breakfast. They're air-con and have fridges and tea/coffee facilities and you can also use the laundry and kitchen facilities but showers and toilets are shared. At 4 Harriet Place, just across Daly St from the centre, the *Crystal Motel* (tel 81 5694) is definitely misnamed — it's just a very basic guest house at $10 per person for a share room, $15 for a single.

Back on Cavenagh St, a little further along from the Windsor Lodge at the corner with Whitefield St, the *Tiwi Lodge* (tel 81 6471) is a very centrally located motel with rooms at $27.50/33. It's air-con and has the usual motel facilities. Also fairly central the *Aspa City Motel* (tel 81 6695) is at 38 Dashwood Crescent but it's rather more expensive at $36/40. Directly across from the airport on the Stuart Highway the *Leprechaun Lodge* (tel 84 3400)

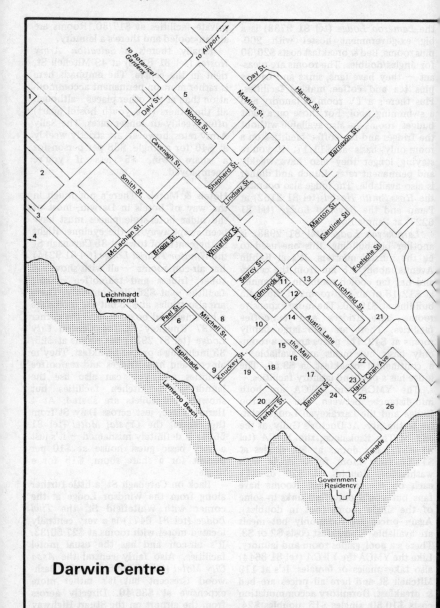

Darwin Centre

1 Larrakeyah Lodge	14 Bookworld
2 YWCA	15 Darwin Plaza
3 to YMCA	16 Tourist Office
4 to Aquascene	17 Victoria Hotel
5 Warung Pojok	18 Ansett
6 Lameroo Lodge	19 Salvation Army Hostel
7 Tiwi Lodge	20 Darwin Hotel
8 Qantas	21 Chinese Temple
9 National Trust	22 TAA & Garuda
10 GPO	23 Bus Terminal
11 Windsor Tourist Lodge	24 Government Information Centre
12 Arnhemland Aboriginal Art	25 Brown's Mart
13 Greyhound Terminal	26 Christchurch Cathedral

cost $34/38 for singles/twins, $40 for a double. In Parap the *Shangri-La Motel* (tel 81 2163) at 52 Gregory St is another cheapie with rooms at $15/20 for singles/doubles or $24/30 with air-con. Darwin, as you can see, is not a great place for motel bargains.

In the motel/hotel category there are a couple of places rather further out from the city centre. The *Berrimah Hotel* (tel 84 3999) is on the Stuart Highway out at Berrimah, close to the youth hostel. Doubles here are $30, they're modern motel-style. Across at Nightcliff you could try *Lim's Rapid Creek Hotel* (tel 85 3000) on Casuarina Drive where singles cost $20 to $25, doubles $27 to $30. The Chinese restaurant here is supposed to be pretty good.

Camping At first glance Darwin would appear to be very well equipped with camping sites but closer inspection reveals a different story. For a start many of them are quite a distance out from the centre — 20 to 30 km down the track. Secondly a number of the more conveniently situated only take caravans — no tent campers. Most conveniently situated are the Shady Glen Caravan Park on the Stuart Highway at Winnellie (across from the airport) and the Overlanders Caravan Park at Berrimah (close to the youth hostel).

Some of the sites include:

Bloodwood Caravan Park (tel 83 1068), 22 km south at Yarrawonga turnoff, camping $2.50 per person.
Coolalinga Caravan Park (tel 83 1026), 30 km south on Stuart Highway, camping sites 16, on-site vans $68 per week.
Howard Springs Caravan Park (tel 83 1169), 22 km south at 290 Whitewood Rd, Howard Springs, camping sites at $4, on-site vans at $66 per week.
Nook Caravan Park (tel 83 1048), 23 km south at Morgan Rd off Stuart Highway, no camping but on-site vans at $25 per night.
Overlander Caravan Park (tel 84 3025), 13 km south at corner of McMillans Rd & Stuart Highway, Berrimah, camping sites at $4, cabins at $10 per night, on-site vans from $10 per night, flats at $65 per week.
Shady Glen Caravan Park (tel 84 3330), 9 km south at Stuart Highway, Winnellie, camping sites at $3 for two, $4 for three, on-site vans $12 to $18.

Places to Eat
Fast Foods Darwin has always been a pretty cosmopolitan place to eat and the new glossy Darwin carries on that pattern. It's also a place for fast foods and takeaways. For a quick snack or meal at lunchtime or early evening on the late night shopping night try Darwin

Plaza off Smith St Mall. There's a good little collection of fast food counters here — the *Sheik's Tent* for Lebanese, the *Taco House* for Mexican, the *Thai Kitchen* for Thai/Chinese, *Energy Foods* for health foods and *Dairyland* for yoghurts and ice cream.

Across the other side of Smith St the *Little Lark Cafe* is another fast food specialist, open a bit later in the evening. Here it is mainly Chinese food, not bad at all at $3.50 to $4, but also drinks, sandwiches, fish & chips and breakfasts. In The Track, another arcade/mall off Smith St, *Simply Foods* is a popular health food place. Here you'll find fruit juices, teas, fruit salads, exotic cakes, sandwiches and so on. It's a very popular meeting place, a good place to sit down and relax.

Counter Meals For counter meals there are a couple of good places right in the centre. The *Darwin Hotel* stretches from the Esplanade to Mitchell and the Bistro Room does meals in the $6 to $7 bracket — 12 to 2 and 6 to 8. Or in Smith St Mall the *Victoria Hotel's* Colonial Bar also has meals around the $7 mark — similar opening times too. Both of them offer that Darwin speciality, buffalo steaks! At the *Parap Hotel* Jessie's Bistro does counter lunches and teas for around $7. You can also get counter lunches Monday to Friday and counter teas on Saturday from 6 pm to 9 pm at the *Berrimah Hotel's* Stuart Bistro. The Chinese restaurant at *Lim's Rapid Creek Hotel* is reputed to be fairly good.

Ethnics *Warung Pojok* at 90 Woods St is open 9 am to 9 pm and does good Indonesian food. There are no prices up because they'll adjust the size to your appetite. You can have a small nasi goreng (fried rice) for $2 or a big nasi campur (rice with everything) for $5 or $6. At Shop 12 in the Track, off the Smith St Mall, *Christo's* is a popular

Greek restaurant either eat there or take-away. At 37 Knuckey St, the *Capri Restaurant* has both a restaurant section and a coffee lounge section. All the usual pizza and pasta dishes from around $4 plus main courses in the $6 to $9 bracket. *Loong Foong's* at 22 Cavenagh St is a Chinese restaurant in the old fashioned bare floor and formica school. The food is also pretty basic but then most dishes are $5 or less so you can't complain. Good pizzas at *Enzrio's* on the corner of Cavenagh and Seeray Sts.

Otherwise — well there are a string of French restaurants in Darwin, some said to be pretty good. Plus steakhouses, seafood specialists, Greek and Italian restaurants and, of course, a number of Chinese.

Darwin has plenty of supermarkets just like anywhere else in Australia. Food is, of course, rather more expensive than 'down south' but the difference is not as great as it used to be and the quality difference has also been narrowed. You've got to expect higher costs when even the milk comes all the way from the Atherton Tableland near Cairns in Queensland. In summer Darwin is simply too hot for cows.

The Darwin Thirst
Darwin has a reputation as one of the hardest drinking towns in the world. In a dry year an average of 230 litres of the amber fluid disappear down each Darwinian throat. The Darwin thirst is summed up by the famed 'Darwin stubby' — a beer bottle that looks just like any other stubby, except that it contains two litres instead of 375 ml. The record for downing a Darwin stubby is one minute two seconds — but that was the pre-83 Darwin stubby which was a mite larger at 2.25 litres!

The Darwin beer thirst gets another go at the annual beer can regatta in June. A series of boat races are held for boats constructed entirely of beer cans. Apart from the racing boats some unusual special entries generally turn up. Like a beer can Viking longboat or a beer can submarine. Constructed by an Australian navy contingent the submarine actually submerged! The races have also their controversial elements — on one occasion a boat turned up made entirely of brand new cans, delivered straight from the brewery, sealed but empty. Unfair cried other competitors, the beer must be drunk!

Entertainment

There are bands at the *Victoria Hotel* on Smith St Mall and at the *Berrimah Hotel*. *Lim's Hotel* has a disco. On Sunday nights the Darwin folk music club meets at 8 pm at the gun turret at East Point Reserve, bring along your guitar. There's also a folk dance club which meets on Tuesday nights at the water-ski club near the museum. The Darwin Film Society meets the first and third Tuesday of each month at 8 pm at the Darwin High School theatrette — temporary membership at the door. Films are also shown regularly at the various city libraries.

Soon after this edition emerges the Darwin casino will move from its temporary location at the *Don Hotel* to its new home at Mindil Beach. So long as you're 'properly dressed' it's quite good entertainment to watch people cast away large sums of money. Callow youths at the door adjudicate if the style of your shirt collar and the cut of your trousers is to their master's liking.

Two-Up

The Alice and Darwin casinos offer plenty of opportunity to watch the Australian gambling mania in full flight. You can also observe a true piece of Australia's cultural heritage, the all-Australian game of two-up. The essential idea of two-up is to toss two 'coins' and obtain two heads. The 'players' stand around a circular playing area and bet on the coins falling either two heads or two tails. The 'spinner' uses a 'kip' to toss the coins and the house pays out and takes in as the coins fall — except that nothing happens on 'odd' tosses (one head, one tail) unless they're thrown five times in a row. In which case you lose unless you've also bet on that possibility. The spinner continues

Belly up to the bar in Katherine Northern Territory

tossing until he or she either throws tails, throws five odds or throws three heads. If the spinner manages three heads then he or she also wins at 7½ to one on any bet placed on that possibility and he or she then starts tossing all over again. When the spinner finally loses the next player in the circle takes over as spinner.

Getting There

Air You can fly to Darwin from all the other states and Darwin is also an international arrival and departure point — principally for Indonesia and Singapore. The Darwin-Denpasar (Bali) flight, once an extremely popular arrival or departure point to Australia, is now rather over-priced at $398 one-way or $420 to $578 for a seven to 28-day excursion ticket. Garuda operates the flight three times a week and visas are available for Indonesia in Darwin in about three days for $3.

From other states the usual route is either via Mt Isa or Adelaide with TAA and Ansett. From WA there are TAA and Ansett flights from Perth via Port Hedland or Alice Springs while Airlines of Western Australia fly Perth-Darwin with services through all the intermediate ports — Karratha-Port Hedland-Broome-Derby-Kununurra. Airlines of Northern Australia also fly via Nhulunbuy to Cairns.

See the Northern Territory introductory Getting There section for air fares within the Northern Territory. Some fares to or from other states include Perth $299, Port Hedland $206, Cairns $221 (most direct route), Mt Isa $182, Brisbane $298 ($224 standby).

Buses You can reach Darwin by bus on three routes -- the Western Australia route from Port Hedland, Broome, Derby and Kununurra; the Queensland route from Mt Isa to Three Ways and up the track or straight up the track from Alice Springs. In the Northern Territory Greyhound generally have

more frequent services than Ansett Pioneer but Aussiepass and Eaglepass travellers can use either service on the Western Australia route. Ansett Pioneer (tel 80 3333) operate from the Ansett terminal on Mitchell St. Greyhound (tel 81 8055) have a terminal on the corner of Cavenagh and Knuckey Sts.

Fares to or from Darwin include Alice Springs $100, 21 hours; Mt Isa $81, 26 hours; Townsville $113, 38 hours, Port Hedland $120, 36 hours.

Bus/Rail Greyhound do a special ticket deal with Australian National Railways so you can be ticketed on the ghan from South Australia to Alice Springs then continue by bus up through the Northern Territory. From Adelaide fares are: Alice Springs $83, Tennant Creek $126, Katherine $153, Darwin $175, Kununurra $184, Halls Creek $195, Fitzroy Crossing $208, Derby $214, Perth $313, Mt Isa $133, Cairns $197. Extra costs for an economy sleeper on the rail sector is $34, for first class travel it's $79.

Getting Around

Bus Darwin has a fairly good bus service — Monday to Friday. On Saturday the services are very limited and on Sunday they shut down completely. The city services start from the small terminal on Harry Chan Avenue where you can get bus timetables. You can also phone 81 2150 or 27 9446 for information. Except for services way down the track (some of the route 8 buses) anywhere in Darwin costs a standard 30c. Route 5 is particularly useful, running from the city via the airport to Berrimah (for the youth hostel) and then up to Casuarina. On weekdays there are 12 services a day from 6 am to 8.55 pm (ex-city) but only four on Saturday mornings and none at all on Saturday afternoons or Sundays. Route 8 also operates from the city via Berrimah to 21 km, 10 times a day but only twice on Saturdays. Two or three times a day (once on Saturdays) it runs right out to Howard Springs and Humpty Doo. Weekends are obviously a problem but Mondays to Fridays you've got 20-plus buses a day between the city and the airport or the youth hostel and for just 30c.

Cars Budget, Letz and Hertz are at the airport. Thrifty and National are also represented in Darwin which is classified as a 'remote' area and therefore rather expensive if you plan to drive very far. There are also a string of local car rental organisations, many of them renting Mokes which are very popular in Darwin. Moke rentals (tel 81 8896 and several other numbers) is typical at $14 a day plus $5 insurance per day plus 14c a km. Others can be cheaper — try Sampan Trading on Smith St or at the Greyhound terminal.

Bicycles Darwin is surprisingly good for bike riding and there is a fairly extensive network of bike tracks. It's a pleasant ride out from the city to the botanic gardens, Fannie Bay, the East Point Reserve or even, if you're feeling fit, all the way to Nightcliff and Casuarina. The youth hostel rent bikes for $4 a day. So do Sampan Trading (tel 81 3708) at 55 Smith St, opposite Woolworths, where they cost $3.50 a half day or $5 a day for pretty good 10-speed bikes.

Airport Darwin airport is only about six km from the centre of town, very conveniently central. The airport handles international flights as well as domestic ones, it's quite a busy airport. Hertz, Budget and Letz have rent-a-car desks at the airport. Taxi fare into the centre is about $4 to $5. Keetley's

Bus Service runs a bus for all incoming flights into the city for $2. It will drop you off pretty well anywhere you want in the centre. To be picked up for departing flights just ring 81 4422. You can also get out to the airport on a bus 5 or 8 for 30c. These same buses run right out to the youth hostel at Berrimah. In the city Ansett (tel 80 3333) are on Mitchell St, TAA (tel 82 3333) are at 16 Bennett St.

Tours There are all sorts of tours from Darwin including short afternoon city tours (around $17 to $20), tours further out to Yarrawonga Zoo and Howard and Berry Springs as well as the city sights ($35), lots of wildlife tours to see the buffaloes and the birdlife ($25 to $80 depending on the duration and the distance covered) or tours down the track as far as Adelaide River or on to the Arnhem Highway ($40 to $80). As you can see Darwin tours are not cheap.

Further afield you can make day tours by air to the Kakadu National Park or over Arnhem Land. Tours to the Aboriginal reserves on Bathurst and Melville Islands cost from $100 for a half-day tour. Various boats can be hired around Darwin. Crocodile enthusiasts can make night time croc-spotting excursions for $18.

Things to Buy
Darwin has a number of souvenir shops and galleries but easily the best place is the Arnhemland Aboriginal Art Gallery at 35 Cavenagh St — on the corner of Knuckey St. They've got all sorts of fine examples of Aboriginal art particularly, of course, bark paintings from Arnhem Land but also interesting carvings by the Tiwi people of Bathurst and Melville Islands.

THE TOP END
There are a number of places of interest fairly close to Darwin. A group of people can hire a Moke and get out to them quite economically. There are also many tours operated out of Darwin to the sites along the track. The youth hostel warden also makes some interesting excursions for hostellers.

Yarrawonga Zoo
Situated 20 km down the track the zoo has a variety of top end wildlife including buffaloes, emus, brolgas, dingoes and crocodiles.

Howard Springs
Turning off just beyond Yarrawonga the springs are 30 km from the city. The forest surrounded swimming hole is rather clogged by weeds and because the reserve is so convenient for the city it can get uncomfortably crowded. Nevertheless on a quiet day it's a pleasant spot for an excursion from the city and there's lots of birdlife.

Arnhem Highway
Thirty-three km south of Darwin the Arnhem Highway branches off to the south-east. Only 10 km down the road you come to the Humpty Doo Hotel, a colourful hotel with some real 'territorian' character. They do counter lunches and teas here all week, Sunday is particularly popular. The Fogg Dam, 60 km out, is a great place for bird watching. This was the site of the unsuccessful Humpty Doo rice project — the planners hadn't reckoned with the birds' appetite. The Bark Hut Inn is a pleasant place to eat near a billabong at Annaburroo Station, 85 km along the Arnhem Highway. The billabong is good for swimming and you can also camp there. The South Alligator Motor Inn is 180 km down the highway, just before the Kakadu National Park. From here

you can make trips on the *Kakadu Princess* along the South Alligator River. Cruises usually cost $30 but on Fridays there are shorter two hour trips for $15.

Darwin Crocodile Farm
On the Stuart Highway, just a little south of the Arnhem Highway turn-off and 40 km from Darwin, the recently opened crocodile farm has a lake full of saltwater and freshwater crocodiles including some real biggies. There's also a display of Northern Territory snakes. The farm is open 9 am to 5.30 pm daily.

Berry Springs
The turn-off to Berry Springs is 46 km down the track and it's then 10 km further to the reserve. It's not so crowded as the Howard Springs reserve, principally because of its greater distance from the city. There's a good walking track here. The sealed road ends soon after Berry Springs but it is possible to continue on all the way to Mandorah on the Cox Peninsula. It's far easier to simply take the ferry across Darwin Harbour.

Rum Jungle
Seventy-seven km south of Darwin the road turns off to Batchelor and the abandoned uranium mine at Rum Jungle.

Mandorah Resort
It's only 10 km across the harbour by boat to this popular holiday resort — you can also reach the resort on the tip of Cox Peninsula by road but that's nearly 140 km, about half of it on unsealed roads. The ferry across to Mandorah costs $7 return and the crossing takes about half an hour. It departs from Stokes Hill Wharf at 10 am and 12 noon on weekdays, also at 2 pm on weekends and public holidays. If you want to stay at the holiday resort

you're looking at $40 or more a night for a double.

Kakadu National Park

Only recently established the Kakadu National Park is one of the most spectacular in Australia. It consists of two distinct regions — the floodplains, billabongs and lagoons drained by the Alligator Rivers and the soaring, rocky Arnhem Land escarpment, cut by fantastic gorges, waterfalls and streams. Apart from the amazing scenery the park also has much wildlife and some superb examples of Aboriginal art. In fact the Aboriginal art is probably the best to be seen in any park in Australia.

The park is 220 km east of Darwin, between the South and East Alligator Rivers. The park headquarters are near Jabiru which is reached by a sealed road, the Arnhem Highway, from Darwin. There is also a uranium mining project at Jabiru and the close proximity of the uranium mines around the Kakadu park has caused much controversy. The park can also be reached by unsealed roads from Oenpelli and Pine Creek but these are often closed in the wet.

Highlights of the park include the Aboriginal art at Nourlangie Rock and Obiri Rock. The Jim Jim Falls (which drop 215 metres) and the Twin Falls in the south-east of the park are spectacular and there is much birdlife to be seen at the Yellow Water billabong. Cruises on the South Alligator River, on the park's western boundary, are also popular. Although the roads in the park are unsealed they are generally quite accessible by conventional vehicles during the dry season. There are campsites at a number of locations in the park, the site at Muirella Park on the Nourlangie Creek is particularly pleasant.

Alternatively there are a variety of tours into the park from Darwin. They range from one-day fly-drive tours for around $150 to two and three-day

CONSERVATION COMMISSION

tours in the $180 to $350 bracket. You can also make four-wheel drive camping trips from the park headquarters for around $150 for two days. There are a number of operators into the park. Uranium enthusiasts can tour the Ranger Uranium Mines at Jabiru for $5.

Crocodiles

The Northern Territory has a fair population of crocodiles and since they are now protected their numbers are increasing. There are two types of crocodiles in the territory — freshwater and saltwater. The smaller freshwater or Johnston's crocodile are found in freshwater rivers and billabongs while the larger (meaner and nastier) saltwater crocodiles are also found in the tidal region of rivers. Freshwater crocodiles are generally thought to be harmless to man but saltwater crocodiles are definitely not. And they can grow to a very large size. It is wise to always enquire locally before swimming in rivers and billabongs in the top end. The NT Conservation Commission has signposted

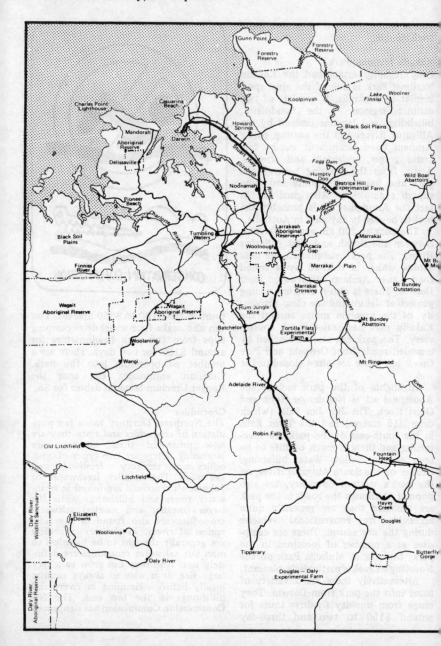

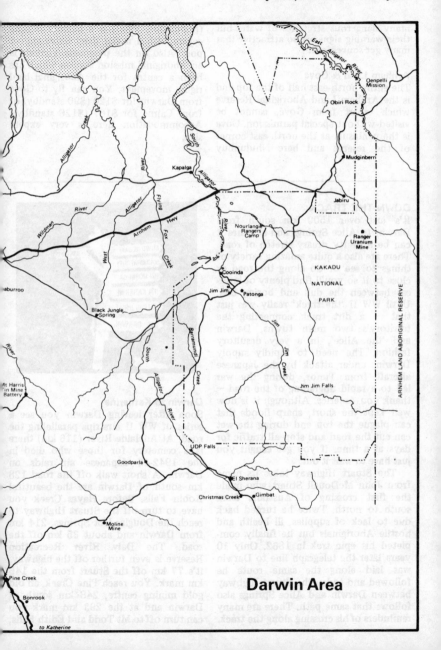

Darwin Area

many dangerous stretches of water but their warning signs are so attractive that many get souvenired.

Arnhem Land & Gove

The entire north-east half of the top end is the Arnhem Land Aboriginal Reserve which, apart from Gove, cannot be visited without special permission. Gove is the peninsula at the north-east corner of the reserve and here Nhulunbuy (population 3600) is a bauxite mining centre with a major deep water export port. Also on the peninsula Yirrkala is an Aboriginal mission station which has been a centre for the Aboriginal land rights movement. You can fly to Gove from Darwin for $120 ($90 standby) or from Cairns for $167 ($126 standby). Accommodation here is very expensive.

DOWN THE TRACK

It's just over 1500 km south from Darwin to Alice Springs and at times it can be a pretty dreary stretch of road. There are also a quite amazing variety of things to see or do along the road or close to it so you'll find plenty of interest between the dull and boring bits. Until WW II 'the track' really was just that — a dirt track connecting the territory's two main towns, Darwin and 'the Alice', in a very desultory fashion. The need to rapidly supply Darwin, under attack by the Japanese aircraft from Timor, during the war led to a rapid upgrading of the road — thank you America. Although it is now well kept the short, sharp floods that can plague the top end during the wet can cut the road and stop all traffic for days at a time. If you get caught you just have to wait it out.

The Stuart Highway takes its name from John McDouall Stuart who made the first crossing of Australia from south to north. Twice he turned back due to lack of supplies, ill health and hostile Aboriginals but he finally completed his epic trek in 1862. Only 10 years later the telegraph line to Darwin was laid along the same route he followed and today the Stuart Highway between Darwin and Alice Springs also follows that same path. There are many reminders of his crossing along the track.

Darwin to Katherine

Soon after leaving Darwin you see a series of WW II airstrips paralleling the road. At Adelaide River (116 km) there is a cemetery for those who died in the 1942-43 Japanese air raids on Darwin. A short walk off the road 128 km south of Darwin are the beautiful Robin Falls. Before Hayes Creek you have to turn off the Stuart Highway to reach the Douglas Hot Springs, 214 km from Darwin and about 35 km off the road. The Daly River Recreation Reserve is even further off the highway, it's 77 km off the Stuart from the 146 km mark. You reach Pine Creek, an old gold mining centre, 248 km south of Darwin and at the 293 km mark you can turn off to Mt Todd and Edith Falls,

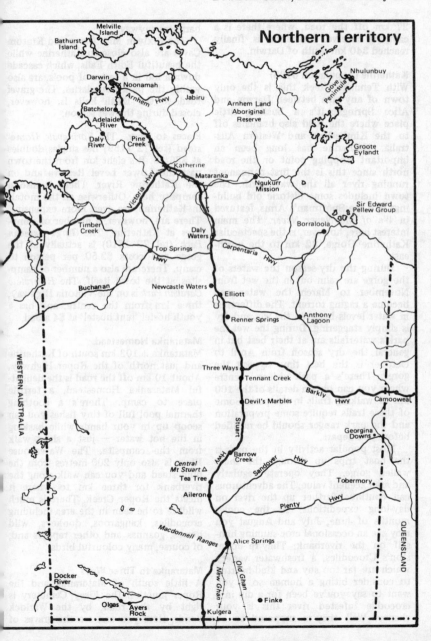

Northern Territory

Melville Island

Bathurst Island

Nhulunbuy

Darwin

Noonamah

Jabiru

Gove Peninsula

Arnhem Hwy

Batchelor

Arnhem Land Aboriginal Reserve

Adelaide River

Daly River

Pine Creek

Groote Eylandt

Katherine

Mataranka

Ngukurr Mission

Sir Edward Pellew Group

Victoria Hwy

Timber Creek

Daly Waters

Borraloola

Carpentaria Hwy

Top Springs

Buchanan

Newcastle Waters

Elliott

Renner Springs

Anthony Lagoon

Three Ways

Tennant Creek

Barkly Hwy

Camooweal

Devil's Marbles

Georgina Downs

Barrow Creek

Sandover Hwy

Tobermory

Central Mt Stuart △

Tea Tree

Aileron

Plenty Hwy

Macdonnell Ranges

Alice Springs

WESTERN AUSTRALIA

QUEENSLAND

Stuart Hwy

Docker River

Olgas

Ayers Rock

Finke

New Ghan

Old Ghan

Kulgera

27 km off the road, where there is a camping reserve. Katherine is finally reached 340 km south of Darwin.

Katherine (population 3100)

With Tennant Creek this is the only town of any size between Darwin and Alice Springs. It's a bustling little place where the road also branches off to the Kimberleys and Western Australia. Katherine has long been an important stopping point on the road north since this is the first permanent running river all the way north. The town includes some historic old buildings like the Sportman's Arms, featured in *We of the Never Never*. The main interest here, however, is the spectacular Katherine Gorge, 32 km to the north-east.

During the dry-season the waters of the gorge are calm but in the wet from November to March the water can become a raging torrent. The difference in water levels between the wet and dry is simply staggering. During the wet the park's waterfalls are at their best but in general the dry season from April to October is the best time to visit the gorge. There's a park visitors' centre where you can obtain details of the 100 km of walking trails in the park. Some of these trails require some preparation and the park ranger should be notified before you depart.

Most popular activity in the park is the boat trips up through the sheer walled gorge. They operate regularly and are excellent value. The adventurous can continue further up the river on day-long expeditions. In the cooler months of June, July and August you may see an occasional croc sunning himself on the riverbank. They're Johnston's Crocodiles, a freshwater variety which are far too shy and kind-hearted to consider biting a human so if you want to say you've been for a dip in a crocodile infested river this is your chance. Well they're supposed to be harmless anyway.

The Sixteen Mile Caves and Kintore Caves are also close to Katherine while the beautiful Edith Falls, which cascade down a hill in a series of pools, are also within the park boundaries. The gravel road to the Edith Falls is, however, closed during the wet season.

Places to Stay The *Springvale Homestead* (tel 72 1159) has singles/doubles at $26/36. It's eight km from the town past the Lower Level Reserve and on the Katherine River. There is also a campsite here. Otherwise all the motels in Katherine are even more expensive. There are, however, a number of campsites at Katherine. The *Gorge Caravan Park* (tel 72 1810) is actually at the gorge and costs $2.50 per person to camp. There are also a number of campsites at the town itself. The *Riverview Caravan Park* is on the Victoria Highway, three km from the centre, and has a youth hostel 'tent hostel' at $4 a bed.

Mataranka Homestead

Mataranka is 103 km south of Katherine and just north of the Roper Highway. About 10 km off the road is the delightful Mataranka Homestead, a terrific place to camp. There's a soothing thermal pool full of tiny fishes you can scoop up in your hands while basking in the hot water — just a short walk from the campsite. The Waterhouse River is also only 200 metres from the homestead and you can walk along the riverbank for three km to where it meets the Roper Creek. There is much wildlife to be seen in the area including crocodiles, kangaroos, donkeys, wild horses, goannas and other reptiles and, of course, many colourful birds.

Mataranka to Three Ways

A little south of Mataranka and the Roper junction the Elsey Cemetery is right by the road, by the Warlock Ponds. Here you can see the graves of characters like 'the Fizzer' who came to life in the turn of the century classic of outback life — *We of the Never Never*. The foundations of the homestead can be seen across the road from the cemetery.

Continuing south you pass through Larrimah — at one time the railway line from Darwin terminated here but it was abandoned after cyclone Tracy. Then there's Daly Waters, Newcastle Waters and Elliott and at all of them the land gets drier and drier. A large rock known as Lubra's Lookout overlooks Renner Springs and this is generally accepted as being the dividing line between the seasonally wet land of the 'top end' and the dry 'dead heart' country of the centre. About 50 km from Three Ways you pass Churchill's Head, a large rock said to look like Britain's wartime prime minister. Soon after there's a memorial to Stuart at Attack Creek. Here the explorer turned back on one of his attempts to cross Australia from south to north, after his party was attacked by a group of hostile Aboriginals. They were running low on supplies at this point and this incident was the final straw.

Three Ways

Situated 537 km north of the Alice, 988 km south of Darwin and 643 km west of Mt Isa, Three Ways is basically a bloody long way from anywhere. Apart from Tennant Creek that is, just 26 km south down the track. This is a classic 'get stuck' point for hitchhikers — fortunately there's a roadhouse at the junction but anybody who has hitched around Australia seems to have a tale about being stuck at Three Ways. The junction is marked by the John Flynn Memorial, to that original flying doctor. A little south of Three Ways there's an old telegraph station from the days of the overland telegraph.

Tennant Creek (population 2200)

Along with Katherine this is the only town of any size along the track between Darwin and Alice Springs. It's just 26 km south of Three Ways, 511 km north of Alice Springs. There's an old tale that Tennant Creek was first settled when a wagon load of beer broke down here and the wagon drivers figured they might as well make themselves comfortable while they consumed the freight. Later Tennant Creek had a small gold rush and you can see the old mines at Warrego and Nobles Nob, which is the largest open cut gold mine in the country. The old telegraph station, just 10 km north of the town by the highway, has a couple of unmarked graves.

About 100 km south of Tennant Creek are the Devil's Marbles, a haphazard pile of giant spherical boulders scattered on both sides of the road. The Rainbow Snake laid them according to Aboriginal mythology. The Rainbow Snake obviously got around because there is a similar collection of boulders in a south island beach in New Zealand and the very similar Devil's Pebbles are only 10 km north-west of Tennant Creek.

Tennant Creek to Alice Springs

After the Devil's Marbles there are only

a few places of interest to pause at on the trip south to the Alice. Near Barrow Creek the Stuart Memorial commemorates John Stuart who, in 1862 made the first south-north crossing of the continent, after several attempts. Visible to the east of the highway is Central Mt Stuart, the geographical centre of Australia. At Barrrow Creek itself there is an old post office telegraph repeater station. It was attacked by Aboriginals in 1874 and the station master and linesman were killed — their graves are by the road. A great number of innocent Aboriginals died in the inevitable reprisals.

The road continues through Tea Tree and finally Aileron, the last stop before the Alice. Although roadhouses and petrol are fairly plentiful (if expensive) along the track, it is wise to fill up regularly, particularly if you have a limited range — like on a motorcycle.

ALICE SPRINGS (population 15,000)
The Alice, as it's usually known, was originally founded as a staging point for the overland telegraph line in the 1870s. The station was built near a permanent waterhole in the bed of the dry Todd River. The river was named after Charles Todd, Superintendent of Telegraphs back in Adelaide, and a spring near the waterhole was named after Alice, his wife.

A town, named Stuart, was first established in 1888, a few km south of the telegraph station, as a railhead for the railway line but then the line didn't get built and the town developed very slowly. Not until 1933 did the town come to be known as Alice Springs. The telegraph line through the centre was built to connect with the undersea line from Darwin to Java, which for the first time put Australia in direct contact with Europe. It was a monumental task laying that line but it was achieved in remarkably short time.

Today Alice Springs is a pleasant, modern town with good shops and restaurants. It acts mainly as a centre for the area and a jumping off point for the many tourist attractions of central Australia. There is also the major US Pine Gap communications base near town and the American influence is very clear.

Alice Springs' growth to its present size has been recent and rapid. When the name was officially changed in 1933 the population had only just reached 200! Even in the 1950s Alice Springs was still a tiny town with a population in the hundreds. Until WW II there was no sealed road leading to Alice Springs and only in the last 10 years has the road south of Alice Springs to Adelaide started to be sealed — there is still a lot of dirt road in that direction.

Information
The Northern Territory Government Tourist Bureau office is at 51 Todd St in the Alice. It's open 8.45 am to 5 pm Monday to Friday and 9 am to 12 noon on Saturday. Just a couple of doors away there's a Yulara information centre, dispensing information about the new tourist village to be built near Ayers Rock. *This Month in Alice* is a useful monthly information booklet produced on the Alice Springs area. Alice Springs has a daily paper *(The Alice Springs Star)* and a weekly *(The Centralian Advocate)*. Marron's Newsagency on Todd St claims to have the best selection of inter-state newspapers at any country newsagent in Australia. The Connoisseur Book Shop in Todd Plaza (opposite the Flynn Church) and

the Arunta Art Gallery at Todd St also have good selections of books.

Summer days can get very hot in the centre but winter nights can be surprisingly cold. Be prepared for that sudden temperature drop with nightfall. Despite Alice Spring's dry climate and low annual rainfall the occasional rains can be quite heavy.

Alice Events

Alice Springs has a string of colourful activities, particularly during the cool tourist months from May through August. The Bangtail Muster takes place in May — it celebrates the old practice of cutting horses tails when they were rounded up and mustered before being shipped out. Today the Bangtail Muster is a colourful parade with floats satirising and making fun of local personalities and events. Also in May there's the Camel Cup, a whole series of races for camels. You'll be surprised at just how many camels they can round up in the centre. All through the cooler months there are a string of country horse races at Alice Springs and surrounding out-stations like Finke, Barrow Creek, Aileron or the Harts Range. They're colourful events and for the out-stations it's the big turn-out of the year.

In August there's the Alice Springs rodeo when for one week the whole town seems to be full of cowboys, swaggering around in their stetson hats, Willie Nelson shirts, Levi jeans, and high heel boots. And all of them bow-legged. Finally in late August there's the event which probably draws the biggest crowds of all — the Henley-on-Todd Regatta. Having a series of boat races in the Todd River is complicated slightly by the fact that there is hardly ever any water in the Todd River. It's as dry and sandy as a desert. Nevertheless a whole series of races are held for sailing boats, doubles, racing eights and every boat race class you could think of. The boats are all bottomless, the crew's legs stick out the bottom and they simply run down the course!

Orientation

The centre of Alice Springs is a conveniently compact area just five streets wide, bounded by the dry Todd River on one side and the railway line on the other. Anzac Hill forms a northern boundary to the central area while Stuart Terrace is the southern end. Most of the places to stay and virtually all of the places to eat are in this central rectangle. Todd St is the main shopping street of the town.

Telegraph Station

Laying the telegraph line across the dry, harsh centre of Australia was no easy task, as the small museum at the old Telegraph Station, two km north of the town, shows. Here too is the original spring after which the town was named. The spring made a good swimming hole in those days and it still does today. It's easy to walk to the station from Alice, just follow the path on the western (left hand) side of the riverbed. Beside the barbecue place you reach after about 20 minutes, there's a path that branches off the vehicle track. Follow that for a more circuitous route to the station. If you can't find it on the way in then pick it up on the way back, following the path around the emu and kangaroo enclosures. You can also walk to the station from Burke St in the east side of town, or you can drive there. There's another pleasant circular walk from the station out by the old cemetery and Trig Hill.

In the May to September tourist season rangers give half-hour tours of the station at 11 am and 3 pm daily. The station, one of 12 built along the telegraph line in the 1870s, was built of local stone in 1871-72. The station continued in operation until 1932. The NT Conservation Commission has an interesting pamphlet on the station reserve.

Around Town

At the north end of Todd St you can make the short sharp ascent to the top of Anzac Hill (or you can drive there). From the top you have a fine view over modern Alice Springs and down to the MacDonnell Range that forms a southern boundary to the town. There are a number of other hills in and around Alice Springs which you can climb but Anzac Hill is certainly the best known and most convenient. Right at the end of the Todd St the picturesque signpost indicating how far Alice Springs is from almost anywhere makes a popular photographic subject.

The National Trust produces a useful walking tour guide to the town's historic buildings, all of them concentrated in the compact central area. Before you stroll down Todd St Mall note the footbridge over the Todd River from Wills Terrace. The road here crosses by causeway but until the bridge was built the Todd's infrequent flow could cut one side of the town off from the other. Todd St is the main shopping street of the town and the one way section has wide pavements to encourage relaxed strolling. Along the street you can see Adelaide House, built in the early 1920s it's one of Alice Spring's earlier buildings. Originally it was the town's first hospital and now it is preserved as a museum. Across the road is Marron's Newsagency, one of the oldest shops in town it's a fine verandahed building. Flynn, the founding flying doctor, has a John Flynn Memorial Church on Todd St. In the back of the church there is a small museum of items relating to the setting up of the flying doctor service.

There are a number of interesting old buildings along Hartley St including the old stone jail built in 1907-08. There's also the court house which was in use until 1980 and the Hartley St school. The Residency, on the corner of Parsons and Hartley Sts, now houses a museum. There's another museum, the

Old Timers Museum, at the old folks home south on the Stuart Highway. It concentrates on the pioneering days in the centre and is open daily from 2 to 4 pm.

Flying Doctor & School of the Air

You can visit both these cornerstones of Australian outback life. The Royal Flying Doctor Base is close to the town centre on Stuart Terrace. It's open 9 to 11.30 am, 2 to 3.30 pm Monday to Friday and 9 to 11 am on Saturday. The half-hour tour costs $1. The School of the Air, which broadcasts school lessons to children on remote outback stations, is on Head St. It's open 1.30 to 3.30 pm Monday to Friday.

Aviation Museum

Alice Springs has an interesting little Aviation Museum housed in the former Connellan hangar on Memorial Avenue, where the town's airport used to be in the early days. The museum includes a couple of poignant exhibits which pinpoint the dangers of outback aviation. In 1929 pioneer aviator Charles Kingsford-Smith went missing in the north-west in his aircraft 'Southern Cross'. Two other aviators, Anderson and Hitchcock set off to search for Kingsford-Smith in their tiny aircraft 'Kookaburra'. North of Alice Springs they struck engine trouble and made an emergency landing. Despite their complete lack of tools they managed to fix the fault but repeated attempts to take-off all failed due to the sandy, rocky soil. They had foolishly left Alice Springs not only without tools but also with minimal water and food. By the time an aerial search had been organised and their plane had been located both had died of thirst. Kingsford-Smith turned up, completely unharmed, a few days later.

Their bodies were recovered but the aircraft, intact and completely undamaged, was left there until, in 1961, it was rediscovered, completely accidentally, by a mining surveyor. In the '70s it was decided to collect the remains and exhibit them but they proved strangely elusive and finding them again was to take several years. They were finally located in 1978 by Sydney electronics whizz Dick Smith. Fifty years of exposure and bushfires had reduced the aircraft to a crumbled wreck but it's an interesting display only a few steps from where the aircraft took off on its ill-fated mission. A short film tells the sad story of this misadventure.

Nor is such a tragedy a long forgotten incident for the museum also displays a Wackett which went missing in 1961 on a flight from Ceduna in South Australia. The pilot strayed no less than $42°$ off course, put down when he ran out of fuel and an enormous search failed to find him since he was so far from his expected route. The aircraft was discovered, again completely by accident, in 1965. The museum is not all tragedy — there are also exhibits of pioneer aviation in the territory and, of course, the famous flying doctor service. The museum is open Monday to Saturday from 9 pm to 10 am and 2.30 pm to 4.30 pm but closed in the mornings from November to March. Admission is $1.50.

Other Attractions

Panorama Guth, at 65 Hartley St in the centre, is a huge circular panorama which you view from an elevated central observation point. It depicts almost all of the points of interest around the centre with uncanny reality. Painted by a Dutch artist, Henk Guth, it measures about 20 metres in diameter and admission is $1 — whether you think it's worth paying money to see a reproduction of what you may also see for real is a different question! On the outskirts of town on Larapinta Drive the Diarama is a recently constructed 'tourist attraction'. It's open from 10 am to 5 pm daily and admission to this rather hokey collection of three-dimensional illustrations of various Aboriginal legends is $1.50. Children love it and there is an excellent art collection in the foyer — the prize winners in the annual Alice Springs art contest. Eventually they will be housed in an Alice Springs art gallery.

Just beyond the Aviation Museum there's a cemetery with a number of interesting graves including those of Albert Namatjira, the renowned Aboriginal artist, and of Harold Lasseter who perished while searching for the fabled gold of 'Lasseter's Reef'. Alice Springs also has some pioneer graves in the small Stuart Memorial Cemetery on George Crescent, just across the railway lines.

Pitchi Ritchi

Just south of the Heavitree Gap causeway is Pitchi Ritchi ('gap in the range'), a flower and bird sanctuary and sculptures by Victorian artist William Ricketts — you can see more of his interesting work in the William Ricketts' Sanctuary in the Dandenongs near Melbourne. The pleasant sanctuary is open 9 am to 5 pm daily and the admission cost is $1.

Date Garden & Camel Farm

On the Old South Rd, just beyond the Heavitree Gap, is Australia's only date garden. It's open daily from 10 am to 5 pm and there are tours on the hour. The Camel Farm is on Emily Gap Rd and is open 8 am to 5.30 pm daily. Here's your chance to ride a camel. It was these strange 'ships of the desert' and their Afghani masters which really opened up central Australia. There's also a museum here on camels and on early radio communications in the outback. Admission is $2.

Antique Motor Museum

Just south of Heavitree Gap the motor

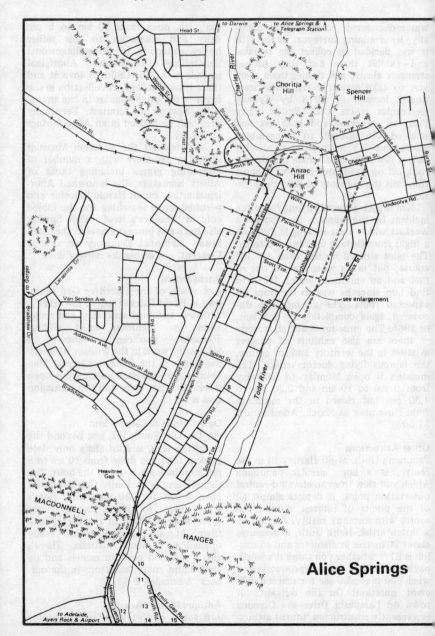

Alice Springs

1 Diaorama	9 Casino
2 Aviation Museum	10 Heavitree Gap Caravan Park
3 Lasseter's & Namatjira's Graves	11 Pitchi Ritchi
4 Stuart Memorial Cemetery	12 Old Timers' Museum
5 Aruna Guest House	13 Auto Museum
6 Left Bank Guest House	14 El Mimi Date Farm
7 Desert Sands Motel & Campsite	15 Camel Farm
8 Toddy's Cabins	

museum has a number of old cars and some interesting exhibits on pioneer motoring in the Northern Territory. They include the tale of the first car to cross the Northern Territory, way back in 1907. The museum is open 9 am to 5 pm daily and admission is $1.

Chateau Hornsby

Alice Springs actually has a winery, it's 11 km out of Alice Springs, five km off the road before you get to the airport turn-off. The wine they produce here (moselle, riesling-semillon and shiraz) is actually not at all bad although most of it gets sold to people intrigued at the novelty of a central Australian wine. Last year 12,000 bottles were produced. There's also a pleasant restaurant here and it makes a nice lunchtime excursion from town — it's open for a lunchtime barbecue Thursday to Monday (steaks $7.50, desserts $2) and for dinner on Friday and Saturday. You can pedal out to Chateau Hornsby by bicycle, after a little free wine tasting the distance back seems much shorter.

Places to Stay

Hostels & Guest Houses Alice Springs has a pretty similar story to Darwin in this category. There's a youth hostel, a privately run ex-government hostel, a YWCA and several other similar places. The *Alice Springs Youth Hostel* (tel 52 5016) is right in the centre at the corner of Todd St and Stott Terrace. Nightly costs are $4 but there is only room for 28 so it tends to fill up pretty rapidly. Fortunately there are a few overflow

places like the popular Left Bank Guest House.

Although it's across the Todd River the *Left Bank Guest House* (tel 52 4859) is no distance from the centre. Cross the river on the Todd Bridge from Stott Terrace and it's the second place you come to at 6 Kharlic St. They've got dorm beds at $5 a night plus rooms at $9 single, $18 double or $12 per person in self-contained flats. It's a simple, straightforward, friendly sort of a place. The rooms are all air-con and there's cooking and laundry facilities. Another hostel overflow place is the *Arura Lodge* at 4 Mueller St ($6 dorm or rooms at $12/18 for singles/doubles) and the *Pine Lodge* at 73 Railway Terrace ($4.50 dorm).

On the corner of Todd and Stott (right across the road from the youth hostel) the big *Melanka Lodge* (tel 52 2233) is an ex-government hostel with 200-plus rooms, all air-con and with fridges and tea/coffee making facilities. None of them have private facilities and recently prices have zoomed at this establishment so it's no longer particularly good value although it is central and convenient and has a swimming pool. Bed & breakfast costs $25/35 for singles/doubles, it is a pretty filling breakfast and other meals are available.

Just round the corner from the Melanka Lodge is the *YWCA Stuart Lodge* (tel 52 1894) on Stuart Terrace. Again the rooms are air-con, there's tea and coffee making facilities, a laundry and TV lounge. The YWCA takes men or women and costs $15/22 room only.

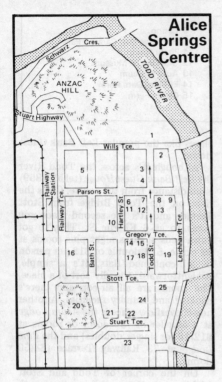

Alice Springs Centre

1 Signpost
2 Old Riverside Hotel
3 Papa Luigi's
4 Stuart Arms
5 Anglican Lodge
6 The Residency
7 Ansett
8 TAA & Greyhound
9 Pioneer Theatre (open air cinema)
10 Mia Pizza, Chopsticks & The Italian Restaurant
11 Post Office
12 Adelaide House
13 NTGTB
14 Telford Alice Motel
15 La Casalinga
16 Pines Homestead
17 Panorama Guth
18 Centre for Aboriginal Artists & Craftsmen
19 Library & Civic Centre
20 Billy Goat Hill
21 Salvation Army Hostel
22 YWCA
23 Royal Flying Doctor Base
24 Melanka Guest House
25 Youth Hostel

It also has a number of fairly straight-forward and simple rooms at $16/24 room only. The restaurant here is said to be pretty good but is also rather expensive.

There's an associate youth hostel at Hamilton Downs, it costs $4 plus $4 for transport out there.

Breakfast is available for $3.50 to $4.50. A couple of doors down Stuart Terrace is the *Salvation Army Red Shield Hostel* (tel 52 1960) on the corner with Hartley St. It's more for long term occupants though.

The *Anglican Lodge* (tel 52 3108) on Bath St, however, is excellent value at $15/22 or $26 for a double with its own facilities. Weekly rates are especially good value since they're only about 3½ times the daily rate. The rooms have all the usual facilities but there is also a communal kitchen so you can fix your own food. *Pines Homestead Lodge* (tel 52 1104) at 73 Railway Terrace is mentioned above as a hostel overflow centre.

Hotels & Motels Down Gap Rd, not too far south of the town centre, *Toddy's Cabins* (tel 52 1322) are at number 41. They have a wide variety of rooms starting with standard rooms with shared facilities at $15 single, $20 double, $30 triple or family. With attached facilities the equivalent prices are $22, $30 to $32 and $36. They also have fully self-contained holiday flats and family units at $25 single, $35 to $40 double and $40 to $45 for triples. The complex also has laundry facilities and a communal kitchen for those not in the self-contained units. Plus there's a swimming pool, barbecue and a small shop on the site. All in all it's quite a convenient and reasonably-priced place.

At 17 Gap Rd, not quite so far from the centre as Toddy's, are the *White Gum Holiday Units* (tel 52 5144). They're not really for one-night stands since there's a minimum booking of three nights but the rooms are fully equipped, air-conditioned, have kitchens with cooking facilities, utensils and a fridge, plus there's a swimming pool. The rooms will sleep four and cost $40 a night.

Amongst the cheaper motels is the *Elkira Court Motel* (tel 52 1222) at 134 Bath St in the centre. Singles/doubles cost $33/35 or $37/39 for the more expensive de-luxe units. Motels in Alice Springs are not cheap. The *Oasis Motel* (tel 52 1444) at 10 Gap Rd is $33/40 or $38/46. They're both comfortable, fully-equipped motels. Just across the Todd River on Khalic St the *Desert Sands Motel* (tel 52 6788) has good motel units at $32/43. The *Stuart Arms Hotel* (tel 52 1811) is on Todd St and costs $29/42.

Camping Alice Springs camping sites and their distance from the town centre are:

Carmichael Tourist Park (tel 52 1200), 3 km west on Larapinta Drive, camping $2.50 per person, cabins $20, on-site vans $18.
Emily Gap Camel Farm (tel 52 4498), 4 km south on Emily Gap Rd, camping $2.50 for one, $5.50 for two, on-site vans $16 single, $20 double.
Greenleaves Tourist Park (tel 52 4603), 2 km east on Burke St, camping $2.50 per person, on-site vans $22 single or double.
Stuart Caravan Park (tel 52 2547), 2 km west on Larapinta Drive, camping $4 for two people, on-site vans $20.
Wintersun Caravan Park (tel 52 4080),

2 km north on the Stuart Highway, camping $2.50 per person, on-site vans $20.
Desert Sands (tel 52 6788), just across the Todd River on Khalic St, camping $2.50 per person.

Places to Eat
Snacks & Fast Food For a sandwich, a burger or a hot dog *Grandads*, in the arcade across from the supermarket on Todd St, is good value. You can sit outside and they also have a good selection of gelati ice cream flavours. Back down at 80 Todd St the *Eranova Caffetteria* (yes, that is how it's spelt) does pizzas for $4 to 5, snacks, meals, even Greek take-aways. It's quite a popular and pleasant place. If you just want a good sandwich try *Dawn's Deli* over on Railway Terrace.

Pub Meals On Todd St the *Stuart Arms* does reasonably priced counter style meals at lunchtime. Steaks and the like are in the $4 to 5 range. On Gregory Terrace at the corner with Hartley St is the *Telford Hotel* where the *Ghost Gum Bistro* does fairly standard counter food in cafeteria style. Meals are in the $5 to 6 bracket, they're filling and really pretty good. There's also a more expensive restaurant here.

Restaurants Down at the Anzac Hill end of Todd St is *Papa Luigi's Bistro* with a variety of meals — schnitzels, chicken, steaks and so on — all at $5.50. Plus other meals like pastas and a fairly comprehensive selection of gelati ice creams. This is a popular place to eat at lunchtime or in the evenings. Round behind it is *Il Sorrentino*, a rather more expensive Italian eatery.

There seems to be quite an Italian influence in Alice Springs and one of the best is *La Casalinga* at 105 Gregory Terrace, just off Todd St. It's a three part restaurant — first a take-away section, then a quite pleasant restaurant section where you can order from the take-away part at the same prices, finally there's a tablecloths and candles section right at the back. In front pizzas cost from $3 to 4 small up to $8 to 9 large. Main courses are $5.50 to 7, pastas $3 to 4. They make a damn good pizza too. The proper restaurant section is a bit pricier — a couple of dollars more for pizzas or main courses. There's also a bar but it's a bit expensive — beers $1.40, house wine $5.50 a litre.

Over on Hartley St you'll find several places in the Ermund Arcade — like the Mia Pizza Bar, the 'pizza palace in the Alice'. Small pizzas cost $3.60, spaghettis, lasagnas and other pastas are available, meals cost from $5 and up. Next door is the Italian Restaurant with pastas at $5 to 7, ($3 to 4 as entrees) and main courses at $6 to 9.

Alice Springs is better for Italian food than Chinese but the Ermund Arcade also has Chopsticks if sweet & sour it has to be. Other places include the Overlanders Steakhouse at 72 Hartley St which specialises in steaks and Mexican food. Prices are in the $6 to 8 bracket for main courses. Bojangles at 76 Todd St costs $6 to 8 for main courses too and a 'dress code' applies. Finally the Old Riverside Hotel has the Other Place on Leichardt Terrace, slightly higher prices than the other counterstyle hotel places.

Entertainment
The Stuart Arms Hotel and the Old Riverside Hotel are both good places for drink. There's often entertainment in

these two places, the Old Riverside has the popular Hitching Rail Bar and also a disco (Sylvester's). Or try the pleasant upstairs bar in the Telford Alice Hotel where you can stand out on the verandah and look out over the town.

On Parsons St between Todd St and the river the old Pioneer Open Air Theatre shows films each Saturday night for $3.50. They show the feature which will be appearing at the drive-in for the coming week. Open air theatres (you could almost call them walk-ins as opposed to drive-ins) were once common in rural Australia but are now a dying relic, definitely worth a visit for the experience. Alice Springs has a casino if you want to watch the Australian gambling enthusiasm in an unusual setting.

Getting There
Air You can fly to Alice Springs with TAA or Ansett from a variety of places. Ansett (tel 52 4455) and TAA (tel 50 5222) face each other across Todd St on corners of Parson St.

See the Northern Territory introductory Getting Around section for details of air fares within the territory. To or from Alice Springs Adelaide is the usual jumping off point and the fare is $184 (standby $138), Perth is $238 direct ($179 standby) but more expensive via Adelaide or Darwin, Mt Isa $121 ($90), Sydney $241 ($181).

Train The ghan between Adelaide and Alice Springs costs $70 in coach class (no sleeper and no meals) or $117 in

Northern Territory

A	
B	C

a. The Henley on Todd Regatta in Alice Springs gets over the small problem that the Todd River rarely ever has any water by using boats that have no bottoms.

b. Close to the 'track' which connects Alice Springs with Darwin is the magnificent Katherine Gorge.

c. In the 'top end' magnetic termite mounds are taller than a Land-Rover, and all aligned north-south.

economy, $162 in first, both including meals and a sleeper. There are departures from Adelaide on Thursday and Sunday morning at 10.40 am, arriving in Alice Springs the next morning at 10.30 am. From Alice Springs the departures are on Friday and Monday at 3.30 pm arriving the next afternoon at 5.35 pm. Cars can also be transported between Port Augusta in South Australia and Alice Springs for $210 for a car up to 5.5 metres long, $315 for larger cars.

Buses Ansett Pioneer and Greyhound both have bus services to Alice Springs on all three routes — Mt Isa to Three Ways and down the track, straight down from Darwin or straight up from Adelaide. In the Northern Territory Greyhound generally have the more frequent services. In Alice Springs Ansett Pioneer (tel 52 2422) operate from the Ansett office on Todd St. Greyhound (tel 52 1700) can be found at the CATA/TAA office also on Todd St.

Fares to or from Alice Springs are Adelaide $84, 24 hours; Mt Isa $54, 17 hours, Darwin $100, 21 hours. From Adelaide Briscoes (tel 268 9444) at 8 Taminga St, Regency Park also have a bus service between Adelaide and Alice Springs. They operate three times weekly and the fare is the same as Ansett Pioneer and Greyhound.

Driving & Hitching The basic thing to remember about getting to Alice Springs is that it's a very long way from anywhere. From Adelaide it's 1983 km and about half of those km is over unsealed road which can easily be cut by rain. Fortunately the road is now sealed from the South Australia-Northern Territory border all the way to Alice Springs but it's still a long, long stretch of dirt to be covered before you get to that point. Coming in from Queensland it's 1180 km from Mt Isa to Alice Springs or 537 km from Three Ways, where the Mt Isa road meets the Darwin-Alice Springs road, 'the track'. Darwin-Alice Springs is 1525 km. Fortunately the road from Mt Isa and from Darwin are both sealed all the way, they're just a very long way.

These are outback roads but you're not in the real outer-outback where a breakdown can mean big trouble. Nevertheless it's wise to have your vehicle well prepared since getting someone to come out to fix it should it break down is likely to be very expensive. Similarly you're not going to die of thirst waiting for a vehicle to come by should you break down but it's still wise to carry water with you — waiting for help can get thirsty. Petrol is also readily available from stops along the road but the price tends to be high and variable. Some fuel stops are notorious for charging well over the odds so carrying an extra can of fuel with you can easily save you a few dollars by allowing you to bypass these places. Even the sealed road can sometimes be cut by a short sharp rainfall and in that case the only thing is to sit and wait for the water to recede. Usually it's not long on the sealed road but waiting for the dirt roads to dry out can be rather longer.

Northern Territory

a. Lesser known than Ayers Rock, the nearby Olgas are equally spectacular.
b. Ayers Rock is renowned for its enormous size, its immense isolation and its deep red colour.
c. Near Alice Springs, Palm Valley is a strange lost valley of primaeval palm trees in the dry centre of Australia.

Hitching to Alice is not the easiest trip in Australia. Traffic is light and getting up the road from South Australia is likely to be very difficult. Coming the other way Three Ways is a notorious bottleneck for hitchers. You can spend a long time there. The noticeboard in the Alice Springs youth hostel is a good place to look for lifts.

The Ghan

Plenty of countries seem to have their great railway adventures and Australia's would have to be the 'ghan'. The ghan went through a major change in 1980 and although it's now a rather more modern and comfortable (dare I say 'safe') adventure it's still a great trip.

The ghan saga started in 1877 when it was decided to build a railway line from Adelaide to Darwin. It eventually took over 50 years to reach Alice Springs and they're still thinking about the final 1500 km to Darwin, over a century later. The basic problem was that they made a big mistake right at the start, a mistake that wasn't finally sorted out until 1980. They built the line in the wrong place.

The grand error was a result of concluding that just because all those creek beds from Marree north were bone dry, and because nobody had seen rain,

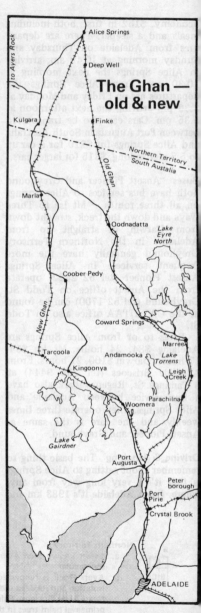

The Ghan —
old & new

THE GHAN

there wasn't going to be rain in the future. In actual fact they laid the initial stretch of line right across a flood plain and when the rain came, even though it soon dried up, the line was simply washed away. In the century or so that the original ghan line survived the tracks were washed away as a regular occurrence.

The wrong route was only part of the ghan's problems. At first it was built wide gauge to Marree then extended narrow gauge to Oodnadatta in 1884. And what a jerry built line it was — the foundations were flimsy, the sleepers were too light, the grading was too steep and it meandered hopelessly. It was hardly surprising that right up to the end the top speed of the old ghan was a flat out 30 km per hour! Early rail travellers went from Adelaide to Marree on the broad gauge line, changed there to narrow gauge as far as Oodnadatta and then had to make the final journey to Alice Springs by camel train. The Afghan led camel trains had pioneered transport through the outback and it was from these Afghans that the 'ghan' took its name.

Finally in 1929 the line was extended from Oodnadatta to Alice Springs but great adventure though the ghan might have been it simply didn't work. At the best of times it was chronically slow and uncomfortable as it bounced and bucked its way down the badly laid line. Worse it was unreliable and expensive to run. Worst of all a heavy rainfall could strand it at either end or even in the middle. Parachute drops of supplies to stranded train travellers became part of outback lore and on one occasion the ghan rolled in 10 days late!

In the early '70s the South Australian state railway system was taken over by the commonwealth government and a new line to Alice Springs was projected. The A$145 million line was to be laid from Tarcoola, west of Port Augusta on the trans-continental line, to Alice Springs — it was to be standard gauge and it would be laid where rain would not wash it out. In 1980 the line was completed in circumstances that would be unusual for any such major project today, let alone an Australian one — ahead of time and on the cost budget. In late '80 the old ghan made its last run and the old line has subsequently been torn up. Whereas the old train took 140 passengers and, under ideal conditions, made the trip in 50 hours the new train takes twice as many passengers and does it in 24 hours. It's still the ghan but it's not the trip it once was.

At present extension of the line further north from Alice Springs to Darwin is still under consideration. There's really no way the line would make economic sense but its value as a 'connection' between the top end and the rest of the country plus the smooth construction of the ghan line has kept the plan as a firm possibility.

Getting Around

There is no public transport around Alice Springs apart from taxis. Fortunately the town centre is quite compact enough to get around on foot but if you want to go further afield you'll either have to take a tour, rent a car or closer in attractions could be tackled by bicycle.

Car Hertz, Budget and Avis all have counters at Alice Springs airport. Alice Springs is classified as a remote area so car hire can be a bit pricey. Moke rental, however, is not too bad. Typical charges are $14 a day, $5 for insurance plus 14c a km for a Moke from Moke Rentals (tel 52 1405) on Parsons St, opposite Ansett. The big rental firms also hire Mokes here and their charges are usually inclusive of 100 or more km — get your calculators out and you may find they are equally good value. If you're hiring a Moke in the Alice check about distance restrictions. Some companies specify that you cannot take them more than 50 km from town. This is OK for the closer places but there are plenty of attractions around Alice Springs which are quite accessible by any reasonable vehicle but which are more than 50 km out. Between a group of people a Moke is a fine way of exploring around the town.

Bicycles Alice Springs also has a number of bicycle tracks and, particularly in the winter, a bike is a great way of getting around town and out to the closer attractions. While researching this edition I biked it as far out as Chateau Hornsby quite easily. Thrifty Bike Hire at the Thrifty car rental office on Todd St hires good bikes out for $6 a day ($10 a 24-hour day) and they're open every day of the week. Or bikes are available for the same price from the Tip Top Jean Shop on Gregory Terrace by La Casalinga. They're only open weekdays and Saturday mornings but at other times on the weekend you can hire their bikes from the Heavitree Gap Caravan Park.

Airport Alice Springs airport is some distance south of the town, about $12 by taxi. The bus fare was $3.40 and since this was a well used bus service it's possible that Ansett and TAA may keep their service. Or that a private one may replace it. The airport is quite a busy one and the terminal is fairly small so when, as often happens, several aircraft arrive at once, it can get extremely crowded and chaotic. In town the Ansett and TAA terminals face each other across Todd St at the corners of Parsons St. Phone numbers are TAA 50 5222 and Ansett 52 4455. Airlines of Northern Australia are with Ansett.

Tours The NTGTB can tell you about all sorts of organised tours from Alice Springs. Typical prices and times are town tour (3 hours, $20), Heavitree range (3 hours, $20), Standley Chasm (6 hours, $25), Namatjira tour (9 hours, $42), Palm Valley (12 hours, $48), Ross River (2 days, $112). As you can see tours from Alice Springs are not cheap. The YMCA organise a regular walking

tour for $25. You're bussed to Standley Chasm from where you walk to Hamilton Downs where you overnight in the youth hostel. Leaving Alice Springs at 7 am in the morning you arrive back at 5 pm the next day. Check at the youth hostel for details. For around $110 to $120 you can go along on the Chartair outback mail runs and visit a string of outback stations to collect and deliver the mails. Phone 52 2421 or 52 2544 for details.

Things to Buy

Alice Springs has a number of art galleries and craft centres. If you've got an interest in central Australian art or you're looking for a piece to buy then visit the Centre for Aboriginal Artists & Craftsmen at 86-88 Todd St. They have a fine display of bark paintings, 'sand' paintings, carvings, weapons, didgeridoos and much else plus excellent descriptions of their development and meaning. It's non-profit making and designed both to preserve the crafts and to provide an outlet for quality work. The prices aren't necessarily cheap but the artefacts are generally good. Out at the Diorama centre on Larapinta Drive the Outcrop Gallery also has quite a good collection of Aboriginal crafts.

Aboriginals

You could easily spend a long time in the southern states of Australia and never see an Aboriginal. But up in the north and particularly in the Northern Territory they're much more visible. The territory has a substantial Aboriginal population and in Darwin or Alice Springs you'll see many Aboriginals. Much of the Northern Territory is reserved for Aboriginals and you cannot visit these often remote areas without special permission. There are a number of reasons for this exclusion but the unhappy result of the collision between our civilisation and theirs is certainly one of them. The great tribes of the centre — the Arunta, the Pintjantjarra or the Gurindji — certainly still exist but the people camping in the sandy bed of the Todd River in the centre of Alice Springs are a sad reminder of their former days of wandering the open land. Australia's modern record of dealing with the country's original inhabitants may not be perfect (although it's a thousand times better than that of the early colonialists) but a great deal of time, effort and money has been expended on trying to do the right thing — without a great deal of success. Integrating the Aboriginals into our still very alien way of life and finding a replacement for their way of life, which we have almost totally destroyed, is going to be a serious and long term problem.

AROUND ALICE SPRINGS

Outside of the town itself there are a great number of places within day-trip distance or with overnight stops thrown in if you have the time and inclination. Generally they're found by heading east or west along the MacDonnell Range which runs east-west directly south of Alice Springs. Places to the south of town are usually visited on the way to Ayers Rock. The scenery along the ranges is quite superb. There are many gorges that cut through the rocky cliffs and their sheer rock walls are often extremely spectacular. In the shaded gorges there are often rocky waterholes and much wildlife if you're quiet and observant. The gorges are often alive with wildflowers in the spring. You can get out to these gorges on group tours or with your own wheels — some of the closer gorges are even accessible by bicycle or on foot. A major advantage of having your own transport around the centre is the immense solitude and quietness you'll experience at many of these places. By yourself the centre's eerie emptiness and peacefulness can get through to you in a way that is completely impossible in a big group.

EASTBOUND

The Ross River road is only sealed for the first 39 km but it continues in pretty good condition most of the way to Arltunga, about 100 km from Alice Springs. From here the road loops back west and rejoins the Stuart Highway 50 km north of Alice Springs but it's a much rougher road and sometimes may require four-wheel drive.

Emily & Jessie Cap

Heading south from Alice Springs you're only just through the Heavitree Gap when the sign points to the road east by the Heavitree Gap campsite. Emily Gap, 16 km out of town, is the next gap through the ranges — it's narrow and often has water running through it. Jessie Gap is only eight km further on, like the previous gap it's a popular picnic and barbecue spot. On one visit to the Alice I was sitting there, having a lunchtime sandwich, when a huge flock of birds swished smoothly through the gap, tightening their formation as they passed by. I heard them coming long before they appeared in sight.

Corroboree Rock

Shortly after Jessie Gap the surfaced road ends at the Undoolya Gap, but it's still quite acceptable for a regular car or a Moke. Undoolya Gap is another pass through the range and here a road runs through. Corroboree Rock is 43 km out, there are many strangely-shaped outcrops of rocks in the range and this one is said to have been used by Aboriginals for their corroborees.

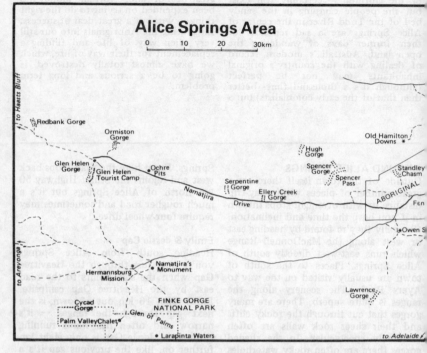

Alice Springs Area

0   10   20   30km

to Haasts Bluff

Redbank Gorge

Ormiston Gorge

Old Hamilton Downs

Glen Helen Gorge
Glen Helen Tourist Camp
Ochre Pits

Hugh Gorge
Spencer Gorge
Spencer Pass

Standley Chasm

to Areyonga

Serpentine Gorge
Ellery Creek Gorge

ABORIGINAL

Fen

Namatjira Drive

Owen S

Hermannsburg Mission
Namatjira's Monument

Lawrence Gorge

Cycad Gorge
Palm Valley Chalet
Glen of Palms

FINKE GORGE NATIONAL PARK

Larapinta Waters

to Adelaide

Trephina Gorge

About 75 km out, and a few km north of the road, is Trephina Gorge. It's wider and longer than the other gaps in the range — here you are pretty well north of the main MacDonnell Range and in a new ridge. A few km west of the gorge, reached by a track which can sometimes be unsuitable for conventional vehicles, are the delightful John Hayes Rockholes. A sheltered section of a deep gorge provides a series of waterholes which retain their water long after it has dried up in more exposed locations. You can clamber around the rockholes or follow the path to one side up to a lookout above the gorge — perhaps you'll see why it is also called the Valley of the Eagles.

Ross River & N'Dhala Gorge

Beyond Trephina Gorge it's another 15 km to the Ross River Tourist Camp, much favoured by coach tours. Rooms cost $35/44 for singles/doubles. The N'Dhala Gorge is about 10 km south of the homestead and has some ancient Aboriginal rock carvings. You may also be able to see rock wallabies here. It's possible to drive through the gorge and return to Alice Springs by the Ringwood Homestead road but you may require four-wheel drive.

Arltunga

At the eastern end of the MacDonnell Ranges, 92 km north-east of Alice Springs, Arltunga is an old gold-mining ghost town. Gold was originally discovered here in 1887 and 10 years later

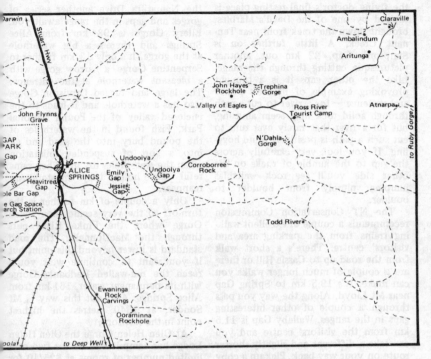

reef gold was also discovered but by 1912 the mining activity had petered out. A few old buildings, a couple of cemeteries and the many deserted mine sites are all that remains here now. Alluvial (surface) gold has been completely worked out in the Arltunga reserve but there may still be gold in the area but further afield. The Ross River Highway from Alice Springs is formed gravel until just beyond the Trephina Gorge turn-off but the rest of the way to Arltunga it is just a graded track and rain can make the road impassable. You can look right round and join the Stuart Highway 50 km north of Alice Springs but this route is just a graded track all the way and can be rough going. With sidetrips off the road a complete loop from Alice Springs to Arltunga and back

would be something over 300 km, a fair drive on outback roads.

WESTBOUND

Heading west the Larapinta Drive is sealed for about 50 km out of town. The sealed road ends where the road divides into the Larapinta Drive heading slightly south-west and the Namatjira Drive continuing more directly west. There are many spectacular gorges out in this direction and also some fine walks. To visit Palm Valley, one of the prime attractions to the west of Alice Springs, requires four-wheel drive.

Simpson's Gap

Westbound on Larapinta Drive you start on the northern side of the MacDonnell Range. You soon come to Flynn's Grave;

the flying doctor's final resting place is topped by one of the Devil's Marbles, brought down the track from near Tennant Creek. A little further on is Simpson's Gap, 22 km out, another picturesque cutting through the range. Like the other gaps it is a thought provoking example of nature's power and patience — for a river to cut a path through solid rock may seem amazing, but for a river that rarely ever runs to cut such a path is positively mind boggling. If you look very carefully across the gap to the jumble of rocks on the other side you'll see rock wallabies jumping nimbly from boulder to boulder.

The NT Conservation Commission recommends a couple of excellent walking trains from the parking area and visitors' centre. There's a short walk from the road up to Cassia Hill or there are a couple of much longer walks you can make. It's 19.5 km to Spring Gap near Mt Lloyd. Along the way you pass through a couple of other interesting gaps in the ranges. Wallaby Gap is 11.5 km from the visitors' centre and you can take a different and slightly shorter route on your way back. Pick up a copy of the 'Nature Walks' pamphlet.

Standley Chasm

Standley Chasm is 51 km out and is probably the most spectacular gap around Alice Springs. It is incredibly narrow, the near vertical walls almost seem to close together above you. Only for a brief instant each day does the noonday sun illuminate the bottom of the gorge — at which instant the Instamatics click and a smile must appear on Mr Kodak's face!

Namatjira Drive

Not far beyond Standley Chasm the surfaced road peters out and you must choose whether to carry on along the Namatjira Drive or take the more southerly Larapinta Drive. Further west along

the Namatjira Drive another series of gorges and gaps in the range await you. Ellery Gorge is 93 km from Alice Springs and there's a big waterhole at the gorge. It's only 13 km further to Serpentine Gorge, a narrow gorge with a pleasant waterhole at the entrance. The large and rugged Ormiston Gorge also has a waterhole and it leads to the enclosed valley of the Pound National Park. Fish found in the waterholes of the pound bury into the sand and go into a sort of suspended animation when the waterholes dry up. When rains refill the holes they mysteriously reappear.

Only a couple of km further is the turn-off to the very scenic Glen Helen Gorge where the Finke River cuts through the MacDonnells. The road standard is lower beyond this point but if you want to continue west you'll reach the red-walled Redbanks Gorge with its permanent water, 161 km from Alice Springs. Also out this way is Mt Sonder, at 1340 metres the highest point in the territory.

At Glen Helen Gorge the Glen Helen Lodge has campsites at $3 for two or a limited number of rooms at $25/40 for singles/doubles, bed & breakfast. From here you get a fine view of the sunrise on Mt Sonder.

Larapinta Drive

The Larapinta Drive crosses the Hugh River and then Ellery Creek before reaching the Namatjira Monument. Today the artistic skills of the central Australian Aboriginals are widely known and becoming increasingly widely appreciated. This certainly wasn't the case when Albert Namatjira started to paint his central Australian landscapes using western equipment and techniques but with a totally Aboriginal eye for the colours and scenery of the red centre. His paintings spawned a host of imitators and the 'Namatjira-style' watercolour has become almost a cliche of Australian art but you'll certainly see what he was painting in these drives out from Alice Springs. Namatjira's paintings became collectors' pieces but unhappily his new found wealth prompted a clash with Alice Spring's staid European society of the time and he died an unhappy man. Only eight km further on you reach the Hermannsburg Mission, 125 km from Alice Springs. If you wish to continue further you'll need four-wheel drive.

Palm Valley

From Hermannsburg the trail follows the Finke River south to the Finke Gorge National Park, only 12 km further on. The track crosses the sandy bed of the river a number of times and four-wheel drive is required to get through. In the park Palm Valley is a gorge filled with some geographically misplaced palm trees — a strangely tropical find in the dry, red centre.

SOUTH TO AYERS ROCK

You can make some interesting diversions off the road south to Ayers Rock. The Henbury Meteorite Craters are only a few km off the road but you've got further to go to get to Ewaninga, Chambers Pillar, Finke or Kings Canyon.

Ewaninga & Chambers Pillar

Following the 'old south road', which runs close to the old ghan railway line, it's only 35 km from Alice Springs to Ewaninga with it prehistoric Aboriginal rock carvings. The carvings found here and at N'Dhala gorge are thought to have been made by Aboriginal tribes who pre-date the current tribes of the centre. Chambers Pillar, an eerie sandstone pillar, is carved with the names and visit dates of early explorers. It's 130 km from Alice Springs and four-wheel drive is required to get there. Finke is a tiny settlement, further down the line.

Henbury Meterorite Craters

A few km off the road, 130 km south of Alice, are the Henbury Meteorite Craters, a cluster of 12 age old craters which are amongst the largest in the world. The largest of the craters is 180 metres across and 15 metres deep. From the car park by the site there's a walking trail around the craters with features signposted. There are no longer any fragments of the meteorites at the site but the Residency Museum in Alice Springs has a small chunk which weighs in at a surprisingly heavy 46.5 kilograms. The road in to the crater site is the start of the Kings Canyon Rd, a gravel road which can be rather slippery after rain.

Kings Canyon

From the meteorite craters the road continues west to Wallara Ranch Tourist Chalet and Kings Canyon, 323 km from Alice Springs. This is an alternative, and rougher, route to Ayers Rock although you have to backtrack the 89 km between Wallara and the canyon. Dubbed 'Australia's Grand Canyon' it's a spectacular canyon with natural features like the 'Lost City' with its strange building-like outcrops or the lush palms of the 'Garden of Eden'. There are fine views over the canyon from its rim but it's a steep climb to the top. The walls of the canyon soar over 200 metres high. At Wallara Ranch camping sites are $4 for two or rooms cost $27/40 for singles/doubles.

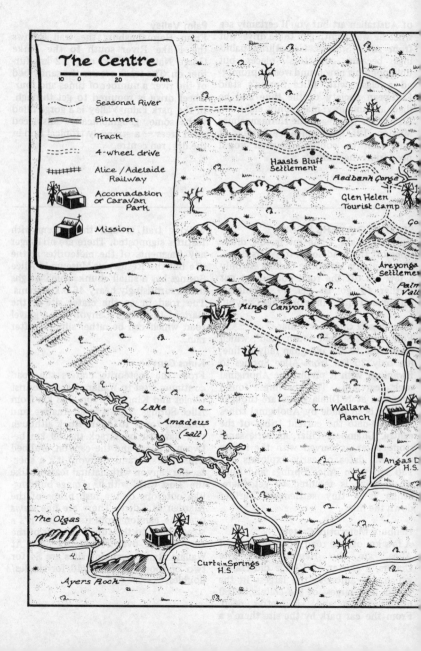

The Centre

10 0 20 40 Km.

——— Seasonal River
≈≈≈ Bitumen
——— Track
----- 4-wheel drive
+++++ Alice / Adelaide Railway
Accomadation or Caravan Park
Mission

Haasts Bluff Settlement

Redbank Gorge

Glen Helen Tourist Camp

Go

Areyonga Settlement

Palm Vall

Kings Canyon

Te

Wallara Ranch

Lake Amadeus (salt)

Angas D H.S.

The Olgas

Curtain Springs H.S.

Ayers Rock

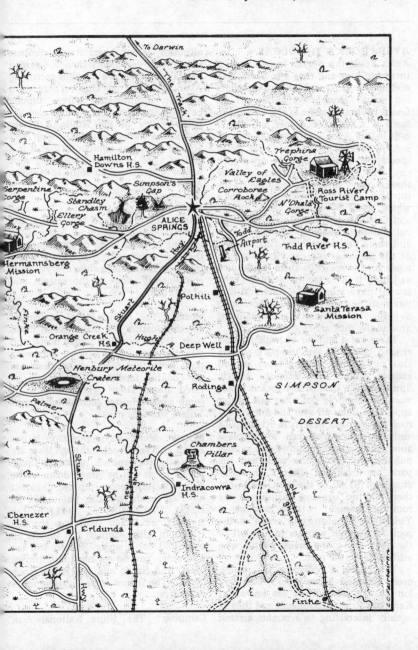

AYERS ROCK & THE OLGAS

Ayers Rock, the world's largest rock, is three km long and rises a towering 348 metres from the pancake flat surrounding scrub. Everybody knows of its famous colour changes as the setting sun turns it a series of deeper and darker reds before it fades into grey each evening. A reverse repeat, with far fewer spectators, is performed at dawn each day. The mighty rock offers far more than a heavy breathing scramble to the top and some pretty colours — it has a whole series of strange caves, gulleys and erosions; the entire area is of deep cultural significance to the Aboriginals and there are many interesting theories of the paintings and carvings they have made on the rock. To them it is known as Uluru. It is no trouble at all to spend several days around the rock and it is likely to become even more interesting as the commercial encroachments around the rock are cleaned up.

There are a number of walking trails around the rock and the park rangers also run guided walking tours around various points of interest. Maggie Springs at the base of the rock is a permanent waterhole but after rain, water appears in holes all over and around the rock in countless waterfalls. At the park visitors' centre you can see displays about the park; slide shows and various publications about the rock and the park are available. There's an entry charge of $1.50 to the park. Note that there are no banking facilities at the rock at present — there may be at Yulara. Just before you arrive at the rock Mt Connor appears to the left of the road — fooling many people who mistake it for the rock.

The Olgas, a collection of smaller, more rounded Ayers Rocks, stand 32 km to the west. They are known as Katatjuta to the Aboriginals and they're equally interesting to scramble around

although, as on Ayers Rock, climbers should take care. More than one person has taken a fatal tumble while ascending Ayers Rock or the Olgas. There are a number of interesting gorges running between the Olgas and there is also the larger Valley of the Winds. A lonely sign at the western end of the loop road around the Olgas points out that it is a hell of a lot of nothing travelling west before you reach Kalgoorlie in Western Australia.

Places to Stay

During the lifetime of this edition the accommodation picture at Ayers Rock is going to make some major changes as the new resort village of Yulara comes into operation. Meanwhile everything is conveniently close to the eastern end of the rock.

Hostel The *Inland Motel* has hostel accommodation for 50 at $5 in dorm beds. It's an associate youth hostel and you can also use the motel swimming pool and other facilities but there are no cooking facilities. Bicycles can be hired here. There will probably be some sort of hostel accommodation at Yulara when it opens.

Motels Motel accommodation is not cheap at Ayers Rock although there are currently four motels operating there. All of them will be closed down as the Yulara facilities come into use. Cheapest are *Red Sands* (booking phone 089 52 1237), *Uluru* (089 51 3411) or the *Ayers Rock Chalet* (bookings through CATA in Alice Springs) but they're all over $30 for a single, $40 to $50 for a double. You do get breakfast thrown in at Red Sands and the Ayers Rock Chalet. The *Inland Motel* is rather more expensive.

Camping The Ulura National Park

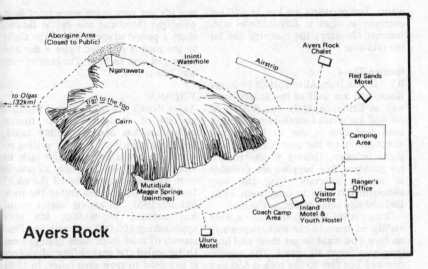

Ayers Rock

camping site has good facilities which for two people costs just $1 a night for tent campers or caravanners. If you're not hostelling then you really have to have a tent at Ayers Rock! There's a shop and fast food centre and free gas barbecues are provided. Wood is scarce at the park and if you want to build a fire you should bring firewood in with you. Remember that it can get very chilly at night in the winter months even though the days will be pleasantly

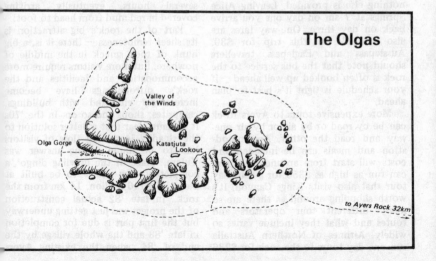

The Olgas

warm. Temperatures are low as 4°C are common at night in July while in mid-summer (January) the mercury can hit the mid-40s.

Getting There

It's 448 km from Alice Springs to Ayers Rock, 246 km west of the Stuart Highway at Erldunda. Only one section of 50 odd km is still unsealed on this entry road and that is due to be finished about the time the new Yulara village starts to open. Driving to the rock is no problem, fuel supplies are available at regular intervals along the way although it is wise to carry some extra fuel and also some water, just in case.

From Alice Springs there are a wide variety of tours to the rock, depending on how you want to get there and how long you want to spend. The regular one-way bus fare to the rock is $50 and the trip takes about 7½ hours. The cheapest way of getting there and back by bus is a regular tour which can be booked through various agents including the youth hostel. Leaving four days a week this tour costs just $55 per person round trip but it's purely transport — nothing else is provided. Leaving Alice Springs at 7 am on day one you arrive back on day three. One-way fares are also available on this trip for $30. Aussiepass and Eaglepass travellers should note that the bus service to the rock is often booked up well ahead - - if your schedule is tight it's best to plan ahead.

More expensive tours to Ayers Rock can be by road or by air or by air one-way and road the other. Accommodation and meals can be included and costs will start from around $100 and can run as high as $350 for a four day tour that also visits Kings Canyon. It's worth shopping around as there are so many different tour operators and routes and what they include varies so widely. Airlines of Northern Australia run one day tours to the rock for $236

but it's not very much more to at least overnight there and one day is far too short a period to spend there. The flight to the rock is operated twice a day and takes just over an hour. The regular one-way fare is $80.

YULARA

Ayers Rock's rise to its current position as one of Australia's major tourist attractions has been incredibly rapid. Until comparatively recently getting to Ayers Rock was often a major task. In fact from 1931 to 1946 only 22 people were known to have climbed the rock! In 1970 25,000 people visited the rock but by 1981 the annual visitor count had zoomed to 80,000. It's now approaching 100,000 and with the final stretch of road from Alice Springs soon to be sealed the annual flow of visitors is expected to grow even faster. In 1983 the last 55 km of road will be surfaced — in 1974 when I first went to the rock there was only a short stretch out of the Alice sealed and then it was dirt all the way. A sudden rainstorm had Maureen and me pushing our motorcycle in and out of mudholes on the final stretch for several hours, eventually arriving covered in red mud from head to foot!

Part of the rock's big attraction is its sheer remoteness — there it is, a big hunk of rock smack in the middle of nowhere. But more visitors require more accommodation and facilities and the rock's surroundings have become increasingly cluttered with buildings, campsites, shops and so on. In the '70s it became clear that a better solution to the steadily increasing flow of visitors had to be found — the answer was Yulara, 'place of the howling dingo', a completely new village to be built at a cost of $110 million, 14 km from the rock. In late '82 actual construction of the project was just getting underway but the first part is due for completion in late '83 and the whole village by the end of '84, when the existing Ayers

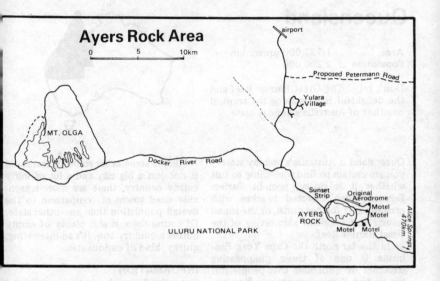

Rock facilities will all be removed.

The concept of Yulara sounds terrific. It's going to be on the edge of the Uluru National Park and will be as closely as possible integrated into the dune landscape of the desert. The low buildings are designed to use as much natural cooling as possible and borrow many design elements from desert towns of the Middle East. Eventually the town will be able to accommodate nearly 5000 people in everything from a campsite and hostel to an 'international standard' hotel. There will also be a supermarket, a visitors' centre, a swimming pool, restaurants and fast food outlets and, of course, a pub. It is intended that a bus service will run between Yulara and the rock so you shouldn't have to worry about being marooned there, at the mercy of tour buses. They also intend to hire bicycles. The first parts of the complex to be opened should be the campsite and one of the more expensive hotels. Not only will all the current motels and camping facilities at the rock be razed the existing airstrip has already gone. Yulara's airport is able to handle small F28 jets.

Queensland

Area 1,727,000 square km
Population 2,200,000

Don't miss: The Great Barrier Reef and the delightful islands along the tropical coastline of Australia's holiday state.

Queensland is Australia's holiday state — you are certain to find something to suit whether it is glossy, neon-lit Surfers Paradise, long deserted beaches with crashing surf further north, or the island resorts and excellent skin diving of the Great Barrier Reef.

In the far north the Cape York Peninsula is one of those disappearing stretches of wilderness that people still try to test themselves against. You can get an easy taste of that frontier in Cooktown, Australia's first (involuntary) British settlement and once a riotous goldrush town. Inland from Cairns there is the lush Atherton Tableland with countless beautiful waterfalls and scenic spots. Further inland is the outback mining town of Mt Isa or in the south-west corner of the state you'll find Birdsville with its famous track.

Queensland started up as yet another 'ship them off out of the way' penal colony in 1824. As usual the free settlers soon followed and Queensland became independent of New South Wales in 1859, less than 10 years after Victoria.

In Queensland today agriculture and mining are the two major activities, the state has a substantial chunk of the nation's mineral wealth. Queensland is also easily Australia's most controversial state — whether it is views on the environment or Aboriginal land rights, censorship of films and magazines, or even how the country should be run, you can count on Queensland to take an opposite stand to everybody else.

Unlike some other states, Queensland is not just a big city and a lot of fairly empty country, there are more reasonable sized towns in comparison to the overall population than any other state. Of course there is also plenty of empty outback country too. It's an interesting, quirky, kind of curious state.

INFORMATION
Queensland is probably the most tourist conscious state so there are plenty of offices of the Queensland Government Tourist Bureau (QGTB) both around the state and in other states. The interstate offices are:

ACT	28-36 Ainslie Avenue, Canberra City 2600 (tel 48 8411)
NSW	516 Hunter St, Newcastle 2300 (tel 26 2800)
	149 King St, Sydney 2000 (tel 232 1788)
South Australia	12a Grenfell St, Adelaide 5000 (tel 51 2397)
Victoria	MLC Building, corner of Elizabeth & Collins Sts, Melbourne 3000 (tel 61 2611)

The RACQ has a series of excellent maps covering the whole state, region by region. They're very detailed and packed with information on the reverse side. Available from RACQ offices.

GEOGRAPHY
Queensland has a series of distinct regions, generally running north-south

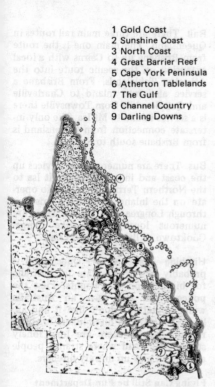

1 Gold Coast
2 Sunshine Coast
3 North Coast
4 Great Barrier Reef
5 Cape York Peninsula
6 Atherton Tablelands
7 The Gulf
8 Channel Country
9 Darling Downs

agricultural land running to the west. This fertile area extends furthest west in the south where the Darling Downs have some of the most productive grain growing land in Australia. Finally there's the vast inland area, the barren outback fading into the Northern Territory further west. Rain can temporarily make this desert bloom but basically it's an area of sparse population, of long empty roads and tiny settlements.

There are a couple of variations from these basic divisions. In the far north Gulf Country and the Cape York Peninsula are huge empty regions cut by countless dry riverbeds which become swollen torrents in the heavy wet season when the whole region is a network of waterways and road transport comes to a complete halt.

GETTING AROUND

Air Ansett and TAA both fly to the major centres of Queensland, connecting them to the southern states and across to the Northern Territory. Within Queensland there is also a very comprehensive network of flights operated by Air Queensland, some of their flights go into tiny missions and outback stations. Around the Gulf of Carpentaria their flights are often the only means of getting in or out during the wet season. Until 1982 Air Queensland was known as Bush Pilot Airways, BPA or 'bushies' — certainly a far more evocative name than the new one, it's a shame they changed it. Bushies came into operation in the early '50s and gradually spread to cover the whole state. Apart from regular and charter flights around the state the airline also operates a number of tours and day trips both to the Queensland outback and to Barrier Reef resorts — mainly to Lizard Island which they operate. The Air Queensland fleet today includes light aircraft, STOL aircraft, small airliners like Metro Propjets and F27s plus a number of venerable DC-3s.

parallel to the coast. First there's the coastal strip — the basis for Queensland's booming tourist trade. Along this strip you've got beaches, bays, islands and, of course, the Great Barrier Reef. Much of the coastal region is green and productive — lush rainforest, endless fields of sugar cane, stunning national parks.

Next comes the Great Dividing Range, the mountain range which continues right down through New South Wales and Victoria. In Queensland the mountains come closest to the coast and are the most spectacular in the far north (where you'll also find Queensland's highest mountains, near Cairns) and in the far south (where they provide a superb backdrop to the Gold Coast).

Then there's the tablelands — flat

The chart below details fares around Queensland.

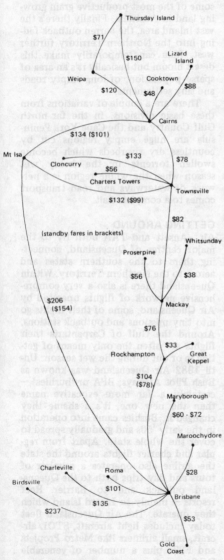

Thursday Island

$71

$150

Weipa

$120

Lizard Island

Cooktown

$48

$88

Cairns

$134 ($101)

Mt Isa

$133

Cloncurry

$56

$78

Charters Towers

Townsville

$132 ($99)

$82

(standby fares in brackets)

Whitsunday

Proserpine

$56

$38

$206 ($154)

Mackay

$76

$33

Rockhampton

Great Keppel

$104 ($78)

Maryborough

$60 - $72

Maroochydore

Charleville

Roma

$28

Birdsville

$101

Brisbane

$135

$237

$53

Gold Coast

Rail There are three main rail routes in Queensland. The main one is the route from Brisbane up to Cairns with a local extension on the scenic route into the Atherton Tablelands. From Brisbane a service also runs inland to Charleville and Quilpie while from Townsville there is a service inland to Mt Isa. The only interstate connection from Queensland is from Brisbane south to Sydney.

Bus There are numerous bus services up the coast and inland through Mt Isa to the Northern Territory. Buses also operate on the inland route from Brisbane through Longreach to Mt Isa. There are numerous local services like Cairns-Cooktown or Brisbane-Gold Coast.

Hitching Take care — Queensland is probably the worst state in Australia for hitching on two counts. First the police (who also have an Australia wide reputation) don't like it and are likely to jump on hitch-hikers for little reason. Second there are long lonely stretches of road where strange people are said to pick up unwary hitchers.

Flying Can Still be Fun Department
The Ansett or TAA flight between Mt Isa and Cairns takes one hour 10 minutes. In the course of researching this new edition I managed to take nearly seven hours to make that flight and it was hands down the most enjoyable flight I've ever made in Australia. My magic carpet was an Air Queensland (or Bush Pilot Airways as they used to be known) DC-3. We flew north from the Isa to Doomadgee, an Aboriginal reserve, where we dropped off some Aboriginal passengers and picked up some more. Then we flew north again to Mornington Island in the Gulf of Carpenteria, another Aboriginal reserve.

As we took off from Mornington every inhabitant of the town seemed to be out in the street to wave goodbye as we flew over. Then it was across the Gulf to the prawning port of Kuranda where we picked up a bunch of people

from the prawl trawlers and the crew off an oil tanker going on leave. From there it was the longest two hour leg across the Cape York peninsula to Cairns. The parched land gradually rising into the lush tablelands then dropping dramatically down to the coast. I even got half an hour on the flight deck on that leg (no they didn't know I was going to write about it). All three of our stops were on dirt strips, we flew low enough and slow enough to plot the route on a road map and we even saw the crashed remains of a WW II Liberator bomber down below. Furthermore the flight was just like you'd hope a far north Queensland airline would be — beers came in stubbies in styrofoam coolers! A great flight.

I'm sure that I'm not the only person who likes this old style flying and for those with the money to spare Air Queensland offers you a 14-day round north Australia tour starting and finishing in Brisbane. You actually take the same old DC-3 and crew all the way round, stopping in a different place each night and next day flying on to your next stop. At $2299 (travel,

accommodation and food) it's certainly not cheap but it sounds like a terrific experience and if I had the time and money to spare I'd love to give it a try.

ACTIVITIES

Bushwalking A popular activity in Queensland year round — there are a number of bushwalking clubs in the state and several guidebooks to bushwalks. If you intend to camp in the national parks you must first obtain a permit although this can sometimes be arranged over the phone.

Popular walking areas include the Lamington National Park, 112 km south-west of Brisbane and inland from the Gold Coast — with rain forests, waterfalls and nearly 150 km of graded walking tracks. Fraser Island also offers good bushwalking possibilities and there are plenty of places in the north around Cairns.

Fossicking There are lots of good fossicking areas in Queensland — get a copy of the QGTB's *Gem Fields* brochure. It tells you the places where you have a fair chance of finding gems and the types you'll find. You'll need a 'miners right' before you set out.

Swimming & Surfing Well what else does one come to Queensland for? There are plenty of swimming beaches close to Brisbane on sheltered Moreton Bay. Popular board surfing beaches are found south of the capital on the Gold Coast and north on the Sunshine Coast. North of Fraser Island the beaches are sheltered by the Great Barrier Reef so they're great for swimming but no go for the surf fans.

The clear, sheltered waters of the reef hardly need to be mentioned but from late November to March care should be taken on beaches where those unpleasant sea wasps may hang out. There are also innumerable good fresh water swimming spots around the state.

Skin Diving Plenty of opportunity for this activity in Queensland too. The reef islands, Moreton Bay and the Sunshine Coast all have good diving spots. Evidence of qualifications must be shown when hiring equipment.

Other Watersports There are some popular canoeing places in Queensland, particularly on the Noosa River on the Sunshine Coast, on the Brisbane River and in the far north. Townsville is another popular canoeing centre. Sailing enthusiasts will also find plenty of opportunities and many places which hire boats both along the coast and inland.

THE GREAT BARRIER REEF
Facts & Figures
The Great Barrier Reef is 2000 km in length. It starts slightly south of the Tropic of Capricorn, somewhere out from Bundaberg or Gladstone, and it ends in the Torres Straits, just south of Papua New Guinea. This huge length makes it not only the most extensive reef system in the world but also the biggest structure made by living organisms. At its southern end the reef is up to 300 km from the mainland but at the north it runs much closer to the coast and has a much more continuous nature. Here it can be up to 80 km across and in the 'lagoon' between the outer reef and the coast the waters are dotted with smaller reefs, cays and islands. Drilling on the reef has indicated that the coral can be over 500 metres thick.

What is It?
Coral is a primitive animal, closely related to the sea anenomes and jellyfish of the family *Coelenterata*. The vital difference is that coral forms a hard exterior surface by excreting lime. When coral dies its hard 'skeleton' remains and these gradually build up the reef. New corals grow on their dead predecessors and continually add to the reef. Coral needs a number of preconditions for healthy growth. First the water temperature must not drop below 17.5°C — thus the Barrier Reef does not continue further south into cooler waters. The water must be clear to allow sunlight to penetrate and it must be salty. Coral will not grow below 30 metres depth because the sunlight does not penetrate and it will not grow around river mouths. The Barrier Reef ends around Papua New Guinea because the Fly River's enormous water flow is both

fresh and muddy — two antagonistic factors for reef growth.

Reef Types

Basically reefs are fringing or barrier. You will find fringing reefs around many of the Barrier Reef islands. Barrier reefs are further out to sea and usually enclose a 'lagoon' of deep water. The Great Barrier Reef is out at the edge of the Australian continental shelf and the channel between the reef and the coast can be as deep as 60 metres. At places the reef rises straight up from that depth. Which raises the question of how the reef built up from that depth when coral cannot survive below 30 metres? One theory is that the reef gradually built up as the seabed subsided, the reef was able to keep pace with the sinking. The alternative theory is that the sea level gradually rose — again the coral growth was able to keep pace.

Reef Inhabitants

The Barrier Reef would just be a very big breakwater were it not for the colourful and highly varied reef life starting, of course, with the coral itself. Coral is highly varied in its types but almost all the coral skeletons are white — it's the living coral 'polyps' which give the coral its colourful appearance. Equally colourful are the many clams which appear to be embedded in the coral. Each seems to have a different colour fleshy area. Other reef inhabitants include starfish, sea urchins, sea cucumbers and fish.

Crown-of-Thorns Starfish One reef inhabitant which has enjoyed enormous publicity is the notorious crown-of-thorns starfish — the starfish that tried to eat the Barrier Reef! For a time in the '70s it seemed like these starfish might do just that but the problem now appears to have receded. At one time vast efforts were made by divers to clear stretches of the reef of these starfish but

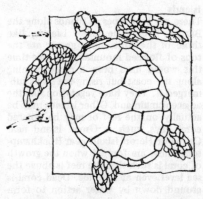

now they appear to have lost their strange appetite for corals and turned to more normal starfish food. It is thought that the crown-of-thorns starfish develop their taste for coral when the reef ecology is upset — as, for example, when the bivalves (oysters, clams) which comprise their normal diet are over-collected.

Nasties Hungry sharks are the usual idea of an aquatic nasty but the Barrier Reef's most unpleasant creatures are generally much less dramatic. For a start there are scorpion fish with their highly venomous spines. The butterfly cod is one scorpion fish and a very beautiful one — it relies on its colourful, slow-moving appearance to warn off possible enemies. In contrast the stonefish lies hidden on the bottom, looking just like a stone, and is very dangerous to step on. Fortunately they're rather rare but it's a good idea to wear shoes when walking on the reef. Stinging jellyfish are a danger only in coastal waters and only in certain seasons. They're not found out to sea around the islands. These deadly box jellyfish are known as sea wasps. As for sharks, well there has been no recorded case of a visitor to the reef islands meeting a hungry one.

Islands

There are two types of islands along the Barrier Reef. The larger islands, like those of the Whitsunday group, are the tops of flooded mountains. At one time this would have been a range running along the coast but rising sea levels submerged it. They have vegetation like the adjacent mainland. Other islands may be actually on the reef or may be isolated coral cays, such as Green Island near Cairns or Heron Island near Rockhampton. These are formed when the growth of coral is such that the reef is above the sea level even at low tide. Dead coral is ground down by water action to form sand and eventually hardier vegetation takes root. Coral cays are low-lying, unlike the often hilly islands closer to the coast.

Queensland has a great selection of islands but don't let the catchword 'reef island' suck you in. Only a few of the islands along the coast are real coral cays on the reef. Most of the popular resort islands are actually continental islands while some of Queensland's islands are actually south of the Great Barrier Reef itself. It's not important since many of them will still have fringing reefs and in any case a bigger continental island will have other attractions that a tiny, dot-on-the-map coral cay is simply too small for — like hills to climb, bushwalks and secluded beaches where you can get away from your fellow island lovers.

The islands vary considerably in their accessibility — Heron is a $100+ helicopter ride, others are just a few dollars by ferry. If you want to stay on an island rather than just day trip from the mainland that too can vary widely in costs. Accommodation is generally in the form of expensive resorts where most visitors will be staying on all-inclusive package deals. There are a few exceptions to this rule plus on many of the uninhabited islands and also on a few of the resort ones it is possible to camp. A few islands have proper sites with toilets and fresh water on tap while at the other extreme on some islands you'll even have to bring drinking water with you. From south to north a brief run down on the islands follows, see the relevant sections for more details.

South Stradbroke — a large sand island, mainly a day-trip from the Gold Coast.

North Stradbroke — a larger sand island, usually a day or weekend trip from Brisbane but also has a variety of fairly reasonably priced accommodation, cheap to get out to.

Moreton Island — sand island, day-trip by plane from Brisbane at fairly reasonable cost or take the longer launch service. One small and fairly expensive resort.

Bribie Island — sand island at the north end of Moreton Bay, another day-trip island but also with accommodation and connected to the mainland by a bridge.

Fraser Island — a huge sand island, very much a get-away-from-it-all place. Either difficult (four-wheel drive) or expensive (fly) to get to but also day and longer trips, wide variety of accommodation from camping through holiday flats to one resort.

Heron Island — tiny coral cay, first island on the reef and also first real reef island. Expensive to get to and also expensive accommodation, mainly for scuba diving enthusiasts.

Great Keppel — continental island, lots of variety, walks, beaches, entertainment, a resort but also cheaper accommodation and camping — can then use some of the resort facilities.

Brampton Island — small continental island, resort is fairly expensive, excellent beaches.

Whitsunday Islands — continental islands, more than 70 in all from tiny dots to 100 square km, resorts on Lindeman, Daydream, South Molle, Long Island and Hayman, resorts all fairly expensive although also a cheaper resort on Long Island. Lots of nice beaches, secluded spots, can camp on uninhabited islands, possible to day-trip to many islands, particularly the resort ones.

Magnetic Island — fairly large continental island, very accessible and lots of day-trippers, wide variety of accommodation, possible to stay cheaply. Not at all a reef island but you can get away from the crowds quite easily.

Orpheus Island — continental island, resort reasonably expensive.

Hinchinbrook Island — very large continental island, one fairly simple resort which is better value for larger groups, couple of camping places but not much in the way of facilities, fairly easy to get out to.

Dunk Island — small continental island (actually volcanic), very very pretty and with very expensive resort but a cheap island for day-trips.

Bedarra Island — tiny continental island close to Dunk Island, very expensive resort.

Fitzroy Island — continental island with recently opened resort, popular for day-trips.

Green Island — tiny coral cay, reasonably cheap for day-trips but rather crowded, fairly expensive resort on island.

Low Island — tiny coral cay, no more than a dot, very pretty but strictly a day-trip.

Lizard Island — continental island but right on the reef, expensive to get to and very expensive to stay there, can camp but facilities very spartan, mainly for game-fishing enthusiasts.

BRISBANE (population 900,000)

When Sydney and the colony of New South Wales needed a better place to store its more recalcitrant cons the tropical country further north seemed a good place to drop them. Accordingly in 1824 a penal settlement was established at Redcliffe on Moreton Bay, but soon abandoned due to lack of water and hostile Aboriginals. The settlement was moved to Brisbane and as Queensland's huge agricultural potential, and more recently the state's mineral riches, were developed Brisbane grew to be a town, then a city with a population today approaching a million, the third largest in Australia.

The skyscraper fever that has gripped Melbourne and Sydney is also taking over Brisbane but to some it's still a little of the 'large country town' which detractors have always been keen to label it. Brisbane is one of those places where you can always find something to see and do but basically there's nothing you absolutely cannot afford to miss. It's really just a gateway to Queensland's other attractions.

Information

The Queensland Government Tourist Bureau (tel 31 2211) is on the corner of Adelaide and Edward Sts. It has the usual comprehensive selection of maps, leaflets and helpful info. Opening hours are 8.30 am to 5 pm weekdays, 8.30 to 11.15 am on Saturdays. The RACQ (tel 221 1511) is at 190-194 Elizabeth St - - see the Queensland introductory comments about their excellent maps. The National Parks office is in the MLC Centre, 239 George St. The YHA (tel 221 2022) is at 462 Queen St in the centre and is open from 8.30 am to 4.30 pm Monday to Friday. The Adventurers' Club (tel 391 7309) at 1 Annie St, Kangaroo Point has entertainment, accommodation and organises a variety of trips and outings. The GPO is on Queen St between Edward and Creek Sts. There are a number of give-away information guides circulated in Brisbane including the useful entertainment guide *Time Off*.

Queensland Aboriginal Creations at 135 George St has a good collection of Aboriginal and Torres Strait islanders artefacts for sale. The Artefact Shop in the university's Anthropology Museum also has a good collection. It's open 10 am to 12 noon and 1 to 4 pm Monday, Wednesday and Friday. Queensland Book Depot, on Adelaide St opposite the City Hall, is Brisbane's biggest traditional bookshop. Other good bookshops include Angus & Robertson on Edward St, Folio Books on Elizabeth St and the American Bookstore on Elizabeth St. Jim the Backpacker in Queens Arcade, Queens St sells backpacking books and outdoor equipment.

Brisbane's city council is unusual in

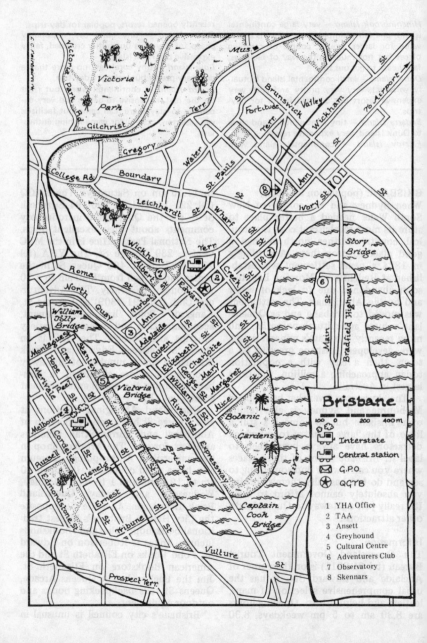

Brisbane

Scale: 100 0 200 400 m

- Interstate
- Central station
- G.P.O.
- QGTB

1 YHA Office
2 TAA
3 Ansett
4 Greyhound
5 Cultural Centre
6 Adventurers Club
7 Observatory
8 Skennars

that it covers the whole city, instead of a host of local government councils covering the city areas and suburbs. You don't have to be in Brisbane long to realise that it's a lot warmer than down south — in the summer it can get rather sticky and humid but in the winter the temperatures are very pleasant, especially when the southern capitals are shivering.

Orientation

The centre of Brisbane is situated on a loop of the Brisbane River, the Botanic Gardens are the actual turn of the river. Once or twice when the river has flooded the water has tried to take a short cut right through the city centre. The main streets run uphill from the river or parallel to it. You'll find the big shops along Adelaide, Queen and Elizabeth Sts or on Albert and Edward Sts which run across them. The Queen St Mall occupies the block from Albert St to Edward St. The Mall was hurriedly completed in late '82 in time for the Brisbane Commonwealth Games but proved an immediate success. It's hoped that the mall will also feature some open air eating places. King George Square, the large open square in front of City Hall, is a popular place to sit and watch the world pass by. Anzac Square by the Central Railway Station is another central city square.

If you continue up Ann St from the city you'll arrive in Fortitude Valley ('the valley') which is Brisbane's restaurant and entertainment centre. The University of Queensland is at St Lucia, upriver from the city centre. Like Sydney, Brisbane has a Paddington and it's also one of the older city suburbs but the Brisbane 'Paddo' isn't a centre for Victorian architecture like Sydney's. The terrace house architecture of the southern capitals only pops up in odd isolated pockets in Brisbane but you'll find the real tropical Queensland stilt houses with their wide verandahs all over the

place. Brisbane's airport at Eagle Farm is conveniently central. The city is surrounded by hills, many of them with fine lookouts.

City Hall

Brisbane's City Hall has gradually been surrounded by modern skyscrapers but the observation platform atop the tower still provides one of the best views across the city. It's open 9 am to 4 pm and the lift to the top is 30c. The City Hall also houses a museum and art gallery on the ground floor. A large open square fronts the City Hall and makes the building look even more grandiose and impressive — at least by daytime it does, by night the backlighting and palm trees make it look positively exotic. Day or night the 1930 building is one of the biggest city halls in Australia.

The Old Windmill

The Old Observatory and Windmill is one of Brisbane's earliest buildings, dating from 1829. It was intended to grind grain for the early convict colony but due to a fundamental design error it did not work properly — but no worries, cheap convict labour was freely available and it was quickly converted from windmill to treadmill. A later supervisor made it work as originally intended in 1837 but the building was then converted to a signal post and then a meteorological observatory. In 1864 a disastrous fire swept Brisbane and the windmill was one of the few early buildings to survive. It stands on Wickham Terrace, overlooking the city.

Other City Buildings

The National Trust's *Historic Walks* brochure will guide you round the most interesting early city buildings. The National Trust have their headquarters in the Old Government House building, built in 1862 at the end of George St. The State Parliament House is in George

St overlooking the Botanic Gardens, it dates from 1868 but there is also a new Legislative Assembly annex. The original parliament building is in French Renaissance style and has a roof of Mount Isa copper. St John's Cathedral at 417 Ann St is still under construction, work started in 1901. You can take a guided tour at 11 am on Wednesday. Queensland's first Government House, built in 1853, is now the Deanery for the Cathedral. The declaration of Queensland's separation from the colony of New South Wales was read here.

Queensland Museum

At the corner of Gregory Terrace and Bowen Bridge Rd in the valley the museum is old-fashioned but has a number of intriguing exhibits. Starting with the absolutely enormous WW I German tank displayed outside - - it carried a crew of 18 and this is the only known example to survive. Also outside are life-size models of a Tyrannosaurus and Triceratops. The museum is open 10 am to 4.55 pm Monday to Saturday, 2 to 4.55 pm Sundays and public holidays. Get there on a Chermside 172, Stafford 144 or Grand 126 bus.

Queensland Cultural Centre

Directly across the river from the city centre, in South Brisbane, this superb new complex houses the Queensland Art Gallery with an excellent collection. Other features will be added to the centre as time goes on but there's already a 500-seat auditorium and a restaurant looking out on the city.

Other Museums

On Stanley St in South Brisbane the Queensland Maritime Museum displays include an 1881 dry-dock, working models and the frigate *HMAS Diamantina*. It's open Wednesday, Saturday, Sunday and public holidays 10 am to 4.30 pm. Doll enthusiasts might like to visit Panaroo's Playthings at 401 Lut-

wyche Rd, Windsor — open rather odd hours. Or postal enthusiasts could try the GPO Museum at 261-285 Queen St. It's open Tuesday and Thursday from 10 am to 3.30 pm. Brisbane's trams no longer operate but you can see some early examples at the Tramway Museum at 2 McGinn Rd, Ferny Grove, 11 km from the centre. Guided tours at 3.30 pm Sunday.

Parks & Gardens

Brisbane has a number of parks and gardens including the Botanic Garden, on a loop of the Brisbane River, almost in the centre of the city. The park occupies 18 hectares and it's a popular spot for bike riding. The riverbanks here are a popular mooring spot for visiting yachts.

Newstead Park is a pleasant riverside park where you'll also find one of the oldest houses in Brisbane, see Newstead House below. Further downriver at New Farm, the New Farm Park is noted for its rose displays and Devonshire teas. Other parks include the small city Roma Street Park, Wickham Park, Bowen Park and Albert Park. Bulimba Creek is a popular recreation area with a variety of walking tracks and barbecue areas.

Lone Pine Sanctuary

The koala sanctuary at Fig Tree Pocket is one of Australia's best known and most popular animal sanctuaries because of its 'cuddle a koala' offer! Well, I guess koalas simply do look very cuddly. The sanctuary also has wombats, emus, Tasmanian devils, platypuses and a variety of other Australian animals. It's open 9.30 am to 5 pm daily and admission is $4. The platypuses are only on view from 11.30 am to 12 noon and 3 to 4 pm. You can get there on a boat cruise for $8 or on a Lone Pine 84 bus from Adelaide St. It's 11 km from the centre.

Other Brisbane sanctuaries include the Alma Park Zoo at Kallangur which has a large collection of palms and Australian and overseas wildlife. It's 28 km from the city centre. Or there's Bunya Park on Bunya Park Drive, Eatons Hill, turn-off just past Albany Creek. The Oasis Gardens at Sunnybank are another possibility.

Mount Coot-tha Forest Park

This large park with lookouts is just eight km south-west of the city centre. The top is distinguished by a confusion of TV transmitter towers but the views from up here are superb. On a clear day you can see the distant line of Moreton and Stradbroke Islands, the Glasshouse Mountains to the north, the mountains behind the Gold Coast to the south and Brisbane with the river winding through it at your feet. The view is particularly superb at night.

The new Botanic Gardens are in the foothills of the park. The gardens include an enclosed tropical display dome and an arid zone collection. There are also some good walks around the park like the walk to the J C Slaughter Falls. Here you'll also find the Sir Thomas Brisbane Planetarium, the largest in Australia. Admission is $3 and there are shows at 3.30 and 7.30 pm Wednesday to Friday, 1.30, 3.30 and 7.30 pm Saturday, 1.30 and 3.30 pm Sunday. You can get to the Mt Coot-tha lookout on a 10C bus or to the Botanic Gardens and planetarium on a Toowong 39 bus.

Eagle Farm Airport

Brisbane's airport, which handles domestic and international flights, is fairly central. A glass-walled building houses one of Australia's most famous aircraft — the tri-motor Fokker Southern Cross which made the first Pacific crossing with Brisbane's own Sir Charles Kingsford Smith at the controls.

Newstead House

On Breakfast Creek Rd, Newstead this is the headquarters for the Royal Historical Society of Queensland — it's the oldest historic home in Brisbane, built in 1846, and delightfully situated overlooking the river. It's open 11 am to 3 pm Monday to Thursday, 2 to 5 pm on Sundays and public holidays. Admission is by donation. You can get there on an Airport 160 bus, or a Toombul 170, 171 or 190 bus. Newstead Park, where the house is situated, has a memorial to US WW II servicemen who passed through Brisbane and also, believe it or not, a memorial to Lyndon Johnson.

Other Old Houses

There are a number of interesting old houses or period re-creations around Brisbane. Early Street Historical Village is on McIlwraith Avenue, off Bennetts St in Norman Park, six km from the centre. It's a re-creation of early Queensland colonial life and is open daily from 11 am to 4.30 pm. Get there on a Seven Hills 8A, 8B bus or a Carina 8C, 8D, 8E bus. At 31 Jordan Terrace, Bowen Hills the Miegunyah Folk Museum is housed in an 1884 building, a fine example of early architecture. It has been restored as a memorial to the pioneer women of Queensland and is open 10.30 am to 3 pm Tuesday and Wednesday, to 4 pm on weekends. Get there on an Airport 160 or Toombul 170, 171 or 190 bus. At Grindle Rd, Wacol is Wolston House, the first National Trust acquisition in Queensland. Built in 1852 of local materials it's open 10 am to 4.30 pm from Wednesday to Sunday and on public holidays. The Joss House, near Albion Park Raceway, on Higgs St, Breakfast Creek, is the only Chinese temple in Brisbane. It was built in 1884.

Other Attractions

Yes, Queensland has a water slide amusement centre — it's Mirage at 2098 Ipswich Rd, Oxley where there is also a go-kart track and other amusements.

Places to Stay

Brisbane is not the best city for accommodation by a long shot — even the solitary hostel is a long way out from the centre although it's a popular place. Plus you can't camp within a 22 km radius of the centre, a curious city council regulation, so the more convenient caravan parks do not permit tent campers. There are, however, a number of guest houses and hotels with fairly reasonable prices both in the centre and close to it.

Hostel The *Brisbane Youth Hostel* (tel 57 1245) is at 15 Mitchell St, Kedron, eight km from the city centre. Get there on a 172 Chermside bus, getting off at stop 27A by the Ho Ho Chinese Pagoda Restaurant. Bookings should be made to the city YHA office at 462 Queen St. Although it's some distance from the centre it's a modern, popular and pleasant hostel with room for 60 and nightly costs of $5.

Although neither are hostels two other very low price accommodation possibilities are worth considering. The

YMCA Youth Centre (tel 57 6482) is at 387 Lutwyche Rd, Windsor. Right across the road from the *Adventurers Club* (tel 391 7309) at 1 Annie St, Kangaroo Point the club has some rock-bottom priced accommodation.

Central Hotels & Guest Houses A bit pricey for budget travellers but very central and convenient the *Hotel Can-*

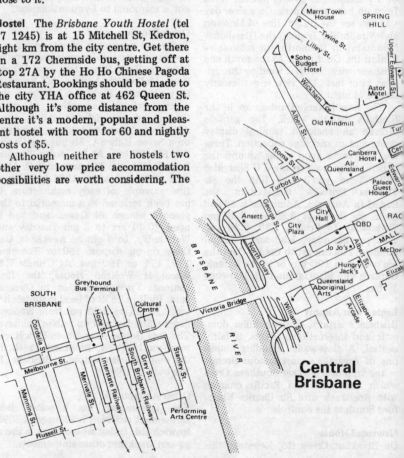

Central Brisbane

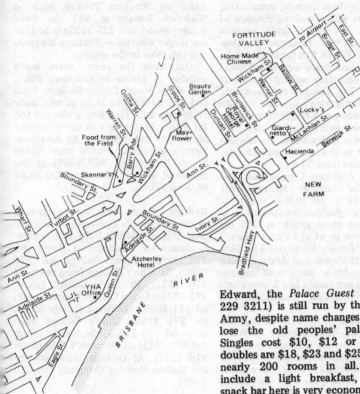

berra (tel 32 0231) is on the corner of Ann and Edward Sts. It's a well-run Temperance Union hotel, with basic rooms without private facilities at $18 single, $32 double. Singles are a bit small but rooms all have tea/coffee making equipment and wash basins. With attached bathroom the rates are $38/46 but on Saturday and Sunday $38 is the top rate, even for triples and rooms for four. All rates include a solid breakfast, ask about discounts for bus pass holders.

Right across the road from the Canberra, also on the corner of Ann and Edward, the *Palace Guest House* (tel 229 3211) is still run by the Salvation Army, despite name changes to try and lose the old peoples' palace image. Singles cost $10, $12 or $15 while doubles are $18, $23 and $25. There are nearly 200 rooms in all. All rates include a light breakfast, the small snack bar here is very economical.

The *Atcherley Hotel* (tel 31 2591) is up at 513 Queen St, the junction with Adelaide St, and has rooms at $16/24. Keep heading up this way to Fortitude Valley where the *Hacienda* (tel 52 4344) on Brunswick St is a small modern place with rooms at $25/32. The *Royal George Hotel* (tel 52 2524) is on the corner of Ann and Brunswick St in the valley. Singles cost $15 or $17 with private facilities, a dollar less without breakfast.

Other Hotels & Guest Houses There are a number of other good value guest houses and hotels away from the central area. *Marrs Town House* (tel 221 5388) is at 391 Wickham Terrace, overlooking the city but within walking distance of the centre. It's a big, fairly modern place housed in ex-nurses'-quarters. Rooms cost $16 to $18 for singles without private bathrooms but with a washbasin and tea/coffee making equipment and radio. The cheaper rooms simply have an inferior view! Doubles are $28 or with air-con and a fridge they're $33. With attached bathroom costs are $28/38 or $2 more with air-con. There's also a restaurant in this modern guest house, breakfast costs from $3.

Also on Wickham Terrace, but a bit closer to the centre at 193, the *Astor* (tel 221 9522) has budget rooms at $20/22 for singles/doubles (shared facilities) or '1st class' rooms at $45 for doubles. Close by at 413 Upper Edward St the *Yale Private Hotel* (tel 31 1663) is a straightforward and fairly spartan guest house style place with nightly costs of $12 per person bed & breakfast. Rooms have fridges, washbasins and fans.

The *Tourist Private Hotel* (tel 52 4171) is at 555 Gregory Terrace, directly opposite the museum. Including breakfast the standard rooms are $12/23 for singles/doubles. They have fans, washbasins and there's a TV room, kitchen and laundry. There's also a motel section at $18/30 again including breakfast. Get there on a number 7 bus from the centre. Only a few doors down at 527 is the *Mornington Private Hotel* (tel 52 4204), right on the corner with Brunswick St. Rooms cost $12/20 including breakfast in the older section while, just like its near neighbour, there is also a more modern motel-style section where rooms cost $16/24, again including breakfast.

Motels Some of the guest house places spill over into the motel category and these are generally the best value to be found -- places like the *Tourist* or the *Mornington* by the museum or the

Astor on Wickham Terrace. Also on Wickham Terrace at 333 the *Soho Budget Motel* (tel 221 7722) is $31/37 for singles/doubles — Brisbane is expensive this close to the centre.

Out from the centre there are a number of places in Kangaroo Point, like the *Carmel Lodge Holiday Flats* (tel 391 4106) 819 Main St with daily costs from $25. Hamilton is also not too far from the centre and the *Riverview Motel* (tel 268 4666) at 20 Riverview Terrace is $29/33. Similar prices at the *South Pacific* (tel 358 2366) at the corner of Bowen Terrace and Langshaw St, New Farm.

Colleges If you want to try your luck at the colleges the University of Queensland places offering individual accommodation are International House (tel 370 9593), Union College (tel 371 1300), St John's College (men only, tel 370 8171), St Leo's College (ditto, 371 1534), Grace College (women only, tel 371 3898), Duchesne College (ditto, tel 371 1148), King's College (men only, tel 370 1125), Cromwell College (tel 370 1151) and Women's College (tel 370 1177). At Griffith University try the Nathan Housing Company (tel 275 7575).

Camping Brisbane is not at all good in this department. The curious Brisbane council regulations forbid tent camping within a 22 km radius of the centre and in any case there are few sites very close in. In fact all in all the camping picture around Brisbane is so miserable you're probably best forgetting it. It's a much better story south on the Gold Coast or north on the Sunshine Coast. It's a drag for the traveller because there's not much alternative at the bottom end in Brisbane. Even Cairns can boast more hostels than Brisbane for example. What little there is in the camping and caravan park list (and most of this is for on-site vans only) is listed below:

San Mateo Caravan Park (tel 341 5423), 2481 Pacific Highway, Eight Mile Plain, 16 km south, no camping, on-site vans from $12 daily.

Sheldon Caravan Park (tel 341 6601), 27 Hilmead Rd, Eight Mile Plains, 16 km south, no camping, on-site vans from $14 daily.

Amaroo Gardens (tel 397 1774), 771 Logan Rd, Holland Park, eight km south, no camping, on-site vans from $10 daily.

Alpha Caravan Park (tel 263 4442), 1434 Gympie Rd, Aspley, 13 km north, no camping, on-site vans from $18 daily.

Oxley Caravan Park (tel 375 4465), Kimberley St, Oxley, 13 km west, no camping, on-site vans from $16 daily.

Newmarket Gardens Caravan Park — forget it!

Wellington Point Caravan Park (tel 207 2722), Birkdale-Wellington Point, 29 km east, camping $5.50 daily, on-site vans $10 daily.

Greenacres Caravan Park (tel 206 4113), corner Mt Cotton & Greenfield Rds, Capalaba, 23 km east, camping $4 daily.

Redlands Caravan Park (tel 207 2752), Collingwood Rd, Birkdale, 21 km east, camping $5 daily, on-site vans from $11 daily.

Belcaro Caravan Park (tel 396 3163), 1893 Wynnum Rd, Wynnum West, 21 km east, camping $4.50 daily.

Carina Caravan Park (tel 398 3081), 1497 Creek Rd, Carina, nine km east, no camping, on-site vans from $12.

Brisbane Caravan Park (tel 399 4878), 18 Scott Rd, Hawthorne, five km east, no camping, on-site vans from $8.

Places to Eat

Although Brisbane certainly hasn't got anything like the reputation of Sydney or Melbourne when it comes to food there are still plenty of good places to try. You'll find restaurants around the city, up the hill in Fortitude Valley and, of course, out at St Lucia near the university. Brisbane is particularly well-known for seafood, the famed Queensland mud-crab above all. Unfortunately like so many other places in Queensland very little advantage is taken of Queensland's sunshine and balmy weather. Not only is there a real paucity of places where you can eat outside there's also a real shortage of places where you can eat moderately late in the evening. Apart from the places featured below Brisbane also has the usual selection of Colonel McPizza Huts.

City You'll find a bit of everything around the central city area from good lunchtime sandwiches to flashy night time splurge places. In the former category you could definitely do much worse than trying *The Source*, a long running favourite in the vegetarian and health food department. It's in the Elizabeth Arcade at 99 Elizabeth St and has everything from tasty hot dishes to a tempting selection of exotic cakes. It's open lunchtimes and until 9 pm on Fridays.

A new and very popular addition to the Brisbane dining scene is *Jo Jo's*, a large place upstairs at the corner of Queen and Albert Sts. In the Perth section of this book you can read about my enthusiasm for the Singapore style 'food-centres', well this is a rather different interpretation of the same excellent idea. Jo Jo's offers a whole collection of fast food counters with everything from French, Greek, Lebanese, Italian, Chinese and Mexican food to beer, wine, coffee, tea, desserts and so on. Tables are scattered in between, and prices range from $3 right up to $8 or $9. It's open until 12 midnight and if you really fancy Mexican while your partner just wants a salad then this is just the place.

There are all sorts of other places to try around the city. Just down beyond the Source in Elizabeth Arcade the *Tortilla Cantina* is a long running Spanish-Mexican favourite which offers pleasant food and surroundings at reasonable prices. Or there's fast food at *Mexican Mick's* on Albert St, main courses at $4 to $7, entrees at $1, $2 and $3. The *Munich Steakhouse* on the corner of Albert and Edward Sts is a close relation to the Bavarian Steakhouse in Surfers. It's straightforward in the extreme — steaks, schnitzel and no messing about. Around $7 to $9 for main courses. The *Arcade Bistro* is in the Brisbane Arcade in the centre and does equally straightforward food with the accent on good value. Steaks, a serve-yourself salad bar, pay as you enter, around $20 for two.

Another of the national pancake house chain the *Pancake Manor* is at 18 Charlotte St. As usual things are just 'lovely' and, also as usual, one of its major virtues is that it's open to midnight every night and 24 hours on Friday and Saturday nights. Right in the centre at 254 Edward St the *Shingle Inn* is a genteel tea house for a genteel morning coffee.

Fortitude Valley If Brisbane has a restaurant centre then it has to be up the hill from the city centre in Fortitude Valley. On the way up there you could try *Food from the Field* at 76 Wickham St, just round the corner from the Skennar's bus depot. It's a vegetarian place offering take-aways and sandwiches at lunch time plus dinner in the evening — when main courses are around $5.50 and nice desserts cost $2.50. Really good food and very convenient if you're just waiting for a bus.

Up in the valley itself there are lots of places to try along Brunswick St or on Ann and Wickham Sts, close to where they cross Brunswick St. Like the popular *Giardinetto's* at 366 Brunswick St. It's a small, pleasant little Italian

---

A BIG OFFER

There's some sort of national mania in Australia for constucting big 'things', like the big pineapple opposite. Elsewhere around the country you can find other superb examples of Australian kitsch ranging from a big lobster (in South Australia) to a big trout (in New South Wales). Not to mention big strawberries, big oranges, big shells, big stubbies, big potatoes, big sugar cane, big codfish and even a big Captain Cook! So we're making a big offer — anybody who sends us a postcard of a big something which we haven't already got gets a free copy of any Lonely Planet title they choose. And we're starting from scratch so the first postcard of the big pineapple opposite will also win. But it's strictly first card only.

Queensland

a. Surfers Paradise, a beautiful beach backed by a real estate agent's dream.

b. Brisbane's Town Hall is a grandiose structure by day, floodlit by night it's positively exotic.

c. When it comes to 'big' objects Queensland has some of the best, this is the 'Big Pineapple' at Nambour.

place with main courses in the $5.50 to $7.50 bracket and also pizzas from around $3.50 for small ones. Round the corner at 683 Ann St the atmosphere is equally pleasant in *Lucky's Trattoria*, a fine little Italian restaurant where two can eat for around $20, very similarly priced to its near neighbour.

At 257 Wickham St the *Home Made Chinese Meal Kitchen* is a minute Chinese place about 100 metres across Brunswick St from the real restaurant block. The size has no relationship to the restaurant's reputation which is definitely on the large size! Excellent food and low prices (say $15 for two) can't be beat.

Other Places Continue up beyond Fortitude Valley to Breakfast Creek to find one of Brisbane's best known seafood specialists and a worthwhile place to consider for a splurge. The *Coral Trout* at 192 Breakfast Creek Rd, Newstead, just before the bridge across the creek, has a high reputation for its seafood, not least the coral trout. Around $30 for two people and don't go there for any other reason than to eat seafood. It's closed Sundays.

Gino's at 470 Kingsford Smith Drive, Hamilton is out towards the airport and does high quality pasta dishes and other Italian food along with the usual pizzas. Around $20 for two.

Counter Meals Brisbane has a good selection of the traditional steak and salad places, one of the best known being the famous *Breakfast Creek Hotel*

at 2 Kingsford Smith Drive, Breakfast Creek. This is a real Brisbane institution with a public bar where beer is still drawn from real wooden kegs. It's a rambling old place right by the creek and has long been a Labor Party and trade union hang-out. It's renowned for its superb steaks which cost in the $6 to $8 bracket. They also do fine sandwiches from a dollar and up plus there's a good beer garden to eat and drink in.

Dead centre in the city the *City Plaza Tavern* in the Plaza Square at the corner of George and Elizabeth Sts does counter meals for $6 to $7. You'll see the tell-tale blackboards at lots of other places around the city. Like the *Carlton Hotel* at 103 Queen St which does cheap counter food. Very cheap counter food ($2 to $3) in *La Cantina* in the *Hacienda Hotel* on Brunswick St, Fortitude Valley. It's open 5.30 to 7.30 Monday to Saturday. At 100 Leichhardt St the *Federal Hotel* does plain and simple pub food at rock bottom prices. Just follow up Upper Edward St to get to it.

Entertainment

Brisbane has all the usual pubs featuring live music, you'll find the full run down on what's on and where in the weekend papers or in the give-away entertainment paper *Time Off*. Rock specialists include the *Mansfield Tavern* in Mt Gravatt and the *Sunnybank Hotel* in Sunnybank. Right in the centre of town the *City Plaza Tavern* on the corner of Adelaide and George Sts features a disco and other entertainment at reason-

Queensland

a. The Millstream Falls in the Atherton Tableland are the widest in Australia, a mini-Niagara only 13 metres high.

b. Towards the end of the dry the rivers running into the Gulf of Carpentaria make intricate patterns. This picture was taken on a flight from Doomadgee to Mornington Island.

c. The Great Barrier Reef off the Whitsunday Islands rears up suddenly from 50 metres or more depth.

able prices. The *Melbourne Hotel* in South Brisbane is one of a number of pubs featuring jazz. The *Adventurer's Club* at Kangaroo Point, across the river, has a variety of entertainment — jazz some nights, disco others, folk on others.

Getting There

Air There are numerous Ansett and TAA flights daily to Brisbane from the southern capitals and north to the Queensland regional centres. All flights to Sydney are direct, of course, while to Melbourne and Adelaide some flights go direct, some through Sydney. Fares include Sydney $121 ($91 standby), Melbourne $180 ($135 standby), Adelaide $196 (direct, more expensive via Sydney or Melbourne) ($150 standby). See the relevant sections for details of the flights up the coast to regional Queensland centres. There are no TAA or Ansett flights between Brisbane and Coolangatta, the airport for Surfers and the Gold Coast. Travellers on round Australia tickets can fly in to one port and out from the other, however, travelling between the two by surface.

Brisbane is also a busy international arrival and departure point with frequent flights to Asia, Europe, the Pacific Islands, North America, New Zealand and Papua New Guinea.

Rail You can reach Brisbane by rail from Sydney and continue north to Cairns or inland to Roma and Charleville. The daily Brisbane Limited Express (I guess that must mean that as an express it's very limited, it certainly isn't fast) takes 16 hours between Sydney and Brisbane. The fares are $75 in 1st, $53 in economy. You can also travel north from Sydney on the Gold Coast Motorail Express to Murwillumbah, just south of the Queensland border. It's popular for people bringing their cars up to Queensland, and not wanting to drive all the way. The trip takes 16½ hours and costs $45 in 1st

($30 more for a sleeper), $32 in economy. That's quite a saving on the fare to Brisbane, particularly if you want to start your Queensland travels on the Gold Coast. There's a connecting bus service to the Gold Coast and Brisbane. It costs $84 for your car to come along for the ride from Sydney to Murwillumbah.

The Sunlander runs between Brisbane and Cairns, 1681 km and 37 hours to the north, six days a week. See the relevant sections for more details. Inland to Roma, Charleville and Cunnamulla the Westlander runs twice a week. See the relevant sections for details. For information on trains in Queensland phone Queensland Railways (tel 225 0211) at 305 Edward St.

Bus There are a lot of buses through Brisbane — particularly to Sydney. Ansett Pioneer (tel 229 4455) are at 16 Ann St and Greyhound (tel 44 7144) at 79 Melbourne St, south of the river from the centre. Both operate regular Sydney-Brisbane services, Ansett Pioneer go daily while Greyhound have two daily via the coastal Pacific Highway and one daily via the New England Highway. Sydney-Brisbane fare is $44.50 and the trip takes about 17 hours.

Both companies also operate daily up the coast to Rockhampton, Mackay, Townsville and Cairns — see the relevant sections for details. See the Gold Coast section for details on buses between Brisbane and Surfers Paradise. Three times weekly Greyhound have a direct Brisbane-Melbourne service via the New England and Newell Highways — 29 hours, $83. They also operate direct between Brisbane and Adelaide three times weekly — 36 hours, $95. Ansett Pioneer have direct Melbourne-Brisbane services via Toowoomba or Surfers, three times weekly on each route. There are also direct services between Brisbane and Mt Isa with either company — see

Mt Isa for details.

Ansett Pioneer and Greyhound are far from the only bus companies operating to and from Brisbane. There are a number of cut price operators like VIP Tours and Intercapital Coachlines offering Sydney-Brisbane for $39. Or there's McCafferty's (tel 44 4015) at the South Brisbane Railway Station, Grey St, South Brisbane. They have services between Sydney and Brisbane either via the Pacific Highway or the New England Highway. Brisbane is linked to Toowoomba and hence to St George (further inland) or to Rockhampton and Mackay up the coast. You can also reach Rockhampton from Brisbane via the coastal Bruce Highway with McCafferty's.

Skennars (tel 221 8610) are at 22-34 Barry Parade, just off Wickham St about half-way up the hill from the city centre to Fortitude Valley. They have a comprehensive service round Queensland including buses to the Gold Coast, the Sunshine Coast, to various places in the New South Wales, New England area, to Port Macquarie on the coast, to the far south-west of Queensland (Charleville, Roma, etc) and to the north-west (Longreach, Mt Isa, etc). Connections also operate from Port Macquarie to Sydney and Tamworth. Including overnight accommodation in Port Macquarie, Skennars will transport you between Brisbane and Sydney for $76.

Getting Around

Buses Brisbane has a comprehensive bus network and a number of special fares. For a start you can buy a $2 Day Rover Ticket which allows unlimited use of the city bus service for a whole day. You can buy them from nominated newsagents or, for 20c more, on board the bus. There's also a Concession Rover ticket for $1 which does not permit use on certain express buses. You can also get Fare Saver Cards which give you 10 tickets for $3.30 (single zone), $5.50 (two zones) or $6.60 (three zones). Regular bus tickets cost 40c for one zone, 60c for two, 80c for three.

For information on city buses it's worth visiting the information centre in the City Plaza behind the town hall. They can answer any queries you might have or supply timetables. Or phone 225 4444. Some useful buses include the 172 Chermside bus for the youth hostel. The 162 also runs by the hostel and the 202 Chermside Express but this does not stop at the youth hostel stop, 27A. For Mt Coot-tha take a 10C bus from Adelaide St. For the airport take a 160 Airport bus for 60c.

Rail Brisbane has a suburban rail network too. There have recently been some extensive additions of new equipment but no doubt some of the old railway carriages are still of such amazing antiquity that you'd think this was where Indian railways retired their rolling stock!

Car Rental All the big car rental operators have offices in Brisbane plus a number of more economical local operators like Manx Rent-a-Car at 325 Wickham St in Fortitude Valley. Manx rates start from $7 plus 15c a km for Mokes, $24 including unlimited km for a Corolla or Gemini. Shoestrings Rent-a-Car (tel 371 8312) claim an unlimited km flat rate of $20 a day. Inedell are another local company with economical flat rates.

Bicycle Rental At 214 Margaret St, near the Botanic Gardens, Brisbane Bicycle Hire is open 9 am to 5 pm daily to hire bicycles. Rates are $3.20 for an hour, $5 for two, $6 for three or all day for $9. A week costs $19.

River Brisbane doesn't make as much use as it might of its river but there are a number of popular day trips out and about on the river. Ferries do, however, run from Eagle St to East Brisbane and Hawthorne every half hour and across the river from Alice St by the Botanic Gardens. Fares across the rivers are just 30c. Probably the most popular cruise is the trip to the Lone Pine Koala Sanctuary. It departs from the Hayles Wharf on Queens Wharf Rd every afternoon at 1.30 pm, returning at 5.30 and on Sunday mornings and costs $8, plus the sanctuary admission. There's a one hour scenic river cruise from the Creek St Ferry Terminal for just 80c. It operates up to 20 times daily on weekdays, plus four times on Saturday mornings.

Sundays and public holidays a cruise runs down the river to the mouth at Moreton Bay. Departures are from the Botanic Gardens at 2 pm and return at 5, the cost is $5. Other cruises include a visit to the Moreton Bay islands for $22 or a day-trip to Stradbroke Island for $33. A day-trip to the Tangalooma resort, including lunch, costs $20, departs daily except Monday and Tuesday from the Hamilton Game Fishing Wharf.

Airport You can get to or from the airport on a 160 public bus for just 60c. By taxi it costs about $5 from the airport to the city, $4 to Fortitude Valley. Avis, Budget and Hertz have desks at the airport. In the city Ansett (tel 226 1111) are at 16 Ann St down by the river. TAA (tel 223 3333) are on the corner of Adelaide and Creek Sts.

Tours There are plenty of bus tours around Brisbane, they typically cost $6 or $7 for a half-day tour, $13 and up for a day tour. Around Brisbane tours visit all the city sites, the Mt Coot-tha lookout and other attractions. Tours out of the city, costing $13 to $18, include the Tamborine Mountains, Gold Coast and the Sunshine Coast. Or you can cross the Great Dividing Range and visit the Darling Downs for $22. Boomerang Tours have the widest range of Brisbane bus tours. See the river transport section for details of river trips.

GIRDED FOR BATTLE with the outback, a family Holden equipped with all the options that spell survival. "Longer, lower, wider be damned!"

Radio - no top 40... weather reports & sports - only the essentials

Roll bar & Sun visor

Space petrol -

Flatbed option for larger families

Mesh grill to fend off windscreen damage.

'Roo bars: heavyweight armour against kangaroos loitering in the roadway at night.

Plenty of light to mesmurise kangaroos at night (see 'roo bars)

"Queensland - sunshine state" at 110° in the shade in understatement.

Lots of extra mirrors... look back and say 'struth, we've made it!'

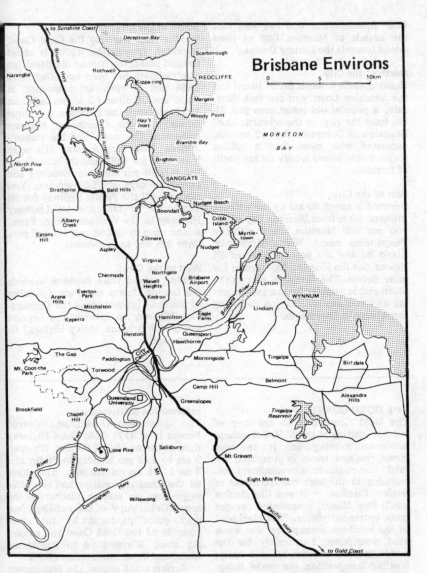

Brisbane Environs

0   5   10km

AROUND BRISBANE

There are many places of interest around Brisbane, in fact several of Queensland's major tourist attractions, places worth visiting in their own right, are also within day-trip distance of the city. The Gold Coast and the Sunshine Coast, for example, are an easy drive from Brisbane and you can also visit the islands of Moreton Bay or head inland towards the Darling Downs.

North of the City

Heading north towards Bribie Island and the Sunshine Coast you can visit Sandgate, a popular old resort area just 19 km from the city, or the eccentric Shell Bungalow at Deception Bay, 32 km out, decorated with more than a million shells. Bribie Island is only 58 km north of Brisbane.

East of the City

Brisbane is about 30 km up the winding Brisbane River from Moreton Bay where you can visit Moreton Island with the Tangalooma resort, North Stradbroke Island or the old penal colony of St Helena. See the Moreton Bay section for more details. The Redlands area to the south-east is popular for market gardening and you can see the (oh dear) Big Strawberry in Thornlands.

South of the City

On the road south to the Gold Coast, Beenleigh (population 4200) is about the mid-point. The famous old Beenleigh rum distillery has been operating since 1884 and is open for inspection at 11.30 am, 12.30 and 2.30 pm daily. An 1897 molasses tank makes a unique housing for the Charthouse Museum collection. The town also has Bullen's African Lion Park & Zoo. It's open 9 am to 5 pm daily and the animals are fed at 2.30 pm daily, on Sundays and public holidays at 11.30 am too. You can turn off the Pacific Highway for Mt Tamborine or take the Mt Lindesay Highway to the Woollahra Dairy Farm, a farm open to visitors and you can continue this way to Beaudesert.

West of the City

Heading inland from Brisbane towards the Darling Downs there are a number of places of interest along the Cunningham Highway to Ipswich and beyond and on the Brisbane Valley Highway to Toowoomba.

THE GOLD COAST

The Gold Coast is a 35 km strip of beaches starting at the NSW-Queensland border and running north. It's the most commercialised resort in Australia, virtually one continuous development culminating in the high rise splendour of Surfers Paradise - 'if you like Surfers you'll love Miami' commented one not quite entranced visitor. 'The Blackpool of the southern hemisphere' was a less kind description. Fortunately for the budget-minded traveller all that nasty, hustling competition can make things surprisingly economical, despite the neon glitter. Particularly if you avoid coming at the worst (school holiday) time.

Information & Orientation

The Queensland Government Tourist Bureau is at 3177 Gold Coast Highway right in the middle of Surfers. It's open 9 am to 4.45 pm Monday to Friday and 9 to 11.15 am on Saturday. They have all the usual information and can offer suggestions on accommodation on the coast. Get a copy of the excellent free map guide produced by the shire councils of the Gold Coast and adjoining areas. It covers up to Stradbroke Island and down into northern NSW.

Surfers is, of course, the best known of the Gold Coast towns but the strip also includes Burleigh Heads, Palm Beach, Coolangatta and Tweed Heads — across the border in NSW. The Gold

Coast airport is at Coolangatta, right at the southern end of the strip. To make it even more interesting the country inland includes some of the most spectacular mountain scenery in Australia in the MacPherson Ranges. The beaches along the Gold Coast are really excellent but the various tourist attractions are basically artificial creations which your life will not be frantically the worse for if you skip.

Surfers Paradise

The centre of the Gold Coast is a real high rise jungle with more buildings still under construction despite the dramatic drop the long running Gold Coast property boom suddenly took in the early '80s. In fact there's such a skyscraper conglomeration that in the afternoon much of the beach here is cast into shadow! Still you can always go a little further north or south to find more of the magnificent Gold Coast beach and with the sun shining upon it. In 1936 there was just the brand new Surfers Paradise Hotel here, a handy little hideaway nine km south of Southport. It's still there on the corner of Gold Coast Highway and Cavill Avenue and its beer garden still operates but it's somewhat lost amongst the big buildings today.

The Gold Coast Highway is the main road right through Surfers, only a couple of blocks back from the beach. Traffic along the highway is non-stop, crossing the road can be quite a feat. Cavill Avenue has a pedestrian mall down towards the beach. Surfers has a number of 'attractions' like a waxworks and the huge Grundy's amusement arcade. Right down by the beach there's one of those water slide thingos — $4 for a half hour.

If you want a place that somehow sums all that the Gold Coast is you need look no further than 'Grundy's, right off the Cavill Mall in Surfers. Only a few steps

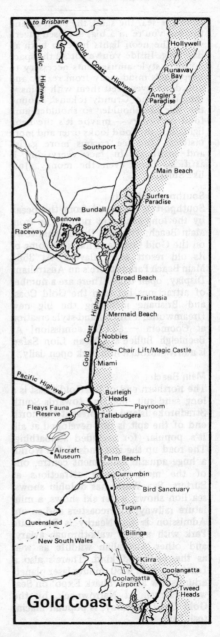

Gold Coast

from the sea, the sand, the open air and the sun you're in a big, enclosed cavern where the neon lights have to burn all day long. Inside you've got all the space invaders style amusements necessary to keep one's mind away from reality and you don't even feed them with coins — they consume 'Grundy tokens'. Around the side are shoulder to shoulder junk food purveyors — maybe it's the neon lights but the food looks drier and more tasteless, the ice creams more garish and artificial. In fact everything is artificial here, even the money. Just like Surfers?

Southport & North
Southport is sheltered from the ocean by the long sand spit running up from Main Beach. This was the original town on the Gold Coast and has kept some of its old resort town flavour. At 3563 Main Beach Parade there's an Australiana Display, open daily. There are a number of attractions between the Gold Coast and Brisbane including the big new Dreamworld — a Disneyland-style creation at Coomera — $11.50 admission! At Beenleigh Bullen's African Lion Safari is a drive through lion park open daily.

Main Beach
The northern end of the Gold Coast is a long sand spit, pointing towards South Stradbroke Island. At present the north end of the spit is not developed at all. It's popular for secluded sunbathing. The road up the spit ends at Sea World, a huge aquatic amusement centre, one of the most popular attractions at Surfers. Sea World has dolphin shows, sea lion shows, water ski shows, a miniature railway, rollercoasters and so on. Admission is $8. Nearby is Bird Life Park with a huge walk-through aviary. and other Australian wildlife as well as the feathered kind. There's also a Laserama with a 50 minute laser planetarium show and a 'Shark Expo' on Seaworld Drive. At Narrowneck, by the Gold Coast Highway, is popular Macintosh Park.

Down the Coast
South of Surfers, Cascades Gardens at Broadbeach is a good barbecue spot and the Pacific Fair shopping centre is the biggest shopping centre on the Gold Coast. At Mermaid Beach, Traintasia has a huge model train collection with 200 metres of track. It's at 2480 Gold Coast Highway and is open Monday to Saturday from 9 am to 5 pm. Continue to Nobbies Beach where there's a chairlift to a fairytale castle on a cliff top over the ocean. At Burleigh Heads the small Burleigh Heads National Park has picnic tables, walking tracks and koalas and wallabies. West Burleigh is just inland from the heads and here Fleay's Fauna Reserve has an interesting collection of native wildlife. The platypus display is particularly interesting, this was the first place where this peculiar marsupial was bred in captivity. The reserve is open daily.

Morning and afternoon flocks of technicoloured lorikeets and other birds flutter in for a free feed at the Currumbin Bird Sanctuary. You can flutter in for $3. The sanctuary is just 500 metres south of Currumbin Creek and is open daily from 8 am to dusk. Other creations here are the Land of Legend, Santaland and the Sea Shell Museum on Millers Drive. At Kirra, south of the airport, Yesteryear World features a large vintage and veteran car collection. There's also a zoo here at Natureland on Appel St. Finally Coolangatta marks the southern end of the Gold Coast and the border to NSW. Coolangatta actually merges right in to Tweed Heads in NSW and you have to see the border marker to know you've gone from one state to the other.

Inland
There are plenty of other attractions just inland from the coast. At Nerang, just in from Surfers, horse enthusiasts might like The Palms where miniature horses are bred, admission is $2.50.

Near Judgeeraba on Springbrook Rd you can brush up on your boomerang technique at Hawes Boomerang Farm & Factory. Also near here war and carnage enthusiasts can try out the Gold Coast War Museum & Battle Playground. There are lots of military vehicles, open 9 am to 5 pm daily. The Air Museum at Chewing Gum Field on Guineas Creek Rd, Tally Valley, six km in from Currumbin Bridge has an interesting collection of old and very old aircraft. Everything from Tiger Moths to jet fighters of the '50s. Wednesday to Sunday the Talley Valley market is held near here.

Places to Stay

The Gold Coast strip is virtually a continuous line of motels — broken only by junk food vendors. The QGTB has accommodation leaflets which list a vast number of places strung out along the highway. They'll also book places for you. Similarly the NSW tourist office in Tweed Heads, at the other end of the strip, has accommodation information but neither these nor the motoring club booklets are totally comprehensive. There are simply too many places to hope to list them all.

One of the easiest ways to find a place to stay is simply to cruise along the Gold Coast Highway and try a few places that look cheap and have the 'vacancy' signs hanging out. They're really all much of a muchness — more money simply gets you a newer (colour) TV, better location or bigger swimming pool. Prices are very variable with season along the Gold Coast. They'll rise during the Christmas and May and August school holidays and over Easter. Some motels push prices higher over Christmas than at other holiday peaks while if there's a cold snap in May or August prices may not rise at all. As a rule of thumb a little searching should find a place at around $20 a double almost anytime of year.

A better bargain than motels, particularly if you're staying for longer, are the flats (apartments) which can also be found all along the coast. Again the lists from the tourist offices are not comprehensive. Basically a flat will have a kitchen, fridge, cooker, etc so you can fix your own food — but it won't have bed sheets, towels, soap or be regularly serviced. Particularly during the peak seasons flats will be rented on a weekly rather than overnight basis but don't let that frighten you off. Even if they won't negotiate a daily rate a $100 a week two bedroom flat is still cheaper than two $20 a night motel rooms even for just three days.

Finally there are other accommodation possibilities — hotels, guest houses even hostels. There are so many places along the Gold Coast (an estimated 3000 different places to stay) that what follows is just a tiny sample. You'll find lots of places just by wandering around.

Hostels The *Gold Coast Youth Hostel* is up at Southport — the Bellevue Youth Centre (tel 32 1777) at 103 Nerang Rd. There's room for 60 at $4 a night. There's talk of building a new youth hostel closer to the centre of Surfers.

Hotels & Motels There are some cheaper, older places right in the heart of Surfers. They're relics of Surfers' earliest days and simply haven't been over-run by the later boom years. One is, of course, the old *Surfers Paradise Hotel* (tel 59 3311) on the corner of Cavill Avenue and Gold Coast Highway. It's a straightforward old-style Australian hotel with rooms from $15/24 for singles/doubles including breakfast.

Down at the other end of Cavill Avenue, right by the seafront, is the *Ocean Court Motel* (tel 39 0644) with rooms at $18/25. It's an older motel and looks a little threadbare but the rooms are OK, you've got a balcony

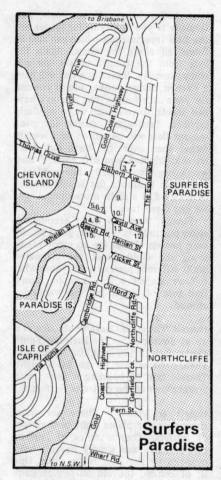

1 to Sea World
2 Bike Hire (three places)
3 Wintersun Motel
4 River Inn Motel
5 Tien Loong
6 East-West Airlines
7 Bavarian Steak House
8 TAA
9 QGTB
10 Post Office
11 Ocean Court Motel
12 Ansett & Grundy's
13 Surfers Paradise Hotel
14 Greyhound
15 Skennars

Surfers Paradise

looking right out over the beach and it certainly couldn't be any more central. Also on Cavill Avenue is *The Hub Motel* (tel 31 5559) at 21 with rooms at $25/33.

The *Hawaiian Village Motel* (tel 31 7126) at 11 Cavill Avenue is $20/26, a couple of dollars more in the high season. Frankly all prices in Surfers seem to be dependent on demand, the current temperature and what the mood of the day is. Also very central is *Hanlan Court Motel* (tel 31 5031) at 48 Hanlan St, a block over from Cavill Avenue. Here rooms are $20/25. A block over from the Gold Coast Highway at 32 Ferny Avenue is the *River Inn Motel* (tel 31 6176), another somewhat flashier motel with rooms at $22/26.

There are countless motels along the Gold Coast Highway, north and south of Surfers. Some are conveniently close to the centre. At 3205 Gold Coast Highway, just on the Southport side of the Surfer's centre, the *Winter Sun Motel* (tel 39 0833) is another straightforward motel, with a swimming pool. Nightly costs are just $18/24 and after night one it drops by a dollar a night. Some other lower priced motels around the centre of Surfers include the *Siesta Motel* (tel 39 0355) at 2827 Gold Coast Highway with rooms at $20 a double. At 2923 the *Kyora Motor Inn* (tel 31 7745) is a little more luxurious and costs $25/30. At 2985 there's *Silver Sands Motel* (tel 38 6041) at $18/22.

Down the Coast A few randomly selected places to consider, moving down the coast from Surfers: In Broadbeach the *Whitehall Motor Inn* (tel 39 9003), on the corner of Elizabeth St and the Gold Coast Highway, has rooms at \$20/30. The *Motel Casa Blanca* (tel 39 9076) at 2649 Gold Coast Highway is \$22/26.

At Palm Beach there's a string of reasonably priced places. The *Moana Motel* (tel 35 1131) at 1461 Gold Coast Highway is just \$20/22 while at 1500 the *Tally-Ho Motel* (tel 35 2955) is even cheaper at \$17/20. On the corner of 10th Avenue is the Tenth Avenue Motel (tel 35 6133) with rooms at \$20/24. The very simple *Tiki Flats* (tel 35 5001) at 1244 Gold Coast Highway has rooms from just \$8.

There's a string of low priced motels along the Gold Coast Highway at Bilinga, near the airport — all with doubles around the \$20 mark. You could try the *Surfside* at 351, the *Sundowner* at 329, *Shipmates* at 281 and *Costa Rica* at 263. There are more places at Kirra and a whole collection of places at Coolangatta including some old-fashioned guest houses like the friendly *Hillside Guest House* (tel 36 2422) at 45 McLean St, just up the hill overlooking the centre of town. Nightly cost per person is \$13 including breakfast or \$16 with dinner too. At the old *Port O'Call Hotel* (tel 36 3066) at the corner of Griffiths and McLean you can get a room for \$8, or a counter meal for \$3.

Camping There are also dozens of camp sites along the Gold Coast strip. The Gold Coast city council operates six sites from Coolangatta to Labrador, just north of Southport. Their Main Beach site is very convenient, just north of Surfers. Just south is the *Broadbeach Island Caravan Village* beside the Gold Coast Highway at Broadbeach. Camping sites along the Gold Coast are typically around \$5 to \$6 a night. Many places have on-site vans, usually from around \$12 a night. Pick up a Gold Coast and hinterland camping leaflet from the QGTB.

Places to Eat
There's plenty of junk food all along the Gold Coast but you can also find some pretty pleasant places to eat in between. What you cannot find very easily is places to eat outside. It's almost a crime that with all that sun and sea air you're almost always sitting inside listening to the air conditioning. Cavill Mall is one of the few places where dining al fresco is possible — you could even take you *McDonalds* outside into the mall here.

Or try a pizza from *Reggio Pizzeria* — small from \$5, meals from \$6 to \$7, pasta dishes from \$3.60 to \$5. *Tamari Bistro* is almost next door and somewhat similar — pastas as main courses from \$4 to \$6, regular main courses from \$6 to \$8. *Cavill Avenue Seafood* at 5 Cavill Avenue in the mall does good fish & chips which you can then take out to eat in the mall. Up at the corner of Gold Coast Highway is the *Bavarian Steak House* — straight-forward steak and chips style food, \$7 to 9. On the opposite corner you can get counter meals in the *Surfers Paradise Hotel* beer garden.

Other popular places include the *Mexican Kitchen* at 3094 Gold Coast Highway with all the usual Mexican specialities, about \$22 for two. Down at the TAA end of Cavill Avenue, *Tien Loong* (at number 57) has some of the best Chinese food on the coast and also some of the lowest prices — about \$22 for two. Still in sweet & sour land there are a couple of places in Southport. *Tum Tum* is at 50 Marine Parade, *Four Seas* is in Brighton Mall at 88 Brighton Parade. Both straightforward and reasonably priced. On West Burleigh Rd in West Burleigh you'll need a car to get to *Gunter's Farmhaus*. It serves plain, solid, down-to-earth German food and at very reasonable prices for a real restaurant meal out.

Surfers, indeed the whole Gold Coast, has plenty more places to choose from including all those junk food centres and lots of 'sophisticated' French style places offering loads of pretentiousness and prices to match. And a warning, in the off-season in particular Surfers closes down remarkably early — eat early or starve. Don't forget Tweed Heads, just across the border in NSW.

Entertainment

The *Paradise Room* in the *Surfers Paradise Hotel* is the local rock centre with low cover charges (nothing some nights, $2 on weekends) and music most nights. Down the Gold Coast Highway at Tallebudgera Bridge the *Play Room* is the local big rock scene where you can catch the top Australian rock bands. Continue to Tweed Heads where the *Twin Towns Services Club* makes lots of money from those nasty poker machines which NSW has plenty of and Queensland none at all. The profits go to putting on some big name shows.

Getting There

Air The Gold Coast is only an hour to two hours (depending on the traffic) from the centre of Brisbane by road but it also has its own busy airport with direct flights by Ansett and TAA from Sydney ($121, $91 standby), Melbourne ($185, $139 standby) and Adelaide ($209, $156 standby). You can also fly between Brisbane and Coolangatta for $53, rather a lot of money compared to the bus fare! East West Airlines have some rather cheaper fares to Sydney, they fly daily.

Bus Greyhound operate a Brisbane-Gold Coast service running down to Tweed Heads with up to 15 departures daily. The trip takes about 1½ to two hours to Surfers and costs $6.10. Note that arriving or departing Brisbane the bus does a city loop and will drop you off or pick you up at stops around the city. The Greyhound terminal is across

the river in South Brisbane. There are a half dozen services a day between Coolangatta and Murwillumbah including buses connecting with the Motorail train service from Sydney. There are also connecting Greyhound services through to Toowoomba. In Coolangatta the Greyhound terminal is on Warner St. In Surfers it's on Beach Rd in the Cavill Park Building (tel 36 2366).

Skennars have an equally frequent Brisbane-Gold Coast service and they continue down the coast to Port Macquarie and Sydney. Their Coolangatta office is on Griffith St (tel 36 2574) while in Surfers they're in the Islander Motor Inn (tel 38 9944). McCafferty's operate between the Gold Coast and Toowoomba. In Tweed Heads they're on Boundary St (tel 36 1700). You'll find Ansett Pioneer at the Ansett terminal on Cavill Avenue.

Rail You can book rail tickets at the Greyhound office in Surfers. There's a daily train service between Sydney and Murwillumbah and a connecting bus between there and the Gold Coast.

Getting Around

Bus There's a regular bus service running right up and down the Gold Coast between Southport at the north end and Tweed Heads at the south. It takes about an hour and 20 minutes from end to end and there are around 40 services a day from 7 am to past midnight. Surfers to Tweed Heads is $1.20.

Car Rental There are stacks of rent-a-car firms along the Gold Coast, particularly in Surfers. So many that making any specific recommendations or even trying to list them is pointless — just pick up any of the give-away Gold Coast guides or scan the yellow pages. All the big companies are represented here plus a host of local operators both in the Moke and small car field and in the rent-a-wreck category. Budget give you a wodge of free and reduced entry tickets with every car you rent.

Bike Rental Bob Panter's at 19 Elkhorn Avenue in Surfers rent out 10-speed bikes at $2 for the first hour and $1 for subsequent hours or $8 for the day. Or try Silly Scycles at 3102 Gold Coast Highway; at Scotty Car Rental, also in Surfers; and at Mikes Bikes, Miami. They cost $1.80 an hour, $7 a day, $15 a week. Tandems are $3, $12, $22 respectively. You can also hire motorcycles on the Gold Coast. Biking along the car crazy Gold Coast sounds a little suicidal but with a little care it's not too bad.

Airport Coolangatta Airport is the seventh busiest in Australia, right behind the state capitals. Hertz, Budget and Avis have desks at the airport but otherwise the plethora of rent-a-car agencies in Surfers are almost all unhappy about pick-ups or drop-offs from the airport.

TAA's office (tel 38 1188) is at 40 Cavill Avenue in Surfers. East West (tel 39 0877) are right across the road at 45 Cavill Avenue. Ansett (tel 38 3699) are also on Cavill Avenue but across the Gold Coast Highway, right down at the beach end of the Mall.

Tours There are all sorts of tours in and around Surfers whether it's visiting various tourist attractions or just cruising the canals along which the Surfers' richies live. Bus trips up into the mountains behind the coast cost around $18 to $20 or for $20 to $25 you can make a boat trip to Stradbroke Island. Or there are joy flights over the coast including flights in old biplane Tiger Moths.

BACK FROM THE COAST
The Gold Coast is more than just the coastal strip and the mountains of the MacPherson Ranges are probably the nicest thing about the coast.

Tamborine Mountains
Just 45 km north-west of the Gold-Coast there are spectacular waterfalls, like the Witches Falls or Cedar Creek Falls, and many small national parks in this pleasant green area. The turn off into the mountains is from Oxenden, north of Southport on the road to Brisbane. Places of interest in the mountain include Jasper Farm, a commercial fossicking site at Upper Coomera or Thunderbird Park where you can fossick for thunder eggs. At Butterfly Farm butterflies are bred in captivity, it's open in the summer months.

Nerang & South
Only nine km in from Southport this pleasant town (population 1500) in the Gold Coast hinterland has become almost a suburb of the coastal strip. Beyond here is the Advancetown Lake and Hinze Dam, named after Russ Hinze, the grossly corpulent right wing Queensland politician who is the one thing that could make almost anybody love Joh Bjelke Petersen. In the Advancetown Hotel grounds is Pioneer House, a slab wall pioneering home restored as a small museum. South of the lake is Springbrook where there's the Canyon, the 'Alpine Panorama' at the end of the road and the 'English Garden' with lots of 'old country' flavour. Natural Bridge is close to the Nerang-Murwillumbah road, an intriguing natural feature reached by a km long walking track.

The Lamington Plateau
This was one of Queensland's first national parks with forests, beautiful gorges and a great many waterfalls. It's only about 30 km in from the coast and has lots of walking tracks, many leading to superb views. There's also a walking track for the blind, equally interesting to sighted people who'd like to give their other senses a chance at communing with nature. Much of the plateau is incorporated in the Lamington

National Park which runs along the NSW border. O'Reilly's Green Mountain tops the western summits of the park. There's a tourist centre at Binna Burra Lodge, overlooking the Numinbah Valley. You can camp in the park with a permit from the ranger at Binna Burra. Information on the many walks in the park is available at Canungra.

MORETON BAY ISLANDS

In all there are said to be 365 islands in Moreton Bay, an island for every day of the year. Actually most of them are little more than sandbanks barely rising out of the water but there are a few larger islands of interest. Moreton Bay is at the mouth of the Brisbane River and the bay islands shelter this stretch of the coast. The south end of South Stradbroke is only just north of Southport, at the end of the Gold Coast, while the north end of Bribie Island is only just south of Caloundra, at the beginning of the Sunshine Coast.

North & South Stradbroke Island

Until 1896 the two Stradbroke Islands were one but in that year a storm cut through the sand spit joining the two at Jumpinpin. Today South Stradbroke is virtually uninhabited but it's a popular day-trip from the Gold Coast with a number of operators making cruises there. North Stradbroke (Straddie to its friends) is a large island with a permanet population, it's a popular weekend escape from Brisbane, despite which it is still relatively unspoilt. In 1828 Dunwich was established on the island as a quarantine station for immigrants but in 1850 an arriving ship brought cholera and the cemetery tells the sad story of the 28 victims of the outbreak that followed. Dunwich, Amity Point and Point Lookout are the three main centres on the island. The island has plenty of beaches, good surfing, some bays and inlets around Point Lookout, 18 Mile Swamp with lots of wildlife and Blue Lake and Brown Lake, the former lake in a national park.

All three centres on the island have camp sites but the only hotel is at Point Lookout. Ferries cross to North Stradbroke from Brisbane, Cleveland and Redland Bay. The vehicular ferry service from Redland Bay to Dunwich operates four to six times daily and takes about an hour to make the crossing.

Moreton Island

Further out in the bay Moreton Island is still virtually a wilderness and little visited. Apart from a few rocky headlands the island is all sand dunes with Mt Tempest, towering to 280 metres, probably the highest sandhill in the world. The island has prolific birdlife and at the northern tip of the island there's a lighthouse built in 1857. With all that sand it's hardly surprising that the sand miners have been looking at its potential and there is some controversy about whether sand mining will be permitted. Sand mining has gone on on North Stradbroke for some time.

Access to Moreton Island is by air (15 minutes, $28) or sea (2½ hours, $10) from Brisbane. Stradbroke Ferries operate from Cleveland to the south end of the island on Saturdays (returning Sunday) and from Bulimba to Korringal on Tuesdays and Fridays, from Manly on Saturdays and Sundays. There are day trips run to the island resort from Brisbane for $20 including lunch — see the Brisbane section. Tangalooma, on the western side of the island, is a popular tourist resort sited on an old whaling station. There are a number of bushwalking tracks around the resort

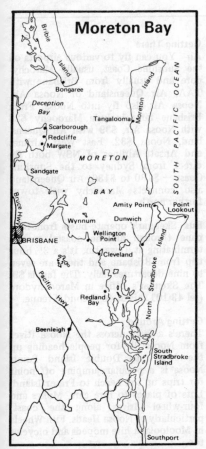

Moreton Bay

main town and buses run there from Caboolture and Brisbane three times daily.

The Bayside — north

Redcliffe (population 40,000), to the north of Brisbane, was the first settlement in Queensland as the original penal colony was established here in 1824. It was moved to Brisbane a year later, chased out by local Aboriginal opposition. The Aboriginals called the place Humpybong or 'dead houses' and the name is still applied to the peninsula. Redcliffe is now an outer suburb of Brisbane. South of Redcliffe, Sandgate is another long-running seaside resort which is now more of an outer suburb. At Beaufort Place on Deception Bay, north of Redcliffe, the Shell Bungalow is a curious house decorated with more than a million shells.

The Bayside — south

South of Brisbane is the Redland Bay area, a fertile market garden area for Brisbane. The (oh dear) Big Strawberry is at Boundary Rd, Thornlands. There's an old 1864 lighthouse at Cleveland Point and the 1853 Cleveland Courthouse is now a restaurant. The Redlands Museum is on Long St, Cleveland but is not open regular hours. Ormiston House is a very fine home built in 1862 and now open for inspection Sunday afternoons between March and November. The first commercially grown sugarcane in Queensland came from this site. At Wellington Point, Whepstead is another early home. Built in 1874 it is open on the first Sunday of the month from May to September.

There are many smaller islands in the bay including St Helena Island, once Moreton Bay's 'Alcatraz' although today only ruins of the prison buildings remain. There's a tour launch to the island every Wednesday, Thursday and on weekends at 10 am — phone 396 5113 or 266 7712 for details.

area apart from the usual resort attractions. Daily accommodation costs at the resort range from $50 to $80 per person.

Bribie Island (population 4500)

At the north of Moreton Bay, Bribie Island is 31 km long but little developed. There's a bridge across Pumicestone Passage to the island at Bellara at the southern end but little else of the island has been touched. There's good surfing on the ocean side and a calm channel towards the mainland. Bongaree is the

THE SUNSHINE COAST

The stretch of coast from Bribie Island to Tin Can Bay near Gympie is known as the Sunshine Coast. It's a far less commercial and neonlit competitor for the Gold Coast. The Bruce Highway does not run through the coast resort area, to get there you have to leave the highway from Caloundra and then turn away from the coast again at Noosa. North of Noosa it's possible to drive up the long beach to Double Island Point and Rainbow Beach, the jumping off point for Fraser Island. The coast is renowned for fine surfing and secluded beaches while inland there are extensive tropical fruit plantations and the scenic hills of the Blackall Range.

Places to Stay

There's no shortage of places to stay along the Sunshine Coast including a couple of youth hostels. The *Maroochydore Youth Hostel* (tel 43 3151) is on Schirrman Drive, Maroochydore and costs $6 a night. The Noosa or *Sunshine Beach Hostel* (tel 47 4793) is on the beach behind the Duke St shops, a beach south of Noosa itself. It costs $6 a day. Otherwise there's all sorts of camping sites, motels, guest houses, holiday flats and what have you. The *Noosa Woods council campsite*, right at Noosa Heads, is very popular with travellers.

Information

There's a Queensland Government Tourist Bureau office on Alexandra Parade, Alexandra Headland. It's open weekdays and Saturday mornings. In Noosaville there's the Noosa Information Centre on the Noosa-Tewantin Rd. There's a Sunshine Coast promotion organisation which produces a good map and information folder on the coast.

Getting There

Air You can fly to various airports on the Sunshine Coast, usually Maroochydore and usually from Brisbane with TAA, Air Queensland or Noosa Air. Noosa Air also fly into Noosa. From Brisbane fares include Maroochy $28 with Noosa Air, $39 with Air Queensland, Noosa $32. East West Airlines and Ansett Airlines of NSW both fly direct from Sydney to the Sunshine Coast — $130 to $136. Air Queensland also connects Maroochy with towns further north.

Bus Skennar's operate buses from Brisbane through all the coastal resorts terminating at Tewantin. It's a 3½ hour trip from Brisbane and there are seven to nine departures daily. The fare is $9. The Skennar's office in Maroochydore (tel 43 1011) is at 40 Second Avenue.

Getting Around

There's a ferry across the Noosa River from Noosaville for people heading up the beach to Double Island Point. Noosa is a popular jumping off point for trips up the beach to Fraser Island. Lots of places to hire cars, Mokes and four-wheel drives along the coast, particularly at Noosa Heads. Fun Wheels in Mooloolaba hire mopeds and bicycles too.

Glasshouse Mountains

Shortly after Caboolture (population 4600), a prosperous dairy centre in a region which once had a large Aboriginal population, the Glasshouse Mountains are a dramatic visual starting point for the Sunshine Coast. They're only 72 km north of Brisbane and the 10 strangely shaped volcanic outcrops were named by Captain Cook. Depending on whose story you believe he either noted the reflections of the glass-smooth rock sides of the mountains or he thought they looked like glass-furnaces in his native Yorkshire. They are popular with rockclimbers.

Caloundra (population 11,000)

At the southern end of the beach strip Caloundra's quite a fair sized town with a number of good beaches. Points of interest include the two thirds scale model replica of the *Endeavour*, on display from 9 am to 5 pm daily at 3 Landsborough Parade, Seafarer's Wharf. A replica of the Bass and Flinders boat *Tom Thumb* is also on display. Caloundra also has a Military Museum on Caloundra Rd and the World of Matchcraft with amazing models made out of hundreds of thousands of matches.

Around Maroochydore (population 10,600)

The three centres of Mooloolaba, Alexandra Headland and Maroochydore are the main growth centre for the Sunshine Coast. Mooloolaba was the landfall for the Pacific La Balsa expedition. On the corner of River Esplanade and Brisbane St there's a Shell & Marine Display while the House of Dolls is at 31 First Avenue. Alexandra Headland has a long sandy beach, good for sunbathing. At Maroochydore there's more good surfing and swimming, the Gallery of Sand Paintings at 209 Bradman Avenue and lots of pelicans on the Maroochy River. Cotton Tree is a popular camping and picnic area on the river while at Bli Bli, 10 km north, there's a 'replica' of a Norman castle. Aptly dubbed Fairyland Castle (well it does have dungeons and a torture chamber) it's open daily. A couple of km further north is Suncoast Pioneer Village; open daily it has vintage cars and Australiana. There is a long string of beaches north from Maroochydore to Noosa Heads. Beaches like Coolum, Peregian, Marcus Beach and Sunshine Beach. There are enough quiet little spots in between that you

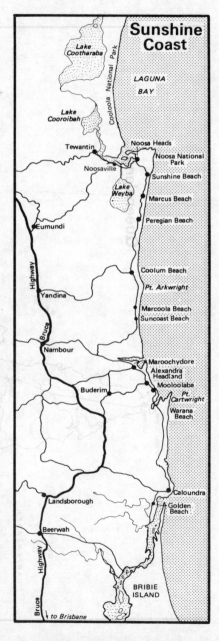

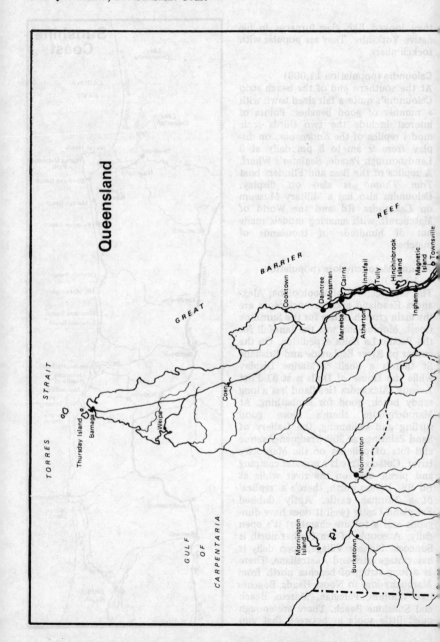

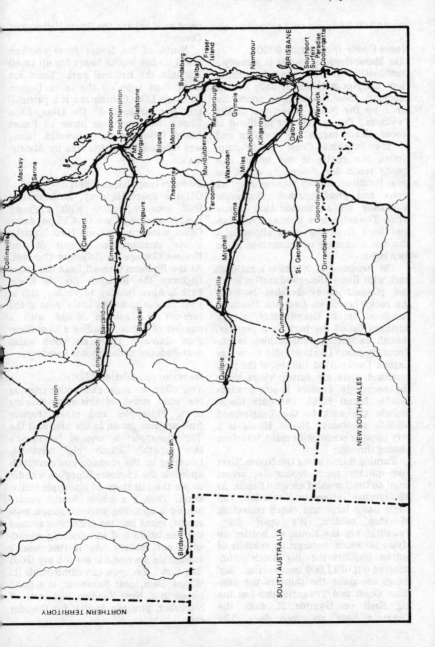

can usually find your own private beach.

Noosa Heads (population 6000)
Like Maroochydore, Noosa is actually a combination of three separate centres. Here it's Noosa Heads actually on the headland, then Noosaville a short distance up the Noosa River, and finally Tewantin. The spectacular headland at Noosa Heads marks the northern end of the Sunshine Coast beach strip. Noosa, the centre at the heads, is a trendy resort and deservedly so. It has great locations, lots of atmosphere, fine views and great beaches. Noosaville is mainly an accommodation centre while Tewantin is a quieter town further back from the coast although it also has a number of attractions in its own right.

The headland at Noosa is a national park with fine walks, good surfing spots and pleasant sandy beaches between the rocky headlands from the Heads to Sunshine Beach. Granite Bay, at the northern tip of the park, is a popular, though unofficial, nude-bathing beach. From Tingirana Lookout (also known as Laguna Lookout) at the top of the park headland there are superb views along the seemingly endless beach towards Double Island Point. The park tracks include the walk to the Tanglewood wildlife sanctuary. Noosa Heads is a very popular centre with many travellers passing through.

Turning inland along the Noosa River you quickly reach Noosaville, access point to the Teewah Coloured Sands. At 82 Gympie Terrace in Noosaville, Tall Ships has a large and varied collection of ship models, it's open daily. Tewantin has the House of Bottles on Myles St which amongst its exhibits of bottles includes the 'Big Bottle', constructed out of 17,000 beer bottles. 'Big' things are quite the thing in the Sunshine Coast and Tewantin also has the Big Shell on Gympie St. Both the Tewantin 'bigs' are open daily. The

coast road rejoins the Bruce Highway at Cooroy.

North of the Noosa River you can travel up the Noosa Lakes for up to 50 km into the national park. There are many boat trips on the lakes. Boreen Point on Lake Cootharaba is a particularly popular spot on the lakes. Eliza Fraser, who gave her name to Fraser Island following her shipwreck there, was held captive at the lake by Aboriginals.

Buderim (population 2900)
Off the Bruce Highway, Buderim is a fruit growing centre with a ginger factory open 8.15 am to 4.15 pm daily. Other attractions include Hans Wetzel's Movie Museum on Burnett St and Pioneer Cottage on Ballenger Crescent. At the Buderim turn-off from the Bruce Highway the Buderim Zoo & Koala Park is open Sunday to Friday, this is your chance to hold a koala. Also at the turn-off is Tanawah World with a number of sights including a huge fiberglass dinosaur. There are good walks near Buderim in the Footes Sanctuary.

Nambour (population 7500)
You often see sugar cane trains crossing the main street of this sugar-growing town. Pineapples and other tropical fruit are also grown in the area and the 'Big Pineapple' is one of Nambour's two superbly kitsch 'big' creations. Looming by the roadside you can climb up inside the 15-metre fibreglass wonder to see the full story of pineapple cultivation. There's a whole tourist centre behind it including souvenir shops, restaurant, snack bar, toy train rides around the plantation and an adjoining macadamia nut factory. As if that wasn't enough six km north is the (oh my God) 'Big Cow'. Yes, you can climb inside it! Wappa Dam, near Nambour, is a good picnic spot. Near Yandina, just north of Nambour, you can fossick for thunder eggs.

Cooloola Coast

North of Noose Heads, and separated from the Sunshine Coast strip by the Noosa River, is the long beach by the Cooloola National Park and running north to Double Island Point. Four-wheel drive vehicles can drive the entire length of the coast along the 50 km beach and round to Wide Bay from where you cross to Fraser Island. The beach is noted for the Teewah Coloured Sands with 200 metre high cliffs of coloured sands.

Just south of Double Island Point is the *Cherry Venture*, a 3000 tonne freighter swept on to the beach during a cyclone in 1973. It was totally undamaged but proved completely impossible to refloat despite many attempts. There's more to Cooloola park than just the coastline and beach and the inland part can be reached without the aid of four-wheel drive. There's a string of lakes connected by the Noosa River which can be explored by boat. You can also reach Lake Cootharaba, the largest lake, by road and you can hire boats at Boreen Point. Boats cross the lake from here and it's then a two-km walk to the Teewah Coloured Sands.

Inland from the Sunshine Coast

The mountains rise up fairly closely behind the coast and you can take the scenic Mapleton-Maleny road right along the ridgeline of the Blackall Range. Parks in the range include the Mapleton Falls National Park and the Kondalilla National Park with the 75 metre high Kondalilla Falls. The small town of Flaxton, eight km south of Mapleton, has a model English village and the Flaxton Inn in Tudor-style. A little south, Montville has a whole series of tourist attractions including an art gallery, a comprehensive model train collection in The Dome on Main St (daily except Wednesday) and a variety of local museums. On the road from Maleny to Kenilworth, Little Yabba Creek is a great picnic spot. Lots of birdlife up here. Continue north to Imbil with an unusual little museum and the Borumba irrigation dam nearby.

Further inland the South Burnett region includes Australia's most important peanut growing area, Kingaroy (population 5000) almost means 'peanuts' in Australia, not least because Joh Bjelke Petersen, Queensland's big peanut himself, hails from here. Near Kingaroy is Nanango (population 1100), another peanut town but with an earlier history of gold mining. North of Kingaroy, Murgon (population 2400) is the main town of the region.

HERVEY BAY AREA

North of the Sunshine Coast is the Hervey Bay area and Fraser Island. Extending from Maryborough to Bundaberg, Hervey Bay is the wide, sheltered bay in the lee of Fraser Island. There are several fair sized towns along the Bruce Highway plus the locally popular beach ports on the bay. Inland from the coast is the Burnett region, one of the earliest farming areas in the state although gold was also found here. Grains, fruit and peanuts are all grown here and Kingaroy is the home of the big peanut himself, Queensland's wonderful Joh Bjelke-Petersen.

Gympie (population 11,300)

Gympie came into existence with an 1867 goldrush and gold continued to be mined here right up to 1920. There's a 'heroic' statue to those early gold miners in the town and for a week each October there's a big Gold Rush Festival in Gympie. There's a Gold Mining & Historical Museum in the town (open

1 to 4 pm daily, 9 am to 5 pm on public holidays) and nearby is the cottage home of early Australian prime minister Andrew Fisher. From Gympie a road leads through extensive pine plantations to Tin Can Bay (population 750) and Rainbow Beach, the gateway to Fraser Island. On the Bruce Highway through Gympie there's also (ho hum) another big pineapple where you can get tourist information; also available at 204 Mary St.

Maryborough (population 20,700)

Although to most people Maryborough is simply a pause on the route north, or a jumping-off point for Fraser Island, it's actually an interesting town in its own right and well worth looking around. Today timber and sugar are Maryborough's major industries but its earlier importance as an industrial centre and seaport led to a series of imposing Victorian civic buildings, many of which survive in fine shape today. The National Trust has a free booklet detailing a walking tour around the centre and a longer driving tour. Even if you're just driving through the walking tour is an interesting and educational hour's diversion.

The town has two fine parks — Queen's Park with its unusual domed fernery, its waterfall and the National Trust classified band rotunda. Elizabeth Park is noted for its roses. The imposing post office is just one of the buildings which reflect Maryborough's early prosperity — it was built in 1869. Some of the old hotels (a number of which have good counter meals in the evenings) are also fine pieces of Victoriana and you'll find other reminders of Maryborough's early history as a port down by the river.

Maryborough's tourist information centre is located just after you cross the Mary River from Brisbane, get a copy of the walking tours booklet there. The town has a youth hostel in the City Caravan Park and a quite amazing collection of fine old pubs which do counter meals.

Hervey Bay (population 9300)

Hervey Bay also refers to the string of small towns along the coast of the bay. There's no surf here so swimming is safe for small children and the area is packed with camping and caravan parks. The coast towns include Urangan from where barges cross to Fraser Island. There's also an Aquarium at Dayman Point. On Tavistock St in Torquay there's the Urimbirra Park, a wildlife sanctuary and museum of Aboriginal and other artefacts. Pialba and Scarness both have historical museums while at Gatakers Bay there's the Parraweena Bird Sanctuary where flocks of lorikeets fly in for daily feeds at 7.30 am and 4 pm. Tourist information is available at the Hervey Bay Town Council Chambers, Torquay, from 8.30 am to 4.45 pm, Monday to Friday.

Bundaberg (population 16,000)

At the north end of Hervey Bay, a 50-km detour off the Bruce Highway, Bundaberg is a major sugar producing centre although tobacco, fruit and peanuts are also grown in the area. Some of that sugar ends up in the famous Bundaberg Rum and you can tour the local rum distillery as well as several of Bundaberg's sugar mills. Bundaberg's Historical Museum is in the School of Arts Building on Bourbong St. Boyd's Antiquatorium is open 2 to 4 pm daily and amongst the exhibits is a replica of Stephenson's original steam locomotive the Rocket. Bundaberg also has an art gallery and a doll museum.

Pioneer aviator Bert Hinkler was born in Bundaberg and made his first flight at the age of 19 in a home-made glider on Mon Repos Beach in 1912. In 1928 he made the first solo flight between England and Australia. There are a number of Hinkler memorials around the town including a cairn on top of the Hummock — a 100 metre high hill, actually an extinct volcano, which is about 10 km out of Bundaberg and is the only hill in the area. Bundaberg's Alexandra Park Zoo has a tortoise which records indicate was brought to Australia from Madagascar back in 1847. Just a couple of km out of town at 12 Ryan St, North Bundaberg, Tropical Wines produces a variety of tropical fruit wines.

Around Bundaberg there's the Dream Time Reptile Park four km out. There's good surf at Bargara (13 km) and Moore Park (23 km) while turtles nest at Mon Repos Beach, 14 km from the city. Three types of turtles lay their eggs at this beach, it's unusual since turtles generally prefer sandy islands off the coast. The season is from October to March and you're most likely to see the turtles laying their eggs around the time of the high tide at night. The turtles and their eggs are totally protected. There's a bus service operating from the city out to the various beaches.

FRASER ISLAND

The world's largest sand island is off Tin Can Bay — it measures 120 km long by about 15 km wide. The island takes its name from Eliza Fraser, the wife of the captain of a ship which was wrecked off Rockhhampton in 1836. Making their way south to look for help a party from the ship, including the captain and his wife, were captured by Aboriginals on Fraser Island (at that time known as Great Sandy Island). Only Eliza Fraser was to survive their captivity. Much more recently the island has been the subject of a controversial dispute between conservationists and sand-miners. The decision went to the conservationists after a bitter struggle.

The island is a delight for fishing, bushwalking, four-wheel drive and trail bike exponents and for lovers of nature in general. There are superb beaches, towering sand dunes and clean, clear fresh water lakes and streams. The northern part of the island is a national park. The island is sparsely populated although there were once two to three thousand Aboriginals living here. Except for 20 km of sealed road in the extreme south the island tracks are not suitable for conventional vehicles — it's four-wheel drive or motorcycles only. It's possible to drive right along the ocean beach, with occasional detours for creeks, but vehicles must be suitably equipped for travelling over soft sand. Don't let this talk of sand, sand, sand fool you. The island is carpeted in a lush rainforest and there are major pine plantations. The island also has a considerable number of lakes, creeks and streams varying from clear water lakes, some of them very deep, to marshy heathland. The island is chiefly popular for fishing, swimming can be dangerous due to severe undertows. Wildlife on the island includes dingoes and brumbies — wild horses.

Starting from the south, Hook Point, you first cross Fourth, Third, Second and First Creek, all of which drain the southern heathland. Dilli Village, the former sand-mining HQ, is between Third and Second. The beach here is aptly titled 75 mile beach, before you reach The Cathedrals, 25 km of coloured sand cliffs. Eli Creek is the largest creek on the east coast and just north of here is the wreck of the *Maheno*, a 5000 tonne liner which was blown on shore while being towed to the scrapyard in Japan in 1935. There are a number of other wrecks around the island. More than 99.9% of the island is

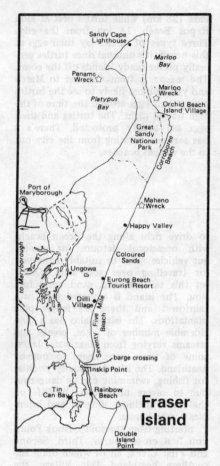

pure sand, the few outcrops of rock are all at the most easterly point — Waddy Rock, Middle Rock and Indian Head; great views from the top of the latter.

Places to Stay

Most people staying on Fraser Island will be camping although whatever your plans you should come well equipped since supplies on the island are limited and only available in a couple of places.

Starting from the south there's a *National Fitness Council* camp at Dilli Village (book in Brisbane, or tel 07 221 4905) with rooms from $7.40 per person, bed & breakfast. Eurong has supplies and petrol and motel-style accommodation at the *Eurong Beach Resort* with weekly rates. Happy Valley, where again you can get petrol, is the main accommodation area on the island with a half dozen holiday flats all with rates around $24 a day for a unit. Right up at the north, just beyond Waddy Rock, the *Orchid Beach Island Village* is a rather more expensive holiday resort — nightly costs with meals are around $50 per person. There's a campsite in the national park where camping is free with a permit from the park ranger.

Getting There & Around

If you're planning on travelling around the island solo and haven't got suitable transport you can rent four-wheel drive vehicles in Brisbane and Maryborough or at Eurong on the island. If you're going to drive through the state forest (not along the beach) you'll need a permit but this can be obtained over the phone by ringing Maryborough (07) 21 2408 or Gympie (07) 82 2244. The alternative is to take a day or longer tour — try John & Robby (tel 071 49 7018) who do tours by Land-Rover from Noosa, $35 for a full day from 6.30 am to 5.30 pm. The usual crossing point to the island is the 10 minute barge crossing from Inskip Point, reached by driving along the beach for 12 km from Rainbow Beach. To Rainbow Beach you can either take the road from Gympie or drive up the beach after crossing the Noosa River at Tewantin. You can also ferry across from Urangan on Hervey Bay — usually to Ungowa. Bus tours of the island run from here and there are a variety of cruise-bus trips available. Ring (071) 28 9370, 28 9120 or 28 9217 for details from the various operators.

Buses and trains run to Urangan from Maryborough, Monday to Friday and the trip takes 1½ to two hours. There are regular buses from Gympie to Rainbow Beach, 1¼ hours. From there you can get a bus-ferry service to the island via Inskip Point. Maryborough-Gympie buses take 1½ hours and run Monday to Friday. Islandair fly to Orchid Beach five times a week from Brisbane and Maroochy and five times a week from Maryborough and Hervey Bay. Fares are Brisbane $45, Maroochy $35, Maryborough $30, Hervey Bay $25.

NORTH TO ROCKHAMPTON
Gladstone (population 22,000)
Only recently has Gladstone attained great importance as a port, it's now one of the busiest ports in Australia handling mineral and agricultural shipping from this area of Queensland. Coal is the major mining export but alumina is also produced and exported from here. Bauxite ore is shipped to Gladstone from Weipa on the Cape York peninsula and then processed here in the world's largest alumina plant. Small Quoin Island is virtually in the harbour at Gladstone and this is also the jumping off point for Heron Island. On the Bruce Highway near Bundaberg is Gin Gin (population 900), an old pastoral town. The strange Mystery Craters are 17 km along the Bundaberg road from Gin Gin.

Heron Island
Well offshore, 70 km east of Gladstone or about 100 km from Rockhampton, Heron Island is right on the Barrier Reef. It's almost the most southerly of the reef islands. Heron is a real coral cay and noted for its many sea birds and for the turtles which lay their eggs here from October to April of each year. The baby turtles hatch out from December to May. The tiny island, only a km across, is a national park with a vast variety of marine life on its surrounding reefs but due to its great distance from the mainland it's one of the more expensive islands to visit. The chopper trip out to the island will set you back $125 return for starters. When you get there you're up for a minimum of $60 a day per person for accommodation with meals and the accommodation standards are better described as 'adequate' rather than 'luxurious'. But it's not creature comforts or easy accessibility which brings people here. Heron Island is famed for its superb skindiving and each November the Barrier Reef Divers Festival takes place here over four weeks.

Burnett Highway Route
As an alternative to the Bruce Highway route you can travel north on the Burnett Highway, further inland. If you turn inland from Gympie you soon reach Gayndah (population 1600), one of the oldest towns in the state and the citrus growing centre of Queensland The District Historical Museum is open on weekends and public holidays. On the way to Gayndah you pass by or can divert to Kilkivan, a popular fossicking area, the Kinbombi Falls with a series of swimming pools and the Ban Ban Springs. You can also reach Gayndah from Gympie or Maryborough via Biggenden, passing the volcanic crater lakes of the Coulston Lakes National Park on the way. Biggenden was once a gold mining centre. On the way to Biggenden from Maryborough you can visit the Woocoo Historical Society Museum in Broweena, open Sunday afternoons or borrow the keys

from the post office.

North of Gayndah is Mundubbera (population 1100), another citrus centre and from here you can also reach the Auburn River National Park. Eidsvold (population 600) was a prosperous gold town for 12 years from 1888. Monto (population 1600) is in the heart of Rockhampton's cattle country. The spectacular Cania Gorge is 25 km north of the town. Just 142 km from Rockhampton is Biloela (population 4600) a busy irrigated agricultural centre. Mt Scoria, 14 km from the town, is a solidified volcano core. From here you continue through Mt Morgan to Rockhampton.

ROCKHAMPTON (population 56,000)

Australia's 'beef capital' sits astride the Tropic of Capricorn, there's a marker beside the road as you enter Rocky from the south. Rockhampton had a relatively small early gold rush but cattle soon became the big industry in this area. A statue of a Braford bull marks the southern approach to the city and a Brahman bull to the north.

Information & Orientation

The QGTB is at 119 East St. There's also a Capricorn Tourist Organisation at the junction of the Bruce, Burnett and Capricorn Highways in Curtis Park near the Tropic of Capricorn spire. The RACQ is at 134 William St. Rockhampton straddles the Fitzroy River with the city centre along the river to the south. The long Fitzroy Bridge connects the old central part of Rockhampton with the newer suburbs to the north.

Around Town

There are many fine early buildings in the town to remind of those pioneer days — particularly on Quay St where you'll find one of the best Victorian street frontages in Australian. More than 20 old buildings along the street bear National Trust classification and there's a National Trust walking tour brochure on Rockhampton. There's an art gallery in the Pilbeam Theatre complex on Victoria Parade. Rockhampton also has one of those water slide complexes (just like almost every other fair sized town on the Queensland coast). It's in North Rockhampton.

Near the airport St Aubin's Herb Farm is in an old 1870 homestead. There's an excellent tropical collection in the Botanic Gardens on Spencer St on the edge of the Athelstane Range. It overlooks Murray Lagoon, just three km from the city centre to the south, near the airport. Established in 1869 it's said to be the finest tropical garden in Australia and has a walk-through aviary and a small zoo.

Places to Stay

Hostel The *Rockhampton Youth Hostel* (tel 27 5288) costs $5. It's a new building across the river to the north of town — about a 20-minute walk from the centre. Cross the bridge, turn right then left and keep walking along Musgrave St (parallel to the main highway) until you hit Macfarlane St. Except on Sundays you can also get there on a High St bus. Note that travelling south, Ansett Pioneer and Greyhound buses arrive in Rocky at terrible hours of the night. You can also book the Great Keppel hostel through the Rocky Hostel but the island hostel tends to be heavily booked so you have to plan ahead.

Hotels & Motels There are plenty of old fashioned hotels around the centre but nothing of great value in the motel line. On Quay St by the bridge the *Criterion Hotel* (or rather Bonaparte's Criterion Hotel) (tel 2 1225) is a magnificent old building, one of the finest of the Quay St frontages. Hotel rooms here are $16/24 but there is also a new motel section at $26/30, about the best motel value in Rocky.

On the corner of East and Denham Sts the *Oxford Hotel* (tel 2 12837) is a straightforward central hotel with rooms at $13 per person, breakfast costs $3.50. On 49 William St, at the corner with Bolsover, the *Crown Hotel* (tel 2 1684) is a bit cheaper at $13/24 but although the rooms are OK in a threadbare sort of way in other respects it's rather shoddy. The *Scariff Hotel* (tel 27 1433) is on Fitzroy St at the corner with Bolsover. It's not special, once again, but OK, once again, at $12 per person. Breakfast and other meals are available.

You'll find lots of motels and camp sites on the Bruce Highway into Rockhampton from the north and south. On the south side the *Lodge Motel* (tel 27 3130) is at 100 Gladstone Rd and has rooms at $27/31. On the north side there's the *Post Office Hotel/Motel* (tel 27 3899) on the corner of Musgrave and Burnett Sts with rooms at $21/26. The *Kalka Hotel/Motel* (tel 28 5666) is at the corner of Lakes Creek Rd and Water St on the 'back road' to Yeppoon. Rooms here are $27/32. Finally the *Park Avenue Hotel/Motel* (tel 2 4251) is on 30 Main St, Park Avenue, north of the river also, and has rooms at $23/33.

Camping There are half a dozen campsites in Rocky including the attractively sited *Municipal Caravan Park*, just across the river from the centre and right beside the bridge. Camping here costs $3.50. Most of the other sites also have on-site vans as well as camping facilities although camping is generally a bit more expensive and none of them are so conveniently situated. There are a clump of them on the Bruce Highway north of town towards the Yeppoon turn-off. *Ramblers Caravan Park* has camping at $5, on-site vans at $17 and holiday units at $31.

Places to Eat
Rocky's a counter meal centre, it's also an early closer. So if you're after a meal out make it reasonably early and you'd better be thinking of making it a steak — this is cattle country after all. Starting at the top there are several places offering slightly flashier and more expensive versions of the counter meal staples. Main courses are in the $6 to $8 range, desserts $2.50 in the *Heritage Tavern* on the corner of Quay and Denham Sts. This used to be the Commercial Hotel before it went through a total restoration-renovation. Much the same food is available for a couple of dollars cheaper in the public bar.

Also on the Quay, by the bridge, the *Criterion Hotel* has the usual counter meal menu and prices from $3.50 to $5.50 (lobster $8) — most dishes are around $5 and desserts $1.50. You can eat in the 'restaurant', the lounge bar or, for a dollar or so less, in the public bar. It's reasonable, not excellent, counter food and is open until 9 pm.

Winsall's on Alma St call their counter meal section the Spanish Restaurant but it too has all the standard dishes with prices in the $5 to $6 bracket. You can find counter food at almost every other hotel in town. The *Scariff Hotel* on the corner of Fitzroy and Bolsover Sts is $3.50 to $5 for most main courses, some like fish & chips or chicken in the basket are only $2.50. In the lounge bar section it's about a dollar more. They're open lunchtimes

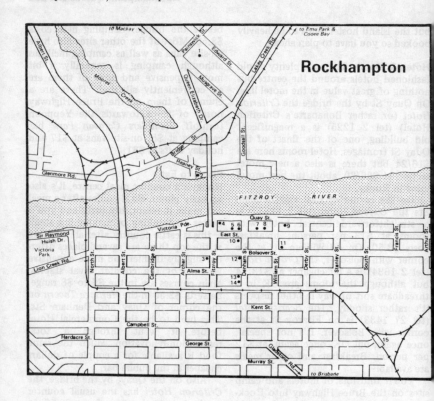

Rockhampton

FITZROY RIVER

Monday to Friday and in the evenings every day of the week. Or try the *Oxford Hotel* or the *Crown Hotel*, both with cheap counter meals in the $3 to $4 bracket.

Pubs apart there's the *Texacana Burger Bar* next to Winsall's, where you can get all manner of burgers, fast food and pizzas. Not bad.

Getting There

Air You can fly to Rocky from all the usual places along the coast. Fares include Brisbane $104 ($78 standby), Mackay $76, Townsville $113 and Cairns $144. In Rockhampton TAA (tel 31 0555) are at 75 East St. Ansett (tel 31 0755) are at 137 East St.

Rail The six times weekly Sunlander runs from Brisbane through Rockhampton to Cairns. Brisbane-Rockhampton takes 9½ hours, it's another 24 hours north to Cairns. Twice weekly the Midlander runs between Rockhampton, Longreach and Winton. It's five hours to Emerald ($15 in economy), 16 hours to Longreach ($47) and 20 hours to Winton ($78).

Bus Greyhound and Ansett Pioneer both travel up the Queensland coast

1 Youth Hostel
2 Municipal Caravan Park
3 Scariff Hotel
4 Criterion Hotel
5 TAA
6 Oxford Hotel
7 QGTB
8 Ansett

9 Heritage Tavern
10 Post Office
11 Crown Hotel
12 Leichardt Hotel
13 Winsall's Hotel
14 Texacana
15 Railway Station

between Brisbane and Cairns, and vice versa, on a daily basis. Brisbane-Rocky takes about 12 hours for $45. Coming south from Cairns it's 18 hours for $65, from Townsville about 12 hours, from Mackay about 5½ hours. Note that the southbound buses arrive at an ungodly hour in the middle of the night with either operator. Greyhound also operate inland from Rockhampton to Longreach — four times weekly, nine hours, $36. McCafferty's also operate buses on the coast between Brisbane and Rocky, twice daily. Their service between Rocky and Mackay operates inland through Emerald and Moranbah, rather than the direct route closer to the coast.

Getting Around

Rocky's airport is fairly conveniently situated about five km from the centre, $3 by taxi. Avis, Budget and Hertz all have desks at the airport. Rocky has a fairly modern railway station with luggage lockers, it's a fair walk from the city centre. From the centre take a High St bus for the youth hostel, north of the river. Rockhampton has a reasonably comprehensive local bus network — timetables from the town hall for 20c.

Buses operated by Young's Bus Service run to Yeppoon via Emu Park and Cooee Bay. There's up to five services daily on weekdays, only two or three on weekends and the fare is $2.40. They also operate a bus to Mt Morgan, see Mt Morgan for more details.

AROUND ROCKHAMPTON
North of the City

The rough and rugged Berserker Range starts 26 km north of Rocky, here you'll find several limestone caves. There are regular tours around Olsen's (or the Capricorn) Cave and Cammoo Cave, both just a few km off the Bruce Highway. Entry to either cave group is $1.75. Nearby you can also visit the Gangalook Museum with everyday items from the pioneering period. Gemland is just past the Yeppoon turn-off and has a rock and gemstone collection and gem cutting and polishing displays. The

Queensland gem fields are inland from Rockhampton.

Mt Morgan (population 4000)

The Mt Morgan mines are 38 km southwest of Rockhampton. The gold and copper mine is open cut and this is one of the biggest holes in the ground in Australia. The mine has been worked off and on for a century and is now nearly 300 metres deep. The town's population was much larger earlier this century. Inspections of the mine take place at 9.30 am and 1.30 pm daily. There's a museum on East St (10 am to 1 pm weekdays, 10 am to 12 noon Saturdays and 2 to 4 pm Sundays) and a Tourist Information Centre in the School of Arts on Morgan St. Young's

Bus Service operates a regular bus from Rockhampton three times daily on weekdays, twice on Saturdays. The fare is $3.

CAPRICORN COAST
The 47 km stretch of coast east of Rockhampton is known as the Capricorn Coast. The main town is Yeppoon (population 5600) which has a small Shell Museum. North of Yeppoon the Japanese Iwasaki Resort is under development — it's planned to be 'big'. There's a flora and fauna sanctuary at Cooberrie Park, 15 km north of Yeppoon (open daily). At Cooee Bay, a couple of km south of Yeppoon, the annual Australian cooeeing (and husband calling) championships are held each August — the judges row out to sea to determine who can 'cooee' the furthest. Rossyln Bay Harbour is the jumping off point for Great Keppel island. At Double Head there's a blowhole, good views from Wreck Point and Bluff Point, and at Emu Park, 14 km from Yeppoon, there's the 'Singing Ship' — a series of drilled tubes and pipes which emit a low, moaning sound when there's a breeze blowing.

Places to Stay
If you're planning to just day trip to Great Keppel you may decide that it's better to stay in Yeppoon, 40 km from Rockhampton. It's a quiet seaside resort with cheaper accommodation and in summer it's much cooler than Rock-

hampton. There are half a dozen caravan parks along the coast from Yeppoon to Emu Park. The *Island View Park* at Kinka Beach, *Cool Waters* at the Esplanade and *Lakeside* at Causeway all have on-site vans or cabins. The *Poinciana Tourist Park* at Cooee Bay has cabins for $18 and holiday flats for $20.

Yeppoon doesn't have Rocky's range of old hotels but it's much better equipped for motels. Try the *Sail-Inn Motel* (tel 39 1130) on James St with rooms at $20/27 for singles/doubles. The pleasant *Tidewater Motel* (tel 39 1632) is on Normanby St right down by the seafront. It's similarly priced and rooms have cooking facilities, some units for four or more are also available. There are also lots of holiday flats and units all along the Capricorn Coast — the best routine is just to cruise along the coast and look for them.

Places to Eat
There are quite a few places to eat around Yeppoon including the *Reef 'n Beef* on Normanby St. It's just a takeaway place with a few tables but does good quality and well-prepared food. The *Railway Hotel*, further up James St has an extensive menu but the food can be rather erratic.

GREAT KEPPEL ISLAND
Owned by TAA, Great Keppel has been heavily promoted as the young peoples'

resort — 'get wrecked on Great Keppel', 'after a holiday on Great Keppel you'll really need a holiday', etc. TAA has a

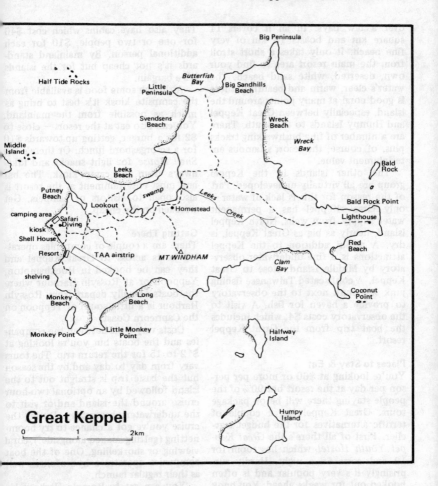

Great Keppel

0   1   2km

variety of package tours to Great Keppel, seven days there will cost you around $500 to 650, plus the air fares to Rockhampton. The package price includes the short flight Rockhampton-Great Keppel and back, all accommodation and meals. Great Keppel is heavy on entertainment — a resident rock band, lots of planned activities, guaranteed exhaustion! People who go there usually reckon it's a lot of fun.

Great Keppel is, however, also one of the easiest and cheapest islands to visit and although it's not actually on the reef it's the equal of most other islands up the coast. Plus, and this is a very big plus, Keppel is an island where it's actually possible to stay really cheaply. The island is 13 km offshore and it's one of my favourites — big enough that you won't see the whole place in an afternoon but small enough to explore over a few days. In all it covers 14 square km and boasts 18 km of very fine beach. It only takes a short stroll from the main resort area to find your own, deserted, white sand beach. The water's clear, warm and beautiful, there is good coral at many points around the island, especially between Great Keppel and Humpy Islands to the south. There are a number of fine bushwalking tracks plus, of course, the resort's famous entertainment value.

The other islands in the Keppel group are all virtually undeveloped. Part of the reason for this is lack of water — only Great Keppel has a permanent water supply from wells. North Keppel island, nearly as big as Great Keppel, is dry. A recent addition to the Keppel attractions is a fine underwater observatory by Middle Island, close to Great Keppel. A confiscated Taiwanese fishing junk was sunk next to the observatory to provide a haven for fish. A visit to the observatory costs $4, which includes the boat trip from the Great Keppel resort.

Places to Stay & Eat
You're looking at $60 or more per person per day at the resort but 90% of the people staying there will be on package tours. Great Keppel has a couple of terrific alternatives for the budget traveller. First of all there's the *Great Keppel Youth Hostel* which has room for 12 and costs $5 a night. Hardly surprisingly it's very popular and is often booked out for weeks ahead. You book the island hostel through the Rockhampton YH but if you want to be certain of a berth it's wise to book through the YH headquarters in Brisbane.

The other alternative is the *Wapparaburra Haven Caravan Park* (tel 39 1907) where you can camp for $5 for two people, $3 for each additional person.

They also have cabins which cost $40 for one or two people, $10 for each additional person. By mainland standards it's not cheap but for the islands it's a bargain.

Although some food is available from the campsite kiosk it's best to bring as much as possible from the mainland. You can also eat at the resort — close to $2 for a burger, getting up towards $10 for a smorgasbord lunch. Or there's the *Shell House* for light snacks and takeaways from the camp kiosk. The bar and most entertainment at the resort is also open to visitors or campers. Get wrecked on the cheap.

Getting There
There are a couple of companies operating boats across to Great Keppel and they can be booked in Rockhampton, Yeppoon or at Rossyln Harbour where the boats actually depart from. Rossyln Harbour is a little south of Yeppoon on the Capricorn Coast.

Costs vary a bit between the companies and the boats but you're looking at $12 to 15 for the return trip. The tours vary from day to day and by the season but the basic trip is straight out to the island followed by an optional two-hour cruise around the island and/or visit to the underwater observatory. During the cruise you've got a chance to try boomnetting (getting soaked alongside!), coral viewing or snorkelling. One of the boat companies operates a hydrofoil as well as their regular launch.

You can get to Rossyln Harbour by car (there's a daily car parking charge), by bus to Yeppoon from Rockhampton ($2.40) and then by taxi, or by a connecting bus to the boat service, which adds about $3 to the tour cost.

Flying to Great Keppel costs $33 from Rockhampton one-way. There are also flying day trips from about $40.

CAPRICORNIA

The country stretching inland from Rockhampton takes its name from its position, straddling the Tropic of Capricorn. There's a road that runs inland, virtually along the tropic, as far as Longreach (562 km inland) before turning north-west to meet the Townsville-Mt Isa road at Cloncurry. Although the area first began to be opened up by miners, chasing gold and copper around Emerald and sapphires around Anakie, it is cattle that provides the area's living today plus the enormous coal deposits starting to be exploited. The region straddles the central highlands and there are some interesting Aboriginal rock paintings to be found south in the Carnarvon Ranges.

Emerald (population 3200)

Directly inland from Rockhampon, Emerald is known as the hub of the central Queensland highlands. It's an attractive town with streets lined with Moreton Bay Figs and a 1901 railway station classified by the National Trust. Cattle raising and agriculture are the main industries. The country west of Emerald is noted for sapphires and other gems found around Anakie and other small towns in the region. There's an arts and crafts centre in Rubyvale and the Desperado Mine can also be visited. On the way to Emerald from Rocky you pass through the coal mining centre of Blackwater (population 4600). North of Emerald is Clermont (population 1600) with the huge Blair Athol open-cut coal mine. There are a number of other coal mines in the Capricornia area or near to Mackay. South of Emerald is Springsure, near which is the Old Rainworth Fort at Burnside.

Carnarvon National Park

Reached from Rolleston, south of Emerald, or from Injune, north of Roma, the rugged Carnarvon National Park is noted for its many Aboriginal rock paintings and carvings, some of which are very large. The park is in the middle of the Great Dividing Range and has some of the most spectacular scenery in Australia. The Carnarvon Gorge is particularly impressive.

Around Barcaldine

Barcaldine (population 1400), between Emerald and Longreach, is another cattle centre and the town also has a historical museum. North of here is Aramac (population 400), another small pastoral centre, while south is Blackall (population 1600). Near Blackall is Black's Palace, an Aboriginal site with burial caves and rock paintings.

Longreach (population 3300)

A modern and prosperous country town, Longreach's human population is considerably outnumbered by the neighbouring sheep population which is close to a million; there are a fair few cattle too. Although the Queensland and Northern Territory Air Services, perhaps better known as Qantas today, commenced operations in Winton it was in Longreach that it got into its stride. The first aircraft 'factory' in Australia was also here — six DH-50 biplanes were assembled here in 1926. The original Qantas hangar still stands at the airport.

Longreach was also the starting point for one of Queensland's most colourful early crimes when in 1870 a bushranger sporting the title 'Captain Starlight' rounded up 1000 head of cattle (not his own needless to say) and trotted them a mere 2400 km south through impossibly inhospitable country to South Australia where he sold them. He then made his way back to Queensland, was arrested and, unbelievably, acquitted. Perhaps for sheer nerve.

There is a youth hostel in Longreach.

Winton (population 1300)

On the road from Rockhampton via Emerald and Longreach to Mt Isa, Winton today is a major sheep raising centre and also the railhead from which cattle are transported out after being brought here from the channel country by road train. The small town has two claims to fame. Back in 1895 Australia's most famous poet-songwriter Banjo Patterson was on a station near here when he wrote Australia's best known ditty — Waltzing Matilda. Later Qantas started its operations here. These two diverse influences are united in the Qantilda pioneer museum! The countryside around Winton is rough and rugged with much wildlife, particularly brolgas, and sites with Aboriginal paintings.

ROCKHAMPTON-MACKAY

The 343 km from Rockhampton to Mackay is one of the most boring stretches of the entire east coast Highway 1 run. For over 200 km from Marlborough north there is virtually nothing apart from a handful of roadhouses and a camp site at Lotus Creek. Finally the road drops down over the range to the much more lush country around Sarina. This is the start of the sugar producing area around Mackay and there are also some fine beaches near the town. The main highway from Marlborough to Sarina is not the Bruce Highway — that runs closer to the coast and is actually a little shorter but since the first 80-odd km are very rough it has not been used so much. Sealing of this route is, however, nearing completion and more people will probably use it in the future.

Sarina (population 2800)

On the Bruce Highway, just 37 km south of Mackay, Sarina is noted for its excellent beaches and for the sugar growing carried out so extensively around here. The Hay Point bulk loading terminal for coal is between here and Mackay. The coal produced from the gigantic coal fields inland from Mackay is railed down to the coast and exported from here.

MACKAY (population 31,600)

Australia's 'sugar capital', Mackay is surrounded by sugar cane and processes a third of the total Australian sugar crop. The sugar is then loaded at the world's largest bulk sugar loading terminal. Sugar has been grown here since 1865. It's also a major coal port where a large part of Australia's coal production is shipped out, principally to Japan. The attractive town centre has many trees introduced from Sri Lanka.

Information

Mackay's tourist information centre is a Mackay attraction all by itself — located on the Bruce Highway on the south side of town it's housed in a Taiwanese fishing junk which was seized in 1976 when it was caught poaching clams within Australian territorial waters. The centre is open seven days a week from 9 am to 5 pm. The QCTB (tel 57 2292) is on River St, just down from the Forgan Bridge. It's open weekdays and Saturday mornings. The RACQ is at 214 Victoria St.

Orientation

Mackay is situated on the Pioneer River,

the main streets of the town are laid out in a simple grid on the south side of the river. The railway station is only a few blocks back from the centre and the airport is also fairly close to the city. The newer suburbs of Mackay are north of the river. Mackay's popular beaches are further north of the city.

Around Town

Good views over the harbour can be found at Mt Basset or at Rotary Lookout on Mt Oscar in North Mackay. Bayersville Zoo, by Harbour Rd, allows visitors to help feed the animals at 3.30 pm daily. There are Botanic Gardens on Goldsmith St. From Mt Basset there are good views over the city and harbour. The Rotary Lookout on Mt Oscar also gives good views.

On weekdays at 3 pm you can make a 1½ hour tour of the Pleystowe Sugar Mill, 19 km from Mackay, during the mid-June to December cane crushing season. At 10.15 am and 3 pm you can also visit the Mackay Harbour sugar bulk terminals. Mackay is a jumping off point for Barrier Reef cruises — particularly to Brampton Island. Mackay has good beaches at Blacks, Bucasia, Illawong, Lamberts and Shoal Point.

Places to Stay

Hostel Mackay's *youth hostel* (tel 59 3209) is rather inconvenient. It's 10 km from the city at Fairleigh, on the Bruce Highway across from a sugar mill and next to a church. There's very little else out there! Nightly cost is. $4 and Greyhound and Ansett Pioneer buses will drop you off at the hostel on request. Alternatively you can get there on Mackay-Seaforth buses from River St. The *Tropical Caravan Park* (tel 52 1211), about a km beyond the junk info centre on the south side of the city, has a couple of on-site vans held for hostelers until 9 pm. A bed costs $5 or $6 if you end up with the whole caravan to yourself.

For women only there's a *CWA Hostel* centrally located at 43 Gordon St. Nightly costs are $6 in a share twin or $10 for a single room.

Hotels There's the usual selection of older hotels around the centre. The *Ambassador Hotel* (tel 57 2368) is at 2 Sydney Rd and has singles/doubles at $14/17. *McGuires* (tel 57 2419) is on Wood St between Victoria and River St and costs $17/22. On the corner of Victoria and Peel Sts the *Austral Hotel* (tel 57 2639) costs from $12/18.

Motels The *Paradise Lodge Motel* (tel 51 1348) is conveniently central at 19 Peel St and pleasantly economical at $18/24 for singles/doubles. The rooms are straightforward but they're all aircon and have a TV and tea/coffee making facilities. A couple of blocks over at 40 MacAlister St the *International Lodge* (tel 51 1022) is even more central, similarly equipped and costs $19/26.

There's a whole string of motels along Nebo Rd, the main highway out of Mackay which runs past the junk and on to Rockhampton. Some cheaper motels along here include *Cool Palms* (tel 57 5477) at 4 Nebo Rd, fairly close to the centre. Nightly costs are $27/32 including a 'tropical' breakfast. Further along *Hi-Way Holiday Units* (tel 52 1172) on the corner of Webberley St and Nebo Rd is good value at $20/24 and there's a pool. Opposite the junk on Nebo Rd, the *Boomerang Hotel* (tel 52 1755) has motel units at $21/26.

Camping The *Central Caravan Park* (tel 57 6141) is at 15 Malcomson St, just across the river in North Mackay. Camping costs $4 and there are also on-site vans for $12 and cabins for $14. At 152 Nebo Rd on the way out of town the *Premier Holiday Village* is well-equipped with camp sites at $4, on-site vans at

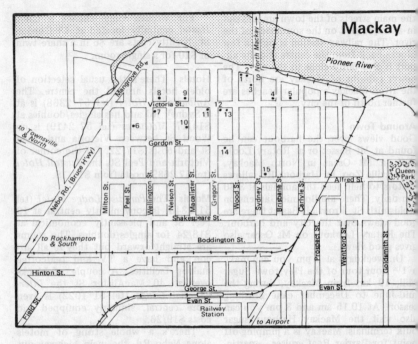

Mackay

$15, cabins at $20 and holiday units at $29. There are quite a few other sites in and around Mackay, at the beach suburbs and up the Hibiscus coast.

Places to Eat

Counter Meals The *Hotel Mackay* on the corner of Wellington and Victoria Sts, does cheap counter meals ($3.50 to $4) at lunch time Monday to Sunday and evenings too Wednesday to Sunday. The *Ambassador Hotel* overlooks the river from the corner of River and Sydney Sts. There's a terrace upstairs which is a popular place for a drink and the hotel does counter style food every night of the week in the $6 to $8 bracket.

The big *Hotel Whitsunday* on the corner of Victoria and Macalister Sts does pretty basic counter meals for $3 to $4 in the public bar or fancier food

with a serve-yourself salad table in the *Bistro Room*. Other pubs with counter food in the $3 to $5 range include *McGuire's* on Wood St and the *Metropolitan Tavern* on Gordon St.

If you're staying in one of the motels or campsites along Nebo Rd there are a couple of places which do counter meals. The *Shamrock Hotel* is at 12 Nebo Rd and does meals at $4 to $5. Further along at the *Boomerang Hotel* opposite the junk, meals are slightly more expensive.

Snack Bars & Take-Aways On Wood St the *Gourmet* does good looking sandwiches with pitta bread and other nice things. *Number 7* at 7 Wood St does straightforward snacks and sandwiches. Further from the river at 94 Wood St the *Tourist Snack Bar* is a big place with good burgers and other fast foods. C

1 Post Office	9 Hotel Whitsunday
2 QGTB	10 International Lodge
3 Ambassador Hotel	11 Ian Wood Travel (buses)
4 Hideaway Restaurant	12 TAA
5 Pizza Napoli	13 Ansett
6 Paradise Lodge Motel	14 CWA Hostel
7 Hotel Mackay	15 Al Pappas
8 RACQ	

try the *Capitol Cafe* at 36 Sydney St for sandwiches, fruit salad and the like.

Restaurants *Al Pappas* on the corner of Alfred and Sydney Sts, a couple of blocks back from the central area, is a pleasant little place with pizzas and other Italian food to eat there or take-away. The pizzas are really very good, small in the $3.50 to $4 bracket, large in the $4 to $5 range. Plus there are pastas dishes from $4 and up. Similar food can be found at *Pizza Napoli* at 42 Victoria St which again has a take-away and eat there section. Main courses here are around $6.50.

Hideaway at the corner of Brisbane and Victoria Sts is a pleasant although pricier place with main courses at $7.50.

Entertainment
The *Ambassador Hotel*, with its pleasant rooftop terrace, is a popular place for a drink. Entertainment and no cover charge at the *Hotel Mackay*. There's a disco in the evenings at the *Metropolitan Tavern* on Gordon St. The *Pacific Hotel* out at the beach at Eimeo also has entertainment.

Getting There
Air Mackay is on the regular Brisbane-Cairns coastal route. Fares include Cairns $116, Townsville $82, Rockhampton $76 and Brisbane $134 (standby $100). In Mackay Ansett (tel 57 1555) are at 97 Victoria St, TAA (tel 57 1444) are at 105-109 Victoria St.

Rail The six times weekly Sunlander between Brisbane and Cairns goes through Mackay, either at 4 am northbound or just before 11 pm southbound. The fare from Brisbane is $62 in 1st class, $42 in economy and the trip takes 21 hours. Southbound it takes 16 hours from Cairns.

Bus Ansett Pioneer and Greyhound both operate through Mackay on their daily services along the coast. From Brisbane it takes 17 hours for $55, from Cairns it's 13 hours for $49, from Townsville five hours for $28. McCafferty's also operate Brisbane-Mackay but their service operates by the inland route from Rockhampton, through Emerald and Moranbah. Rockhampton-Mackay is $30. Ian Wood Travel (tel 57 2858) on Victoria St handle all three companies in Mackay.

Getting Around
Airport Mackay's airport is conveniently close to the centre, count on about $2 to $2.50 for a taxi to the city. Avis, Budget and Hertz have counters at the airport.

Tours There are lots of half day and day tours in and around Mackay to the sugar mills, the national parks around Mackay and other local attractions. Broughs Scenic Tours (tel 51 2150) are the main operators. Air tours include scenic flights out to the reef, flights landing on Bushy Atoll and on alternate Mondays you can go along on regular station runs to remote stations and coalfields inland from Mackay.

MACKAY TO PROSERPINE

There are a number of places of interest along the road from Mackay to Townsville but the main attraction is the beautiful Whitsunday Island group. To reach the Whitsundays you turn off the Bruce Highway at Proserpine and drive down to Shute Harbour, the jumping off point for Whitsunday cruises. See the Whitsunday section for more details. You can, if you've got the dollars to spare, fly to the Whitsundays from Mackay, also to Brampton Island which is about mid-way between Mackay and the Whitsundays.

Coal Mines

The massive open cut Queensland coal mines are about 200 km inland from Mackay at Blackwater, Goonyella and Peak Downs. Much of the coal is exported from the Hay Point coal terminal, 40 km south of Mackay. Free tours of the mines are available but it is usually necessary to phone ahead and book. The Blackwater tour bus departs from the main office on Wednesday at 10 am (tel 82 5166). The Goonyella tour bus departs from the Moranbah Town Square at 10 am Tuesday, the Peak Downs bus from the same location at 10 am Thursday. Ring 50 7122 for Goonyella, 50 7233 for Peak Downs.

Near Mackay

The Eungella National Park is the largest national park in Queensland, it's directly inland from Mackay straddling the Clarke Range. There are fine lookouts in the park, 85 km from Mackay and this is one place where you've got a good chance of seeing platypuses. The Eungella road runs through the Finch Hatton Gorge. Cape Hillsborough National Park is 55 km up the coast and

has walking tracks through the rainforest plus good beaches and camping areas. One of the most popular walking tracks is the Hidden Valley trail. To get to the park turn off just before Seaforth from where it is 10 km on a gravel road to the park entrance.

Brampton Island

Mountainous Brampton Island covers eight square km — the island is a national park and wildlife sanctuary with lush forests and surrounded by coral reefs. The island is part of the Cumberland group and is connected to nearby Carlisle Island by a reef which you can walk across at low tide. Accommodation on Brampton costs $40 to $70 per person. The island is reached by air or launch ($20 return) from Mackay. There are day trips from Mackay to the island.

Newry Island

There are day trips three days a week from Victor Creek to pleasant Newry Island — a little known tropical island with good swimming, bushwalks and plenty of koala bears. Departures are at 11 am on Wednesday, Saturday and Sunday, accommodation is available on the island.

Sugar Growing

Sugar is easily the most visible crop from Mackay right past Cairns up the Queensland coast. Sugar was a success almost from the day it was introduced in the region back in 1865 but the early days of the Queensland sugar industry had a distinctly unsavoury air as the plantations were initially worked by Pacific islanders who were virtually shanghaied to work on the canefields. 'Blackbirding', as this slave trading was known, took a long time to be stamped out. Today cane growing is a highly mechanised business and visitors are welcome to inspect the crushing plants during the harvesting season from August. The most spectacular part of the operation is the firing of the cane-fields in which rubbish is burnt off by spectacular night time fires — which also have the advantage of chasing off snakes and other unwelcome inhabitants of the fields.

Mechanical harvesters cut and gather the cane which is then transported to the sugar mills, often on narrow gauge railway lines laid through the canefields. These lines are a familiar sight through-out the cane country. The cane is then shredded and passed through a series of crushers. The extracted juice is heated and cleaned of impurities and then evap-orated to form a syrup. The next process reduces the syrup to molasses and low grade sugar. Further refining stages end with the sugar loaded into bulk containers for export. Sugar pro-duction is a remarkably efficient pro-cess. The crushed fibres, known as bagasse, are burnt as fuel; impurities separated off from the juice are used as fertilisers and the molasses are used either to produce ethanol or as stock feed.

PROSERPINE (population 3000)

A sugar growing centre on the Bruce Highway, 195 km north of Mackay, this is the jumping off point for Airlie Beach and hence the Whitsunday Islands. That's really Prosperpine's function in life, a place where you turn off the main road. From 9 am to 5 pm on weekdays during the sugar season (June to Novem-ber) you can take a guide-yourself tour of the Proserpine Sugar Mills. There's also a Folk Museum in Marathon St, open 9.30 am to 12 noon, 2 to 5 pm from Friday to Wednesday.

Places to Stay

Hostels There are a couple of youth hostel listed places although neither of them are official hostels. *Plaza Lodge* (tel 45 1396) is at 9 Hinschen St, oppos-ite the railway station. Nightly cost is $6 but there's no kitchen. The *Avalon Motel* (tel 45 1200) at 32 Herbert St keeps some beds for YHA members until 7 pm. Nightly cost is $5 if you share a room (an extra dollar if you've not got a sheet sleeping bag), $9 for a single. Again there are no kitchen facilities.

Other Accommodation The *Palace Hotel* (tel 45 1026) at 31 Main St has rooms from $13/20. Cheaper motels include the *A&A Motel* (tel 45 1888) and the *Solaris Motel* (tel 45 1288) both on the Bruce Highway and both at around $27/33. Or there are campsites.

Getting There

Air Proserpine has an airport but it is not on the TAA and Ansett itineraries. this is important for travellers on round Australian tickets since they cannot fly through Proserpine without extra charges for the Air Queensland flights. Air Queensland fly Townsville-Proser-pine ($70) and Mackay-Proserpine ($56). The small Whitsunday airstrip near Shute Harbour is mainly used for joy flights but there is an Air Queens-land service between Mackay and Whit-sunday for $38.

Rail Proserpine is on the six times weekly Brisbane-Cairns Sunlander ser-vice. The fare from Brisbane is $66 in 1st, $44 in economy. It takes 2½ hours between Mackay and Proserpine.

Bus Ansett Pioneer and Greyhound both run through Proserpine on their daily Brisbane-Cairns service. The fare from Brisbane is $60, from Cairns $42, from Townsville $21. Mackay-Prosperpine takes less than two hours.

There is also a regular bus service between Prosperine and Airlie Beach and Shute Harbour. It's quite feasible to stay in Proserpine and make day trips from Shute Harbour as buses are scheduled to connect with the boat departures. There are three or four departures a day, one-way fare is $4.40 Proserpine-Airlie Beach ($7 return), $1.10 Airlie Beach-Shute Harbour ($2 return). Departures are from Filby's Motors in Main St, Proserpine.

AIRLIE BEACH & SHUTE HARBOUR

Airlie Beach is the main accommodation centre on the mainland from the Whitsundays. If you plan to stay on the mainland and see the islands by day-tripping out to them you can either stay here or in adjoining Cannonvale (back towards Proserpine) or along towards Shute Harbour. There's a National Park camping site between Airlie Beach and Shute Harbour. It's 25 km from the Bruce Highway turn-off at Proserpine to Airlie Beach and another eight km from here to Shute Harbour. The town has a wide variety of accommodation and loads of ticket agents selling all the tours and trips out to the reef. Airlie Beach has grown phenomenally over the past 10 years.

There's a wildlife sanctuary and an adjoining aquarium up from Airlie Beach. The sanctuary has a collection of Australian wildlife and birds, the lorikeets fly in to be fed at 3 pm daily. Admission to the aquarium is $3. Mandalay Coral Gardens have fish, and coral on display in tanks. Other attractions in and around the town include Cedar Creek Falls, fine falls, a walk off the road eight km along from Proserpine. The pools above the falls are popular for skinny dipping. The Conway National Park is densely forested and relatively unspoilt. There are some limited walking trails and some fine views across the Whitsunday Passage, the highest point is 563 metres. The park separates the passage from Repulse Bay, named by Captain Cook who strayed in to the bay thinking it was the main passage. There are some good beaches in the Whitsunday vicinity — Conway Beach to the south, Earlando and Dingo Beach to the north.

Airlie Beach is the centre of activities during the annual Whitsunday Village Fun Race (for cruising yachts) each August or September. The festivities include a Miss Figurehead competition where the contestants traditionally are topless! A more regular event is Tuesday and Thursday night toad races at the Airlie Beach Hotel. Rent-a-toad will hire you a steed if you haven't got your own. Beware of marine stingers in the water at Airlie Beach from October to April.

Places to Stay

Hostels The *Cool Palms Youth Camp* (tel 43 6132) is on Mandalay Point Rd, about six km from Airlie Beach. Nightly cost for YHA members is $4.50 but phone first and check that there's room.

Hotels, Motels & Holiday Flats Airlie Beach's rapid expansion has put a bit of a squeeze on accommodation. Finding reasonably priced places to stay can sometimes be a bit difficult. Apart from

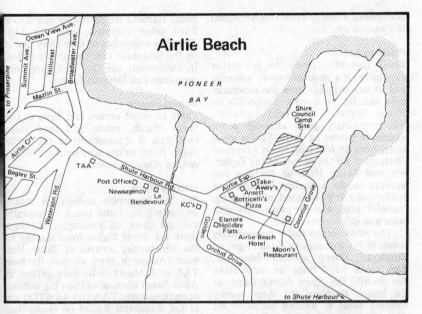

the regular advertised places there are also quite a few holiday flats around in the $30 to $35 bracket.

At Harper St, Airlie Beach, just a few steps back from the main road, *Elanora Holiday Units* (tel 46 6482) are simple and straightforward but well-equipped with cooking facilities and other mod cons. For singles/doubles the nightly cost is $20/26 or $30/35 depending on the season but there are also rates for larger groups — in the low season a unit for five is just $35. And there are cheaper weekly rates. Excellent value and lorikeets and other wildlife pay regular visits to the feeding station established on the balcony upstairs.

The *Airlie Beach Hotel* (tel 46 6233) offers the usual motel facilities at $22/33. Back in Cannonvale you could try *Cannonvale Villas* (tel 46 6177) where compact little units with kitchen facilities cost $25 for two, $5 for each additional person — a bit of a squeeze

for four. See camping below for more possibilities in cabins and on-site vans. There are a lot of other motels around Airlie Beach but you'll be pushed to find anything with doubles for under $30 — most are in the mid-30s, quite a few go to $50 and above.

Camping Fortunately camping is much more straightforward. There are quite a few camp sites in Cannonvale and Airlie Beach and more strung along the road to Shute Harbour. Come early though, they're often packed out. The National Park camp, almost down at Shute Harbour, is probably the best bargain although its range of facilities is not so wide. In Jubilee Pocket on the Shute Harbour Rd the *Island Gateway Village* (tel 46 6228) costs $5 to camp and there are on-site vans at $18. *Island Trader Cabins* are $22/24, good value.

There's a municipal campsite right in Airlie Beach where camping costs $3.70. Amongst the other popular sites is the convenient *Pioneer Park* (tel 46 5266) in Cannonvale.

Places to Eat

Food generally tends to be rather expensive, it's probably more economical to buy supplies from the supermarkets and fix your own. *Botticelli's* on Shute Harbour Rd, behind Ansett, has surprisingly good although a bit expensive pizzas at from $5 for small ones, from $6 for large. *Moon's Seafood Restaurant* on the corner of the Esplanade and Shute Harbour Rd is a real attempt to do a quality restaurant at Airlie Beach. It's a licensed, nice looking, 'tasteful' place and for two people with wine you can count on $40.

The *Airlie Beach Hotel* does counter meals in the evenings to 8 pm (7 pm on Sundays). Cheap specials from $2, ham steak $4, T-bone or rump steak for $5.50. The *Spice Island Bistro* at 66 Shute Harbour Rd does mainly Chinese food at around $6.50 — eat there or take-away. Other pricier restaurants include *KC's Chargrill* (no relation to KC's in Kathmandu!) on Shute Harbour Rd, Airlie Beach. Steaks for around $8. *Le Rendezvous*, also on Shute Harbour Rd, is pricier but does a fixed price complete meal for $10. There's a collection of take-away places on the Esplanade near the Ansett office. In Cannonvale the *One-Way Cafe* does vegetarian and Mexican food.

Entertainment

There are night cruises and visits to the resort islands, music and toad races (well this is Queensland) at the Airlie Beach Hotel or the Whitsunday Village, various other activities.

Getting There

See the Proserpine section for details on getting to Airlie Beach — basically you get there via Proserpine although there are direct flights from Mackay to the Whitsunday airstrip at Shute Harbour. Although they do not fly here TAA and Ansett both have offices in Airlie Beach because of their big holiday operations here. TAA (tel 46 6273) are in the Wanderers Resort on Shute Harbour Rd, Ansett (tel 46 6255) are on the Esplanade. Almost all the island tours leave from Shute Harbour, see the Whitsunday Island section below.

THE WHITSUNDAY ISLANDS

The 70-odd islands of the Whitsunday group are probably the best known and most developed of the Barrier Reef islands. The group was named by Captain Cook who sailed through here on Whitsunday, 1770 — 3 July. They're scattered on both sides of the Whitsunday Passage. All the islands in the group are within 50 km of Shute Harbour, the jumping off point for the many cruises through the group. The actual barrier reef is at least 60 km out from Shute Harbour, Hook Reef is the nearest part of the reef.

Camping on the Islands

Although accommodation on the resort islands, is expensive there is one cheaper location — Happy Bay on Long Island. Plus you can camp on any of the uninhabited islands except those with a grazing lease, with a free permit from the National Parks office. The office is located opposite the National Park campsite, about a km before Shute Harbour. Only a few islands have water supplies, on the others you'll have to bring your own water. Those with water are North Molle (two camping sites, one

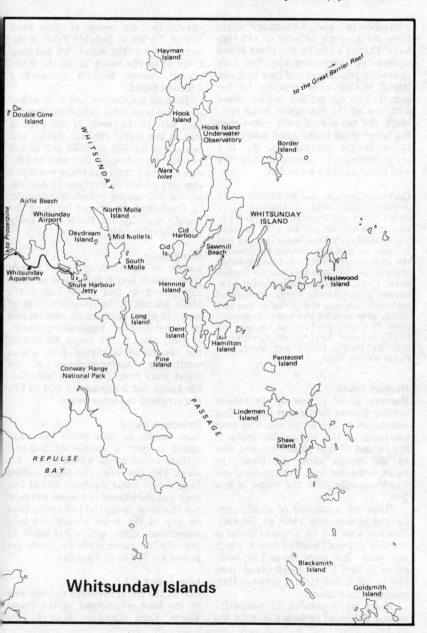

Whitsunday Islands

with showers) and Whitsunday where there are a couple of sites on Cid Harbour. There's a site by the Hook Island underwater observatory too. You have to specify your island and how long you intend to stay when applying for the permit. You can get out to your island with one of the day cruise boats (generally the sail-around ones rather than the island resort boats) or by water taxi. If you've got camping gear give it a try — Robinson Crusoeing on your very own island can be a lot of fun.

Curiously enough the Whitsundays are probably misnamed — Captain Cook didn't really sail through them on Whitsunday. When he got back to England his meticulously kept log was a day out because he had not allowed for crossing the international date line! As he sailed through the Whitsundays and on further north Cook was also unaware of the existence of the Barrier Reef, although he realised there was something to the east of his ship making the water unusually calm. It wasn't until he ran his boat on to Endeavour Reef, near Cooktown, that he finally found out about the Great Barrier Reef.

Hayman Island
Hayman Island is one of the longest running Barrier Reef resort islands, first established in the early '50s. The most northerly of the Whitsunday group it has an area of four square km and rises to 250 metres above sea level. The resort is fronted by a wide, shallow reef which emerges from the water at low tide.

There are a number of small, uninhabited islands very close to Hayman. You can walk out to Arkhurst Island at low tide or from Langford Island, which has some fine coral around it, walk across to Bird Island. Black Island (they like to call it Bali Ha'i) is between Hayman and Hook Island.

There are a number of bushwalks around the island including an eight km circuit, two km across to Blue Pearl Bay or 3.5 km to Dolphin Point at the northern tip of the island. It's less than a km from the resort up to the Whitsunday Passage lookout overlooking Arkhurst Island.

Because the shallow reef is so extensive a toy train takes visitors in from the long jetty to the resort. If you want to stay at the Royal Hayman Resort you can count on $60 to $100 per person per day depending on the room and the season. Apart from the cruise boats you can also go out to Hayman by helicopter for $35 return — including transfer to Proserpine airport and lunch on the island. Basically for those who really like helicopter rides.

South Molle
Largest of the Molle group of islands (four square km) South Molle is virtually joined to Mid Molle and North Molle Islands. It has long stretches of sandy or coral beach and is criss-crossed by a network of bushwalking tracks. Highest point is 198 metre Mt Jeffrey but the climb up Spion Kop is also worthwhile. Accommodation at the resort costs from $45 in the basic Sealife Lodge but it's generally $60 to $70 per person in the other rooms.

Daydream Island
Also known as West Molle this small island is only a couple of hundred metres across at its widest point. It's about two km long. The island suffers from severe water shortages and at one time was abandoned as a resort but now has the most delightful swimming pool on any of the resort islands — a long convoluted affair with a bar-island in the middle. Accommodation costs per person are $50 to $70 per day.

Long Island
One of the closer in islands and also one of the least commercial of the resort islands, Long Island is about 11 km

long but no more than 1½ km wide and covers 18 square km. It was named by Matthew Flinders. There are actually two centres on the island. Happy Bay is the main resort with a long expanse of the properly tropical-island sort of beach. This is where the cruise boats come to but it's not a flashy international sort of resort, more a quiet family type of place and the prices are all somewhat lower.

There are 13 km of walking tracks around the island and if you head south you'll soon come to the other centre, Palm Bay, which is probably the cheapest island resort on the Whitsundays. Here there are fairly simple separate little units with cooking facilities. You can get some supplies here or bring them over from the mainland. At Happy Bay daily costs per person are $50 to $70 including all meals. At Palm Bay (tel 46 9400) a unit for four to six people costs $45 to $50 a day, it's wise to book well ahead. Guests at Palm Bay are able to use facilities of the Happy Bay resort.

Lindeman Island

This is the oldest of the Barrier Reef resorts, it was first established back in 1929 and covers eight square km. Lindeman is another family-style resort with lots of entertainment for kids. The island has 20 km of walking trails. The highest point on the island is 210-metre Mt Oldfield. There are a lot of small islands dotted around Lindeman and it's easy to get across to some of them. With plenty of little beaches and secluded bays it's no hassle at all to find one all to yourself. Per person cost including all meals is $55 to $80 per day depending on the room and the season. Regular flights to Lindeman cost $74 return from Mackay, $62 from Proserpine or you can day-trip to Lindeman from Mackay by air for $40, contact Lindeman Aerial Services (tel 57 3226) for details.

Hook Island

Second largest of the Whitsunday Group, Hook Island has an area of 53 square km and rises to 450 metres at Hook Peak and 376 metres at Mt Sydney. There are a number of beaches dotted around the island but no resort development. It does, however, have the Hook Island Underwater Observatory, one of the most popular attractions in the Whitsundays. You descend to a viewing area in the reef, 10 metres below the surface. It's the next best thing to diving since you're right in there with the fish — not just looking down from above, as with glass-bottom boats. Hook Island also has a camping area near the observatory. If you want to stay out on the islands without the resort costs and without doing the Robinson Crusoe, away from the world, bit then this is a good place to go. Once the day-trip crowds have gone back to Shute Harbour it's very peaceful and pleasant. The beautiful, fiord like Nara Inlet on Hook Island is a very popular deep-water anchorage for visiting yachties.

Whitsunday Island

The largest of the Whitsunday Islands, Whitsunday covers 109 square km and rises to 438 metres at Whitsunday Peak. There is no resort development on the island but Whitehaven Beach on the north-east coast is probably the longest and finest in the group and at Sawmill Beach on the south-east side there is a national park camping area which has fresh water available.

Cid Island

East of Whitsunday Island the Cid. Harbour, wedged between the two islands, was the deep-water anchorage used by part of the US Navy fleet before the Battle of the Coral Sea, turning point in the Pacific theatre of WW II. Today visiting ocean cruise liners anchor here.

Other Islands

There's a kerosene lit lighthouse on Dent Island, guiding ships through the passage. Hamilton Island, nearby, is on a grazing lease but there are plans to build another resort here. Near Lindeman Island, Pentecost Island was named by Captain Cook and has a 208-metres high cliff face shaped remarkably like an Indian head.

Getting Around

Land There are a number of land based tours around the peninsula although it's out on the water that has the real interest. You can rent bikes from Toys & Books on the corner of Shute Harbour Rd and the Esplanade in Airlie Beach — it's open Monday to Saturday and Sunday mornings. The usual rent-a-car agencies operate in Shute Harbour. Mokes are popular with typical costs around $12 a day, $6 for insurance, 12c a km or $30 including 100 km.

Sea There are all types of boat trips out to the islands of the Whitsundays and beyond them to the Barrier Reef. The trips all depart from Shute Harbour, the end of the road from Airlie Beach. You can bus there from Airlie Beach or leave your car in the car park for $1. Tours can be divided into several categories. First of all there are the straightforward go-see-the-islands cruises. You go to resort island A, have an hour or two there to sample the beach, pool and bar, then carry on to do the same at island B. Somewhere along the line you usually get a barbecue lunch thrown in. An excursion to the underwater observatory at Hook Island is usually also part of the picture. Typical prices for these cruises are $20 to $30. Great if you want to make on the spot assesments of the resort swimming pools. A variation on these resort island trips is one that just takes you out to one island and leaves you there for the day. A day on Happy Island, for example, for $15

including lunch or South Molle for $15 or $20 including lunch. There are similar day-out trips to Daydream and Hayman.

Category two is the nowhere in particular trips. Usually in small boats you stay away from the resort islands, perhaps try a beach here, a bit of snorkelling there, maybe some fishing somewhere else. Many of the boats operating these trips are yachts. A day on the former America's cup contender Gretel is yours for $25 for example, other boats can be cheaper.

Then there are the outer reef trips where you power out to the outer reef for a spot of walking on the reef itself, a look-see from a glass bottom boat and perhaps a bit of snorkelling too. For these trips you need a fast boat to get out to the reef in the minimum time possible. Departure times vary with the tides because you want to be on the reef at low tide, when it comes clear of the water. At high tide the reef can be five or more metres underwater. These trips are generally more expensive (you're looking at $50) but getting out to the reef is really an other-worldly experience and, if you can afford it, certainly not to be missed. It's quite eerie suddenly coming upon the long sweep of reef, way out from the mainland and shelving rapidly up from 50 metres or more depth. The coral and fish are, naturally, superb. The most important piece of equipment you'll need for visiting the reef are shoes — an old pair of sneakers are ideal, thongs are not really suitable.

Finally there are all sorts of do-your-own-thing odds and ends. You could get yourself dropped off at an uninhabited island from one of the nowhere in particular boats or by the Water Taxi (tel 469 438). Or go out for a fishing trip. Or charter a boat and sail yourself. You can get small fishing dinghies with outboard motors from $20 to $40 a day, 22 foot yachts for $80 a day, catamarans at Airlie Beach for $10 an hour, big cruising yachts for a small fortune!

Air Scenic flights over the Whitsundays can run from $15 or $20 all the way up to $60 for a flight right out over the Barrier Reef — check with Coconut Airways or Air Whitsunday. For $85 Air Whitsunday will fly you out to Hardy Lagoon on the reef in their amphibious aircraft, there they have a glass bottom boat anchored and you get an hour and a half of coral viewing, reef walking and snorkelling before flying back.

WHITSUNDAYS TO TOWNSVILLE

Bowen (population 6700)

The first settlement in north Queensland, dating from 1861, Bowen has a good historical museum at 22 Gordon St with exhibits relating to the town's early history. It's open from 10.30 am to 4 pm on weekdays, 3 to 5 pm on Saturdays. Beaches around Bowen are Queens Beach, Greys Bay, Murray Bay, Horseshoe Bay, Rose Bay and Kings Beach — there are lots of beaches around Bowen and some of them are really excellent, beautiful beaches and often as secluded as you could ask for.

Ayr (population 8600)

On the Burdekin delta Ayr is, once again, a sugar town and it also grows rice. On Wilmington St the House of Australian Nature has displays of orchids, shells, butterflies and beetles. It's open 8 am to 5 pm daily. Across the Burdekin River is Home Hill (population 5200) with a historical museum. Between Ayr and Townsville you pass the Australian Institute of Marine Science on Cape Ferguson — phone 78 9211 to arrange to visit it. Mt Elliot National Park, only 25 km south of Townsville, has good swimming holes in the Alligator Creek Gorge. There are also walking tracks, camping areas and an information kiosk here. Alligator Creek Antique Museum is open Sunday to Thursday from 9 am to 5 pm.

TOWNSVILLE (population 80,000)

The third largest city in Queensland and the main centre in the north of the state, Townsville is the port city for the agricultural and mining production of the vast inland region of northern Queensland. The town was founded in 1864 by Robert Towns, a sea captain who foresaw the need for a port for the growing cattle stations inland. Today Townsville is the site of the James Cook University. The city is dominated by Castle Hill with a lookout perched on top, 290 metres above the city on the Ross Creek. From the lookout you get a fine view of the centre and across to Magnetic Island.

Information

The Townsville Tourist Organisation has a large information centre (tel 71 2724) at the corner of Sturt St and Stokes St. It's open 9 am to 5 pm Monday to Friday. Amongst the material they have available is a National Trust walking tour brochure, leading you around the city's main fine Victorian buildings. There is also a Queensland Government Tourist Bureau office in Flinders Mall. The RACQ is at 711-717

Flinders St (tel 71 2168). The GPO is at the end of the Mall, on the corner of Denham St, and the library is next door. Mary Who at 143 Flinders St is an excellent bookshop. Aboriginal artefacts can be found in the Aboriginal Gallery at 137 Flinders St, also in the same Magnetic House complex, a group of early Townsville buildings.

Orientation

The town is situated astride Ross Creek, a rather larger river than its name might suggest. The city centre is immediately to the north of the river and Flinders Mall, the main shopping street of Townsville, is pedestrian only. You can easily get around the centre on foot — it's no distance to the railway station from the centre or along the river to the wharf for Magnetic Island. Most of the accommodation centres, including the youth hostel, are also conveniently central.

Around Town

Townsville has one of the best city malls in Australia. It's bright, breezy, full of interest and a great place to wander or simply sit and watch the passing scenery. Giant games of chess, backgammon and snakes and ladders are part of the mall activities. The Strand is a long beachfront drive with parks and gardens, lots of bougainvilaea, the Tobruk swimming pool and an impressive artificial waterfall. Beside the Strand the old Queens Hotel on the corner of Wickham Terrace is now a TV and broadcasting station with glassfronted studios so passersby can look in and see what's happening. There's a coral display at Coral Gardens (9.30 am to 5 pm daily) on Tomlin St, just across from the town centre. Admission is $2.50, not really worth it.

Townsville's main landmark is Castle Hill, towering over the town and river. There's a road up to the top and you can also walk there though it is quite a climb. There's a Townsville organisation

dedicated to making Castle Hill into a mountain by adding the few metres of dirt necessary for its reclassification. Several years work has only resulted in a few cm of additional height. Queen's Gardens on Gregory St, North Ward, is the original botanic gardens in Townsville. They're clearly visible below Castle Hill. Ho hum, Townsville has a water slide like almost every other big Queensland town, Crystal Cylinders is on Kings Rd.

Old Buildings

There are many fine old buildings in the town centre but Buchanan's Hotel, at 12 Sturt St with its superb iron lacework verandahs, burnt down in 1982. This was Townsville's finest building and one of the finest in far north Queensland. While discussion was going on about whether it could be rebuilt or simply the facade saved and a new building built behind, the demolition squad moved in and in true Queensland fashion down it went. At the bottom of Stokes St, Victoria Bridge is one of the few remaining swing bridges in Australia. It's not in use but there are plans to restore it.

Galleries

There are quite a few galleries around town including the Perc Tucker Regional Gallery at the corner of Denhan and Flinders Sts — 'one of the best regional art galleries in Australia'. There's also the Martin Gallery at 475 Flinders St and the Magnetic House Art Gallery also on Flinders St, down towards the Magnetic Island wharf. The latter has an eclectic collection of paintings, antiques, books and some really beautiful carpets.

Further Out

Four km out of the city the Jezzine Military Museum is on Mitchell St, North Ward and is open Wednesday to Sunday, 12 noon to 4 pm. The new botanic garden, the Anderson Park &

Kokoda Pool, is six km out on Hugh St, Mundingburra. The Tropicforest Garden Estate is seven km out at 56 Bowen Rd, Rosslea and apart from rainforest walks it also has Australia's largest freshwater aquarium. On the Town Common, only four km from the centre, you can see a wide variety of wildlife, particularly early in the morning. During the winter there are sometimes thousands of the stately brolgas here as well as many other waterbirds. On the second Sunday of the month there are ranger guided tours on the common. At Stuart, about 11 km out of the city, there are free tours of the large copper refinery at 10.30 am and 1.30 pm on weekends. A couple of km south of Stuart a road climbs to the top of Mt Stuart. There are good natural swimming holes at Mt Elliott National Park.

Further out from Townsville is the Mt Spec-Crystal Creek National Park, a pleasant day-trip from the city. There are fine panoramic views, swimming holes, bushwalks and camping areas. The turn-off to the park is 69 km north. The Jourama Falls National Park is nine km off the road, 89 km north of Townsville, it's also a popular outing from Ingham. More good swimming holes here — very pleasant in the summer heat.

Places to Stay

Hostel The *Townsville Youth Hostel* (tel 72 2820) is at 23 Willis St, conveniently close to the centre but a hell of a long climb up steps from the street. Your efforts are rewarded with a superb view over the town. Nightly cost is $5, there's a cramped kitchen, an over-loud TV set and an excellent noticeboard.

Hotels & Guest Houses There are several conveniently central hotels and guest houses in Townsville. The old *People's Palace* (tel 71 6874) is at the corner of Sturt and Blackwood Sts. The four

storey building has nearly 100 rooms and nightly costs for the standard singles/doubles is $13/24 including a light breakfast. There are also more luxurious singles with attached bathrooms at $16 or rooms with carpet, air-con and colour TV for $21/30.

There are several guest houses/private hotels close to the centre. Across the road from the People's Palace at 10 Blackwood St the *Sunseeker Private Hotel* (tel 71 3409) has rooms at $14/20 (triples are also available) plus $2 or $4 for breakfast. Or go back a block to *Civic House* (tel 71 5381) at 262 Walker St where nightly cost is $9 per person — quite a good place with kitchen facilities, TV lounge and laundry. Weekly cost is $45. Another couple of blocks back at 32 Hale St there's *Coral House* (tel 71 6337) with singles at $12, share twins at $9 each, self-contained units at $25.

Then there are a number of the traditional old hotels like the *Great Northern* (tel 71 6191) at 500 Flinders St down by the railway station. Nightly cost is $10.50 per person, another $3 for breakfast. Also some rooms with attached bathroom for an extra $3. The *Seaview Hotel* (tel 71 5005) on the Strand has singles at $10 a night, $14 including breakfast.

Motels The *Coachman's Inn* (tel 72 3140) is on top of the Greyhound Terminal at the corner of Flinders and King Sts, by the river. Singles/doubles in this modern motel are $28/33. Other cheaper motels include *Motel 16* (tel 72 4166) at the corner of Queens Rd and Railway Avenue on Route 16. Singles/doubles are $26/32. Or there's the *Strand Motel* (tel 72 1977) at 51 The Strand with singles/doubles at $24/29 and the very central *Rex City Motel* (tel 71 6048) at 143 Willis St with rooms at $27/31.

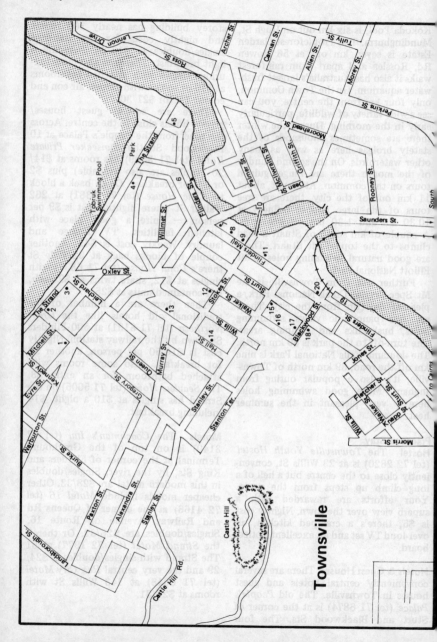

1 Allen Hotel	11 Ansett & Ansett Pioneer
2 Seaview Hotel	12 Townsville Tourist Office
3 Strand Motel	13 Youth Hostel (up steps)
4 Waterfall	14 Coral Guest House
5 Greyhound Terminal	15 Ansett & Ansett Pioneer (again)
6 Magnetic Island Ferry	16 Civic House
7 GPO	17 People's Palace
8 QGTB	18 Sunseeker Guest House
9 Townsville International Hotel	19 Railway Station
10 Historic Swing Bridge (not used)	20 Great Northern Hotel

Camping Townsville has a number of camping sites on the roads into the town, particularly on the Bruce Highway.

Places to Eat

Counter Meals There are lots of places in this category but no real standouts. The three that follow are pretty good places to consider. The *Exchange Hotel* is one of a string of hotels along Flinders St, opposite the Hayles' wharf. The pub part is a bit rough but go through to the back where the *Courtyard Bistro* has good counter meals for $4 to $6 — pick your own steak from the chiller display.

On the waterfront Strand the *Seaview Hotel* has an outdoor eating area — it's a bit drab but then opportunities to eat in the open air are pretty rare in Queensland. You've got to wend your way right through to the *Garden Bistro* at the back. It's open 12 noon to 2 pm and 6 to 8 pm, ham steak is $3.50, rump steak $5.50, most meals in that sort of bracket.

One floor up in the big *Townsville Hotel* (the circular one on the Mall) is the *Copper Gate Bistro*. It's semi-self-service, cafeteria-style and a little bit bland but not bad for all that and it's open to 10 pm. Main courses are $5.50 to $7. There's a confusing mish-mash of bars and restaurants on the floor.

Other places include the *James Cook Tavern* on Flinders St. Counter meals are in the $3.50 to $4.50 range at

the *Great Northern Hotel* by the railway station.

Other For snacks and lunches you could try the *Fruit & Nut Shop* in the Cat & Fiddle Arcade. Or at 438 Flinders St the *Mango Tree* has vegetarian and health foods at lunchtime. More health food at *Mr Natural's Garden Cafe*, way down Flinders St past the railway station at 829. *Pizza Sorrento* is also up this end of town at 815.

Up at the post office end of the Mall the *Canadian Kitchen* is open from 8 am every day of the week for breakfast, lunch and dinner. Straight-forward no-nonsense food and tables out in the mall. On the Strand the *Ozone Cafe* is a popular take-away spot.

For a night out you could do worse than try *The Balcony* at 287 Flinders Mall. It's a pleasant open-air balcony looking out over the mall, main courses a dollar either side of $6, desserts very reasonably priced and generally a nice relaxing place to eat.

Entertainment

Quite a few pubs around Townsville feature music. There's jazz on weekends at *Tattersalls* and at the *James Cook Tavern*. Rock at *Lang's*, the *Seaview Hotel* and the *Exchange*, also at *The Warehouse* at the *Mansfield Hotel*, Flinders St — small cover charge. *Lowth's* has a disco on the top (5th) floor with a $4 cover charge. There are lots of bars in this hotel, music in the basement bar. *Pickers & Pluckers* features acoustic music for $2 on Wednesday nights at Personalities Theatres Restaurant, just across the river. Acoustic music also features at the *Mingus Cafe*, 2 Blackwood St, from 7 pm to 2 am. *Banks*, at the wharf end of Flinders St, is a nightclub with a $5 cover charge.

Getting There
Air Yes you can fly to Townsville from anywhere you care to mention. It's on the regular east coast run up from Brisbane to Cairns and also connected to Mt Isa and through to Darwin and Alice Springs. Some typical fares are Brisbane $156 (standby $117), Rockhampton $106, Mackay $78, Cairns $75 and Mt Isa $152.

Rail The Brisbane-Cairns Sunlander rail service operates through Townsville. The service operates six times weekly and it takes about 30 hours from Brisbane to Townsville at a fare of $56 in 1st, $37 in 2nd. A sleeping berth is an extra $9 per night in 1st, $4.50 in economy. It's 7½ hours between Cairns and Townsville by rail.

The Inlander operates twice weekly from Townsville to Mt Isa. Travel times and fares are Charters Towers three hours, $12.30 1st or $8.20 economy; Cloncurry 17 hours, $52.70 1st or $35.10 economy; Mt Isa 21 hours, $62.40 1st or $41.60 economy. Sleepers cost an extra $12 in 1st, $6 in economy per night. Note the amazing trees in the Townsville railway station car park.

Bus Ansett Pioneer and Greyhound both operate through Townsville on their services between Brisbane and

Cairns and also from Townsville inland to Mt Isa and from there to Alice Springs or Darwin. It's 24 hours from Brisbane to Townsville ($73), six hours from Cairns ($25), 12 hours to Mt Isa ($59). In Townsville Ansett Pioneer (tel 81 6611) are on the corner of Sturt and Stanley Sts; Greyhound (tel 71 2134) are on the corner of Flinders and King Sts, down beyond the Hayles wharf.

Getting Around
Bus & Rental Vehicles There are a variety of local bus services around Townsville. The regular rent-a-car operators are all represented here including Natcar plus smaller firms like Brolga Moke Hire or Sun City Rent-a-Moke. You can rent bikes from Townsville Bike Hire at Graham Bourke, the chemist at 342 Flinders Mall. Costs are $2.50 for a half day, $4.50 for a day.

Airport Townsville airport is fairly convenient for the city, about $4 by taxi. TAA (tel 81 6222) are on the corner of Flinders and Stokes Sts in the mall. Ansett (tel 72 3333) are on Sturt and Stanley Sts although they also have an office on the mall. Avis, Hertz and Budget have desks at the airport.

Tours There are various town tours and also reef and island tours such as to Palm Island Reef for $27 (10% discount to YHA members) or a reef trip to Wheelers Reef — check with Sun Bird Island Cruises by the Hayles wharf. Or Sea Safari do day snorkelling trips for $18.

MAGNETIC ISLAND (population 1800) Magnetic is one of the most popular reef islands for travellers because it's so cheap and convenient to get to and has such a great selection of cheap places to stay. It's also big enough and varied enough to offer plenty of things to do and see including some really fine bushwalks. Only 13 km offshore from Townsville (a 35-minute ferry trip), Magnetic Island is almost a suburb of Townsville and a popular day trip from that city. The island was given its name by Captain Cook, who thought his ship's compass went funny when he sailed by in 1770. Nobody else has thought so since! The island has some fine beaches, lots of bird life, bushwalking tracks, a koala sanctuary and an aquarium. It's dominated by 500-metre Mt Cook. There are several small resort towns along the coast and a variety of accommodation possibilities. Since the island is a real year round place it has quite a different atmosphere to the purely resort islands along the reef. This is one of the larger islands (52 square km) and about 70% of the island is national park, much of the wildlife is extraordinarily fearless.

Information & Orientation
Magnetic island is roughly triangular in shape with Picnic Bay, where the ferry runs from Townsville, at the bottom (southern) corner of the triangle. There's a road up the eastern side of the island to Horseshoe Bay and a rough track along the west coast but along the north coast it's a walking track only. Picnic Bay is the main town on the island and has shops, bicycle, motorcycle and Moke rental agencies and the Hotel Magnetic.

Picnic Bay to Nelly Bay
Many travellers stay in Picnic Bay because it's the most convenient for the ferry, has a good selection of shops and places to eat and has one of the most popular places to stay. There's a lookout above the town and just to the west of Picnic Bay is Cockle Bay with the wreck of the *City of Adelaide*. Heading around the coast from Picnic Bay you soon come to Rocky Bay where it's

a short, steep walk down to a beautiful and secluded beach.

Next round the coast is Nelly Bay with the Marine Observatory, also billed as 'Shark World'. It's really a bit dismal, just a bunch of fairly small sharks swimming around in an oval swimming pool. The labelling and explanation on the adjoining aquarium tanks is minimal. All in all it could do with a good clean up and some major improvements. If you must it's open 8.30 am to 5 pm daily and admission is $2.50. The sharks get their daily feed at 2 pm. Nelly Bay has a good beach with shade, barbecue areas and a reef at low tide. At the far end of Nelly Bay there are some pioneer graves.

Arcadia
Round the headland you come to Geoffrey Bay with shops and a walking track then there's Arcadia with the Arcadia Hotel and, just round the headland, the very pleasant Alma Bay beach. Arcadia also has the Mountain View Fernery & Orchid Display on Rheuben Terrace. Admission to the fernery is $2.50 which includes a half hour guided tour.

Radical Bay & The Forts
From here the road runs back from the coast until you reach the junction to the Radical Bay road. There's a choice of routes here. You can take the road which runs down to the Radical Bay resort with tracks leading off to Arthur Bay and Florence Bay or you can take the track via the Forts. On the Radical Bay road there's also a track leading off to the old searchlight station on a headland between Arthur and Florence Bays. Fine views from up here and the bays are also pleasant and secluded.

Alternatively you can take the track to the forts, starting from right at the Horseshoe Bay-Radical Bay junction. You can drive most of the way down to the WW II forts but it's also a pleasant

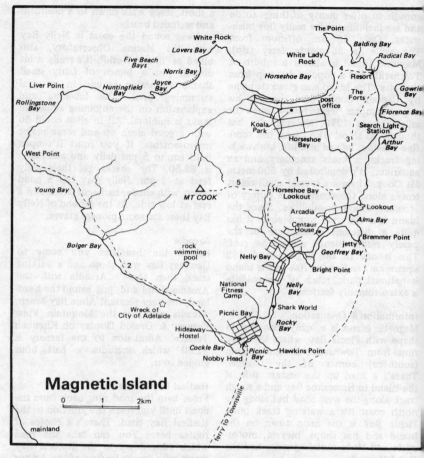

Magnetic Island

White Rock
Lovers Bay
Five Beach Bays
Norris Bay
Liver Point
Huntingfield Bay
Joyce Bay
Rollingstone Bay
West Point
Young Bay
Bolger Bay
MT COOK
rock swimming pool
Wreck of City of Adelaide
National Fitness Camp
Hideaway Hostel
Cockle Bay
Nobby Head
Picnic Bay

0 1 2km

mainland

ferry to Townsville

The Point
Balding Bay
White Lady Rock
Radical Bay
Horseshoe Bay
Resort
post office
The Forts
Gowrie Bay
Koala Park
Florence Bay
Horseshoe Bay
Search Light Station
Arthur Bay
Horseshoe Bay Lookout
Lookout
Arcadia
Alma Bay
Centaur House
Bremmer Point
jetty
Geoffrey Bay
Nelly Bay
Bright Point
Nelly Bay
Shark World
Rocky Bay
Picnic Bay
Hawkins Point

stroll and the views from the top are very fine. The forts comprise a command post and signal station, gun sites and an ammunition store. As an alternative to backtracking to the road junction you can continue downhill from the forts and rejoin the Radical Bay road just before the resort. From here you can walk across the headland to Balding Bay and Horseshoe Bay.

Horseshoe Bay

Whether you continue along the road from the junction or walk across from Radical Bay you eventually end up at Horsehoe Bay, the end of the road and the other end of the island from Picnic Bay. Here there are more shops and accommodation possibilities, a long stretch of beach, a lagoon bird sanctuary and a koala park, a long drive off the main road, where admission is $3. You can also walk from here to Maud

Bay, round to the west, or down the beach and across the headland to Radical Bay. Along the Radical Bay track another trail branches off down to pretty little Balding Bay, a popular place for skinny dipping.

Bushwalks

The National Parks produce a walks leaflet for Magnetic Island's excellent bushwalking tracks. Possible walks include:

1 Nelly Bay-Arcadia	5 km	1½ hrs
2 Picnic Bay-West Point	8 km	2 hrs
3 Horseshoe Bay road		
-Arthur Bay	2 km	½ hr
-Florence Bay	2 km	½ hr
-The Forts	2 km	1½ hrs
4 Horseshoe Bay		
-Balding Bay	3 km	¾ hr
-Radical Bay	4 km	¾ hr
5 Mt Cook	8 km	all day

Except for the long Mt Cook ascent none of the walks require special preparation. You can string several walks together to make an excellent day's outing. Starting from Nelly Bay walk directly inland along Mandalay Avenue and follow the signpost to Horseshoe Bay lookout from where the trail drops down and around to Aracadia. This is about a five km walk taking an hour and a bit. Towards the end of the track there's a choice of routes. Take the longer track via the Sphinx Lookout which brings you on to the Horseshoe Bay road beyond Arcadia. You've then only got a short walk to the Radical Bay junction from where you can walk down to the Forts and on down to the Radical Bay resort. From here it's up and over to Horseshoe Bay, via Balding Bay if you wish. From Horseshoe Bay you can take the bus back to the other end of the island.

If you want to make the Mt Cook ascent a compass and adequate water supply should be carried. There is no marked trail but it's fairly easy to follow a ridge line from the saddle

on the Nelly Bay-Arcadia track. After heavy rain there's a waterfall on Peterson Creek. You can also hike along the west coast from Picnic Bay to Young Bay and West Point.

Places to Stay

Hostels One reason Magnetic Island is so popular with travellers is the excellent accommodation possibilities — there are no less than four hostels! Only a minute's walk from the ferry pier at Picnic Bay is the *Hideaway Hostel* (tel 78 5110). They've got a variety of rooms — $5 in the bunkrooms, $6 in rooms for four, $7 in a twin share (ie a double would cost $14), plus there are family rooms. If you've not got a sheet bag there's a $1 bed linen charge. It's a friendly, busy place with kitchen and laundry facilities and a TV room — the kitchen is very cramped though.

Also in Picnic Bay is the *National Fitness Camp* (tel 78 5280), a short walk from the pier. There's room for only 20 here, nightly cost is $4.50. Possibility three is *Camp Magnetic* (tel 78 5151), the Uniting Church Camp at Nelly Bay. There's also a swimming pool here and nightly charges are $3.50.

Finally at 27 Marine Parade, Arcadia, right by the sea, is *Centaur House*. There's no phone here so you just have to front up and take your chances. Non-smokers are preferred and you have to vacate the premises daily but only from 10 am to 1 pm. Nightly costs are $4.50 in this popular hostel.

Hotels & Holiday Flats There are two hotels and several resorts and motels on the island plus more than a dozen holiday flats. At certain times of year they can be rather packed so it's wise to phone ahead, check the situation and book if necessary. Right by the pier in Picnic Bay the *Magnetic Island Hotel* (tel 78 5166) has double rooms at $30, $35 and $40. The *Arcadia Hotel* (tel 78 5177) is in Arcadia and has doubles in the old units at $25, the new ones are $50. The beach resorts are all in this price bracket or more expensive.

Then there are all sorts of holiday flats, most of which quote weekly rates although it's always worth asking if you want to stay for a shorter period. Prices vary with the season and with demand — even in the season you may find bargains if there just happens to be a room vacant. Single bedroom flats are typically in the $100 to $200 bracket per week. Two bed-room flats are generally not that much more expensive. Check with the QGTB for a full list of flats. One cheaper place which also quotes daily rates is the *Pamray Guest House* (tel 78 5252) at 40 Horseshoe Bay Rd, Horseshoe Bay. Per person the cost is $16 a day, $65 for a week. *Foresthaven* (tel 78 5153) at 11 Cook Rd, Arcadia, is also cheap.

Places to Eat

Both hotels do counter meals — at the *Arcadia* counter lunch in the *Bosun's Grill* is $5.95. The *Tropical Inn* on the Esplanade in Picnic Bay is a good place for a meal, either take-aways or eat there. Food is reasonably expensive but the fish & chips are really excellent and just $1.60 if you eat there. And you're entertained by the pet possums who appears on a shelf by the ceiling and drive the dogs crazy! *Crusoe's*, next door, is a bit more expensive.

There's also a snack bar by the Arcadia Hotel, another place doing take-aways and light meals just around the headland at Alma Bay and the *Bee Ran Cafe* in Horseshoe Bay. The seafood place next door to the Bee Ran is, once again, reasonably expensive. Good bread and other bakery products at the *South Pacific Bakery* at Arcadia which also does pizzas.

Getting There

Ferries across Cleveland Bay to the island leave from the Hayles Magnetic Island wharf (tel 71 6927) at 168 Flinders St. They go to Picnic Bay and sometimes to Arcadia as well. There are about eight to 10 departures a day on weekends and Saturdays, a dozen on Sundays and public holidays. A round trip ticket costs $4.60 per person. Tickets are also available including a day's bus travel on the island, and also with entry to Shark World, but they're no saving on paying as you go along. You can also take cars across on a vehicle ferry to Arcadia which operates twice daily on weekdays, once on Saturdays. It costs $10 return for a motorcycle, $36 for a car — fairly expensive so unless you're staying for long you'll probably find it cheaper to hire a Moke there — or use the bus service.

Getting Around

The Magnetic Island Bus Service operates a delightful open-sided bus back and forth between Picnic Bay and Horseshoe Bay about half a dozen times a day. You can either get tickets from place to place or get a $3 tour ticket which lets you get on and off the bus anywhere you choose for the day.

Alternatively you can hire bicycles, motorcycles or Mokes. Magnetic Island would be an ideal size for biking around if only the bikes available were a bit better. They're hired from Picnic Bay (tel 78 5374) and cost $4.50 per day, $8 for tandems and are really not much use for going very far. Much better are motorcycles — a couple of places in Picnic Bay hire them. The Hideaway hostel has quite a collection with daily rates of $10 for 50cc mopeds, $14 for 80cc step-throughs or $19 for a 100cc motorcycle. You certainly don't need anything bigger than that to explore the island. The rates include insurance, unlimited km and petrol plus a crash helmet. You must have a motorcycle licence. If you're a YHA member you get a $2 discount.

Finally you can hire Mokes — in fact

you soon get the impression that 90% of the vehicles on the island are Mokes, there seem to be nothing else. There are several Moke hire places in Picnic Bay, the other towns or from the various accommodation centres. Typical rates are $9.50 for day one plus 10c per km. Insurance is $3 per day, additional weekdays cost $7.50. Cheaper rates are available for longer periods, varying if they include a weekend or not. The minor hassle with Mokes that there is no safe place to leave things is no problem at all on Magnetic Island, where you can't go far enough from home base to need very much!

TOWNSVILLE TO CAIRNS

It's 374 km from Townsville to Cairns and there's plenty of interest along the way — lush rainforests, several towns, a number of islands offshore and from Innisfail an alternative route on to the Atherton Tableland.

Ingham (population 5900)

There's a lot of Spanish and Italian influence in this important sugar producing town. The Ingham Cemetery has some impressive Italian mausoleums. Lucinda, 24 km from Ingham, is the port from which the sugar is shipped and it has a jetty nearly six km long! There are a number of places to visit around Ingham including the Wallaman Falls, 48 km inland, where the water falls 278 metres, the longest single drop in Australia. Only seven km off the highway is the Victoria Mill, the largest sugar mill in the southern hemisphere. You can see a large display of Queensland gemstones at Jack Fraser Gemstone Gallery in Trebonne, eight km from Ingham. Forrest Beach and Taylors Beach, both 17 km out, have good swimming.

Orpheus Island

North of Townsville and a little south of Hinchinbrook, Orpheus is a small 14 square km volcanic island surrounded by a coral reef. It's about 20 km offshore from Lucinda Point near Ingham and only 15 km from the Great Barrier Reef. The island, which is a national park, is heavily forested and there is lots of birdlife. Turtles also nest on the island and at this point the outer barrier reef is relatively close. It's a quiet, secluded, small resort with nightly costs from $120 per person! You can get there from Tully by helicopter for $80 return or by launch for $25 return.

Cardwell (population 900)

The road south of Cardwell climbs high up above the coast with tremendous views down across the winding waterways known as the Everglades which separate Hinchinbrook from the coast. There are good views across Rockingham Bay too. From Cardwell there are boat trips to Hinchinbrook, the Everglades and other islands. This is the only town on the Bruce Highway all the way from Brisbane to Cairns which is actually on the coast. At 235 Victoria St the Wishbone Tree is a local gallery, museum and even Devonshire teas! Near Cardwell are the Murray Falls with fine rock pools for swimming and the Edmund Kennedy National Park.

Hinchinbrook Island

Halfway between Townsville and Cairns and usually reached from Cardwell, the entire large 374 square km island of Hinchinbrook is a protected reserve. The island is only separated from the mainland by a narrow channel. There's one resort on the island, on the northern peninsula, Cape Richards, but there are also a couple of camp sites. The

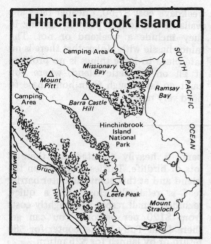

Hinchinbrook Island

Camping Area

Missionary
Bay

Mount
Pitt

Camping
Area

Barra Castle
Hill

Ramsay
Bay

Hinchinbrook
Island
National
Park

Bruce

Leefe Peak

Mount
Straloch

SOUTH PACIFIC OCEAN

to Cardwell

HWY

terrain of the island is very variable — lush tropical forests on the mainland side, towering mountains in the middle and long sandy beaches and secluded bays on the eastern side. The island covers 635 square km and the highest peak, Mt Bowen, is 1050 metres. There are a number of walks around the resort and much wildlife, especially prettyfaced wallabies. Zoe Bay, with its beautiful waterfall, is one of the most scenic spots on the island.

The Hinchinbrook Island Resort (tel 8585) operates a launch service across to Cape Richards from Cardwell for $18 return. It operates six days a week except in March, April, November and December when it only operates three times a week. The resort is a fairly simple and straightforward place and guests can prepare their own meals — the units have kitchens — although there's also a dining room with meals available. If you want to fix your own food there's a small shop at the resort. Daily cost is $75 for units which take up to four people, room only ($4 extra at peak seasons). All meals would cost $26 per day per adult.

The island campsites, for which permits must be obtained from the park rangers at Cardwell, Cairns or Townsville, are at Haven (water available from Pages Creek) and Machushla (bring drinking water with you).

Tully (population 2800)
The wettest place in Australia gets a drenching average of 440 cm a year, about 14 feet. There are some fine beaches around Tully, generally backed by lush (would you believe) rainforest. They include Mission Beach, an eight km long stretch of sand with a memorial to the ill-fated Edmund Kennedy Cape York expedition at Tam O'Shanter Point at the southern end of the beach. Day-trips operate from Mission Beach to Dunk Island and there are a number of camp sites and caravan parks along the beach. Other places of interest around Tully include Clump Point, Bignil Bay, Kareeya Gorge and the Murray Falls.

Dunk Island
One of the flashier Barrier Reef resorts is off Tully at Brammo Bay on Dunk Island. From 1897 to 1923 E J Banfield lived here and wrote his book *The Confessions of a Beachcomber*, the island is remarkably little changed from that early description. The five square km island has more than 19 km of walking tracks through the rainforest and is noted for its prolific birdlife (nearly 150 species are seen here) and many butterflies. There are superb views over the entrances to the Hinchinbrook Channel from the top of 271 metre Mt Koo-taloo. Launches run daily to Dunk Island, only five km off the coast, from Clump Point for $9 return or you can travel by air from Townsville or Cairns. Nightly costs at the Dunk Island resort range from $70 per person. At tiny Bedarra Island there's a very small resort on this heavily wooded island only six km from Dunk. Including meals nightly costs at

Bedarra are $135 per person!

Innisfail (population 8000)

A sugar city for over a century Innisfail has a large Italian population although on Owen St you can also find a joss house. It's a busy town which produces a large proportion of the state's sugar. From here you can visit Australia's only tea plantation at Nerada, 35 km to the west (open Tuesday to Sunday) or climb Mt Bartle Frere, the highest mountain in Queensland. There's a good road from here up on to the Atherton Tableland. Mourilyan, seven km south of Innisfail, has a tourist office and also a sugar museum. Just north of Innisfail is Babinda (population 1500), close to the Bellenden Ker National Park. Popular swimming and picnic spots around here are the Boulders, just 10 km inland, and Josephine Falls in the national park. Further north Gordonvale (population 2100) is almost at Cairns. The winding Gillies Highway leads from here up on to the tableland.

CAIRNS (population 39,500)

The 'capital' of the far north and probably the best known city up the Queensland coast, Cairns is a colourful and easy-going place with plenty of interest and variety to offer. Off-shore from Cairns is Green Island, a coral cay resort. Inland are the beautiful, cool and fertile rainforests of the Atherton Tableland. North stretches the string of superb beaches leading to the delightful little town of Port Douglas while further north again is historic Cooktown and then the wild 'last frontier' of the Cape York Peninsula.

Cairns marks the northern terminus of the Bruce Highway and the end of the railway line from Brisbane. It came into existence in a half-hearted manner in 1876, initially as a port for the gold and tin mines developing inland. Earlier the bay had been used as a shelter for beche-de-mer gatherers. At first it was known as Trinity Bay and engaged in a fierce rivalry with Port Douglas. Later sugar growing became the major activity of the region and it remains so today. Cairns is at its best from May to October, it gets rather sticky in the summer. The annual 'Fun in the Sun' festival takes place in October.

Information

The Visitors' Information Centre is at 44 McLeod St, right across from the railway station, and is open from 9 am to 5 pm daily. The Queensland Government Tourist Bureau is at 12 Shields St. The RACQ have their Cairns office at 112 Sheridan St, see them if you want information about the road to Cooktown or if you're contemplating a Cape York expedition. The National Parks & Wildlife Service is in Moffat St, off Sheridan St, near the airport. The Civic Centre is Cairns arts and cultural centre on the corner of Florence and Sheridan Sts. The GPO with its very busy poste restante counter is on the corner of Spencer and Abbot Sts. 'Cairns' is pronounced in a manner that sounds suspiciously like 'Cannes' to non-Australians.

There are a number of give-away information sources in Cairns with maps and listings of accommodation, restaurants, rent-a-car agencies and so on. Walker's Bookshop at 96 Cairns is the best bookshop in town. Absell's Newsagency, on Lake St opposite Ansett, has charts and survey maps of the far north. The Cairns Bushwalkers organise regular bushwalks and can probably arrange transport if you want to go along. Contact them on 55 1865 in

Cairns, 92 1491 in Mareebra. Kouda
Traders at 52 Shields St have a fine
collection of Aboriginal art and artefacts
for sale.

Orientation

The centre of Cairns is a relatively compact area running back from the waterfront. The railway station is within
walking distance from the centre of
town and the airport is only a few km
to the north. Cairns is surrounded to the
south and north by mangrove swamps
and the sea right in front of the town
is shallow and at low tide becomes a
long sweep of mud — lots of interesting
waterbirds though. Along the waterfront is the Esplanade and a pleasant
strip of parkland, nice for a stroll.

Around the City

The earliest part of the port of Cairns
is down around the junction of Wharf St
and the Esplanade. Part of this colourful
area was known as the 'Barbary Coast'.
Here you'll find many fine old buildings
with typically tropical wide verandahs.
There's an interesting National Trust
walking tour brochure to guide you
around the old part of Cairns. Walk
along the pleasant Esplanade and look
for the colourful posters illustrating
all the birds you might spot here. Further along is the rather sad Catalina
memorial to the aircrew who operated
from Cairns during WW II.

Cairns Reef World is on the Esplanade and is open 8.30 am to 5.30 pm
daily, it displays a wide variety of fish
and coral. Feeding time is 2 pm daily,
admission is $2.50. Orchid growing is a
big business in Cairns, as you can see
at Limberlost Nursery (113 Old Smith-
field Rd, Freshwater) or Roraima
Orchids (342 Sheridan St, Cairns North).
In Edge Hill the Royal Flying Doctor
Service, 1 Junction St, is open to
visitors 10 to 11.30 am and 1.30 to 3.30
pm on weekdays. You can see coral
jewellery and a free Barrier Reef film at

Laroc on the corner of Aumuller and
Comport Sts, Portsmouth. Cairns has
one of those water slide operations
which seem to have proliferated up and
down the Queensland coast — $1.50
entry then $2.50 a half hour for the
slides. It's at the end of Lake St. You
can tour the Carlton & United Brewery
at 113 Spence St, on Tuesday and
Thursday afternoons and see NQ Lager
and Cairns Draught in production
Tickets from the tourist office at 44
McLeod St.

On the corner of Lake and Shield
Sts the Cairns Museum is housed in the
old School of Arts building of 1907
a fine example of early north Queensland architecture. The museum, only
opened in 1980, has exhibits of Abor
iginal artefacts, a display on the con
struction of the Cairns-Kuranda railway
the contents of a now demolished Chin
ese joss house, exhibits on gold mining
in the area and natural history displays
It's open Monday to Friday from 10
am to 3 pm and admission is $1.

Further Out

There are arrowed walks around the
Flecker Park Botanic Gardens of
Collins Avenue, Edge Hill. In all the
blue and red arrow walks cover about
10 km. The walk up to Mt Whitfield
provides fine views over Cairns. It'
open daily. Centenary Lakes in North
Cairns is another, more recently opened
gardens with a variety of birdlife on the
park lakes.

At Smith Creek you can tour the
Bulk Sugar Terminal at 3.30 pm on
weekdays from late-July to early
December. There are short cruise
around the mangrove swamps off Smith
Creek, daily from the Marlin Jetty
Marlin are caught off Cairns from Sep
tember to December and major catche
are weighed at the game fishing whar
on the Esplanade. Perhaps in another
century big-game fishing will be looke
upon with the same distaste as Africa

big-game hunting is now.

Places to Stay

Cairns has hostels, motels, hotels (not too many surprisingly enough), quite a few pleasantly old-fashioned guest houses, lots of holiday flats and a wide selection of campsites. It's also quite a travellers' centre, there is so much to see and do around Cairns and it's also an Australian arrival or departure point for Papua New Guinea. The seafront Esplanade is one of the best places to look for accommodation in Cairns — you'll find an example of almost every accommodation possibility going along the Esplanade, including both hostels. There are also quite a few places along the beaches north of Cairns, particularly holiday flats. Note that the accommodation scene in Cairns is extremely competitive. If you're there in a slack season there's likely to be a lot of price cutting and you can often find some real bargains.

Hostels Cairns has a couple of hostels although neither is an official youth hostel. The popular *Cairns Tropical Hostel* (tel 51 2323) is at 123 Esplanade, conveniently central. It's a big, rambling old place with plenty of open garden area where you can sit out and talk or just collect a suntan. The kitchen facilities are a bit cramped but it's a popular place and that doesn't appear to bother most people. Nightly costs are $4.50 per person and there are quite a few rooms for two so couples can effectively have a double room for $9. The hostel also rents out bicycles for $5 a day and does probably the cheapest tour out to the reef you'll find anywhere.

At 77-79 Esplanade the *Seaview Hostel* (tel 51 2159) is a guest house recently converted to hostel-style operations. With a YH card a bed costs $5.50, otherwise it's $6 and accommodation is all in rooms for two, three or four, there are no dorms. Between the two Esplanade hostels most people seem to prefer 123.

Guest Houses, Private Hotels & Holiday Flats There's lots of overlap in this segment and quite a few places seem to have rooms that fall into more than one category. The Esplanade is again the best hunting ground for guest houses. The *International Private Hotel* (tel 51 2225) at 67 Esplanade is an excellent example — it's convenient and good value. Singles cost $12 or 15, doubles $24 or 28 — none of these rooms have private facilities but the more expensive rooms are brighter and have tea/coffee making equipment. There are also some $30 doubles with attached bathrooms. All prices include breakfast (a substantial one) plus it's a friendly place and there are laundry facilities and a TV lounge.

At 89 Esplanade, *Warana* (tel 51 2376) costs $12/20 for singles/doubles with shared facilities, tea/coffee making equipment plus a TV lounge and a small swimming pool. Further down the Esplanade at 149 is *Sans Souci* (tel 51 2431), a cheap guest house at $9 per person, room only. At 153 is *Silver Palms* (tel 51 2059) where rooms cost $15/22 including use of kitchen facilities, laundry and a TV room. There is a whole string of guest houses on the Esplanade between Minnie and Upward Sts. At 179 there's *Ocean View Holiday Flats* and further along at 223 *Linga Longa* (tel 51 3013) is excellent value with holiday flats at just $16 a day (for two) or $81 a week.

Moving back from the Esplanade you could try the *Parkview* (tel 51 3573) at 174-180 Grafton St. The guest house section has rooms with shared facilities at $10 per person. There is a kitchen, barbecue, laundry, pool and the inevitable TV lounge. You could easily get the impression that all Cairns has to offer in the evening is the idiot box! Parkview also has holiday flats, all self-contained and with cooking facilities,

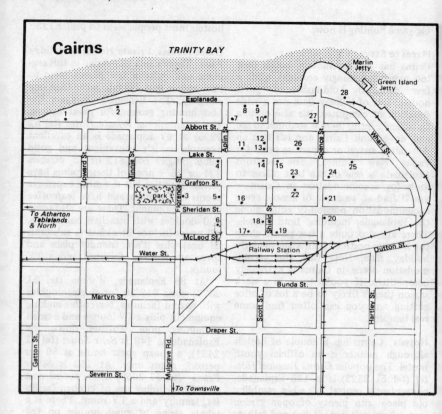

Cairns

TRINITY BAY

Marlin Jetty

Green Island Jetty

Esplanade

Abbott St.

Aplin St.

Lake St.

Grafton St.

Florence St.

park

Sheridan St.

McLeod St.

Water St.

Upward St.

Minnie St.

Science St.

Wharf St.

Railway Station

Dutton St.

To Atherton Tablelands & North

Bunda St.

Martyn St.

Scott St.

Hartley St.

Draper St.

Gatton St.

Mulgrave Rd.

Severin St.

To Townsville

1 Catalina Memorial
2 Tropical Hostel
3 Civic Centre
4 Trinity Cycles
5 RACQ
6 Mangrove Jacks, Trinity Fish & Chips
7 Air Queensland
8 Seaview Hostel
9 International Guest House
10 Air Niugini
11 Walker's Bookshop
12 QGTB
13 TAA
14 Cairns Museum

15 Hides Hotel
16 Budget Accommodation
17 Cairns Tourist Office
18 Strawbs
19 Grand Hotel
20 Mamma Maria's
21 Mexican Pete's
22 Rusty's Bazaar
23 Greyhound Terminal
24 Pizza Corner
25 Cairns Waterworks
26 Ansett
27 GPO
28 Reef World

for $24 a double. It's a pleasantly run place and good value.

Also on Grafton St there are more holiday flats at *Coral Court* at 194-196 or at 151 there's the *Grafton Lodge Guest House* (tel 51 6638) which costs $10 single, $16 double with pool, communal kitchen, the inevitable TV room and fans in the room. There are cheaper rates by the week in this convenient place. Over at 86 Abbott St, *Central House* (tel 51 2869) costs $17/25 for fan-cooled rooms, again there's a pool, laundry and communal kitchen.

A bit out from the centre at 158C Martyn St the *Tropicana Lodge* (tel 51 1729) has rooms at $15/25 for singles/doubles or $27/32 with private facilities. All rooms have tea/coffee making equipment, there's a laundry and pool and the prices include breakfast. Finally at 100 Sheridan St, just round the corner from the railway station, *Budget Accommodation* (tel 51 1264) used to be the old Sally Army People's Palace. Nightly costs are just $11/20 for singles/doubles including continental breakfast. There's a laundry and use of kitchen facilities.

Motels The *Cairns Motel* (tel 51 2771) at 48 Spence St is about as central as you could ask for. Rooms are fan-cooled, singles/doubles cost $25/30.

Like everything else there are quite a selection of motels along the Esplanade. At number 81 Esplanade the *Esplanade Motel* (tel 51 2326) is a small, two-storey place with tea/coffee making facilities, fridge, TV and fan cooling for $28/32.

Acacia Court (tel 51 5011) at 230-238 Lake St is really holiday flats but there's a pool, laundry facilities, rooms are fully-equipped and nightly costs are $32 for a double, $36 with kitchen facilities. The *Reef Motel* (tel 51 3540) at 215 Abbott St is a new motel with singles/doubles at $20/30 including a 'tropical' breakfast. *Hollywood Inn* (tel

51 3458) at 239 Sheridan St has singles/doubles at $22/30 and cheaper rates by the week — they have one and two bedroom holiday flats and smaller 'flatlets' but there's a three night minimum.

There are quite a few motels along the Bruce Highway, which runs right through the city. Cheaper places include the *Glenlee* (tel 54 1009) at 560 Bruce Highway with singles/doubles at $26/30. Or at 43-45 the *Sun Scene* (tel 55 4357) is $23/27.

Camping There are about a dozen campsites in and close to Cairns and others up the coast. Almost without exception they take campers as well as caravans. Some of the more central sites include:

Cairns Golden Key Caravan Park (tel 54 1222), 532 Mulgrave Rd, camping $4.60, on-site vans $15, holiday flats $31.

City Caravan Park (tel 51 1467), corner of Little & James Sts, camping $4, on-site vans $14.

Coles Caravan Park (tel 53 1163), 28 Pease St, camping $4.60, on-site vans $15.

First City Caravilla Caravan Park (tel 54 1403), Kelly St, camping $4.60, on-site vans $15.

Four Seasons Caravan Park (tel 54 1479), 495 Mulgrave St, camping $5.50, on-site vans $17.

White Rock Cabina Trailer Court (tel 54 1523), corner Skull Rd & Bruce Highway, camping $3.50, on-site vans $13, holiday flats $16.

Places to Eat
For a town of its size Cairns has quite an amazing number (and even more important variety) of restaurants. Unfortunately they suffer from the same problem you'll find south in Surfers — a tendency to close early and virtually no attempt to take advantage of the climate by providing open-air-dining. A

great waste!

Snack & Fast Food Lots of places
around town do good sandwiches, fast
foods and takeaways including a
number of health food places. In
Rusty's Bazaar at 89 Grafton St, *Good-
ings* does excellent sandwiches or if you
fancy croissants for breakfast they're
open from 8 am. In Andrejec's Arcade,
from 55 Lake St through to Grafton St,
Nibbles is another good place for sandwiches. Or try *Happy's*, on Sheridan St
almost on the corner of Spence, open at
6.30 am so they're good for an early
breakfast. *Trinity Fish & Chips* at 49
Aplin St do excellent fish & chips.

Counter Meals Most of Cairns' counter
meal places tend to be very straightforward but also very cheap. You can get
a meal for $3 to $4 in quite a few of
Cairns many old hotels — some to try
include *Fitzgerald's Pub* on the corner
of Grafton and Shields, the *Great
Northern Hotel* at 69 Abbott St or the
Railway Hotel on McLeod St, opposite
the railway station.

Also opposite the railway station is
the *Grand Hotel*, where there's a fancier
counter meal section (it's also open to
8.30 pm, later than Cairn's norm). Here
meals are in the $5 to $7 bracket (generally at the cheaper end) and there's a
serve-yourself salad bar. Right in the
city centre *Hides Hotel* has the *Tropical
Lounge Bistro* with some of the best
counter food in Cairns. It's open 6 pm
to 9 pm, main courses are in the $5.50
to $8 range (mostly around $6 to $6.50)
and there's a serve yourself salad table.

Restaurants *Strawbs* at 74 Shields St is
great value with entrees around $2.50,
main courses around $4.50 (lots of veal
dishes, scallops at $5.50, prawns and so
on) and desserts for around $2.50. You
can have an excellent three-course meal
here for $10, and it's a pleasant, relaxed,
friendly place to eat. A little less of a

place for a night out but also very economical, *Mangrove Jack's* is next door to
Trinity Fish & Chips at 49 Aplin and is
really a sit down fish & chippery — but
it's bright and cheerful and offers a
straight forward fixed-price meal for
just $4. That gets you a choice of main
courses (with the accent on fish of
course), dessert and tea or coffee. Both
of these places are highly recommended
for pleasant and economical eating in
Cairns.

A few doors down from Mangrove
Jacks is *Thuggee Bills* at 42B Aplin.
If your Indian history isn't good enough
the Thugs were a gang of ritual mur-
derers who plagued parts of India during
the days of the Raj — until they were
finally wiped out by a British officer,
Thuggee Bill. Good curries but rather
more expensive at $7 to $9 for main
courses. *Mexican Pete's* at 61 Spence
St has terrific decor and good food,
main courses $4 to $7.50. On some
nights there is also live music, in which
case there's a 50c surcharge. Across the
road at 42 Spence is *Toko Baru*, good
Indonesian food but again it's slightly
more expensive.

Cairns has a bunch of places of the
faster food variety. Like *Pizza Corner*
on Grafton and Spence where you can
get pizzas from $4.20 to $5.20 for small
ones, $5.80 to $6.80 for large ones, plus
pastas in the $3.50 to $5.50 range. A
few doors down at 43 Spence the *Pancake House* is also popular, main courses
around $4. In Rusty's Bazaar at 89
Spence, *Eggcetera* is a pleasant place
with lots of different omelettes in the
$3 to $6 bracket.

Mamma Maria's is a long-runner, a
pleasant, old, outdoorsy sort of place on
the corner of Spence and Sheridan. The
menu is pizzas and general Italian and
the main courses are in the $5 to $6
bracket. At 67 Esplanade the *Inter
national Guest House* has a restaurant
downstairs, open to the sea breezes
in front. They do a $6 soup-main course

dessert-tea or coffee meal with a nightly special at $5.

Entertainment
Radio 4CA have the run down on who is playing where around the Cairns pubs. Facing each other across Lake St down by Spence St the *Great Northern* in the Tudor Room and the *Central Hotel* both have live music in the evenings. *Hides Hotel* also often has live entertainment. Cairns Folk & Jazz Club meets on Sunday evenings at the Theatre Shop, sort of behind the Water Works on Grafton St, costs $1.

Getting There
Air Ansett and TAA both fly to Cairns from all the regular places. In particular there are as many as eight to 10 flights daily coming up the east coast from Brisbane and the southern capitals. Some typical fares include Melbourne $294, Sydney $252 (standby $189), Brisbane $193 ($145), Alice Springs $198 ($149), Townsville $78, Mt Isa $134 ($101), Darwin $221 ($167). The Darwin fare varies considerably, depending on the route you take. The cheapest fare, listed above, is via Gove with Airlines of Northern Australia. In Cairns TAA (tel 50 3777) are on the corner of Shield and Lake Sts. Ansett (tel 51 3366) are at 84 Lake St.

Air Queensland (tel 51 6511) live at 62 Abbott St. Cairns is their HQ and they have a comprehensive network around north Queensland — see the introductory Getting Around section. Cairns is also an international airport with regular flights to and from Port Moresby in Papua New Guinea. Air Niugini (tel 51 4177) is at 4 Shields St and the Port Moresby flight costs $155.

Rail The Sunlander from Brisbane to Cairns operates six days a week. The train takes about 40 hours to make the 1681 km trip. The fare from Brisbane is $81.20 in 1st, $54.10 in economy.

Sleeping berths cost $12 per night in 1st, $6 in economy. You can break your journey anywhere along the way, within certain guidelines. By rail it's about 7½ hours to Townsville, 16½ to Mackay, 24 to Rockhampton.

Bus Greyhound and Ansett Pioneer both operate daily on the coast route from Brisbane. Fares vary slightly between the two carriers. From Brisbane it's 30 hours ($92), Rockhampton 18 hours ($66), Mackay 13 hours ($49), Townsville six hours ($25). Ansett Pioneer (tel 51 2411) are at 58 Shields St and Greyhound (tel 51 3388) at 78 Grafton St.

Getting Around
Bus There are a number of bus services in and around Cairns. The northern beach bus service (tel 55 3079 for details) operates from Cairns as far as Ellis Beach above five times a day on weekdays, twice only on Saturdays and Sundays. The fare to Ellis Beach is $1.50. On weekdays there are a couple of other trips which don't run all the way north to Ellis Beach.

Other bus services include Mossman twice a week, up through the Atherton Tableland to Herberton and also to Cooktown twice a week. Plus, of course there's the famous Kuranda train trip. See the relevant sections for more details.

Car Rental Cairns is another place where it's worth considering renting a car if you don't already have your own transport. There are places of interest in the town itself and most visitors manage to get out to at least one of the islands off the coast, but there is also plenty to see and do around Cairns whether it's making the beach crawl up to Port Douglas or exploring the Atherton Tablelands. As in other areas of tropical Australia Mokes are about the cheapest cars to rent and they're also ideal for the sunny climate and for relaxed, open-air sightseeing. Almost all the rental firms in Cairns have Mokes.

All the major firms are represented in Cairns, you'll find most of them along Lake St, where Hertz, Budget and Avis all live within a stone's throw of each other. Other local firms include Mini Car Rental at 142 Sheridan St with Mokes at $9.50 a day plus 11c a km or Lasers at $11.50 plus 12c. Lasers are also available at $28 a day with unlimited km. At Sheridan Rent-a-Car at 196A Sheridan St, Mokes are $8 and 11c while VW beetles and 'oldies' go from $6.50 plus 11c. Cairns Rent-a-Car at 67 McLeod St also have the ubiquitous Mokes at $10 plus 13c and if you want to go bush bashing they hire Suzuki four-wheel drives at $12.50 plus 15c.

Note that most Cairns rental firms on most of their cars specifically prohibit you from taking them up the Cape Tribulation road, on the road to Cooktown, or on the Chillagoe Caves road. A sign in the car will announce this prohibition and the contract will threaten dire unhappiness if you do so. Of course lots of people ignore these prohibitions but if you get stuck in the mud half-way up to Cape Tribulation it could be a little embarrassing.

Bike & Motorcycle Rental Trinity Cycles on the corner of Aplin and Lake Sts rent bikes for $4 a day ($15 a week) with back-pedal brakes, $6 and $20 for bikes with gears. You can rent motorcycles from Cairns Motorcycle Hire at 134 Sheridan St from $15 a day.

Airport Cairns' airport at Aeroglen is fairly convenient for the city, about $5 to $6 by taxi. If the airport bus service has not been replaced you could always try going out to the main road and getting a northern beaches bus as it comes by — phone 55 3079 for timetable details. Cairns airport is an old-fashioned place, well overdue for a new terminal building. At the moment all the airlines operate from different buildings scattered indiscriminately around. Avis, Budget and Hertz have desks at the airport.

Tours There are a vast number of tours in and around Cairns. Day tours include the city sights, up on the Atherton Tableland or to Kuranda, or up the coast to Port Douglas. There are also bus trips up to Cape Tribulation or three day tours to Cooktown ($120). Of course there are numerous kinds of trips out to Green and Fitzroy Islands off Cairns or Low Island off Port Douglas. Scuba diving trips, reef cruises, fishing trips and Cairns' famous game fishing are other possibilities. You're looking at $300 a day for game fishing!

If you want to get out to the outer reef one of the cheapest ways of doing it is through the Tropical Hostel at 123 Esplanade. They have fairly regular reef trips costing $23, or $25 if you're not staying there. There are also cruises up the mangrove creeks around Cairns, $7 for two hour cruises from the Marlin Jetty. Or for $27 you can make a day's canoeing trip on the Mulgrave River.

Aerial trips are another possibility. The North Queensland Aero Club have a whole collection of flights from brief scenic flights for $20 on up. Air Queensland also have a number of standard tours out of Cairns. A day trip to Cooktown is $70, a day tour to Cooktown and Lizard Island is $125, a three day tour of the Cape York Peninsula, taking in Cooktown, Lizard Island, Weipa, Thursday Island and the Edward River will set you back $500.

GREEN & FITZROY ISLANDS

There are two popular islands off from Cairns, both of which attract lots of day-trippers (too many some think) and some overnighters too. Just up the coast off Port Douglas there's another reef island, popular for day-tripping although nowhere near as commercialised as Green Island. North of Green Island, Michaelmas Cay is a popular rendezvous for trips out to the Barrier Reef. Further still, although also reached from Cairns, is Lizard Island an expensive and exclusive hideaway and certainly not over-run by tourist hordes at all.

Green Island

Offshore from Cairns, 27 km to the north-east, Green Island is a true coral cay and the island and its surrounding reef is all national park. Green Island is a popular day trip from Cairns although it also has overnight accommodation. It's a really beautiful island and although somewhat marred by casual, shonky development it's easy to get away from it. A 10-minute stroll down to the other end of the island and you can forget the tourist development is even there. The beach, right around the island, is beautiful, the water fine, the fish prolific.

The man-made attractions start at the end of the pier with the underwater observatory ($2.40) with lots of fish to be seen around the windows five metres below sea-level. On the island there's the Barrier Reef Theatre ($1.50) with a Barrier Reef film and Marineland Melanesia ($2.50) with a wide variety of fish and corals in aquarium tanks plus larger creatures (sharks, turtles, stingrays, crocodiles) in pools or enclosures and a display of PNG art.

Places to Stay At the *Coral Cay Resort* (tel 070 51 4644) nightly cost including dinner, bed and breakfast is $32 to $50 per person in the off-season, $35 to $60 in the tourist-season.

Fitzroy Island

Six km off the coast and 26 km south-east of Cairns, Fitzroy Island has only developed as a resort island since 1981. It's a larger continental island with some fine beaches and good coral only 50 metres off the beach in the resort area. Day trips to the island operate from Cairns and you can also make day-trips which combine Fitzroy and Green Islands.

Places to Stay Including meals a double at the island resort costs $75 a day.

Getting There

There is a wide variety of day-trips to the two islands, either to one island or the other or combining both islands. Check departure times and return times and the travelling time when choosing your boat. Typical trips are the regular Green Island cruise for $11 return, 1½ hours travel each way. The faster catamaran makes the trip in just 45 minutes and costs $17 return. Or there's a trip to both Green and Fitzroy Islands with 1½ hours on Fitzroy, three hours on Green, $15. Another cruise includes lunch and a glass-bottom boat trip at Green Island for $20. Or you can go out to both islands on a slower boat for $15 including a barbecue lunch. Or there's a Fitroy Island only trip for $12. The cruises leave from the Marlin Jetty or Green Island Jetty.

ATHERTON TABLELAND

Inland from the coast between Innisfail and Cairns is the lush, rolling countryside of the Atherton Tableland and the Evelyn Tableland. From the coast the land rises up sharply then rolls gently back towards the Great Dividing Range. here the altitude tempers the tropical heat and abundant rainfall and rich volcanic soil combine to make this one of the greenest places in Queensland. It's an easy-going area yet little more than a century ago this peaceful, pastoral region was still a wild jungle.

The first explorers came here in 1874 to '76, looking for a repeat of the Palmer River goldrush, further to the north, a few years before. The Aboriginal population was violently opposed to this intrusion but they were soon over-run. Some gold was found and rather more tin but though mining spurred the development of roads and railways through the rugged, difficult land to the plateau it was farming that soon became the principal activity.

Today the tableland is a pleasant escape from the coastal heat and it also offers beautiful scenery and some of Australia's most appealing waterfalls. In the southern section of the Evelyn Tableland are Queensland's two highest mountains — Mt Bartle Frere (1656 metres) and Mt Bellenden-Ker (1591 metres). Getting there is half the fun in the tablelands and the railway ride to Kuranda is one of the region's major attractions.

Getting There

The most popular route up to the tablelands is the incredibly scenic railway line that winds up from Cairns to Kuranda, with its famous station. The fare is $3 one-way, the train runs daily, ring 51 1111 for details. White Car Coaches operate buses from the Ansett Pioneer terminal up into the tablelands every day. Fares are Kuranda $2.60, Mareeba $7.85, Atherton $11.85, Herberton $15.

Kuranda (population 500)

The railway line from Cairns climbs through superb scenery to Kuranda, at the top of the Macalister Range, 34 km away. The line was completed, at great expense, in 1888 and goes through 15 tunnels during its steep ascent. The final stretch is through the spectacular Barron Falls gorge — it's even more spectacular after heavy rain although hydro-power generation has detracted from its magnificence. Kuranda's picture postcard railway station, decked out in tropical flowers and ferns, is justly famous.

Other attractions include the colourful Sunday morning market with produce and local arts and crafts on display — there's quite a large alternative establishment up here. There are a couple of short jungle walks in the same area while the Honey House Motel, in front of the market site, has a variety of honeys on sale plus glass-fronted beehives so you can see the busy little workers doing their stuff. On the main street there's a small Aboriginal museum and crafts centre — admission 50c. Just off the highway, on Black Mountain Rd, there's a jungle walk at the Tropical Sanctuary & Wildlife Garden. Close to Kuranda the Rainforest World tourist park has rainforest tours in WW II army amphibious vehicles for $3. Down on the plains, where the Kennedy Highway branches off for Kuranda, there's a monument to the trail blazers who cut the difficult roads into the tableland.

Places to Stay Kuranda has one of Australia's most popular *youth hostels* (tel 93 7355) at 6 Arara St. It's in a fine old building, run by Mrs Miller, and accommodates no less than 120. Nightly cost is $3.60 and the guys' quarters are better than the girls' — say the girls!

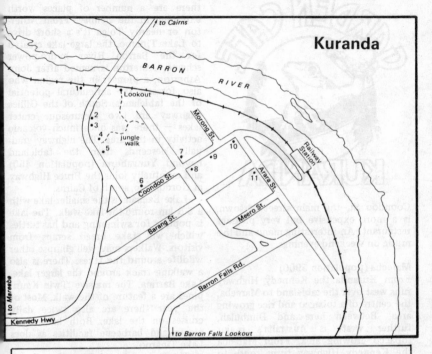

Kuranda

1 Pioneer Cemetery	7 Post Office
2 Garden Cafe	8 Top Pub (Fitzpatrick's)
3 Kuranda Inn	9 Aboriginal Museum
4 Kuranda Market	10 Bottom Pub (Kuranda Hotel)
5 Honey House	11 Mrs Miller's Youth Hostel
6 Frog's Restaurant	

Alternatively the *Honey House Motel* (tel 93 7261) is small, right in the centre and costs $20/27 for singles/doubles. The *Bottom Pub* also has accommodation. There's a caravan park just beyond the town. Note that there is no bank in Kuranda.

Places to Eat Plenty of places to eat in Kuranda including counter meals at the hotels — the top pub and the bottom pub. The *Kuranda Rainforest Restaurant* is in the youth hostel — open 6 to 10 pm it does mainly vege-

tarian food. Main courses are around $4, it's not just for hostellers. The *Kuranda Garden Cafe* is a pleasantly breezy place — you can eat inside (cane blinds) or out in the open. Burgers for $1.30, main courses from around $5.50 (rump steak) to $7 (barramundi). Delicious strudel here too. It closes at 6 pm, all day on Monday. Next door the *Kuranda Inn* does curries and pizzas (a good combination!), it's closed Thursdays.

Honey House is excellent for scones, cream and honey. And you can do a honey tasting session! *Frogs* on

Coondoo St, the main street of town, is a more expensive but very pleasant restaurant. An interesting menu and live music on weekend evenings.

Mareeba (population 5900)
From Kuranda the Kennedy Highway runs west over the tableland to Mareeba, the centre of a tobacco and rice growing area. Between here and Dimbulah, further west, is Australia's major tobacco growing area. From Mareeba the Kennedy Highway turns south to Atherton in the centre of the tableland.

Chillagoe
From Mareeba you can continue 140 km to the Chillagoe Caves — the road is dirt but it's a very interesting trip. Check road conditions before departing, the road can be difficult after Dimbulah. There are tours, usually twice daily, at 9 am and 1 pm, of the extensive limestone caves. Other caves you can explore yourself but you'll need a torch. Chillagoe itself also has a museum with reminders of its heyday as a mining town.

Atherton (population 3700)
Although it's a pleasant, prosperous town, Atherton, like Mareeba, has little of interest in its own right although there are a number of places worth exploring in the vicinity. From Atherton or nearby Tolga it's a short drive to Lake Tinaroo, the large lake created for the Barron River hydro-power scheme. Atherton is named after John Atherton, a pioneer in the region who also foresaw the agricultural potential of the tablelands. South of the Gillies Highway are two picturesque crater lakes — there was once much volcanic activity in this area. The highway gradually descends from the tableland beyond Yungaburra (population 450) and eventually joins the Bruce Highway at Gordonvale, south of Cairns.

Lake Eacham is the smaller lake with a 6.5 km round-the-lake walk. The lake is popular for swimming and has turtles which will take bread scraps from visitors. Walkers may well glimpse other wildlife around the lakes. There is also a walking track around the larger lake, Lake Barrina. The massive 'Twin Kauri' pines are a feature of the walk. Most of the year there are also twice daily cruises on the lake. Both lakes have picnic and barbecue facilities as does Lake Tinaroo.

The western road from Yungaburra to Malanda passes by the massive 'Curtain Fig Tree', a fig tree curtained by a huge strangler palm.

Malanda
Malanda claims to have the longest milk-run in Australia since its dairy industry supplies milk all the way to Mt Isa, Darwin and even the north of Western Australia and across to Papua New Guinea. An equivalent in the US would be a dairy in California supplying milk to a town in New York state! Just north of the town are the Malanda Falls which drop into a pleasant swimming hole. There's a good four km walk along the riverside and through the rainforest.

Millaa Millaa (population 350)
South of Malanda the 15 km gravel

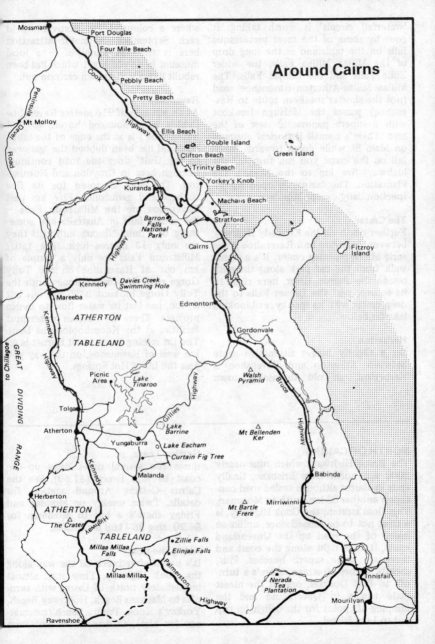

Around Cairns

Mossman
Port Douglas
Four Mile Beach
Cook
Highway
Peninsula
Pebbly Beach
Pretty Beach
Mt Molloy
Ellis Beach
Double Island
Clifton Beach
Trinity Beach
Yorkey's Knob
Kuranda
Machans Beach
Stratford
Barron
Falls
National Park
Cairns
Green Island
Fitzroy
Island
Davies Creek
Swimming Hole
Kennedy
ATHERTON
Edmonton
Mareeba
TABLELAND
Gordonvale
Walsh
Pyramid
Picnic
Area
Lake Tinaroo
Bruce
Highway
Tolga
Lake
Barrine
Mt Bellenden
Ker
Atherton
Yungaburra
Lake Eacham
Curtain Fig Tree
Herberton
Malanda
Babinda
ATHERTON
Mirriwinni
TABLELAND
Mt Bartle
Frere
The Crater
Zillie Falls
Elinjaa Falls
Millaa Millaa
Falls
Millaa Millaa
Nerada
Tea
Plantation
Innisfail
Ravenshoe
Highway
Mourilyan

GREAT DIVIDING RANGE

Kennedy Highway

Gillies Highway

Palmerston Highway

to Chillagoe

Mt Molloy Mossman Road

'waterfall circuit' is worth taking. It goes by some of the most picturesque falls on the tableland — the long drop of the Millaa Millaa Falls, the wider Zillie Falls and the Elinjaa Falls. The Millaa Millaa-Atherton/Ravenshoe road (not the shorter southern route to Ravenshoe) passes the McHugh Lookout with a superb panoramic view of the area. There's a small Historical Museum on Main St while down towards Innisfail on the coast you can turn off the highway five km to the Nerada Tea Plantation. The factory is open for inspection daily except Mondays.

The Crater
Further north on the Kennedy Highway between Atherton and Ravenshoe is the eerie Mt Hypipamee crater. It's a scenic walk from the car park along the path beside the Barron River, here close to its source, past the Dinner Falls to the deep crater with its spooky, evil-looking lake far below.

Herberton
On a slightly longer alternative route between Atherton and Ravenshoe is Herberton, an old tin-mining town where a colourful Tin Festival is held each September. A major attraction here is the Tin Pannikin — a local museum in an old hotel which has been rebuilt like a well known cartoon pub.

Ravenshoe
At an altitude of 915 metres Ravenshoe (which is pronounced 'ravens-ho' not 'raven-shoe') is at the edge of the tableland and has been dubbed the 'gateway to the Gulf' since the road continues through here to Croydon and Normanton. The area is noted for its fine timbers and gemstones. Five km past Ravenshoe are the Millstream Falls — the widest falls in Australia and something of a mini-Niagara although they are only 13 metres high. The Little Millstream Falls are only a couple of km out of Ravenshoe on the Tully Gorge road. If you continue south the Tully Gorge lookout is 25 km out but it, too, has lost its water flow to hydro projects. There are various watersport facilities at the Koombooloomba Dam. The tin mining town of Mt Garnet is 47 km west of Ravenshoe, on the way you pass the Innot Hot Springs.

NORTH OF CAIRNS
The Bruce Highway, which runs nearly 2000 km north from Brisbane, finally ends in Cairns although sealed road continues another 80 km north to Mossman. This final stretch, the Cook Highway, is a treat not to be missed since, unlike so much of the road up the Queensland coast, it runs right along the coast and there are some superb beaches. Plus, shortly before Mossman, there's a turn-off to Port Douglas, one of the nicest little towns in Queensland and the jumping-off point for the delightful trip out to Low Island.

Getting There
Buses run several times daily up the coast to Ellis Beach ($1.50). See the Cairns Getting Around section for details. Twice weekly on Monday and Friday there's a bus to Mossman for $6.20, ring 98 1168 for details.

Along the Coast
It's beach after beach all the way along the Cook Highway. They start almost immediately north of Cairns with turn-offs to Machans Beach, Holloway Beach, Yorkey's Knob, Trinity Beach (catamarans for hire), Clifton Beach and Palm

Cove where there is the Australian Bird Park (open daily 9 am to 5 pm, admission $3). Catamarans can also be hired here. Then round the headland from Buchan Point the road runs along the coast and hugs it the rest of the way to Port Douglas. Ellis Beach is an unofficial nude-bathing beach at its southern end while at the central part of the beach there's a campsite and place to eat. Further north there's Pretty Beach and Pebbly Beach before the superb sweep of Four Mile Beach which stretches south from the headland at Port Douglas.

Soon after Ellis Beach you reach Hartley Creek Jungle Reserve with a collection of native Australian wildlife of the far north. Frankly, as a reserve it's no great shakes, most of the enclosures are a bit shoddy and dull, but the sheer showmanship of the proprietor makes it one of the most interesting reserves in Australia. When he feeds Charlie the crocodile you know for certain why it's not wise to get bitten by one! And you've never seen anything eat apples until you've seen a cassowary knock back a dozen of them. The park is open daily (at least during the winter season) but you want to go there at crocodile feeding time so check the times in Cairns. Entry cost is $2.50, an extra dollar at showtimes. More crocs can be seen at the Australian Crocodile Park at Palm Cove.

Port Douglas (population 500)

In the early days of the far north's development, Port Douglas was actually a rival for Cairns, or Trinity Bay as Cairns was then known, but Cairns got the upper hand and Port Douglas became a sleepy little backwater. It was just a quiet little fishing town until people began to realise what a delightful, laid back little place it was. Now it's quite a busy tourist centre but still a great place to visit with a string of interesting little shops and restaurants to

wander around when the magnificent beach, the boats and the lookout get dull. If you've spent a long time travelling up the coast this is a great place to sit back and recharge your batteries before heading on somewhere else.

The two old hotels on the main street have to be the best part of Port Douglas. It's hard to imagine a nicer country pub than the Central Hotel and Court House Hotel on the corner is just about as pleasant. A recent addition to the Port Douglas attractions is the Ben Cropp Wreck Museum on the old wharf. There's a collection of bits and pieces of junk salvaged from various wrecks plus a continuous film show. It's open 9 am to 5 pm daily and admission is $2 — one for the wreck freaks.

Barrier Reef Shells on Macrossan St have a good display of shells while up the hill the Nautilus Boutique produces rather beautiful shell jewellery. There's a fine view over the coastline and out to sea from Flagstaff Hill lookout. You can hire bikes for $6 a half-day,. $8 a day, from beside Mocka's Pies on Macrossan St, the main street.

Places to Stay There are a number of campsites along Four Mile Beach into Port Douglas, some of them within easy walking distance of the centre. Cheapest of the motels is the *Port Douglas Motel* (tel 98 5248) on Davidson St at $27/32. On the corner of Macrossan and Garrick Sts the *Balboa Holiday Flats* (tel 98 5354) are just $22 for a double but there are only three of them. There are also holiday flats at *Whispering Palms* (tel 98 5128) on Langley Rd from $27 for two. Or check the noticeboard by the post office if you're looking for longer term accommodation.

Places to Eat There are plenty of places to eat in Port Douglas including the famous *Mocka's Pies* on the main road. Pie connoisseurs have claimed their 75c pies are absolutely the best anywhere in

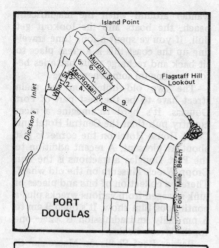

PORT DOUGLAS

1 Ben Cropp Museum
2 Catalina Restaurant
3 Court House Hotel
4 Central Hotel
5 Post Office
6 Nautilus Enterprises
7 Mocka's Pies, Los Romanos
  Restaurant & Pizzas, Bike Hire
8 Island Carvings
9 Barrier Reef Shells

Australia. You'll have to judge for yourself but I've got to admit I'm on the connoisseurs' side! Next door is the slightly expensive *Los Romanos Restaurant* and the adjoining pizza section — with pizzas from $2 (mini) to $6.

You can get counter lunches and teas in both of the delightful pubs on the main street — the *Central Hotel* and the *Court House Hotel*. In the latter there's a pleasant outdoor eating place and prices are generally around $5. Port Douglas also has other more expensive eating places, including the nice outdoorsy *Catalina Seafood Restaurant*. But a pie from Mocka's, sitting in the park by the waterfront, is hard to beat.

Low Island

Offshore from Port Douglas is a fine

little coral island topped by an incredibly well kept old lighthouse. This is a very different sort of reef island from the hyped-up Green Island off Cairns and worth making the trip out to see. The *MV Martin Cash* goes out every day at 10.30 am and the cost is $22.50. There are also trips available including transport from Cairns for $28.

Mossman (population 1600)

The far north sugar town of Mossman is almost the end of the road. Sidetrack five km to visit the beautiful river and waterfalls at Mossman Gorge. This is the furthest north sugar town in Australia and during the July to November crushing season you can tour the sugar mills. The old steam train Bally Hooley makes $5 trips daily on the narrow gauge railway lines through the canefields.

Daintree

The road continues north-west to the real end of the sealed road at Daintree but before there you can turn off the road to the ferry crossing on the Daintree River and continue up the dirt road to Cape Tribulation. Between Mossman and the ferry turn-off is the fine beach at Wonga. From the Daintree Ferry the Crocodile Express makes daily trips up the river to Daintree for $10.

Cape Tribulation

After Port Douglas the road turns away from the coast to Mossman and then Daintree but shortly before Daintree you can branch off the road, on a small dirt road that runs down to the Daintree River. These, beside the 'Beware of Crocodiles' sign, a cable ferry crosses the river to the start of the Cape Tribulation road. It's 41 km to Cape Tribulation on a dirt road all the way, there are a number of creek crossings to be made but except after periods of heavy rain it's no problem in conventional two-wheel drive cars.

In the '70s this was a hippie outpost

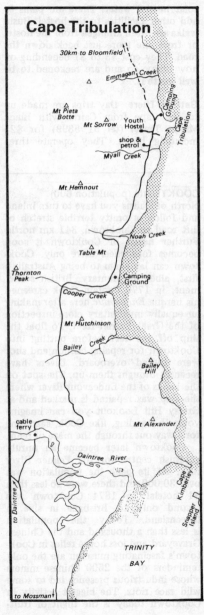

Cape Tribulation

with a number of settlements, particularly at the infamous Cedar Bay, further north towards Cooktown. There the Queensland police mounted a raid on the unfortunate inhabitants in search of the dreaded weed, burnt down their homes and charged them with, would you believe it, vagrancy! Today, with improvements to the road, Cape Tribulation is becoming more and more popular for visitors. It's hardly surprising since this stretch of coast is incredibly beautiful. It's one of the few places in Australia where the rainforest still runs right down to the waterline. The cape itself was named by Captain Cook, since it was a little north of here that his troubles and tribulations really started when he ran his ship on to the Endeavour Reef. The mountain rising up behind the cape was also named by him — Mt Sorrow! On the road up to the cape stop at the lookout point high above the mouth of the Daintree River and further on pause at the bouncing rocks — a beach where the unusually smooth stones bounce to a great height if thrown down.

Places to Stay There's a campsite by Cooper Creek, about half way up to the cape. *Palm Beach Camp* is right up by the cape, you can camp there for $2.50 and there are cabins for $21. Just before the cape and right underneath Mt Sorrow is a new *Youth Hostel*. Nightly costs in this very pleasant place are $4.50, there's a modern kitchen and solar heated water. There are plans to add other facilities to the hostel. Bushwalks are often arranged from the hostel or from the store just back down the road. They cost $3 to $7 depending on how many go and are reckoned to be well worth it.

Getting There Day trips are made up to the Cape from Cairns with Black Marlin Travel (tel 51 5899) for $25 including lunch. They operate three a week and it may be possible to get up there on the tour bus. It's quite easy to hitch since when you've crossed the Daintree ferry there's nowhere else to go but up the road. Note that most Cairns hire cars specifically prohibit their use on the Cape Tribulation road which does not stop lots of people from doing just that! The ferry costs $3 for car and driver plus $1.20 per passenger — the return trip is free.

COOKTOWN (population 600)

North of Cairns you have to turn inland and follow a pretty terrible stretch of dirt road to Cooktown, 341 km north. Further north of Cooktown it soon becomes four-wheel drive only. Cooktown can lay claim to being Australia's first, albeit involuntary, British settlement. In 1770 Captain Cook careened his barque *Endeavour* here after making an equally involuntary close inspection of the Great Barrier Reef. To float the ship off the reef before putting into Cooktown for repairs, cannon and shot were hurled overboard. Divers have recently brought them up. The spot on the banks of the Endeavour River where the ship was repaired is marked and at Grassy Hill Lookout you can imagine yourself standing, like Cook, searching for a way out through the maze of reefs.

Cooktown later became an unruly goldrush centre for the Palmer River rush. At its peak the population was over 30,000 and there were no less than 94 hotels! In 1874 Cooktown was second only to Brisbane in size in Queensland. Today the population is less than a thousand and the Chinese Graveyard and joss house relics in Cooktown's fascinating museum are the only reminders of the 2500 Chinese miners whose industrious presence led to some wild race riots. The biggest activity in Cooktown today is the flight of fruit-

NATIONAL TRUST OF QUEENSLAND
JAMES COOK HISTORICAL MUSEUM
COOKTOWN, N.Q.

Souvenir Ticket

bats that head out from the swamps every night.

Quiet though it is (only three pubs remain open today), Cooktown is a quite delightful place and if you can get there it's a place not to be missed. Apart from just taking in the atmosphere you can visit the James Cook Museum in the Sir Joseph Banks Gardens, inspect the fine old Bank of NSW building or perhaps hitch a ride on a yacht heading north for Thursday Island and the South Pacific. While in Cooktown Banks collected 186 plant species and the first kangaroo seen by the expedition was spotted here. Cooktown has a memorial to Cook, of course, but there's also a cairn to the unlucky explorer Edmund Kennedy and to the equally tragic Mary Watson (see Lizard Island) who is buried in the Cooktown Cemetery. On the way to Cooktown you pass the black granite boulders known as Black Mountain or to Aboriginals as Kalcajagga — the mountain of death. Helenvale, just south of here and off the road, has the colourful old Lion's Den Hotel, an old mining pub.

Places to Stay

There are half a dozen motels in Cooktown, cheapest is the *Hillcrest Holiday Lodge* on Hope St where rooms cost $9 single or $15 double. The *Seaview Motel* on Charlotte St costs $25 for a room-only double. There are also several campsites in Cooktown, a couple of them with on-site vans.

Good counter meals are available at several of Cooktown's hotels.

Getting There

McGrath's Cooktown-Cairns Bus Service (tel 51 1064) operates via Mareeba on Friday, via the Cook Highway and Julatten on Tuesday. The trip takes a little over eight hours and the fare is $25. The Cooktown-Cairns trip is made on Sundays and Thursdays. Air Queensland fly to Cooktown five times a week, the fare is $48.20. By road it takes about eight hours, the road is sealed to a little beyond Mt Carbine, about a quarter of the way there. The RACQ in Cairns can advise you on road conditions.

There are a variety of tours available from Cooktown both locally and further afield into Cape York. Daily river cruises for $5 also operate along the Endeavour River from Cooktown.

CAPE YORK PENINSULA

The north of Queensland ends in a huge triangle pointing like a finger towards Papua New Guinea. The tip of Cape York is the furthest north point on the mainland of Australia and from here a scatter of islands dot the Torres Straits. This is one of the wildest and least populated parts of Australia away from the great deserts of the centre. As you head further north a few cattle stations, small work parties along the overland telegraph line to Bamaga and a number of Aboriginal communities and reserves are all you will find. Getting up to the north along the rough and rugged Peninsula Development Road is still one of Australia's great road adventures — it's a trip for the tough and experienced since even at the height of the dry the main river is to be forded barely drops below a metre in depth.

Driving to the Top

Every year a handful of hardy travellers,

equipped with four-wheel drive vehicles or trail motorcycles, make the long haul up to the top of Cape York. Apart from being able to say you've been as far north as you can get in Australia you also test yourself against some pretty hard going and see some wild and wonderful country into the bargain. It's no easy trip — for a start from December to March, during the wet seaon, nothing moves by road at all. Even if you could move in the mud the rivers would be totally impassable at this time of year. From May to November conventional vehicles can usually travel north of Laura as far as Coen and with care and skill even across to Weipa on the Gulf of Carpentaria. If you want to continue north from the Weipa turn-off to the top of the cape, however, then you're going to need four-wheel drive, a winch and plenty of strong steel wire.

August to October is usually the only time you can get to the very top. The major problem is the many river crossings; even as late as June or July they will still be swift flowing and frequently alter their course. The rivers often have very steep banks on entry and exit and the Jardine River only drops below a metre in depth at the very height of the dry season. The Great Dividing Range runs right up the spine of Cape York and rivers run to the Coral Sea on the east side and to the Gulf of Carpentaria on the west. Although the rivers in the south of the peninsula only flow in the wet season those further north flow year round.

The ideal for a Cape York expedition is two four-wheel drive vehicles travelling together — one can then haul the other out where necessary. Motorcycles also make it up to the top, floating the machines across the wider rivers. There are usually large truck inner tubes left at the river crossings for this purpose. Beware of crocodiles. Apart from Weipa on the coast there is no regular supply of petrol north of Coen. You must either carry enough with you for the round trip Coen-Cape York-Coen or arrange to have fuel sent from Thursday Island to Bamaga, about 40 km south of the cape. The round trip from Coen is close to a thousand km so you'd need a pretty large fuel tank! Permission must be obtained before visiting any of the Aboriginal communities or reserves on the cape.

Cape York Tours

A number of companies operate four-wheel drive trips to the top of Cape York. The QGTB can advise you on latest prices and departure dates but the trips typically take 12 to 14 days and cost from around $550 to 1000 from Cairns to the top and back to Cairns. There have also been trail bike tours to the top you have to provide your own trail bike but the operators provide a support vehicle, food and fuel.

Lakeland & Laura

The Peninsula Development Road turns off the Cooktown road at Lakeland. There are facilities here including a general store, petrol and a hotel-motel. From Lakeland it's 734 km north to Bamaga, almost at the top of the cape. The first stretch to Laura, where again there is petrol and a hotel, is not too bad but it gets steadily worse as you continue north.

Coen

This small town is the last place north for mechanical repairs, petrol or supplies, apart from Weipa which is 153 km off the Peninsula Development Road. The rest of the way to Bamaga the only habitation is a few telegraph stations — the road generally follows the telegraph line. Coen has an airstrip and a race course where picnic races are held each August.

Weipa (population 2900)

This modern mining town works the world's largest bauxite deposits. Bauxite is the ore from which aluminium is processed. The mining company Comalco operates tours of the mining operations. The town has a wide range of facilities including a motel and a camp site. There are direct flights to Weipa from Cairns but outside the town the roads are as bad as ever.

Jardine River National Park

At the top of the peninsula this was where explorer Edmund Kennedy was killed by Aboriginals in 1848. The Jardine River has the second greatest flow of any river in Queensland and it flows year round. Only in August, September or October is it possible to get a vehicle across the river.

Bamaga

There are limited facilities at this Aboriginal community at the top of the peninsula. There's a motel (advance

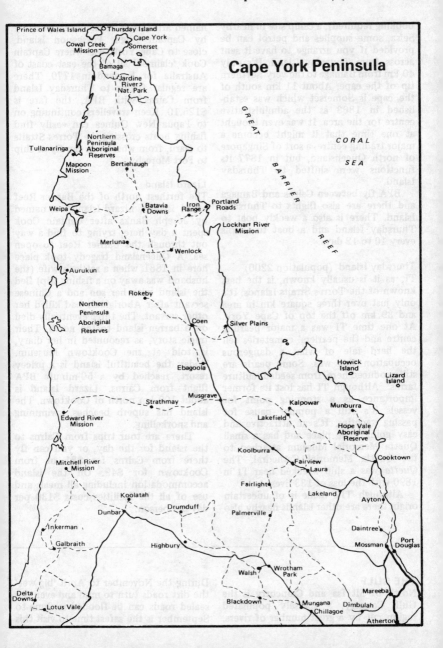

Cape York Peninsula

Prince of Wales Island
Thursday Island
Cowal Creek Mission
Cape York
Somerset
Bamaga
Jardine River Nat. Park

GREAT BARRIER REEF
CORAL SEA

Northern Peninsula Aboriginal Reserves
Tullanaringa
Mapoon Mission
Bertiehaugh

Weipa
Batavia Downs
Iron Range
Portland Roads
Lockhart River Mission

Merluna
Wenlock

Aurukun

Rokeby
Northern Peninsula Aboriginal Reserves
Coen
Silver Plains
Howick Island
Lizard Island

Ebagoola
Kalpowar
Munburra

Musgrave
Lakefield
Hope Vale Aboriginal Reserve

Strathmay
Edward River Mission
Koolburra
Fairview
Laura
Cooktown

Mitchell River Mission
Koolatah
Fairlights
Lakeland
Ayton

Drumduff
Palmerville
Daintree

Dunbar
Highbury
Palmerville
Mossman
Port Douglas

Inkerman
Galbraith
Walsh
Wrotham Park

Delta Downs
Lotus Vale
Blackdown
Mungana
Chillagoe
Dimbulah
Mareeba
Atherton

booking required), a camp site in nearby Seisa, some supplies and petrol can be provided if you arrange to have it sent across from Thursday Island. It's only 40 km from Bamaga to the very northern tip of the cape. About 11 km south of the cape is Somerset which was established in 1863 as the administrative centre for the area. It was even thought at one time that it might become a major trading centre, a sort of Singapore of north Queensland, but in 1877 its functions were shifted to Thursday Island.

BPA fly between Cairns and Bamaga and there are also flights to Thursday Island. There is also a weekly boat to Thursday Island and a boat to Cairns every 10 to 12 days.

Thursday Island (population 2200)

TI, as it is usually known, is the best known of the Torres Straits Islands. It's only just over three square km in area and 39 km off the top of Cape York. At one time TI was a major pearling centre and the pearlers' cemeteries tell the hard tale of what a dangerous occupation this was. Some pearls are still produced here, from seeded 'culture farms'. Although TI has lost its former importance as a stopping point for vessels it's still a popular pause for passing yachties. It's an attractive and easy going little place and has a small Quetta Memorial Museum attached to the Quetta Memorial Cathedral. The *Quetta* was a ship wrecked near TI in 1890 with the loss of 133 lives.

Although TI's name is of uncertain origin there are other islands nearby also named after day's of the week, possibly by Captain Bligh. Possession Island, close to Cape York, was where Captain Cook 'claimed' all of the east coast of Australia for England in 1770. There are regular flights to Thursday Island from Cairns with BPA, the fare is $125.10. Keen travellers continuing on to Papua New Guinea can easily find fishing boats crossing the Torres Straits to Daru, from where you can fly or ship to Port Moresby.

Lizard Island

The furthest north of the Barrier Reef resort islands, Lizard Island was named by Joseph Banks after Captain Cook spent a day here, trying to find a way out through the Barrier Reef to open sea. A Queensland tragedy took place here in 1881 when a settler's wife (the husband was away on a fishing trip) fled the island with her son and a Chinese servant after Aboriginals had killed her other servant. The three eventually died on a barren island to the north. Their tragic story, as recounted in her diary, is told at the Cooktown Museum. Today the beautiful island is a pricey resort, reached by a 50-minute BPA flight from Cairns. Lizard Island is about 100 km north of Cooktown. The island has superb beaches, swimming and snorkelling.

There are tour trips from Cairns to the island for the day, or you can fly there from Cairns for $81 or from Cooktown for $49. On the island accommodation including all meals and use of all the facilities costs $130 per day per person.

THE GULF

North of Mt Isa and Cloncurry is the Gulf Country, a sparsely populated region cut by a great number of rivers. During the November to April 'big wet' the dirt roads turn to mud and even the sealed roads can be flooded so June to September is the safest time to visit this area. Burke and Wills were the first Europeans to pass through the Gulf Country but the coast of the Gulf of Carpentaria had been chartered by Dutch explorers even before Cook's visit to Australia. The actual coastline of the Gulf is mainly mangrove swamps which is why there is little habitation right on the coast — Burke and Wills did not actually manage to reach the sea but knew they were close to it because of the tidal movement on the rivers.

The main roads into the Gulf region are from Cloncurry to Normanton (sealed all the way) with a turn off to Burketown at the point where the road from Julia Creek (also all sealed) meets it. Between Cloncurry and Normanton the flat plain is interrupted by a single, solitary hill beside the road. It's colourfully named Bang Bang Jump-up. The Gulf Developmental Road also runs to Normanton from the Atherton Tableland area. The last stretch into Normanton on this route can be made on the famous (though a little pointless!) Gulflander rail service which runs once weekly in each direction between Croydon and Normanton. The 151-km trip, in a very vintage looking railmotor which bounces and bucks down the old line, is made from Croydon on Thursday and from Normanton on Wednesday.

Burketown
This tiny town is probably best known for its isolation — when the rains come it can be cut off for weeks at a time. In the centre of a cattle raising area

Happy
The Hungry Shire of Burke

Burketown is 65 km south of the Gulf and can be reached by road from Cloncurry, Julia Creek or Camooweal. The 332 km trip to Camooweal from Burketown only passes one supply stop the whole way, tiny Gregory Downs. Small, remote, isolated and forgotten though Burketown is the Shire of Burke has made considerable efforts to ensure that it's not forgotten. Amongst their efforts they will issue (for $5) a Burketown passport which grants you 'citizenship' of the shire and (more important) three free beers — at the Albert Hotel, the Gregory Hotel and the Escott Barramundi Fishing Lodge (12 km out of town) — plus a free meal from the Saltpan Store.

Normanton (population 800)
The main town in the gulf region had a population of 3000 at the peak of its goldrush days in 1891. Karumba, 69 km from Normanton and actually on the gulf, is the prawn fishing centre for the gulf region. Croydon, connected to Normanton by that curious rail-car service, is an old gold-mining town and has many historic and interesting old buildings.

TOWNSVILLE TO MT ISA
It's 887 km from Townsville inland to Mt Isa and they're generally pretty boring km although there are several points of interest along the way.

Getting There
The Inlander railway service and the Ansett Pioneer and Greyhound bus services both operate through Charters Towers and the other towns on the

route to Mt Isa. You can also fly — Townsville to Charters Towers is $53, Charters Towers to Mt Isa $93. By train it's $8.20 in economy, $12.30 in 1st from Townsville to Charters Towers. The Inlander takes a bit over three hours and operates twice a week but there is also a slightly faster Rail-Motor Service which operates from Townsville only as far inland as Charters Towers every weekday. By bus it's less than two hours to Charters Towers for $11.30. By planning your trip it is possible to day trip to Charters Towers from Townsville on some days of the week.

Charters Towers (population 7900)

Only 130 km inland from Townsville, this interesting old town's principal activities today are fruit growing and cattle raising but from 1872 to 1916 this was a fabulously rich gold mining town with a peak population of 30,000. The beautiful old buildings with their classic verandahs and lacework are a living reminder of those days.

There's a War Museum at 61 Gill St and on Mosman St there's the restored 1887 Stock Exchange Arcade. In the same building is the Assay Room Mining Museum while Mosman St also has a Folk Museum and the Zara Clark Museum with a number of historic vehicles. The old Venus Battery is about four km from town off Millchester Rd. Ore was first crushed here in 1872 and it continued operating right into the 1970s. Charters Towers also has the Rotary Lookout on Buckland's Hill and a small wildlife sanctuary in Lissner Park.

There's a Tourist Information Centre at 61 Gill St.

On the way to Charters Towers from Townsville you can turn south at Mingela (95 km out) to Ravenswood. This was a class boom-and-bust goldrush town where gold was first discovered in 1868. Fossickers still find gold in the creek beds near this intriguing almost-a-

ghost town.

Charters Towers to Mt Isa

It's about 750 km on from Charters Towers to Mt Isa, a fairly unexciting trip although, fortunately, the last stretches of unsealed road were finally surfaced in 1976. Towns you pass through along the way are:

Hughenden (population 1800) An early explorer camped here in 1862 while in search of the ill-fated Burke and Wills expedition. Hughenden is on the main road and rail route to Mt Isa and the Porcupine Gorge National Park, a sort of Grand Canyon in miniature with walls rising sheer over 120 metres, is about 50 km north.

Richmond (population 900) and Julia Creek (population 650) are two more small towns. From Julia Creek a sealed road turns off north to Normanton on the Gulf.

Cloncurry (population 2100) The centre for a copper boom in the last century, Cloncurry was the largest copper producer in Australia in 1916 but the mines and smelters declined soon after. Today it's a pastoral centre and a major base for the flying doctor service. Points of interest in the town include the old Chinese and Afghani cemeteries, the court house, the indoor museum on Scarr St (with Burke and Wills relics) and the outdoor museum on Ramsay St. It's a rough trip about 100 km south of Cloncurry to the ghost town of Kurilda.

Mary Kathleen (population 800) At Corella River, just before you reach Mary Kathleen, there's a memorial cairn to the Burke and Wills expedition. Only 55 km from Mt Isa, Mary Kathleen is a controversial small town due to its uranium mine — which is not open to visitors.

MT ISA (population 25,000)

Mt Isa is a one activity town — an immensely rich copper, silver, lead and zinc mine. The town is a comparative oasis in the wilderness — travelling east or west you'll feel a considerable relief when 'the Isa' finally hoves into sight. It's a kind of rough and ready town, the image of an outback mining place despite its shiny new buildings. The deposits here were discovered in 1923 and today this is the major town of north-west Queensland. Virtually the whole town is run by Mt Isa Mines and ore produced is railed 900 km to Townsville on the coast.

Information & Orientation

There's a tourist office on Camooweal St, open Monday to Friday from 9 am to 5 pm. The Crusade Bookshop at 11 Simpson St is the best bookshop between Townsville and Darwin. The town centre is a fairly compact area, immediately south of the Leichhardt River which separates it from the mining area.

Around Town

There's a major new Civic Centre in the city and the August Rotary Rodeo is quite an occasion but the mines are the major attraction. Daily surface working tours take place from the Visitors Centre, Kings Cross at 8.30 am and 1.30 pm, Monday to Friday. The underground tours tend to be booked well ahead — write to the General Manager, Mt Isa Mines if you want to be certain of getting on a tour. Tours take place at 7.30 am (for men) and 12.30 pm (for women), nobody under 16 allowed.

Above Marian and Hilary Sts there's a lookout with a signpost giving directions all over the world. A more recent addition is the Frank Aston Museum, an underground complex cut into a hill close to the town centre. It's open 10 am to 3 pm daily with a display of mining equipment and other exhibits from the pioneering days.

Lake Moondarra, 20 km north of Mt Isa, is an artificial lake popular for water sports activities but the main water supply for the town comes from Julius Dam, 105 km out.

Places to Stay

Hotels, Motels & Lodges The *Boyd Hotel* (tel 43 3000) on the corner of West and Marian Sts is shabby and run down but also very central (perhaps too central when the pubs close!) and reasonably cheap at $15/23 room-only.

Otherwise head along Marian St where there are a variety of places within a km or so of the centre. At 97 Marian St the *Copper Gate Motel* (tel 43 3233) is $20/28. The rooms are a little old-fashioned but they're self-contained, air-con, have a TV, fridge and cooking facilities so they're pretty good value. Only a stone's throw away at the corner of Marian St and Doughan Terrace the *Silver Star Motel* (tel 43 3466) is $25/30 and also has a pool.

In and around the centre there are a number of very basic accommodation places — several of them single-sex. The *Queensland CWA Hostel* (tel 43 2216) at 5 Isa St takes women and children only at $5 a night. There's a kitchen and laundry facilities. Behind the Verona Motel on the corner of Marian and Camooweal Sts is the *Tourist Inn* (tel 43 3024) with scenic views of the Verona's undercover car park. It's just a long wooden hut, singles at $14, men only. At 10 Marian St there's *Star Accommodation* (tel 43 4079) which again is men only and costs $10 for a single. It does have a kitchen and TV lounge and the rooms are air-con.

Low priced but not single-sex, the *Boomerang Lodge* (tel 43 2019) is rather a long way out from the centre at 11 Boyd Parade. Rooms are $16/20 and

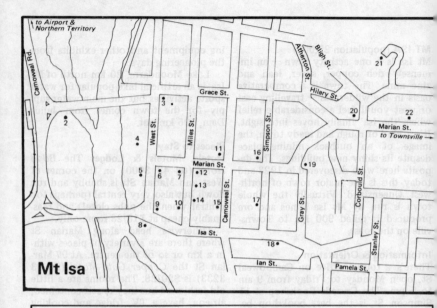

Mt Isa

1 Railway Station
2 School of the Air & Flying Doctor
3 Bonanza Restaurant
4 Civic Centre
5 City Cafe
6 Boyd Hotel
7 Mt Isa Hotel
8 Queensland CWA Hostel
9 Argent Hotel
10 TAA
11 Verona Motel & Tourist Inn

12 Post Office
13 Greyhound
14 Ansett
15 Tourist Information Centre
16 Kentucky Fried
17 Crusade Bookshop
18 Tavern
19 Frank Aston Museum
20 Star Accommodation
21 Lookout
22 Boomerang Lodge

they're air-con, have shower and toilet, plus there's a communal kitchen and TV lounge and a swimming pool. Much closer in, it's easy to walk to from the centre, *Budget Accommodation* (tel 43 4004) is at 28 Marian St and costs $10/16 including a light breakfast. Facilities are shared. Finally there's *The Welcome Inn* (tel 43 2241) at 118 Camooweal St with rooms at $14/22. The rooms don't have private facilities but they are air-con and have tea/coffee making equipment and fridges.

Camping Mt Isa also has a string of camping sites, a number of them conveniently close to the city centre. On Marian St the *Townview Caravan Park* (tel 43 3328) has sites at $5 and cabins at $12/15. There's a laundry and pool. Only a little further along Marian St the *Mt Isa Caravan Park* (tel 43 3258) has tent sites at $1.50 per person. There are a number of other sites around town.

Places to Eat
Excellent counter meals at lunch time or in the evenings at the *Tavern* and

also at the *Argent Hotel* — both on Isa St. At either place there is a variety of main courses in the $5 to 6 bracket, a serve yourself salad table plus cheaper dishes and entrees.

Or you could try the *Bonanza Family Restaurant* on the corner of West and Grace Sts. It's a very glossy, American style place (part of a Queensland chain) serving meals in cafeteria fashion. Next door is the rather more expensive *Phoenix Centre* and, of course, there are a number of pizzerias, cafes and so on including the *City Cafe* on West St which offers no less than 19 varieties of burgers!

Getting There

Air Ansett and TAA both fly through Mt Isa with non-stop flights to and from Alice Springs $121 ($90 standby), Brisbane $206 ($154), Cairns $134 ($101) and Darwin $182. There are also many flights with stops to other main centres but note that the fares vary depending on the route taken. The Brisbane-Mt Isa fare, for example, is more expensive via Cairns or Townsville than direct. If you're on a round Australia ticket note that Mt Isa can be a bit of a problem — getting in from, say, Alice Springs and then out to Cairns can be a little difficult since flights through the Isa are not terribly frequent. Air Queensland also have a number of flights through the Isa on their interesting outback routes. Ansett (tel 44 1711) and TAA (tel 44 1222) are both on Miles St in the town centre.

Rail The Inlander operates Townsville-Hughenden-Cloncurry-Mt Isa. Departures are on Tuesday and Friday at 4.45 pm, arriving in the Isa 21 hours later, a stunning 42 kph pace. From Mt Isa departures are on Friday and Sunday at 10.30 am and 6.30 pm respectively. Townsville-Mt Isa costs $62.40 in 1st, $41.60

in economy. Sleeping berths cost an extra $12 in 1st, $6 in economy.

Bus By bus it takes 11½ hours from Townsville to Mt Isa, the fare is $62 from Townsville. Continuing on it takes another 7½ hours to Three Ways where connecting buses travel north to Darwin and south to Alice Springs. Fares to Mt Isa are $54 from Alice Springs, $81 from Darwin. Ansett Pioneer operate three times weekly on this route, Greyhound four times.

Both companies also operate a more direct route between Brisbane and Mt Isa via Charleville. This takes about 27 or 28 hours and costs $94 with Greyhound (three times weekly) or $106 with Ansett Pioneer (once weekly). Ansett Pioneer (tel 43 4888) are on the corner of Pamela and Stanley Sts. Greyhound (tel 43 6655) have a terminal on Miles St.

Getting Around

There is little public transport around Mt Isa. A taxi to the airport costs around $5. Hertz, Budget and Avis have airport desks. Campbell's Coaches do a day tour around Mt Isa for $18 including lunch.

Mt Isa to Three Ways

If you thought the road from Townsville to Mt Isa was pretty long and dull wait until you hit this stretch. There's nothing much for the whole 650 km to the Three Ways junction in the Northern Territory. Camooweal (population 300) is 188 km from Mt Isa, just before the Queensland-Northern Territory border and it's the only place of any size on this stretch. The unique feature along this road are the 'goals' thoughtfully erected for passing drivers to hurl their beer cans at — hopefully containing the empty can debris to a small area.

DARLING DOWNS

West of the Great Dividing Range, inland from Brisbane, stretch the extensive plains of the Darling Downs, some of the most fertile and productive agricultural land in Australia. In the state's early history the Darling Downs were something of a back door into the region. Nobody was allowed within a 50 mile radius of the penal colony of Brisbane but settlers gradually pushed their way north from NSW through this area.

Places to Stay

There are youth hostels and hostel-style accommodation in the Darling Downs region at Jondaryan, Lost World near Beaudesert, Roma, Toowoomba and Warwick.

Getting There

Rail The Westlander runs from Brisbane to Roma and Charleville twice a week. From Charleville it turns south to Cunnamulla or you can change trains and continue west to Quilpie. It's 777 km from Brisbane to Charleville and the trip takes 17 hours. Fares from Brisbane are Roma $37 1st, $25 economy; Charleville $53 1st, $35 economy; Cunnamulla $62 1st, $42 economy; Quilpie ditto. Sleeping berths cost an additional $12 in 1st, $6 in economy.

Ipswich (population 72,500)

Virtually an outer suburb of Brisbane this was a convict settlement as early as 1827 and is now a gateway to the Darling Downs, either to Warwick or Toowoomba. The Redbank Railway Museum is 10 km back towards Brisbane while at Wacol the Wolston House historic homestead can be visited from Wednesday to Sunday.

Toowoomba (population 64,000)

On the edge of the Great Dividing Range and the Darling Downs, 138 km inland from Brisbane, this is the largest city in the region. It's a pleasant, gracious city with parks, tree-lined streets and many early buildings. They include the National Trust Bull's Head Inn on Drayton Rd and the Early Settler's Museum on Parker St. There's also a Cobb & Co Museum on the corner of James and Water Sts, a Teddy Bear Museum in Bell St and various art galleries.

Near Toowoomba is Oakey (population 2400) where the Brookvale Park is a picnic and barbecue spot with visiting wildlife. Shearing demonstrations can be seen at the 1859 Jondaryan Woolshed where there is also a youth hostel. The woolshed once handled 200,000 sheep a season. Pittsworth (population 1700) is another typical Darling Downs town with a folk museum.

Warwick (population 9200)

South-west of Brisbane, 162 km inland and near the NSW border, this is the oldest town in Queensland after Brisbane itself. It's a busy Darling Downs farming centre noted for the roses that grow in its parks and for its annual rodeo in October. There are various parks and lookouts in the area and Pringle Cottage in the town, dating from 1863, has been preserved as a local museum. There is a Tourist Information Centre in the Warwick Town Hall.

Between Warwick and Goondiwindi is Inglewood (population 1000) while east of Warwick near the NSW border is Killarney (population 750), a pretty little town in an area of fine mountain scenery with a number of scenic waterfalls. Texas (population 900) is another small border town with a historical museum in the old police station. South of Warwick is Stanthorpe (population 3900) near the NSW border. At an altitude of 915 metres it's the coolest town in the state and a popular area for fruit production and winemaking. There are good bushwalks and rock-climbing opportunities in the Girraween National Park and on Mt Lindesay.

Goondiwindi & Further West

Continuing west from Warwick you reach Goondiwindi (population 3700), right on the NSW border and Macintyre River. It's a popular stop on the Newell Highway route between Melbourne and Brisbane. There's a small museum in the old customs house and a wildlife sanctuary at the Boobera Lagoon. If you continue inland from Goondiwindi you reach St George (population 2100), where cotton is grown on irrigated land. Much further west is Cunnamulla (population 1900), 254 km north of Bourke in NSW and very definitely out in the outback. This is another sheep raising centre and is noted for its wildflowers after rain. The Yowah opal fields are about 150 km further west.

Other Towns

Near Toowoomba other agricultural towns include Gatton (population 4000) and Dalby, a crossroads town in what is probably the richest grain growing area in Australia. About 20 km south-east of Gatton is the pioneer village at Laidley, open on Sunday afternoons. South of Toowoomba towards Warwick, Allora (population 700) also has a historical museum, open Sunday afternoons. Cunningham's Gap National Park is 50 km east of Allora and has extensive bushwalking tracks. Boonah (population 2000) is just off the Brisbane-Warwick road, near the Fassifern Valley National Park, and Clifton (population 700) is another town in the same area. North of Toowoomba is Crows Nest (population 900) which took its name from a local Aboriginal, Jim Crow, who lived in a hollow tree near the town site. Follow the Valley of Diamonds signs to the Crows Nest Falls

National Park where there are good walking trails to the gorge and falls.

Roma (population 5900)

An early Queensland settlement and now a sheep and cattle raising centre, Roma also has some curious small scale industries. There's enough oil around Roma to support a small refinery, producing just enough petroleum for local use. Gas deposits here are rather larger, Roma supplies Brisbane through a 450 km pipeline. Plus Roma has a small local winery, the Romavilla Winery, open daily! Roma is a crossroads town for travellers heading north, south, east or west.

On the way to Roma from Toowoomba and Dalby you pass through Chinchilla (population 3200). In the western part of the Darling Downs, 355 km from Brisbane, Chinchilla is yet another busy agricultural town and it has an interesting folk museum. Just beyond Chinchilla is Miles (population 1400) with a historical museum and brilliant wildflowers in the spring. West of Roma towards Charleville is Mitchell (population 1300) from where an interesting but rugged unsealed road leads north into the Carnarvon Range National Park in the Great Dividing Range.

Charleville (population 3200)

Way inland from Brisbane, about 800 km from the coast, Charleville is the terminus of the Westlander railway service and the centre for a huge cattle and sheep raising region. This was an important crossroads for early explorers and something of an oasis in the outback, it was a real frontier town around the turn of the century. There are various reminders of the early explorers around the town and a historical museum in the 1880 Queensland National Bank building on Albert St.

THE CHANNEL COUNTRY

The remote and sparsely populated south-west corner of Queensland, bordering the Northern Territory, South Australia and NSW, takes its name from the myriad channels which criss-cross the area. In this inhospitable region it hardly ever rains but the water from the northern monsoon pours into the channel country along the Georgina, Hamilton and Diamantina Rivers and the Cooper Creek. Flooding towards the great depression of Lake Eyre this mass of water arrives on this huge, virtually flat plain and meanders aimlessly about, eventually drying up in waterholes or salt pans or simply sinking back into the ground. Only on rare occasions (the early '70s was one occasion during this century) does the vast amount of water that pours west actually manage to reach Lake Eyre and fill it. For a period after each wet season, however, the channel country does achieve a short fertile period and cattle are grazed here. Soon the land returns to its barren, dusty dryness.

During the October to May wet even sealed roads are often cut and the dirt roads become quagmires. In addition the summer heat at that time is unbearable so a visit to this region is best made in the cool, dry winter period from May to September. Visiting this area requires a sturdy vehicle, four-wheel drive if you want to get off the beaten track, and some experience of outback driving. West of Cunnamulla and Quilpie you should always carry plenty of petrol and drinking water and you should notify the police so that if you don't turn up at the next town the necessary steps can be taken.

Mt Isa to Charleville

The main road through the channel country is the Diamantina Development Road that runs south from Mt Isa through Dajarra and Boulia to Bedourie and then turns east through Windorah and Quilpie to Charleville. In all it's a long and lonely 1340 km although, fortunately, about half of the road is sealed.

Boulia (population 300) is the 'capital' of the channel country and near here the mysterious 'Min Min' light, a sort of earthbound UFO, is sometimes seen. Burke and Wills passed through here on their long trek. Windorah is either very dry or very wet but it's a welcome stop in the middle of nowhere. Quilpie is the railhead from which cattle, grazed here during the fertile wet season, are railed to the coast. Charleville is a comparatively large town.

Other Routes

The Kennedy Development Road runs from Wilton to Boulia, partly sealed and with a couple of stops on the way. From Quilpie to Birdsville you follow the Diamantina road through Windorah but then branch off south to Betoota. It's 394 dull, dull, dull km from Windorah to Birdsville and Betoota, wth one store and one pub, is absolutely all there is all the way. South of Quilpie is Thargomindah from where camel trains used to cross to Bourke in NSW. Nocundra was once a busy little community, now it consists of a hotel (where you can get fuel, food and accommodation) and a permanent population of three!

Birdsville

The tiny settlement of Birdsville, with a population of less than 200, is the most remote place in Queensland and possesses one of the most famous pubs in Australia — the Birdsville Pub. Birdsville is only 12 km from the South Australian border and it's the northern end of the Birdsville Track — see the South Australia outback section for

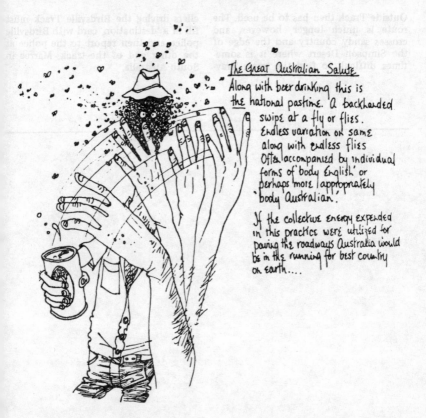

The Great Australian Salute

Along with beer drinking this is the national pastime. A backhanded swipe at a fly or flies. Endless variation on same along with endless flies. Often accompanied by individual forms of 'body English' or perhaps more appropriately 'body Australian'.

If the collective energy expended in this practice were utilized for paving the roadways Australia would be in the running for best country on earth....

more details. At one time Birdsville was quite a busy little place as cattle were driven south to South Australia and a duty charge was made on each head of cattle leaving Queensland. With federation the charge was abolished and now railways and roads carry the cattle so Birdsville has become almost ghost-like — the Royal Hotel is a reminder of what once was.

Birdsville's big day is the annual Birdsville Races in August or September when as many as 3000 racing and boozing enthusiasts make the long trip to Birdsville and get through as many as 50,000 cans of beer! Birdsville gets its water from a 1219 metre deep artesian well which delivers the water at near boiling point and also drives a hydro-electric turbine to provide Birdsville's electricity. Birdsville takes its name from the many birds which can be seen along the Diamantina River. The Diamantina River never completely dries up and waterholes can usually be found near Birdsville.

The first stretch of the Birdsville Track, south of Birdsville, has two alternatives. The usual Inside Track crosses the Goyder Lagoon, the 'end' of the Diamantina River, but a big wet will sometimes cut this route and the

Outside Track then has to be used. The route is much longer, however, and crosses sandy country and the edge of the Simpson Desert where it is sometimes difficult to find the track. Travellers driving the Birdsville Track must fill in a 'destination' card with Birdsville police and then report to the police at the other end of the track, Marree in South Australia.

South Australia

Area   984,000 square km
Population   1,300,000

Don't miss: Beautiful Adelaide, the wine country to north and south, the mighty Murray River and the terrific Flinders Ranges.

South Australia is the most urbanised and also the driest of the states. Even Western Australia doesn't have such a large proportion of desert. Adelaide, the capital, once had a reputation as the 'wowser's' capital and was contemptuously referred to as 'the city of churches'. The churches may still be there but otherwise times have changed.

Today the city's cultural spirit is epitomised in the biennial Adelaide Arts Festival. The death of wowserism is nowhere better seen than in the Barossa Valley Wine Festival which takes place on alternate years. South Australia's relatively liberal attitude is demonstated in Australia's first legal nudist beach, just a short drive south of the city.

Outside Adelaide the state is best known for its vineyards and wineries. The famous Barossa Valley, north of the city, is probably the best known wine producing area in the country, even though the amount of 'Barossa wine' produced annually far exceeds the grape growing capacity of the valley! South Australia also has the fine Clare and Coonawarra Valleys and the southern vineyards are within minutes drive of the city. Wine festivals in South Australia are frequent and fun.

Further north the rough and rugged Flinders Ranges make an ideal area for all sorts of outdoor activities — this is another of my favourite Australian places. The far north and west of the state has some of the most barren and inhospitable land in Australia although several years of unexpectedly heavy rain turned some of the inland salt lakes at least temporarily into the real, water-filled, thing in the mid '70s.

The drive across the Nullarbor used to be one of the more accessible of Australia's driving adventures but the new road opened in '76 (it was already paved westward from the South Australia-Western Australia border) hase civilised even that long drive. The road actually runs close to the cliff tops along the Great Australian Bight. That still leaves you the Murray River, the interesting coast towards the Victorian border, fascinating Kangaroo Island, plus the Eyre, Yorke and Fleurieu Peninsulas to explore.

GEOGRAPHY

South Australia is Australia's most urbanised state — once you get out of Adelaide there's not a lot of population elsewhere in the state. Adelaide, the Fleurieu Peninsula to the south and the country to the north with the well known wine producing Barossa and Clare Valleys are green and fertile but most of the rest of the state is definitely not. As you travel further north it

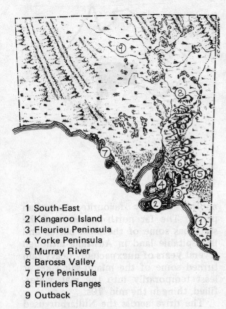

1 South-East
2 Kangaroo Island
3 Fleurieu Peninsula
4 Yorke Peninsula
5 Murray River
6 Barossa Valley
7 Eyre Peninsula
8 Flinders Ranges
9 Outback

becomes progressively drier and more inhospitable and most of the north is a vast area of desert and dry salt lakes with only scattered, tiny settlements.

One area of this dry land is not to be missed, however. That's the magnificent Flinders Ranges, a desert mountain range of exceptional beauty and great interest. South Australia is also notable for its peninsulas and coastline. Starting from the Victorian border there's the south-east region with Mt Gambier, the wine producing Coonawarra area and the long coastal lake of the Coorong. Then there's the Fleurieu Peninsula with nearby Kangaroo Island, the Yorke Peninsula and finally the remote Eyre Peninsula fading into the Great Australian Bight and the Nullarbor Plains which lead to Western Australia.

INFORMATION

The South Australian Government Travel Centre has offices in Melbourne and Sydney as well as in Adelaide. They have a series of regional brochures which are amongst the most useful literature produced by state tourist offices in Australia. These brochures have maps, sightseeing and accommodation details, even restaurants. The travel centres can also supply more basic leaflets on travel details, accommodation costs and so on.

NSW 402 George St, Sydney 2000 (tel 232 8388)
South Australia 18 King William St, Adelaide 5000 (tel 212 1644)
Victoria 25 Elizabeth St, Melbourne 3000 (tel 61 2431)

GETTING AROUND

Air Ansett-owned Airlines of South Australia is the main regional operator in South Australia. They operate F27s on routes which principally fan out from Adelaide to places like Mt Gambier, Kangaroo Island, Port Lincoln, Streaky Bay and Ceduna. They also fly over the NSW border to Broken Hill. There are a number of other local operators in South Australia including a whole collection who fly to Kangaroo Island.

Trans Regional Airlines, contact them via TAA in Adelaide, have an extensive outback network including flights to Oodnadatta, Innamincka, Birdsville, Hawker and Broken Hill. TRA have standby fares to Port Augusta ($35). The chart opposite shows the main South Australian air fares.

ACTIVITIES

Bushwalking Close to Adelaide there are many good walks in the Mt Lofty Ranges. Good walks can be found in the Belair Park, Cleland Park, Morialta Park, Deep Creek Park, Bridgewater-Aldgate, Barossa Reservoir and Parra Wirra Park.

In the Flinders Ranges, 400 km from Adelaide, there are excellent walks in the Wilpena Pound area as well as furth-

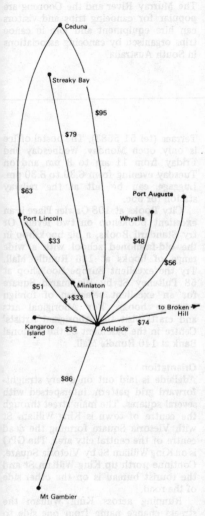

be extreme. Get a copy of *Flinders Ranges Walks*, produced by the Conservation Council of South Australia.

The Heysen Trail is a walking trail from Encounter Bay at the bottom of the Fleurieu Peninsula up to the Barossa Valley. It's hoped to link this up with a series of walking trails right up into the Flinders. There are several bushwalking clubs in the Adelaide area who organise weekend walks in the Mt Lofty Ranges or longer weekend walks in the Flinders. Information can also be obtained from bushgear shops like Thor Adventure Equipment, 40 Weymouth St, Adelaide.

Swimming & Surfing There is no surf at popular city beaches like Glenelg, but as you travel further south there are plenty of good beaches and good surf. Seacliff, Brighton (sailing too), Somerton, Glenelg, West Beach (oily looking sea report some), Henley Beach, Grange, West Lake, Semaphore, Glanville and Largs Bay are all popular beaches. Legal skinny-dipping at Maslins Beach, 40 km south of the city. You have to get over to Pondalowie on the Yorke Peninsula for SA's best board riding. Other good surf areas can be found along the Eyre Peninsula or, close to Adelaide, at Boomer and Chiton, between Victor Harbor and Port Elliott and near Goolwa.

Skindiving There are lots of diving possibilities around Adelaide and you can hire equipment in the city, with evidence of diving proficiency. Several of the shipwrecks off Kangaroo Island are within easy reach of scuba divers. Port Noarlunga reef marine reserve (18 km south) and Aldinga (43 km south) are good centres for boat diving. The reefs around Schnapper Point are suitable for snorkelling. At Rapid Bay (88 km south) you can dive from the jetty and there is much fish life. Wallaroo on the Yorke Peninsula, Port Lincoln on the Eyre Peninsula and Second Valley (65

er south in the Mt Remarkable National Park or further north in the Arkaroola-Mt Painter Sanctuary area. Some of the walks in this area are for the more experienced walker since conditions can km south of Adelaide) are other good areas.

Sailing & Canoeing There is good sailing all along the Adelaide shoreline of St Vincent's Gulf — lots of sailing clubs.

The Murray River and the Coorong are popular for canoeing trips and visitors can hire equipment and join in canoe trips organised by canoeing associations in South Australia.

ADELAIDE (population 900,000)

Adelaide is a solid, dare I even say, gracious city. It even looks solid — when the early colonists built they generally built in solid stone. It goes further than architecture, however, for despite all the liberalism of the Dunstan years Adelaide is still an inherently conservative city, an 'old money' place. In part that's due to Adelaide's role in Australia. It can't compete with Sydney or Melbourne in the big city stakes nor with Perth or Brisbane as a go-go centre for the resources boom. So Adelaide goes its own way and for the visitor that's one of the nicest parts about it. Adelaide is civilised and calm in a way no other Australian city can match. What's more it has a superb setting, the city centre is surrounded by green parkland and further out the whole metropolitan area is rimmed by a fine range of hills, the Mt Lofty Range, which crowd the city against the sea.

Information

The South Australian Government Tourist Board (tel 212 1644) is at 18 King William St, right in the centre of Adelaide. It's open 8.45 am to 5 pm on weekdays, 9 to 11.30 am on Saturdays, 10 am to 2 pm on Sundays and public holidays. On Wednesday evenings at 8 pm they show films about South Australia. The Royal Automobile Association of SA (tel 223 4555) is also very central at 41 Hindmarsh Square — they have a good bookshop section. The Adelaide YHA office is at 72 South

Terrace (tel 51 5583). The hostel office is only open Monday, Wednesday and Friday from 11 am to 3 pm and on Tuesday evening from 6.30 to 8.30 pm. Luggage can be left at the railway station for 55c.

City Books at 108 Gawler Place is an excellent bookshop on two levels. Or try Standard Books, a big bookshop in the old-fashioned school with a wide range of books at 136 Rundle Mall. Try the excellent Europe Bookshop at 58 Pulteney St by Hindmarsh Square for an excellent selection of foreign language books. For Aboriginal arts and crafts visit the Aboriginal Artists' Centre in the basement of the National Bank at 140 Rundle Mall.

Orientation

Adelaide is laid out on a very straightforward grid pattern, interspersed with several squares. The main street through the centre of town is King William St with Victoria Square forming the dead centre of the central city area. The GPO is on King William St by Victoria Square. Continue north up King William St and the tourist bureau is on the other side of the road.

Running across King William the streets change name from one side to the other. The main shopping and restaurant street is Hindley on the west side changing to Rundle St on the east. Rundle St is a mall from King William through to Pulteney Sts. The next block up 'is North Terrace with the railway station just to the west and a string of major public buildings including the university and the museum to the east. Continuing north you're in the North Parklands with the Festival Centre, then it's across the Torrens River and into North Adelaide, also laid out in a straight-forward grid pattern.

Around the City

Adelaide's most interesting streets are Rundle Mall and Hindley St. Rundle Mall was one of Australia's first city malls and is certainly one of the most successful. It's colourful and always full of activity and you'll find most of the big city shops along the mall. Street buskers add to the fun. Cross King William St, the main drag in Adelaide, and Rundle Mall becomes Hindley St. This is the Adelaide left bank/sin centre if such a solid place as Adelaide can be imagined to have such a centre. Well you'll find the odd strip club and dirty book shop along here, together with plenty of reasonably priced restaurants and snack bars. Running parallel to both these streets is North Terrace, a fine old boulevard with city buildings on one side and the university, State Library, Art Gallery, Museum and Government House on the other.

South Australian Museum

On North Terrace the fine museum is an Adelaide landmark with huge whale skeletons exhibited in the front window. In front of the building there's a three thousand year old Egyptian column thought to have been erected by Ramses II. The museum has a huge Aboriginal collection and excellent collections from New Guinea and Melanesia. It's a fine museum, not to be missed. Opening hours are Monday to Friday 10 am to 5 pm except Wednesday when it does not open until 1 pm, Sunday 2 to 5 pm. Admission is free.

Other Museums

On North Terrace, by the railway station, the Constitutional Museum is the only political history museum in Australia. It features an hour and a half audio-visual on the state's history. The museum is housed in the old Legislative Council Building and is open Monday to Friday 10 am to 5 pm, weekends 1.30 to 5 pm. Admission is $2.50. Behind the Art Gallery of SA on North Terrace the South Australian Historical Museum was erected in 1867 and is open Monday to Saturday from 10 am to 5 pm (Wednesday to 9 pm) and on Sundays from 1.30 to 5 pm.

There's a Railway Museum on Railway Terrace off West Beach Rd at Mile End South. It tells the history of railways in the state and displays early railway engines. Admission is 60c and it's open on the first and third Sunday of the months from 2 to 5 pm. At Electra House, 131 King William St there's a Telecommunications Museum open weekdays from 10.30 am to 3.30 pm. St Kilda, 30 km from the centre, has an Australian Electrical Transport Museum with historic transport vehicles, open Sundays 1 to 5 pm. There's a Shipping Museum (open by appointment) on the corner of Causeway and Semaphore Rds in Glanville. Plus a Gallery of Vintage Fashions at 284 Rundle St and the Australian Wine Museum on Russell St, Belair.

Art Galleries

On North Terrace the Art Gallery of South Australia has a good contemporary section both of Australian and overseas artists. The South-East Asian ceramic collection is also of particular note. The gallery has a pleasant little coffee shop with outside tables. Other galleries include the Festival Centre gallery near the playhouse, the Aboriginal Artist Centre at 140 Rundle Mall and a number of private galleries around town.

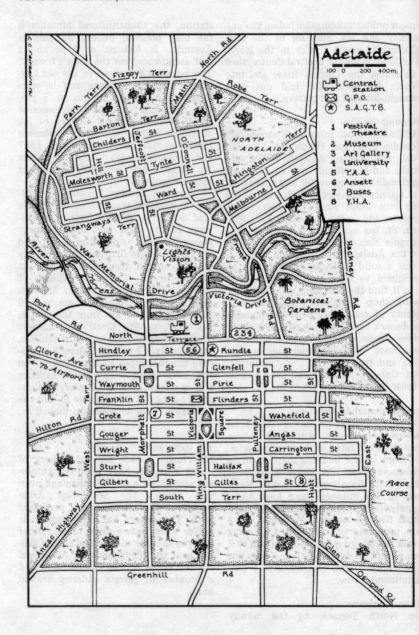

Adelaide

100 0   200 400m.

🚂 Central station
✉ G.P.O.
★ S.A.G.T.B.

1 Festival Theatre
2 Museum
3 Art Gallery
4 University
5 T.A.A.
6 Ansett
7 Buses
8 Y.H.A.

Ayers House & Edmund Wright House

On the North Terrace, close to the city centre, this fine old mansion was originally constructed in 1846 but added to and extended over the next 30 years. Completely restored it now houses two restaurants but is open for visitors on weekends between 2 and 4.30 pm. There are also tours on the hour between 12 noon and 4 pm Tuesday to Friday. The elegant bluestone building serves as the headquarters of the SA National Trust. At 59 King William St, Edmund Wright House was originally built in 1876 for the Bishop of South Australia in an elaborate Renaissance style with intricate decorations. It is now used as government offices and for official functions.

Other City Buildings

The imposing town hall, built in 1863-66 in 16th century Renaissance style, looks out on King William St. Faces of Queen Victoria and Prince Albert are carved into the facade. The post office across the road is almost as imposing. On North Terrace Government House was built between 1838 and 1840 with a later addition in the centre in 1855. The earliest section is one of the oldest in Adelaide. Parliament House on North Terrace is fronted by 10 Corinthian marble columns. It was commenced in 1883 but not completed until 1939.

Holy Trinity Church, also on North Terrace, was commenced in 1838, the first Anglican church in South Australia. Other early churches are St Francis Xavier Cathedral on Wakefield St (commenced between 1856 and 1858) and St Peter's Cathedral in Pennington Terrace, North Adelaide (built between 1869 and 1876). St Francis Xavier Cathedral is beside Victoria Square, where you will also find a number of other important early buildings — the 1847-50 Magistrate's Court House (originally used as the Supreme Court), the 1869 Supreme Court and the Treas-

ury Building. Adelaide's Central Market, open on Tuesdays, Fridays and Saturdays, has all sorts of food and bargains.

Festival Centre

The Adelaide Festival Centre stands close to the Torrens River, looking uncannily like a squared off version of the vastly more expensive Sydney Opera House. It performs a very similar function with its variety of auditoriums and theatres. The complex was completed in 1977 and there are tours Monday to Friday hourly from 10 am to 3 pm and on Saturdays at 10.30 am, 11.30 am, 2 and 3 pm. They can be changed without notice so it's wise to phone 51 0121 and check. The tours cost $1.50. One of the most pleasant aspects of the Festival Theatre is its riverside setting, people picnic on the grass in front of the theatre and there's a very pleasant open air bistro overlooking the river. You can also hire pedal paddle boats from right in front of the centre.

Adelaide Arts Festival

South Australia enjoys two of Australia's major festivals — the Barossa Valley Vintage Festival on odd numbered years and the Adelaide Arts Festival on the even years. The three-week festival of the arts attracts culture-vultures from all over Australia to dance, drama, music and other live performances, plus a writers' week, art exhibitions, poetry readings and other activities with guest speakers and performers from all over the world. Today the festival boasts 300 or more separate performances and next takes place in 1984 and 1986 in February-March.

Botanic Gardens & Other Parks

On North Terrace the botanic gardens have pleasant artificial lakes and are only a short stroll from the city centre. The glass Palm House was made in Germany in 1871. The central area of Adelaide is completely surrounded by green parkland and the Torrens, itself bordered by park, separates Adelaide from North Adelaide which in turn is also surrounded by park.

Rymill Park in the East Parkland has a boating lake and a 600-metre jogging track can also be found here. The South Parkland contains Veale Gardens with streams and traditionally arranged flowerbeds. To the west are a number of sports grounds while the North Parkland borders the Torrens and also surrounds North Adelaide. The Adelaide Oval, site for cricket test matches, is north of the Torrens River in this part of the park. The North Parkland also contains Bonython Park, Pinky Flat and Elder Park which adjoins the university and Festival Centre.

Light's Vision

On Montefiore Hill, north of the city centre across the Torrens River, stands the statue of Light's Vision. Here Adelaide's founder is said to have stood and mapped out his plan for the city. It makes a good place to start your exploration of the city since you get a good bird's eye view of the modern city, with green parkland and the gleaming white Festival Centre at your feet.

Adelaide Zoo

On Frome Rd the zoo has a noted collection of Australian birds as well as other important exhibits including sloths, giant ant-eaters, spider monkeys and ringtailed lemurs. The zoo is open Monday to Saturday from 9.30 am to 5 pm and on Sunday from 10 am to 5 pm. Admission is $3. The best way of getting to the zoo is to take a cruise downriver on board the *Popeye*. The trip costs just 80c and departs from Elder Park, in front of the Festival Centre. The return trip is 60c.

North Adelaide

Interesting old bluestone buildings and pubs abound in North Adelaide, only a short bus ride through the park to the north. It's one of the oldest parts of Adelaide and Melbourne St is Adelaide's swankiest shopping street with lots of interesting little shops and expensive restaurants.

West Beach Airport

Very centrally located, Adelaide's airport is between the city and Glenelg. The Vickers Vimy which made the first flight between England and Australia, way back in 1919, is on display in a showroom in the car park. At the controls were Sir Keith and Sir Ross Smith and the flight took 27 days — with numerous stops along the way. A similar aircraft made the first nonstop Atlantic crossing in the same year. The Vimy was a WW I twin-engined biplane bomber of surprisingly large size.

Glenelg

The suburban seaside resort of Glenelg has a couple of attractions. First of all it's an excellent place to stay — there are many guest houses, hotels and holiday flats here if you can't find something suitable in the city. Secondly it's one of the oldest parts of Adelaide, the first South Australian colonists actually landed here, so there are a number of places of historic interest. As a bonus to either reason for a visit Glenelg is exceptionally easy to get to. Adelaide's only tram runs from Victoria Square in the centre right to Glenelg Beach. It costs 70c and since it runs, like a railway train, on its own separate line it's commendably fast.

In Glenelg pick up the two part walking or cycling tour brochures from the information centre by the beach, in front of the town hall and opposite the tram stop. You can also rent bicycles here before you set off to explore. Glenelg is one of the most popular of the Adelaide beaches which stretch in a long chain south of the city. On Macfarlane St the Old Gum Tree marks the place where the proclamation of South Australia was read in 1836. Governor Hindmarsh and the first colonists landed on the beach near here. Apart from Glenelg's fine collection of early buildings it also has a popular amusement park behind the beach including one of those all-the-rage waterslides.

The boat harbour shelters a large yacht population and Glenelg's premier attraction, a reproduction of *HMS Buffalo*, the original settlers' conveyance. Used as a rather expensive restaurant it's also open to visitors for $2, from 10 am to 5 pm daily (closed 12 noon to 2.30 pm on Wednesdays). The original *Buffalo* was built in 1813 in India.

Marineland Park

Just north of Glenelg and adjoining Adelaide airport is the dolphins-through-the-hoops marine park on Military Rd, West Beach. The seals and dolphins go through their paces at 11 am, 12.30 and 3 pm daily. The park also has an aquarium with sharks and rays and a 360° audio-visual show. Admission is $5.

Other Suburbs

In Jetty St, Grange you can see Sturt's Cottage, the home of the famous early Australian explorer. Preserved as a museum it's open Wednesday to Sunday and public holidays from 1 to 5 pm. In Semaphore there's Fort Glanville, built in 1878 when Australia was having its phase of Russia-phobia, as a result of the Crimean War. It's open during the summer. In Port Adelaide you can make boat trips from North Parade Wharf except during July.

Places to Stay

Adelaide is not the best city in Australia for cheap and central accommodation. The only hostel is the small youth hostel which is often packed out. There's also a very reasonably priced YMCA right in the centre but apart from the usual collection of old hotels and guest

houses you'll have to move out from the centre — particularly to the beach suburb of Glenelg.

Hostels Adelaide's *Youth Hostel* (tel 223 6007) is centrally located at 290 Gilles St, walking distance from the centre. It has a major drawback though, there's room for only 16 hostellers and in a city the size of Adelaide that's plainly inadequate. So it's hardly surprising that the hostel is usually full. Furthermore it's not exactly the most popular hostel in Australia. Still it's all Adelaide has to offer so you can like it or lump it! Nightly cost is $5.50, 50c less if you have your own regulation sheet sleeping bag. If the hostel is full there's a list of alternatives posted up outside. One possibility, for women only, is the *Salvation Army Sutherland Lodge* (tel 223 3423) which costs $5.

The Y Adelaide's *YMCA* (tel 223 1611) is at 76 Flinders St, very centrally located indeed. It takes guests of either sex. Dorm beds cost $4 or there are singles at $8, with shower at $9. Doubles are $6 per person. Weekly rates are five times the daily rate. The Y also has a very economical cafeteria serving breakfast and supper, a TV lounge and a laundrette, plus sporting facilities including squash courts and a sauna.

City Hotels The *Metropolitan Hotel* (tel 51 5471) at 46 Grote St is central and cheap at $10 for bed and breakfast. It's a 'help yourself' breakfast which means 'you can gorge yourself if you feel so inclined' reported one traveller. And they give a discount to bus pass travellers.

Just round the corner from the youth hostel the *Afton Private Hotel* (tel 223 3416) at 260 South Terrace costs $11 including breakfast but with a YHA card you get a special room-only rate of $8, going down to $6 on subsequent nights. Weekly rates are also available and there are also kitchen facilities. If you arrive after 8 pm phone ahead before turning up. It's a big place with 100 rooms but also rather unfriendly, on the rude side of unfriendly in fact.

Other central hotels include the *Plaza Private Hotel* (tel 55 6371) at 85 Hindley St. Rooms cost from $18/27 — a bit more expensive but the Plaza is an old but well kept place built around a very pleasant palm filled central courtyard. The rooms have washbasins. Or there's the *Angas Hotel* (tel 223 5649) at 78 Angas St where the room only rate is $12/20. At 205 Rundle St the *Austral Hotel* (tel 223 4660) gives a 10% discount to Aussie and Eaglepass travellers. Bed & breakfast costs $15/28 for singles/doubles.

The *Criterion Hotel* (tel 51 4301) at 137 King William St is conveniently close to the Central Bus Station and costs $13 per person room-only. At 437 Pulteney St the *Hotel Hanson* (tel 223 2442) costs $15/27 for singles/doubles including breakfast. This is a flashier place with air-con, colour TV and tea and coffee making facilities but there are only seven rooms. Finally the *Centralia* (tel 51 4536) at 65 North Terrace costs $12/20 and the *Somerset Hotel* (tel 223 2768) at 197 Pulteney St is $14 per person, both room-only.

City Motels & Guest Houses Right in the city centre is the *Clarice City Motel* (tel 223 3560) at 220 Hutt St, also just around the corner from the youth hostel. There are some rooms here from $20/26 but the motel units are $26/33. Across the East Parkland from the city centre at 22 Wakefield St, Kent Town is the *Kent Town Lodge* (tel 31 7568). Singles/doubles cost $15/20 or with self-contained facilities $26/32.

Other Motels Although you'll find motels all over Adelaide — some are also covered under Glenelg — there's a 'motel alley'. It's along Glen Osmond

Rd, the road that leads in to the city centre from the south-east for people coming from Melbourne or Sydney. This is quite a busy road so some places can be a bit noisy but there's a good selection right along the road.

Powell's Court (tel 271 7995) is only two km from the centre at 2 Glen Osmond Rd, Parkside. Rooms are $30/32 which doesn't sound like great value but they all have kitchens and there are also rooms big enough for three or four for not much more than the price of a double. All the usual mod-cons (TV, air-con) are there as well as the fridge and cooking facilities.

The *Sunny South Inn* (tel 79 1621) is four km out at 190 Glen Osmond Rd, Fullerton and offers the usual sort of motel standards at $24/28 and up. Across the road is *Princes Highway* (tel 79 2993) at 199 Glen Osmond Rd, Frewville which costs $23/26 and up.

Or there's the *Sands* (tel 79 6861) at 198 Glen Osmond Rd, Fullarton which costs $24/27 and the *Motel 277* (tel 79 9911) at 277 Glen Osmond Rd, Glenunga, four km from the centre. It's excellent value at $25 for a double for a standard room (there are also twin rooms with kitchens) but prices go up at holidays and long weekends. Weekly rates are five times the daily rate.

Glenelg Accommodation Glenelg is the main city beach suburb, just 10 km from the city centre on the other side of the airport. It's easily reached by Adelaide's one remaining tram line, a popular 15 minute, 70c excursion. There's a lot of accommodation here — a couple of old hotels, a number of good guest houses, a handful of reasonably priced motels and a lot of holiday flats. The main road down to the sea in Glenelg is Jetty Rd, along which the tram runs. Running along the seafront is South Esplanade and on the other side of the boat harbour entrance it becomes North Esplanade.

Down on the seafront at 2 Jetty Rd is the spacious old *Glenelg Pier Hotel* (tel 295 4116). This is a seaside hotel of the old school and rooms are $16/25 or $26/34 with private facilities. The tariff includes a 'light breakfast'. At 16 South Esplanade the old fashioned *Oriental Private Hotel* (tel 295 2390) costs $14/24 including a substantial breakfast.

Russell Court (tel 295 2545) at 5 Olive St has room-only rates of $14/24 and other rooms with private facilities at slightly higher prices. *Colley House* (tel 295 7535) is at 22 Colley Terrace, opposite the reserve, offers serviced apartments all the way from $18 to 48. There are a lot of holiday flats and serviced apartments in Glenelg. Most of them quote weekly rather than daily rates. Pick up a copy of the holiday flats leaflet from the tourist bureau.

At 7 North Esplanade the *Alkoomi Holiday Motel* (tel 294 6624) has rooms from $20 singles, $25-35 doubles. All with private facilities, fridges and tea-coffee making equipment. The adjoining *Wambini Lodge* (tel 295 4689) is similarly priced. The *Norfolk Motel* (tel 295 6354) is at 69-71 Broadway, a few blocks south of Jetty Rd. It's a fairly small motel with 20 units at $26 to 28 for singles, $30 to 32 for doubles, including breakfast. The *Bay Hotel Motel* (tel 294 4244) is $26/32 with air-con, colour TV and tea/coffee making facilities. It's at 58 Broadway, about a half km from the beach. The hotel section does counter lunches. There are lots of restaurants and take-away places down Jetty Rd; Glenelg is noted for its Greek food.

Other Beach Suburbs Glenelg isn't the only beach suburb with accommodation possibilities. You can also find plenty of places to stay at West Beach and Henley Beach, a little further north. West Beach in particular has a variety of holiday flats while at Henley Beach there are

holiday flats and the reasonably priced *Del Monte* private hotel (tel 356 8664) on the Esplanade with rooms at $17/30.

University Colleges The usual vacation only, students preferred rules apply but the Adelaide universities are no longer such good places to try for a room. Phone the University Welfare officer at 223 4333, extension 2915 Monday to Friday from 9 am to 5 pm if you want to give it a try. You can also try the Flinders University Halls of Residence.

Camping There are quite a few camping sites around Adelaide although some of the more convenient ones do not take tents, only caravans. The tourist bureau have a useful brochure on camping and caravan parks around the city. The following are within a 15 km radius, all camping charges are per site.

Recreation Caravan Park (tel 278 3540), National Park, Belair, 13 km south, camping sites $4 per day, on-site vans $15.

Sturt River Caravan Park (tel 296 7302), Brookside Rd, Darlington, 13 km south, camping $5 per day, on-site vans from $15 per day.

Adelaide Caravan Park (tel 42 1563), Bruton St, Hackney, only two km north-east and by the Torrens River, camping $5.50 per day but limited number of tent sites, on-site vans from $14 per day.

Glenbrook Caravan Park (tel 42 2965), Portrush Rd and River St, Marden, five km north-east, camping $4 per day, on-site vans from $12 to 18 per day.

Marion Caravan Park (tel 276 6695), 323 Sturt Rd, Bedford Park, 12 km south, camping $5 per day, on-site vans $20 to 22 per day — vans take five or six people.

Brownhill Creek Caravan Park (tel 271 4824), Brownhill Creek in the foothills of the Mount Lofty Ranges at Mitcham, eight km south, camping $3 per day, on-site vans $14.

Norwood Caravan Park (tel 31 5289), 290 Portrush Rd, Kensington, three km east, no camping but cabins from $16 per day for two people.

Levi Trust Caravan Park (tel 44 2209), Lansdowne Terrace, Walkerville, five km north-east, camping $4 per day, on-site vans from $14 per day.

West Beach Caravan Park (tel 356 7654), Military Rd, West Beach, eight km west, camping $4.30 to 5.30 per day depending on season.

Marineland Caravan Village (tel 353 2655), Military Rd, West Beach, eight km west, no camping, on-site vans $17 to 20 per day depending on season.

Windsor Gardens Caravan Park (tel 261 1091), 78 Windsor Grove, Windsor Gardens, six km north-east, camping $3.80 per day.

Places to Eat

Although Adelaide does not have the variety or quality range that Melbourne or Sydney can offer it certainly has quite enough to ensure survival with style! Furthermore Adelaide is well equipped with places you can eat outside. Licensing laws are more liberal in South Australia than in Sydney or Melbourne so a higher proportion of restaurants are licensed. Those which claim to be BYO are often just licensed restaurants which allow you to bring your own if you wish.

Open Air & Lunch Adelaide is one of the best cities in Australia for al fresco dining — the climate is dry so you're unlikely to get rained on, it's sunny so being outside is nice, and yet it's not so super-hot that for much of the year you're risking sunstroke. Best of all there are many places where you can have lunch, or other meals, in the open air.

One of the finest, for setting at least, is the *Festival Centre* where you can look out over the Torrens River while

you eat. There's a small kiosk with pies, hot dogs and pasties or the flashier bistro where you get a table and chair on the 'balcony' above the park. The food there may not be knockout but it's certainly OK and also fairly reasonably priced and the ambience is unbeatable. Prices range from $3.50 for a spaghetti bolognese with most dishes in the $5 to 6 bracket — including excellent serve yourself salads. Salad only costs $2.50, good value for vegetarians. With a carafe of wine this is a very fine place to eat.

Hindmarsh Square is another great place for city lunches and also another good place for dining out. There's a collection of snack bars and restaurants around the square and tables with umbrellas to complete the picture. On the north Pulteney St corner *Carrots* is a long running health food place although it has had the odd name change over the years. It's a nice, airy place to sit and look out over the square while you're

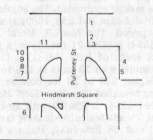

Hindmarsh Square

1 Hungry Jacks
2 Europa Bookshop
3 Carrots
4 Liberty Books
5 Inn on the Park
6 RAA of SA
7 Crank's Salad Bowl
8 TW's Coffee Shop
9 Jasmin Restaurant
10 Cafe Patron
11 Coalyard Restaurant

munching on a slice of hunza pie or carrot cake or sipping a fruit juice. On the west side of the square, with the tables and umbrellas, you can try *Crank's Salad Bowl* for fried brown rice, vegetable pies, soya bean pizzas and the like — mainly in the $1 to 1.80 range. Next door is *TW's Gourmet Coffee Shop* — nothing to do with me but nice sandwiches!

Then there's the *Jasmin Indian Restaurant* with main courses generally in the $4 to 5 bracket. You can also eat here in the evenings but note that it is not licensed at all. Next up is *Cafe Patron*, a nice looking place with lunch dishes in the $2 to 5 bracket — fancy sandwiches, quiches, etc. A bit further around the square is the more expensive *Coalyard Restaurant* which also does a complete $8 lunchtime buffet.

Snacks, Fast Foods & Late at Night If you're after late night eats then the *Pie Carts*, which appear every night from 6 pm till the early hours, are an Adelaide institution. If a pie floater (the great Australian meat pie floating on a thick pea soup) is your thing then look for their vans at the railway station on North Terrace and on Norwood Parade in Norwood. If a floater does not sound like your thing (and I sincerely hope it does not for your stomach's sake) then they also have other, more straightforward pies.

The *Pancake Kitchen* (see below) and *Bertie's Pancake Factory* at Imperial Place (close to the Grenfell and King William Sts intersection) are open late.

Adelaide has McDonalds and other front runners in the fast food stakes but *Hungry Jacks* is a similar chain which almost seems to be an Adelaide-only operation. Their burgers and the like are really pretty good and they've got one branch right in the centre on the corner of Pulteney and Rundle Sts. The railway station has a cafeteria and the YMCA's restaurant is very econom-

ical. Adelaide University's union building is also conveniently close to the city centre — try the Tavern there.

On Frome St, between North Terrace and Rundle St, *Govinda's* is a Hare Krishna run vegetarian place offering an all-you-can-eat vegetarian lunch plus fruit juice or lassi for $3.50. The modern Southern Cross Arcade runs through to St James Place from King William St, just down from Rundle Mall. There are lots of fast food and take-away places here, good for a quick lunch. *Rita's Health Foods* is particularly good with Indian snacks like samosas from 80c. More Indian take-aways at *Rani's* at 83 Gouger St. At 285 Rundle St, *Mezes* is a pleasant little snack bar place with a Mediterranean flavour.

Just a cup of tea or coffee? Head for *Kappy's* in Stephen Place, just off Rundle Mall in the city. It's a delightfully old-fashioned and very genteel tea house where you can get a nice cup of tea and slice of raisin toast! Or try the much more modern *Left Bank* at 165 Pulteney St, just down from Hindmarsh Square. They have coffee, tea, light snacks, sandwiches and so on in very pleasant surroundings. The *Al Fresco Gelateria* at 260 Rundle St has tables out on the sidewalk, a good place for a gelati or capuccino.

Counter Meals Adelaide is very well represented in this category, particularly at lunchtime. Just look for those telltale blackboards standing outside. A few blocks from the centre they don't come any cheaper than the *Old Queen's Arms* at 88 Wright St. It's straightforward food at prices that can't be beat — meals for around $3.

Move a block north to Gouger St, where all the seafood specialists can be found. The *Talbot Hotel* at 104 Gouger St has a nice deal with the Gouger Cafe next door. You get their excellent seafood at $5 to 7 for main courses in the hotel's pleasant beer garden. Another block over brings you to Franklin St where you'll find the Central Bus Station and a couple of hotels including the *Hotel Franklin* at 92 Franklin St which also does $2 breakfasts.

Hindley St and Rundle St have a number of pubs with good food. On the corner of Rundle St and East Terrace *The Stag* is a regular looking pub with a high reputation for its pub food. Main courses are generally $5 to 7. On the corner of Grenfell St and Hindmarsh Square the *Inn on the Park* is a ritzily done up pub with a bistro where you'll pay $7 to 10 but also a cheaper counter meal section where you can eat for $3 to 4.

Across to North Adelaide where *The British* at 58 Finniss St has a 'touch of the British' about it — plus a pleasant beer garden where you can grill the food yourself at the barbecue. Main courses are $5 to 6. Out at Glenelg the *Glenelg Pier Hotel* does low price and filling meals at lunchtime.

Hindley Street If Adelaide has a food centre, and a cheap food centre at that, it has to be Hindley St. Down there you'll find a whole series of Italian, Greek, Lebanese, Chinese and eastern European restaurants, interspersed with Adelaide's small and seedy collection of strip clubs, not to mention the 24-hour Third World Bookshop.

At 33 Hindley St you'll find *Chinatown* down in the basement. It's an unpretentious looking place with most dishes in the $5 to 7 bracket and the food really is good. Across the road at 68 Hindley St the *Feed Bag* is strictly American fast food style but it's cheap, clean, open reasonably late and not bad at all, plastic though it may be. The daily specials are good value.

Pagana's at 101 Hindley St does pastas for $4, 5 and 6 or main courses from $6 to 8 to 10. Good authentic Italian food and wine at 65c a glass. Then there are a string of steak/charcoal grill

places. The *Grecian Bar-B-Q* at 182, the *Barbecue Inn* at 196 and *Lubo's Barbecue* at 108A. *Athens*, a narrow little place and very Greek, is at 121 while at 139 you'll find *Hindley's Olympic Restaurant* with souvlaki, spiced lamb and the like. These places are all Greek or Yugoslav and main courses are in the $5 to 7 bracket.

The Middle East is represented here too — the *Jerusalem Shishkebab House* is at 133 and further down is the Lebanese *Cedar's* (rather flashier) at 179. Or a straightforward pizza at the *Pizza House* at 169A and at 123 you can turn to Malaysia at *Shah's* where main courses are $5 to 6.

Around the City Lots more places can be found around the city. The other end of Rundle St, for example, has quite an Italian flavour — just go down Hindley St, through Rundle Mall and at 201 Rundle St, *Don Giovanni's* is still a very popular Italian eatery — reasonable prices, a $3.50 lasagna is BIG and the calzone rustica is superb.

Or feel the sea breeze and head across to Gouger St which is the fish and seafood centre of Adelaide. Some of the places here have been running for many years and recently a lot of new places have appeared to join them. There's *Paul's* at 79 and the *Gouger Cafe* at 98. Main courses in the latter are $5 to 7, it also handle the counter meals next door in the Talbot Hotel. Or there's *George's* at 111 and *Stanley's* at 76.

Right in the centre you can stick with seafood at the rather plastic and fast-food flavour *Chief Charley's* at 12 Grenfell St which does a $4.80 'all you can eat' fish special. *The Hungarian* at 135 Cardwell St, a hop, step and jump from the youth hostel, is a bit pricier at around $7 for main courses but it's good, filling food for goulash or stuffed pepper enthusiasts. At 69 Grote St *Ellinis* is a Greek restaurant specialising in seafood — excellent food and reasonably priced.

Gilbert Place, a small lane, across the corner of King William and Hindley Sts in the centre, has several places worth a look. The *Pancake Kitchen* is notable for being open 24 hours a day, seven days a week and it's also pretty good value. But where else but Australia would you find 'steak & pancakes'? Next door is the *Omelet Pan* which is only open lunchtimes and weekend evenings but does lots of omelets and does them well — good value, cheap, plus nice salads. Round the corner is *Lino's City Spaghetti House* — a pleasant Italian place with dishes (schnitzels, parmagianas, etc) in the $4 to 6 range and pastas a bit cheaper. The long running but more expensive *Arkaba Steak Cellar* is also in this compact little group.

Finally you can make your way up to North Adelaide just to look at the *Pink Pig* at 52 O'Connell St, the *Black Bull* next door and for fish & chip takeaways the *White Whale* across the road. All with large models of the animals in question. Round the corner at 103 Tynte St the *Das Cafe* looks nice and is pretty reasonably priced. At 133 Glen Osmond Rd, Glen Osmond (south-east of the centre) *Fiore Pizza* is good value. The *Glenelg Barbecue* on Jetty Rd, Glenelg is good for steaks, kebabs and other straightforward food. It's one of many places along Jetty Rd.

Entertainment

There are lots of pubs with entertainment in Adelaide and a host of 'what's on' information, including a regular news-sheet put out by the SAGTB.

The usual rock pub circuit operates around Adelaide. It includes places like the *Arkaba* at 150 Glen Osmond Rd or the *Highway Inn* on the Anzac Highway in Plympton. The *Findon Hotel* on Grange Rd, Findon also has rock bands.

Popular city pubs with regular rock music include the *Angas Hotel* on Angas St, the *Producers Hotel* at 235 Grenfell St and the *Tivoli* at 261 Pirie St. On trendy Melbourne St, North Adelaide the *Old Lion Hotel* is a trendy hotel with everything from bars and dining room (expensive) to a disco and more rock music. Adelaide University often has big name rock bands on at the union.

Adelaide also has a string of places with folk and jazz, particularly on Friday and Saturday nights. You'll find them in the 'what's on' guides too. There's always something on at the Adelaide Festival Centre, the SAGTB's 'what's on' guide tells all.

There is a good selection of interesting film centres in Adelaide. The university film club often shows good films in the union or check out the Chelsea at 275 Kensington Rd, Kensington Park — good films and student discounts.

Getting There

Air Ansett and TAA fly to Adelaide from all the other state capitals and Adelaide is also the major departure point for Alice Springs and Darwin. All flights from Melbourne and most flights from Sydney for the Northern Territory go via Adelaide. Fares to or from Adelaide include Brisbane $209 ($156 standby), Sydney $170 ($168), Melbourne $117 ($88), Perth $249 ($186), Alice Springs $184 ($138), Darwin $283 ($212)

Rail Adelaide is connected by rail with Sydney, Melbourne, Perth, Broken Hill, Alice Springs and other centres. To Melbourne the daily overnight Overland has 1st class sleeping berths and 1st and economy sitting passengers. The trip takes about 13 hours and fares are $59 in 1st ($79 with sleeper) or $42 in economy. You can travel between Sydney and Adelaide either via Melbourne (daily) or via Broken Hill on the Indian Pacific (four times weekly). On the latter you connect with the Indian Pacific at Peterborough. Fares in 1st are $134 via Melbourne, $154 via Broken Hill, add $20 for a sleeper. In economy it's $95 via Melbourne, $118 via Broken Hill and sleepers are available on the Broken Hill route for $16.

Between Adelaide and Perth you can travel on the four times weekly Indian Pacific or the three times weekly Trans-Australian. The latter originates at Port Pirie so in either case you have to change trains from Adelaide. Fares are $281 in 1st, $216 in economy, including sleeping berth and all meals. On some Trans-Australian services there are also economy seats available at a cost of $95 not including any meals. The Adelaide-Perth trip takes about 42 hours.

The ghan between Adelaide and Alice Springs operates weekly and takes 24 hours. The fare is $174 in 1st, $125 in economy including sleeping berth and meals. An economy seat without meals is $90. You can also go by train to Broken Hill by taking the daily train to Peterborough to connect with the four times weekly Indian Pacific. State rail services also operate to Port Pirie, Mt Gambier and Victor Harbor. Rail bookings in Adelaide are made by phoning 212 6699. It's wise to book ahead, particularly on the ghan which is very popular.

Bus Ansett Pioneer and Greyhound both operate to Adelaide from Sydney, Melbourne, Perth, Alice Springs and other main centres. From Melbourne it's 11 hours and $35, Sydney is 22 hours and $69, Perth 35 hours and $79. There are also a whole collection of direct buses, particularly on the Perth route. To Alice Springs takes 27 hours and costs $77. Ansett Pioneer (tel 51 2075) and Greyhound (tel 212 1777) both operate from the Central Bus Station at 101-111 Franklin St. You'll also find Stateliner, Briscoes and other South Australian operators here. Briscoes have services to Alice Springs, Stateliner to other parts of South Australia and across the NSW border to Broken Hill. See the appropriate sections for details.

Getting Around
Bus, Train & Tram Adelaide has an integrated local transport system operated by the STA (State Transport Authority). For information you can ring 218 2345 until 10.30 pm seven nights a week. Adelaide is divided into three zones, travel within one zone costs 40c, two zones 70c, three zones 90c. The 70c and 90c zones cover unlimited travel for up to two hours. You could, for example, come into Adelaide on the Glenelg tram, take a bus to the station and go out the other side by train, all on the same ticket. In fact the ticket lasts from the start of the next hour so if you buy a ticket at 9.05 am your two hours isn't up until two hours from 10 am, to 12 noon.

Between 9 am and 3 pm on weekdays the 90c fare drops down to 70c, the 70c to 40c. In the city centre there are also a couple of free bus services. The 99B Bee Line service basically runs down King William St from the Glenelg tram terminus at Victoria Square and round the corner to the railway station. It operates 8 am to 6 pm weekdays, to 9 pm on Fridays and 8 am to 12.15 pm on Saturdays. The 99C City Loop does a loop around the central city area. It operates from 8 am to 6 pm Monday to Friday. The 99B operates every five minutes, the 99C every 10 minutes.

Day Tripper tickets are available for unlimited use from 9 am daily. A single ticket covers two adults and (unlimited?) children under 15 throughout the Adelaide metropolitan area for $2.50.

Apart from buses and trains there's also a solitary tram service — the Glenelg tram which will whisk you out to the seaside suburb from Victoria Square for 70c. You can get a useful route guide and map from the STA. Buses are colour coded — silver for the plains, brown and cream for the hills and for express services, orange and white for the circle services. The free buses have fancier colours.

Airport Adelaide's airport has recently gone international and all sorts of renovation took place as a result. What didn't change is its very convenient central location. There's an airport bus service operating between major hotels and the airport every hour. The fare is $2, phone 381 5311 for details. You can get out to the airport entrance on a 27B or 27c public bus. Otherwise count on about $5 for a taxi. Budget, Hertz and Thrifty have rent-a-car desks at the airport. There's a reasonably priced coffee bar/restaurant at the airport — get a spaghetti for $4 or a pepper steak for $7, most dishes in the $5 to $6 bracket. In the city TAA (tel 217 3333) are at 144 North Terrace, Ansett (tel 212 1111) are at 150 North Terrace.

Tours Half-day tours around the city include the Festival Centre or go out to Glenelg and cost around $10. You can go out further to Hahndorf in the Adelaide Hills or to Birdwood Mills and the Torrens Gorge or to the Mt Lofty Ranges and the Cleland Reserve for around $14. Day tours, such as those out to the Barossa Valley, or to the valley and Kapunda, or to Goolwa and the Murray Mouth, cost around $20 to $24. Other tours include day excursions to Victor Harbor (transport only) for $10, flying day trips to Kangaroo Island for up towards $100 and in summer there are historic steam locomotive rail tours organised by the Australian Railway Historical Society.

Car Rental The major firms — Avis, Hertz, Budget and Thrifty — are all represented in Adelaide. Action Rent-a-Car (tel 352 7044) must be unique in Australia for renting Alfa Romeos! Including unlimited km an Alfa Sud TI or a Ford Laser costs $25. Cut Price Car Rentals (tel 21 7359) is on the corner of Morphett and Gouger Sts and has cars from $10 a day. Adelaide has a selection of the Rent-a-Wreck, Hire-a-Hack folk, find them in the yellow pages.

Bicycle Rental You can hire bikes from Elliotts at 230 Rundle St. Three-speed machines cost $5 a day or $10 a week. Out at Glenelg there's a bike hire place right next door to the information centre at the seashore end of Jetty Rd. They cost $2 to $3 a day.

AROUND ADELAIDE

Adelaide is fortunate to have so much so accessible to the city — the Barossa is an easy day-trip, the wineries of the southern vales are a morning or afternoon visit and the Adelaide Hills are less than half an hour from the centre.

Adelaide Hills

Adelaide is flanked by hills to the south and east. The highest point, Mt Lofty at 771 metres, is just 30 minutes drive from the city and offers spectacular views over Adelaide, particularly from Windy Point at night. The hills are scenic and varied with tiny villages seemingly transplanted from Europe. The Montacute Scenic Route is one of the best drives through the hills. Walking tracks, 1000 km of them in all, also criss-cross the hills.

Parks in the hills include the Cleland Conservation Park, just 19 km from the city on the slopes of Mt Lofty. The park has a wide variety of wildlife and is open from 9 am to 5 pm daily. On the way out to the Princes Highway for Victoria you'll pass the Old Toll House at Glen Osmond, at the foot of the hills. Tolls were collected here for just five years from 1841. There are walking tracks, barbecues, waterfalls and a rugged gorge at the Morialta Park near Rostrevor. Other parks include the Parra Wirra Park to the north of the city and the Belair Recreation Park to the south.

Birdwood

Less than 50 km from Adelaide. Birdwood Hill Museum has the largest collection of old cars and motorcycles in Australia. The collection, which includes other pioneering exhibits, is housed in an 1852 flour mill and is open daily from 10 am to 5 pm. The town was once a gold mining centre and has various other old buildings. You can get to Birdwood via Chain of Ponds and

Gumeracha or via Lobethal. Gumeracha has a toy factory with a 20-metre high rocking horse — yes another of those Australian 'big' attractions. Lobethal has a fine little historical musem open on Tuesday and Sunday afternoons.

Hahndorf

The oldest surviving German settlement in Australia, Hahndorf is 29 km southeast of Adelaide and a popular excursion from the town. Settled in 1839 by Lutherans who left Prussia to escape religious persecution, the town took its name from the ship's Captain Hahn, dorf means 'town'. Various German festivals and celebrations are held in the town including the annual mid-January Schuetzenfest beer festival, and the German Arms Hotel at 50 Main St dates from 1834. The Hahndorf Academy, established in 1857, houses an art gallery and museum.

FLEURIEU PENINSULA

South of Adelaide is the Fleurieu Peninsula, so close that most places on it can be seen on easy day-trips from the city. The Gulf of St Vincent coast has a series of fine beaches down to Cape Jervis, looking across to Kangaroo Island. The southern coast of the peninsula, from Cape Jervis to the mouth of the Murray, is pounded by the high seas of the Southern Ocean. There are some good surfing beaches along this rugged coastline. Inland there's rolling countryside and the fine vineyards of the McLaren Vale area. The peninsula was named by Frenchman Nicholas Baudin after Napoleon's Minister for the Navy who financed Baudin's expedition to Australia. In the early days settlers on the peninsula ran a busy smuggling

business into Adelaide but in 1837 the first whaling station was established at Encounter Bay and this grew to become the South Australian colony's first successful industry.

Places to Stay

The Fleurieu Peninsula is a popular holiday area so there are plenty of places to stay whether you're looking for campsites, motels, hotels or guest houses. There's a youth hostel in the Inman Valley, near Glacier Rock and 20 km from Victor Harbor.

Getting There

Australian National Railways (tel 212 6699 in Adelaide) have a daily and twice on Friday service from Adelaide to Strathalbyn, Goolwa, Port Elliot and

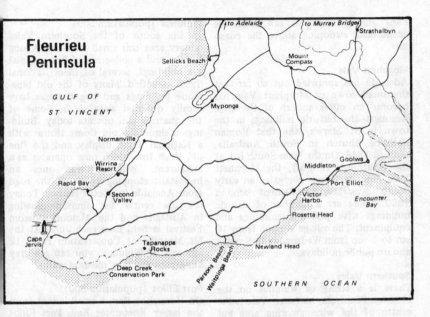

Victor Harbor. It takes about three hours all the way to Victor and fares are $4 to Strathalbyn, $5 to Goolwa and $6 to Port Elliot and Victor Harbor.

Alternatively you can get down to the peninsula by bus, all of which operate from the Central Bus Station on Franklin St. Premier Roadlines (tel 217 0777) have one to three services daily Adelaide-McLaren Vale-Willunga-Victor Harbor-Port Elliot. It takes about two hours all the way and fares are McLaren Vale $1.85, Willunga $2, Victor Harbor $4.80 and Port Elliot also $4.80. Brierly Coachlines (tel 264 1487) operate twice weekly to Cape Jervis via Aldinga, Yankalilla and other stops. Fares are Aldinga $2, Yankalilla $4, Cape Jervis $5.40 and the trip takes two hours to the cape. Johnsons Motor Services (tel 51 5959) operate weekdays to Goolwa, a two hour trip costing $4.

Gulf St Vincent Beaches

There is a string of fine beaches along the Gulf St Vincent coast of the peninsula, south of Adelaide. The beach stretch extends from Christie's Beach, with a good beach below red sandstone cliffs. Then there's Port Noarlunga, Seaford Beach and Moana Beach before you reach the best known beach on the peninsula — Maslins Beach where the southern end of the beach was the first legal nude bathing beach in Australia.

Further south, beyond Aldinga Beach and Sellicks Beach, the coastline is rockier but there are still good swimming beaches at Myponga, Normanville and a number of other places. The coast road eventually runs through the small town of Delamere and ends at Cape Jervis at the tip of the peninsula. From here you can look across the narrow Backstairs Passage to Kangaroo Island, 13 km away. At one time ferries ran across the straits from Cape Jervis. Near Cape Jervis there's a 12 hectare fauna park. The cape, with its high cliffs and strong sea breezes, is a popular spot for hang gliding and you can often see enthusiasts swooping above the coastline.

Morphett Vale

Adelaide has sprawled out so far that the small town of Morphett Vale has become an outer suburb of the city. Amongst the historic buildings in the town is St Mary's, the first Roman Catholic church in South Australia, built in 1846. On the Main South Rd, at the Noarlunga turn-off, the Morphett Vale Pioneer Village recreates an early South Australian settlement around 1860. There are a number of historic buildings with period furnishings and equipment. The village is open from 10 am to 5 pm from Wednesday to Sunday and on public holidays.

Southern Vales

There is a string of wineries on the Fleurieu Peninsula. McLaren Vale is the centre of the wine growing area but you'll also find winemakers at Reynella, Willunga and Langhorne Creek. The area is particularly well suited to red wines. There are around two dozen wineries in the McLaren Vale area alone and about 40 in the whole region. Many of them have tastings and also sell their wines — you can make a pleasant tastings crawl around the various wineries. The first winery in the area, in Reynella, was established in 1838 and some of the wineries date back to the last century and have fine old buildings. Most of them are open to the public Monday to Saturday, many of them on Sunday as well. A number have picnic or barbecue areas near to the cellar door sales.

The McLaren Vale Wine Bushing Festival takes place over a week in late October, early November each year. It's a busy time of wine tastings, tours and the whole thing is topped by a grand Elizabethan Feast. At McLaren Flat, near McLaren Vale, there's the Manning Fauna & Flora Reserve.

Willunga (population 500)

In the south of the Southern Vales winery area this small town has a long history and a collection of fine colonial era buildings, several of them National Trust classified. Many of the old bluestone buildings and pug cottages have locally quarried slate roofs. Some of the quarries still operate today. Buildings include the old Court House with a National Trust display and the fine old Bush Inn which now operates as a restaurant. Willunga was once an important stopping point on the road from Adelaide to Victor Harbor. Today it's the centre for almond growing in Australia and the Almond Blossom Festival is held here each July. At the Mt Magnificent Conservation Park, 12 km east of Willunga, you can see grey kangaroos and take pleasant walks.

Port Elliot (population 800)

On Horseshoe Bay, a small indent from the larger Encounter Bay, Port Elliot was originally established as the sea port for the Murray River trade and was the first town on Encounter Bay. At the time it was established in 1854 nearby Victor Harbor was still just a whaling station. Port Elliot proved less than ideal as a port, however, and in 1864 its functions were shifted to Victor Harbor where Granite Island provided a safer, more sheltered anchorage. Today the town is a popular holiday resort with fine views along the coast to the mouth of the Murray and the Coorong. Horseshoe Bay has a sheltered, safe swimming beach with a good cliff-top walk above it. This stretch of coast is particularly popular with surfers and Boomer Beach, on the edge of town to the west, is one of the best surfing beaches. Middleton Beach, to the east of town towards Goolwa, is another beach that attracts the boardriders.

Victor Harbor (population 4300)

The main town on the peninsula, 84 km south of Adelaide, Victor Harbor looks out on to Encounter Bay where Flinders and Baudin made their historic meeting in 1802. Up on the headland known as the Bluff there's a memorial to the 'encounter' which took place on the bay below. It's a steep climb up to the Bluff from where there are fine views.

The port is protected from the high southern seas by Granite Island, a small island out in the bay which is connected to the mainland by a causeway. A tourist tractor-train trundles visitors across to the island between November and May. On the island there's a chairlift up to the top from where there are fine views across the bay. You may see fairy penguins and seals on the shores of Granite Island.

Victor, as the town is often referred to, was established early in South Australia's history as a sealing and whaling centre. South of the town at Rosetta Bay, below the Bluff, is Whaler's Haven with many interesting reminders of those early whaling days. The first whaling station was established here in 1837 and another followed soon after on Granite Island but whaling ceased here in 1864, only 27 years later.

Other historic buildings in the town include St Augustine's Church of England from 1869, the Museum of Historical Art and the Cornhill Museum & Art Gallery. There are also a number of interesting excursion points around the town. The Urimbirra fauna park, with a nocturnal house, is only five km out. You can make pleasant bushwalks around the Hindmarsh Valley Falls. Spring Mount Conservation Park is 14 km to the north-west. Also in this direction is the Myponga Conservation Park with many grey kangaroos and Glacier Rock, 19 km out. Along the coast from Victor Harbor towards Cape Jervis, Waitpinga Beach is another popular surfing beach and updrafts from

the cliffs attract hang-gliders. It's no good for swimming though.

The Victor Harbor Tourist Office is on Ocean St.

Goolwa (population 1150)

On Lake Alexandrina, near the mouth of the Murray, the town initially rose to prominence with the growth of trade along the mighty Murray. Then the Murray mouth silted up and large ships were unable to get up to Goolwa so a railway line, the first in South Australia, was built from Goolwa to nearby Port Elliott but in the 1880s a new railway line to Adelaide spelt the end for Goolwa as a port town.

Today Goolwa is a popular resort with a number of interesting old buildings including the National Trust museum in the first house built in the area, back in 1852. The old paddle steamer *Captain Sturt* can be seen in the town and on the main street there's a horse-drawn railway carriage from the early days of the railway line. Goolwa is an access point to the Coorong Park, the long stretch of the beach to the actual mouth of the Murray can be driven along and there's a ferry crossing over to Hindmarsh Island. You can also take cruises on Lake Alexandrina on the *MV Aroona*. Goolwa is the departure point for upriver cruises on the *Murray River Queen*. Milang, on Lake Alexandrina was a centre for the river trade even before Goolwa. In the early days of the river shipping business bullock wagons carried goods overland between here and Adelaide.

There's a Goolwa Tourist Office at 52 Hutchinson St.

Strathalbyn (population 1700)

Situated on the Angas River, well inland from the coast, this picturesque town was settled back in 1839 by Scottish immigrants. St Andrew's Church, the original 'kirk', is one of the best known country churches in Australia. It was built in 1848 and its tower overlooks the river. There's also an attractive Memorial Gardens on the riverbanks with a large contingent of resident waterbirds. The town has many old buildings with a distinctly Scottish flavour to them — there's a National Trust pioneer museum, an old police station and court house, a historical folk museum, the Angas flour mill of 1852 and in all enough reminders of the region's early history to qualify Strathalbyn as a 'heritage town'.

THE BAROSSA VALLEY

South Australia's most famous wine producing valley vies with the Hunter Valley in NSW as the best known in Australia. The gently sloping valley is about 40 km long and five to 11 km wide. The Barossa turns out a quarter of all the wine in Australia and since the valley is only about 50 km from Adelaide it's a very popular place to visit. The Barossa still has some German flavour from its original settlement in 1842. Fleeing religious persecution in Prussia and Silesia those first settlers weren't wine makers but fortunately someone soon came along and recognised the valley's potential. The name, curiously enough, is actually a misspelling of Barrosa in Spain, close to where the Spanish sherry comes from. Prior to WW I the Barossa probably sounded even more Germanic because during the war many German place names were patriotically Anglicised. When the jingoistic fervour died down some changed back.

There are a variety of places to stay in the Barossa and a leisurely tastings crawl around the various wineries is a popular activity for visitors as well as people from Adelaide. The valley is initially a little disappointing since it's rather wide and flat and from the central road doesn't really appear very valley-like at all. Furthermore that main road through Lyndoch, Tanunda and Nuriootpa, the main valley towns, is rather busy and noisy, not at all like the peaceful valley you might expect. Get off the main road or take the scenic drive between Angaston and Tanunda and you'll begin to appreciate the Barossa.

Information

There's a tourist information centre in Coulthard House at 66 Murray St, Nuriootpa.

Wineries

The Barossa has something over 30 wineries around the valley and many of them are open to the public, offer guided tours or free wine tastings. Get a copy of the SAGTB's Barossa leaflet for full details of location and opening hours. Just some of the most interesting wineries include Chateau Yaldara (1) at Lyndoch. Established in 1947 in the ruins of a 19th-century winery and flour mill it has a notable art collection which can be seen on conducted tours.

Gramp's Orlando (2) at Rowland Flat, between Lyndoch and Tanunda, was established in 1847, one of the oldest wineries in the valley. Krondorf (3) at Tanunda is currently one of the glamour wine makers with a high reputation for their wine. Chateau Tanunda (4), also in Tanunda, is a magnificent old bluestone building built in 1889 but it is not open to the public at all. Leo Buring Chateau Leonay (5) is also in Tanunda and is another winery fantasy with turrets and towers although it dates only from 1945.

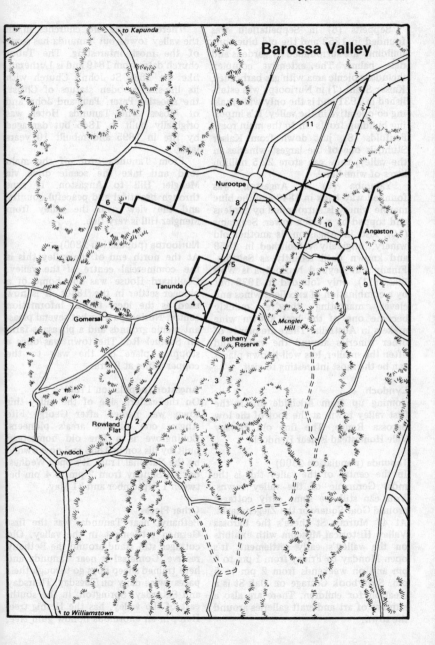

Seppelts (6) in Seppeltsfield was founded in 1852 and the old bluestone buildings are surrounded by gardens and date palms. The extensive complex includes a picnic area with gas barbecues. Kaiser Stuhl (7) in Nuriootpa was established in 1931 and is the only wine-making co-operative in the valley. It's imposing building fronts on to the main road. Penfolds (8), just down from Kaiser Stuhl, is one of the largest wineries in the valley, they can store 22.5 million litres of wine here!

Yalumba (9) in Angaston was founded way back in 1849 and the blue marble winery is surrounded by gardens and topped by a clock tower. Seagrams (10), also in Angaston, is another old winery, originally established in 1859 and known until recently as Saltram. Finally out beyond Nuriootpa is Wolf Blass (11), only founded in 1973 but by a combination of excellent wines and clever marketing they've quickly become one of the best known wine makers in Australia. There are plenty of other wineries around the valley and often the smaller, less well-known places can be the most interesting to visit.

Lyndoch

Coming up from Adelaide this is the first valley town, at the foot of the low Barossa Range. The fine old Pewsey Vale Homestead is near Lyndoch.

Tanunda (population 2300)

In the centre of the valley this is the most Germanic of the valley towns. You can still see some early cottages around Goat Square or the Ziegenmarkt. At 47 Murray St there's the Barossa Valley Historical Museum with exhibits on the valley's early settlement. It's open Monday to Friday from 1 pm to 5 pm and on weekends from 2 pm to 5 pm. Storybook Cottage on Oak St is a creation for children. There are also a number of art and craft galleries around the town.

There are fine old churches in all the valley towns but Tanunda has some of the most interesting. The Tabor church dates from 1849 and is Lutheran, like the 1868 St John's Church with its life-size wooden statues of Christ, the apostles Peter, Paul and John and of Moses. The Tanunda Hotel was originally built in 1845 but damaged by fire in 1895 and rebuilt 10 years later.

From Tanunda turn off the main road and take the scenic drive via Mengler Hill to Angaston. It runs through beautiful and peaceful country and the view over the valley from Mengler Hill is very fine.

Nuriootpa (population 2800)

At the north end of the valley this is the commercial centre of the valley. Coulthard House was the home of a pioneer settler in the 1840s. It is now used as the local tourist information centre. Nuriootpa also has several pleasant picnic grounds and a pheasant farm on Samuel Rd. The town was once a stopping place on the way to the copper mines at Burra.

Angaston (population 1750)

On the eastern side of the valley this town was named after George Fife Angas, one of the area's pioneers. Collingrove is a fine old homestead built by his son in 1853 and now owned by the National Trust. It's open Wednesday to Sunday from 2 pm to 4 pm between 1 September and 31 May.

Other Places

Bethany, near Tanunda, was the first German settlement in the valley. Old cottages still stand around the Bethany reserve. Gomersal is near Tanunda and here trained sheep dogs go through their paces twice daily on Tuesday, Thursday and Saturday. Springton, in the southeast of the valley, has the Herbig tree. Here, in an enormous hollow gum tree,

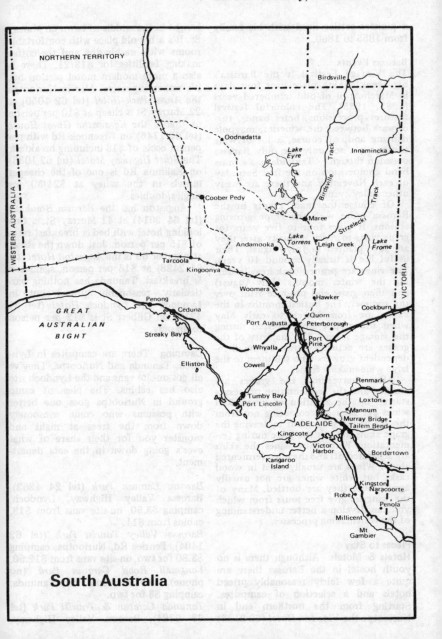

NORTHERN TERRITORY

WESTERN AUSTRALIA

VICTORIA

Birdsville

Oodnadatta

Lake Eyre

Innamincka

Birdsville Track

Coober Pedy

Marree

Strzelecki Track

Lake Torrens

Andamooka

Leigh Creek

Lake Frome

Tarcoola

Kingoonya

Woomera

Hawker

Cockburn

Penong

Ceduna

GREAT AUSTRALIAN BIGHT

Port Augusta

Quorn

Peterborough

Streaky Bay

Whyalla

Port Pirie

Elliston

Cowell

Renmark

Tumby Bay
Port Lincoln

Loxton

Mannum

ADELAIDE

Murray Bridge
Tailem Bend

Kingscote

Victor Harbor

Bordertown

Kangaroo Island

Kingston

Naracoorte

Robe

Penola

Millicent

Mt Gambier

South Australia

a pioneer settler lived with his family from 1855 to 1860.

Barossa Events

The Vintage Festival is the Barossa's big event, taking place over four days in March-April of odd numbered years (1983, 1985). The colourful festival features processions, brass bands, tug-of-wars between the wineries, maypole dancing and, of course, a lot of wine tasting. It's not only the only Barossa occasion though — Tanunda has a brass band competition on the first Saturday of each November and there are many other valley events.

Of course the main events in the Barossa move with the grape growing seasons. It takes four to five years for grape vines to reach maturity after they are first planted in July-August. Their useful life is usually around 40 years. The vines are pruned back heavily during the winter months (July-August) and then grow and produce fruit over the summer. The busiest months in the valley are from March to early May when the grapes are harvested during the vintage season. The majority of the grapes are actually grown by small independent growers who sell them to the large wine-making firms.

After harvesting, the grapes are crushed and the fermentation process is started by the addition of yeast. Red wines get their red colouring not from the use of red grapes but by leaving the grape skins in with the juice during fermentation. With white wines the skins are separated off and the juice fermented alone. Wines are usually aged in wood casks but white wines are not usually aged before they are bottled. Many of the wineries give free tours from which you can develop a better understanding of the winemaking processes.

Places to Stay

Hotels & Motels Although there is no youth hostel in the Barossa there are quite a few fairly reasonably priced hotels and a selection of campsites. Starting from the northern end in Nuriootpa the *Vine Inn Hotel* (62 2133) is right in the middle of town on Murray St. It's a big old place with comfortable rooms with washbasins and tea/coffee making facilities for $13/21. There is also a more modern motel section but it's rather expensive. Also in Nuriootpa the *Angas Park Hotel* (tel 62 1050) at 22 Murray St is cheap at $10 per person or there's the *Karawatha Guest House* (tel 62 1746) on Greenock Rd with per person costs of $13 including breakfast. The *Sturt Highway Motel* (tel 62 1033) on Kalimna Rd is one of the cheaper motels in the valley at $24/30 for singles/doubles.

Angaston has the *Barossa Brauhaus* (tel 64 2014) at 41 Murray St, a fine looking hotel with bed & breakfast rates of $15 per person. Just down the street at number 59 is the *Angaston Hotel* (tel 64 2428) at $16 per person, again bed & breakfast. Tanunda has nothing particularly reasonably priced but in Lyndoch the *Lyndoch Hotel* (tel 24 4211) on Gilbert St is $12 per person room only.

Camping There are campsites in Lyndoch, Tanunda and Nuriootpa. They've all got on-site vans and the Lyndoch site also has cabins. The pleasant camp ground in Nuriootpa goes one better with possums who come winsomely down from the trees at night and monster you for their share of whatever's going down in the eats department.

Barossa Caravan Park (tel 24 4262), Barossa Valley Highway, Lyndoch, camping $3.50, on-site vans from $13, cabins from $14.
Barossa Valley Tourist Park (tel 62 1404), Penrice Rd, Nuriootpa, camping $3.80 for two, on-site vans from $12.50.
Langmeil Road Caravan Park (no phone), two km from PO, Tanunda, camping $3 for two.
Tanunda Caravan & Tourist Park (tel 63 2784), Barossa Valley Highway,

Tanunda, camping $3.50 for two, on-site vans from $12.

Places to Eat

The valley is renowned for its solid, German-style eating places but most of them tend to be decidedly expensive. One definite exception is the *Heinemann Park Restaurant*, just on the Adelaide side of Tanunda, directly opposite the caravan park. It's simple and straight-forward with good solid food at reason-able prices — most main courses around $6. At 51 Murray St in the town the *Tanunda Hotel* has a nice lounge with counter meals in the $4 to $5.50 range.

In Nuriootpa meals are in the $6 to $8 bracket in the *Vine Inn* on Murray St. Angaston has a couple of hotels with good counter meals. The *Angaston Hotel* at 59 Murray St has most meals in the $4 to $5 bracket. Or try the

Barossa Brauhaus with its very pleasant lounge area and meals in the $6 to $8 range, most at $7. The valley is famed for its fine bakeries and bread and one of the best is *Linke's Bakery* at 40 Murray St, Nuriootpa.

Getting There & Around

It's $3 by Briscoes' bus from Adelaide to the valley. You can book valley tours from the tourist office in Nuriootpa where you can also enquire about hiring bicycles. Otherwise a car is nice to have in the valley — but don't plan on very much wine tasting if you're driving too. There are several routes from Adelaide to the valley. Most direct is via the Main North Rd through Elizabeth and Gawler. More picturesque routes go through the Torrens Gorge, Chain of Ponds and Williamstown or via Chain of Ponds and Birdwood.

NORTH OF ADELAIDE

Two main routes run north of Adelaide. One runs north to Gawler, where you can turn off east to the Barossa Valley and the Riverland area. Continuing north you'd pass through Burra and near Peterborough have the option of turning north-west to the Flinders Ranges or continuing on the Barrier Highway as it bends off to the north-east and makes the long, dull run to Broken Hill in NSW. The other route from Adelaide heads off slightly north-west through Wakefield then to Port Pirie and Port Augusta on the Spencer Gulf. Again you can then choose be-tween the Flinders, the Eyre Peninsula or simply heading west towards Western Australia.

This area to the north of Adelaide includes some of the most fertile and pleasant land in the state. Sunshine, rainfall and excellent soil combine to

make this a prosperous agricultural region with excellent wine making areas, like the Clare Valley, thrown into the bargain. Apart from the two main routes north there are a network of smaller roads running across this region.

Adelaide to the Barossa

On the way north to the Barossa or Clare Valleys you pass through Elizabeth (population 34,000), an industrial satell-ite city of Adelaide with major auto-motive manufacturing plants. Just after the turn-off from the Sturt Highway to the Barossa, Gawler (population 8700) is on the edge of the valley. Like Adelaide it was planned by Colonel Light and the old telegraph station, built in 1860, now houses a Folk Museum which is open Tuesdays to Thursdays from 2 pm to 4 pm. There is also a National Trust Telecommunic-ations Museum in the same building —

open the same hours plus on Sundays from 2 pm to 5 pm.

Kapunda (population 1400)

About 80 km north of Adelaide and a little north of the Barossa Valley, Kapunda is actually off the main roads north but you can take a pleasant backroads route from the valley, through Kapunda and join the Barrier Highway a little further north. Copper was found here in 1842 and Kapunda became the first mining town in Australia and for a while was the biggest country town in South Australia. At its peak it had a population of 10,000 with 22 hotels but the mines closed in 1888. There's a lookout point in the town with views over the old open cut mines and mine chimneys. Kapunda has a Historical Museum with old mining relics plus the old courthouse and jail tearooms — a good place for a country-style tea. It's a pleasant drive northeast of Kapunda to Eudunda.

Burra (population 1200)

This really pretty little town was a copper mining centre from 1847 to 1877. The district Burra Burra takes its name from the Hindi word for 'great great'. Pick up a guide-yourself leaflet from the tourist office by the centre of town (40c) and explore the town with its many solid, old stone buildings and tiny Cornish cottages. A couple of old miners' dugouts have been preserved by the riverbank.

The town has a folk museum on Market Square, in the tourist office building. The 33 cottages at Paxton Square were built for Cornish miners in the 1850s and are being restored by the National Trust. Other old buildings include Redruth Jail, the Bon Accord Mine Building, and the courthouse and jail at Burra North. Burra Gorge is north of the town.

After Burra the country rapidly becomes drier and more barren and

along the road to Broken Hill the number of dead roos is phenomenal — they're almost continuous all the way to the NSW border. Over one five km stretch I counted 47 recently killed. Fortunately not everything is dead, you may also see the odd emu and plenty of galahs.

Clare (population 3600)

This pleasant little town, 135 km north of Adelaide, is another important wine producing centre although it is far less commercial than the Barossa. It was originally settled in 1842 and named after County Clare in Ireland. The first vines were planted here in 1848 by Jesuit priests and communion wines are still produced here today. There are lots of wineries in the valley including the well-known Stanley Wine Company, dating from 1894.

The town has a number of interesting buildings including, in what seems to be a South Australian norm, a police station/courthouse, dating from 1850, which is preserved as a National Trust museum. The Wolta Wolta Homestead dates from 1864 while Christison Park has a fauna and flora reserve and picnic grounds. At the Pioneer Memorial Park there are walking trails and barbecue facilities.

You can visit the Barossa on your way north to the Clare Valley and in turn Clare can be visited en route to the Flinders Ranges. There's a daily bus to Riverton which connects to trains to Adelaide. There's a Tourist Office in the Town Hall at 229 Main St.

Port Pirie (population 15,000)

Just 84 km south of Port Augusta at the northern end of Spencer Gulf, this is a major port and industrial centre with huge lead smelters that handle the output sent down by rail from Broken Hill. There are tours of the smelters on weekday afternoons. It's also an important port for shipping of agricultural production. Port Pirie has lots of interesting old buildings including some fine hotels down the main street of the town. On Ellen St the National Trust Museum includes the ornate old railway station and customs house. Near to Port Pirie there's an interesting museum on Weerona Island, 13 km out, and the Telowie Gorge park is also within easy reach.

Other Towns of the Mid-North

Balaklava (population 1250) is a picturesque town on the northern edge of the Adelaide plains. There's a National Trust Museum open on Sundays only and it's a short trip from here to Wakefield at the northern end of Gulf St Vincent. Jamestown (population 1300), north of the Clare Valley and at the southern edge of the Flinders Ranges, is a country town with a Railway Station Museum open Sundays from 2 to 4 pm.

Peterborough (population 2800) is another gateway town to the Flinders. This is an important railway centre and also a place where the problems railway engineers in Australia have to cope with are clearly illustrated. The colonial bungling which led to Australia's mixed up railway system managed to run three different railway gauges through Peterborough! Steamtown is a working railway museum and on holiday weekends narrow gauge steam train trips are made from Peterbough to Orroroo ($6.60) or Eurelia ($11). The old town hall in Peterborough is now a museum and art gallery.

North from here into the Flinders a land boom in the 1870s took place as settlers established farming towns, encouraged by easy credit from the South Australian government. Sturdy farms and towns sprung up but the wet seasons that had encouraged hopes of wheat farming soon gave way to the normal dry conditions and as the land dried out the towns tumbled into ruins. Some of the most interesting reminders of those days can be seen in the southern Flinders.

KANGAROO ISLAND (population 3000)

The third biggest island in Australia (after Tasmania and Melville Island off Darwin in the Northern Territory), Kangaroo Island is a popular holiday resort from Adelaide. It's about 110 km from Adelaide to Kingscote, the main town on the island, but the north-east corner of Kangaroo Island is actually only 10 km off the southern tip of the Fleurieu Peninsula. Kangaroo Island is about 150 km long by 30 km wide but sparsely populated. It offers superb scenery; pleasant, sheltered beaches along the north coast; a rough, rugged and wave-swept south coast plus lots of native wildlife. There are no foxes, rabbits or the other introduced wildlife that have upset the balance on the main-

land. The island also has excellent fishing.

Like other islands off the south coast of Australia, Kangaroo Island has a rough and ready early history with sealers, whalers and escaped convicts all playing their often ruthless part. Many of the names around the island have a distinctly French flavour to them since it was first charted by the French explorer Nicholas Baudin. He had just met Matthew Flinders, who was in the process of circumnavigating Australia, at nearby Encounter Bay off Victor Harbor. Flinders had already named the island after the many kangaroos he saw there but Baudin went on to name many other prominent features on the island. Apart from beaches, bushwalks and wildlife the island has also attracted

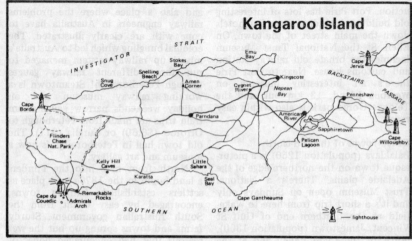

Kangaroo Island

more than its fair share of shipwrecks and there are a number of these of interest to skindivers.

Places to Stay

There is a very wide variety of accommodation all over the island — hardly surprising with such a popular holiday resort. *Guestward Ho Holiday Cottages* is an 'alternate accommodation' youth hostel in Penneshaw. Nightly cost is $4. Otherwise there are plenty of camping sites and caravan parks, some with on-site vans, and a wide selection of holiday flats with costs in many cases under $20 a night in places with room for four to six. On a weekly basis costs are even lower.

Getting There

Ferry The *MV Troubridge* crosses to Kingscote from Port Adelaide three times weekly. The crossing takes 6½ hours. Once weekly it continues on to Port Lincoln on the Eyre Peninsula and returns. There are some seasonal variations in summer, over school holidays and on public holidays. Fares to Kingscote from Port Adelaide or from Port Lincoln are $20 for adults. Cars cost

$27 to 46 depending on size but in the November 30 to March 1 period the cost jumps by $20. Motorcycles cost $12, bicycles $1.50 — in all cases these vehicle costs are for accompanied vehicles. Shipping agents are R W Miller (tel 47 5577), 3 Todd St, Port Adelaide. In Kingscote you can find R W Miller (tel 22 273) on Commercial Rd.

You can also get to Kangaroo Island on the *Philanderer II* from Cape Jervis. The crossing takes about an hour and there are two services a day at $28 return. Another route is from North Haven, near Glenelg, from where there are services on Friday, Saturday, Sunday, Monday for $45 return.

Air Airlines of South Australia (tel 217 7332) are booked through Ansett at 150 North Terrace. They fly Adelaide-Kangaroo Island up to three times daily and the cost is $33. The flight takes just half an hour and student discounts are available if you're under 26. Apex return fares at $46 are also available on certain 'off-peak' flights.

You can also fly to American River, Kingscote and Parndana with Emu Air (tel 352 3128). Fares are $25 to any of the three stops and there are two flights daily. Trans Regional Airlines (tel 212 3355) are booked through TAA at 144 North Terrace. They fly to Kingscote and Penneshaw up to four times daily and the fare is $33. Albatross Airlines have one or two flights daily between Adelaide and Kingscote and their fare is $30.

Getting Around

There is no public transport on Kangaroo Island apart from taxis. There are, however, a variety of hire cars and motorcycles and you can also hitch. The SAGTB has a car hire leaflet for the island. Budget Rent-a-Car have two agencies there and there are a number of independent operators with typical charges being a Moke at $12 a day plus 17c a km, a Sigma for $16 plus 12c or a Corolla at $16 plus 18c. Abacar (tel 22 390) at Dauncey St, Kingscote rent older Valiants at $8.50 plus 12c or Falcons at $10 plus 12c.

Tours around the island cost about $10 for half-day tours, $18 for full-day tours. There are also a variety of launch cruises.

Kingscote (population 1100)

The main town on Kangaroo Island, Kingscote is also the arrival point for the ferries and flights to the island. This was actually the first settlement in South Australia although it was soon superseded by Adelaide and other mainland centres. It was formally settled in 1836 and all but abandoned a few years later but there were other Europeans on the island many years earlier. Kingscote has a rock pool for swimming and Brownlow Beach is also a good swimming place. The old cottage 'Hope', built in 1858, is a National Trust museum and the headstones in Kingscote's cemetery make interesting reading.

American River

Between Kingscote and Penneshaw the small settlement of American River takes its name from the group of American sealers who built a boat here in 1803-04. The town is situated on a small peninsula and shelters an inner bay, named Pelican Lagoon by Flinders, which today is a bird sanctuary. American River is a popular tourist resort, good for sailing and fishing.

Penneshaw

Looking across the narrow Backstairs Passage to the Fleurieu Peninsula, Penneshaw is a quiet little resort town with a pleasant beach at Hog's Bay and the tiny inlet of Christmas Cove as a boat harbour. You can sometimes see penguins on the rocks below the town. Frenchman's Rock is a monument housing a replica of the rock Baudin left here in 1803. The actual rock he marked to note his visit is now in the South Australian Art Gallery. The Dudley Peninsula, the knob of land on the eastern end of the island on which Penneshaw is located, has several other points of interest. There's surf at Pennington Bay and the sheltered waters of Chapman River are very popular for canoeing. The Cape Willoughby lighthouse, first operated in 1852 -- it's the oldest in South Australia, is open from 1.30 to 3.30 pm on Monday to Friday.

North Coast

There are a series of fine sheltered beaches along the north coast of the island. Near Kingscote, Emu Bay has a beautiful long sweep of sand. Other good beaches include Stokes Bay, Snelling Beach and the sheltered sandy stretch of Snug Cove.

Flinders Chase National Park

Occupying the whole western end of the island the Flinders Chase park is the largest national park in South Australia. The park has beautiful forests of eucalyptus plus koalas, wild pigs and possums plus kangaroos and emus which have become so fearless with humans that they'll come up and brazenly badger you for food. The popular picnic and barbecue area at Rocky River Homestead is actually fenced off to protect park visitors from these free-loaders. On the north-west corner of the island Cape Borda has a lighthouse built in 1858 with guided tours Monday to Saturday from 10 am to 12 noon and 2 to 4.30 pm. The lighthouse is on a cliff 150 metres above the sea. There's an interesting little cemetery nearby at Harvey's Return. In the southern corner of the park Cape du Couedic (named by Nicholas Baudin of course) is wild, remote and rugged. An extremely picturesque lighthouse built in 1906 tops the cape and you can follow the path from the car park down to Admiral's Arch — a natural archway pounded by towering seas. You can often see seals and penguins here. At Kirkpatrick Point, only a couple of km east of Cape du Couedic, the Remarkable Rocks are a series of bizarre granite rocks on a huge dome stretching 75 metres down to the sea. You can camp at the Rocky River park headquarters, or elsewhere with a permit.

South Coast

The south coast of the island is rough and wave-swept in comparison to the north coast. At Hanson Bay, close to Cape du Couedic at the western end of the coast, there's a colony of fairy penguins. A little further east you come to Kelly Hill Caves, a series of limestone caves discovered in the 1880s when a horse, appropriately named Ned Kelly, fell through a hole in the ground. There are tours daily at 10 am to 12.30 pm and 1.30 to 4.30 pm. Vivonne Bay has a long and beautiful sweep of beach and there is excellent fishing here but swimmers should exercise great care. The undertows here are fierce and swimmers are recommended to stick close to the jetty or the river mouth. Seal Bay is another sweeping beach with plenty of resident seals. They're generally quite happy to have two-legged visitors on the beach but a little caution is required, don't let them feel threatened by your presence. Nearby and close to the south coast road is 'little Sahara', a series of enormous white sand dunes, ideal for playing Lawrence of Arabia.

THE SOUTH-EAST

The South-East of South Australia is the area through which most travellers between Melbourne and Adelaide pass. Travelling between the two cities you can either take the Western-Dukes Highway or the Princes Highway through the south-east region. The Western-Dukes is the most direct route between the two cities (729 km) but the Dukes Highway stretch in South Australia is not terribly exciting -- it just runs through a lot of flat, dull, agricultural land. South of this route

there is some rather more interesting country and you can take slightly longer detours off the usual route but the Princes Highway, along the coast, is of greater interest. Along this road you pass through Mt Gambier, with its impressive crater lakes, and then run along the extensive coastal lagoon system known as the Coorong.

Getting There

Air Ansett fly from Melbourne to Mt Gambier most days of the week and twice on some days. The flight takes just over an hour and costs $86, Airlines of South Australia have a similar schedule between Adelaide and Mt Gambier, again it's about an hour and a quarter flight and the fare is $67.

Rail Phone 212 6699 for rail bookings in Adelaide. There are daily services between Adelaide and Mt Gambier, twice daily on some days. The trains follow the Melbourne line to just beyond Bordertown before turning south to Naracoorte and Mt Gambier. By day Adelaide-Mt Gambier is about eight hours but overnight services take about 11 hours. Fares from Adelaide are Bordertown $11, Naracoorte $13, Mt Gambier $15.

Bus Mt Gambier Motor Service (tel 217 0777) operate from the Central Bus Station in Adelaide to Mt Gambier six days a week. The trip takes about six hours and fares are Kingston $17.60, Robe or Millicent $18.40, Mt Gambier $19.20. Ansett Pioneer operate from Melbourne to Mt Gambier daily. The trip takes about six to eight hours (varies from day to day) and the fare is $28.35.

Meningie (population 700)

On the southern edge of Lake Albert and at the north of the Coorong this small town is a popular gateway to the Coorong. A wide variety of watersports are available on Lake Albert and there are also good bushwalks in the area. The birdlife around Meningie is prolific and a wide range of waterbirds can be seen.

The Coorong

The Coorong is a unique national park, a long narrow strip curving along the coast for 145 km south of Adelaide. The northern end of the Coorong is marked by Lake Alexandrina where the Murray reaches the sea and the southern end is marked by the small town of Kingston SE. The Coorong consists of a long, narrow, shallow lagoon and a complex series of salt pans, all separated from the sea by the huge sand dunes of the Younghusband Peninsula, more usually known as the Hummocks. The Coorong is a superb natural bird sanctuary with a vast number of waterbirds to be seen. Cormorants, ibis, swans, terns, shags, ducks and other waterbirds can all be seen but it is the pelicans for which the Coorong is best known. The film *Storm Boy*, about a young boy's friendship with a pelican, was filmed on the Coorong. At Salt Creek you can take the nature trail turn-off from the Princes Highway and take the old road which runs along the shore of the Coorong for some distance.

Kingston SE (population 1300)

At the southern end of the Coorong Kingston is a popular beach resort and a good base for visits to the Coorong. The town was originally named Maria Creek after a ship which was wrecked at Cape Jaffa on the Coorong in 1840. Nobody lost their lives in the actual shipwreck but as the 27 crew and passengers made their way south towards Lake Albert they were all massacred by Aboriginals. There's a memorial to the Maria in Kingston, but it's said that Policeman's Point was named after the point where white man's retribution caught up with the Aboriginals.

Other attractions are the National Trust Pioneer Museum and the nearby Cape Jaffa lighthouse which is open from 2 pm to 5 pm daily. Kingston is a centre for rock lobster fishing but Kingston's best known lobster, and a major landmark in its own right, is hardly edible. Towering by the roadside is 'The Big Lobster', a superb piece of Australian kitsch the amazingly realistic lobster is made of fibreglass and steel and marks a tourist centre with restaurants, souvenirs, information and other touristic needs. You can, however, buy crayfish freshly cooked at the jetty.

The **Jip Jip National Park** is 45 km north-east of Kingston and features huge granite outcrops in the bush. From Kingston conventional vehicles can drive 16 km along the beach to 'The Granites' while with four-wheel drive you can continue right along the beach to the Murray River mouth.

Robe (population 500)
A small port, steeped in history, Robe was one of South Australia's first settlements, dating from 1845. Early buildings include the old Customs House which is now a National Trust Museum. There is also an old jail up on the cliffs and a small arts and crafts gallery. The citizens of Robe made a colourful fortune in the late 1850s due to the Victorian gold rush. The Victorian government instituted a £10 head tax on Chinese goldminers in 1855 and 16,000 ingenious Chinese circumvented the tax by getting to Victoria via Robe in South Australia. 10,000 arrived in 1857 alone. The 'Chinamen's Wells' in the region are a reminder of that time. There are fine views along the coast from the Obelisk at Cape Dombey.

Beachport (population 400)
South of Robe this quiet, little seaside town is, like other places along the coast, a busy lobster and crayfishing centre. There's a small National Trust museum in the old wood and grain store plus a couple of other old buildings. There's good surfing near Beachport at the 'blowhole' and a nearby salt lake called the 'Pool of Siloam'.

Millicent (population 5500)
At Millicent the 'Alternative 1' route through Robe and Beachport rejoins the main road. The town has a central swimming lake and there's a National Trust Museum and the Admella Gallery both on George St. A narrow gauge steam engine is also on display nearby. There's also a Historical and Maritime Museum in the town.

The **Canunda National Park**, with its enormous sand dunes, is 13 km west of Millicent. Tantanoola, 21 km away, has the stuffed 'Tantanoola Tiger' on display in the Tantanoola Tiger Hotel. This beast, actually a wolf, was shot in 1895 after a lot of local publicity. Tantanoola also has limestone caves which are open 9 am to 5 pm daily.

There's a National Trust Tourist office at 7 Mt Gambier Rd.

Mt Gambier (population 19,400)
The major town and commercial centre of the south-east, Mt Gambier is 486 km from Adelaide. The town is built on the slopes of the volcano which gives it its name. The volcano has three craters, each with its own lake. The beautiful and spectacular Blue Lake is the best known although from about March to November the lake is more grey than blue. In November it changes back to blue again, just in time for the holiday season! The lake is 70 metres deep and there's a five km scenic drive around the lake.

Mt Gambier also has many parks including the Cave Park with its deep 'cave', actually more of a steep-sided hole, which is right in the centre of the city. Mt Gambier is in a rich agricultural area but timber and limestone, cut in blocks for use as a building material, are the main products. The poet Adam Lindsay Gordon who commited suicide in 1870, is also connected with Mt Gambier where he lived for some years.

Black's Museum, open daily, has displays of Aboriginal artefacts. On Sunday afternoons you can also visit the museum in the old courthouse. There are tours of the sawmills around Mt Gambier, check with the Mt Gambier Tourist Information Centre on Casterton Rd.

Port MacDonnell (population 700)
South of Mt Gambier this quiet little fishing port is a centre for rock lobster fishing. At one time it was a busy shipping port, hence the surprisingly big 1863 customs house, now used as a restaurant. Adam Lindsay Gordon's home, Dingley Dell, is now a museum. There are some fine walks around Port MacDonnell including the path to the top of Mt Schank, an extinct volcano crater. On Wednesdays and Thursdays from 2 pm to 4 pm you can visit the Cape Northumberland Lighthouse on the superb coastline west of the port.

Along the Dukes Highway
The Dukes Highway, the main Melbourne to Adelaide route, is not terribly exciting, particularly from the South Australian border through to Tailem Bend. Bordertown (population 2000), just across the border, is in a prosperous agricultural area. There's a good picnic area by the stream on the east side of town with a small wildlife sanctuary nearby.

Keith (population 1200) is another farming town and it also has a small museum and the Mt Rescue Conservation Park 16 km north. This area was once known as 90-mile desert. Tintinara (population 400) is the other town of any size and also an access point to the Mt Rescue park. Coonalpyn (population 300) is a tiny township and jumping off point for the Mt Boothby Conservation Park.

Naracoorte (population 4600)
Settled in the 1840s, Naracoorte is one of the oldest towns in South Australia and one of the largest country towns in the south-east. The town has the Old Mill Museum, a National Trust Museum and the Naracoorte Art Gallery. On Jenkins Terrace the Naracoorte Museum & Snake Pit (!) has gems, antiques and a reptile park. It's open daily from 10 am to 5 pm except Sundays when it's open 2 to 5 pm. Pioneer Park has restored locomotives and the town also has a swimming lake.

Naracoorte Caves are 11 km out of town — Fossil Cave has ice age fossils and there are three others with stalactites and stalagmites. It's open daily. Bat Cave, wiith lots of bats which make a spectacular departure every evening, is 17 km out of the town. At a similar distance from the town you can see lots of waterbirds at the Bool Lagoon Reserve. The type of birds vary during the year.

The Naracoorte Tourist Information Centre is at 128 Smith St.

Coonawarra
A fine wine producing area, 10 km north of Penola, there are 10 wineries in the area. Wynn's Coonawarra Estate is the best known of the wineries here although it is not open to the public, like some of the smaller wineries. Most of them are open Monday to Friday, some also on Saturdays and Sundays. Penola (population 1300) is the main town in the area. Bushman's Inn in Penola North has displays of coins and Aboriginal artefacts.

MURRAY RIVER
Australia's greatest river starts in the Snowy Mountains in the Australian Alps and for most of its length forms the boundary between NSW and Victoria.

It's in South Australia that the Murray comes into its prime, though. First it flows west through the Riverland area, a region where the wonders of irrigation has turned an unproductive land into an important region of wineries and fruit growing. Although names like the Barossa and the Hunter are better known, this area actually produces 40% of Australia's wine. Then at Morgan the river turns sharply south and flows through the Lower Murray region to the sea. In all it is 650 km from the South Australia/NSW-Victoria border to the sea.

The Murray has lots of water sport possibilities, plenty of wildlife (particularly water birds) and, in the Riverlands section, a positive surfeit of wineries to visit. This, however, is also a river with a history for until the advent of the railways the Murray was the Mississippi of Australia with paddle-wheel steamers carrying trade from the interior down to the coast. Many of the river towns still have a strong flavour of those riverboat days and if you've the cash and inclination you can still ride a paddle-steamer, forging its leisurely way on a cruise down the mighty Murray.

Life on the River

The Murray River region has plenty of conventional accommodation including a youth hostel by the Riverfront Caravan Park in Loxton, but to really get to grips with the Murray the ideal way is, of course, out on the river. You can do that by a number of methods. Simplest and cheapest are day trips such as those operated by the *MV Barrangul* from Renmark, the *MV Kookaburra* from Murray Bridge or the *MV Pelican* which operates across Lake Bonney to Chambers Creek where there is much birdlife.

If you've got a family or a group of people a very pleasant way to explore the Murray is to rent a houseboat and set off along the river by yourself. These can be hired in Morgan, Waikerie, Loxton, Berri, Renmark and other river centres but they are very popular so it's wise to book well ahead. The SA travel centre offices can advise you about prices and make bookings. The cost depends on what you hire, where you hire it and, most important, when you hire it. Typical sorts of prices are around $300 a week for a four-berth houseboat, around $400 for larger eight or 10-berth boats. These costs can drop in low seasons.

Finally there are the river trips on riverboats such as the huge paddlewheeler *Murray River Queen* which makes five-day trips from Goolwa to Swan Reach and back. Or you could take the *Murray Explorer* from Renmark up into the NSW-Victoria stretch of the Murray, then back down to Loxton and finally up to Renmark again. These trips cost around $420 per person in a share twin — not cheap!

Getting There

Air Murray Valley Airlines (tel 217 7711) can be found at TAA, 144 North Terrace, Adelaide. They fly to Renmark from Adelaide twice daily Monday to Friday. The fare is $65.

Bus Alternatively you can get there by bus. Briscoes (tel 217 0777) operate to Morgan daily from Monday to Friday for $8. Stateliner (tel 217 1777) operate Adelaide-Blanche Town-Barmera-Berri-Renmark daily. The fare to Blanche Town is $8, to Barmera and beyond it's $13. They also operate daily Adelaide-Blanche Town - Waikerie - Loxton with fares of $10 to Waikerie, $13 to Loxton. Briscoes and Stateliner are both at the Central Bus Station, Franklin St, Adelaide.

Renmark (population 3400)

In the centre of the Riverland irrigation area, 295 km from Adelaide, this was not only a starting point for the great irrigation projects that revolutionised the area but also the first of the river towns. Irrigation was started by the Canadian Chaffey brothers in 1887 and you can see one of their original wood-burning irrigation pumps on Renmark Avenue. Olivewood, Charles Chaffey's home, built around 1890, is also on Renmark Avenue. It's open daily except Wednesday from 2.30 to 4 pm.

Today the area earns its living from vineyards, orchards and other fruit growing. In the town you can inspect the 1911 paddle-steamer *Industry* which is now a museum. There are several art galleries in the town centre while Goat Island in the river is a wildlife sanctuary with many koalas.

Around Renmark there is Bredl's Reptile Park & Zoo with lots of snakes and crocodiles, five km out of town. And, of course, there are plenty of wineries in the area which provide free tastings.

There's a tourist office on Murray Avenue.

Berri (population 2900)

At one time a refuelling stop for the wood-burning paddle-steamers, the town takes its name from the Aboriginal words 'berri berri' — 'big bend in the river'. It's the economic centre of the Riverland and there are a number of wineries in the area. Berri Estates Winery, at Glossop 13 km to the west, is the biggest winery in Australia if not in the whole southern hemisphere.

Berri also has a large fruit juice factory with tours four times a day on weekdays. Lovers of Australian kitsch should visit the 'big orange', four km out of Berri on the road to Renmark. This 16 metre diameter fibreglass 'orange' houses exhibits telling the economic story of the Riverland region. There's also a display of vintage cars and motorcycles in the adjacent Riverland Display Centre. It's open 9 am to 5 pm daily.

In the town you can climb up to the lookout on Fiedler St for views over the town and river. There's a koala sanctuary near the Martins Bend recreation area on the river. Near Berri the small town of Monash has a huge children's playground with no less than 120 differ-

ent children-amusers! Annual big event in Berri is the Berri'Rodeo which takes place each Easter Monday. Punts still cross the river from the Berri Hotel on Riverside Avenue to Loxton.

There's a tourist office on Vaughan Terrace.

Loxton (population 2800)

From Berri the Murray makes a large loop south of the Sturt Highway and Loxton is at the bottom of the loop. It's an additional 38 km to follow this loop off the main road. The town follows the usual Riverland activities of fruit growing and winemaking. The town has expanded dramatically since WW II due to a land settlement scheme instituted for returned servicemen.

The town's major attraction is the Historical Village on the riverbank. The village includes a replica of the town's first house, a pine-and-pug hut built by William Charles Loxton in 1878. In all over two dozen buildings re-create a working village of the Riverland district at the turn of the century. It's open daily from 10 am to 4 pm on weekdays, to 5 pm on weekends.

There's a tourist office — the Loxton Tourist & Travel Centre — in the Loxton Hotel on East Terrace.

Barmera (population 1900)

On the shores of Lake Bonney, where English record holder Donald Campbell made an attempt on the world water speed record in 1964, Barmera was once on the overland stock route along which cattle were driven from NSW. The ruins of Napper's Old Accommodation House, built in 1850 at the mouth of Chambers Creek, is a reminder of that era as is the Overland Corner Hotel, on the Morgan road, 19 km out of town. It is now preserved as a National Trust Museum but is open rather odd hours.

There's also a National Trust Art Gallery & Museum in the town. Lake Bonney, with sandy beaches, is popular for swimming and watersports. There's even a nude beach at Pelican Point.

There's a Barmera Tourist Office on Barwell Terrace.

Waikerie (population 1600)

The town takes its name from the Aboriginal word for 'anything that flies', after the teeming bird life on the lagoons and river around Waikerie. Curiously, anything that flies also includes gliders for Waikerie has the most active gliding centre in Australia. You can arrange to take a joy ride in a glider here. Wine tasting, Pooginook Conservation Park (12 km north-east) which has echidnas and hairy-nose wombats and the Kangaroo Park and Holden Bend Reserve are other attractions in the town or nearby.

There is a Tourist Centre at 20 McCoy St.

Morgan (population 350)

In its prime this was the busiest river-port in Australia and the massive wharves, towering 12 metres high, may be quiet today but they're certainly still there. Morgan is off the Sturt Highway to the north and from here a pipeline pumps water to Whyalla on Spencer Gulf.

Blanche Town

The site of the first river lock on the Murray, built in 1922, Blanche Town also has the small Portee wildlife reserve near town, specifically intended for the hairy-nose wombat.

Swan Reach

This sleepy little old town has very picturesque river scenery and, hardly surprisingly, lots of swans. Just down-river the river makes a long, gentle curve lasting 11 km in all. The bend is appropriately known as Big Bend and there's a picnic reserve here and many white cockatoos. The *Murray River Queen* ends its up-river cruise at Swan Reach.

Mannum (population 2100)

The *Mary Ann*, Australia's first riverboat, was built here and made the first paddle-steamer trip up the Murray from Mannum in 1853. The river is very wide here and there are many relics of the pioneering days on the river to be seen, including the 1898 paddle-wheeler *Marion*, now a floating museum, open daily 10 am to 4 pm.

You can also see a replica of Sturt's whaleboat and relics of the *Mary Ann*. The Halidon Rd Bird Sanctuary has pelicans, ducks, swans and other water birds. The Cascade Waterfalls, 11 km from Mannum on Reedy Creek, are also worth visiting. Off Purnong Rd there's a lookout tower.

Murray Bridge (population 8800)

South Australia's largest river town is only 82 km from Adelaide. It's a popular area for fishing, swimming, water-skiing and barbecues and from here you can make day cruises on the *MV Kookaburra*. There's a Folk Museum at Johnston Park and the Murray Bridge Folk Museum has 600 antique dolls and toys

South Australia

a. Adelaide's Festival Centre is pleasantly situated beside the Torrens River in the city centre.

b. The Rundle Mall is the main shopping street in Adelaide and a centre for city activities.

c. The wine growing Barossa Valley plays heavily on its German background.

and a wide range of Australiana. In the Sturt Reserve by the river there's a 20c coin in the slot bunyip!

Near Murray Bridge is Monarto — the town that never was. A grandiose plan was drawn up to build a second major city for South Australia by the turn of the century. This site was chosen and land purchased in the early 1970s but nothing further happened and a few years ago the project was totally abandoned.

Tailem Bend (population 2000)
At a sharp bend in the river, Tailem Bend is near the mouth of the river. After Wellington the Murray opens into huge Lake Alexandrina — lots of waterbirds but sometimes tricky boating. The river mouth is near Goolwa — see the Fleurieu Peninsula section. You can take a ferry across the river at Jervois from where it's 11 km to the interesting old town of Wellington.

YORKE PENINSULA
Located an easy drive from Adelaide the Yorke Peninsula is a popular holiday area with some pleasant beaches along both sides of the peninsula, plenty of opportunity for fishing and the Innes National Park on the tip of the peninsula. The Yorke Peninsula originally based its economy on the copper mines of 'little Cornwall', as they declined agriculture took mining's place and much of the land is now devoted to growing barley and other grains.

Places to Stay
There are campsites, hotels, motels and a variety of holiday accommodation all over the peninsula. Port Vincent has an associate youth hostel.

Getting There
Bus There are a number of bus services

between Adelaide and towns on the Yorke Peninsula. They all depart from the Central Bus Station, 111 Franklin St. Premier Roadlines (tel 217 0777) operate Adelaide - Kadina - Wallaroo - Moonta-Port Hughes-Moonta Bay. The fare is $5.90 and the journey takes from two to three hours depending on where you get off. There are two services daily Monday to Friday, one each on Saturday and Sunday.

Briscoes (tel 268 9444) have a couple of routes to the peninsula. Monday to Friday and on Sunday a bus runs from Adelaide to Ardrossan ($7), Port Vincent ($9.50), Stansbury ($9.70), Edithburgh ($10) and Yorketown ($10). The trip takes from 2½ hours to Ardrossan to four hours to Yorketown. Their other service goes from Adelaide to Maitland ($7), Minlaton ($9.50) and Warooka ($10). It takes four hours to

South Australia

a. The sheer walls of Wilpena Pound show the beautiful colours and shadows typical of the Flinders Ranges.
b. Fording a river crossing on a Flinders Ranges' outback road.
c. Seals on the beach at Kangaroo Island.

Warooka and also operates daily except Saturday.

Air Commodore Airlines (tel 212 3355), at the TAA office on North Terrace, have daily flights from Adelaide to Minlaton and on to Port Lincoln and return. Adelaide-Minlaton or Port Lincoln-Minlaton costs $32.50.

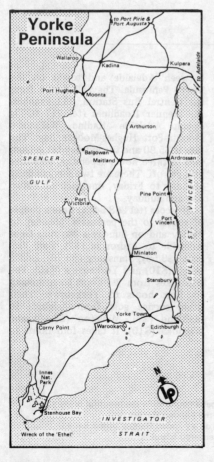

Cornwall & Copper Mines

In the early 1860s copper was dicovered in the Moonta-Kadina-Wallaroo area of the Yorke Peninsula and within a few years a full scale copper rush was on. The majority of the miners who worked these copper deposits were from Cornwall in England and they left a distinctly Cornish flavour to the land. There are still many old cottages and churches which look for all the world as if they have been transplanted straight from Cornwall. The mining boom continued right through into this century, reaching its peak around the turn of the century, but in the early 1920s a slump in copper prices, rising labour costs and competition from mines abroad forced the closure of all the peninsula copper mines. There is still a strong Cornish element in the area, however, and over the long holiday weekend in May in odd-numbered years a festival known as the Kernewek Lowender is held in 'little Cornwall'. It's a chance to try Cornish pasties or watch a wheelbarrow race. There are National Trust museums in each of the towns of the 'Cornish Triangle' and they're open on Wednesdays, Saturdays, Sundays, school holidays and certain other days during peak holiday seasons.

Kadina (population 2800)

The largest town on the peninsula, Kadina was once the centre of the copper mining activities. The old Wallaroo mines are beside the town. The National Trust's Kadina Museum includes a number of buildings, one of which was the former home of the Matta Matta mine manager, known as Matta House. There is also a blacksmith's workshop, a printing museum, displays of early agricultural equipment and the Matta Matta mine. Kadina has some fine old hotels with laceworked balconies and wide verandahs. There's a Tourist Office on Graves St.

Wallaroo (population 2000)

The second part of the Yorke Peninsula's 'Cornish triangle' this port town was a major centre during the copper boom. One of the great chimneys from the copper smelters, 'the big stack' built in 1861, still stands but today the port's main function is as an export port for agricultural products. Situated in the original town post office the National Trust Maritime Museum has many ship models and items from the town's early history as a port. There are other interesting old buildings in the town and good beaches.

Moonta (population 1750)

A little south of Wallaroo the copper mine here was once said to be the richest mine in Australia. The town grew so fast that its school once had over a thousand students — the building now houses the largest country museum in the state. Other sights include numerous old Methodist churches, the town had 14 at one time, a National Trust restored Cornish miner's cottage, the Arts & Crafts Centre in the old railway station and ruins of the various mining works. Moonta Bay, the port for Moonta, is three km west of the town.

Maitland (population 1000)

In the centre of the peninsula this agricultural commercial centre also has a National Trust Museum.

Minlaton (population 800)

Another agricultural commercial centre, Minlaton was the home town of pioneer aviator Harry Butler. His 1916 Bristol monoplane, nicknamed the 'red devil', is on display in the Harry Butler Museum. Nearby is the National Trust Museum on Main St while close to town there's an arts and crafts centre at the Gum Flat Homestead Gallery (two km out) and the Koolywurtie Museum with pioneer exhibits (11 km out). Minlaton was originally known as Gum Flat.

Innes National Park

The southern tip of the peninsula, marked by Cape Spencer, is all part of the Innes National Park. Stenhouse Bay, just outside the park, and Pondalowie Bay, within the park, are the principal settlements. Pondalowie Bay is the base for a large crayfishing fleet and also has a fine surf beach. The park has fine coastal scenery and camping is permitted with permits from the park rangers who are located at Stenhouse Bay. The main landmark in the park is the wreck of the barque *Ethel*, a 711 ton ship which was driven ashore on the beach in 1904. Despite an almost successful attempt to refloat her later that year she has remained, rusting away, high and dry ever since. The ship's anchor is mounted in a memorial on the clifftop above the beach.

West Coast

The west coast, looking out onto the Spencer Gulf, also has plenty of beaches but the road does not, generally, run so close to the coast. The main port towns are Port Broughton and Wallaroo and Moonta Bay in the 'little Cornwall' area.

East Coast

The east coast road, from the top of Gulf St Vincent right down to Stenhouse Bay close to Cape Spencer, closely follows the coast. There are many pleasant sandy beaches and secluded coves along the coastline. Port Clinton is the northernmost beach resort while a little south is Price, where salt is produced at salt pans just outside town. Ardrossan (population 800) is 150 km from Adelaide and is the largest port on the east coast. There's the Ardrossan & District Historical Museum on Fifth St and ploughing enthusiasts will be delighted to hear that Ardrossan was the place where the 'stump jump plough' was invented. Continuing south the road runs through Pine Point, Black Point, Port Julia and Port Vincent in the next 50 km, each with a sandy beach. The road continues to hug the coast through Stansbury, Wool Bay, Port Giles and Coobowie before turning away from the coastline at Edithburgh. Edithburgh has a rock swimming pool in a small cove and from the clifftops

you can look across to the small islands of the Troubridge Shoals where there is good scuba diving. The town also has a small Maritime Museum and nearby Sultana Bay is a good spot for swimming. The southern part of the peninsula is sparsely populated but the road from Edithburgh to Stenhouse Bay is very scenic.

EYRE PENINSULA

The wide Eyre Peninsula points south between Spencer Gulf and the Great Australian Bight. It's bordered on the north side by the Eyre Highway from Port Augusta to Ceduna. The coastal run along the peninsula is in two parts — first the Lincoln Highway south-west from Port Augusta to Port Lincoln and then the Flinders Highway north-west to Ceduna. It's 468 km from Port Augusta direct to Ceduna via the Eyre Highway while making the loop south totals 763 km. This is a popular beach resort area with many fine beaches, sheltered bays and pleasant little port towns. Further along the Port Lincoln-Streaky Bay-Ceduna stretch there are superb surf beaches and some of Australia's most spectacular coastal scenery. Off shore further west is home to the great white shark — this is a popular area for making shark films, some of the scenes from *Jaws* were filmed here. The Eyre Peninsula also has a flourishing agricultural sector while the iron ore deposits at Iron Knob and Iron Baron are processed and shipped from the busy port of Whyalla.

The stretch of coast from Port Lincoln to Streaky Bay had one of the earliest European contacts. In 1627 the Dutch explorer Peter Nuyts sailed right along the north and west coasts of Australia in his ship the *Gulden Zeepard*. He continued along the south coast,

crossed the Great Australian Bight but finally gave up at Streaky Bay and turned back to more hospitable climes. It was left to Tasman, 15 years later, to complete the circumnavigation of the continent and not until Cook, over a century after that, was the fertile east coast finally 'discovered'.

In 1802 Matthew Flinders charted the peninsula and named many of its prominent features during his epic circumnavigation of Australia. The peninsula takes its name from Edward John Eyre, the hardy explorer who made the first east to west crossing of the continent.

Places to Stay

There are plenty of places to stay on the Eyre Peninsula since many of the coastal towns are popular resorts — lots of camping grounds, holiday flats, hotels and motels.

Getting There

Ferry The *MV Troubridge* sails once weekly from Adelaide via Kangaroo Island to Port Lincoln. It takes 6½ hours Adelaide-Kangaroo Island and another 9½ hours on to Port Lincoln. Fares are from Adelaide $28, from Kangaroo Island $20. Cars cost $36 to 58 from Adelaide depending on size, $27 to 46 from Kangaroo Island. During the peak period of December, January and February car costs go up by

$20. A motorcycle costs $19 from Adelaide, $12 from Kangaroo Island, a bicycle costs $1.50 from either. Port Lincoln services stop between mid-December and early January when extra trips are made to Kangaroo Island from Adelaide. Agents for the ferry are R W Miller (tel 47 5577) at 3 Todd St, Port Adelaide. In Port Lincoln they are at Patrick Agencies (tel 82 1011) at 33 Edinburgh St.

Air Airlines of South Australia (tel 217 7442) are at the Ansett terminal at 150 North Terrace, Adelaide. They fly to Port Lincoln ($51), Streaky Bay ($79) and Ceduna ($95) on the Eyre Peninsula. The Port Lincoln flights operate several times daily. There are also flights from Adelaide to Whyalla and other towns at the head of the gulf. Commodore Airlines fly between Minlâton on the Yorke Peninsula and Port Lincoln every day for $33.

Bus Greyhound and Ansett Pioneer services to Perth operate through Port Augusta ($12) and Ceduna ($27). It takes 9½ hours from Adelaide to Ceduna. Stateliner (bookings and departures from the Greyhound terminal) operate to Port Lincoln ($22.50), Streaky Bay ($23.50) and on to Ceduna.

Port Augusta (population 13,000)
At the head of Spencer Gulf this busy port city is a crossroads for travellers. From here roads head west across the Nullarbor to Western Australia, north to Alice Springs and Darwin in the Northern Territory, south to Adelaide and east to Broken Hill and Sydney in New South Wales. It is also on the main railway line between the east and west coast and serves as the terminus for the Ghan service to Alice Springs. Apart from its importance as a supply centre for goods going by rail or road into the outback it's also a major electricity generating centre, burning coal from the Leigh Creek open-cut mines. You can take a tour of the Thomas Playford Power Station or the Australian National Railways workshops, the latter at 2 pm from Monday to Friday.

Other city attractions include the Curdnatta Art & Pottery Gallery located in what was Port Augusta's first railway station. Old buildings include the Greenbush Gaol from 1869, the old town hall, the Grange from 1878 and Homestead Park pioneer museum which also includes a railway museum and is on the corner of Elsie and Jaycee Sts.

Whyalla (population 33,500)
The largest city in South Australia after Adelaide, Whyalla is a major steel producing city and also a busy deepwater port for shipping the steel and iron production elsewhere and overseas. The town was originally known as Hummock Hill. Whyalla also had a major shipyard but it was closed down during the '70s. There are free tours of the steel works in Whyalla at 9.30 am on weekdays and 11 am on Saturdays — they start at the visitors' reception centre on Steelworks Rd. Ore comes to Whyalla from Iron Knob/Iron Monarch and from Iron Baron and there are also tours of the Iron Knob mining operation at 10 am and 2 pm on weekdays and at 11 am on Saturdays. Iron Knob was the first iron ore deposit in Australia to be exploited. For safety reasons visitors on either of the Whyalla area tours must not wear sandals, thongs or other open shoes.

Apart from its industrial face Whyalla also has fine beaches and a Fauna & Reptile Park on the Lincoln Highway near the airport. On Ekblom St there are historical exhibits in the National Trust Mt Laura Homestead Museum which is only open on Sundays and public holidays from 2 to 4 pm. Studio 41, on the corner of Wood and Donaldson Terrace, includes an exhibit of local art. The Whyalla Tourist &

Information Centre is at 3 Patterson St.

Whyalla to Port Lincoln

It's 280 km from Whyalla to Port Lincoln at the tip of the peninsula and there are quite a few places of interest along the way. Cowell (population 600) is close to a very large jade deposit and jade is cut and polished here. There's a jade workshop on West Terrace and the town also has a small National Trust museum in the old post office. Cowell has good beaches on Franklin Harbour, an expanse of water which is only open to the sea through a very narrow inlet. Cleve, 43 km inland from Cowell, has an interesting fauna park with a nocturnal house. Continuing 47 km further south, Arno Bay is a popular little beach resort.

South again you reach Port Neill, another beach resort, and then Tumby Bay (population 900) which has a long, curving, white-sand beach and a number of interesting old buildings around the town. The Sir Joseph Banks group of islands are 15 km offshore from Tumby Bay and there are many attractive bays and reefs here plus a wide variety of sea birds which make their homes on the islands.

Port Lincoln (population 10,300)

At the southern end of the Eyre Peninsula, 662 km from Adelaide by road but only 250 km as the crow flies, Port Lincoln was named by Matthew Flinders in 1801. The first settlers arrived in 1839 and the town has grown to become the tuna fishing capital of Australia — the annual Tunarama Festival in January of each year signals the start of the tuna fishing season with boisterous merriment over the Australia Day weekend.

Port Lincoln is pleasantly situated on Boston Bay with a variety of opportunities for watersports. There are a number of historic buildings in the town including the Old Mill on Dorset Place

which houses a small pioneer museum. The Lincoln Hotel dates from 1840, making it the oldest hotel on the peninsula. On the Flinders Highway Mill Cottage is another museum, open from 2 to 5 pm daily. There are also a number of islands off Boston Bay.

At one time Port Lincoln was considered as an alternative to Adelaide as the state capital. It still operates as an important deep-water port today. There is a Tourist Office (tel 82 3781) at the Town Hall, Tasman Terrace — the main street.

Around Port Lincoln

Cape Carnot, better known as Whalers' Way, is 32 km south of Port Lincoln and a permit to enter the conservation reserve must be obtained in Port Lincoln before you travel down there. A 15 km drive around the reserve takes you past stupendous cliffs, pounded by huge surf. It has some of the most impressive coastal scenery in Australia and at Sleaford Bay there is the remains of an old whaling station. Also south of Port Lincoln is the Lincoln National Park, again with a magnificent coastline. You can visit off-shore islands like Boston Island, Wedge Island or Thistle Island — the Tourist Office will help you find a boat to get out to them. Just north of Port Lincoln Poonindie has an unusual old church.

Port Lincoln to Streaky Bay

Soon after leaving Port Lincoln the road passes by Coffin Bay, a sheltered stretch of water with some fine beaches. Coffin Bay itself is a tiny township and from here you can find spectacular coastal scenery at Point Avoid, Almonta Beach and Yangie Bay. There's a 25 km trail to Yangie Bay but you need four-wheel drive from there to Point Sir Isaac. You can see emus, Cape Barren geese and other wildlife at the Kellidie Bay Conservation Park. Elliston, further along the coast, is another beach resort and from here you can get out to a number of offshore islands. There are good swimming beaches around Waterloo Bay while Blackfellows has fine surf. Talia, further up the coast, has impressive granite rock faces and the limestone Talia Caves.

At Port Kenny on Venus Bay there are more beaches, and whales are often seen off the coast in October, when they come here to breed. Venus Bay has an active fleet of prawn trawlers. Shortly before Streaky Bay the turn-off to Point Labatt takes you to the conservation park where you can see the only permanent colony of sea-lions on the Australian mainland. There's magnificent coastal scenery from here to Streaky Bay, 40 km north.

Streaky Bay (population 1000)

This popular little resort town takes its name from the 'streaky' water, caused by seaweed, in the bay. The town is surrounded by bays, caves and high cliffs. It was at Streaky Bay that the Dutch explorer Peter Nuyts gave up and turned back. Curious granite outcrops known as inselbergs are found at numerous places around the Eyre Peninsula. You can see a particularly good group in the wheatfields close to the highway about 20 km south-east of Streaky Bay. They've been nicknamed 'Murphy's Haystacks'.

Ceduna (population 2300)

Just past the junction of the Flinders and Eyre Highway, Ceduna marks the end of the Eyre Peninsula area and also the start of the long, empty stretch of highway across the Nullarbor Plains into Western Australia. The town was founded in 1896 although a whaling station had existed on St Peter Island, off nearby Cape Thevenard, back in 1850. There is an overseas telecommunication earth station, 34 km north of Ceduna, from where microwave communications are bounced off satellites. Tours are made every two hours from 10 am to 4 pm from Monday to Friday. There are many beaches and sheltered coves around Ceduna while 13 km out of town you can see the old McKenzie Ruin at the earlier township site of Denial Bay. On the way from Streaky Bay you pass Smoky Bay, a small coastal fishing town. Near Point Sinclair, 95 km beyond Ceduna, is Cactus Beach with huge sand dunes and strong surf that draws enthusiasts to this remote surfing spot.

Other Places

Cummins, inland and north of Port Lincoln, is a small town with the Koppio Museum showing early agricultural equipment. Along the Eyre Highway the road passes through Kimpa, Kyancutta and Wudinna, all important as agricultural centres but of little other interest. Kimba (population 800) is on the very edge of the outback and you can visit Lake Gilles and the Gawler Ranges from here. Mt Wudinna, near Wudinna (population 500), is the second largest rock in Australia — nowhere near as well known as the largest! Tortoise Rock, also near Wudinna, looks much like a tortoise.

THE FLINDERS RANGES

Rising from the northern end of Gulf St Vincent and running north for 800 km into the dry outback region the Flinders Ranges is a desert mountain range offering some of the most spectacular scenery in Australia. It's a superb area for bushwalks, wildlife or simply taking in the ever changing colours of the Australian outback. In the far north of the

Flinders region the mountains are hemmed in by barren salt lakes.

The ranges, like so much of Australia, are geologically ancient but worn though the peaks may be the colours are amazing — this area has always been a favourite of artists. Like other dry regions of Australia the vegetation is surprisingly diverse and colourful and in the spring the ranges are carpeted with wildflowers. At that time of year rain is most likely and the country is at its greenest. In summer the nights are cool but the days can be searingly hot. Winter, is, overall, the best time for a Flinders visit although there are attractions for any time of the year.

When Flinders first touched on the ranges that were named after him, back in 1802, there were a number of Aboriginal tribes in the Flinders region and you can still see evidence of these people. Amongst the Aboriginal sites you can visit are the rock paintings at Yourambulla (near Hawker) and Arkaroo (near Wilpena) and the rock-cut patterns at Sacred Canyon (near Wilpena) and Chambers Gorge. Particularly in the early mornings and evenings you've got a good chance of spotting wildlife in the ranges including emus, a variety of kangaroos and many different types of lizards. The birdlife is especially prolific with colourful parrots, galahs, rosellas and many other birds — often in great numbers.

Bushwalking is one of the main attractions for the area and the winter months from June to October are the best time to hit the trail. Campers can generally find water in rock pools during those months and the daytime temperatures are pleasant. This is wild and rugged country and care should be taken before setting out. Wilpena Pound, the Arkaroola-Mt Painter Sanctuary and the Mt Remarkable National Park all have excellent walks, many of them along marked trails.

Information

It's definitely worth getting a good map of the Flinders Ranges since there are so many back roads and such a variety of road surfaces. The SAGTB's Flinders leaflet is quite good and the RAA, SA Department of Tourism and the National Parks office all put out maps of the whole ranges area and of Wilpena Pound. *Touring in the Flinders Ranges* is a good little book produced by the RAA and available from their offices. If you're planning on doing more than just the standard walks in the Flinders look for a copy of *Flinders Ranges Walks* for more information.

Getting There

Bus Stateliner (tel 217 0777) have buses to Wilpena Pound on Wednesday, Thursday and Friday. The trip takes 6½ hours and costs $20. On Wednesday and Saturday they have a service via Quorn, Hawker and Parachilna to Arkaroola. It takes 12 hours all the way to Arkaroola and the fare is $30. Students get a 25% discount.

Rail Australian National Railways (tel 212 6699) operate from Adelaide to Quorn daily except Saturday. It takes seven hours to Quorn and costs $14.

Air Trans Regional Airlines (tel 212 5733) fly to Hawker and on up to Leigh Creek four times weekly. The fare to Hawker is $67 and the flight takes nearly two hours. Four times weekly there are flights to Balcanoona, near Arkaroola, for $99.

Road If you're driving yourself to the Flinders it's good sealed road all the way north to the Wilpena Pound itself but the dirt road begins as soon as you leave there. If you take the Marree road that skirts the western edge of the Flinders the road is sealed up to Parachilna. There are three routes to Arkaroola. Fastest is to continue up the Marree road beyond Parachilna and turn off at Copley, near Leigh Creek. An alternative is to travel up the Barrier Highway towards Broken Hill as far as Yunta and then turn north and follow the long dirt road via Frome Downs, skirting the edge of Lake Frome. There is no petrol or water available along this road and it's best to do it earlier in the day because the sun in your eyes can be unpleasant in the late afternoon. Probably the most interesting route is to go via Wilpena Pound and take the road via Chambers Gorge, meeting the Frome Downs road south of Balcanoona. This road does tend to be difficult after rain, however.

Getting Around

You can make a loop that takes you around an interesting section of the southern part of the Flinders. From Port Augusta you go through the Pichi Richi Pass to Quorn and Hawker and on up to Wilpena Pound. From the pound you continue north through the Flinders Range National Park to Blinman then down through the Parachilna Gorge to Parachilna, back on the plains and back south to Hawker — thus looping right round Wilpena Pound. From the pound you can also make loops north into the Flinders Range National Park through Bunyeroo Gorge and the Aroona Valley.

Tours There are plenty of tours from Adelaide to the ranges and also tours out from Wilpena Pound and Arkaroola. Air tours made from the Pound include day trips to Arkaroola. Road tours go to the Aroona Valley, Blinman and Parachilna Gorge, Chambers Gorge or to Arkaroola.

Mt Remarkable National Park

South of Port Augusta and in the southern stretch of the Flinders Ranges, the Mt Remarkable National Park is near Wilmington and Melrose. From Wil-

mington you enter the park through narrow Alligator Gorge — in places the walls of the gorge are only two metres apart. Hancock's Lookout, near Horrock's Pass just north of the park, offers excellent views of Spencer Gulf.

Melrose

This tiny town is the oldest settlement in the Flinders Ranges. It's on the southern edge of the Mt Remarkable National Park, at the foot of Mt Remarkable itself. There's a walking trail to the top of the mountain. The old police station and court house now houses a National Trust Museum while the North Star Hotel of 1854 is the oldest hotel in the Flinders. The Mt Remarkable Hotel is only a few years younger and its exterior has scarcely changed over the past 125-plus years. There are a number of other interesting and picturesque old buildings in this enjoyable little town. Pleasant walks lead alongside the creek through the town and there's a good campsite on the riverbanks.

Other Towns

Other towns in the south of the Flinders include Carrieton where a major rodeo is held each October. Bruce and Hammond, near Wilmington, were both railheads at one time but have now faded away. Bruce is just a ghost town today. Orroroo is an agricultural centre and nearby Black Rock Peak has good bushwalks and terrific views over the surrounding countryside. You can see Aboriginal rock carvings at Pekina Creek by the town and the ruins of the nearby Pekina Station Homestead are also worth visiting.

Quorn (population 1000)

The 'gateway to the Flinders' is about 330 km north of Adelaide and only 46 km from Port Augusta. This was once an important railway town after the completion of the Great Northern Rail-

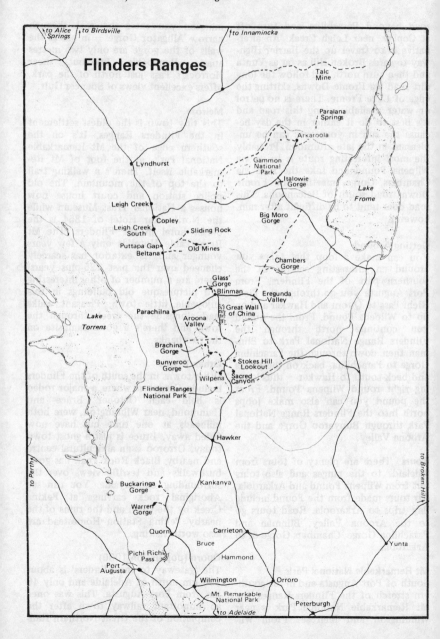

Flinders Ranges

to Alice Springs

to Birdsville

to Innamincka

Talc Mine

Paralana Springs

Arkaroola

Gammon National Park

Lyndhurst

Italowie Gorge

Lake Frome

Leigh Creek

Big Moro Gorge

Copley

Leigh Creek South

Sliding Rock

Puttapa Gap
Beltana

Old Mines

Chambers Gorge

Glass' Gorge
Blinman

Eregunda Valley

Parachilna

Great Wall of China

Lake Torrens

Aroona Valley

Brachina Gorge

Bunyeroo Gorge

Stokes Hill Lookout

Wilpena

Sacred Canyon

Flinders Ranges National Park

Hawker

to Perth

Buckaringa Gorge

Kankanya

Warren Gorge

Quorn

Carrieton

Bruce

Hammond

Yunta

Pichi Richi Pass

Port Augusta

Wilmington

Orroro

Mt. Remarkable National Park

Peterburgh

to Broken Hill

to Adelaide

way in 1878 and the town still has a lot of the flavour of the old pioneering days. The railway line was closed down in 1957 but since 1974 parts of the line have been re-opened as a tourist attraction by railway enthusiasts. On weekends and public holidays a vintage steam engine makes a 25 km round trip from Quorn to the scenic Pichi Richi Pass.

The town, picturesquely sited in a valley in the ranges, has a couple of art galleries and the small Flinders Museum in an old bakery and flour mill. From Quorn you can make four-wheel drive trips into the Flinders and visit the nearby Warren Gorge (which has good rock climbing) and the Buckaringa Gorge (good for picnics). Closer to the town you can follow walking trails to the top of Devil's Peak and Dutchman's Stern.

North of Quorn, about half-way to Hawker, are the ruins of the old Kanyaka settlement. Founded in 1851 it supported 70 families at its peak before being abandoned in the 1870s. Only the ruins of the solid, stone-built houses remain to remind of the high hopes that early settlers had for this harsh area.

If you're coming from the north don't be fooled by the signs for the Kanyaka settlement. All there is here is a solitary gravestone by the creek bed. The ruins are further south, deserted except for roos and galahs. There are two groups of the ruins, the second group is a couple of hundred metres away along the dirt road, a rise obscures them from view. The first group also has an old graveyard and note the solid stone dunnies, they were clearly built to last. It's about a km along the creek to the cookhouse and shearing shed. The track continues around 1½ km to a picturesque permanent waterhole, overlooked by the Kanyaka Death Rock.

Hawker (population 400)

In a sprawling, sheep-raising area the country town of Hawker has a tiny museum of minerals in the Mobil station. There are a number of places of interest which can be conveniently visited from here, including the Kanyaka ruins to the south, and Wilpena Pound is only a short drive north. Willow Waters is another old property abandoned in the 1890s when crops failed. There are Aboriginal rock paintings south of Hawker at Yourambulla Cave, a hollow in the rocks, high up on the side of Yourambulla Peak.

Places to Stay The *Royal Hotel* costs $14/20 for old-fashioned, but quite OK, small rooms. In the new motel part rooms are $27/34 for singles/doubles. Counter meals cost $4.50, they're certainly filling. There's also a campsite in Hawker.

Wilpena Pound

The best known feature of the ranges is the huge natural amphitheatre known as Wilpena Pound. This vast basin covers about 80 square km, ringed in by a circle of cliffs and accessible only by the narrow opening at Sliding Rock, through which the Wilpena Creek sometimes flows. From outside the pound the cliff face is almost sheer, soaring to 1000 metres, but inside the basin floor slopes gently away from the peaks. There are many excellent walks within the pound including the climb to 1190 metres high St Mary's Peak with superb views over the pound. There are day walks on marked trails in the pound including the climb up St Mary's Peak. Other popular walks are the one to Endeowie Gorge and Malloga Falls or the one to Mt John.

There is much wildlife to be seen in the pound, particularly the prolific birdlife which includes everything from rosellas, galahs and budgerigars to wedge-tailed eagles. You can make scenic flights over the pound (booking at the Wilpena Pound Motel) or make

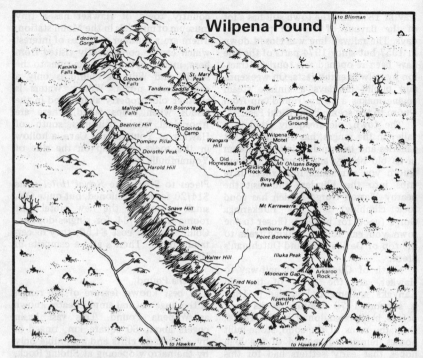

Wilpena Pound

to Blinman

Edeowie
Gorge

Kanalla
Falls

Glenora
Falls

St. Mary
Peak

Tanderra Saddle

Malloga
Falls

Mt Boorong

Attunga Bluff

Landing
Ground

Beatrice Hill

Cooinda
Camp

Wangara
Hill

Wilpena
Motel

Pompey Pillar

Dorothy Peak

Old
Homestead

Sliding
Rock

Mt Ohlssen Bagge
(Mt John)

Harold Hill

Binya
Peak

Snave Hill

Mt Karrawarra

Dick Nob

Tumburru Peak

Point Bonney

Walter Hill

Illuka Peak

Moonarie Gap

Arkaroo
Rock

Fred Nob

Rawnsley
Bluff

to Hawker

to Hawker

excursions to other places of interest in the vicinity. Sacred Canyon, with rock-cut patterns, is off to the east. North of the Wilpena Pound is the Flinders Range National Park where scenic attractions include the Bunyeroo and Brachina Gorges and the Aroona Valley.

Walks You can make an excellent day-long walk from the campsite to St Mary's Peak and back. The walk can be made either as an up-and-down or a round trip expedition. Up and back it's faster and most interesting to take the route outside the pound and then up to the Tanderra Saddle since the scenery is much more spectacular. The final climb up to the saddle is fairly steep and the stretch to the top of the peak is a real rock scramble. From the saddle and the peak the view's are simply superb.

The white glimmer of Lake Torrens is visible off to the west and the long Aroona Valley stretches north of the pound. Descending from the peak to the saddle you can then head back down on the same direct route or take the longer round trip walk through the pound via the homestead and Sliding Rock. This is the same track you take to the Edeowie Gorge.

There are a series of bushwalks in the park, clearly marked by blue triangles along the tracks. Pick up a copy of the Wilpena leaflet issued by the National Parks & Wildlife Society or the similar leaflet from the tourist office — either have maps which are quite OK for day walks on the marked trails. It is recommended that you do not walk solo and that you are adequately equipped — particularly with drinking water and sun protection in the summer. Most of the walks start from the campground and the walking times indicated are for a reasonably easy pace. The St Mary's Peak walk is probably the most interesting but there are plenty of others worth considering including walks taking more than a day.

Places to Stay Unless you've got a tent there is no cheap accommodation at the pound. If you're equipped for camping there's a campsite at the pound entrance with facilities including a pretty well stocked store. Costs are $3.50 for a car including two people, $1.50 for a motorcycle. Otherwise the *Wilpena Pound Motel* has all mod cons including a restaurant and swimming pool but you can count on $38 to $40 for singles and doubles.

You can get pies and pasties in the shop, as well as food to fix yourself, or counter lunches are available and there's the motel restaurant.

Blinman
From the 1860s to the 1890s this was a busy copper town but today it's just a tiny country town on the circular route around Wilpena Pound. It's a useful jumping off point for visits to many of the scenic attractions in the area and the delightful *Hotel North Blinman* has the real outback pub flavour — bed & breakfast is $15 per person. The beautiful Aroona Valley and the ruins of the Aroona Homestead are to the south of Blinman. Further south is the Brachina Gorge, another typically spectacular gorge of the Flinders. Between Blinman and the pound is the Great Wall of China, a long ridge capped with ironstone. Between Parachilna and Blinman it's a scenic drive through the Parachilna Gorge where there are good picnic areas.

North on the Oodnadatta road Beltana is almost a ghost town today but you can turn east here and visit the old copper mines at Sliding Rock. At one time Beltana was a major camel breeding station and much of the town is now being restored. You can get a guide to the town from the old railway station which is now a museum. It's a long drive from anywhere to Chambers Gorge, well to the north-east towards Lake Frome. The deep gorge has rock carvings and from Mt Chambers you can see Lake Frome and the Flinders Ranges all the way from Mt Painter to Wilpena. There are camping facilities at Mt Chambers.

Leigh Creek (population 1000)
North again along the Oodnadatta road, Leigh Creek is the biggest town between Port Augusta and Alice Springs. The huge open-cut coal mine here supplies the Port Augusta power station. Tree planting has transformed this once barren town and you can do a drive-yourself tour of the coal works by following the green arrow signs. From Leigh Creek you can visit the Aroona Dam and the Gammon Ranges National Park, 64 km to the east, are also reached from Leigh Creek but they're a remote and rugged area, for experienced bushwalkers only. In 1982 the whole town was shifted south a few km because the site of the original town is now being mined.

Arkaroola
The tiny settlement of Arkaroola, in the northern part of the Flinders, was only established in 1968. It's a privately operated wildlife sanctuary in rugged and spectacular country. From the settlement you can take a four-wheel drive along the 'ridge-top' through rugged mountain country and there are also scenic flights and many walking tracks. The ridge-top tour costs $22.50. Arkaroola used to be a mining area and old tracks cut during the mining days lead to rockpools at the Barraranna Gorge and at Echo Camp and to waterholes at Arkaroola and Nooldoonoold-

oona. Further on is the Bolla Bollana Springs and some ruins of an old copper smelter.

Mt Painter is a well known and very scenic landmark in the region while there are fine views from Freeling Heights across Yudnamutana Gorge or from Siller's Lookout from where you can see across to the salt flats of Lake Frome. This is the real, red outback country and Mt Painter is a visually spectacular example of that outback landscape. The Arkaroola area is of geological significance since Paralana Hot Springs is believed to be the site of the last volcanic activity to have taken place in Australia.

THE OUTBACK

North of the Eyre Peninsula and the Flinders area stretches the vast, empty area of South Australia's far north. Sparsely populated and difficult to travel through yet with much of interest. Large parts of the far north are prohibited areas — either Aboriginal reserves or the Woomera military area — and without four-wheel drive or camels it's not possible to stray far from the main roads. There is virtually no sealed road in the far north. The main Stuart Highway stretches nearly 1100 km from Port Augusta to the Northern Territory border but only the first 79 km are sealed although from the territory border the road is sealed all the way to Darwin. The alternative road to the Northern Territory, also not surfaced of course, runs from Port Augusta through the Flinders to Marree, Oodnadatta and eventually joins the Stuart Highway not far south of the territory border. For most of the way it runs close to the old railway line route.

The two other routes of interest in the far north are the famous Birdsville Track and the Strzelecki Track. These

Places to Stay The resort campsite costs $1.50 per person and there are also a variety of other accommodation possibilities here. In the bunkhouse, bunk beds are $3 but these are intended mainly for groups. Same price, however, in the 'Shearers' Quarters'. There are also a number of holiday flat style units — $60 a night in a unit for six, $50 in a unit for five. Plus there are some double rooms without private facilities at $20. Finally there are motel units — $36 for a double in the Greenwood Lodge and $42 in the Mawson Lodge.

routes are only possible in good conditions and with the right equipment. The South Australian outback includes much of the Simpson Desert and the harsh rocky land of Sturt's Stony Desert. There are also huge salt lakes which every once in a long while fill with water. Lake Eyre, used by Donald Campbell for his attempt on the world's speed record in the '60s, filled up for a time in the '70s; it was only the second occasion since the white men first reached this area. When the infrequent rains do reach this dry land the effect is amazing. Flowers bloom, plants grow and multiply, all at a breakneck pace in order to complete their life cycle before the dry returns. There is even a species of frog that goes into a sort of suspended animation, remaining in the ground for years on end only to pop up with the first sign of rain. On a much more mundane level roads can be washed out and the surface turned into a sticky glue. When this occurs vehicles on the road are often stuck for days, even weeks on end.

Places to Stay

Although Coober Pedy has a number of

motels, in most other outback towns accommodation is rather limited. If you want to stay it's wise to book ahead. Camping is no problem and although there are no youth hostels in the region if you enquire at the bus station in Coober Pedy they'll put you on to places where hostellers get a special deal.

Getting There

Air There are a variety of flights to outback stations from Adelaide and Alice Springs. Opal Air (tel 217 7222) at the Ansett office at 150 North Terrace, fly to Woomera for $87 and Coober Pedy for $133. Trans Regional Airlines (tel 212 5733) can be found at the TAA office at 144 North Terrace. They fly from Adelaide to Andamooka ($92), Innamincka ($168), Birdsville ($190) and Oodnadatta ($160). Chartair fly to Oodnadatta from Alice Springs for $75.

Bus Stateline (tel 217 0777) at the Central Bus Station, 111 Franklin St, operate once or twice daily to Woomera ($22), Pimba ($22), Kingoonya ($34), Coober Pedy ($49) and Marla ($64). It takes 15 hours to Coober Pedy. There's a once weekly service to Maree which takes 12 hours and costs $30. To Andamooka is twice weekly, taking eight hours and costing $30. The Stateliner service continues through from Coober Pedy and Marla to Alice Springs daily — these are operated for Greyhound. Ansett Pioneer also operate on the Adelaide - Coober Pedy - Marla - Alice Springs run three times weekly with Briscoes. Fares vary slightly from Greyhound/Stateline.

Rail The new ghan operates from Adelaide to Tarcoola, Marla and up to Alice Springs rather than along the old Maree, Oodnadatta route. Fares are $41 to Tarcoola, $52 to Manguri and $64 to Marla.

Coober Pedy (population 1900)

On the Stuart Highway 935 km north of Adelaide, Coober Pedy is one of the best known towns in the outback. The name is Aboriginal and means 'white fellow's hole in the ground', which aptly describes the place as a large proportion of the population live in dugouts to shelter from daytime temperatures that can soar over $50^{\circ}C$ and winter nights which can get uncomfortably cold. Coober Pedy is in an extremely inhospitable area, even water has to be brought in to the town. The town survives from opals which were first discovered here in 1911. Here, as in Andamooka, keen fossickers can have a go themselves having acquired a prospecting permit from the Mines Department in Adelaide. There are literally hundreds of mines around Coober Pedy and there are tours, opal cutting demonstrations and polished stones and jewellery on sale.

Coober Pedy is about the only place to get petrol between Kingoonya (285 km south and 162 km beyond Pimba) and Kulgera just across the Northern Territory border (478 km north).

Opals

Australia is the opal producing centre of the world and South Australia is where most of Australia's opals come from. Opals are hardened from silica suspended in water and the colour in an opal is produced by light being split and reflected by the silica molecules. Valuable opals are cut in three different fashions. Solid opals can be cut out of the rough into cabochons — domed top stones. Triplets consist of a layer of opal sandwiched between an opaque backing layer and a transparent cap. Doublets are simply an opal layer with an opaque backing. In addition some opals from Queensland are found embedded in rock and these opals are sometimes polished while still incorporated in the surrounding rock.

An opal's value is determined by its colour and clarity — the brighter and clearer the colour the better. Brilliance of colour is more important than the colour itself. The type of opal is also a determinant of value — black and crystal opals are the most valuable, semi-black and semi-crystal are in the middle, milk opal in the bottom. The bigger the pattern the better and lack of visible flaws, certainly no cracks, also have a bearing on the opal's value. Shape is also important in as much as a high dome is better than a flat opal. Finally, given equality in other aspects, the size is important. As with any sort of gemstone don't expect to find great bargains unless you clearly know and understand what you are buying.

Woomera

During the '50s and '60s Woomera was used to launch experimental British rockets and conduct tests of the abortive European project to orbit a satellite. The projects were later abandoned and Woomera is once again just a large area of nothing much. What remains of the township of Woomera is six km off the Stuart Highway from the tiny town of Pimba.

Andamooka (population 400)

Off the Stuart Highway, north of Woomera and west of Lake Torrens, Andamooka is a rough and ready little town devoted to opal mining. Many of the residents live in dug-out homes to give some relief from the temperature extremes. It's about a 100 km from Pimba to Andamooka and although the road is fair it very quickly becomes impassable after rain. Uranium has been discovered at Roxby Downs, near Andamooka.

Marree (population 300)

On the rugged alternate road north through Oodnadatta, Marree is a tiny township once used as a staging post for the Afghan led camel trains of the last century. There are still a few old date palms, standing as reminders of those days. Marree is also the southern end of the Birdsville track and just six km

north of here is the Frome Creek, a normally dry creek bed that with rain can cut the track for weeks on end. Marree is likely to get even smaller in the future, with the closing of the old railway line to Alice Springs.

Birdsville Track

Years ago cattle from the south-west of Queensland were driven down the Birdsville Track to Marree where they were loaded aboard the train — these days they're trucked out on the 'beef roads'. It's 481 km between Marree and Birdsville, just across the Queensland border. Although in good conditions the track can even be managed by conventional vehicles it's worth bearing in mind that it's a long way to push if you break down. And that traffic along this road isn't exactly heavy. There is, however, petrol usually available at Mungeranie, about 200 km north of Marree and 280 km south of Birdsville. The track is more or less at the meeting point between the sand dunes of the Simpson Desert to the west and desolate wastes of Sturt's Stony Desert to the east. There are ruins of a couple of old homesteads scattered along the track and artesian bores gush out boiling hot and very salty water at many places. At Clifton Hill, about 150 km south of Birdsville, the track splits and one route or other may be better — seek local advice. The last travellers to die on the track took the wrong route, got lost, ran out of petrol and died before they were discovered.

Strzelecki Track

The Strzelecki Track is even more rough and rugged than the Birdsville and at 494 km it's even longer. The track starts from Lyndhurst, about 80 km south of Marree, and runs to the tiny outpost of Innamincka. There's nothing by the way of supplies, petrol or help from one end to the other. Natural gas deposits have now been discovered near Moomba so there is likely to be much development here in the future. The new Moomba Strzelecki track is better kept but longer and less interesting than the old track which follows the Strzelecki Creek. Innamincka is near Cooper's Creek, where the Burke and Wills expedition of 1860 came to its tragic conclusion. From Innamincka you can visit the Burke and Wills 'dig' tree, their graves and several memorials to them and to Sturt.

Oodnadatta (population 200)
A tiny town and like Marree likely to get even tinier with the old ghan track's closure, Oodnadatta is at the point where the road and railway lines diverge. Oodnadatta was an important staging post during the construction of the overland telegraph line and later was the railhead for the line from Adelaide from its original extension to Oodnadatta in 1884 until it finally reached Alice Springs in 1929.

The Ghan
See the Northern Territory section for details of the famous train line from Adelaide to Alice Springs.

Tasmania

Area	68,000 square km
Population	450,000

Don't miss: Historic old Hobart and the wild and rugged country where you'll find some of Australia's best bushwalks.

Tasmania was Australia's second settlement; fairly soon after Sydney was securely on its feet the authorities decided that a second settlement further south had better be made pretty quick before some other European power decided to muscle in. After a cursory glance at Port Phillip Bay in Victoria (no good was the report) they decided on Hobart and it soon grew to be a rival city to Sydney.

Later, as the vast potential of the huge expanses of land in NSW started to be utilised, Hobart began to slip behind but this has had the beneficial effect of preserving many of the old places of historic interest in Tasmania, not sweeping them aside in the name of progress.

The convict days are especially evident in Tasmania — the worst of the cons were often shipped off to Van Diemen's land (Tassie's early name) which was soon dubbed 'that isthmus between earth and hell'. There are a number of interesting old penal settlement ruins — Port Arthur being the best known — and many examples of convict-built bridges and buildings. Early mining also left its mark and Tasmania has a number of fascinating ghost towns not to mention some more modern mining sites to visit.

For many visitors Tasmania's real fascination won't be charming old buildings or ruins but the wild natural scenery. Spectacular stretches of coast, excellent bushwalking trails and some of the best parks in Australia — and the smaller, almost un-Australian, scale of Tassie brings it all within easy reach.

INFORMATION

The Tasmanian Government Tourist Bureau has a head office in Hobart and branch offices in Launceston, Devonport, Burnie and Queenstown. On the mainland they have a comprehensive collection of offices at:

ACT	5 Canberra Savings Centre, City Walk, Canberra 2600 (tel 47 0070)
NSW	129 King St, Sydney 2000 (tel 233 2500)
Queensland	217-219 Queen St, Brisbane 4000 (tel 221 7411)
South Australia	32 King William St, Adelaide 5000 (tel 211 7411)
Victoria	256 Collins St, Melbourne 3000 (tel 63 6351)
Western Australia	55 William St, Perth 6000 (tel 321 2633)

There are also offices in Auckland and Christchurch, New Zealand. The offices have information on the usual tourist sights plus accommodation, restaurants and travel. Every two months the bureau produces *Tasmanian Travelways*, a very comprehensive newspaper covering facilities, accommodation, public transport and current costs throughout the state. It's free.

The Tasmanian Tourist Council has info at a variety of shops and restaurants plus Golden Fleece garages — look for a TAS sign. They produce an annual *Visitors Guide to Tasmania* — $1.50 from tourist bureau offices or newsagencies. This is an excellent publication with information on most places in Tasmania and good maps in the back. The council also produces a whole series of 'Let's Talk About' brochures. These are excellent for more comprehensive local information on towns, areas of larger towns, wildlife, parks and so on.

The Royal Automobile Club of Tasmania produce a tourist map of the island for $1 (free to members and reciprocal members). They also put out an accommodation guide and they have offices in most larger towns.

GEOGRAPHY

Tasmania is a varied and in places quite un-Australian island. Despite its compact size and relatively (by Australian standards) dispersed population it also has some areas of very light population. And not, as in most other unpopulated Australian regions, because of lack of rainfall; Tasmania's south-west enjoys abundant rainfall but it's simply very wild.

The population of Tasmania is mainly in the east and along the north coast. Here the land is rolling and fertile, the midlands region is almost a recreation of the green England so beloved of early settlers. The east coast and north coast are both inviting and interesting with many beaches, coves and bays.

By contrast the south-west and the west coast are amazingly wild. The coast here is virtually untouched, Strahan is the only port of any size on the whole coast and its bay, difficult though it is to get in to, is virtually the only safe harbour on the whole coast. The entire coast is often assaulted by raging seas. Inland the forest and mountains of the south-west are dense but delightful. Unfortunately this is also the region which has become a battlefield between conservationists and the 'profits today, to

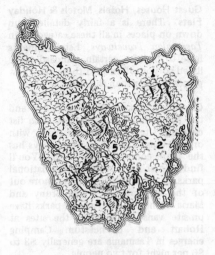

1 North-East
2 East Coast
3 South & South-West
4 North-West Coast
5 Midlands
6 West Coast

hell with tomorrow' developers intent on flooding more and more of the most beautiful rivers in the quest for hydroelectric power.

PLACES TO STAY

Hostels There are 18 youth hostels scattered around the island but in the peak holiday periods Tasmania is very popular with hostellers and it may be advisable to book ahead. You'll find the hostels at Bicheno, Coles Bay, Cygnet, Hobart, Devonport, Deloraine (summer only), King Island, Launceston, Maydena, New Norfolk, Oatlands, Port Arthur, Scamander, Sheffield, St Marys, Swansea and Wynyard.

Guest Houses, Hotels, Motels & Holiday Flats There is a fairly detailed run down on places in all these categories in *Tasmanian Travelways*. Establishments have to be of a certain standard to be listed so you often find there are a few places cheaper than the ones they list.

Camping Tasmanian Travelways and the automobile clubs' guides both list camping sites and caravan parks with on-site vans. *Tasmanian Travelways* has the more comprehensive listing. You'll find sites at most towns, in the national parks, at some beaches and at more out of the way places — like Bruny and Maria Islands. Many caravan parks have on-site vans — including the sites at Hobart and Launceston. Camping charges in Tasmania are generally $3 to $6 per night for two people.

GETTING THERE

Air TAA and Ansett fly to Hobart and Launceston from Melbourne and Sydney, some of the Sydney flights go direct to Launceston then Hobart. Ansett and East-West fly from Melbourne to Wynyard (for Burnie) and Devonport and East-West also fly Sydney-Hobart direct. Regular fares and standby fares are available on these routes. If you're under 25 you can join East-West's Club 25 (it's free) and get 20% off their fares to Hobart (from Sydney) or to Wynyard and Devonport (from Melbourne). This brings the ticket price almost down to standby level without having the uncertainty of standing by. East-West also have special deals for youth hostellers including one or two weeks youth hostel accommodation and (if you want it) a rent-a-car. You can also fly to Tasmania via King and Flinders Island but this is somewhat more expensive — see the Getting Around by air section for fare details. The chart below shows these main routes to Tasmania by air.

You can also fly between Tasmania

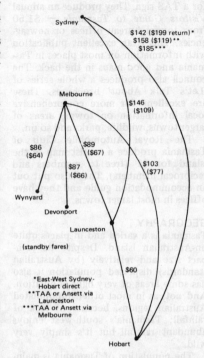

Sydney

$142 ($199 return)*
$158 ($119)**
$185***

Melbourne

$146 ($109)

$86 ($64) $89 ($67)

$87 ($66) $103 ($77)

Wynyard

Devonport

Launceston

(standby fares)

$60

*East-West Sydney-Hobart direct
**TAA or Ansett via Launceston
***TAA or Ansett via Melbourne

Hobart

and New Zealand — TAA fly Hobart-Christchurch and Christchurch-Hobart twice weekly and they've recently been joined on the route by Air New Zealand. The regular one-way economy fare is A$280 (NZ$384). Advance purchase fares vary from A$320 to 438 return (NZ$438 to 600). The flight takes a bit under three hours.

Ferry You can reach Tasmania from the Australian mainland by sea as well as by air. The regular shipping service between Melbourne and Devonport is particularly popular with people who want to bring their vehicles to Tasmania with them. Apart from a couple of its annual overhaul the 8196 tonne *Empress of Australia* makes three crossings each way. Departures from Williamstown

Rd, Port Melbourne are at 7.30 pm on Monday, Wednesday and Friday arriving 14 hours later at 9.30 am the following morning. The return trips depart Devonport at 7.30 pm on Sunday, Tuesday and Thursday arriving at 10 am the following morning. There is a free bus service between the Melbourne city centre and the docks for departing and arriving services.

Fares vary between the high season (mid-December to end of May) and low season (beginning of June to mid-December). Cheapest fares are on a sleeper chair for $52 ($44 low season). Then there are a whole host of cabins starting from four-berth cabins, then two-berth, then cabins with private facilities and finally the luxury suites. They cost $62, $77, $83, $105, $114 or $124 per person in the high season; $53, $66, $70, $89, $98 or $106 in the low season. The high and low seas-

ons for vehicles vary slightly from those for passengers. Cars cost $157 to $274 depending on their size in the high season; $147 to $256 in the low season. You can take a motorcycle across for $33 or a bicycle for $15. All vehicle rates are two-way, so long as you bring them back within 12 months.

One important point to consider if you plan to take the ferry in the peak summer season — from December to April — it's very heavily booked and you must plan well ahead.

GETTING AROUND

Air Airlines of Tasmania and Kendell Airlines operate a fairly extensive network around Tasmania and also fly between Tasmania and Melbourne's Essendon Airport. You can fly from Melbourne to Tasmania via Flinders Island at not a great amount more than

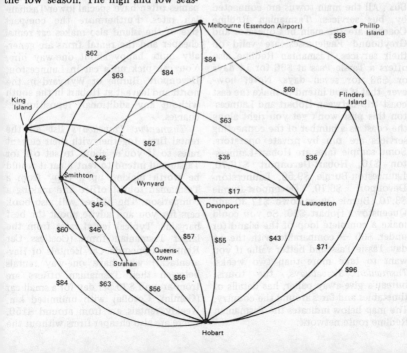

a regular Melbourne-Tasmania flight. The chart on the previous page shows the main routes and costs with the smaller airlines. Students aged 19 to 26 get a 25% discount with Air Tasmania.

Stop Press Phillip Island Air Charter fly between Phillip Island (near Melbourne) and Smithton every Friday. The fare is $58 or $39 standby. Phone 059 56 7316 for more details.

Rail There are no longer any passenger rail services in Tasmania — the Hobart-Launceston line stopped passenger services 'for economic reasons'. The Emu Bay run also no longer takes passengers although you may be able to arrange to get on it privately. It's run by mining companies and operates through some exciting mountain passes between Burnie and Roseberry.

Bus All the main towns are connected by bus services. Tasmanian Redline Coaches are the main bus operator and Greyhound Eaglepasses are valid on their services. Tasmanian Redline. also offers a Tassie Pass at $66 for 14 days or $53 for seven days. Note, however, that if you intend to make the east coast trip between Hobart and Launceston this pass won't get you right along the coast as a number of the connecting services are run by private operators. Some sample fares are Hobart-Launceston $10, Hobart-Devonport $16.70, Launceston-Burnie $9.50, Launceston-Devonport $6.70, Devonport-Burnie $3.70, Burnie-Queenstown $17.30 and Queenstown-Hobart $20. So you could make a complete loop of the island for under $60 — comparable with the 14 day Tassie Pass and better value if you want to take more than two weeks. *Tasmanian Travelways*, the tourist bureau's give-away paper, has details of timetables and fares around the country. The map below indicates the Tasmanian Redline route network:

Car Many people bring their cars from the mainland to Tasmania by the ferry service but for a short visit it's not particularly economic to do this so Tasmania has a comprehensive collection of rent-a-car operators. The main national firms are all here but they face stiff competition from the host of local firms — rates are generally lower than on the mainland and even the big companies often have special lower Tasmanian rates. Furthermore the compact size of the island also makes car rental cheaper and the rental firms are generally quite happy about one-way hire. You can pick up a car in Launceston, Devonport, Burnie or Wynyard in the north and leave it at Hobart in the south without any additional 'repositioning' charges.

Tasmanian Travelways list all the rental firms together with their current rates so if you're about to set off for Tassie and intend to rent a car it would be worth picking up a copy from a Tasmanian tourist office and making a comparison. The offices will also book cars for you and advise about the best bargains. Typical rental rates from the larger Tasmanian firms (Costless Car Rentals, Concorde Car Rentals or Havarentacar) who have one-way rentals between their Tasmanian offices are from around $30 per day for a small car (Gemini, Corolla) with unlimited km. Weekly rentals are from around $150. There are also cheaper firms without the one-way facilities (Elite in Launceston, Ambassador in Hobart and Launceston) who have similar cars from around $20 to $25. Extra charges are made for insurance (typically about $6) and sometimes for one-day rentals. Cheapest of all are the companies renting older cars. Jalopy Car Rentals in Launceston and Devonport have early-70s Falcons, Holdens and Valiants from around $15 to 20 a day with unlimited km. Rent-a-Rocket do a similar deal in Hobart.

You can also hire campervans (typically from around $40 a day) from a whole host of companies. Several companies rent motorcycles (Abel Car Rentals in Hobart and Launceston, Mike's Rent-a-Bike in Launceston, Kingston Rent-a-Car in Hobart and Launceston) at costs from $15 a day. Weekly rentals ($65 for a Yamaha 125, $85 for a Kawasaki 250) are also available.

Tasmania is just the right size for exploring on a small motorcycle. Or at least you'd think so — an entry in the Launceston youth hostel log book warned that's 'all you would be travelling bikers, unless you're on a 650cc or bigger, pannier bags, heavy wet weather gear, a pillion passenger to talk to, and you're slightly mad — don't consider riding around Tassy!' The note added that rental motorbikes are available but they're generally not worth it — you could rent a car for the same price and the condition of the bikes is not always good. Hmm.

Tasmanian roads don't all have too good a reputation. The highway from Hobart to Wynyard via Launceston, Devonport and Burnie is very good. Some other highways can be quite narrow and winding in places while the back roads vary from reasonable to very rough. Fortunately the distances are usually fairly short!

Hitching Travel by thumb is generally pretty good in Tasmania, some people say it is the best in any state of Australia. It can get a bit hard on both the east and west coasts though, especially during the off-season when there is very little traffic. The back roads, which often lead to the most interesting places, suffer from the same problem. King's Bus, reported Simon Hayman, would not stop when he gave up hitching and tried to flag it down!

Tours Many of the TGTB tours don't operate unless there are sufficient numbers or you pay extra to charter a taxi. This means that trips in the off-season tend to be non-existent, especially away from the major centres like Hobart and Launceston.

Cycling Tasmania

Tasmania is the only state in Australia that can realistically be cycled around. Yes I know lots of people ride bikes right round Australia but lots of madmen do all sorts of crazy things! There are some long hills and some steep hills in Tasmania (more of both variety if you're on a bicycle) but the distances are relatively short and on many routes the traffic is light enough to make bike riding a pleasure.

Getting There Many people hire bicycles in Tasmania and a number of bike hire places are set up to cater for bicycle touring. Otherwise you've got to get your bike over there. By the ferry service it's no problem so long as you've booked far enough in advance to ensure you get aboard. By air the two airlines will carry one item of baggage free and that one item can be your bike. If you travel light enough it's even possible to make that your only item of baggage. Pack it well, if possible wrap it so that the baggage loaders aren't tempted to lift it by the wheel spokes or commit similar indignities upon it. It's probably easier to get your bike over to Tassie on the flights to Hobart or Launceston rather than the Wynyard or Devonport flights, because they use larger jet aircraft, not small F27s. I've put a 250cc motorcycle on an F27 from Darwin to Timor many years back so they're not that small.

Gear Make sure your carrier rack is strong and that pannier bags are firmly attached. Try to balance the load about a third to the front, two thirds to the rear. As many first time bicycle tourers soon discover carrying capacity is absolutely not the problem on a bike — it's very easy to carry far too much gear with you. Travel as light as possible, if it's not 100% necessary leave it behind.

Getting Around Count on 10-14 days for a half-way round trip — Launceston-Hobart by east or west coast for example. For a full circuit of the island allow 14-28 days. Bikes can travel cheaply on the local bus services as freight and a short bus ride, even just 20 or 30 km, can make life a whole lot easier in some hilly sections. You're likely to suffer fewer headwinds if you travel around anti-clockwise. Many of the youth hostels are keen promoters of bicycle touring, the Launceston hostel in particular.

Renting a Bike *Tasmanian Travelways* has the latest information on bike hire and rates. Launceston is probably the best starting point as there are two hire places both set up for renting machines for touring. They're Launceston Rent-a-Cycle at the youth hostel and R&W Cycle Hire. Typical rental rates are $5 a day, $30 a week for a 10-speed bike. There are also bike renters in Devonport, Hobart, St Helens and on Flinders Island but some of these are more for the one-day local visitor rather than the long distance tourer.

AROUND TASMANIA

History and the bush are Tasmania's attractions: there's plenty of both. Although Tasmania was not settled until after Sydney its relatively rapidly achieved prosperity and its small size means that there are plenty of solid reminders of those pioneering days. In Tasmania the settlers had the resources to build for posterity — their bridges, homes, churches and public buildings are all solidly constructed of brick and stone. Tasmania's wilderness is equally solid, or at least it should be if the dam builders can be stopped from flooding the place. Despite the dam building that has already gone on Tasmania has a lot of parks, reserves and plain wilderness. You can still get yourself thoroughly lost in Tasmania despite its small size. If you want to get to grips with Australia on foot you'll find some of the classic bushwalks in Tasmania, including the popular Cradle Mountain to Lake St Clair walk.

You can make a very handy loop around Tasmania, seeing a fair amount of the country and not doing too much backtracking. Whether you come to Tasmania by air or sea it's best to commence your loop on the north coast since flights are cheaper to the north coast airports than to Hobart and the only shipping route also runs there. So if you fly in to Launceston, Devonport, Wynyard or Smithton or ship to Devonport you could start your circuit by travelling along the north coast where there are a number of interesting little towns, some excellent beaches and fine scenery. Then head south to the wild west coast with the historic mining town of Queenstown and the old port of Strahan. Keen bushwalkers could take an alternative route south by travelling to Waldheim and then making the walk to Lake St Clair.

From the west coast you head down

the Derwent Valley through some of the prettiest and most 'English' country in Tasmania to Hobart, the pleasant and historically intriguing capital of the state. Hobart is compact, easy-going and in many ways one of Australia's nicest cities. From Hobart you can make excursions out to the early colonial towns in the area like Richmond or south to the Huon peninsula. You certainly shouldn't fail to travel down to the Tasman Peninsula to see the early penal colony ruins at Port Arthur. This is Tasmania's number one tourist attraction and an eye opener to the sort of treatment meted out to Australia's early convict population — even in a so-called 'model prison'. Finally you can complete the loop from Hobart to the north coast either by one of the two central Midland routes, again through pastoral English-like country, or by taking the less frequented road up the east coast. By the time you get back to your starting point you'll have seen plenty of what Tasmania has to offer.

ACTIVITIES

Bushwalking Not unexpectedly Tasmania, with its rugged mountainous country — much of it still barely touched by man, is ideal for bushwalking. It has some of the finest bushwalking to be found in Australia and one walker commented recently that the superb Cradle Mountain-Lake St Clair walk is the equal of any of the better known walks in New Zealand.

Good information sources on bushwalking include the Federation of Tasmanian Bushwalking Clubs in Hobart and the National Parks & Wildlife Service also in Hobart. They can supply maps and guides to popular walks. Other good information sources are the book *100 Walks in Tasmania* and the excellent bushgear shops such as Paddy Pallins in Hobart, or Allgoods in Launceston, The Tasmanian Wilderness Society at 28 Criteron St, Hobart is dedicated to protecting Tasmania's superb wilderness and they're also a good information source.

Summer is the best time for Tasmanian bushwalks although even then the mountain country can spring some nasty surprises on the unwary. Be prepared for sometimes viciously changeable weather.

Cradle Mountain-Lake St Clair with its 80 km long track is one of the classic long bushwalks in Australia — see the separate section on this walk. Frenchman's Cap National Park is for the experienced bushwalker only — there are shelter huts at Lake Vera and Lake Tahure. South West National Park with Lake Pedder and the peaks of the Arthur Range is also mainly for the knowledgeable walker although there are shorter, easier paths. The Hydro-Electric Commission (HEC) has several lodges.

On the east coast the Freycinet National Park has good year-round coastal walks and a popular 27 km walking circuit. Ben Lomond National Park, south-east of Launceston, also has good walks and one shelter hut.

Water Sports There are good bayside beaches near Hobart including Bellerive, Long Beach, Kingston and Nutgrove. Good surf beaches are found on all the coasts but on the east coast many of the surf beaches are unpatrolled while the west coast surf is ferocious and there are very few access points to the coast. Canoeing is a popular activity on several of the state's rivers.

The often rugged Tasmanian coast provides some fine skin-diving opportunities. Equipment can be rented in Hobart and Launceston and good diving can be found on the north-east, east and south-west coast.

Skiing Tasmania has two ski resorts which offer cheaper, although less developed, ski facilities than the major resorts in Victoria and NSW. Despite its southerly latitude Tasmania's snowfalls tend to be fairly light.

Ben Lomond is 60 km from Launceston and in the ski season a bus departs every morning from Tasmanian Redline Coaches' depot in Launceston. The fare is $15 round trip on a daily basis, less for longer term tickets. From Jacob's Ladder to the ski village car park, the last four km up to the snow, you can also take a four-wheel drive bus for $6 return — if you want to drive most of the way there yourself. Mt Mawson, the other resort, is 96 km from Hobart. It's rather smaller and lower key and the snow coverage is often not very good but the ski-touring can be exceptional.

Tasmanian Aboriginals

The story of Australia's Aboriginals has not been a happy one since the European arrival but nowhere has the story been sadder than in Tasmania. The first British settlement was made in Tasmania in 1803 and in less than one hundred years the settlers had managed to completely wipe out the Tasmanian Aboriginal race. The last one died over a hundred years ago. Tasmania's Aboriginals became separated from the Aboriginals of the mainland over 10,000 years ago when rising ocean levels following the close of the last ice age cut Tasmania off from the mainland. From that time their culture diverged from that of the mainland population. They lived by hunting, fishing and gathering, sheltered in bark or leaf lean-tos and despite Tasmania's cold weather they went naked apart from a coating of grease and charcoal.

They were doomed as soon as the first Europeans arrived for Tasmania was fertile and easily divided and fenced to make farms. Soon they were losing their hunting grounds and then hunted and shot like animals by ruthless convicts, bushrangers and farmers. Finally from the 1830s the pitiful remnants of a race were rounded up and shipped to a reserve (read 'prison') on Flinders Island where, with nothing to do except exist, they gradually died off from sheer boredom. It had taken just 25 years to reduce the entire Tasmanian Aboriginal population to this miserable group on Flinders Island. The final 44 survivors were moved back to the mainland in 1847 but in 1874 the last surviving male full-blood died in the Dog & Partridge Taven in Hobart. In 1876 Truganini, the last surviving Tasmanian Aboriginal, died and the race had been wiped out.

HOBART (population 167,000)

Established in 1804, just 16 years after Sydney, Hobart is Australia's second oldest capital city. It's also the smallest state capital and the most southerly — in winter temperatures in Hobart often drop to near freezing and even in summer, sunny though it is, the temperature rarely climbs above 25°C. Hobart is picturesquely situated at the mouth of the Derwent River and backed by mountains which provide a fine view over the city and are often dusted with snow in the winter. It's a pretty little place and pleasantly easy-going — you never have problems getting around and about Hobart, it's small enough to be manageable. Most important Hobart is a town that not only has a history but has also managed to preserve it. It has been around long enough to have plenty of interesting and historic old buildings but has not grown so fast and so extensively that the sense of history has been swamped. The combination of old, time-worn buildings, the busy and colourful harbour and the pleasant atmosphere all go together to make Hobart one of my favourite Australian cities.

Information

The Tasmanian Government Tourist Bureau (tel 34 6911) is at 80 Elizabeth St and is open Monday to Friday from 8.45 am to 5.30 pm, weekends and holidays from 9 to 11 am. The Royal Automobile Club of Tasmania (tel 34 6611) is on the corner of Murray and Patrick Sts. Colony 47 (tel 23 6159) at 47 Davey St is an info and referral centre and coffee shop. The Tasmanian Youth Hostel Association office (tel 34 9617) is at 133A Elizabeth St and is open on Tuesdays and Thursdays between 12.30 and 5 pm and on Wednesday and Friday from 12 noon to 2 pm. The Tasmanian Wilderness Centre is in Bathurst St. The National Parks & Wildlife Services has its head office at 16 Magnet Court, Sandy Bay (the shopping centre). They have lots of information on Tasmania's many parks and reserves and are an essential contact for would-be-walkers.

Orientation

Hobart is an easy city to find your way around. It's small enough to be manageable and it's also very simply laid out. The central streets are in a straightforward grid pattern with Liverpool St the main shopping street. Both TAA and Ansett have their city terminals along this street while the tourist office and the GPO are on Elizabeth St which runs across it. Salamanca Place, the old warehouse area, is along the waterfront while south of this is Battery Point, the delightful early colonial area of Hobart which has been maintained largely in its early form. Follow the river around from Battery Point and you'll come to Sandy Bay, site of the University of Tasmania and the Wrest Point Casino which has quick-

ly become Hobart's major landmark. The northside of the centre is bounded by the Queen's Domain and the Royal Botanical Gardens, then the Derwent River. From here the Tasman Bridge crosses the river to the northern suburbs and the airport.

Walking Tour

One of the best ways of getting a feel for Hobart's interesting history is to take the Saturday morning walking tour. Organised by the National Trust and the TGTB it starts at 9.30 am during the summer and school holidays. Cost is $2.50 including morning tea. You can make a similar do-it-yourself tour with the aid of a leaflet from the TGTB. The walk centres around historic Battery Point and includes the small Maritime Museum and ends at the colonial warehouses at Salamanca Place.

Around Town

You'll find some of Hobart's best Georgian architecture around Macquarie and Davey Sts. Close to the centre St David's Park, with its lovely old trees and pioneer cemetery with graves dating from the earliest days of the colony, is a good place to pause and relax. Built by convicts between 1835 and 1841 and originally used as a customs house, the old Parliament House is on Murray St, across from the park. At 29 Campbell St the Theatre Royal dates from 1837, it's the oldest theatre in Australia and has a delightful Georgian interior.

In the centre the Cat & Fiddle Arcade is one of Hobart's most popular shopping areas. On Davey St you can see one of only three royal tennis courts in the southern hemisphere. The other two are just down from the Lonely Planet office in Richmond, Victoria! You can look in at the courts on the walking tour. Hobart's waterfront area, very close to the centre of the city, is still a colourful scene although no

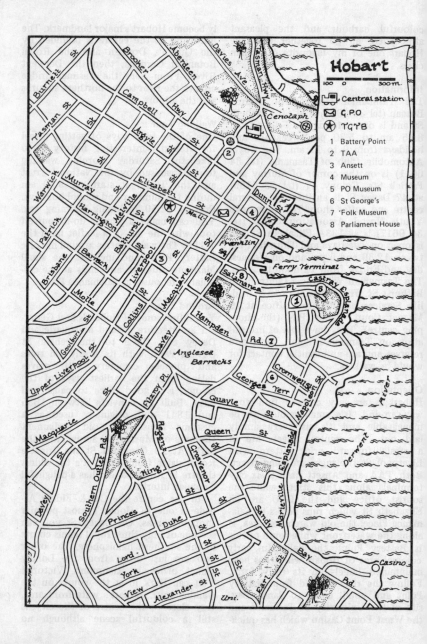

Hobart

100   0   300 m.

- Central station
- G.P.O
- TGYB

1 Battery Point
2 TAA
3 Ansett
4 Museum
5 PO Museum
6 St George's
7 'Folk Museum
8 Parliament House

longer the roughhouse, brawling place it was in the early whaling days. It really comes alive around Constitution Dock at the finish of the annual Sydney to Hobart Yacht Race over Christmas-New Year each year.

Anglesea Barracks

Australia's oldest military establishment, the Anglesea Barracks on Davey St are still used by the army. They were built in 1811 and are open weekdays from 9 am to 5 pm, admission is free.

Van Diemen's Land Folk Museum

Housed in Narryna, a fine old home furnished as in early colonial days, at 103 Hampden Rd, Battery Point, the museum re-creates the early pioneering days in Tasmania. It's open Monday to Friday from 10 am to 5 pm and on weekends from 2 to 5 pm. Admission is $1.50. You can easily walk to it from the centre or take a Sandy Bay bus.

St George's Anglican Church & Maritime Museum

Only a short stroll from Narryna, the church is on Cromwell St, Battery Point. Construction was commenced in 1836 but the tower was not completed until 1847. It was designed by two of the best known Tasmanian colonial architects — James Blackburn and John Lee Archer (see Stanley). Behind the church there's a fascinating little Tasmanian Maritime Museum.

Museums

The excellent Tasmanian Museum & Art Gallery has a particularly emphasis on Tasmania's unfortunate Aboriginals and equally unfortunate whales. There are also many exhibits on Tasmania's early colonial history and the gallery has a large collection of early colonial paintings. It's open daily and admission is free. The Allport Library & Museum of Fine Arts has a collection of rare

books on Australasia and the Pacific region. The museum is open Monday to Friday from 9 am to 5 pm and admission is free.

Down at 19-21 Castray Esplanade the Post Office Museum has an interesting display on the development of the post and telegraphic services. It's open from Monday to Friday from 9 am to 5 pm and on Saturday from 9 to 11 am, again admission is free.

Battery Point

Behind the city docks and north of Sandy Bay is the historic centre of Hobart, the old port area known as Battery Point. It takes its name from the gun battery which stood on the promontory by the 1818 guard house, the oldest building on Battery Point. In Hobart's early days this was a colourful area of pubs, homes, churches and narrow, winding streets. It has been lovingly preserved and is a real delight to wander around with glimpses of the harbour seen between the many interesting buildings.

Some of the interesting places in Battery Point include Arthur's Circus, a small circle of quaint little cottages built around the former village green. The old warehouses of Salamanca Place, the National Trust house Narryna and old pubs like The Shipwright's Arms and The Lord Nelson are other attractions.

Salamanca Place

The old colonial warehouses on the harbour front at Salamanca Place are probably the best to be seen in Australia. A popular open-air market is held here each Saturday morning during the summer. In winter it moves inside one of the old warehouses. The buildings also house a string of galleries and restaurants while nearby there's the Post Office Museum on Castray Esplanade. From Salamanca Place you can climb up the precipitious Kelly's steps, wedged between two warehouses, into Battery Point.

Further Afield

Hobart is dominated by the 1270 metre Mt Wellington, often dusted with snow in the winter. There are fine views over the city and the Derwent River from the summit and there are also many walking tracks in the area but it can get very cold up there. The Old Signal Station on top of Mt Nelson, above Sandy Bay, also gives good views. The city is on both sides of the Derwent, spanned by the Tasman Bridge which collapsed disastrously in 1975 after being rammed by a runaway cargo ship. Government House and the Botanical Gardens are at the base of the ridge on the city side.

If you head away from the centre past Battery Point on the coast road towards the west you soon come to the University of Tasmania and then the Wrest Point Casino at Sandy Bay. The hotel and casino, Australia's first (well first legal one, anyway) quickly became a symbol of the town. Tasmania has very successfully capitalised on Australia's gambling mania!

Beyond Sandy Bay, on the way to Taroona, is the Model Tudor Village at 827 Sandy Bay Rd, Lower Sandy Bay. It's open daily from 9 am to 5 pm and you can get there on a Taroona bus from Franklin Square. North of the city at 61 Bay Rd, New Town, Runnymede is a finely restored old National Trust house with good views over the surrounding country. Built in 1844 it's open 1.30 to 4.30 pm and admission is $1.50. Another popular short trip from the city is the guided tour of the Cadbury chocolate factory — it costs $4 or $9, including transport, if you go on a TGTB tour. At Kangaroo Bluff there are the ruins of an old fort, built to repel a feared Russian invasion — similar forts can be seen in Sydney and Newcastle, NSW. Near here Lauderdale,

Seven Mile Beach and Cremorne are popular Hobart beaches. Go to Clifton for surf.

Places to Stay

Hostels Hobart has two *youth hostels* although one is only for groups or for use as an overflow for the main hostel (tel 44 2552) which is across the river at 52 King St, Bellerive. It's an interesting old stone schoolhouse dating from 1859 and charges $3 a night. When it is full the Woodlands Hostel comes into operation; find it at 7 Woodlands Avenue, New Town, which is about three km from the centre. Charge there is $4 a night. You must check with the Bellerive Hostel first though. Woodlands is only open from mid-December to late-February and then only when Bellerive is full.

Guest Houses There's not a lot available at a reasonable price in this category in Hobart. There are a few places to check out in the city, mostly at the south-west end, and a few at Sandy Bay, a short distance from the centre towards the university and the casino. Scan the Hobart Mercury for cheaper, longer term accommodation.

Buckingham Accommodation (tel 72 9826) at 51 Davey St costs only $10 a night per person including a cooked breakfast, or $50 a week per person including dinner. Also in the city, *Narrara Guest House* (tel 34 3928) at 88 Goulburn St has singles at $11 a night and doubles from $18. Breakfast costs an extra $2 to $3, dinner $4 to $5. By the week it's $35 or $65 full board and it's a modern place with a pleasant atmosphere.

At Sandy Bay *Number 27* is, as you might expect, at 27 Red Chapel Avenue (tel 25 2273) and a single costs $15 bed & breakfast or a double $25. It's an old-fashioned sort of place but pleasantly, not coldly, so. Other guest houses tend to be more expensive. The *Astor*

Private Hotel (tel 34 6384) at 157 Macquarie St has keen new owners and bed & breakfast costs $20/36 for singles/doubles. It's an old fashioned sort of place in the process of being restored — some rooms have showers, most don't. It does have the advantage of being very central.

Hotels The Hobart hotels are all a bit featureless and drab — some to try include the pleasant *Good Women Inn* (tel 34 4796) at 186 Argyle St where bed & breakfast costs $14/24 for singles/doubles. The *Black Prince Hotel* (tel 34 3501) at 145 Elizabeth St near the Mall is a good, clean place with rooms at $18/24 and an extra $3 for a cooked breakfast.

The *Aberfeldy* (tel 23 7218) at 124 Davey St costs $16/26 for bed & breakfast. The *Brunswick* (tel 34 4981) at 67 Liverpool St is $15/25 again for bed & breakfast. The *Customs House* (tel 34 6645) at 1 Murray St is $15 per person for bed & breakfast. The *Globe* (tel 23 5800) at 178 Davey St is $14/24 room-only. *Hadleys* (tel 23 7521) at 34 Murray St is $13/24 room-only. The *Theatre Royal* (tel 34 6925) at 31 Campbell St is $16/27 for bed & breakfast.

Motels & Holiday Flats The *Marina* (tel 28 4748) at 153 Risdon Rd, New Town is about the cheapest motel around at $20/28 for singles/doubles. The *Argyle Motor Lodge* (tel 34 2488) is a comfortable motel at 2 Lewis St on the corner with Argyle St, about two km from the centre in North Hobart. Rooms are $26/30. *Motel Mayfair* (tel 34 1670) is very central at 17 Cavell St, West Hobart and costs $25/30. If none of these cheaper motels appeal you could always opt for the Wrest Point Casino where a single in the tower block will set you back $62 per night.

Hobart has a number of self-contained places where you are left to fend for yourself. In town the *Domain View Holiday Apartments* (tel 28 0690) at 352 Argyle St costs $20 for two, $4 for each extra person. There is a one night surcharge. *Clendon Court* (tel 23 7087) at 30 Corby Avenue, West Hobart is similarly priced and has a two night minimum. In Sandy Bay at 2 Earl St there's the *Earl Street Holiday Flat* (yes flat, not flats) which costs just $18.

Colleges During the December-February summer vacation and in the May and August vacs you can stay at the residential halls at the University of Tasmania. *Christ College* (tel 23 5190) has a whole range of charges, depending on whether you are a student or not and what meals you want included. Room-only rates are $7 for students ($12 for non-students), with breakfast $9 ($14.50), with all meals $14.50 ($23.50). Other colleges to check are *St John Fisher* (tel 23 1106) and *Jane Franklin* (tel 23 2421).

Camping The handiest camp is *Sandy Bay Caravan Park* (tel 25 1264) less than four km from the centre at 1 Peel St, Sandy Bay. It's uphill from the casino intersection and a 54 or 55 bus will get you there. Camping costs $6 for two, on-site vans are $17.50 for two. Other less convenient sites are located in the northern suburbs at Glenorchy and Berriedale.

Places to Eat

Hobart has a surprising variety of restaurants for a town of its size — although they display a uniformly deplorable aversion to putting menus or prices on view outside (with a couple of honourable exceptions). This Australian habit of making you guess what they have and what it costs could definitely do with changing, it certainly doesn't happen to anything like the same extent in Europe. If there were a constant stream of people stomping in, demanding to look at a menu and then stomping out again, restaurants might wake up a little.

To ease restaurant hunting you can divide Hobart into three main food areas — the city itself (where you'll find a variety of places although you'll have to hunt around a bit), Sandy Bay (close to the university) and Battery Point (the historically interesting area of Hobart where you'll find the smaller and more intimate places and most of the exotica, and the prices to go with it. You can easily walk from the city to Battery Point and even Sandy Bay if you're feeling mildly energetic. Don't expect to find anything much apart from greasy spoon stuff or expensive meals on Saturday or Sunday afternoons.

Plain & Simple If it's plain, plebian food you want then try the *Piccadilly* at 136 Collins St, a popular lunch time snack sort of place. The *Domino* at 55 Elizabeth St is another good place for an economically priced lunch. *Chequers* at 53A Murray St also dishes out plain, straightforward and low-priced food at lunchtime. There is also a whole selection of eateries across the river in Bellerive, near the youth hostel.

There's the usual selection of pizzerias and Italian food specialists. *Etna Pizza House* is also an eat there or takeaway place, a short stroll from the centre at 201 Elizabeth St. They're a little more varied than straightforward pizza. You can get good value at the *Commonwealth Government Cafeteria* in the Commonwealth Centre at 188 Collins St. Or for wholefood try the

Pumpkin Eater at 181 Liverpool St — restaurant and take-aways. The *Carlton Restaurant* at 50 Liverpool St (corner with Argyle) is another straightforward and no-nonsense sort of place but it has the considerable virtue of staying open until reasonably late in the evening. At Constitution Dock you can buy fresh fish from floating stalls.

Counter Meals There are lots of these and, of course, for down to earth value they are the places to head for. You can get a huge meal for around $3 at the *Queen's Head* at 400 Elizabeth St, North Hobart. Similar prices at the *Brunswick* at 67 Liverpool St (schnitzels, etc); the *Wheatsheaf Hotel* at 314 Macquarie St; and the *Telegraph Hotel* at 19 Morrison St. You can get a steak or similar meal for around $3.50 at the *Shamrock* on the corner of Liverpool and Harrington Sts.

More expensive, but excellent food, at the *Iron Duke Steak Bar* in the *Duke of Wellington Hotel*, 192 Macquarie St. The *Bavarian Tavern* has good solid food in sombre surroundings with stern waitresses and a rollicking band to complete the German feel! Find it at 281 Liverpool St but you'd better book ahead on Thursday-Friday-Saturday when the band is on. Actually the Bavarian Tavern is more a restaurant than a counter food specialist in the evenings and the prices fall between pub and restaurant levels.

Up a Notch *Barton Cottage*, at 72 Hampden Rd, Battery Point, is a nice

Tasmania

a. Port Arthur was once the prison 'hell' of Tasmania, today its ruins make a peaceful scene.

b. Arthur's Circus is a small circle of quaint little cottages in Hobart's historic Battery Point.

c. At Taroona, just outside Hobart, the old shot tower is a local landmark.

old house serving Devonshire teas for $2. For pasta lovers *Romano's* at 112 Liverpool St is right in the city centre. It's fully licensed and open later than most Hobart restaurants. *Beards* is an old brick cottage in town at 101 Harrington St with an interesting blackboard menu and open fires in winter time. It's byo, main dishes are around the $6 mark and it's generally a nice place.

Tattersall's Bistro & Bar is another Hobart favourite, more about it under entertainment. The food here is really steakhouse style but it's the pleasant atmosphere which attracts people to Tattersalls. It's at 112 Murray St and main courses are around $6. The *Astor Grill* is a new restaurant at the Astor guest house and main courses are around $6.50 to 8.

Exotica Well for Japanese food there's *Sakura*, next door to the Ball & Chain at 85 Salamanca Place (around $8 to 9 for a main course). *Taco Bill*, at 41 Hampden Rd, Battery Point, is Mexican, of course. Back in town you can find Indian food at *Kashmir*, 109 Elizabeth St. The *Mandarin* at 177 Elizabeth St is a Chinese restaurant of the bare tables and straightforward food variety. It's another place which is open every day of the week. If you like Italian food *Don Camillo's*, in the Sandy Bay shopping centre, has a good reputation in Hobart. Main courses are in the $7 to 9 bracket — good veal dishes and saltimbocca. There's a cheaper coffee bar section in the front as well as the pricier licensed restaurant behind. The walls are hung with paintings by local artists which are for sale.

Top End Hobart has some very pleasant, if sometimes rather pricey, restaurants around Battery Point. *Mure's Fish House*, at 5 Knopwood St, is reputed to be one of the best fish restaurants in Australia. Main courses are around $6 to 9 at lunchtime, $7 to 10 for dinner. With Hobart's seafaring tradition it's not surprising that fish is popular here.

Dirty Dick's Steak House, on the corner of Hampden Rd and Francis St, is no relation to the mainland Dirty Dick's (thank God). It's quite a nice byo place. The *Ball & Chain* is pseudo-colonial style (the staff dress up) and is situated in the fine old warehouses of Salamanca Place. Olde English food in olde worlde surroundings but distinctly modern prices! The *Red Fox* at 47 Hampden Rd, Battery Point also specialises in traditional old English. They're open for lunch on weekdays and dinner every night. It'll cost you $12 to 16 depending on how many courses you have.

Entertainment

Check the *Hobart Mercury* for a guide to what's on and where. You tend to run into the 'no jeans, no running shoes' nonsense at quite a few of Hobart's entertainment spots, especially discos.

For jazz head to the *Dog House* on the corner of Barrack and Goulburn Sts. They have something on every night except Sunday; no cover charge, no hassles and counter meals available. The *Ingmar Hotel* at 34 Patrick St also has jazz. *St*

Tasmania

a. The bare hills around Queenstown are a stark reminder that pollution and wanton destruction of our environment are nothing new. Will the Franklin River be the next to go?

b. The 1824 Richmond Bridge is the oldest in Australia.

Ives, on Sandy Bay Rd, has jazz, folk and rock.

The *Fern Tree Tavern* is pleasant while *Ye Old Red Lion* at 19 Macquarie St usually has good rock bands. For folk there's the Bothy Folk Club on Fridays and Saturdays in the *Sir William Don Hotel*, 304 Elizabeth St, North Hobart. *Tattersalls*, at 112 Murray St, have a wine bar come night club called Pip's. They have laid-back music, a solo guitarist till midnight Monday to Saturday and country rock on Sunday afternoons.

The *Foreshore Tavern* is another venue to check. The *Portlight Bar* in the *Wrest Point Casino* has rock (and expensive drinks). Others include the university union, of course. Saturday morning the market at Salamanca Place is a great place to visit, especially during the summer.

Getting There

Air You can fly to Hobart from Melbourne or Sydney on the mainland as well as from other places in Tasmania. Hobart is even an international port — there are two flights a week between Hobart and Christchurch in New Zealand. See the introductory Getting There section for more details.

Bus See the various sections for more details on buses and their schedules. The two main bus depots in Hobart are Tasmanian Redline Coaches (tel 34 4577) at 96 Harrington St and Cape Country Coaches (tel 34 9081) at Hobart Railway Station. Services in brief are:

Hobart-Port Arthur You can travel there and back with Richardson's Coach Service (the mail bus) for $5 single, $8 return. Or with the Peninsula Coach service from the Tasmanian Redline depot for $6 single, $11 return. It is not possible to day-trip to Port Arthur except on tours.

Hobart-Launceston Direct Tasmanian Redline and Cape Country Coaches operate about five services a day between them Monday to Friday, two on weekends. The trip takes about 2½ to 3½ hours and fares are $9.70 on Tasmanian Redline, $13 on Cape Country.

Hobart-Launceston East Coast Via the east coast it takes at least a couple of days because there are a number of bus trips to be made by a number of operators and connections are not always good. See *Tasmanian Travelways* for the latest schedules. Total fare is about $25.

Hobart-Queenstown Monday to Saturday there are daily departures, the trip takes nearly seven hours and costs $20.

Hobart-North-West Coast Some of the services to Launceston continue through to the coast, or there are connections from Launceston. Typical fares from Hobart include Devonport $16.40 with Tasmanian Redline ($20 with Cape Country), Burnie $19.20 ($25), Smithton $30 with Cape Country.

Getting Around

Buses Local buses are run by the Metropolitan Transport Trust (MTT) and depart from various central city streets. For only $1 (although it may go up soon) you can get an unlimited travel bus ticket for use between 9 am and 4.45 pm and after 6.30 pm on weekdays, all day on weekends. The tourist bureau have free timetables. For the youth hostel catch a Tranmere bus from outside Fitzgerald's in Collins St. The ones that go via the Bluff stop very close to the hostel but if they don't you can walk it. For Mt Wellington the alternative to taking a tour is to catch a Fern Tree bus from Franklin Square, Macquarie St, to the base of the mountain — after which it's a 12 to 13 km walk! You might be lucky enough to get a ride.

For getting out of town to hitch north a Bridgewater bus could be your best bet, but they don't run very often so you may have to be content with a bus to somewhere like Glenorchy. In the south there are bus services to Huonville and Dover.

Ferry There's a ferry service across the river from Hobart to Bellerive for 50c, a pleasant way to get to the youth hostel but it operates only on weekday rush hours. There's even a bar on board! Departures from Hobart are between 6.40 to 7.55 am and 4 to 5.45 pm. From Bellerive they leave 7 to 8.10 am and 4.15 to 6.30 pm.

Cars See the introductory Getting Around section for information on the many car rental firms in Hobart. *Tasmanian Travelways* gives you a comprehensive run down on the latest hire rates. Rent-a-Rocket (tel 34 4512 or 34 4390) probably have the cheapest rental cars but they get mixed reports from users. Some complain about the mileage you get from them, breakdowns, large deposits and age restrictions. But on the other hand another traveller wrote that 'three of us hired an XB Falcon wagon, by negotiation we got it for $120 for the week and we covered 2500 km including some very rough roads'. They must have driven right round the island twice!

Bicycles You can hire bikes in Hobart from the Sandy Bay Caravan Park. Straightforward pedal brake bikes cost $8 a day, 10-speed bikes are $10, tandems $14, plus a security deposit. These bikes are really intended more for day use than bicycle touring but longer term rentals can be negotiated. If you want a bike on the weekend it's necessary to book ahead.

Airport Hobart's airport is some distance from the town centre, across the river. Tasmanian Redline Coaches run an airport bus service for $3. It departs from their depot at 96 Harrington St an hour before the flight departures. Alternatively a taxi costs about $11. In Hobart TAA (tel 38 3333) are at 4 Liverpool St. Ansett (tel 38 1111) are at 178 Liverpool St on the corner of Elizabeth St.

Tours There are a variety of tours in and around Hobart. Typical half day local tours include trips to Richmond, New Norfolk, Mt Wellington or the Cadbury factory — fares are $8 to $10. Longer day trips cost $18 to $20 and include Lake Pedder, Port Arthur, the Huon Valley and Hastings Cave or Maria Island. There are also boat trips out on the Derwent River and around Hobart's harbour. They cost from $5 for a two-hour harbour cruise to $9 for a five-hour harbour and river cruise including a stop for lunch (extra cost for lunch). The Bellerive ferry *Kangaroo* makes Sunday cruises for $2.50.

AROUND HOBART

Roads fan out from Hobart in a number of directions and there are a number of interesting places you can day-trip to from the capital city. They include Richmond on the way to Port Arthur, New Norfolk on the way up the Derwent Valley towards the west coast and a number of good beaches within easy driving distance of the city.

Taroona (population 3300)
Continue on beyond Wrest Point and you'll soon see Taroona's famous shot tower. Completed in 1870, the top of the tower gives a fine view over the river

estuary. The small museum at the base of the tower was built in 1855 and the adjoining residence in 1835. The tower and museum are open daily until dusk. Lead shot used to be produced in the high towers like these by dropping molten lead from the top. On the way down the globule of lead formed a perfect sphere and had solidified before it reached the bottom.

Kingston (population 6300)
Only 11 km south of Hobart there are good beaches here and south at Blackmans Bay. From Mt Louis at Piersons Point there are fine views across to Bruny Island.

Bridgewater (population 2800)
Only 19 km north of Hobart at the main river crossing of the Derwent, the causeway here was built by 160 convicts who managed to move two million tonnes of stone while still in chains. At Granton, on the other side of the river, the Old Watch House was built in 1838, once again by convincts, to guard the causeway. It's now a petrol station.

Pontville (population 800)
Further north on the Midlands Highway, Pontville has a number of early buildings dating back as far as 1819. There are other old towns in the vicinity. Pontville's quarries supplied much of the freestone for early buildings in other Tasmanian towns and two of the quarries are still working today.

New Norfolk (population 7000)
On the Derwent River, just 38 km from Hobart, this is one of the oldest and most historically interesting towns in Tasmania. Beer enthusiasts may be pleased to hear this is also the centre of hop growing in Australia and there are many oast houses, the conical buildings used to store hops, around the area. The Oast House has a museum devoted to hops and also does Devonshire teas.

Paper production is the other major industry of the area.

New Norfolk took its name from Norfolk Island; when the island settlement was abandoned in 1808 the settlers were transferred here and gave their new home a familiar name. There are many old farms with a very English look about them, the New Norfolk area also has many poplar trees and is said to resemble Kent in England — where English hops come from. Interesting old buildings in New Norfolk include the Bush Inn which dates from 1815 and is claimed to have the oldest licence in Australia (you wouldn't know it was so old, it's been well hacked around) but the Launceston Hotel disputes its claim. On Montague St the Old Colony Inn is a fine old building dating from 1835. It has an antique collection and does lunches and, yet again, Devonshire teas. St Matthew's Church of England was built in 1823 which makes it Tasmania's oldest church; there's a craft centre next door.

In 1864 the first rainbow and brown trout in the southern hemisphere were bred at the Plenty Salmon Ponds, 11 km west of New Norfolk. From this beginning streams and lakes in Australia and New Zealand were stocked with trout. There is now a picnic area and other facilities here plus a museum of freshwater fish.

Rokeby (population 3500)
Across the Derwent River from Hobart, Tasmania's first apple exports were made from here. Rokeby has a village green and a few historic buildings still remain including the old St Matthew's Church. There are good beaches south of Rokeby at South Arm and good surfing at Clifton Beach.

Richmond (population 400)
Another of Tasmania's historic attractions the old town of Richmond is 27 km from Hobart and a convenient side-

trip on the way to Port Arthur. Originally founded in 1824 Richmond has many early buildings from that era including the fine old stone Richmond Bridge of that year. It's probably Australia's most photographed bridge as well as its oldest.

The classic photos of the bridge all show St John's Church framed by an arch. Built in 1836 it's Australia's oldest Catholic Church. The jail, dating from 1825 is now open to visitors and has a resident guide. Other old buildings from the 1820s and 30s include the court house, St Luke's Church, the old post office, the Bridge Inn, Saddlers Court (with craft displays), the Richmond Arms Hotel and several others.

South of Richmond, at the junction of the Tasman and Arthur Highways, Sorell (population 2200) is the centre of an agricultural area that at one time was one of the most important in Australia. In the Carlton and Dodges Ferry area there are many beaches which are a popular weekend escape from Hobart.

SOUTH OF HOBART

South of Hobart is the Huon Peninsula (a centre for Tasmania's apple growing industry), Bruny Island and the Hartz Mountains National Park. Around January and February there's work available picking apples and hops but a lot of people come here to look for work. The Channel Highway runs out of Hobart past the Taroona Shot Tower and through Kingston right around the Huon Peninsula.

Kettering (population 300)

Several times daily (more often during peak holiday periods) the car ferry crosses from the small port of Kettering to Bruny Island. Things to do and see in the vicinity include the good walking track along the Snug Falls Track and the nearby beach at Coningham, both to the north. South of Kettering there's a monument to the French navigator d'Entrecasteaux at Gordon.

Bruny Island (population 300)

The sparsely populated islands of North and South Bruny, joined by a narrow isthmus, were visited by Furneaux, Cook and Bligh but were named after Bruni d'Entrecasteaux who explored the area in 1792. The channel between the islands and mainland, D'Entrecasteaux Channel, also takes its name from him. On one of William (Mutiny on the Bounty) Bligh's visits to the island the first Tasmanian apple tree was said to have been planted here. There's an interesting little Bligh Museum (open daily) in Adventure Bay and nearby there's a memorial to early explorers. On South Bruny the lighthouse is the second oldest in Australia, it was built in 1836. A walking trail circumnavigates Mt Bruny on the southern peninsula.

Cygnet (population 700)

Port Cygnet, on which this small town stands, was named by d'Entrecasteaux for the many swans (cygne in French) seen on the bay. There are some good beaches in the area plus a winery four km out of town.

Huonville & South

Huon pine was first discovered near the busy small town of Huonville (population 1300). Today it's a centre for apple growing. A little further south is Franklin (population 500), also an apple

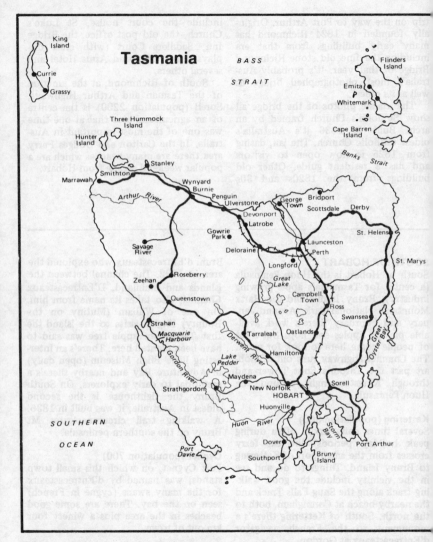

growing town although timber milling is the main activity here. Franklin was first settled in 1804, making it the oldest place in the Huon area. Continuing south through Port Huon brings you to Geeveston (population 900)

another timber town and also the jumping off point for trips into the wild Hartz Mountain National Park. Much of Australia's paper is produced at the Australian Paper Mills centre at nearby Hospital Bay.

Dover (population 400)

Further south on the Huon Highway this very attractive little fishing port has curious old houses, fine beaches and some excellent bushwalks in the vicinity. If you're heading further south this is the last chance to get provisions and petrol. Southport, 24 km beyond Dover, is the end of the main road. It's another pretty little town which has been here since the era of the whalers and sealers.

Hastings

The tiny town of Hastings is a popular tourist attraction due to the limestone caves about 10 km from the town and the scenic railway. There are daily guided tours around one of the caves. Just south of the Lune River, beyond Hastings, is the Ida Bay Railway which now operates as a tourist run on the seven km trip to Deep Hole.

TASMAN PENINSULA

The old penal settlement of Port Arthur, 150 km south-west of Hobart, is probably Tasmania's number one attraction. Originally built in 1830 to house all the prisoners from the colony's scattered jails it was finally abandoned in 1877. You can see the gloomy ruins of the guard house with its stone turrets, the prison and the interesting museum with records of the early settlement of the colony and prison tools and clothing. Ruins include the convict-designed church, the wheel-shaped 'model prison', the house of Irish rebel William Smith O'Brien and the restored lunatic asylum. On the Island of the Dead, in Port Arthur Bay, are the graves of 1769 prisoners who died while imprisoned here. Not one of the prisoners' graves are marked although there are 180 other graves of prison staff and military guards.

In mid-winter there may be just one tour per day around the settlement but the rest of the year there will probably be five or six, every day of the week except Thursday. The tours cost $2.50.

Eaglehawk Neck is at the narrow point of the isthmus to the Tasman Peninsula, 19 km north of the prison. Escapees were inevitably recaptured here unless they were very good swimmers because a line of ferocious guard

Tasman Peninsula

to Hobart

Arthur Hwy

Tasman Memorial

Cape Frederick Henderson

Dunalley

FORESTIER

PENINSULA

Norfolk Bay

Saltwater River

Tesselated Pavement

Eaglehawk Neck

Tasman Arch

Blow Hole

Nubeena

TASMAN PENINSULA

Cape Hauy

Port Arthur

Remarkable Cave

Munroe Bight

Maingon Bay

Cape Pillar

TASMAN SEA

0 5 10 15km

dogs were chained up right across the isthmus and armed guards were also on patrol. No escapee ever got away by land. Within a few km of the neck are several interesting natural features — Tasman's Arch, the Blowhole, the Devil's Kitchen and a stretch of tesselated pavement. There are some excellent walks around Port Arthur so it's easy to spend more than a day here.

On the way down the peninsula to Port Arthur you pass the Tasmanian Devil Park at Taranna. They have excellent displays of Tasmanian wildlife, particularly those evil looking Tasmanian devils. The park is open daily from 9 am to 5 pm and admission is $2.50.

Places to Stay
The *Port Arthur Youth Hostel* (tel 50 2311) is behind the motel in the town of Port Arthur. Nightly costs are $3. Motels and hotels in Port Arthur tend to be uncomfortably expensive. You can camp at the *Garden Point Caravan & Camping Park* for $5 for two people.

Getting There
The only way to day-trip to Port Arthur (if you haven't got your own transport) is on a TGTB tour from Hobart for $20. Otherwise two bus services operate, both requiring an overnight stop-over at Port Arthur.

Richardson's Coach Service (tel 65 2295) operates the mail bus from Hobart to Port Arthur. Departing from the rear of the tourist bureau at 7.45 am Monday to Friday it goes by the Bellerive roundabout (if you're staying at the youth hostel) about five minutes later. Arrival at Port Arthur is at 10.40 am and the fare is $5 single or $8 return. Return departures are at 10.40 am, arriving at Hobart 3 pm.

The alternative is the Peninsula Coach Service from the Tasmanian Redline Coach office (tel 34 6954) at 96 Harrington St. It departs five days a week at 4 pm and arrives at Port Arthur at 6 pm. The fare is $6 single or $11 return and return departures are at 7.45 am, arriving Hobart at 9.45 am.

EAST COAST & NORTH-EAST
The east coast, with its beaches and fishing, is probably the least visited region of Tasmania. Although exploration and settlement of the coast started soon after the establishment of Hobart it has always remained a quiet backwater. The largest town on the coast, St Helens, has a population of less than a thousand. It's quiet.

Buckland (200)
This tiny township was once a staging post for coaches, it's 61 km from Hobart. The old stone church of St John the Baptist, dating from 1846, has a stained glass window with an interesting history. The east window is said to come from 14th century Battle Abbey at the site of the Battle of Hastings in England. It was rescued from the abbey before Cromwell sacked it in the 17th century and somehow found its way to Tasmania.

Orford & Triabunna
Orford (population 350) is a popular little seaside resort surrounded by tall hills. A little further north the larger town of Triabunna (population 850) was once a whaling station early in the last century. It still has a busy fishing industry and is also the jumping off point for boat charters to neighbouring Maria Island.

Maria Island
Named by Dutch explorer Abel Tasman after the wife of the Batavia governor Van Diemen, Maria Island is a National Park today. It's very quiet (the only car on the island is used by the park rangers) and has plenty of wildlife and magnificent scenery, particularly the

cliffs on the north and east coasts. At one time the island was used as a penal settlement, actually predating Port Arthur. Later half-hearted efforts were made to produce wine here or to establish farms but today it's just a very untouched park. The tiny settlement of Darlington is very well preserved due to its isolation.

Swansea (population 400)
On Oyster Bay, at the mid-point between Hobart and Launceston via the east coast, there are many historic buildings in this old town including a log cottage dating back to the 1820s. 'Good Old Days' is a pioneer exhibit in the old Mechanic's Institute Building. It includes old farm equipment, the oldest car in Tasmania and a 'full size' billiards table which weighs a tonne!

Coles Bay & Freycinet National Park
The tiny town of Coles Bay (less than 200 population) is approached through the Hazards, 300 metre high hills of solid red granite. It serves as the gateway to the many good beaches, coves, cliffs, bays and walks of the Freycinet National Park. In the park Wineglass Bay has spectacular scenery and Moulting Lagoon is a breeding ground for black swans. There is a 27 km walking circuit of the park.

Bicheno (population 400)
This old whaling port on a grassy cape was first used by whalers in 1803. There are lookouts on the hills over the town, from which watch used to be kept for passing whales. Crayfishing is now a major occupation here. You can get out to Diamond Island, with its fairy penguins, at low tide while on the foreshore the Sealife Centre has a variety of fish. The youth hostel here is nicely situated on the beach.

St Mary's (population 700)
Situated 10 km inland and reached through the Elephant Pass, St Mary's is at the headwaters of the South Esk River which runs down to Launceston. On the coast nearby Falmouth is an historically interesting small town with some early convict built buildings and good beaches. From St Helens you make a fine descent through St Mary's Pass to St Helens. From St Mary's the Esk Main Road turns inland through Fingal, with a number of early historic buildings, to join the Midlands Highway at Conara.

St Helens (population 800)
The largest town on the east coast is a popular beach resort on George Bay. Once again fishing, particularly for crayfish, is a major business — you'll find good fresh fish in the restaurants here. From here you can make excursions to Beaumaris and Scamander, pleasant beach resorts back towards St Mary's. Or visit the fishing village of Binalong Bay or Sloop Rock or the St Columba Falls.

Gladstone
About 25 km off the main Tasman Highway between St Helens and Scottsdale, the tiny town of Gladstone is one of the few tin-mining centres still operating right up in the north-east corner of Tasmania. At one time there were a number of mining communities in the area and a large Chinese population. Today most of them are ghost towns or near ghost towns — like Boobyalla and Moorina.

Scottsdale (population 1800)
The major town in the north-east is a quiet place in a beautiful setting. Bridport (population 700) is a beach resort 21 km north on Bass Strait. There's a fine old 1839 homestead there. You can also get to the pine forests en route to Branxholm and the beaches of Tomahawk.

George Town (population 5300)

At the mouth of the Tamar River, George Town is one of Tasmania's earliest settlements, dating from 1811. Today it's a popular industrial and fruit growing centre. There's a popular beach at Low Head, five km north of the town.

Getting Around the East Coast

It's 358 km on the east coast route between Hobart and Launceston if you turn off the coast from St Mary's to Fingal and Avoca. If you continue up to St Helen's and Scottsdale it's 434 km. Further still if you go north to Bridport and George Town or branch off to the Tasman Peninsula and Port Arthur in the south.

Travelling by bus along this route involves a number of changes and it takes a couple of easy going days — longer if

the weekend intervenes. Tasmanian Redline Coaches operate Launceston-Scottsdale-Herric and Launceston-Conara-St Marys but along the coast you have to use a number of private bus companies. Check *Tasmanian Travelways* for the latest timetables and fares. Starting from Hobart there are about five companies operating overlapping services along this route. Fares and approximate travel times are Hobart-Swansea $7.90 to $9.25, 2½ to four hours; Swansea to St Marys $4.80, one to 2½ hours; St Marys to St Helens $1.80, one hour; St Helens to Winnaleah $3, two hours; Winnaleah to Launceston $6.50, three hours. Therefore the total fare is about $25 but you have to sit down with the timetables, a pen and a piece of paper to work out your schedule since the services and departures vary from day to day.

THE MIDLANDS

The rolling midlands of Tasmania have an almost English look about them due to the diligent efforts of early settlers who planted English trees and hedgerows. They set out to create an antipodean England and they certainly succeeded. It was the fertility and agricultural potential of the central part of the island that led, in large part, to Tasmania's rapid settlement and early prosperity. The growth of agriculture here was a clear contrast to the struggle early settlers in the Sydney area had faced. A string of solid little towns soon sprang up between Hobart and Launceston, either along the Midlands Highway or the alternative Lake Highway. The Midland Highway is one of the earliest routes on the island and using this road it's just 199 km from Hobart to Launceston.

Oatlands (population 600)

Once a dreaded hideout for bushrangers, Oatlands, 84 km north of Hobart, is in a popular fishing area and has many historic old buildings from the 1830s including the even earlier convict-built court house of 1829. North of town St Peter's Pass has hawthorn hedges cut and shaped to look like animals.

Ross (population 300)

This old coach staging post, 120 km from Hobart, was established in 1812 to protect travellers on the route between Hobart and Launceston. The convict-built Ross Bridge, while not as old as the Richmond Bridge, is said to be the best example of bridge building from that era still remaining. Like other classic early Tasmanian structures it was designed by John Lee Archer (see Stanley). Amongst other important early buildings in Ross is the restored

Scotch Thistle Inn which was originally built in 1826. It's now an expensive restaurant. The Beaufort Deer Park, six km from Ross, has native wildlife as well as deer and is open daily except Tuesday and Wednesday.

Campbelltown (population 900)
A further 12 km from Ross and 66 km south of Launceston, once again there are (ho hum) lots of early colonial buildings. They include the large brick and stone building known as The Grange, the Campbell Town Inn, Balmoral Cottage and St Luke's Church. All date from the late 1830s and early 1840s.

Bothwell (population 400)
On the alternative Lake Highway, Bothwell is 72 km north of Hobart and is a popular base for fishing on the lakes. Hardly surprisingly Bothwell also has the usual Tasmanian quota of historic buildings including a colonial museum in the Coffee Palace, the fine 1831 St Luke's Church and the restored 'Slate House' plus other old homesteads and mills in the vicinity.

Lake Country
The Lake Highway continues north through the Tasmanian lakes area, centre for the state's hydro-electric project. Miena, a tiny town on the southern tip of Great Lake, is a good base for visits to other lakes in this area. Poatina, south-west of Launceston, was the construction centre when the hydro-power stations were under construction and guided tours are available of the underground power station about five km away.

HYDRO-ELECTRIC POWER
Tasmania has the largest hydro-electric power system in Australia — it's larger than the far better known Snowy Mountain scheme in NSW and generates about 10% of Australia's total elect-

ric power output. Dam building for the hydro power station is, however, a subject of considerable controversy due to the great potential these dams have to harm the environment. The first hydro-electric dam was constructed on Great Lake in 1911 and subsequently the Derwent, Mersey, Forth and Gordon Rivers were also dammed. Visitors can inspect the power schemes and visit the Tungatinah, Tarraleah, Liapoorah Trevallyn power stations along the extensive Derwent scheme between Hobart and Queenstown.

The smaller schemes on the Mersey and Forth Rivers are close to the north-west coast and although not so large are much more spectacular than the Derwent system. The flooding of Lake Pedder raised the first outcry against uncontrolled damming of Tasmania's magnificent rivers and currently there is a major dispute over the projected damming of the Franklin and Lower Gordon Rivers. Construction of this series of dams would do irreparable damage to Australia's last great wild river and lose forever some of the most superb scenery in Australia. The majority of Tasmanians are opposed to the construction of these dams and if you can try to support the Tasmanian Wilderness Society in their brave fight against the powers of big business.

LAUNCESTON (population 65,000)

Tasmania's second city, Launceston is nearly as old as Hobart but it remains a sleepy, quiet little town. Settlements were established in the area in 1804 and the city was officially founded in 1805, at first named Patersonia. Launceston is on the upper reaches of the Tamar River, 64 km south of the Bass Strait and 200 km north of Hobart. Victoria, and its capital Melbourne, owes some debts to Launceston. It was from here that early settlers first went out to the ports along the Victorian coast and John Pascoe Fawkner, a founding father of Melbourne, was landlord of Launceston's Cornwall Hotel in 1835 when he introduced his plan to colonise Victoria. It is from Launceston in Cornwall, England that Launceston, Tasmania takes its name.

Information

The Tasmanian Government Tourist Bureau office (tel 31 5833) is on the corner of St John and Paterson Sts. The TAA office (tel 31 4411) and the Ansett office (tel 31 7711) are both on corners of George and York Sts. The Post Office is on the corner of Cameron and St John Sts. Yes, everything does seem to be on corners in Launceston. The Launceston Environment Centre, however, which is a good info source, is in Paterson St. The central section of Brisbane St, between Charles and St John Sts, is a pedestrian mall and the town centres around the mall. The main attractions are all within walking distance of the centre.

Cataract Gorge

Only a few minutes from the centre of Launceston the South Esk River cuts a deep canyon as it approaches its junction with the Tamar River. A 1½ km path on the north face of the gorge leads to a popular picnic and swimming area at First Basin. There's also a hiker's trail along the south face, it takes half an hour as against 10 minutes on the north side. A chairlift also operates across the gorge and a flock of magnificent peacocks lord it over the grounds around the tea house here. This is a popular spot for Devonshire teas! A good walking trail leads further up the gorge to the deserted ruins of the old hydro-electric power station.

Penny Royal Windmill

There's a beautifully reconstructed windmill at this motel/restaurant complex, together with a watermill of similar (1825) vintage. The buildings were originally at Barton and were moved here and reassembled, stone by stone. Admission is $1.25 to each mill or $2 to both. A restored tramway links the complex to the Penny Royal Gunpowder Mill at the old Cataract quarry where there is a foundry used for casting cannons and a model steam railway system. Entry costs are $3.95 and it's really a bit of a tourist rip-off.

Other

Launceston has been dubbed the 'garden city' and has plenty of parks to prove it. They include the City Park with a small zoo, the Royal Park on the South Esk River by the Tamar River junction and the Launceston Wildlife Sanctuary on Punch Bowl Rd. In the Royal Park the Queen Victoria Museum & Art Gallery has interesting exhibits on Tasmania's often unique wildlife and of Aboriginal artefacts as well as a Chinese joss house. On Tamar St at the Brisbane St junction, by the City Park, the Design Centre of Tasmania has a good display of modern Tasmanian craftsmanship. At 60 George St the Old Umbrella Shop was built in 1860 and is now operated by the National Trust as an information centre and gift shop.

There's a good view over the city from the Talbot Rd lookout, south-east of the centre. You can make river cruises from Royal Park, book through the tourist office.

Places to Stay

Hostels The *Launceston Youth Hostel* (tel 31 5839) is close to the centre at 138 St John St and it costs $4 a night. You're actually living in a house with the warden and his family although when it's busy they use another house as well, just up the street. Unfortunately not everybody gets on with the warden very well and this is generally rated as the most unpopular hostel in Tasmania. Tread gently if you stay here.

Guest Houses At *Ashton Gate* (tel 31 6180), 32 High St you get a substantial breakfast for your $11.50 per person but otherwise it's fairly dull. Just a few doors down at 22 High St the *Windmill Private Hotel* (tel 31 9337) costs $12 for a single, $10 each in a double but breakfast is extra. The *Rubina Joy Private Hotel* (tel 46 9900) is at 375 Hobart Rd and bed & breakfast costs $12 a single, $20 for a double.

Hotels Launceston has a quite amazing collection of hotels for a town its size; the cheapest ones, at around $12 per person, are usually not listed in the *Tasmanian Travelways* paper. They include the *Riverview* (tel 31 4857) at 43 Lower Charles St and the *Mowbray* (tel 26 1752) at 254 Invermay which both charge $12 for a bed & breakfast single, a bit over twice that for a double. The *Crown* (tel 31 4137) at 152 Elizabeth St costs $14 per person including breakfast while the *Enfield* (tel 31 4040) at 167 Charles St is the same price but room only.

The following hotels are all in the $15 to $16 bracket for a bed & breakfast single: *TRC* (tel 31 3424) at 131 Paterson St, the *Royal* (tel 31 2526) at 90 George St, the *Richmond* (tel 31 3302) at 32 Wellington St, the *St George* (tel 31 7277) at 119 St John St, and the *Star* (tel 31 9659) at 113 Charles St. In all these places doubles are in the $30 to $32 range.

Motels Despite its 'motel' tag the *Mews Mini-Motel* (tel 31 2861) is a little bit guest-house-like in that there are a couple of non self-contained rooms and you get an excellent breakfast included in the tariff. It's at 89 Margaret St, quite close to the centre, and costs $21/29 for singles/doubles which is good value in the motel field. Cheaper on paper, but then breakfast is not included, is the *Maldon* (tel 31 3979) at 32 Brisbane St which costs $20/28. It's another pleasant place to stay.

Launceston also has some holiday flats and other self-contained accommodation which may be worth checking. The *Frederick St Holiday Flat* (there's just one!) at 79 Frederick St (tel 31 8307) costs $18 per night for two and there's a three night minimum. A little way out at Mowbray *Barton Lodge* (tel 26 2581) is at 11-13 Barton St and costs $24 for two, $5 for each extra person. More central, the *Windmill Hill Flats* (tel 31 9337) at 22 High St costs $28 for a double, $4 for each extra person.

Camping There's a *Treasure Island Caravan Park* (tel 44 2600) in Glen Dhu St, Glen Dhu, just south of the central area of the city. Treasure Island is a chain of well-equipped sites which are a bit more expensive than the general run. Camping here costs $5.50 for two people and there are also on-site vans at $17 for two, $2 for each extra person.

Places to Eat

Launceston has a few more eating places than it used to but there's still rather a gap between the counter food/ pizzerias/Chinese cheapies and the

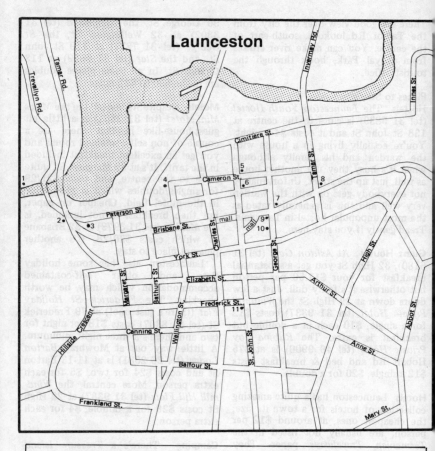

Launceston

1 Cataract Gorge
2 Gunpowder Mill
3 Penny Royal Mills
4 Museum & Art Gallery
5 Post Office
6 Tourist Bureau
7 Ansett
8 Tasmanian Design Centre
9 TAA
10 Tasmanian Redline Coaches
11 Youth Hostel

expensive steak houses and 'flashing out' places. Partly, some say, because the locals don't eat out very often!

Counter Meals There are, however, plenty of places for a good counter meal. The *TRC Hotel* at the gorge end of

Paterson St has a good selection of counter lunches and teas from $2 to $3. Other places to try with good counter food at lunch time or in the evening are the *Hotel Richmond* on the corner of York and Wellington Sts or the *Royal Oak* on the corner of Tamar and Brisbane Sts.

The *Batman Fawkner* in Cameron St has a carvery where you can have as much as you can eat for $6.50 at lunchtime (at night it's a la carte). The *Launceston Hotel's* counter meals are more expensive than most others and the food is not very good.

Bottom End For cheap food during the day *Bobbies* in Quadrant Mall is the place to go — pleasant and low-priced. There are quite a few Italian places of the eat here and take-away variety. *Akka's*, on Brisbane St opposite Kingsway, has good pizzas but the *Capri Pizza Restaurant* at 76 St John St has even better pizzas (around $3 to $4) while the *Pizza House* on George St also has excellent pizzas.

Other places are the *Gobble n' Go* on George St and *Dominic's Pizza Parlour* at 196 York St. Sweet & sour fans can look for the *Canton* at 203 Charles St. The *Sorrento* on Charles St is cheap and straightforward with food in the steak or schnitzel line.

More Expensive *Clayton's Coffee Shoppe* on Quadrant Mall is a little pricey but very nice. They have mouthwatering cheesecake, etc, as well as meals. The *Winton* on York St has steaks and other main courses for around $5. *Pierre's* at 88 George St is also worth trying but prices soon start to jump up in Launceston.

At 107 Brisbane St, *Dicky White's* is in the *Launceston Hotel*, which can lay claim to being the longest running hotel in the country. Dicky White was a convicted highwayman who went straight when he finished his time down under, became a colourful figure in early Launceston and founded the hotel. The bistro bearing his name serves up rather ordinary steak and salad for around $8 but the 'Tasmanian deep-dish apple pie' is positively out-of-sight.

On the corner of York and Kingsway

the *Old Butter Factory* has a very similarly priced steakhouse style menu but here the emphasis is on do-it-yourself. You pick your hunk of steak from the display then grill it yourself and heap the salads on board from the selection on the table. Both Dicky White's and the Old Butter Factory are licensed but wine is very reasonably priced. At Dicky White's you buy your booze at the hotel's bottle shop prices. A carafe of quite reasonable wine at the Old Butter Factory will cost you just $4. Starters and desserts are also reasonably priced.

The Top End Launceston has quite a few places in this category. They include *Rowels* in George St, *Sals* in Brisbane Arcade, *Aces* in Wellington St and *Old Masters* on the corner of Elizabeth and St John Sts. The *Owls Nest* in the olde worlde Penny Royal Watermill has main courses in the $9 to $10 bracket plus very pleasant surroundings.

Entertainment

Lots of pub music around Launceston. *Rock Central* in the *Hotel Tasmania* (entrance from Elizabeth St) has a band or disco Thursday to Saturday. *Nick's Bar*, in the same hotel but enter from Charles St, sometimes has country, folk or rock by local musicians. *Rosie's*, in a nice old building on the corner of George and Elizabeth Sts, has a good guitarist on Tuesday and Wednesday, rock or jazz from Thursday to Saturday. Drinks are rather expensive and it's a bit fussy about clothes. If you've got wheels there's folk music at the *Country Club Hotel* in Longford on the first Saturday night of each month.

In the disco department there's a crowded disco from Thursday to Saturday at the *Old Tudor Inn* at Prospect. *Ragines* is an expensive disco at the casino (free admission Sunday to Thursday though) while *Josephine's* in the *Launceston Hotel* is horribly pretentious and open Wednesday to Saturday. The *Butter Factory* has a disco from Tuesday to Saturday after 9 pm.

Many Launceston venues have an unfortunate tendency to be rather fussy about what you're wearing. If you're staying at the youth hostel beware that you don't get locked out at night, whatever the warden might say about the door being open.

Getting There

Air Ansett and TAA both have a number of flights to Launceston from Sydney and Melbourne daily, some flights from Sydney go direct. From Melbourne it takes just under an hour, from Sydney about 1½ hours direct. Fares are from Melbourne $89 ($67 standby), from Sydney $146 ($109 standby) on the direct flights but $172 on the flights via Melbourne. You can fly TAA or Ansett between Hobart and Launceston for $61 but with H C Sleigh Airlines it's just $43. See the Tasmania introductory Getting Around section for details of air fares around Tasmania and to the Bass Strait islands with H C Sleigh and Air Tasmania.

Bus Tasmania Redline Coaches have a network of services to and from Launceston. To or from Hobart there are three services daily ($10), Burnie is four times daily via Devonport ($9.50), Devonport ($6.50). There are also three services daily to George Town, a one hour trip for $3.50. Buses run to Bell Bay, the north-east coast and St Mary's. Other bus companies also operate between Hobart and Launceston and on to the north-west. See the Hobart section for details of the Hobart-Launceston east coast trip.

Road Launceston is 199 km from Hobart by the direct route, 434 km by the east coast route. It's 89 km from Launceston to Devonport, another 54 km on to Burnie.

Getting Around

Bus The MTT run the local buses and a $1 all-route all-day bus ticket is available from the tourist office, from Teagues at 102 Brisbane St and from the MTT office at 168 Wellington St. Most routes do not operate in the evening and Sunday services can be very sketchy if they operate at all. The Punch Bowl bus leaves from Brisbane St opposite Kingsway but there's no evening service and next to none on a Sunday. A free bus map is available with a route map on the back.

If you're hitching to Devonport and the north-west catch a Prospect bus from outside the Launceston Bank for Savings on St John St. For Hobart and the east coast catch a Franklin Village bus near the HEC on St John St. The Tasman Highway route to the east coast is longer and more scenic but also harder. For this route catch a Waverly bus from opposite Quadrant Mall on St John St. There is no bus service north of George Town on the Tasman Highway apart from the twice daily service to Bridport. There's no traffic either, especially to Tomahawk.

Car & Bicycle See the Tasmania introductory Getting Around section for information on renting cars and bicycles. The major car rental firms all have offices either in Launceston or at Launceston Airport. Jalopy's office is at 332 Hobart Rd (tel 44 8004).

Airport Bus fare out to Launceston Airport on the Tasmanian Redline bus is $2. A taxi would be about $8.

Tours Day and half-day tours operate around Launceston and the northern area. There are also river cruises on the *MV Goondooloo* from the Royal Park Ferry Terminal.

AROUND LAUNCESTON

There are a number of interesting old houses in the vicinity including Franklin House, seven km to the south. It was built by convicts for an early settler and the classic, two-storey Georgian-style house is classified by the National Trust and is open daily, entry is $1.50. At Hadspen, 13 km from Launceston, Entally dates from 1820 and has fine gardens and sheds full of old farm machinery and vehicles.

The National Trust's own property, Clarendon, is at Nile, near Evandale and 18 km south of Launceston. Built in the late 1830s this is one of the grandest Georgian mansions in Australia. Admission is $1.50 and it's open daily but closed in July. Evandale also has Pleasant Banks, an old homestead (open by private arrangement only) plus Horseless Carriage, a colonial store with a miniature car display.

Longford, 27 km south of Launceston, is a National Trust Classified village and Brickenden is another fine old mansion located there. It dates from 1838, is open daily and entry is 50c. The great number of fine, early houses in Tasmania is indicative of the prosperity the new colony quickly developed from its rich agricultural potential. If you've not yet exhausted your appetite for stately homes then Launceston can still find several more to offer. Westbury is 42 km south-west and here the White House, dating from 1841-42, has an antique collection, vintage cars and old carriages. There's also a real village green in Westbury. At Cressy, 33 km south-west, you can visit the old colonial Palmerston House while in George Town, 52 km north, the Grove was built in the 1820s and is yet another lovingly restored old colonial

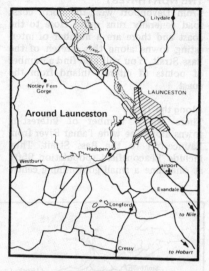

home (daily, closed during July).

As a change from all the old colonial mansions and homesteads you can stroll through the pleasant rain forests of Notley Fern Gorge, 24 km north-east of Launceston. If you continued up the Cataract Gorge you'd come to Trevallyan Dam where the Hydro-Electricity Commission has a pleasant garden and picnic spot at the storage dam. The Longford Wildlife Park is 14 km from the city on the Pateena road. The park has deer, wallabies, kangaroos and wildfowl and is open 10 am to 5 pm except on Mondays and Fridays.

At Lilydale, 27 km to the north-east of Launceston, there are many pleasant walks, picnic areas, a couple of waterfalls and even a local winery. The small town (population 300) stands at the foot of 1187 metre Mt Arthur and there are some scenic walks on the mountain.

THE NORTH-WEST

From Devonport west the north coast road generally runs quite close to the coast and there are a number of interesting towns along this stretch of the Bass Strait. You will also find a number of points of interest inland from the coast.

Along the Tamar

There are a number of interesting towns along the wide Tamar River from Launceston to the Bass Strait. They include Beaconsfield (population 950), at one time a small gold mining centre

called Cabbage Tree Hill, there are still a few old mining buildings standing. Beauty Point (population 1000) was once a port for Beaconsfield and still functions as a port today.

On the mouth of the river Kelso and Greens Beach are popular beach resorts, Kelso dates back to the earliest days of Tasmania's European settlement. Port Sorrell (population 800) is near Devonport, a pleasant little resort town and the oldest on the north-west coast, but unlike many Tasmanian towns few of its historic old buildings have survived.

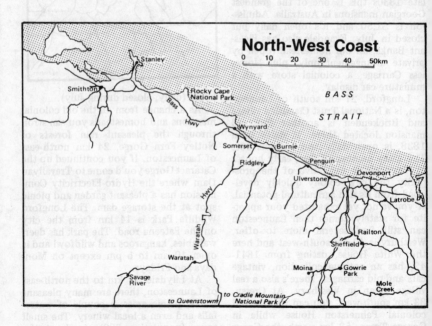

DEVONPORT (population 20,000)

Situated on the Mersey River, Devonport is the arrival point for the vehicle ferry from Melbourne. This is one of the larger towns in Tasmania but it doesn't have a great deal of interest in its own right apart from a couple of museums and Tiagarra, the Aboriginal cultural centre. Otherwise it's more of a base to visit other places. Or an arrival or departure point for Tasmania of course.

Information

The Tasmanian Government Tourist Bureau (tel 24 1526) has its office at 18 Rooke St on the corner of King St and there is also an office at the Ferry Terminal in East Devonport. Phone 24 1431 for the after hours 'dial-a-bed' service. There's a Wilderness Info Centre in the Hub Arcade off Rooke St Mall. You'll find a laundrette at 157 Rooke St (the Victoria Parade end).

Tiagarra

The Tasmanian Aboriginal Culture & Art Centre, known as Tiagarra, is on Mersey Bluff at the north side of Devonport. It's open daily and admission is 80c. The word means 'keep' in the Tasmanian Aboriginal language and the centre is intended to preserve remnants of their culture. Tiagarra consists of a centre showing aspects of the now extinct culture of Tasmania's Aboriginals plus a rare collection of Aboriginal rock carvings. The signs and patterns carved in the rocks here were discovered by a Devonport school teacher in 1929.

Museums

On Gloucester Avenue the Maritime Museum has models of early ships that plied to Tasmania plus other interesting nautical items. It's open Tuesday to Sunday from 1 to 4.30 pm in winter and from 10 am to 4.30 pm in summer (December to April). Admission is 60c.

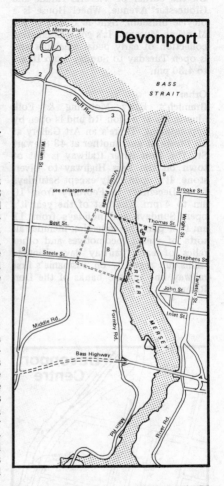

Devonport

BASS STRAIT

MERSEY RIVER

Mersey Bluff

Bluff Rd

William St

Victoria Parade

Brooke St

Wright St

Best St

Thomas St

Steele St

Stephens St

John St

Tarleton St

Inlet St

Middle Rd

Formby Rd

Bass Highway

River Rd

Main Rd

see enlargement

1 Tiagarra
2 Bluff Caravan Park
3 Maritime Museum & Wheel House
4 Youth Hostel
5 Terminal Caravan Park
6 Ferry
7 Bass Strait Ferry Terminal
8 City Centre
9 To Don River Tramway

On the corner of Victoria Parade and Gloucester Avenue, Wheel House is a bicycle museum, right nextdoor to the Maritime Museum. It's got a fascinating collection of early pedal machines and is open Tuesday to Sunday from 10 am to 4.30 pm.

Other

Bramich's Early Motoring & Folk Museum is at 3 Don Rd and is open by appointment. There's an Art Gallery at 46 Steele St and another at 43 Stewart St. The Don River Railway is out of town on the Bass Highway to Ulverstone. It's open daily except Saturdays from December to February from 10 am to 4 pm. The rest of the year it's open Sundays and holidays from 11 am to 4 pm. The collection includes all sorts of steam locomotives and other relics of early railway days. Vintage trains run regularly on Tasmania's first railway line on the banks of the Don River.

Around Devonport

From Braddon's Lookout, near Forth to the west of Devonport you have a fine view along the coast. On the Rubicon River estuary, just 20 km northeast of Devonport, is Port Sorell, a popular seaside resort with a wildlife reserve, picturesque Squeaking Point and the wide sands of Hawley Beach. Only a few km south of Devonport at Latrobe there is a scenic pathway which follows the winding Mersey River through Bell's Parade. Latrobe also has a hydro-electric project.

Places to Stay

Hostels The *Devonport Youth Hostel* (tel 24 7197) is in a wonderful old building at 26 Victoria Parade. It costs $4.

Hotels & Guest Houses *Cara* (tel 24 4364) is a pleasant little guest house at 22 Victoria Parade, before the youth hostel if you're coming from town. Singles/doubles are $12/20 with continental breakfast but, unfortunately, it was up for sale as this goes to press and may no longer be in operation. *Limani Tourist Lodge* (tel 24 4928) at 57 Percy St costs $10 per person room-only. At 44 MacFie St the *Tradewinds Private Hotel* (tel 24 1719) is $12 single then $8 for each additional person, room-only.

There is not much in the way of cheap hotels here but you could try the *Tamahere* (tel 24 1898) at 34 Best St where you'll pay $12 single, $6 for each extra person, room-only. The *Formby* (tel 24 1601) is at 82 Formby Rd and the cheapest singles/doubles are $17/

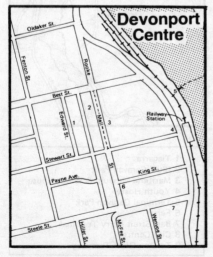

Devonport Centre

1 Tasmanian Redline Coaches
2 Ansett
3 TAA
4 Post Office
5 Ferry to East Devonport
6 Tourist Bureau
7 RAC

26 including breakfast. Both these hotels are very central.

Motels & Holiday Flats The *Sports Centre Lodge* (tel 24 4109) at 34 Forbes St costs $16 for two, $5 for each extra person. *Shoreline Holiday Units* (tel 27 8185) at 3 Brooke St is $18 for two, only $1 for each extra person. The *Mersey Bluff Lodge* (tel 24 5289) at 247 Williams St is very good but a bit more expensive at $28 for two, $4 for each extra person. *Edgewater Motor Inn* (tel 27 8441) is at 2 Thomas St, East Devonport, three km from the centre. Singles are $22 to $25, doubles $26 to $29.

Camping The *Mersey Bluff Caravan Park* (tel 24 2193) is out at the Bluff by Tiagarra and camping costs $3 for two. At the *Terminal Caravan Park* (tel 27 8794) in Terminal Park Rd, East Devonport, the cost is the same. The Terminal site also has on-site vans for $16 single, $2 for each extra person.

Devonport Caravan Park (tel 27 8886) on Caroline St, East Devonport costs $3.50 for two to camp, $16 for an on-site van for two, $1 for each extra person. *Shoreline Caravan Park* (tel 27 8794) at 1-3 Brooke St, East Devonport costs $3.50 for two to camp and has on-site vans also at around $16 for two.

Places to Eat
Apart from counter meals in the pubs there's really just a few coffee lounges and take-aways. *Napoli* in the Mall is a cafe-style place which serves morning and afternoon teas and lunch dishes for around $4 but it closes at 4.30 pm. The *Tamahere* at 34 Best St, the *Elimatta* at 12 Victoria Parade and the *Formby* at 82 Formby Rd all have counter meals for around $3 to $5.

Entertainment
The *Tamahere* at 34 Best St has a disco from Thursday to Saturday from 8.30

pm. Admission is $2 on Thursday, $3 Friday and Saturday and the usual Tasmanian no-denims rules apply. *Joo's Disco* at the *Elimatta* at 12 Victoria Parade runs on Wednesday, Friday and Saturday and is similarly priced. *City Limits* is a nightclub on King St.

Getting There
Air Between Ansett and East-West Airlines there are about half a dozen flights a day between Melbourne and Devonport. Using F27s the flight takes about one hour 15 minutes direct, a bit longer if the flight operates via Wynyard (Burnie). The fare is $75 or $57 standby. You can also fly from Devonport to King Island ($49), Launceston ($17), or Wynyard ($30) with Air Tasmania or H C Sleigh Airlines.

Ferry See the introductory Tasmania Getting There section for full details on the ferry service between Melbourne and Devonport. From Devonport the ferry departs at 7.30 pm on Sunday, Tuesday and Thursday. If you have a car it must be there between 5.30 and 6.30 pm. If you're on foot embarkation is between 6 and 7.15 pm although the terminal is open earlier if you have nowhere to go.

Bus Tasmanian Redline Coaches have four services a day to Launceston and the fare is $6.50. There is no public transport to the caves around Mole Creek — sometimes there are taxi trips organised from Devonport but they rarely get enough people in winter and in any case it's not cheap. See the Cradle Mountain-Lake St Clair section for details on getting there from Devonport.

Getting Around
Morse's Motors run a local bus service but it's so limited you might as well forget it. The buses run from the corner of Rooke and Stewart Sts to East

Devonport, North Devonport via Mersey Bluff and to West Devonport. Fortunately most places are within walking distance anyway. It's a pleasant stroll along the waterfront to most of Devonport's attractions.

There's a ferry across the Mersey (remember the song?!) which operates daytime only from Monday to Thursday and in the evening too on Friday and Saturday. There are no services on

Sunday and public holidays. The fare is 35c, on Saturdays 40c. Don't confuse it with the Bass Strait ferry from East Devonport, very nearby.

The major car rental firms all have offices in Devonport but Jalopy (tel 26 1490) is probably the cheapest in town. You can hire bicycles from Hire-a-Bike (tel 28 6234) — 10-speeds are $8, tandems $16, plus a $10 deposit.

DEVONPORT TO BURNIE
Ulverstone (population 9000)
Only 19 km west of Devonport, at the mouth of the Leven River, is the business centre for the rich agricultural area around here. There are some good beaches particularly at Leith and Turners Beach. You can make an interesting round trip from Ulverstone to the Leven Canyon where a 20-minute walk takes you through some superb scenery. The 105 km circuit takes you out through Sprent, Castra and Nietta to the canyon near Black Bluff (1340 metres) and back via Preston, Gunns Plains and North Motton. There are limestone caves at Gunns Plains which are usually open during the summer months.

Penguin (population 2500)
Further along the coast Penguin is pleasantly situated on three bays with good swimming beaches. There are excellent views from the 465-metre summit of Mt Montgomery, five km from Penguin. Penguin also has a couple of National Trust classified churches. If you're driving between Devonport and Ulverstone don't take the new road, the scenic old Bass Highway, running closer to the coast, offers some fine views of the coastline and across to the small islands known as the Three Sisters. On these islands and also along the coast there is prolific birdlife.

BURNIE (population 20,000)
Tasmania's third largest city is 148 km from Launceston on the shores of Emu Bay. Paper production is the major industry here. In the High St, behind the Law Courts, is Burnie's Pioneer Village Museum, a re-creation of turn of the century commercial activities. It's open Monday to Friday from 10 am to 5 pm and on weekends from 1.30 to 5 pm. Admission is $1. In Burnie Park the Burnie Inn is the oldest building in the

town, it was moved here from its original location and is open during the summer months.

There are a number of waterfalls and viewpoints in the Burnie area including Roundhill Lookout, Fern Glade, just three km from the centre, and Guide Falls, 16 km out. The Emu Bay Railway is the only private railway system in the state, it runs to Rosebery on the west coast and railway enthusiasts should visit the 'Loco Bar' of the Burnie Town House Motor Hotel to learn more about the railway's history.

Information

The Tasmanian Government Tourist Bureau (tel 30 2224) is at 48 Cattley St and is open 8.45 am to 5 pm Monday to Friday and 9 to 11 am on Saturday and public holidays. TAA, for East-West, are on the corner of Cattley and Mount St (tel 31 6222). Ansett (tel 31 5677) are on the corner of Wilmott and Mount. There's a good noticeboard in the Electric Jug snack bar. At 25 Ladbrooke St there's a laundromat which is open every day.

Places to Stay

There is no youth hostel in Burnie, the nearest one is 19 km away in Wynyard. At the *Bay View* (tel 31 2711) at 15 Marine Terrace you can get bed & breakfast for $13 per person while the *Club* (tel 31 2244) at 14 Mount St costs $13 for room-only. Hotels include the *Regent* (tel 31 1933) at 26 North Terrace and the *Burnie Hotel* (tel 31 1922) at 27 Marine Terrace, both with singles for $12 and breakfast for an additional $3. The *Burnie* costs $22 for a room-only double.

Three km west on the Bass Highway at Cooee there's a *Treasure Island* campsite. Camping costs $5 for two while on-site vans are $17 for two or self-contained flats are $24.

Places to Eat

Burnie is short on places to eat — especially on Sundays when the town is very quiet. The *Beach Hotel* on the corner of North Terrace and Wilson St does counter lunches and teas from Monday to Saturday (12 noon to 1.30 pm and 6 to 8.30 pm). Above Fitzgeralds there's a *Napoli*, similar hours and meals to the one in Devonport. At 54 Cattley St, opposite Circular Head Motors, the *Rivoli* is open every day

until... possibly late. It does takeaways and sit-down grill meals for around $4 to $6. You can also try the Electric Jug snack bar.

Entertainment

There's a disco every Sunday to Saturday at the Burnie Hotel from 4.30. Webb Brothers in the corner of Mount and Cattley Sts is a good record shop.

Getting There

Air Ansett and East-West Airlines fly to Wynyard, about 20 km from Burnie, rail times a day from Melbourne. Some flights go via a multi-zone direct. The direct flight time is just over an hour, $97 and the cost is $73 on a Saturday.

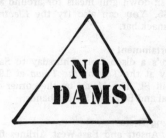

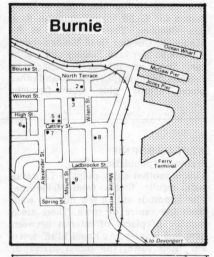

1	Tourist Bureau
2	Webster Travel
3	Ansett
4	TAA (East-West agents)
5	Tourist Bureau
6	Pioneer Village Museum
7	Circular Head Motor Services
8	Post Office
9	Tasmanian Redline Coaches

until reasonably late. It does take-aways and sit-down grill meals for around $4 to $5. You can also try the *Electric Jug* snack bar.

Entertainment
There's a disco from Thursday to Saturday at the *Top of the Town* at 195 Mount St. The *Menai* on the corner of Menai and Edwards Sts has bands.

Getting There
Air Ansett and East-West Airlines fly to Wynyard, about 20 km from Burnie, several times a day from Melbourne. Some flights go via Burnie, some direct. The direct flight time is just over an hour by F27 and the cost is $73 or $55 standby.

Bus There are four buses daily to Launceston for $9.50 with Tasmanian Redline Coaches. Their office is at 93 Mount St. Circular Head Motor Services run out to Wynyard, Stanley and Smithton. There are infrequent services to Penguin, Wynyard, Ulverstone and other places nearby plus more frequent

services to Somerset.

Rail The Emu Bay railway service only takes passengers if it is not carrying explosives. It is also sometimes used for special holiday runs. It runs about twice a week, leaving around 12.30 pm on the way to Roseberry and returning about 4.30 pm, getting in to Burnie between 8 and 9 pm. There's no time to look around Roseberry (unless you want to stay for three or four days!) so it's really just a train enthusiast's trip. If the trip back is in other than daylight saving time it will be mostly in the dark and the lights flicker too much to read! Still, travellers have reported managing to ride part way in the driver's cab. Phone 312 822 for information on the train, round trip fare is about $10.

Getting Around
Local buses are run by MTT and, as in Launceston, you can get an unlimited travel, all-day ticket. There are no bus services in the evenings or on weekends though.

WEST OF BURNIE
Wynyard (population 4500)
This is another entry point to Tasmania with regular flights from Melbourne. The airport is only a few minutes walk from the centre of town. There are a number of places of interest between here and Stanley. At Fossil Bluff, seven km from town, the oldest marsupial fossil found in Australia was unearthed; it's beyond the Wynyard Golf Course. Table Cape has a lighthouse and spectacular views along the coast. Continuing west you'll find one of the best beaches on the entire north coast at Boat Harbour, 11 km from Wynyard. A further seven km along is Sisters Beach where the National Park contains

aboriginal caves. About 31 km from Wynyard, at about the mid-point between there and Stanley, is the small Rocky Cape National Park. There are some excellent short walks in the park — get a copy of the *Let's Talk About Rocky Cape* brochure. An 85 km pipeline runs from Savage River to a bulk loading facility at Port Latta, beyond Rocky Cape. Iron ore is pumped down this pipeline as a slurry and then pelletised and shipped from here to Japan.

Stanley (population 700)
This tiny town is one of the most picturesque and historically interesting in Tasmania. This was the original site for the British based Van Dieman's Land

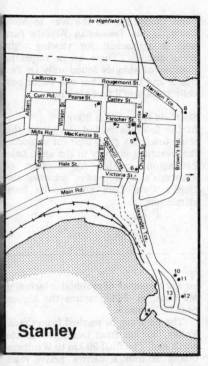

Stanley

1 The Rectory (1842)
2 St James Presbyterian Church (1855)
3 St Paul's Church of England (1880)
4 Stanley Discovery Centre
5 Plough Inn (1842)
6 Union Hotel (1849)
7 Commercial Hotel (1842)
8 Old Stanely Cemetery
9 To the Nut
10 Bay View Hotel (1849)
11 PM J A Lyon's birthplace
12 Poet's Cottage
13 Customs House
14 Old Wharf

Company headquarters and from its wharf whalers and sailing ships used to operate in the Bass Strait. Modern fishing boats, seeking crayfish and sharks, still operate from Stanley today. The old fishing port is dominated by the extraordinary rock formation known as 'the Nut'. Originally sighted by Bass and Flinders during their 1798 circumnavig-

ation of Australia it's a pleasant climb to the top of the huge rock outcrop.

Stanley has many interesting old buildings and it's worth picking up a walking tour map from the Discovery Centre on Church St which contains an amusing little museum. There's a particularly fine old bluestone customs house built in 1843 plus three solid old hotels from the 1840s (the Plough Inn of 1843 is open for inspection, the Union Hotel still does counter lunches). Stanley's old cemetery has many interesting graves including that of John Lee Archer, the architect who designed many of Stanley's old buildings among them the customs house. His home is known as Poet's Cottage.

Smithton (population 3235)
After Smithton, 22 km west of Stanley, the road bends away from the coast. At the end of Massey St there's a look-out tower on Tier Hill.

INLAND

Behind the coastal strip the Great Western Tiers rise up into Tasmania's central mountains and the Cradle Mountain National Park. There are some interesting and scenically attractive spots in this area.

Deloraine (population 1800)
Inland and west of Launceston this picturesque town has a number of interesting old buildings including the old Folk Museum & Cider Bar. There's also a small Military Museum in the town. Out of town you can visit the Bower-

bank Mill Gallery, just two km away. There are also a number of waterfalls in the area including the Montana, Meander and Liffey Falls.

Mole Creek (population 300)
Beyond Deloraine there are a number of limestone caverns in the vicinity of Mole Creek. They include the interesting Marakoopa Cave with its glow-worms, seven km out, and the smaller King Solomon Cave, a further two km away. Mole Creek is a centre for production of Tasmania's leatherwood honey which is produced by bees from the blossoms of the leatherwood tree. Two km be-

yond Chudleigh, on the way to Mole Creek, is the Tasmanian Wildlife Park with a noctarium for viewing night going animals. There are a surprising number of animals found only in Tasmania and this park has one of the best collections you'll find anywhere.

Sheffield (population 800)
In the foothills behind Devonport this small town is a good base for exploring the beautiful country in the area. Lake Barrington, created by another of Tasmania's hydro-power schemes and Devil's Gate Dam are popular local attractions.

CRADLE MOUNTAIN — LAKE ST CLAIR NATIONAL PARK
The 85 km walk from Waldheim to glacial Lake St Clair in the Cradle Mountain — Lake St Clair National Park is one of the finest bushwalks in Australia although walkers should be prepared for often viciously changeable weather. This is the largest park in Tasmania with magnificent scenery, fine fishing and also good opportunities for rock climbing. The walk takes five or six days at an easy pace but it's quite possible to spend longer if you want to make diversions off the track.

The park owes much to an Austrian, Gustav Weindorfer, who fell in love with the area and in 1912 built Waldheim Chalet (waldheim means 'forest home' in German) at the northern end of what was to later become the national park. The 126,000 hectare park provides a wide variety of terrain and shelters an equally wide range of Tasmania's flora and fauna. The north end of the park is dominated by Cradle Mountain while in the south you find the deep, 17 km long Lake St Clair. Within the park boundar-

ies are a number of mountains including Mt Ossa, at 1617 metres the highest peak in Tasmania.

The park can be reached from Cradle Valley, 95 km from Devonport at the north end. The final 30 km to Waldheim Chalet is over a narrow gravel road. From the south Lake St Clair is reached by a six km gravel road off the Lyell Highway at Derwent Bridge. The wallabies that hang around the site here at Cynthia Bay are very tame and will come to you to beg for food; they've discovered that park visitors are an easy touch. The third access route to the park is along the Arm River walking track coming in to the park from the east.

The best time to walk the Overland Track is during the summer when the flowering plants are most prolific and the weather is most predictable. Spring and autumn also have their attractions and you can even walk the track in winter, if you're well prepared and experienced. Even in summer there can be sudden blizzards so adequate clothing and equipment are essential. The short

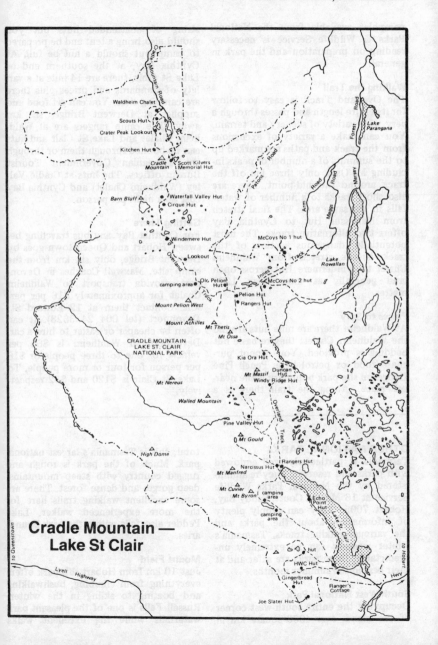

**Cradle Mountain —
Lake St Clair**

pamphlet available from the National Parks & Wildlife Service is necessary reading on preparation and the park in general.

Walking the Trail

The Overland Track is easy to follow for its entire length and passes through a very wide variety of scenery and terrain. You can make a variety of excursions from the track and paths are marked up to the summits of a number of peaks including Mt Ossa, only three km off the track around the mid-point. There are also short tracks to a number of waterfalls in the same area. The final stretch from Narcissus Hut to Cynthia Bay offers two alternative tracks. The most potentially dangerous section of the track is the stretch from Waldheim Chalet to Windermere Hut across open land generally at more than 1200 metres.

Places to Stay

At Waldheim there are nine huts around the Waldheim Chalet; they're basic but bedding is provided. You cannot purchase food or petrol here; Pencil Pine Lodge on the park boundary is the nearest place. Along the trail there is a string of unattended huts but you should also bring a tent and be prepared to camp out should a hut be full. At Cynthia Bay, at the southern end of Lake St Clair, there are 14 huts at a variety of standards and prices plus there are camping sites. You can get food and supplies at Derwent Bridge, six km away. The camp rangers are at Waldheim Chalet and Lake St Clair and huts can be booked through them or through the Tasmanian Government Tourist Bureau offices. The huts at Cradle Valley (Waldheim Chalet) and Cynthia Bay cost $6 a night per person.

Getting There

For Cynthia Bay any bus travelling between Hobart and Queenstown goes by Derwent Bridge, only six km from the camp site. Maxwell Coaches in Devonport provide transport to Waldheim Chalet for approximately $16 per person. Contact them at 12 Edward St, Devonport (tel 004 24 3628). It can often be cheaper or easier to hire a car. Devonport to Waldheim is $60 per vehicle for one to three people or $16 per person for four or more people. To Lake St Clair is $120 and $32 respectively.

OTHER NATIONAL PARKS

Tasmania is particularly well endowed with parks and reserves. They're administered by the National Parks Wildlife Service at 16 Magnet Court, Sandy Bay, Hobart 7005. They can supply plenty of information about the parks and the various walking tracks. Tasmania's winter weather can be extremely unpredictable, these parks are safer and at their best in the summer months.

South-West National Park

Occupying the entire south-west corner of the island, over 4000 square km in total, this is Tasmania's largest national park. Much of the park is rough and rugged country with steep mountains, deep gorges and dense forest. There are some excellent walking trails here for the more experienced walker. Lake Pedder also falls within the park boundaries.

Mount Field

Just 10 km from Hobart this park offers everything from climbing, bushwalking and boating to skiing in the winter. Russell Falls is one of the pleasant park waterfalls while the excellent walks include the popular Lyrebird Walk.

Hartz Mountain

South-west of Hobart this rugged park has snow-capped peaks (in winter) including the 1255 metre Hartz Peak. There are also some beautiful high altitude lakes.

Other Parks

Near Queenstown, Frenchman's Cap National Park is dominated by the unusual 'capped' mountain which gives it its name. Maria Island and Freycinet are both parks on the east coast of Tasmania. Fairy penguins breed on islands off Port Sorell near the mouth of the Tamar in the north. State reserves also include limestone caves, the Gordon River, various Aboriginal sites and a number of other natural features.

QUEENSTOWN (population 4500)

Situated 254 km north-west of Hobart this is the largest town on the coast. The final winding descent into the town is a stark reminder that the problems of pollution are not new — the surrounding hills are totally denuded of vegetation; by 1900 uncontrolled pollution from the early copper smelters had killed all the vegetation that had not already been cut down to feed the furnaces. The rocks then took on dramatic colour stains although since the cleaning up of the smelting process in 1922 vegetation has very gradually started to grow back. The road from the Derwent Valley to Queenstown is scenic and often quite spectacular.

There were once two mining operations in the Queenstown area — the Mount Lyell company in Queenstown, which still continues, and its rival the North Lyell company only a few km away at Linda. Tin and copper were first discovered here in 1879 and 1883, prompting the west coast's mine rush. Gormanston, six km from Queenstown, was the original mining site. Today you pass the derelict buildings that are all that remain of Linda as you descend Mount Owen into Queenstown. The Linda deposits had quickly run out and the mines were closed but Queenstown's deposits of copper, lead and tin plus later finds of iron and zinc are low grade but in massive quantities.

At the height of their rivalry the two companies each built railway lines down to Macquarie Harbour. The Mount Lyell line reached the harbour at Regatta Point near Strahan while the North Lyell line ran through Crotty (named after the mine manager) to Kelly's Basin, also on Macquarie Harbour but much further up. After the closure of the mine the line was torn up but on a trail bike or with four-wheel drive you can still drive down part of the old line and a magnificent railway bridge still crosses the fast flowing King River.

Guided tours of the present day mining operations are available, they depart at 9.15 am and 4 pm on weekends and public holidays only just down the road from the tourist office. Cost per vehicle is $2. Also in Queenstown drop in to the photographic museum on the corner of Sticht and Driffield Sts — the usual collection of old junk but also a vast and fascinating collection of photographs of early Queenstown. Admission is 60c. Queenstown, in its raucous heyday, had 14 hotels of which six still remain.

Information

The Tasmanian Government Tourist Bureau office is at 39 Orr St.

Places to Stay

The Queenstown Youth Hostel has closed down recently — it was on Driffield St. The *Pine Lodge* (tel 71 1852) is a small guest house at 1 Gaffney St. Bed & breakfast singles/doubles are $14-18/$24-28. The more expensive rooms have attached shower and toilet. On Driffield St the *Commercial Hotel* (tel 71 1511) is $18/30 for bed & breakfast while the *Empire Hotel* (tel 71 1699) at 2 Orr St is $18-24/24-30 but room-only. Motels tend to be expensive, the cheapest is probably the *Four Seasons Motor Hotel* (tel 71 1888) at 1 Orr St with rooms at $27.50/33. Be careful — there are three different 'four seasons' motels in Queenstown. If you want to camp you'll have to keep going right through Queenstown to Zeehan or Strahan; there are no campsites here.

WEST COAST

The sparse population and wild scenery of the west coast is a complete contrast to the quiet, pastoral beauty of the rolling midlands of Tasmania. This is definitely not gentle English scenery and were it not for the region's mineral wealth it's probable that it would still be uninhabited today. Indeed it was only in 1932 that the road through to Queenstown was completed from Hobart and only comparatively recently was the road upgraded from a rugged track to a proper sealed surface. Prior to construction of the road access to the west coast was only possible by small boats — there is only one port, Strahan, on the coast and difficulty of access to Macquarie Harbour means that only small boats can use it. Today a second road also links the west coast to Burnie on the north coast. Whatever time of

Getting There

You can fly to Queenstown from various places including Melbourne and Hobart — see the introductory Getting There section for details. By road there are buses between Burnie and Queenstown and between Hobart and Queenstown from Monday to Saturday. The bus from Burnie departs at 1.15 pm while the return trip leaves at 9 am and gets to Burnie at 1.35 pm. The fare is $17.30.

Hobart-Queenstown buses leave at 8 am and arrive at 2.40 pm, return trip at 9 am to arrive Hobart at 3.10 pm. The fare is $20. There is also a bus to Strahan at 3.30 pm Monday to Saturday, arriving at 4.30 pm. The fare is $3.20 and the bus from Strahan leaves at 7.20 am and arrives at 8.45 am. The Queenstown depot of Tasmanian Redline Coaches (tel 71 1011) is on Orr St.

year you visit the west coast be prepared for the exceptionally heavy rainfall.

Strahan (population 400)

On Macquarie Harbour, 39 km from Queenstown, Strahan is the only town actually on the coastline in the west — indicative of just how inhospitable this rough and rugged coast is. It's due to a combination of heavy seas, the extreme rainfall and the lack of natural harbours. Macquarie Harbour looks like a fine harbour at first glance but its entrance is guarded by a formidable bar which allows only shallow depth boats to enter. It's not inappropriate that in the early convict days the entrance became known as Hell's Gate.

Although it was mining that made the west coast and also, for that matter, Strahan, there was activity in the harbour long before the mining boom.

In 1817 the first expedition was mounted here to exploit the Huon pine found along the rivers which flowed into the harbour. This excellent and long wearing wood was extensively used in early colonial Tasmania but it has proved virtually impossible to grow commercially and also is extremely slow growing so that today very little is left in accessible areas and it is also very expensive.

In 1821 a penal colony was estab-lished on Sarah (or Settlement) Island in the harbour. This hell-on-earth features in the early Australian novel *For the Term of his Natural Life*. It was intended to be an escape proof prison for the very worst of the colony's convicts and brutality and sadism were the order of the day. In 1822 of 182 convicts only 13 were not flogged and the 169 who were, shared 7000 lashes between them. In the first 11 years of the colony 112 convicts escaped but once off the island where was there to go? Of that number 62 died in the bush and a further nine were murdered by their desperate comrades.

As the port for Queenstown, Strahan reached its peak of prosperity with the copper boom and the completion of the railway line in 1892 but today it is just a quiet little town. The imposing post office and Union Steam Ship Company building, probably the finest buildings on the west coast, hint at just how important it must once have been. There's an interesting little museum by the caravan park and Strahan also has the Botanical Creek Park. From Strahan it's just six km to the 40 km long Ocean Beach where huge seas crash upon equally huge sand dunes. From here you can see the lonely lighthouse at Cape Sorell, on the opposite side of the harbour.

Harbour Cruises Cruises up Macquarie Harbour are a prime Strahan attraction. They go from Strahan up to the Gordon River and about 15 km up-river then return across the harbour via Sarah Island to Hell's Gate. The all-day tour departs at 9 am and returns at 12.45 pm. The cost is $15 including morning tea. Further up the Gordon are the Marble Cliffs on the riverside.

Zeehan (population 2000)
In 1882 silver-lead was discovered here and Zeehan quickly became a mining boom town. By the turn of the century

the population was 5000 and it peaked at nearly 10,000. It was the third largest town in Tasmania, had 26 hotels and the Gaiety Theatre (which is still there today) was the largest theatre in Australia. Then the mines began to run out, just before WW I they were closed and Zeehan became a virtual ghost town with a population of just a few hundred. Recently it has had a revival with the re-opening of the Rennison Bell tin mine nearby.

Apart from a number of buildings remaining from those boom days Zeehan also has the excellent West Coast Pioneers' Memorial Museum which has a particularly good mineral collection amongst other exhibits. Outside the museum is an exhibit of steam locomotives used on the various west coast railways, a railway line used to connect Zeehan to Strahan. Rough roads leading to Trial Harbour, 23 km away on the coast, and Dundas, a mining town which has now all but disappeared. Zeehan was named after Tasman's ship and is 38 km north of Queenstown.

Roseberry (population 2500)
Mining started here when the Emu Bay Railway from Burnie to Zeehan opened in 1900 but with the closure of Zeehan the mines here also shut down. With new mining processes the mine was re-opened in 1936 and has operated successfully ever since. There's a spectacular series of aerial buckets transporting ore down the mountainside at Williamsford, seven km out, while Tasmania's highest waterfalls, the Montezuma Falls, are five km out. Until the completion of the road from Burnie the old railway line was the only direct route up from the north coast but the line only carries freight now.

Savage River (population 1200)
Ore from this new international mining project is formed into a slurry and pumped down an 85 km long pipeline to the handling port at Port Latta on the north coast. Nearby Corinna is the almost-ghost-town remains of a former gold rush town and a base for Pieman River excursions. While Waratah, a tiny town back towards the main Burnie-Queenstown road, was the site of Tasmania's first mining boom. The Mt Bischoff Mine (see a model of it in the museum in Zeehan) became the richest tin mine in the world but, like other Tasmanian mining towns, Waratah withered away. Today it is having a modest revival principally due to other mining in the area, mainly Savage River, but also the re-opening of mining in Waratah.

BASS STRAIT ISLANDS
Tasmania has two major islands in the Bass Strait — Flinders Island to the north-east of Tasmania and King Island to the north-west. They're rough and rugged places, great if you really want to get away from it all. Both have excellent fishing, bushwalking and scuba diving opportunities. There are a great number of shipwrecks dotted around both islands and these offer plenty of attractions for keen divers. In spring countless mutton birds arrive at the rookeries around the coasts of these islands.

KING ISLAND
The rugged island is 64 km long across at its widest point. When first discovered by European settlers the island was

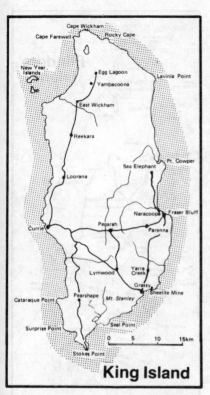

King Island

home to a great number of sea-elephants but they are now virtually extinct. The first permanent settlement on the islands was in 1855. The main towns are Currie and Grassy and the sand mining and the mining of scheelite are the main economic activities on the island.

No less than 57 shipwrecks are charted around the island, including that of the *Catarque*, an immigrant ship which went down in 1845 with the loss of 399 lives. At Cape Wickham the lighthouse is one of the largest in the world. Much of the island is still undisturbed bush and there is a wide variety of wildlife to be seen. The excellent bushwalking includes tracks along the unpopulated north coast.

Places to Stay

The *King Island Youth Hostel* (tel 61 1229) is a simple electricity-less place with room for just six. Advance booking is essential, nights cost $3.25.

In Currie the *Boomerang Motel* (tel 62 1288) costs $29.50 for one person, $38 for two. Or there are the *Naracoopa Holiday Units* (tel 61 1326) at $24 and $4 for each additional person. There are also a variety of private rooms available on King Island. Take a tent and spend a week walking around the coast. Currie has a Chinese restaurant that does takeaways.

Getting There

You can fly to King Island either with Air Tasmania or H C Sleigh Airlines. Both use small aircraft, Cessna 404 Titans in the case of H C Sleigh, on their flights. Air Tasmania fly Hobart-Smithton-King Island-Smithton-Hobart on Monday, Thursday and Friday. Smithton-King Island is $41, Hobart-King Island is $80. Bookings can be made by phoning 34 9577 in Hobart, 52 1677 in Smithton and 62 1322 on King Island. H C Sleigh have a more extensive schedule through King Island flying Launceston-King Island direct or through Wynyard and sometimes Devonport. Fares to King Island are $61.70 from Launceston, $48 from Devonport and $41.80 from Wynyard.

Getting Around

You can rent cars on King Island Auto Rentals (tel 62 1272) in Currie; Georges (tel 62 1297) also in Currie; or from Avis at the same number as Georges. Georges are cheapest with cars from $27.50 per day with unlimited km. Some King Island roads are two wheel ruts of deep sand and either four-wheel drive or lots of digging gear is recommended — the road to Seal Rocks and Martha Lavinia Lake are bad.

FLINDERS ISLAND

Flinders is the largest island of the Furneaux Group and it takes its name from the pioneer explorer Matthew Flinders. The young Lieutenant Flinders was part of an expedition sent from Sydney in 1797 to rescue the survivor of the *Sydney Cove*, wrecked in the island and sheltering on the small Preservation Island. He did not know at the time that the main island of the group was later to bear his name. In all there are around 50 islands in the group and, like King Island, they were intermittently used by sealers until the first permanent settlement in the 1830s. The early sealers were a notoriously cruel and rough lot, thinking nothing of leaving helpless seal pups to die having slaughtered their mothers. Nor were they able to resist the lure of a little piracy from time to time, or luring ships on to the rocks around the island by displaying false lights. It's likely that quite a few of the 120-odd ships wrecked around the Furneaux Group got there with a little outside help.

The first permanent settlement in 1830, was one of the saddest pages from Tasmania's history. In that year the remaining survivors of Tasmania's decimated Aboriginals were settled here at Wybalenna, an Aboriginal word meaning 'blackman's house'. This last ditch attempt to save what earlier Tasmanian settlers had been so keen to wipe out was a dismal failure and in 1847 the last surviving Aborigines were moved to Oyster Cove and the Tasmanian Aboriginal race soon disappeared completely. It was not until 1888 that the island was finally and permanently settled but even so it remained sparsely populated even after WW II. Only since the 1950s has the island really become agriculturally developed.

As on King Island there are beaches and bushwalks but also a variety of other things to do and see. Wrecks of ships are dotted right around the islands and there are plenty of opportunities for diving on them. A couple of the wrecks are clearly visible above water. The *City of Foochow* went down with a load of coal off the east coast in 1877 while the *Farsund* went aground near Vansittart in 1912. At Wybalenna, near Emita, the graveyard tells the hopeless story of the final Tasmanian Aboriginals and the small settlement's chapel has been restored. Emita also has a small museum with items from the days of the sealers and whalers, the Aboriginal settlement and from the many shipwrecks.

Rock climbers will also find plenty of interest on Flinders Island, including 800 metre Mt Strzelecki in the national park south of Whitemark. Gem fossickers can also have a go on Flinders Island, the Killecrankie 'diamonds' found near Palana are actually topaz. Whitemark is the main town on the island and close to the airport but Lady Barron, in the south, has the deepwater port.

Places to Stay

There are a number of hotels and motels on Flinders Island. At Whitemark there's *Bluff House* (tel 59 2034) at $15 per person including breakfast or the *Interstate* (tel 59 2144) also at $15 per person but room only. The more luxurious *Furneaux* (tel 003 59 3521) at Lady Barron is also rather more expensive at $24/36 for singles/doubles but this does include colour TV and other mod cons. Also at Whitemark there's the *Flinders Island Cabin Park* (tel 59 2188) with self-contained cabins. You can also find private accommodation on the island.

Getting There

H C Sleigh Airlines fly between Launceston and Flinders Island three times each weekday, twice on Saturday and once on Sunday. The flight costs $36. On Monday, Wednesday and Friday there are flights to Flinders Island from Melbourne's Essendon Airport for $60. The airport is about five km north of Whitemark.

Getting Around

Flinders Island Car Hire (tel 59 2189), Flinders Island Car Rental (tel 59 2158) and Flinders Island Transport Services (tel 59 2060) all hire cars from Whitemark. Rates range from $34 per day with unlimited km or with Transport Services from $17 plus 20c a km.

Mutton Birds

Each September the mutton birds, stormy petrels or shearwaters, arrive back on Flinders and King Island, as they do on other Bass Strait islands. They have spent the northern summer along the Japanese, Siberian and Alaskan coasts. Having cleaned out and repaired their burrows the birds head out to sea again, returning in late November to breed.

All the millions of eggs are laid in one three-day period and the parents take turns, two weeks at a time, incubating the eggs. Having hatched out their single chick both parents feed the fluffy little bird until, in mid-April, the adult birds all depart, leaving the young to fend for themselves, and eventually follow their parents north. Unfortunately for the well-fed little mutton birds they're tasty little creatures and at this time of year the mutton bird hunters move in for their short season.

The Furneaux Group is also home for the Cape Barren Goose. At one time it was feared that it would be hunted to extinction but the completely protected bird is no longer at risk.

Victoria

Area   228,000 square km
Population 3,800,000

Don't miss: Melbourne, Australia's second largest city, the mountains of the Victorian Alps, the gold country and the ever interesting Murray River.

When the founding fathers up in Sydney decided it was time to get a foothold on some other part of the continent they had a go at establishing a settlement on Port Phillip Bay in 1803 but through bad luck and bad management soon decided it was a lousy place to live and moved down to Tasmania. So it is not surprising that when Melbourne finally did become established a long lasting rivalry was to be the order of the day.

It was 1835 when the first permanent European settlement was made in Melbourne although whalers and sealers had used points along the Victorian coast as shelters or harbours for a number of years previously. The earliest settlers, John Batman and John Pascoe Fawkner, came to Melbourne in search of the land they were unable to obtain in Tasmania. Not until 1837, by which time several hundred settlers had moved in, was the town named Melbourne and given an official seal of approval.

The independent spirit naturally led to clashes with the staid powers of Sydney, the settlers were not interested in the convict system for example and on a number of occasions turned convict ships away. Finally in 1851 the colony of Victoria was formed and separated from New South Wales. At about the same time gold was discovered and the population doubled in little more than a year. As with a number of other Australian gold rushes, few people made

fortunes but many stayed on to establish new settlements and work the land. Some of the most interesting historical areas in Victoria are associated with those gold rush days.

Melbourne, as Australia's second city, is naturally the state's prime attraction. Although it is not as intrinsically appealing as Sydney, Melbourne lays claim to being the fashion, food and cultural centre of Australia and also the financial focus. Victoria is the most densely populated of the Australian states and also the most industrialised.

Of course Victoria is much more than its capital city. The Great Ocean Road runs south-west towards South Australia and has some of the most spectacular coastal scenery in Australia and evocative reminders of the whaling days in some of the small port towns that actually pre-date Melbourne. To the south east of the capital is Phillip Island with its nightly penguin parade. Further south is Wilson's Promontory, the Prom is the furthest south point on the Australian mainland and also one of Australia's best loved national parks with excellent scenery and bushwalks. Continuing east towards the NSW border there's more great coast along the Gippsland region.

Victoria's stretch of the Snowies includes some of the best skiing in Australia and it is much closer to Melbourne than NSW's snowfields are to Sydney.

Skiing on weekends is easy for Melbournians while in summer the mountains are popular for camping, walking and a whole host of outdoor activities. Of course you don't have to go all the way to the Snowies to get into the hills. The ever popular Dandenongs are less than an hour from the centre of Melbourne while the Grampians are another popular hill area, further to the west.

Finally there's the Murray River region in the north with historic river towns like Swan Hill and Mildura. Victoria also has its wine growing areas, particularly in the north on the slopes of the Great Dividing Range. And the gold country certainly shouldn't be forgotten — towns like Bendigo and Ballarat still have a strong flavour of those heady gold rush days and lucky prospectors are still finding gold today.

GETTING AROUND

VicRail has a fairly comprehensive network of InterUrban and InterCity services. The rail services are supplemented by connecting VicRail buses. The principal rail routes fanning out from Melbourne are: 1 — through Geelong to Warrnambool in the south-west. 2 — through Ballarat and on through the central west to South Australia. 3 — also through Ballarat and up to Mildura on the Murray River in the extreme north-west. 4 — through Bendigo and the central highlands up to Swan Hill on the Murray. 5 — up to Shepparton and Numurkah in the Goulburn Valley. 6 — up the Hume Highway route to Albury/Wodonga on the route to Sydney. 7 — through Traralgon and Sale to Bairnsdale in Gippsland. VicRail have a timetable of all their services, available from station bookstands for 50c. *Transport in Victoria* (30c) is a map showing all the country bus services in the state on one side and the rail routes on the other.

CLIMATE

Victoria, Melbourne in particular, has a single major drawback — the bloody climate. It's not statistically that bad — the average temperature summer or winter is only a few degrees less than Sydney and it's certainly far less humid than Sydney or Brisbane. The annual rainfall is also less than either of those damp cities. The trouble with Melbourne's climate is it's totally undependable. You can broil one day and shiver the next. What the hell am I talking about — it's the next minute, not the next day. In Melbourne if you don't like the weather, so they say, just wait a minute. It's not that Melbourne has four distinct seasons it's that they often all come on the same day. You simply can't trust the sun to shine in summer or, for that matter, the winter to be cold. It's totally fickle. Although the weather is basically somewhat cooler in Melbourne you'll still never need more than a light jacket or sweater even in the depths of winter.

GEOGRAPHY

Victoria's geography is probably more complex than any other Australian state as it includes both the final stretch of the Great Dividing Range and associated outcrops plus a swath of the flatter country to the west. The Great Dividing Range reaches its greatest altitude across the NSW-Victoria border and the Victorian Alpine region is a popular area for skiing in the winter, bushwalking in the summer. The mountains run south-west from the NSW border, then bend around to travel more directly west as the range crosses north of Melbourne and finally fades out before the South Australian border.

The Victorian coast is particularly varied, on the eastern side is the mountain backed Gippsland region while to the west is the scenic Great Ocean Road and the spectacular coastline towards South Australia. The north-west of the state, beyond the Great Dividing Range, is flat and often tedious plains, especially dull and dry in the extreme northwest of the state. For most of the length of the border between NSW and Victoria the mighty Murray River forms the actual boundary.

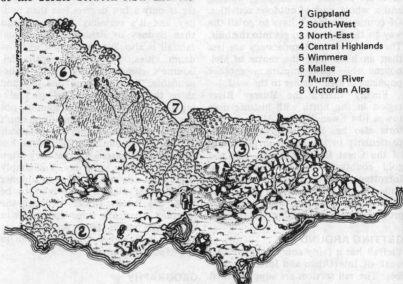

1 Gippsland
2 South-West
3 North-East
4 Central Highlands
5 Wimmera
6 Mallee
7 Murray River
8 Victorian Alps

ACTIVITIES

Bushwalking Victoria has some great bushwalking areas and a number of very active bushwalking clubs. Check the bushgear shops around Hardware and Little Bourke Sts in Melbourne for local club news and magazines. For more information about bushwalking in Victoria look for the handy walking guides *50 Bush Walks in Victoria* and *50 Day Walks Near Melbourne* both by Sandra Bardswell and published by Anne O'Donovan.

Walking areas close to the city include the You Yangs, 56 km to the west, with a notable variety of bird life, and the Dandenongs right on the city edge to the east. Wilson's Promontory, the 'prom', is south-east in Gippsland — the furthest southerly point of mainland Australia. There are many marked trails from Tidal River and from Telegraph Bay — walks can be from a few hours to a couple of days. If you are overnighting in the park a permit must be obtained from the park manager in Tidal River.

The Alpine Walking Track starts at Mt Erica, 144 km east, and ends at Tom Groggin on the NSW border. This is a very long trail for the experienced walker. There are other popular marked trails in the Bright and Mt Buffalo areas of the Alps. The Grampians are 256 km north-west where Victoria's only remaining big red roos hang out. Mallacoota Inlet Park is equally rugged inland but the coastal walks are easier.

Rock Climbing Again the Hardware St bushgear shops are good info sources. If you just want to scramble around in rather crowded conditions there's Hanging Rock (of picnic fame) 72 km northwest. Sugarloaf and Jawbones, the latter more difficult and a longer walk, are 112 km out in the Cathedral Range. The

Grampians, 241 km from Melbourne, have a wide variety of climbs as does Mt Arapiles, 334 km out near Natimuk. At Mt Buffalo, 359 km north in the Alpine area, the hardest climb is Buffalo Gorge.

Swimming & Surfing Although there is reasonably good swimming on the eastern side of Port Phillip Bay you have to get outside the bay to find surf. Some of the bay beaches close to the city are not too special but as you get further round the bay there are some very fine beaches. Along the Mornington Peninsula you have the choice between sheltered bay beaches on one side and the open ocean beaches only a short distance away on the other side of the peninsula.

Further out there are excellent beaches at Phillip Island and right along the Gippsland coast. Ditto for the western side of the state where the area from Point Lonsdale to Apollo Bay is particularly popular surfing ground.

Skin Diving Flinders, Portland, Kilcunda, Torquay, Anglesea, Lorne, Apollo Bay, Mallacoota, Portsea, Sorrento and Wilsons Prom are all popular diving areas. There are clubs and equipment renting organisations in Melbourne.

Boats & Sailing At Studley Park in the Melbourne suburb of Kew you can hire a whole selection of row boats, canoes and kayaks by the hour. Good fun although a fair few people seem to find themselves upside down in the muddy Yarra! Canoes can also be rented by Como Park, further down the Yarra towards the city. At Albert Park Lake you can hire rowboats and sailing boats. There are many sailing clubs all around the bay in Melbourne and on Albert Park Lake. Elsewhere around the state there are many lakes popular for sailing and many sailing clubs.

Running & Bicycling The four km jogging track around the Domain park in central Melbourne is one of the most popular running circuits in Australia. Albert Park Lake is also busy. With its relatively flat terrain Melbourne is very popular with bike riders — I ride a bike to work most days I'm in town. It's easy to hire bicycles along the popular Yarraside bicycle track but not so easy to find bikes for longer term hire in Melbourne. The state as a whole is pretty good for biking, relatively compact and with many good areas for two-wheel travelling — such as along the Great Ocean Road.

MELBOURNE (population 2,700,000) Melbourne has always been the poor relation of Sydney; despite their fierce rivalry Melbourne has always come off second best. It goes right back to their founding, Sydney had nearly 50 years head start on its southern sister and even then the foundation of Melbourne was a rather haphazard affair. The first attempt at establishing a settlement on Port Phillip Bay in 1803 was an abject failure and the colonists soon transferred to the more inviting situation of Hobart. Not until 1835, following exploratory trips from Tasmania, was Melbourne eventually founded by a group of Tasmanian entrepreneurs.

In 1851 the colony of Victoria became independent of NSW and at about the same time Melbourne actually became a rival for Sydney when it was the centre for Australia's biggest and most prolonged gold rush. In just a few years Melbourne suddenly became a real place on the map and the city's solid, substantial appearance essentially dates from those heady days. Having reached parity with Sydney, for a time

Melbourne was actually the larger city, Melbourne was never able to pull ahead and has always been a number two to its glamorous northern sister.

In population there's little between them, they're both large cities in the 2½ to three million bracket. Yet somehow Sydney is far more the metropolis than Melbourne. It's brighter, more active, more hurried than its younger sister. Quite why is hard to pinpoint — Melbourne is certainly less attractively situated, on a flat coastal plain where Sydney rises, dips and curves around its beautiful harbour. Melbourne is certainly better planned — wide, sweeping boulevards against Sydney's narrow and often convoluted streets. Melbourne's much more solid, more permanent, more 'Victorian' in appearance. Even more dull?

Part of Melbourne's inferiority complex is due, no doubt, to the architectural kiss of death the city seems to suffer from. Spend as much as you want, plan as far ahead as you like, nothing seems to work in Melbourne. When every Australian city had to have a central pedestrian mall Melbourne had one too, except trams run through Melbourne's, people huddle to the sides and all in all it's a disaster. Melbourne's city square, the product of much planning and competition was an instant total flop. When Sydney built a performing arts centre they ended up with the opera house. When Melbourne did the same thing they ended up with something that works very well but in appearance is so dull and innocuous you'd barely know it was there. Even its pointy spire is cunningly coloured to blend into a typical cloudy Melbourne sky with such precision as to be invisible. And Melbourne's biggest and most impressive bridge actually fell down during its construction.

Information

The Victorian Government Travel Centre (tel 602 9444) is at 230 Collins St and is open 9 am to 5 pm on weekdays, 9 am to 12 noon on Saturday mornings. It's a place with a rather Victorian atmosphere too! The RACV (tel 607 221) is at 123 Queen St and has a bookshop and information section on the 8th floor. The National Parks Service of Victoria is at 240 Victoria Parade, Victoria has about 40 national, state and coastal parks. The National Trust puts out a useful walking tours leaflet.

The Melbourne GPO is on the corner of Bourke St and Elizabeth St. There's an efficient poste restante here and also phones for interstate and international calls. Phone centres can also be found right behind the GPO on Little Bourke St, right across the road on Elizabeth St and up Bourke St just across Swanston St.

The YHA has its helpful Melbourne office at 122 Flinders St. At 44 Spencer St the Overseas Visitors Centre (tel 62 6991) is a travel agent specialising in young travellers, it's open seven days a week and offers small discounts on some accommodation plus general advice. If you're after bush gear or information on bushwalking the centre for bush gear shops is around the junction of Hardware St and Little Bourke St, close to the GPO. Melbourne has a lot of excellent bookshops including a big Angus & Robertson on Elizabeth St, several Collins Bookshops around the city, the agreeably chaotic McGills on Elizabeth St opposite the GPO (good for interstate and overseas newspapers) and several alternative bookshops. Best of these are Whole Earth at 83 Bourke St and Readings on Lygon St in Carlton. Readings also has an excellent window noticeboard where you'll find all sorts of offers to share accommodation or rides. It's actually mostly accommodation and some of the requirements are quite amazing will that lesbian household really find a vegetarian, cat loving, musician with leftist political leanings? The *Age Weekender*, which comes with the Age newspaper on Fridays, is the best source of info on what's happening around Melbourne for the following week.

Aboriginal Handcrafts is on the 5th floor, 182 Collins St and is open weekdays after 10 am. There are a number of other Aboriginal craft shops and countless junk souvenir places. Melbourne also has a number of delightful Australiana shops including a great one in the Jam Factory in South Yarra and another at 1114 High St, Armadale.

In the city there are a number of intimate and elegant little shopping arcades apart from the glossier modern affairs. The Royal Arcade off Bourke St Mall is noted for its figures of Gog and Magog which strike the hours.

Orientation

Melbourne's city centre, the 'Golden Mile' is deceptively simple. Wide boulevards run south-west to north-east and south-east to north-west but the south-west to north-east roads are interspersed with narrow streets from which a veritable maze of little alleys and lanes run off, giving the otherwise overpoweringly orderly and planned centre a little human chaos. The main streets are Collins and Bourke Sts (south-west to north-east) crossed by Swanston and Elizabeth Sts (south-east to north-west). Swanston St is the real main artery of Melbourne as it crosses straight over the river on the southern side and runs straight out of the city into Carlton on the north. Thus most traffic comes into the city from the south enters by Swanston St while most traffic from the north comes in on parallel Elizabeth St, since this is the direct route in from the airport or from Sydney.

The Yarra River forms a southern boundary to the city area, with railway lines running alongside it and Flinders St the city centre street running closest to the riverbank. Right beside the river at the corner of Swanston and Flinders St is the ornate although rather elderly looking Flinders St Railway Station. This is the main railway station for local city railway services. The other Melbourne station, for country and interstate services, is the Spencer St Station. The Spencer St end of town also has a number of old hotels and cheaper places to stay.

The Collins and Bourke St blocks between Swanston and Elizabeth are Melbourne's shopping centre, the Bourke St block being a pedestrian mall. On the mall you'll find Myers, the biggest department store in Australia, and right next door, on the Bourke and Elizabeth Sts corner, the GPO.

The Yarra River

Melbourne's prime natural feature, the 'muddy' Yarra, is about all the city has to offer as a competitor for Sydney's harbour and it's a loser from the start. There's no way a river which is the butt of countless jokes about its 'running upside down' can win against beautiful Port Jackson. Which is a little unfair because actually the Yarra is very pretty and hopefully, if plans currently held for it come to fruition, will be even more attractive in the future.

When the racing row boats are sculling down the river on a sunny day, or driving along Alexandra Avenue towards the city on a clear night the Yarra can really look quite magical. Best of all there's a bicycle track along the riverbank so you can bike it for miles along the riverside or ride to work without risking being wiped out by some nut in a Holden. The bike track has been gradually extended further upstream and hopefully will soon start to move further downstream as well. On weekends you can hire bicycles from beside the Botanical Gardens and near Como Park. There are also riverside barbecues beside the river and near Como Park in South Yarra you can also hire canoes and rowboats although further upstream at Studley Park, Kew is the most popular place for boating. Two person canoes here cost $8 for the first hour, $9 for three person. Subsequent hours are $4 and $4.50. They also hire kayaks and row boats. A more leisurely way to boat down the river is on one of the pseudo-paddlewheeler tour boats which operate on the river from Princes Walk beside Princes Bridge (across from Flinders St Station). There are some really beautiful old bridges across the Yarra and Alexandra Parade, the riverside boulevard on the south side, provides delightful views of Melbourne by day or night.

Polly Woodside

Close to Spencer St Bridge, immediately south of the city centre, is the *Polly Woodside*. Built in Belfast, Northern Island in 1885 she's an old iron-hulled sailing ship involved in freight carrying in the dying years of the sailing era. Recently restored it's hoped the *Polly Woodside* and the adjacent nautical museum will eventually form the centre for a major redevelopment project on this run down riverside docks area. The ship and museum are open 10 am to 4 pm weekdays, 12 noon to 5 pm on Saturday and Sunday. Admission is $2. Across the river stands the recently completed World Trade Centre office block.

City Square

At the intersection of Collins and Swanston St is Melbourne's disastrous city square. Plans for a city square where discussed for years but despite all the advance planning and architectural competitions the city square still suffered from Melbourne's kiss of death. It's a nice enough square with lots of fountains and even a graffiti wall but for some reason it has simply never worked. The only interest the city square has ever really had for the people

of Melbourne was in the early days of the 'yellow peril'. This big chunk of modern sculpture was intended to give the square a central focus but, unfortunately, it was the sort of thing that makes the 'you call that art' brigade foam at the mouth. Doubly unfortunately Melbourne's city council at that time had absolutely nothing better to do than foam at the mouth and after endless arguments and veritable Zeppelins full of hot air the council got the sack and the yellow peril was spirited away to a new, and obscure, home in a riverside park down towards Spencer St. Now the square has no focus at all although it does have a rather good statue of Burke and Wills looking heroic and unlucky. This statue has had quite an interesting history moving from place to place all over the city.

On Around the City

Continuing up Collins St beside the City Square you come to the 'Paris End' where graceful trees shade the street and do give it something of a Parisian look although callous development has torn down many of the fine old buildings that used to line the street, replacing them with more big office blocks. Up Collins St the other way you come to the Melbourne Stock Exchange at 351. You can visit the 3rd floor visitors' gallery from 9 am to 12 noon and 2 to 5 pm, Monday to Friday. Those interested in the forces of capitalism at work can also have a free tour of the exchange.

Bourke St has more shops/less style than Collins St but it too can boast a Melbourne fiasco. When, in the '70s, every Australian city had to have a pedestrian mall. Melbourne got one too but the Bourke St Mall has been a nonstarter from the very beginning. Melbourne has one big difference to any other Australian city — trams. It soon became very clear that there's no way a pedestrian mall can work if you've got 30 tonne trams barrelling through the middle of it every few minutes. Or at least it soon became very clear to the likes of you and me, it's still not at all clear to the powers that be and several multi-million dollar re-arrangements of the potted plants and the benches still hasn't made it any clearer. In my opinion (and my opinion comes free) there's only two ways to make the Bourke St Mall work. The cheap way is to stop the trams running through the mall by putting the terminus at the Swanston St end of the mall. The expensive way is to stop the trams running through the mall by putting them in a tunnel underneath the mall.

A half block up from Bourke St is something that's much more of a Melbourne success story, the Chinatown on Little Bourke St. This narrow lane was a thronging Chinese quarter even back in the gold rush days and it's now a busy, crowded couple of blocks of often excellent Chinese restaurants (though also often very expensive), Asian supermarkets and shops. The successful touch here was the addition of decorative street lamps and Chinese tiled arches over the lane. Yes, I know they're artificial and garish but they look great. Another half block up to Lonsdale St brings you to the central city's Greek quarter.

City Buildings

Melbourne's an intriguing blend of the soaring new and the stately old. Carrying the 'new' banner are buildings like Nauru House on Exhibition St. Nauru is a tiny Pacific island whose entire population could comfortably be housed in this big office block. Nauru is also an extremely wealthy island since it's basically solid phosphate, hence the building's nickname of 'birdshit house'. Only a sparrow hop away is the equally soaring Regent Hotel with its central atrium, starting on the 35th floor. A great place to stay if you can stretch to

$100 a night.

Just round the corner on Spring St is a hotel of quite another era, the gracious old Windsor. Across the road from there is the imposing State Parliament House, a relic of Melbourne's gold rush wealth. Other old buildings in the centre include the 1853 Treasury Building in the Treasury Gardens, the 1872 Old Royal Mint and the 1842 St James Cathedral both beside Flagstaff Gardens. Victoriana enthusiasts may find some very small Melbourne buildings of interest — scattered around the city are a number of very fine cast iron men's urinals (like French pissoirs). They mainly date from 1903 to WW I and one on the corner of Exhibition and Lonsdale St is classified by the National Trust. Other fine examples include one outside the North Melbourne Town Hall where there is also a notable drinking fountain.

The Melbourne Club, pillar of the Melbourne establishment, is off Spring St up at the Treasury Gardens end of town. Bourke St up at this end is an interesting block with a mixture of excellent restaurants, book and record shops. St Patrick's Cathedral, one of the city's most imposing churches, is also at this end of town. Over the other side of the city the Victoria Market, on the corner of Peel and Victoria Sts, is the city's main produce centre, a colourful and popular scene Tuesdays to Saturdays when the stall operators shout, yell and generally go all out to move the goods. On Sundays the fruit and vegies give way to general goods — everything from cut price jeans to second hand records.

Museum & Library

Extending for a block between Swanston St and Russell St beside La Trobe St, is the inter-connected collections of the National Museum and the Science Museum from Swanston St, but you can actually get to either collection from

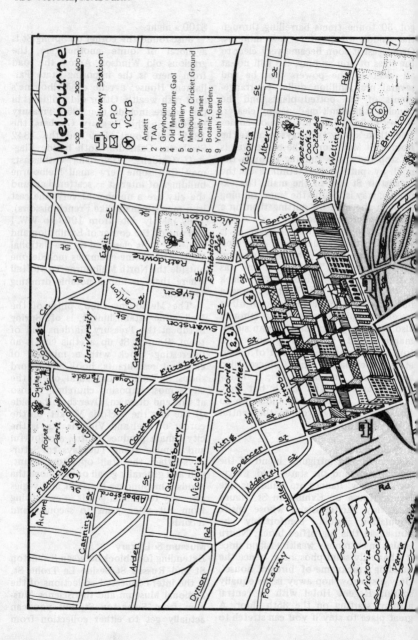

Melbourne

■ Railway Station
✉ Q.P.O
⊗ VGTB

1 Ansett
2 TAA
3 Greyhound
4 Old Melbourne Gaol
5 Art Gallery
6 Melbourne Cricket Ground
7 Lonely Planet
8 Botanic Gardens
9 Youth Hostel

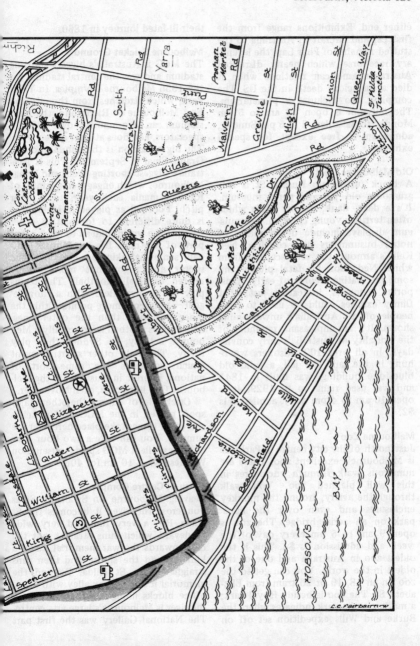

L.C.Fairbairn.w

either end. Exhibitions range from the first car and aircraft in Australia to the stuffed remains of Phar Lap, the legendary racehorse which nearly disrupted Australian-American relations when it died a suspicious death in the US. The complex also includes a planetarium. The museum is open 10 am to 5 pm Monday to Saturday, 2 to 5 pm Sunday, admission is free except for special exhibits.

Old Melbourne Gaol
A block further up Russell St is this gruesome old jail and penal museum. It's a dark, dank, spooky place which often terrifies young children. The museum displays include death masks of noted bushrangers and convicts, Ned Kelly's armour, the very scaffold from which Ned took his fatal plunge and some fascinating records of early 'transported' convicts, indicating just what flimsy excuses could be used to pack people off to Australia's unwelcoming shores. It's an unpleasant reminder of the brutality of Australia's early convict days. In all over 100 prisoners where hung in the jail. The jail, a solid old bluestone building, was built in 1841 and was used right up to 1929. It is open 10 am to 4 pm daily, admission is $2.

Melbourne Zoo
Just north of the city centre in Parkville is Melbourne's excellent zoo. There are numerous walk through enclosures in this well planned zoo. You walk through the aviary, around the monkey enclosures and even over the lions' park on an aerial bridge. The zoo is open 9 am to 5 pm every day of the week and admission is $4. This is the oldest zoo in Australia and one of the oldest in the world. You can get to the zoo on an 18, 19 or 20 tram from Elizabeth St. The zoo is beside Royal Park; a marker in the park indicates where the Burke and Wills expedition set off on their ill-fated journey in 1860.

Melbourne Cricket Ground
The MCG is Australia's biggest sporting stadium and was the central stadium for the 1956 Melbourne Olympics. In Yarra Park, which stretches from the city and East Melbourne to Richmond, the huge stadium can accommodate over 100,000 spectators, and does at least once a year. The big occassion is the annual football Grand Final in September. This is Australia's biggest sporting event and brings Melbourne, which engages in a winter of football mania each year, to a fever pitch. Football as played in Melbourne is quite different to football in other parts of the world, indeed to most other parts of Australia. It's Aussie rules football, somewhat akin to a cross between soccer and rugby but most closely related to Gaelic football. The teams play on an oval field with a 'double' goal — you score more points within the inner goalposts than the outer ones. Aussie rules football is principally a Melbourne activity, in Sydney they play rugby. The only other sporting event which generates the same sort of national interest in Australia is the Melbourne Cup horserace, each November.

Cricket is, of course, the other major sport played in the MCG, test matches and other games take place here over the summer. You can take a two hour tour of the excellent MCG sports museum on Wednesdays at 10 am for 40c.

Cultural Centre Complex
Leaving Melbourne on Swanston St as you cross the river it becomes the St Kilda Rd, a very fine and very wide boulevard which runs straight out the city towards the war memorial, takes a kink around the shrine and then runs straight on to St Kilda. Beyond the memorial it's ad agency alley with many office blocks lining the road. Right by the river is Melbourne's large arts centre. The National Gallery was the first part

of the complex to be completed, back in 1968, and although it's a rather dull cubic building and the 'urinal' front window is something of a local joke, it houses a very fine collection of art. The gallery has local and overseas collections and many excellent temporary exhibits. The stained glass ceiling in the Great Hall is a highpoint of the gallery. I particularly like the strange water fountains in the central courtyard. The gallery is open 10 am to 5 pm Tuesday to Sunday and the regular entry charge (higher for special exhibits) is 80c (students 40c).

Beside the gallery is the recently opened Concert Hall complex. It may look rather like a grounded prison ship from Star Wars but it houses an excellent concert hall, the state theatre, playhouse, studio and a performing arts museum, all topped by that tall pointy spire. Well it does look nice at night. The construction of the centre certainly caused some problems while at the hole in the ground stage. The more they dug the more it filled up with water and the more they pumped the water out the more the whole locality began to sink! Furthermore the water that drained in proved to be acidic and a low voltage has to be fed through the centre's foundations to prevent them rotting away!

Parks & Gardens

Victoria has dubbed itself 'the garden state' and it's certainly true in Melbourne, the city has many swathes of green all round the central area. They're varied and delightful; formal central gardens like the Treasury and Flagstaff Gardens, wide empty parklands like the Royal Park, a particularly fine botanical garden and many others. In the summer months the FEIP (Free Entertainment in the Parks) programme puts on a wide variety of entertainment in city parks on weekday lunchtimes and on weekends.

Royal Botanical Gardens Arguably the finest gardens in Australia and certainly one of the finest in the world this is one of my favourites spots in Melbourne. There's nothing more genteel to do in Melbourne that to have scones and cream by the lake on a Sunday afternoon — and Maureen and I do most Sundays we're in town! The beautifully laid out gardens are right beside the Yarra River, indeed the river once actually ran through the gardens and the lakes are the remains of curves of the river, cut off when the river was straightened out to lessen the annual flood damage when it used to wind back and forth across the flood plain at this point. The garden site was chosen in 1845 but the real development took place when Baron Sir Ferdinand von Mueller took charge in 1852.

There's a surprising amount of fauna as well as flora in the gardens. Apart from the ever present water fowl and the frequent visits from cockatoos you may also see rabbits and possums if you're lucky. In all more than 50 varieties of birds can be seen in the gardens. Recently a large contingent of fruit bats, usually found in the warmer climes of north Queensland, have taken up summer residence. You can pick up guide yourself leaflets at the park entrances, these are changed with the seasons and tell you what to look out for at the different times of year.

Kings Domain The gardens form a corner of the Kings Domain, a park which also contains the Shrine of Remembrance, La Trobe's Cottage, the Sidney Myer Music Bowl and is flanked by the majestic St Kilda Rd, the grand avenue which leads straight out from the heart of the city. The whole park is encircled by the 'tan track', a four km running track which is probably Melbourne's favourite venue for joggers. It's another of my Melbourne regulars, I do a couple of laps every Sunday morning but I must admit I'm slower than I was a year or two ago. The track has an amusing variety of exercise points — a mixture of the stations of the cross and miniature golf someone once said.

Beside the St Kilda Rd stands the massive Shrine of Remembrance, a WW I war memorial which took so long to build that WW II was well underway when it eventually opened. The shrine is another example of the Melbourne architectural jinx — huge though it is and imposing though it was intended to be the shrine somehow manages to look completely anonymous. You can almost forget it is there. It's worth climbing up to the top walkway as there are fine views from there into the city along the St Kilda Rd. From up there you can clearly see how the St Kilda Rd runs so straight out of the city and on to St Kilda, but takes a distinct kink around the memorial. The shrine's big day of the year is Anzac Day; back during the Vietnam era some commendably enterprising individuals managed to sneak up to the well guarded shrine on the night before Anzac Day and paint 'PEACE' across the front in large letters. The shrine is open to visitors Monday to Saturday from 10 am to 5 pm, Sunday from 2 to 5 pm.

Across from the shrine is La Trobe Cottage, the original government house sent out from the mother country in prefabricated form in 1840. It was originally sited in Jolimont, near the MCG, and moved here when the decision was made to preserve this interesting piece of Melbourne's early history. The simple little cottage is open daily and admission is $1.20 (students 60c). Beside the cottage is the Old Observatory and the National Herbarium, where, amongst other things, marijuana samples are tested to make sure they really are the dreaded weed. The imposing building overlooking the botanic gardens is Government House where Vic-

toria's governor resides. It's a copy of one of Queen Victoria's palaces, on the Isle of Wight.

Up at the city end of the park is the Sidney Myer Music Bowl a functional outdoor performance area in a natural bowl. It's used for all manner of concerts in the summer months but rock concerts here sometimes become rather disreputable as young drunks create havoc with the flora and leave mountains of garbage. A real shame.

Treasury & Fitzroy Gardens These two popular formal parks lie immediately to the east of the city centre, overshadowed by the Hilton Hotel. The Fitzroy Gardens with their stately avenues, lined with English elms, are a popular spot for wedding photograhs; on virtually every Saturday afternoon of the year there's a continuous procession of wedding cars pulling up here for the participants to be snapped. From above, the pathways in the park are laid out in the form of a union jack! The gardens contain several points of interest including Captain Cook's cottage. It was uprooted from its native Yorkshire and reassembled in the park in 1934. Actually it's not certain that the good captain ever did live in this house but never mind, it looks very picturesque there. The house is furnished in period style and has an interesting Captain Cook exhibit. It's open 10 am to 4.30 pm daily and admission is 60c. The Brits got a lump of good Aussie rock in exchange.

In the centre of the gardens, by the refreshment kiosk, is a small miniature Tudor village and a fairytale carved tree. Off in the north-west corner of the park is the people's pathway — a circular brick paved path made with individually engraved bricks. Anybody who dropped by here on 5 February 1978 got to produce their own little bit of art for posterity and it's quite intriguing to wander around.

Other Parks The central Flagstaff Gardens were the first public gardens in Melbourne. From a lookout point here, ships arriving at the city were sighted in the early colonial days. A plaque in the gardens describes how the site was used for this purpose. Closer to the seafront is Albert Park Lake, a shallow lake created from a swamp area. The lake is popular for boating and there's another popular jogging track around the perimetre. You can hire boats on the lake, the Jolly Roger Boathouse is at the city end of the lake and rents rowboats for $5 to $7 an hour, sailing boats at $5, $7 and $10 an hour.

On the north side of the city the Exhibition Gardens are the site of the Exhibition Buildings, a wonder of the southern hemisphere when they were built for the Great Exhibition of 1880. Later they served as the Federal Parliament building for 27 years until Canberra's parliament building was finally completed. They're still a major exhibition centre today and a new extension is one of the few really successful uses of the 'mirror building' architectural craze which appears to have gripped Melbourne. There are some fine old fountains around the old building, one of them well reflected in the mirror building.

Trams
If Melbourne has a man made symbol then it's a moveable one — trams. Not those horrible, plastic looking orange things either: real Melbourne trams are green and yellow, ancient looking and half the weight of an ocean liner. Melbourne's trams are the standard means of public transport and they work remarkably well, more than a few cities which once had trams probably wish they still did today. The old trams are gradually being replaced by new ones but the orange colour has proved so unpopular that new ones to be introduced will be in the traditional green and

cream colour. Some of the older trams have been turned into mobile works of art, painted from front to back by local artists. I like the one covered in sheep. If you like old trams then watch out for them on weekends, some delightful old vintage trams are rolled out on summer Sundays and used in place of the modern ones on the Hawthorn run from Princes Gate.

To get to grips with Melbourne and its trams try a ride on number 8. It starts off along Swanston St in the city, rolls down the St Kilda Rd beside the Kings Domain, turns round by the war memorial and on to the Toorak Rd through South Yarra and Toorak. As you near Chapel St on the Toorak Rd look for my 'it should be bombed' prize for ugly monstrosities, the ANZ Bank computer building on your left. Another popular tram ride is number 15 which cruises right down the St Kilda Rd to St Kilda. Trams are such a part of Melbourne life they've even been used for a play — act one of *Storming Mt Albert by Tram* took place from Mt Albert to the city, act two on the way back. The passengers were the audience, the actors got on and off along the way. It wasn't a bad play!

Melbourne trams require a little care for non-users. You can only overtake a tram on the inside and must always stop behind one when they halt to drop or collect passengers. In the city centre there are a number of junctions where a peculiar path must be followed to make right hand turns, in order to accommodate the trams. Note that in rainy weather tram tracks are extremely slippery, motorcyclists should take special care. Bicyclists must beware of tram tracks at all times, if you get a wheel into the track you're on your face immediately. I've done that twice in Melbourne, smashing a pair of glasses on one occasion.

Melbourne Suburbs

Melbourne's inner city suburbs have gone through the same 'trendification' process that has hit Sydney suburbs like Paddington and Balmain. Carlton is the most obvious example of this activity but Parkville, South Melbourne, Albert Park, Richmond and Hawthorn are other popular inner city suburbs with a strong Victorian flavour.

Carlton This is one of Melbourne's most interesting inner city suburbs — partly because here you'll find probably the most attractive collection of Victoriana, partly because the university is here and partly because Carlton is also the Italian quarter of Melbourne with the biggest collection of Italian restaurants in Australia. Lygon St is the backbone of Carlton and along here you'll find enough Italian restaurants, coffee houses, pizzerias and gelateria to satisfy the most rabid pasta and cappucino freak. Carlton is flanked by gracious Parkville and the seedy/trendy mixture of Fitzroy.

South Yarra & Toorak South of the Yarra River, as the name indicates, South Yarra is one of the more frenetic Melbourne suburbs, Toorak one of the most exclusive. The two roads to remember here are Toorak Rd and Chapel St. The Toorak Rd is one of Australia's classiest shopping streets, heavily populated by those well known Toorak matrons in their Porsches and Benzes. Apart from expensive shops and some of Australia's best, though also most expensive, restaurants, the Toorak Rd also has a number of very reasonably. priced places to eat. The Toorak Rd forms the main artery through both South Yarra and Toorak.

Running across the Toorak Rd is Chapel St in South Yarra; if the word for the Toorak Rd is 'exclusive' then for Chapel St it's 'trendy'. The street is virtually wall-to-wall boutiques ranging from punk to Indian bangles and beads, op shop to antique. Plus restaurants, the imaginative Jam Factory shopping centre and, at the Prahran end of the street, the delightful Prahran market. The market is a great place for fruit and vegetables and you'll find me here early every Friday morning. Chapel St fades away into Prahran but take a right turn by the Prahran town hall and wander along Greville St, at one time Melbourne's freak street but now become a little ordinary and dull.

South Yarra also has one of Australia's finest colonial mansions, overlooking the Yarra River from Como Park. Built between 1840 and 1859 Como House is now the authentically restored and furnished headquarters of the National Trust. Aboriginal rites and feasts were still being held on the banks of the Yarra when the house was first built and an early occupant writes of seeing a cannibal feast from her bedroom window. Como is open 11 am to 3 pm Wednesday to Friday, 10 am to 5 pm on the weekends, admission is $2 (students 80c) and you can get there on a number 8 tram from the city.

Richmond As Carlton is to Italy so is Richmond to Greece; this suburb, just to the east of the city centre, is the Greek centre for the third largest Greek city in the world. That's right, after Athens and Thessaloniki, Melbourne is the next largest city in terms of Greek population. Richmond is, of course, the best place for a souvlaki in Melbourne! Richmond is another centre for Victorian architecture, much of it restored or currently in the process of restoration. It's also where I live and where Lonely Planet has its office; yes I know our post office box address is across the river in South Yarra. On the corner of Lennox and Swan Sts is a small post office museum open Monday, Wednesday and Friday from 10 am to 4 pm on Sundays from 1 to 5 pm.

St Kilda This seaside suburb is Melbourne's most cosmopolitan and most lively on weekends, particularly on Sundays. It's also the somewhat feeble excuse for a Melbourne sin centre, if you're after sin you'll do better in Sydney's Kings Cross. St Kilda is, however, most definitely Melbourne's drug centre and a sorrier scene for that. If you want a meal late at night or some activity on the weekends then St Kilda is the place to be. Fitzroy St with its many restaurants, snack bars and takeaways is the main street in St Kilda and also the red light centre. Sunday morning along the Esplanade in St Kilda features an interesting amateur art show while along Acland St gluttons will have their minds blown by the amazing selection of cakes in the coffee shop windows. St Kilda has lots of local Jewish and ethnic colour. The huge old Palais Theatres and the raucous Luna Park amusement centre, with roller-coasters and the like, can also be found here.

Williamstown At the mouth of the Yarra this is one of the oldest parts of Melbourne and has many interesting old buildings. Williamstown remained relatively isolated from developments in the rest of Melbourne until the completion of the Westgate Bridge suddenly brought it to within a few minutes' drive of the centre. *HMAS Castlemaine*, a WW II minesweeper, is now preserved as a Maritime Museum and is open on weekends. Williamstown also has an Historical Museum on Electra St and the Railway Museum on Champion Rd, North Williamstown has a fine collection of old steam locomotives.

Other Suburbs South of the centre are other Victorian inner suburbs with many finely restored old homes, particularly in South Melbourne, Middle Park and seaside Albert Park. Emerald Hill in South Melbourne is a whole section of 1880s Melbourne, still in relatively authentic shape. Wealthier inner suburbs to the west, also popular shopping centres, include Armadale, Malvern, Hawthorn and Camberwell. Sandwiched between the city and Richmond is the compact area of East Melbourne, like Parkville it's one of the most concentrated areas of old Victorian buildings around the city with numerous excellent examples of early architecture.

Ripponlea is at 192 Hotham St, Elsternwick, close to St Kilda. It's another fine old mansion with elegant gardens inhabited by peacocks. Ripponlea is open 11 am to 3 pm Wednesday to Friday, 10 am to 5 pm on weekends, admission is $2 (students 80c). In Eltham, the mud brick and back-to-the-earth suburb, Montsalvat on Hillcrest Avenue (26 km out) is an artists colony open dawn to dusk daily.

Beaches
Melbourne hasn't got fine surf beaches like Sydney, at least not close to the city, but it's still not at all badly equipped for beaches and you can find surf further out on the Mornington Peninsula. Starting from the city end, Port Melbourne, Albert Park and South

Melbourne all have very popular beaches. They're often quite crowded. Elwood, Brighton and Sandringham are not bad and Half Moon Bay is very good for a suburban beach. Beyond here you have to get right round to the Mornington Peninsula before you find the really excellent beaches.

Places to Stay

Melbourne has a fairly wide range of accommodation. It's not centred in any particular area although the old fashioned hotels are found mainly in the city, particularly around Spencer St railway station. The seaside suburb of St Kilda is probably the best general accommodation centre in Melbourne. There you'll find a wide variety of reasonably priced motels, private hotels, guest houses and holiday flats. St Kilda also has an excellent selection of eating places ranging from cheap take-away places to some of Melbourne's finest restaurants. It's the most cosmopolitan area of Melbourne and a bit like a lower key version of Sydney's Kings Cross.

For places to share the university noticeboards, the board in the youth hostel office and the front window of Readings in Carlton are all worth checking. *The Age* classified columns on Wednesdays and Saturdays is the place to look for longer term accommodation. It is much easier to find places to rent in Melbourne than in Sydney. Note that most of the cheaper hotels, guest houses and the like will also offer cheaper weekly rates. These are typically about four times the daily rates so it soon becomes cheaper to stay for a week.

Hostels There are actually two *Melbourne Youth Hostels* these days. Initially one was simply an overflow for the main hostel but these days such is demand that both are in full time operation. They're only about a minute's walk apart and only about three km

from the city centre in North Melbourne, easily accessible by tram 50, 54 or 57 from Elizabeth St. The 500 Abbotsford St Hostel (tel 328 2880) has 44 beds while the 76 Chapman St hostel (tel 328 3595) has 100. The Chapman St hostel is a more modern building with 50 double rooms while the Abbotsford St one is normal dorm style. Both hostels have good noticeboards if you're looking for people to travel with, share lifts, airline tickets going cheap or just general information. Nightly charges are $5.50 at either hostel. If you're coming in from the airport ask the driver to drop you near the YH (the buses go by Abbotsford St along Flemington Rd soon after leaving the Tullamarine Freeway) and he should be obliging. You can also arrange for the airport bus to pick you up from the hostel, to save the trek into town.

The Y The *YWCA Family Motel* (tel 329 5188) is conveniently central at 489 Elizabeth St and very competitively priced. Singles/doubles are $19/26 and rooms all have shower and toilet, heating and cooling and tea making facilities. Outside it's very much '70s bare concrete but inside it's functional and well-equipped. There's also a rather basic cafeteria here. The YWCA is almost directly across the road from the airport bus office.

Hotels Melbourne's cheap hotels tend to be concentrated at the Spencer St end of the city, around the railway station and also close to the Greyhound bus terminal. At 44 Spencer St the *Spencer Hotel/Motel* (tel 62 6991) is making a real pitch for the travellers' market offering information and advice at the adjoining Overseas Visitors Centre as well as accommodation. They have rooms at $10/14 in the older hotel section or motel-style rooms at $25/28 and $28/32. It's rather brighter inside than its somewhat gloomy exterior would indicate.

Close by at 131 King St the *Kingsgate Hotel* (tel 62 4171) used to be the old Peoples Palace. It's still very big (over 200 rooms) with prices including a light breakfast from $15 to $25 single, $22 to $34 double. The rooms vary widely — the most expensive have private facilities, air-con, fridges, and so on. In between there are rooms with attached shower and toilet, or just a washbasin, or right at the bottom they're very bare and basic.

Very centrally located at 215 Little Collins St, *The Victoria* (tel 63 0441) is a notch up market from the cheapest city hotels. It's a big place with no less than 520 rooms. There are 135 basic rooms without private facilities which cost $21/26 for singles/doubles. The majority of the rooms have private facilities, colour TV and other mod-cons and are rather more expensive at around $36/43. The Victoria is one of the most conveniently located hotels in Melbourne, you could hardly ask to be more centrally located.

There are also numerous private hotels in and around the central city area. The *Great Southern* (tel 62 3989) is an old-fashioned place at 16 Spencer St, another reminder of the days of rail travel. With rooms at $10/14 its prices are pretty old-fashioned too. None of the rooms have attached bathrooms and most of them don't even boast a washbasin. Other very basic city cheapies include the *City Lodge* (tel 67 6679) at 235 King St at $10/15, *Purnall's* (tel 329 7635) at 445 Elizabeth St at $14/19 and the *Hotham* (tel 62 2681) at 2 Spencer St which is $9/12 and a bit grotty looking.

Suburban Accommodation — East & West Melbourne

In the inner suburbs around the central city there are a number of places in the private hotel/ guest house/bed & breakfast categories. All these places will quote cheaper weekly rates. In West Melbourne the *Miami* (tel 329 8499) at 13 Hawke St has wash basins with hot and cold water in all the rooms and breakfast is included in the $14/20 nightly tariff. Although it's very simple and straight-forward the Miami is also very well kept and it's an easy walk from here to the centre. The Miami is a big, square block of a place with over 100 rooms.

Similarly convenient and well kept the *Magnolia Court* (tel 417 2782 or 419 4518) is in East Melbourne at 101 Powlett St which is also only a km from the centre. Rooms here are $22/32, room only, for singles/doubles. *Georgian Court* (tel 419 6353) at 21-25 George St, also in East Melbourne, has rooms from $12 a day, cheaper weekly rates and share cooking facilities. George St is a quiet, tree-lined street and the genteel looking Georgian Court is right across the road from the post office. Although East Melbourne is so close to the city centre it's generally a fairly quiet area.

Suburban Accommodation — South Yarra

A little further out in South Yarra the *Westend* (tel 26 3135) is up at 76 West Toorak Rd. There are tea making facilities and rooms cost $13/23 including breakfast. The Westend is pleasantly situated looking across Toorak Rd to Fawkner Park. Right in the heart of the South Yarra shopping area, about midway between the South Yarra railway station and Chapel St, the *Toorak Private Hotel* (tel 241 8652) is at 189 Toorak Rd. It's a big, dark green building and nightly costs are just $10/ 14 for singles/doubles. Weekly rates are $40/56.

Suburban Accommodation — St Kilda

It's very easy to get out to seaside St Kilda, just a straightforward tram ride (number 15) from Swanston St in the city, down the wide, tree-lined St Kilda Rd to Fitzroy St. Alternatively suburban

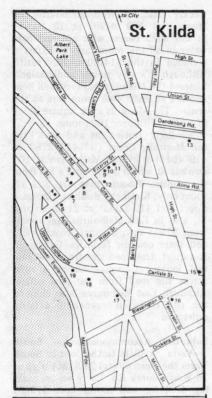

St. Kilda

1 Railway Station
2 Executive Motel
3 Tolarno's
4 Massoni's
5 Cleopatra's
6 Prince of Wales Hotel
7 Leo's Pizza Bar
8 R&M Books
9 Regal Private Hotel
10 Majestic Court Private Hotel
11 Waldorf
12 Hampton House
13 Chapel Motel
14 Linden Court
15 Carlisle Lodge
16 City Gate
17 Cosmos Books
18 Luna Park
19 Palais Theatre

train services run from Flinders St Station to St Kilda where the line terminates right at the junction of Canterbury Rd and Fitzroy St.

Up at the city end of Fitzroy St there's a clump of possibilities. First of all at 155 Fitzroy St there's the rather basic *Waldorf* (tel 534 5039) with daily rates from around $10 or weekly costs of $33 single, $50 double. Next door is the big, genteely old-fashioned *Majestic Court Private Hotel* (tel 94 0561) at 151 Fitzroy St. Rooms here cost $22/30 for singles/doubles with private facilities. Breakfast costs around $2 to $4. Next door again at 149 is the *Regal Private Hotel* (tel 534 5603 or 4053) with bed & breakfast (a 'nice breakfast' they say) at $12 for singles, $20 for doubles. Rooms have hot and cold water but not private facilities.

The restaurants and shops along Fitzroy St start just down from these three places. Just round the corner off Fitzroy St is *Hampton House* (tel 534 5283) at 24 Grey St. Rooms cost $10/18 for singles/doubles including breakfast, it's a rather gloomy place of the run down school. Another block down Fitzroy St and you can turn off on to Acland St where *Linden Court* (tel 534 2396) is a small private hotel in a National Trust classified building at number 26. Bed and breakfast rates start from $12.50 for a single, $22 for a double but there are also more expensive rooms with private facilities from $19/26 for singles/doubles. Once again cheaper weekly rates are available. There are communal tea making facilities and a TV lounge. There are a lot more places in similar style around St Kilda, the above is just a small selection.

Just around the bay from St Kilda is Elwood where the *Bayside* (tel 531 4778) is at 65 Ormond Esplanade, a rather busy road separated by a narrow park from the bay. All rooms have TVs, fridges, and tea making facilities, some have attached bathrooms. Nightly costs including breakfast are $15/25. Again cheaper weekly rates are available, including all meals.

Motels The Spencer Hotel/Motel and the YWCA both offer motel style accommodation in the city centre and are reasonably priced. There's no real motel strip in Melbourne but you can find reasonably priced and fairly central motels in South Yarra and St Kilda in particular. The *Domain* (tel 26 3701) is at 52-54 Darling St in South Yarra and has rooms at $25/31. Rooms have all the usual motel mod cons and it's conveniently close to the tram lines for the centre and to the Yarra River.

In St Kilda *Carlisle Lodge* (tel 534 0416) at 32 Carlisle St is very cheap at $22/26. It's a plain, slightly older motel but rooms have fridges and cooking facilities as well as air-con and the other usual motel facilities. The *Chapel Motel* (tel 51 5371) at 64 Wellington St is also reasonably low priced at $25/30. It's a big block near to the Dandenong Rd and Chapel St. Almost on the corner with Fitzroy St, directly opposite the station, the *Executive* (tel 534 0303 or 04) is at 239 Canterbury Rd and has rooms at $24/29. It's a square, featureless cube looking just like a block of flats rather than a motel, but conveniently close to all the noise and colour on Fitzroy St.

You'll also find some reasonably priced motels in less attractively situated suburbs on the main routes into and out of Melbourne. In Coburg the *Coburg Coach House* (tel 350 2844) is at 846 Sydney Rd (the road from Sydney) has rooms at $27/32. Ditto in Footscray, the route from Adelaide, where the *Mid Gate Motor Lodge* (tel 689 2170) is on 76 Droop St and has rooms at $25/28.

Holiday Flats There are a couple of associated places in St Kilda with motel style rooms which also have cooking facilities. *Melbourne Gate* (tel 51 5870)

is at 87 Alma Rd on the corner with Chapel St while *City Gate* (tel 534 2650) is at 6 Tennyson Rd. Melbourne Gate is a more modern building (and will have also added the adjoining building before this book appears) while City Gate is on a rather quieter street. Typical costs for singles are $24 for motel-style rooms with kitchenettes, $28 for one-bedroom flats. Equivalent weekly rates would be $69/85 while as a double a one-bedroom flat would cost $120 a week. They also have larger holiday flats with two and three bedrooms but the majority are just one bedroom.

Colleges Melbourne has three universities, the long established Melbourne University and two newer 'bush universities' — La Trobe and Monash. Visitors would probably find the latter too far away from the centre to be worth considering. Melbourne University, by contrast, is very central, just to the north of the city centre. Colleges with accommodation in the vacations are Ridley College (tel 387 7555) with non-student rates from $8 a day room only, St Hilda's College (tel 347 1158) at $21.50 including breakfast, Whitley College (tel 347 8388) from $11 per day room only, Ormond College (tel 347 4837) from $20 including breakfast, Trinity College (tel 347 1044) from $18 including breakfast, St Mary's College (tel 347 4311) from $12 including breakfast, University College (tel 347 1073) from $18 room only and finally International House (tel 347 2351) from $12.60 per day including breakfast and dinner plus lunch on weekends.

All these places are conveniently central, most of them in Parkville. There are some other Melbourne University colleges which only offer accommodation to convention groups. Generally the colleges above are available during the vacations although some close over Christmas. Only some require advance booking but almost all of them prefer it. International House is one of the best bets and also has accommodation year round although your chances are best in the vacations.

Camping Melbourne is not too badly off for city campsites although none of them are too close to the city centre. The Coburg East site (10 km north) and the Footscray site (eight km west) are probably the most convenient. The Footscray site only has on-site vans but the Coburg one is quite comprehensively equipped as well as being handily situated. The following are some of Melbourne's closer campsites.

Half Moon Caravan Park (tel 314 5148), corner Geelong & Millers Rd, Brooklyn, 11 km west, camping $5, on-site vans $16 to 18.

Northside Caravan Park (tel 305 3614), corner Hume Highway & Coopers Rd, Campbellfield, 14 km north, camping $6, on-site vans $17.

Sylvan Caravan Park (tel 359 1592), 1780 Hume Highway, Campbellfield, 14 km north, camping $6, on-site vans $15 to 17.

Melbourne Caravan Park (tel 354 3533), 265 Elizabeth St, Coburg East, 10 km north, camping $5, on-site vans $17 to 20, flats $20 to 25.

Crystal Brook Caravan Park (tel 844 3637), corner Warrandyte & Andersons Creek Rd, Doncaster East, 21 km northeast, camping $6.50, on-site vans $19.

Footscray Caravan Park (tel 314 6646), 163 Somerville Rd, West Footscray, eight km west, no camping, on-site vans $14 to 16.

West City Caravan Park (tel 363 3262), 610 Ballarat Rd, Sunshine, 13 km west, camping $4.

Willowbrook Gardens Caravan Village (tel 333 1619), Mickleham Rd, West Meadows, 18 km north-west, camping $6 or 7, on-site vans $17 to 20.

Hobsons Bay Caravan Park (tel 397 2395), 158 Kororoit Creek Rd, Williamstown, 17 km south, camping $6, on-site vans $14.

Places to Eat

The Victorian licensing laws make it very difficult and expensive to get a liquor license but quite simple to obtain a BYO license. The resulting plethora of BYO's are held by staunch Melbournians to be the cornerstone of Melbourne's culinary superiority. There are lots of licensed restaurants too, some of which are actually cheap, but it's the BYO's which you find everywhere around the city. It's very rare to be charged 'corkage' when you bring your own wine to a Melbourne BYO.

Melbourne is so keen about food that you'll also find the best restaurant guide in Australia if you want to read about it as well as eat it! The *Age Good Food Guide*, available from bookshops for $7.95. The Melbourne Yellow Pages phone directory runs to 26 pages of restaurants. There are restaurants all around the city and there are often real national quarters — go to Lygon St, Carlton for Italian food; Swan St, Richmond for Greek food; Sydney Rd, Brunswick for Turkish, Little Bourke St in the city for Chinese.

City — Chinese While elsewhere around Melbourne food tends to be regional by area, in the city you'll find a bit of everything. The city is, however, the centre for Chinese food and you'll find a superb variety along Little Bourke St, the Chinatown of Melbourne. Most of the Little Bourke Chinese restaurants tend to be more expensive, however. You have to dive off into the narrow lanes off Little Bourke, or abandon it altogether, to find the real bargains. Like *Nam Loong* at 223 Russell St where even the blackboard menu is in Chinese. You almost feel like they're condescending to you when they produce an English menu and you can certainly expect nothing but chopsticks. The prices are something to smile about — apart from a few specials at $4 or $5 almost everything on the menu is a standard $2.80 and it's not bad food. Plus excellent Chinese tea comes free. Eat early though, Nam Loong closes at 9 pm.

Peony Gardens at 283 Little Lonsdale is more of a take-away place, less a restaurant. They say you'll find good Chinese food in restaurants patronised by the Chinese. So a restaurant patronised by Chinese students should be not only good but cheap too. At Peony Gardens most dishes are in the $1.80 to $2.80 bracket and at that price you really can't complain about the plastic plates and utensils or having to clear the table off after you've eaten. One catch — it closes promptly at 7.30 pm.

On Little Bourke St there are, of course, some bargains to be found. Like the pleasant *Golden Orchid* at 126 where the service may be rather abrupt but the food is excellent and a couple can eat for around $15. A new place is the big *Asian Food Plaza* on the corner of Little Bourke and Russell Sts. It's got a huge menu featuring all manner of Chinese, Malaysian, Vietnamese, Korean and other Asian food. The kitchens around the dining area are all open so you can see what's going on and the prices are generally in the $4 and $5 range. Around the city you'll also find plenty of Japanese and Korean places.

City — Other Open from 7 am to midnight every day and 24 hours over the weekend the *Pancake Parlour* is the place to go for a meal from breakfast to a late night snack. It's at 25 Market Lane, is fairly fast-foodish in atmosphere and a bit expensive but very popular. There's another branch in Centrepoint on Bourke St. The *Pancake House* is next to the main Pancake Parlour and offers similar fare and an open air courtyard in the back.

Carry on a little further up Bourke St, cross the road past the Whole Earth bookshop and you'll find another late night place at 20 Meyers Place. The *Italian Waiters Club* is totally anonymous, you just climb the stairs, open the door and there it is. It's open Monday to Saturday to midnight and the food is straightforward and not bad. Across Bourke St is another Melbourne institution — *Pelligrini's* at 64. It's a quick meal sort of place with usual pasta dishes. If you want to take things a little easier then go round the corner to Crossley St where you can relax over the same food at slightly higher prices.

Lebanese House at 268 Russell St is one of the longest running Lebanese restaurants in Melbourne and these days it's definitely not one of the best. It's reasonably priced, however, and also fairly central. At 289 Little Lonsdale St, *Orhans Place* is a great Turkish restaurant with a special lunch at $3.80, main courses at $4 to $5 and a set dinner for $8.50. On Friday and Saturday nights there's a belly dancer. *Campari Bistro* at 25 Hardware St, a hop, step and jump from the GPO, is a busy little Italian bistro, which can get very crowded at lunchtime.

Lygon St You can take a 1, 15, 21 or 22 tram from the centre but you can also walk to Lygon St, it's no distance at all from central Melbourne. This is not only the Italian centre of Melbourne it probably also qualifies as the restaurant centre of the city as there are literally dozens of places to eat scattered along Lygon St. Starting from the city end there's *Toto's Pizza House* at 101. They claim to be the first pizzeria in Australia and true or not they certainly make some of the best pizzas in Melbourne — with prices from $3 to $4 for small pizzas, $5 to $7 for large ones it's also great value. Toto's is licensed but drinks are very reasonably priced, a litre carafe of house wine is just $2.80.

As a final plus it's open past midnight every night of the week.

Head on up Lygon St after your pizza for an excellent coffee and cake at *Notturno* at 177-179. There are tables out on the pavement and it's open 24 hours. Or continue to 215 where *Il Gambero* is another long runner. They're a seafood specialist and also do pizzas. The food is a bit variable, some things pretty good, some things pretty awful — like garlic bread made with garlic salt! Nevertheless the seafood can be good, it's open until midnight and two can have three courses here for $20 to $25 and their pizzas are very very good. Better, some say, than *Papa Gino's Pizzas* a couple of doors up. On the other side of the street is the long running *Cafe Sport* at 262 Lygon St. It's one of those hidden places, you have to walk through the coffee bar and up the anonymous stairs at the back. And what do you find there? The Lygon St Italian standard menu — fairly good food at fairly reasonable prices.

Between Faraday and Elgin Sts there's a whole collection of places to eat but first turn off Lygon St to *Johnny's Green Room* at 194 Faraday St. They're another place open 24 hours a day, a place where you can get a cheap bowl of spaghetti and a cup of strong coffee (a game of pool too if you must) at any hour of the night. Back on Lygon St there's *Tiamo's* at 303 — old timers still refer to it as Tamani's. It's a straightforward pasta place with most dishes in the $3 to $5 bracket. Popular with students from Melbourne University, which is only a short stroll up Faraday St.

Right across the road *Cafe Paradiso* at 368 Lygon St is tremendously popular. The blackboard menu reveals nothing out of the Carlton-standard and the food itself is just simple and straightforward but it's a pleasant, relaxed place to be. A place where you can always sit and talk for another half

hour over yet another cup of coffee. Prices here are all very reasonable but the desserts are the Paradiso's crowning achievement — one of their trifles (particularly!), fruit salads or cheesecake is not only delicious but likely to be big enough for two. As an additional bonus there's a superb shady courtyard out back, covered by an enormous grapevine, which in summer is one of the best places in Melbourne to eat. I'm often there on Saturday lunchtime. Unhappily the Paradiso's position is threatened — heartless developers are planning to tear the building down and build some dreary new shopping centre or office block. Protest!

Almost next door to the Paradiso is *Brunetti's Cakes Gelateria* which does superb ice cream. There's a popular theory that hidden somewhere in the middle of Lygon St there's an enormous Italian kitchen that turns out all the food for all the restaurants in Carlton — they're that much alike! There are, however, some different places. At 376 Lygon St, just a few doors down from the Paradiso, the *Pancake Place* does good pancake dishes. Across the road there's *Shakahari* at 329 Lygon St. This is one of Melbourne's longest running and most popular vegetarian restaurants with a really interesting menu. Typical prices for main courses are around $5 to $6, count on around $20 for a complete meal for two in this pleasantly relaxed restaurant.

Almost next door is the famed *Jimmy Watson's Wine Bar* — see pub food. Or turn the corner to 183 Elgin St where *Borbles* is yet another Carlton place which has been running for years. It's rather more of a restaurant and less of a cafe than many other Lygon St places, pleasant inside and the service is friendly. Main courses are in the $6.50 to $8.50 bracket and two can have a complete meal for around $25 to $30.

Back towards the city and a block

over from Lygon St Indian food enthusiasts can consider *Phantom India* at 472 Swanston St. This was the place that kicked off Melbourne's current fad for tandoori food. Food cooked in a tandoori oven emerges with a special and very delicious flavour and this place does it well and at not too outrageous prices — around $30 to $35 for two.

Richmond Take a 70, 71 or 77 tram from Batman Avenue, by the river in the city, and get off on Swan St at the Church St junction in Richmond, the Greek centre of Melbourne. You're now precisely half way between where I live and where Lonely Planet lives, both in Richmond. The hundred metres or so along Swan St away from the city past the Church St junction is virtually wall-to-wall Greek restaurants and the best/most popular has to be the *Laikon* at 272. Remember a Greek L is like an upside down V but you can always recognise the Laikon from the prosperous proprietor's hairy Ford Falcon Cobra in blue and white Greek national colours outside! Inside the Laikon is as plain as you could ask for. Don't fuss around, order zatsiki and taramosalata (both dips), pitta bread to dip in them, and souvlaki (kebabs) which come with salad. A sticky sweet dessert and coffee will leave you change from $10 and the food is as delicious and straightforward as you could ask for. Don't expect somebody to come to your table to take your order, front the counter and ask for what you want. You can also cork your own wine bottle (opener on the end of the counter) and grab the glasses too! The Laikon is open every day of the week until midnight. It's also excellent for take-aways, a souvlaki in pitta to go is just $1.40. In fact all this talking about it has just inspired us to send out for them for lunch!

The Laikon is just one of the many Greek restaurants along here but it's probably the best value for money.

Richmond isn't all Greek, however. There's a variety of cuisines along parallel Bridge Rd including *Enris* at 344, an Argentinian restaurant where steak and garlic are the order of the day. Enri is a great character but you'll pay about $40 for two and it's strictly for big meat eaters. You'll also find a couple of Indian restaurants in Richmond (both so so) and a lot of Vietnamese. In fact Victoria St has been dubbed 'Little Saigon' from the number of Vietnamese who have moved in around here. Back towards Europe and right across the road from the Valhalla Cinema is the *Cyprus Kebab House* at 387 Victoria St. It's got a relaxed coffee bar atmosphere, food with a Turkish flavour and low prices. Also opposite the Valhalla is one of Melbourne's multitude of *Taco Bill's* Mexican restaurants where you get assembly line Mexican food, but pretty good for all that.

Sydney Rd Head directly north of the city centre along that majestic avenue Royal Parade and you suddenly find yourself in the narrow, congested shopping street Sydney Rd, Brunswick. This is indeed the road to Sydney but it's also one of the worst bottlenecks in Melbourne, at least in the rush hours. In the evening it's no problem at all and this is Melbourne's Turkist restaurant area. You can get there from the city centre on an 18, 19 or 20 tram.

If you've not tried Turkish food before it's very straightforward, honest fare, closely related to Greek or Lebanese food. Lots of interesting starters, main courses like kebabs, spiced lamb, various grilled meats, a wide variety of interesting desserts. Best of all it's generally very cheap and the Turkish restaurants along Sydney Rd often bake their own delicious bread on the premises — Turkish bread is superb. The Turkish restaurants along Sydney Rd are a fairly recent phenomenom but most of them are already very popular, though curiously enough the first couple on the scene (both excellent places too) have now disappeared.

You can't miss *Alasya* at 555 Sydney Rd, it's so popular that it's engulfed the places next door and spawned an identical offshoot, Alasya 2, closer to the city at 163 Sydney Rd. Here, as at most of the other Turkish places, you can choose from the menu or opt for a fixed price meal which gets you a dozen (yes!) starters, a mixture of main courses, a selection of desserts, heaps of freshly baked bread, coffee and all for $7 a head. Terrific value and you'd better bring a healthy appetite with you. Quite a bit further up Sydney Rd, the *Golden Teras* (or Terrace) at 820 is a smaller place and equally popular. Just across the road the spacious *Sultan Ahmet* at 835 is more of the same. Fixed price menu for $8 or choose from the menu (which doesn't have prices). Main courses around $4, all the Turkish regulars.

South Yarra Along Toorak Rd you'll find some of Melbourne's most expensive restaurants — places where a couple would have no trouble paying $70 or $100 for a meal. Fortunately there are some more relevant places in between — like *Pinocchio's* at 152 Toorak Rd. This is my favourite pizzeria on this side of town and it also has a blackboard menu of other standard Italian favourites. Pizzas generally cost from $4.60 to $6 for small ones, $6.80 to $8 for large but the take-away prices are much lower ($3.50 to $4.50 and $5.50 to $6.50), a dollar or so more for the specials. It's a pleasant and convenient place to eat and the pizzas are excellent.

Only a couple of doors away at 156 is *Tamani's*, Italian once again, a long running favourite restaurant with good pasta dishes and salads. Prices here are around $3 to $4 for pasta dishes, chicken and veal dishes for around $5 to $6. Just across the railway tracks at

164 *Alfio's* is almost too smoothly trendy looking for its own good but the prices aren't bad, there's a nice sunny courtyard out back and their pasta is superb. Backtrack down Toorak Rd to number 74 where you'll find similar ambience and similar food at the *Barola Bistro* — a pleasant little expresso bar with a blackboard menu and snappy service.

South Yarra's not all Italian, backtrack again to the South Yarra post office and across the road is *Yarra's* at 97, with main courses in the $6 to $7 range and nice desserts. Continue down Toorak Rd and you'll find *Norgen-Vaaz* ice cream at 232 with possibly the best ice cream in Melbourne, possibly the most expensive too. Right turn into Chapel St where you'll find a whole string of restaurants including the 24 hour *Spaghetti Graffiti. Amigo's* at 596 is a pleasant little Mexican place, principally for take-aways but you can also eat there and the food is good and reasonably priced.

Right on down Chapel St almost to Commercial Rd you'll see *Soda Sisters Drugstore* at 382. It's an authentic facsimile of a '50s American soda fountain with ice cream sodas, sundaes, hamburgers and other representatives of American kulcha. The immensely popular Prahran market is back from the Chapel St-Commercial Rd junction — go here for some of the best fresh vegetables, fruit and fish in Melbourne — and here you'll also find *La Brasserie*, excellent food and a pleasant open air dining area overlooking the market square. A fine place to enjoy a leisurely lunch (about $15 to $20 for two) on a sunny Saturday, especially if there's a jazz band playing. Cross Commercial Rd into Prahran and continue down to Greville St beside the town hall. On Greville St right by the railway lines you ll find the pleasantly relaxed *Feedwell Cafe*, a long running health food place, great for a healthy lunch.

Other Places — North of the City Brunswick St in Fitzroy has developed as a whole new restaurant area in the past few years. It's international — everything from Italian to Indian including Melbourne's only Afghani restaurant. The *Kabul Afghan Restaurant* is at 327 Brunswick St, certainly something a bit different and the atmosphere is pleasant but at $7 to $9 the main courses are a bit expensive and they also charge corkage, mumble, grumble. The *Black Cat* at 252 is an ultra-with-it coffee bar, ideal for coffee and a cake at late hours. At 262 *Chieu Vuong* (King's Retreat) is one of Melbourne's many Vietnamese restaurants, displaced from their usual Richmond location. The food is consistently excellent, the quantities decently sized and the management fall all over themselves to be helpful. Main courses are $5 to $6.50.

Round the corner of Johnston St you'll find Melbourne's Spanish quarter with restaurants like the very Spanish *Costa Brava* at 36. Still in Fitzroy at 199 Gertrude St is *Macedonia*, a pleasantly basic and straightforward Yugoslav restaurant offering the central European regulars including excellent schnitzels. A two course meal for two here can be less than $15 and for dessert you've got a choice of pancakes, pancakes or pancakes. Also on this side of town is the popular *Jim's Greek Tavern* at 32 Johnston St, Collingwood (several blocks away from the Costa Brava despite the similar numbers). Typical Greek food but in a rather more 'restaurant' setting, the prices are still low. At 354 Smith St, Collingwood is *Brussio's*, a small Italian bistro with good food at good prices and pleasant surroundings leaning heavily towards the Chianti bottle look.

In North Fitzroy the *Cosmopolitan* at 454 Nicholson St is definitely worth a visit if you like Lebanese/Middle Eastern food. It's disguised by the pizza take-away counter at the front but behind is the spartan restaurant section where they do extremely good Lebanese food at surprisingly low prices. At 359 Victoria St in West Melbourne is *Amiconi's*, another place with a typical Italian menu but the prices are very reasonable and it's got a pleasantly relaxed atmosphere.

Other Places — South of the City Cross town to South Melbourne where you'll find several places worth considering along Clarendon St. The *Old Paper Shop Deli* at 266 is another place where you can eat outside, on the pavement breathing in the traffic fumes. The food is superb but it's wise to keep an eye on the prices — with care you can eat very reasonably but it's quite easy to keep making additions from the counter and end up with a surprising bill. A bit further along at 331 is the *Chinese Noodle Shop* — excellent noodle dishes at reasonable prices in pleasant surroundings. Further again to *Taco Bill's* at 375 — strictly mass-market Mexican food but good value for all that. There's a whole string of Taco Bills around Melbourne, all very similar, check the addresses in the phone directory.

Continue across to Albert Park where *Yin's Wandering Wok* at 116 Bridport St is Chinese with a difference. Set menus start from around $12 per person and the food is sort of nouvelle cuisine, Chinese-style. On again to Fitzroy St, St Kilda where if you were going to have one super splash out meal in Melbourne then *Tolarno's* would be the place to do it. It's licensed and a complete meal and drinks for two will set you back around $40 to $50 but the food and service are the equal of much more expensive places. Still on Fitzroy St but right at the other end of the price scale is *Cleopatra's* at the seaside end at number 1. It's Lebanese (or Egyptian?) and mainly take-aways but they produce some of the best quality Middle Eastern food in Melbourne, right up there with the Cosmopolitan and very reasonably priced.

Pub Food Melbourne has a good assortment of these, ranging from the humble corner place to some trendy, flashy establishments. The *Palace Hotel* at 893 Burke Rd, Camberwell has to be one of the best food bargains in Melbourne. It's worth the trip out there, take a Camberwell tram from Swanston St which loops round through Prahran to run up Burke Rd, or take a train straight to Camberwell Station, right beside the Palace. Inside there's a long menu featuring all the pub food regulars, from steak, fish or schnitzel to veal parmigiana or chicken kiev. The prices are amazingly reasonable, $3.50 to $4.50 covers the majority of dishes and there's a stunning variety of salads to help yourself from. The only drawback is that the Palace is a lot of other peoples' favourite too! Finding a seat can be difficult! It closes at 8.30 pm.

Since it's a wine bar rather than a pub it's probably not correct to put *Jimmy Watson's* in this section, but never mind. At 333 Lygon St this ever popular place does excellent food as well as reasonably priced wine by the bottle. And it's courtyard is packed to capacity on any sunny Saturday morning.

You'll find quite a few pub food places around South Yarra and Prahran. The *Fawkner Club* (which isn't a club) is only a couple of blocks along Toorak Rd from St Kilda Rd. You can get there on any St Kilda Rd tram (walk down Toorak Rd) or the Toorak tram but then you have to walk back to Toorak Rd where the tram joins it. The Fawkner Club's main attraction is the fine open-air courtyard out front — it's not been altered by a recent up-market trendification inside. Counter meal regulars in the $5 to $7 bracket plus a serve yourself salad table. On Argo St the *Argo Tavern* is a popular pub with

an expensive restaurant but also with good counter food until 9 pm. Prices in the $5 to $7.50 bracket and live music Monday to Thursday and on Saturday night.

Cross over to Chapel St and continue to number 270 where the *Court Jester* serves superior pub food in the $5 to $7 range. They have some slightly adventurous dishes amongst the counter regulars and a good reputation for their food. Now U-turn and go right back along Chapel St through South Yarra, across the Yarra River into Richmond and on your right at 481 Church St (Chapel St changes names with the river) is the *Anchor & Hope*. The restaurant part in front is more expensive but the Bugatti Bar in back (with its amazing collection of car badges, number plates and assorted automotive memorabilia) has a grill-it-yourself barbecue area with steak and other similar dishes in the $4 to $5 range. Lonely Planet's local pub is the *London Tavern* at 238 Lennox St, Richmond. It's a pretty straightforward place but with a very good chef so the food is excellent (and reasonably priced) and with a bright and sunny courtyard so you can eat outside. Finally in Albert Park the *Victoria Hotel* at 123 Beaconsfield Parade is upmarket but pretty good.

Entertainment
The best source of 'what's on' info in Melbourne is the *Age Weekender* which comes out every Friday. During the summer months watch out for the FEIP (Free Entertainment In the Park) programme with activities put on in city parks on weekday lunchtimes and on the weekends. There's also often something going on in the City Square. The recently completed cultural centre by the river will probably become more of a focus for concerts and other performances as time goes on. Melbourne has been in dire need of a good, big place for rock concerts — the Festival

Hall is big but barn like, the Dallas Brooks Hall too small for big events.

Rock Music A lot of Melbourne's night time scene is tied up with rock pubs — some of the big crowded places can afford the top Australian bands and it's for this reason that Melbourne is very much Australia's rock music centre. It's on the sweaty grind around the Melbourne rock pubs that Australia's best bands really prove themselves. The *Age Weekender*, and radio stations like EON FM or 3XY will tell you who's on and where. Cover charges at the pubs vary widely — some nights it's free, generally it's from around $5, big names on weekend nights can cost $6 or more. Music generally starts around 9.30 pm. Those that follow are just a few of the places offering a variety of music.

Although it's not what it once was the small *Station Hotel* on Greville St, Prahran still attracts the crowds. It's one of the longest running of the rock pubs, a place with a bit of a Melbourne rock history. The Saturday arvo sessions are popular. At the opposite end of the scale are places like the *Bombay Rock* a monster place on Phoenix St, Brunswick. It's crowded, rough, expensive, impossible to get to the bar, the bands tend to start late and the bouncers are terrible but you do get the big name bands here — if you don't mind paying $9 or $10 for them. In St Kilda, *Earls Court the Venue* is similar though not quite so bad.

Between these extremes are places like the *Armadale Hotel* in Armadale, not a bad place with upstairs and downstairs rooms (harder rock upstairs?). On Toorak Rd, South Yarra is *Macy's*, a smaller place which operates seven nights a week and has rock videos and pretty reasonable bands — plus a fabulous girl on the door said the girl-on-the-door who happens to be laying this book up.

The *London Tavern* in Caulfield caters mainly for students with middle of the road to bland music. Ditto for the *Prospect Hill* in Kew which attracts fairly big bands, the *Central Club* in Richmond is another student type of pub which caters mainly for small bands. In North Fitzroy the *Aberdeen Hotel* is a small, friendly sort of place catering mainly for fringe bands, something a bit different. *The Club* in Collingwood is similar, attracting interesting fringe bands. In St Kilda *The Ballroom* is a larger fringe place which also gets overseas acts. The big *Club Chevron* on St Kilda Rd, Prahran is free some nights and has quite a good atmosphere. Finally in the city there's *Billboard* on Russell St — basically for rich trendies who like looking at themselves not listening to the music.

Folk Music Yes there are also folk pubs. In the *Age Weekender* check the acoustic music listings as well as folk. One of the most popular is *Dan O'Connell's Hotel* on the corner of Princes and Canning Sts in Carlton. For those interested in Irish music they claim 'we sell more Irish whisky than Scotch' as proof of their Irish authenticity. On High St, Malvern the long running *Green Man* is still a popular folk venue. *Hatters Castle* in South Yarra; the *Troubador* on Brunswick St, Fitzroy; the *New Lincoln Inn* in Carlton and the *Renown Hotel* in Fitzroy are others.

Jazz Just like the pubs that specialise in rock or folk there are also pubs that specialise in jazz. Popular ones include the *Anchor & Hope* on Church St in Richmond or the *Beaumaris Hotel* out at Beaumaris. The *Victoria Hotel* in Albert Park, the *Limerick Arms* in South Melbourne and the *Beaconsfield Hotel* in St Kilda are others and at *La Brasserie* at Prahran Market in South Yarra you can, if the weather is co-operating, sit outside and enjoy the jazz.

Discos For those who like their music canned rather than live Melbourne also has its fair share of discos ranging from the absurdly expensive on down. The *Melbourne Underground* on King St, near Flinders St in the city, is a much flashier establishment than the rock pub havens. There are a number of restaurants in this sprawling establishment. Others include *Inflation* on King St, *Sheiks* on Collins St and *Madison's* on Flinders Lane, all in the city.

Pubs & Wine Bars Apart from the music pubs there are quite a few other popular pubs and wine bars. Top of the wine bar list would have to be *Jimmy Watson's* on Lygon St, Carlton — very much a place to see and be seen at, especially around lunchtime Saturday. It has a delightful (when the sun is shining) open courtyard out back.

Other popular Carlton places include the *Weathercock Wine Bar* at 117 Drummond St. Some of the places listed in the pub food places (the *Fawkner* or the *Argo Inn* for example) are also good places to drop in. Other popular pubs include the *Anchor & Hope* on Church St, Richmond with its amazing carbadge decor; *Lord Jim's* (very much a place for pick-ups) at 36 St George's Rd, North Fitzroy or the *Council Club* in South Melbourne. The *Fun Factory Wine Bar* at the corner of Toorak Rd and Chapel St in South Yarra is also popular.

Theatre Restaurants No mention of Melbourne's eating / entertainment possibilities would be complete without a section on theatre restaurants. They've always been a popular idea but Melbourne's particular inspiration is combining eating out with fringe theatre. To a large extent the source of that inspiration is the amazing John Pinder.

John started out with a hole in the wall place called the *Flying Trapeze* and then moved on to greater things with the *Last Laugh*. On the corner of Smith and Gertrude Sts in Collingwood it's an old cinema/dole office done up in a dazzling mish-mash of styles from high kitsch up and down. In fact look up as you come in . . . . . to see the weird and wonderful collection of airplanes hovering in the entrance hall. Everything from a cigar smoking Concorde to a flying vacuum cleaner. Inside there's room for 200 people to have a good time — you arrive, pay your money at the door (it's getting pretty expensive, you can pay over $20 depending on the night and the show), buy drinks at the bar. There's a blackboard menu and food is reasonably good (for a theatre restaurant where food often takes second place to the show). Like other fringe places vegetarians are well catered for. You have time to get through the appetisers, soup and main course before part one of the show and dessert comes up before part two. The shows can be almost anything, one of the best would have to be the repeat visits by Circus Oz where you could consider the possibility of a tightrope walker landing in your lap half way through your meal.

Afterwards the patrons can take their turn to perform as the stage becomes a disco. Upstairs there's the *Last Laugh's* upstairs bar where aspiring acts appear late at night. Good grief, Lonely Planet researcher Alan Samagalski has even played 'atomic folk music' there. The upstairs bar is $5 to $6 most nights although some nights are cheaper. The *Last Laugh* also probably becomes a little too establishment these days but there are other places like the *Comedy Cafe* at Brunswick St in nearby Fitzroy where one show in 1982 consisted of taking the audience off in a bus to invade some of Melbourne's ritzier establishments while dressed in Groucho Marx masks. The *Comedy Cafe* also has its late-night upstairs bar, the Banana Lounge, where fringe-comedy gets a go.

Melbourne's comedy ranges from the awe to the awful; a mish-mash of misfits, idiots, exhibitionists, geniuses (real or imagined). So don't clap too loud, some people will be trying to sleep . . . . .

One of the foremost on the comedy scene are the North 2 Alaskans, the world's first psychedelic cabaret orchestra. What an explosion of molten acid-billy, cabaret vibe, a crystal airship of pure golden light swooping low across the heads of our children . . . . THIS is a celebration, a joyous happening merry-go-round of psychedelia, a vinyl festival of love, peace and cabaret dollar! The North 2s feature Spencer Jones on 16-string fretless sitar, James Williams on bottle-neck farfisa, Johnny Topper on supreme electric bodyless bass, Steve Watsch on templebongs and Frank Savage on double cutaway mediaeval dulcimer. And remember, their Platter's special effects may frighten little kiddies! See them — they're the most entertaining band playing the pubs.

Incidentally, three members of the North 2s used to be part of a band called the Pete Best Beatles (Pete Best on drums, Pete Best on lead-guitar, Pete Best on piano . . . .) until forming their new band. Their drummer went off and formed a group called the Sex Flintstones (well, you've heard of the Sex Pistols haven't you?) but unfortunately, they've disbanded. Dynamic Gary Adams still does a regular Angry Anderson impersonation with the North 2s though. They're also joined by Slim Whittle, a country-and-western superstar-in-his-own-mind, who drawls through some of the worst cow songs ever written . . . . the sacred cowbow of cabaret.

Others, well there's Los Trios Ringbarkus, two gentlemen in the forefront of stage-fright and incompetency. This might be your only chance to hear a heavy-metal version of Eleanor Rigby on one electric-guitar and a piano accordion. Incidentally for $1000 and the legal fees, Los Trios have an open offer to throw a cream pie in Malcolm Fraser's face.

Cinema Melbourne's best alternative cinema centres include the long running *Valhalla* at 216 Victoria St, Richmond which shows a different film every night. In fact they show two films every night and since they also have student discounts it's great value. They produce a superb six monthly film calendar detailing all their shows. The *Carlton Moviehouse* at 235 Faraday St has a similar programme. Various other cinemas around Melbourne specialise in non-mainstream films. They include the *Longford Cinema* at 55 Toorak Rd, South Yarra, the popular *Brighton Dendy*, and the *La Trobe Agora* (same company as Valhalla).

Getting There

Air There are frequent connections between Melbourne and other state capitals — Melbourne-Sydney flights are hourly during the operating hours. Fares include Sydney $124 (standby $93), Brisbane $189 ($142), Canberra $98 ($74), Adelaide $117 ($88), Perth $288 ($216). Connections to Alice Springs are made via Adelaide. Melbourne is the main jumping off point from the mainland to Tasmania. Hobart flights cost $103 (standby $77), Launceston $89 ($67), Burnie $86 ($64), Devonport $87 ($66). Burnie and Devonport are operated by East-West Airlines rather than TAA. TAA and Ansett are almost side by side, up on Franklin St at the top end of the city. TAA (tel 345 3333) at 50 Franklin St, Ansett (tel 342 2222) at the corner of Franklin and Swanston Sts. Both airlines have other smaller offices around town.

Bus Ansett Pioneer and Greyhound both have frequent services to and from Melbourne. Adelaide connections are made daily, the trip takes about 11 hours and costs $38, services connect through to Perth via Adelaide and the fare is $113. Canberra takes about 10 hours for $30. Melbourne-Sydney services go direct (via Canberra), via Wagga Wagga or up the coast along the Princes Highway. The direct trip takes about 15 hours and costs $42. There are also direct services between Melbourne and Brisbane, either via the Gold Coast or via Toowoomba. The trip takes 31 or 32 hours and costs $90. There are also a variety of other services from Melbourne — to Bega, Mildura, Mt Gambier or Deniliquin for example. Ansett Pioneer (tel 342 3144) operate from the Ansett terminal on the corner of Swanston and Franklin Sts. Greyhound (tel 62 2332) are at 667 Bourke St, right up at the Spencer St end.

There are quite a few alternative bus companies operating through Melbourne. Across Australia Coachlines (tel 62 3848) are at 56 Spencer St and offer Sydney for $25 ($21 for students), Adelaide $35 ($30) and Perth $100 ($80). Olympic East-West Express (tel 568 4655) are at 90 Koornang Rd, Carnegie and have similar or slightly cheaper fares. They also go to Brisbane and Surfers for $50. Deluxe Coachlines (tel 347 8144) at 440 Elizabeth St do all the above (at slightly higher prices) plus Canberra for $27 and Noosa for $67.

Rail There are three train services between Melbourne and Sydney. The Southern Aurora and the Spirit of Progress both operate overnight every day of the week. The Intercapital Daylight Express operates by day, Monday to Saturday. The trip takes 13 to 14 hours and costs $53 in economy, $75 in 1st. A sleeping berth is an extra $20 on top of the 1st class fare, there are no berths in economy. You can take a car on the Melbourne-Sydney services for $70. To get to Canberra by rail you take the Intercapital Daylight as far as Yass Junction from where a bus connects for the one hour trip into Canberra.

To or from Adelaide the Overland operates overnight every day of the week. The trip takes 13 hours and costs $42 in economy, $59 in 1st, again with a $20 supplement for a sleeper. The Intercapital Daylight to or from Sydney connects with the Overland. To get to Perth by rail from Melbourne you take the Overland and then the East-West Express to Port Pirie where you connect with the Trans-Australian or the Indian-Pacific. The Melbourne-Perth fare is $258 in economy, $360 in 1st, including sleeping berths and meals on the Port Pirie-Perth sector in economy or 1st.

There is also a rail service between Melbourne and Mildura, the Sunday to Friday Vinelander which takes 10 hours overnight and costs $23.40 in economy, $31.60 in 1st, sleeping berths $14 extra on 1st.

Rail tickets for interstate services can be booked at the Spencer St railway station in Melbourne, from where the interstate services depart. There is also a Railways of Australia office in the Embank Arcade across the corner of Elizabeth and Collins St in Melbourne.

Vintage train enthusiasts should enquire about the Steamrail Victoria monthly excursions in old steam locomotives.

Getting Around
Public Transport Melbourne's public transport system is based on buses, suburban railways and the famous trams. The trams are the real cornerstone of the system, in all there are about 750 of them and they operate as far as 20 km out from the centre. They're frequent and fun. Buses are the secondary form of public transport, supporting the trams where tram lines do not go, even replacing them at quiet weekend periods. There are also a few private bus services as well as the public ones. The train services provide a third link for Melbourne's outer suburbs. There is even an underground city loop but in early '83 not all of the stations were yet in oper-

ation. For information on Melbourne transport contact either the Victorian Government Travel Centre at 230 Collins St or phone the Transport Information Centre (tel 602 9011) between 7.30 am and 10 pm Monday to Saturday or 9.15 am to 10 pm on Sunday.

You've got a choice in Melbourne of either paying a straight fare for distance or getting a day travelcard. On MMTB trams and buses the straight fares range from 30c for one section up to $1.20 for 11 or more sections. Melbourne is also divided into zones — the central city, the inner suburbs (zone 1), the outer suburbs (zone 2) and the way outer suburbs (zone 3). On trains fares vary from $1.10 for a journey within zone 1 only (the inner city is part of zone 1) up to $2 for a journey that traverses zone 1 to 3. Shorter journies are cheaper. Tram lines all terminate within zone 1, suburban rail lines usually in 2.

Travelcards allow unlimited travel on trains, trams and buses for a whole day and can be bought on trams, buses or at railway stations. They range from $1 for central area use only, $2 for zone 1 including the central area up to $3.60 for all three zones. You can also get weekly travelcards from $10 to $18. There are other concession tickets available on trains and trams. Train travellers can get off-peak return tickets for use after 9 am. Or off-peak travelcards which start at a railway station and allow only the one rail journey but also permit tram and bus travel within the central area. Or there are tram concession cards — eight rides in the city centre for $2, five rides in the centre plus one section outside also for $2. There are other deals but we don't want to make this too complicated do we!

The Ministry of Transport put out a leaflet which tries to explain the whole relatively complicated system of tickets and travelcards. The tram board's *See Melbourne by Tram* leaflet shows all the tram routes and indicates the things worth seeing on these various routes. For travel further afield pick up a copy of the 30c *Transport in Victoria* map which not only shows the complete VicRail suburban bus and train network but also details bus routes and operators throughout the state.

Car Rental All the big car rental firms operate in Melbourne. Avis, Budget and Hertz have desks at the airport and you'll also find Thrifty and Natcar in the city. The city offices tend to be at the north end of the city or in Carlton or North Melbourne. Melbourne also has a number of rent-a-wreck style operators, renting older vehicles at lower rates. Their costs and conditions vary widely so it's worth making a few enquiries before going from one firm over another. Typical are Rentabomb (tel 429 4003 or 4095) at 129 Bridge Rd, Richmond. They rent '72 to '76 Holdens and Toranas at $12 to $15 a day plus $4 for insurance and including unlimited km but you're limited to a 50 km radius from the centre. Equivalent weekly rates are $100 to $120. Rentawreck (tel 267 5999) are at 391 St Kilda Rd, directly across from the Australian Tourist Commission. They have a variety of early '70s models with rates of $18 or $28 per day including insurance and unlimited km. Longer term rates are $2 a day less. They also restrict you to the metropolitan area at these rates but you can go anywhere in Victoria for the same daily rate plus 10c a km in excess of 100 km a day. The telephone yellow pages list lots of other firms (like Dam Cheap Hire, Discount Rent a Car, Rent an Oldie and so on) but some rates do not include any free km and you soon get up to the level of the unlimited distance firms.

Bicycle Rental Melbourne's not a bad city for biking — there's that lengthy riverside bicycle track and other bicycle tracks and lanes around the city. Plus it's reasonably flat so you're not pushing and panting up hills too often. Look for a copy of *Weekend Bicycle Rides* ($2.50) for a pleasant introduction to bike rides around Melbourne. There are quite a few rides you can make in the surrounding country by taking one train out of Melbourne then riding across to a different line to get the train back. An example is to take the train out to Gisborne and follow the fine ridgetop ride to Bacchus Marsh from where you can get another train back in to the city.

Unfortunately, if you've not already got your own bike, Melbourne is not a great place for hiring a bike. At least it's not if you want to hire a bike to go very far. If you just want to dawdle along the pleasant riverside bicycle path you can easily get a bike on weekends or holidays. There are hire places opposite the Botanical Gardens, beside Como Park and at the Kevin Bartlett Reserve in Richmond. Bikes cost $2.50 for a half hour, $3.50 for an hour or $9 for four hours. At 502 Swan St, Richmond, Hire a Bicycle (tel 429 3049), one of the riverside hire operators, hires bikes out at other times at the same rates.

Airport Although Melbourne's airport Tullamarine is a fair way, about 20 km, out from the city it's quite easy to get to or from since the Tullamarine Freeway runs almost into the centre. Melbourne's old airport, Essendon, is on the way out to Tulla.

A taxi between the airport and city centre will cost about $12 or $13. There are two privately operated bus services. The Skybus Express costs $3.50, departs from the TAA and Ansett ends of the airport terminal, runs about every half hour through the day and the city terminus is at Spencer St Railway Station. The Skybus VIP service costs $4 and runs less frequently, particularly on weekends. It departs from outside the international part of the terminal, in the middle. At the city end the VIP bus does a loop around the city centre, via the big hotels, the airport bus terminal (up by the TAA and Ansett offices at 440 Elizabeth St) and Flinders St Station. There is also a fairly frequent bus by Gull Airport Service between the airport and Geelong. It costs $10 ($8 for students under 26) one-way, less for return. The Geelong terminus is 45 McKillop St. You can get timetables for these services from the information counter in the international section.

Tullamarine is a modern airport with a single terminal; TAA at one end, Ansett at the other, international in the middle. There's an information desk upstairs in the international departure area. It's the most spacious airport in Australia and doesn't suffer the night flight restrictions which apply to some other Australian airports. Avis, Hertz and Budget have rent-a-car desks at the airport. Tulla's snack bar and restaurant sections are the airport norm for quality and price but if you're stuck at the airport for any reason you can stroll over to the customs agents building, turn right out of the terminal and it's about two hundred metres walk, where there's a cheap snack bar. There's another in the small centre beyond the car park by the Travelodge Motel.

Tours The usual variety of tours are available in and around Melbourne. Typical costs include city tours from around $13, half day tours to the Dandenongs for a similar price, to Healesville for $18. Longer day tours to Ballarat, Phillip Island for the penguins or into the snow country cost from around $25 to $30.

AROUND MELBOURNE

There are places of interest all around Melbourne and in all directions from the city — north and west into the gold country, south-east and south-west around Port Phillip and out to the Dandenongs.

The Dandenongs

Right on the eastern edge of Melbourne the Dandenongs are one of the most popular day trips from the city. They're cool due to the altitude and lushly green due to the heavy rainfall. The area is dotted with fine old houses, classy restaurants, beautiful gardens and some fine short bushwalks — quite apart from Melbourne's TV transmitter towers on 633 metre Mt Dandenong, the highest point in the Dandenongs. You can clearly see the Dandenongs from central Melbourne and they're only about an hour's drive out.

The small Fentree Gully National Park has pleasant strolls and lots of birdlife including, if you're very lucky, lyrebirds for which the Dandenongs are famous. The Sherbrooke Forest Park is similarly pleasant for walks and you'll see lots of rosellas here. The William Ricketts sanctuary on Olinda Rd, Mt Dandenong is named after its delightfully eccentric resident sculptor. The forest sanctuary is filled with his artwork and you can see more of his work far away in Alice Springs.

Puffing Billy One of the major attractions of the Dandenongs is Puffing Billy — a restored miniature steam train which makes runs along the 13 km track from Belgrave to Lakeside at the Emerald Lake Park. Puffing Billy was originally built in 1900 to bring farm produce to market. Emerald (population 2100) is a pretty little town with many crafts galleries and shops. At Lakeside there's a whole string of attractions

from barbecues and waterslides to a huge model railway with over two km of track! At Menzies Creek beside the station there's a Steam Museum open every Sunday and public holiday from 11 am to 5 pm. It houses a collection of early steam locomotives and admission is 60c. Phone 870 8411 for Puffing Billy timetable details, it runs on weekends and holidays — every day through the school holidays. The round trip takes about 2½ hours and costs $5.60 for adults, $3.70 for children. Note that Puffing Billy does not run on days of total fire ban. You can get out to Puffing Billy on the regular suburban rail service to Belgrave, one-way fare is $1.40, a day travelcard is $2.60.

West to Ballarat

The trip out to the old gold town of Ballarat is a favourite excursion from Melbourne and there are several points of interest along the way. Bacchus Marsh (population 5000) is just 49 km from Melbourne and has some fine old National Trust classified buildings. It's a good jumping off point for walks and picnic spots in the vicinity like the Werribee Gorge, Lerderberg Gorge, Wombat State Forest or, a little to the south in the Brisbane Ranges National Park, the Anakie Gorge which is particularly scenic and a popular barbecue spot.

Bacchus Marsh has a tourist office in the Peddlers Shoppe on Main St and a train from Melbourne costs $1.90.

South-West to Geelong

It's a quick trip down the Princes Freeway to Geelong, you can exit Melbourne rapidly over the soaring Westgate Bridge and enjoy the fine views of the city on the way across the bridge. Not far out of Melbourne is Werribee Park with its huge Italianate mansion built between 1874 and '77. The flamboyant

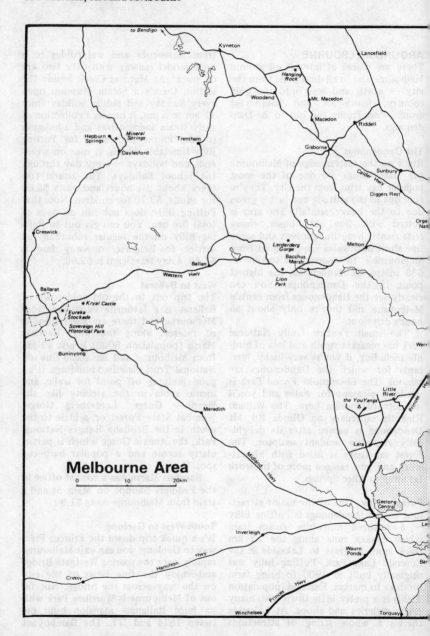

Melbourne Area

0   10   20km

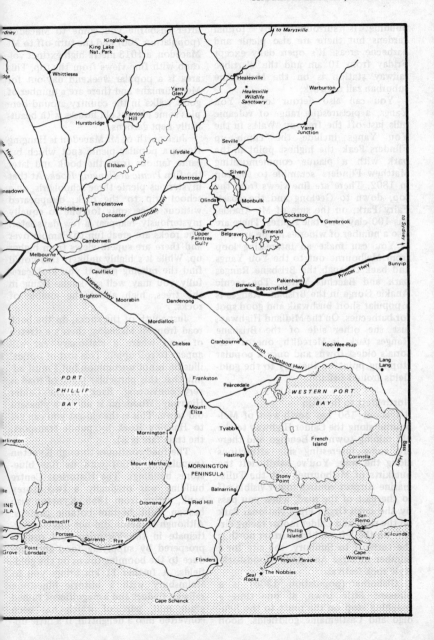

building is surrounded by formal gardens but there are also picnic and barbecue areas. It's open daily except Friday from 10 am and the Werribee railway station is on the Melbourne suburban rail network.

You can also detour to the You Yangs, a picturesque range of volcanic hills just off the freeway. Walks in the You Yangs include the climb up Flinders Peak, the highest point in the park with a plaque commemorating Matthew Flinders' scramble to the top in 1802. There are fine views from the top, down to Geelong and the coast. Fairy Park, on the side of Mt Anakie, has 100 clay fairy tale figures. There are also a number of wineries in the area.

You can make an interesting loop from Melbourne out to the You Yangs and back through the Brisbane Ranges park and Bacchus Marsh. The scenic Anakie Gorge in the Brisbane Ranges is a popular short bushwalk and good spot for barbecues. On the Midland Highway, just the other side of the Brisbane Ranges park, is Meredith, one of Victoria's oldest towns and once a popular stopping point on the way to the goldfields around Ballarat.

North-West to Bendigo

It's about 150 km north-west of Melbourne along the Calder Highway to the old mining town of Bendigo and there are some interesting side attractions along the way. You've hardly left the outskirts of Melbourne, with the Tullamarine Airport control tower visible off to the east of the road, when you pass by the small Organ Pipes National Park on the right and Calder motor racing circuit on the left. A little further north is the turn-off to Sunbury, the site for a number of large Australian Woodstock-style rock festivals.

Gisborne (population 1300) is a pleasant little town, at one time a coaching stop on the route to the Bendigo and Castlemaine goldfields. Soon after Gisborne you come to Macedon (population 700) and the turn-off to Mt Macedon, a 1013 metre high extinct volcano with fine views from the top. This area is a popular weekend day-out for Melbournians and there are a number of good walks in the country around here plus some elegant old houses with beautifully kept gardens.

Just north of Mt Macedon is Hanging Rock, a popular picnic spot which became famous from the book and later the film *Picnic at Hanging Rock*. At that mysterious picnic three schoolgirls, on a school trip to the rock, disappeared without trace, only for one to equally mysteriously reappear a few days later. The rocks are great fun to clamber over and there are superb views from higher up. While it's highly unlikely that you'll find the missing girls, if you look carefully you may well see koalas lazing in the trees, high above the jumble of rocks.

Just south of the rocks, on the back road from Mt Macedon, there's a stretch of road where a stationary car will appear to roll uphill. This sort of optical illusion is not uncommon but I must admit that this particular piece of road is very convincing. Back on the Calder Highway, Woodend is another pleasant old town. This is the closest you can get to Hanging Rock by public transport, the train fare is $4.

The road continues through Kyneton (population 3700) with its fine bluestone buildings. The Historical Centre building was originally a two storey bank, dating from 1855. Kyneton also has an eight hectare botanic gardens. Although Kyneton did not directly participate in the Victorian gold rush it prospered by supplying food and produce to the booming towns on the goldfields. A further 11 km brings you to Malmsbury with a historic bluestone railway viaduct and a magnificent ruined grain mill, part of which has been converted into a delightful, if a little upmarket, restaurant.

Healesville & the Hills

You don't have to travel far to the east of Melbourne before you start getting into the foothills of the Great Dividing Range. In winter you can find snow within a hundred km of the city centre. Healesville (population 3700) is on the outskirts of Melbourne, just where you start to climb up into the hills. There are some pleasant drives from Healesville, particularly the scenic route to Marysville, but the Sir Colin MacKenzie Wildlife Sanctuary is a prime attraction. This is one of the best places to see Australian wildlife in the whole country. Most of the enclosures are very natural, some of the birds seem to just pop in for the day. Some enclosures are only open for a few hours each day so you may want to plan your visit accordingly. The platypus, for example, is only on show in his glass-sided tank from 1.30 to 3.30 pm daily. The nocturnal house, where you can see many of the smaller bush dwellers which only come out at night, is open from 10.30 am to 4 pm while the reptile house is open to 4.30 pm. The whole park is open 9 am to 5 pm and admission is $4. There are barbecue and picnic facilities in the pleasantly wooded park. Healesville is on the regular Melbourne suburban transport network, trains operate to Lilydale from where connecting buses run to Healesville.

Beyond Healesville is Warburton (population 3700), another pretty little hill town in the Great Dividing Range foothills. There are good views of the mountains from the Acheron Way near here and you'll sometimes get snow on Mt Donna Buang, seven km from town. Warburton, in the Upper Yarra Valley, is one of a number of picturesque spots along the upper reaches of the Yarra River. On the Melbourne side of Healesville there are a number of wineries from Yarra Glen along the Yarra Valley.

Marysville (population 600) is a delightful little place and a very popular weekend escape from Melbourne. The one-way bus fare there is $6.75. There are lots of bush tracks to walk, especially to Nicholl's Lookout, Keppel's Lookout, Mt Gordon and Steavenson Falls. Cumberland Scenic Reserve, with numerous walks and the Cumberland Falls, is 16 km east of Marysville. The cross country skiing trails of Lake Mountain Reserve are only 10 km beyond Marysville.

Lake Eildon

Continuing beyond the hill towns of Healesville and Marysville you come to Lake Eildon, a large lake created for hydro-power and irrigation purposes. It's a popular resort area with lots of boats and houseboats to hire. Trout breeding is carried out at Snob's Creek Fish Hatchery, drop in it's very interesting, and there's a fauna sanctuary nearby. The Snob's Creek Falls drop 107 metres. On the shores of the lake the Fraser National Park has some good short walks including an excellent guide-yourself nature walk. On the south side of the lake is the old mining town of Jamieson. Alexander (population 1800) and Eildon (population 800) are the main centres near the lake. One-way bus fare to the lake is $9.85, changing bus at Marysville.

The Goulburn Valley Highway starts from Eildon and runs to Seymour and north. North of Yarra Glen is Yea (population 1100), a good centre for the Kinglake National Party with waterfalls, fern gullies and other attractions including much wildlife. The Gulf Station, a couple of km from Yarra Glen, is only open from time to time but it's an interesting collection of rough old timber buildings, a small rural settlement of the 1850s which has hardly been changed since that time.

MORNINGTON PENINSULA

The Mornington Peninsula is the spit of land down the east side of Port Phillip Bay, bordered on its eastern side by the waters of Westernport Bay. The peninsula really starts at Frankston, 40 km from the centre of Melbourne and from there it's almost a continuous beach strip, all the way to Portsea at the end (almost) of the peninsula, nearly 100 km from Melbourne. 'Almost' because the final tip of the peninsula, looking out across 'The Rip', the narrow entrance to Port Phillip Bay, is a restricted military base.

This is a very popular Melbourne resort area with many holiday homes; in summer the accommodation and campsites along the peninsula can be packed right out and traffic can be very heavy. In part this popularity is due to the peninsula's excellent beaches and the great variety they offer. On the west and north side of the peninsula you've got calm water on the bay beaches (the front beaches), looking out on to Port Phillip Bay, while on the south side there's crashing surf on the rugged and beautiful ocean beaches (the back beaches) which face Bass Strait.

Town development tends to be concentrated along the Port Phillip side. The Westernport Bay and Bass Strait coasts are much less developed and you'll find pleasant bushwalking trails along the Cape Schank Coastal Park, a narrow coastal strip right along the Bass Strait coast from Portsea to Cape Schank. Frankston is the start of the peninsula, linked by rail to Melbourne.

There's a Tourist Information Centre in Dromana, on the coast road down the peninsula and the National Park Service's *Discovering the Peninsula* brochure tells you all you'll want to know about the peninsula's history, early architecture and walking possibilities.

Frankston to Blairgowrie

Beyond Frankston you reach Mornington and Mt Martha, early settlements with some old buildings along the Mornington Esplanade and fine, secluded beaches in between. Dromana is the real start of the resort development, just inland from here a winding road leads up to Arthur's Seat lookout at 305 metres, you can also reach it by a scenic chairlift (weekends and holidays in summer only). On the slopes of Arthur's Seat, in McCrae, the McCrae Homestead is a National Trust property, dating from 1843 and open daily from 10 am to 5 pm from December to Easter and weekends the rest of the year. Coolart on Sandy Point Rd, Balnarring is another historic homestead on the peninsula. Coolart is also noted for the wide variety of birdlife which can be seen on the reserve. Balnarring is on the other side of the peninsula.

After McCrae it's Rosebud, Rye and Blairgowrie before you reach Sorrento. Rosebud has a Marine & Reptile Park open daily from 10 am to 4 pm ($1.50 admission). The Peninsula Gardens Tourist & Fauna Park (sounds a great combination) is also in Rosebud. It's open weekends and holidays from 9 am to 5 pm, admission $2.

Sorrento

Before you enter Sorrento there's a small memorial and pioneer cemetery from the first Victorian settlement at pretty Sullivan Bay. The settlement party arrived here from England in October 1803, intending to forestall a feared French settlement on the bay. Less than a year later in May 1804 the project was abandoned and transferred to Hobart, Tasmania. The main reason for the settlement's short life was a lack of water — they had simply chosen the wrong place as there was adequate water further round the bay. The settlement's numbers included an 11-year-old boy, John Pascoe Fawkner, who 25 years later would be one of the founders of Melbourne. It also included a convict who escaped soon after the arrival in 1803 and lived with Aboriginals for the next 30 years as the 'wild white man'.

Sorrento has a rather damp and cold little aquarium ($1.50 entry) and an interesting small historical museum (50c) in the old Mechanic's Institute building on the Old Melbourne Rd. From the 1870s paddlesteamers used to run between Melbourne and Sorrento. The largest, entering service in 1910, carried 2000 passengers. From 1890 through to 1921 there was a steam-powered tram operating from the Sorrento pier to the back beach. The magnificent hotels built of local limestone in this period still stand — the Sorrento (1871), Continental (1875) and Koonya (1878).

Portsea

Portsea, at the end of the Nepean Highway, offers another choice between the front and back beaches. At the Portsea back beach there's the impressive natural rock formation known as London Bridge, plus a cliff face where hang-gliders make their leap into the void. There are fine views across Portsea and back to Melbourne from Mt Levy Lookout by the back beach.

At the entrance to the government zone at the end of the peninsula are two historic gun barrels which actually fired the first shots in WW I and WW II. In 1914 a German ship was on its way out from Melbourne to the heads when news of the declaration of war came through on the telegraph. A shot across its bows at Portsea resulted in its capture. The first shot in WW II turned out to be at an Australian ship!

Cheviot Beach, at the end of the peninsula, featured more recently in Australian history. In 1967 then Prime Minister Harold Holt went for a swim here and was never seen again. US presidents get shot by nuts, in Australia prime ministers presumably get eaten by sharks. Although the area is closed to the public, tours are operated from the Sorrento Pier (tel 84 2000) — five times daily from 26 December to 1 February, four times daily on weekends from then to Easter.

The Ocean Coast

The southern (or eastern) coast of the peninsula faces Bass Strait and Westernport Bay. A connected series of walking tracks are being developed all the way from London Bridge to Cape Schank and Bushrangers' Bay. Some stretches of the Peninsula Coastal Walk are along the beach, some are actually cut by high tide, but in all the walk extends for over 30 km and takes over 12 hours to walk from end to end. The walks are best done in stages because the park is so narrow and so easily reached at various points.

Cape Schank itself is marked by the 1859 lighthouse and there are good walking possibilities around the cape. The rugged coast further east towards Flinders and West Head has natural features like the Blowhole. Towns like Flinders and Hastings on this coast are not quite as popular and crowded in the summer as the Port Phillip ones. Point Leo, near Shoreham, has a good surf beach. Off the coast in Westernport Bay is French's Island which is virtually undeveloped. A ferry operates between Stony Point and Cowes on Phillip Island.

Places to Stay & Eat

There is a virtual string of campsites along the bay front from Dromana to Sorrento but over the Christmas rush finding a place to set up tent can be very difficult. There are a number of hotels and motels along the peninsula but no travellers' bargains. Counter meals are available at the Sorrento Hotels — the *Lady Nelson Bistro* in the Sorrento, the *Tavern Bar* in the Continental, the *Bistro* in the Koonya. Excellent fish & chips at the *Hungry Eye* in Rye.

Getting There

There's a regular bus service from Frankston through to Portsea (ring 602 9444 for details) and Frankston is reached by rail from Melbourne. During the summer months there's a ferry making the half-hour crossing from Sorrento and Portsea to Queenscliff on the other side of the heads — by road it's a couple of hundred km right round the bay. From 24 December to the end of January it operates 10 times daily, then to Easter five times daily, in November and December it operates three times daily on weekends and it also operates in the May and August school holidays. The return fare is $4 and for the first couple of morning departures there's a connecting bus into Geelong from Queenscliff.

PHILLIP ISLAND

At the entrance to Westernport Bay, 128 km south-east of Melbourne, Phillip Island is a very popular holiday resort for the Melbourne area. There are plenty of beaches, both sheltered and with surf, and a fascinating collection of wildlife including the island's famous fairy penguin colony. The island is joined to the mainland by a bridge from San Remo to Newhaven.

Information & Orientation

There is an excellent information centre just after you cross the bridge to the island. Cowes is the main town on the island. It's on the north side of the island and has a pleasant, sheltered beach. Hotels, motels, camping grounds, restaurants, snack bars and other amenities can all be found here. Cowes also has a Tourist Information Centre at 71 Thompson Avenue.

Penguins, Koalas & Seals

Every evening, at Summerland Beach in the south-west of the island, the tiny fairy penguins which nest there perform their 'parade', emerging from the sea and waddling resolutely up the beach to their nests — totally oblivious of the sightseers. The penguins are there year round but they come in far larger numbers in the summer when they are rearing their young. It's no easy life being the smallest type of penguin, after a few short hours of shut-eye they'll be heading down to the beach again at dawn to start another hard day's fishing.

The parade, which takes place like clockwork a few minutes after sunset each day, is a major tourist attraction so there will be big crowds here in summer. To protect the penguins you're strictly regimented — keep to the viewing areas, don't get in the penguins' way and no camera flashes. There's a $1.50 admission charge to the penguin nesting area of the beach but it's money well spent for this is a unique sight.

Off Grand Point, the extreme south-west tip of the island, a group of rocks rise from the sea. They're known as the Nobbies and are inhabited by a resident colony of fur seals numbering 5000. You can view them through coin-in-the-slot binoculars from the food kiosk in the car park on the headland but unfortunately it shuts its doors quite early in the evening; too early if you come here

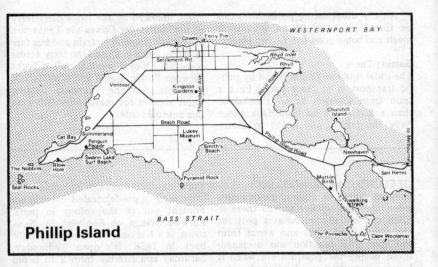

Phillip Island

just before continuing on to the penguin parade.

Koalas are the third wildlife attraction on the island. There are a number of koala sanctuaries around the island where you can see the lazy little creatures close up . Phillip Island also has mutton bird rookeries, particularly in the sand dunes around Cape Woolamai. The birds arrive here in November each year from their migration flight from Japan and Alaska. You'll also find a wide variety of waterbirds including pelicans, ibis and swans in the swampland at the Nits at Rhyll. Kingston Gardens Zoo has a variety of native Australian wildlife and also domesticated animals.

Other

Swimming and surfing are popular island activities and there is also a motor racing circuit, now little used, on the island. The Len Lukey Museum has a fine collection of veteran and vintage cars and racing cars. It's on Back Beach Road and open Fridays, Saturdays and Sundays.

There's a blowhole, spectacular when the seas are running high, at Grant Point. Rugged Cape Woolamai is particularly impressive, there's a real contrast between the high seas on this side of the island and the sheltered waters on the northern, Cowes, side.

Churchill Island is a small island with a restored house and beautiful gardens. It's connected to Phillip Island by footbridge but you have to get to the bridge by a bus through private land. Entry is $2.50 and the bus normally departs from the information centre at Newhaven at 10 am.

Places to Stay & Eat

There are all sorts of guest house, motel and holiday flat accommodation and camp sites in Cowes, Newhaven and San Remo. Alternate hostel facilities are available at the *Anchor Belle Holiday Park*, 272 Church St, Cowes — booking is advisable.

All the usual eating possibilities can be found in Cowes including counter meals and some good fish & chip places.

Getting There
The usual route to Phillip Island by public transport is in three parts. First a train from Flinders St to Frankston, then a bus (once on Saturdays, twice daily the rest of the week) to Stony Point followed by the twice daily ferry service across to Cowes via Tankerton on French Island. The train and bus fare to Stony Point is $2 and the ferry across costs $3. Once a week there's a flight between Phillip Island and Smithton in Tasmania. See the Tasmania Getting There section for more information on this unusual route.

GEELONG (population 172,000)
Geelong began as a sheep-grazing area when the first settlers arrived there in 1836 and initially served as a port for the dispatch of wool and wheat from the area. This function was overshadowed during the goldrush era when it became important as a landing place for immigrants and for the export of gold. Around 1900 Geelong started to become industrialised and that's very much what it is today — a rather dull, unattractive industrial city.

Information
There's a tourist office (tel 97 220) at 83 Ryrie St. They are very helpful, have lots of information to hand and are very useful if you're going down along the coast to the Otways or other areas around Geelong.

Things to See
In general there are no real 'not to be missed' attractions in Geelong although the city has more than 100 National Trust classified buildings including some interesting pre-fabricated buildings brought out to the colony in parts. Barwon Grange on Fernleigh St, Newtown, is a National Trust property built back in 1856. It's open Wednesday, Saturday and Sunday from 2 to 5 pm and admission is $2. That admission will also get you in to a second National Trust property, The Heights at 140 Aphrasia St, which is open the same hours. This 14 room timber mansion is an example of pre-fabricated colonial construction and has an unusual watch-tower. Another pre-fabricated building is Corio Villa, made from iron sheets in 1856. The bits and pieces were shipped out from Glasgow but nobody claimed them on arrival! Osborne House and Armytage House are other fine old buildings.

The Art Gallery on Little Malop St is open daily and has lots of pretty Australiana (when will people stop painting landscapes?) and some interesting mod-art. Admission is 50c. Or you could take

---

1 Kangaroo Hotel	5 Art Gallery
2 Ferry Trip	6 Tourist Office
3 Railway Station	7 Post Office
4 Carlton Hotel	8 Corio Hotel

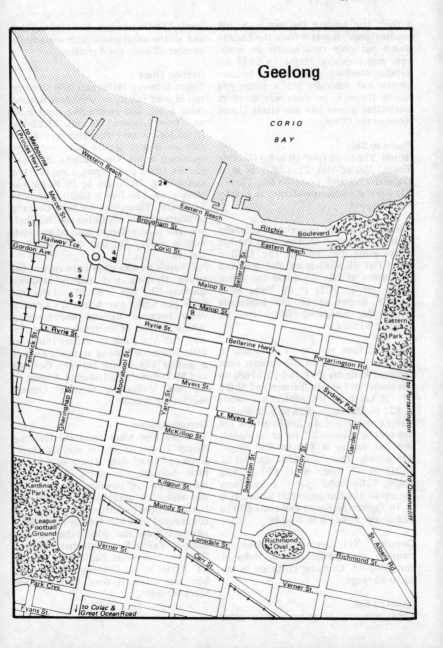

Geelong

CORIO BAY

to Melbourne
(Princes Hwy)

Western Beach

Mercer St.

Eastern Beach

Brougham St.

Ritchie Boulevard

Eastern Beach

Bellerine St.

Corio St.

Railway Tce.

Gordon Ave.

Malop St.

Lt. Malop St.

Ryrie St.

Lt. Ryrie St.

Fenwick St.

Gheringhap St.

Moorabool St.

Yarra St.

Myers St.

Lt. Myers St.

McKillop St.

Bellarine Hwy

Portarlington Rd.

to Portarlington

Sydney Pde.

to Queenscliff

Swanston St.

Fitzroy St.

Garden St.

Eastern Park

Kardinia Park

League Football Ground

Park Cres.

Kilgour St.

Mundy St.

Verner St.

Lonsdale St.

Carr St.

Richmond Oval

St. Albans Rd.

Richmond St.

Verner St.

Evans St.

to Colac &
Great Ocean Road

a ferry trip around the bay with 'Bill the Boatman'. It leaves from the Eastern Beach but only runs hourly on weekends and holidays. Phone 78 1697 for details. Geelong also has a botanic garden but basically it's a place you transit through, on your way to more interesting places like the Great Ocean Road or the Otways.

Places to Stay

Hostel The small (just 16 beds) *Geelong Youth Hostel* (tel 21 6583) is at 1 Lonsdale St and costs $3.50. There's YH alternate accommodation at nearby *Portarlington*.

Hotels There are two cheap, centrally located hotels and another a bit further away along the beach. The *Carlton Hotel* (tel 91 954) is on Malop St and has rooms at $15/25 while the *Corio Hotel* (tel 92 922) at 69 Yarra St is $10/18. Round at 16 The Esplanade South the *Kangaroo Hotel* (tel 21 4022) is $18/24.

Motels There are stacks of motels in Geelong, just some of the cheaper ones include: *Karindia Park* (tel 21 5188) on the corner of Latrobe Terrace and Sharp St, 1½ km from the centre, has rooms at $22 to $26 single, $28 to $32 double. The *Dinosaur* (tel 48 2606) is five km out on the Queenscliff Rd at Newcomb and has rooms at $20 to $22 single, $28 double. The *Colonial Lodge* (tel 21 3521) at 57 Fyans St is $20 to $22 single, $28 double. Only a km from the centre the *Kangaroo* (tel 21 4022) is at 16 Esplanade South and costs $20 to $22 single, $24 to $26 double.

Camping Yes, Geelong has plenty of camping sites, particularly at Belmont and Leopold. Camping costs are in the $2 to $5 range.

Places to Eat

There are lots of pubs with counter meals, McDonalds, a Kentucky Fried and all the usual possibilities including a number of quite good restaurants.

Getting There

Trains between Melbourne and Geelong run at least hourly on weekdays starting from 6 am and continuing until 8.55 pm (from Geelong) or until 11.22 pm (from Melbourne). On Saturdays there's also an hourly service but over more restricted hours. On Sundays there are just six trains daily, from 8 am to 8 pm ex-Geelong, 10.05 am to 10.30 pm ex-Melbourne. The fare is $3.20 economy, $4.30 1st. Trains run on from Geelong to Warrnambool via Colac and Winchelsea. The road between Ballarat and Melbourne is very flat and dull but it is a fast trip.

There's a twice daily railways bus between Geelong and Ballarat railway stations. The fare is $4.80 and the trip takes just under two hours. It's a pretty route between Ballarat and Geelong with a number of small towns along the way, the bus stops to deliver things to little bluestone railway stations. There's a regular bus service between Geelong and Melbourne's Tullamarine Airport — see the Melbourne Getting Around section for details.

Getting Around

You can hire bikes from the Geelong Youth Hostel if you're staying there. Geelong-Otway Bike Tours is a useful little booklet containing routes and information on possible bike-tours in the area. It's available free from the tourist office. Unfortunately there is no commercial bike hire facility in Geelong although you can hire bikes at the Barwon Valley Fun Park, near Barwon River, on weekends. Eagles bike shop at 64 Ryrie St in Geelong occasionally hire out bikes, if they have suitable bikes available.

BELLARINE PENINSULA

Beyond Geelong the Bellarine Peninsula is a twin to the Mornington Peninsula, forming the other side of the entrance to Port Phillip Bay. In summer a ferry makes the crossing of the heads between Portsea and Queenscliff and there's a connecting bus between Queenscliff and Geelong. Like the Mornington Peninsula this is a popular holiday resort and boating venue.

Around the Peninsula

Round the peninsula in Port Phillip Bay is Indented Head where Flinders landed in 1802, one of the first visits to the area by a European. In 1835 John Batman landed at this same point, on his way to buy up Melbourne. At Portalington (population 1800) there's a fine example of an early steam-powered flour mill. Built in 1856-57 the massive, solid building is open from 2 to 5 pm every Sunday. St Leonards (population 700) is a popular little resort just south of Indented Head.

Queenscliff (population 3000)

Fort Queenscliff was built in 1882 and houses the Australian Military College. It's open on weekends and public holidays. Queenscliff was originally established as a fishing port and much fishing is still carried out from here. Queenscliff has a fascinating little Historical Centre beside the post office on Hesse St. It's open daily from 2 to 4.30 pm and over the main school holiday seasons it's also open 10 am to noon. You can get an interesting *Visitor's Guide to Queenscliff* here and explore the town with the walking tour guide. Along the front the Ozone and the Queenscliff are two hotels in the Victorian seaside 'grand' manner, very popular for leisurely weekend lunches. Queenscliff's fort was built during the 1880s Russian scare. The 'Black Lighthouse', dating from 1862, is within the fort. Tours take place on Sundays and public holidays at 2.15 pm, there's a fine ocean lookout below the fort.

Point Lonsdale is almost continuous with Queenscliff. The lighthouse here guides ships through the narrow rip into the bay and below the lighthouse is Buckley's cave. Here the 'wild white man', William Buckley, lived with the Aboriginals for 32 years after escaping from the settlement at Sorrento on the Mornington Peninsula.

Railway enthusiasts will enjoy the Bellarine Peninsula Railway which operates from the old Queenscliff station with a fine collection of old steam trains. On weekends, public and school holidays steam trains make 16 km trips to Drysdale or shorter runs around Swan Bay.

Ocean Grove & Barwon Heads

These resorts on the ocean side of the peninsula offer good skin diving on the rocky ledges of the Bluff at Ocean Grove and further out there are wrecks of ships which failed to make the tricky entrance to Port Phillip Bay. Some of the wrecks are accessible to divers. Barwon Heads has sheltered river beaches.

BALLARAT (population 60,700)

Ballarat is the largest inland city in Victoria. It's 112 km from Melbourne on the main Western Highway to Adelaide. Ballarat was a major centre for Victoria's great gold rush. When gold

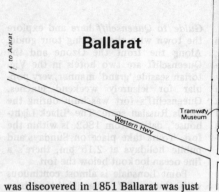

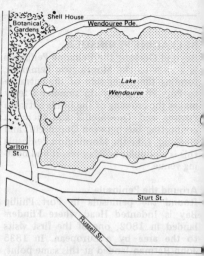

Ballarat

was discovered in 1851 Ballarat was just a small country town but two years later the population had already grown to 40,000. Today there are still many reminders of this gold mining past although Ballarat doesn't have quite the historical flavour as Bendigo, the other large Victorian town from the gold era.

Information

The Ballarat Tourist Office is on Victoria St, just past The Mall. The people are very helpful and they seem to be well-stocked with lots of printed information. The RACV (tel 32 1946) have an office on Doveton St.

Around Town

Even before Ballarat's gold boom the town planners had the foresight to include a wide main street. With Ballarat's gold wealth to spend Sturt St became a magnificent boulevard lined with the lavish buildings so typical of Australian gold towns. A wander along Sturt St takes you by verandahed Australian Victorian buildings, bedecked with lacework; plus a whole series of European styles from Gothic to Renaissance.

Sovereign Hill

Ballarat's major tourist attraction is Sovereign Hill, a fascinating recreation of a gold mining township of the 1860s,

complete with shops, a hotel and theatres along the main street including a post office, blacksmith's shop, printing shop, even a Chinese joss house. The site actually was mined back in the gold era so much of the equipment is still on its original site, including the old mineshaft. There's a variety of above ground and underground mining works — open daily from 9.30 am to 5 pm and admission is $5 for adults. This is one 'attraction' that is definitely worth seeing.

Eureka Stockade

Australia never had a revolution which fired a national consciousness, like America's did. The closest we ever came was the Eureka Stockade rebellion in

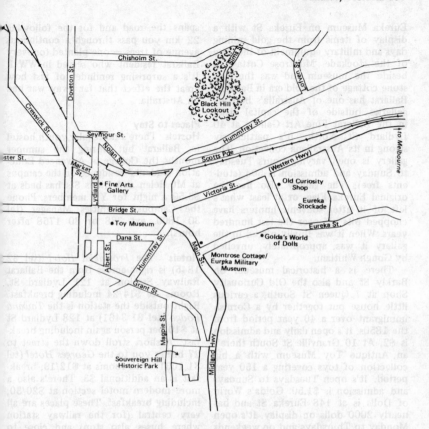

On the map:
Chisholm St
Stawell St
Loreto St
Doveton St
Creswick St
Black Hill Lookout
Hummffray St
(to Melbourne)
Seymour St
Nolan St
Scotts Pde
Market St
(Western Hwy)
ster St.
Lydiard St.
Victoria St.
Old Curiosity Shop
• Fine Arts Gallery
Eureka Stockade
Bridge St.
• Toy Museum
Eureka St.
Dana St.
• Golda's World of Dolls
Albert St.
Hummffray St.
Main St.
Montrose Cottage/ Eurpka Military Museum
Grant St.
Magpie St.
Midland Hwy
Sovereign Hill Historic Park

1854 when disgruntled miners refused to pay a government mining tax and mounted a futile opposition to the far superior government forces. Second time around the redcoats won. Today there's a monument at the stockade site and a action replay of the events and causes of this short lived 'revolt' against British rule. The park is on Stawell St South.

Botanical Gardens

In the city Lake Wendouree is beside Ballarat's excellent 40 hectare Botanic Gardens. A paddle steamer makes tours of the lake and the cottage of poet Adam Lindsay Gordon stands in the gardens. On weekends and holidays there's a tourist tramway operating around the gardens. A little Ballarat joke is the Avenue of Past Prime Ministers, a pathway lined with busts of Australian PMs, there's a Fraser there but no Whitlam! Actually the whole garden is littered with statuary including the glasshouse-like 'Statue House'. There's also a Shell House, admission 50c.

Around the Town

Notable Ballarat buildings include the

Eureka Museum on Eureka St with a display of items from the gold mining days and military equipment of the time of the stockade. Montrose Cottage is beside the museum and was the first stone cottage of the gold era in Ballarat. Ballarat has one of Australia's best art galleries outside of the capital cities in the Ballarat Fine Art Gallery at 40 Lydiard St North. It's particularly strong in its Australiana collection. The gallery is open varying hours Tuesday to Sunday and admission is 50c (students free). The gallery also has the original Eureka Flag, or at least what's left of it after souvenir hunters have chopped bits off over the last hundred years. When it was finally placed in the gallery it was, appropriately, unveiled by Gough Whitlam.

There is a historical museum on Barkly St and also the Old Curiousity Shop at 7 Queen St South, a curious little house put together by a Cornish immigrant over a 40 year period from the 1850s. It's open daily and admission is $2. At 10 Granville St South there's an Antique Toy Museum with a big collection of toys covering a 150 year period. It's open Tuesdays to Sundays and admission is $1.50. Golda's World of Dolls is at 148 Eureka St and has nearly 2000 dolls on display. It's open Monday to Thursdays and on weekends and public holidays. Admission is $1. Or you can climb Black Hill Lookout for the view.

Out of Town

Situated eight km on the Melbourne side of Ballarat, Kryall Castle is a modern bluestone 'mediaeval English castle'. Surprisingly it's a very popular attraction, no doubt helped along by the daily hangings (volunteers called for), 'whipping of wenches' and a weekly jousting tournament — kids love it. It's open 10 am to 5 pm daily and admission is $4.50 for adults. Towards Adelaide an Arch of Victory

spans the road and for the following 22 km you pass through a continuous avenue of trees — one planted for every Ballarat resident who served in WW I. It's a surprising reminder of just how great the effect that far away war had on Australia.

Places to Stay

Hostels There's no regular youth hostel in Ballarat but during the summer months the College of Advanced Education students' residence on the campus at Mt Helen and Gilles Sts has beds at $3.50 a night for YH members. Phone the Campus Amenities Manager (tel 30 1800, ext 388 or 30 1768 after hours).

Hotels The *Provincial Hotel* (tel 32 1845) is right across from the Ballarat Railway Station at 121 Lydiard St. Rooms are $14/24 including breakfast. Right outside the station is the *Tawana Lodge* (tel 31 3461) at 128 Lydiard St at $10 per person again including breakfast. A short stroll down the street to 27 brings you to the *Georges Hotel* (tel 31 1031) with rooms at $12/19, breakfast is an additional $3. There's also a more modern motel section at $20/30, including breakfast. These places are all very central (for the railway station where buses also stop) and close to Cycle City where you can hire bikes. They're about 10 minutes walk from The Mall.

Other hotels include the *Ballarat*

1	Railway Station
2	Provincial Hotel
3	Taurana Lodge
4	Cycle City
5	George Hotel
6	Post Office
7	Criterion Hotel
8	Craig's Royal Hotel
9	Union Hotel
10	Ballarat Hotel
11	Tourist Office

Hotel (tel 31 3132) at 92 Bridge St, the *Union Hotel* (tel 31 3273) at 11 Sturt St, the *Robin Hood Hotel* (tel 31 3348) at 33 Peel St, the *Criterion Hotel* (tel 31 1451) at 18 Doveton St South and *Craigs' Royal Hotel* (tel 31 1377) at 10 Lydiard St South. The Union and the Ballarat are the cheapest at around $12 for singles, $20 for doubles.

Motels Ballarat has plenty of motels too, many of them on the Western Highway on both sides of the centre. The *Ballarat* (tel 34 7234) on the Melbourne side, seven km east, has rooms at $21 to $23 single, $25 to $29 double, including a light breakfast. At 1853 Sturt St, on the Western Highway six km west, the *Arch* (tel 34 1464) has rooms at $20/24. Another reasonably priced motel is the *Eureka Lodge* (tel 31 1900) at 119 Stawell St South, three km out, with rooms at $22 to $24 single, $28 to $30 double, again with a light breakfast.

Camping There are plenty of campsites in and around Ballarat with typical prices in the $3 to $5 a night range.

Getting There

Trains run regularly from Melbourne to Ballarat via Bacchus Marsh and there are also VicRail operated buses. The trip takes two hours direct and the fare is $6.50 in economy, $8.70 in 1st. Ansett Pioneer and Greyhound run through Ballarat on the Melbourne-Adelaide services, the buses go via Geelong so it's a rather roundabout route.

There's a railway's bus from Ballarat to Geelong Railway Station at 6.45 am and 3.30 pm daily. The trip takes one hour 45 minutes and costs $4.80. Tickets are available from the station ticket office. Buses operate to towns all around Ballarat including Maryborough, Hamilton and Bendigo. The Ballarat-Bendigo bus costs $12.20.

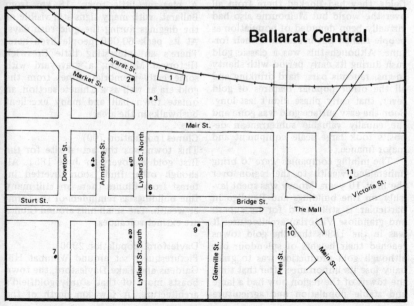

Ballarat Central

Ararat St.

Market St.

Mair St.

Sturt St.

Bridge St.

The Mall

Doveton St.

Armstrong St.

Lydiard St North

Lydiard St South

Glenville St.

Peel St.

Victoria St.

Main St.

Getting Around

There's a tourist bus service which makes four trips a day, each lasting about an hour, around the major sights with a running commentary on their history and the history of the town itself. The bus leaves from the tourist office although bookings can also be made at the railway station. Cost is $3 for adults, $2.50 for students.

Bikes can be hired from Cycle City at 35 Armstrong St, about five minutes' walk from the railway station. The cost is $5 per day, plus an amazing $60 deposit.

GOLD TOWNS

Australia has had several gold rushes but the Victorian rush was the biggest, the longest lasting and the one which has left the most visible reminders. In 1851 gold was first discovered in Clunes, today just a small town 40 km north of Ballarat. Three months later 8000 people had poured into the region in search of the elusive metal and within a year their numbers had swollen to 30,000. Four years later Victoria had over 100,000 men working on the gold fields, they had flocked there from all over the world but Melbourne also had virtually been denuded of population as people rushed out in search of their fortune. Although this was a classic gold rush during its early period with shanty towns, raucous bars, hard drinking and all the other popular features of gold fever, that early phase didn't last long. Soon the easy surface gold was gone and the equally valuable subterranean deposits took large scale equipment and major finance.

The mining companies were to bring unheralded wealth to the region over the next 10 years. Money was spent lavishly on fine buildings and Bendigo in particular is still noted for its superb and grandiose Victorian architecture. It was in the 1880s that the gold towns reached their heights of splendour but although gold production was to gradually lose its importance after that time the towns of the region now had a large and stable population and agriculture and other activities steadily supplanted gold as the economic base for the area.

The major towns of the gold rush era were Bendigo and Ballarat but even in the many smaller towns you'll still find some fine examples of the architecture which gold wealth brought to the region. The buildings here are solid and substantial — often quite unlike the impermanent look of so many Australian country towns.

Creswick (population 2000)

A pleasant little town, 18 km from Ballarat, with many signs still visible of the diggings during the gold rush days. At its peak 60,000 people lived here. There's an interesting little Creswick Historical Museum, a graveyard with some early memorial stones from the gold era as well as a Chinese section, an ornate town hall and many excellent bushwalks in the area.

Clunes (population 700)

This town was the actual site for the first gold discovery in June 1851. Although other finds soon diverted interest from Clunes there are still many fine buildings as reminders of the former wealth. The small hills around Clunes are extinct volcanoes.

Daylesford (population 2900)

Picturesquely set around Wombat Hill Gardens and Lake Daylesford, the town boasts more of that sturdy goldfield's architecture. A few km north of the town is Hepburn Spa which has been noted for its medicinal waters since the last century — bottling mineral water is still big business here. The volcano crater of Mt Franklin is visible from the lookout point in the botanic gardens atop Wombat Hill.

Castlemaine (population 7600)
A larger town, the centre of Castlemaine has been virtually unaltered since the 1860s. Castlemaine's rise to prosperity was rapid but the surface gold was equally quickly worked out. Amongst the Victorian gems here is the fine market building which has been restored and now houses a museum with exhibits and an audio-visual display on the town and district in its gold financed heyday. Castlemaine has numerous other fine examples of goldfield buildings including a couple of elegant hotels, a sandstone jail, an impressive town hall and a substantial CBC bank building.

Near Castlemaine it is possible to visit the Wattle Gully gold mine at Chewton. At Vaughan there's a mineral springs and an interesting Chinese cemetery. Guildford was a centre for the large Chinese constituent amongst the goldminers.

Maldon (population 900)
The current population is a scant reminder of the 20,000 who used to work the goldfields near Maldon. The whole town is a well preserved relic of the era with many fine buildings constructed from the local stone. The interesting buildings along the main street include Dabb's General Store with its authentic shopfront and the restored

hotel with the Eagle Hawk Restaurant. There are some good bushwalks around the town and amateur gold hunters still scour the area with some success. On Phoenix St the Maldon Progress Association has tourist information.

Maryborough (population 7600)
Maryborough was already an established sheep farming town when gold was discovered. It's still a busy town today and its Victorian buildings include a magnificent railway station. In fact a century ago Mark Twain described Maryborough as 'a railway station with town attached'. Bowenvale Timor, a short distance north of Maryborough, was a busy mining town at the height of the rush.

Dunolly (population 600)
This small town was once in the heart of the gold field area. More gold nuggets were unearthed in and around Dunolly than anywhere else in Australia. The largest gold nugget ever found, the 'Welcome Stranger' was found here. There are, hardly surprisingly, some interesting buildings along the main street and the Goldfields Historical Museum (open weekends only) displays replicas of some of the more mouth watering nugget finds!

Buninyong
Just south of Ballarat this was the scene for one of the first gold finds in the state. The impressive, tree-lined main street boasts several fine Victorian buildings from the gold days including the old Crown Hotel, first licensed in 1842.

BENDIGO (population 50,000)

This was once one of the richest gold mining towns in Australia and although the gold days are now just history there's plenty of evidence of the wealth they once brought. The buildings around the town centre are very solid, substantial and imposing. Many of them were designed by William Charles Vahland, a German architect. Bendigo also makes the most of its gold mining past with a number of tourist attractions worth investigating. Gold mining commenced here in 1851 and continued right up into the 1950s.

Information

There's a tourist office at Charing Cross, it's closed for lunch between 12 and 1 pm.

Pall Mall/McRae Streets

There are some fine old buildings along this street including the Shamrock Hotel, the third hotel of this name on the site, it was built in 1897. It's a very large, fully-restored and very fine example of the hotel architecture of the period. Its size gives some indication of how important and prosperous the town must have been in the goldmining era but the interior is a bit disappointing — some nicely carved woodwork around the dining hall bar but nothing spectacular.

Other large buildings along these streets include the Bendigo Technical College, the extremely elaborate post office, the fine fountain at Charing Cross, the war memorial and the town hall at the end of Bull St.

Around Town

Rosalind Park is a pretty little place, in the middle is a lookout tower which was once the mineshaft head of the Garden Gully United Gold Mining Company — good views across the town from the top. The Bendigo Art Gallery on View St has a nice collection — lots of Australian paintings, bush scenes, droving, mining. It's open Monday to Thursday from 10 am to 5 pm and Friday, Saturday from 2 to 5 pm. Admission is 60c.

Bendigo Tram

A vintage tourist-tram makes a regular run from the Central Deborah Mine, through the centre of the city and out to the tramways museum and the joss house with a commentary along the way. It runs hourly on weekends, public holidays and school holidays from 9.30 am. On weekdays it departs from the Central Deobrah at 9.30 am and 2 pm. For enquiries phone 43 8070, fare is $2.50.

Central Deborah Mine

On Violet St this is one of the major gold-mining sites in Bendigo. It was the last mine to close on the goldfields, operating for 103 years from 1851. Now restored and developed as a museum it's well worth a visit, partic-

1 Goldmines Hotel	9 Lookout Tower
2 Fortuna Villa	10 Dai Gum San
3 Stone-crusher	11 Tourist Office
4 Central Deborah Mine	12 War Memorial
5 Sacred Heart Cathedral	13 Post Office
6 Wesley Church	14 Shamrock Hotel
7 City Family Hotel/Motel	15 Fernery & Conservatory Gardens
8 Art Gallery	16 Chinese Joss House

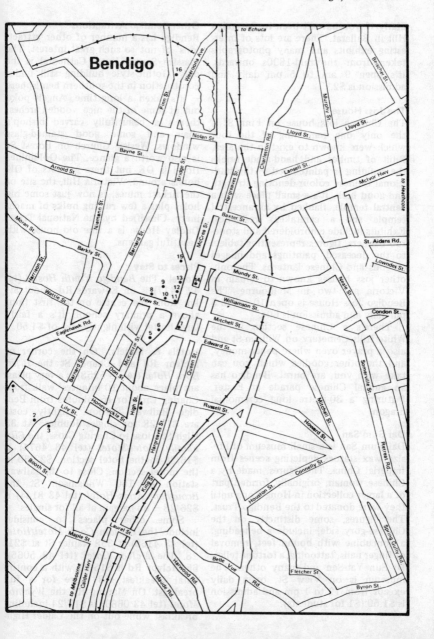

Bendigo

ularly if you haven't been to Sovereign Hill in Ballarat. There are lots of interesting exhibits and many photographs taken from the mid-1800s onwards. It's open 9 am to 5 pm daily and admission is $2.

The Joss House

The Chinese joss house on Finn St is the only one remaining of the four which were known to exist in the area. Built of timber and hand-made bricks the building is painted red — the traditional Chinese colour denoting strength and good luck. It's a small place with a central temple, flanked by an ancestral temple and a caretaker's residence. Exhibits include embroidered and stone-rub banners, figures representing tablets to the deceased, paintings and images of gods and Chinese lanterns. The only other joss houses known to remain in Victoria are two in Melbourne. The Bendigo Joss House is open 10 am to 5 pm daily and admission is 60c.

There's a Chinese section in the White Hills Cemetery on William St and also a prayer oven where paper money, and the other goodies which you can take with you, are burnt. Bendigo has an annual Chinese parade at Easter, featuring a 30-metre long ceremonial dragon.

Dai Gum San

Dai Gum San is a small museum of life-size wax statues depicting scenes from Imperial China. The figures, made by a Chinese woman, originally formed part of a larger collection in Hong Kong until they were donated to the Bendigo Trust. The figures, some distinctly on the Chinese-gory side, include a beheading, a concubine with bound feet, removal of finger nails, tattooing, a fortune teller, Dr Sun Yat-Sen and many others. The museum is on View St, open daily except from 12 to 1 pm and admission is $1.50 ($1 for students).

Other Bendigo Attractions

Bendigo has a number of other 'attractions' of not so such great interest. The massive Sacred Heart Cathedral is the only Gothic-style building still under construction in the southern hemisphere — it's taken a long time. Angels poke out of some of the nice wooden arches, there's a beautifully carved bishop's chair and some good stained-glass windows. Wesley Church on Forest St is also worth a glance. The Goldmines Hotel is OK but there are lots of OK hotels around. Victoria Hill, the site of the richest mines, is now just some big holes plus a few rusting hulks of machinery. Classified by the National Trust, Dudley House is a fine old house with beautiful gardens.

Places to Stay

Hostel The *Bendigo Youth Hostel* (tel 42 1417) is on Edwards Rd, about 3½ km from the centre on the first floor above a primary school. It's a fairly large hostel with nightly cost of $4.50.

Hotels & Motels On the corner of McIvor Rd and Chapel St the *Brian Boru Hotel* (tel 43 5258) is a very pleasant place about 10 minutes' walk from Charing Cross or 15 minutes from Bendigo Railway Station. Nightly costs are $16/28 for singles/doubles. At 33 High St, close to Charing Cross, the *City Family Hotel/Motel* (tel 43 4674) is $16/26 in the hotel section, $22/30 in the motel section. Close to the railway station at 150 Williamson St the *Brougham Arms Hotel* (tel 43 8144) is $26/28 — no bargain at all for singles.

Some other places to consider include the *Captain Cook Motel/Hotel* (tel 43 4168) at 358 Napier St at $21/28. The *McIvor Hotel* (tel 43 5065), 65 McIvor Rd is $15/25 with a continental breakfast, $3 more for a full breakfast. On Marong Rd the *Wyamba Motel* (tel 43 0660) is $17/24 including breakfast while out on the Calder Highway the *Calder Motel* (tel 47 7411) has rooms at $19/24.

Camping There are lots of campsites in and around Bendigo and up at Lake Eppalock. Most sites permit camping and nightly costs are in the $2 to $5 range.

Places to Eat
There are a number of pubs with counter meals, particularly along Pall Mall, including the fine old *Shamrock Hotel*. Pall Mall also has a number of pizzerias. On High St, the Melbourne side of the fountain at Charing Cross, there's a *McDonalds* and across the road is the *Mexican Kitchen*. For splashing out in Bendigo the superlative (but commensurately priced) *Copper Pot* at 8 Howard Place and *Bridgette McGuinty's* at 101 Williamson St are both worth considering.

Getting There
Trains From Melbourne to Bendigo take about 3½ hours and cost $9 in 2nd class, $12.20 in 1st. The first train departs from Spencer St Station at 8.45 am and there are about half a dozen services a day on weekdays. Ansett Pioneer and Greyhound buses operate through Bendigo on the route to Swan Hill and Mildura.

There is a minibus service between Bendigo and Ballarat, it departs from the Houlden Tours office at Charing Cross at 7.45 am and arrives at Ballarat at 10.30 am. The cost is $12.20, tickets from the driver. The route between the two gold towns is rolling and attractive, particularly at the Bendigo end, flattening out close to Ballarat.

AROUND BENDIGO
Close to Bendigo
Sandhurst Town at Myers Flats is a colonial era gold town re-creation which includes a working two-foot gauge railway line. At Epsom you'll find Bendigo Pottery, the oldest pottery works in Australia. There are guided tours of the works and you can buy pieces here. Hartland's Eucalyptus Factory at Whipstick Forest was established in 1890 and the production process can still be inspected today.

Further Afield
The large reservoir Lake Eppalock is about 30 km from Bendigo and provides the town's water supply. It's popular for all sorts of watersports — I learnt to sail there and set some sort of record for capsizing in the process. There are some fine lookouts in the vicinity of Heathcote (population 1100), a quiet little highway town.

GIPPSLAND
The Gippsland region is the south-east slice of Victoria, stretching from Melbourne to the NSW border. It's bordered by the coast to the south and the Great Dividing Range to the north. Gippsland is an area of multiple attractions, the beaches and coastal lakes of the coastal strip, the foothills of the dividing range and Wilson's Prom, one of Australia's

most popular national parks and the most southerly point in Australia. Gippsland was also an early gold rush area and today is the centre for Victoria's huge brown coal deposits. Offshore from Gippsland in the Bass Strait are the oil fields which provide most of Australia's petroleum supply.

Places to Stay

There's a *youth hostel* in Bairnsdale and an associate *youth hostel* in Mallacoota.

Getting There

VicRail operate Melbourne-Traralgon-Sale-Bairnsdale, sometimes by bus from Sale onwards. Fares from Melbourne are $8.50, $11.50, $14.20 respectively in economy, $11.50, $15.50, $19.50 in 1st. Ansett Pioneer have a co-ordinated service from Bairnsdale railway station onwards by bus, costing $17.50 to Lakes Entrance or $21.30 to Orbost. By Greyhound fares are Traralgon $14.50, Sale ditto, Bairnsdale $22.30, Lakes Entrance $23.30, Orbost $24.80. There's no public transport service all the way down to Wilson's Prom, about the closest you can get is Fish Creek, buses run there fairly regularly from Spencer St Station for $8.50.

Dandenong to Sale

Soon after leaving Dandenong the road divides, the Princes Highway continuing east, the South Gippsland Highway diving off to the south-east to Phillip Island and Wilson's Prom. You can take the South Gippsland Highway and rejoin the Princes Highway at Sale. The Princes Highway runs at first through the Latrobe Valley, site of Victoria's huge coal deposits and the electricity generating stations.

Towns along the Princes include Drouin (population 3100) with historical exhibits in the old police station. The Gippsland Regional Tourist Association has its headquarters at 231 Princes Highway, Drouin. A little further along you come to Warragul (population 7400) a dairy farming centre. Trafalgar (population 1900) is another dairy centre before you reach the large town of Moe.

Moe (population 18,800) is a Latrobe Valley coal mining centre and you can visit the Yallourn Power Station here. Old buildings have been collected here and reassembled in the Gippsland Folk Museum on the Princes Highway to re-create a 19th century community. From here there's a scenic road north to Walhalla, an historic old gold mining town, and the road continues north across the mountains. There are good views of the valley from Narracan and Coalville, small towns on a back road between Moe and Trafalgar.

Morwell (population 16,100) has huge coal deposits and electricity generating plants. In all the Latrobe Valley generates more than 85% of Victoria's electricity. Traralgon (population 15,100) is, like Moe and Morwell, a major Latrobe Valley electricity centre.

Walhalla

This tiny ghost gold town is in the mountains 46 km north of Moe. At one time the richest gold mine in Victoria was here, today the Long Tunnel Mine is open for visitors on weekends and holidays. There are a number of National Trust classified and other old buildings in the town so there's plenty of history but the spectacular drive up to the town is an equal attraction.

Sale (population 12,100)

At the junction of the Princes and Gippsland Highways, Sale is a supply centre for the Bass Strait oil fields. There's an Oil & Gas display centre on the Princes Highway on the western side of town. The Port of Sale, also on this side of town was a busy centre in the paddle steamer days and you can still take cruises from Sale into the Gippsland lakes. In the city centre Lake Guthridge has picnic and barbecue spots and the city also has some fine old buildings like the laceworked Criterion Hotel. On Princes Highway there is a Historical Museum.

There are many popular excursions and local attractions around Sale like Seaspray Beach with good surfing south of the city. Lake Wellington is very popular for sailing and boating. Just beyond Sale at Stratford you can turn north on the unsealed road across the spectacular Dargo High Plains to Mt Hotham. There are also exciting roads into the mountains from Maffra (population 3800) and Heyfield (population 1700). The forest road through Licola and Jamieson, near Lake Eildon, is particularly spectacular.

Tourist Information is available from the Oil & Gas centre.

The Gippsland Lakes

The long stretch of sand along 90 Mile Beach separates the sea from the extensive waterways of the Gippsland Lakes — an area offering lakes and sea, beaches and surf, fishing and boating. Bairnsdale (population 9100), at the junction of the Princes and Omeo Highways, is a popular base both for the mountains to the north and the lakes immediately to the south. West of Bairnsdale is Lindenow and the small Glenaladale National Park. The park has good bushwalking tracks and the Den of Nargun, an Aboriginal ceremonial ground in a gorge of the Mitchell River.

Paynesville (population 1200) is a resort on the lakes, you can cross to nearby Raymond Island by punt or to 90 Mile Beach by boat. Between Bairnsdale and Lakes Entrance you can turn off to Metung, a popular place to hire boats on Lake King. This interesting little fishing village has the small Angus McMillan cottage museum nearby at Chinaman's Creek. The Omeo Highway leads north from here onto the Bogong High Plains. Tourist info can be obtained from the Victorian Eastern Development Association at 63 Main St, Bairnsdale.

At the eastern end of the lakes is Lakes Entrance (population 3000) where there's a bridge across to 90 Mile Beach at Cunningham Arm. This is also a busy fishing port and lots of cruise boats operate on to the lakes. There's a Shell Museum on Marine Rd, an

Antique Car Museum on the Princes Highway, and an Aboriginal Art Museum, also on the Princes Highway. You can visit the Buchan Caves from here.

To the NSW Border

From Orbost (population 2800) the Bonang Highway leads up through beautiful hill country into NSW. The route to Buchan and beyond is equally scenic so you can make a fine loop from Orbost around the Snowy River National Park by taking one road north and the other south. Most of this route is on unsealed road. There are a number of limestone caves around the tiny town of Buchan (population 200). Tours take place three times daily at the Royal and Fairy caves.

From Orbost you can also take the road down to the coast at Marlo and on to Cape Conran. Beyond Orbost is Cann River (population 300) and a series of coastal national parks stretching all the way to the NSW border. The Mallacoota National Park around the Mallacoota Inlet is the best known and most popular. Mallacoota (population 600) is the main centre for this area.

South Gippsland

Way back at Dandenong you can opt to take the route south into the south Gippsland area rather than continue east on the Princes Highway to Sale. This route takes you down to Phillip Island and Wilsons Promontory. On the way south to Wilsons Prom you pass Koowee-rup (population 1000) with the nearby Bayles Flora & Fauna Park. Wonthaggi (population 4600), close to the coast, was once a major coal mining centre and from here there are good beaches at the small resort of Inverloch (population 1500), Tarwin Lower and Walkerville. Waratah Bay has good beaches from Walkerville right round to Sandy Point toward the Prom.

Near Korumburra (population 2800) is the Coal Creek Historical Park, a very

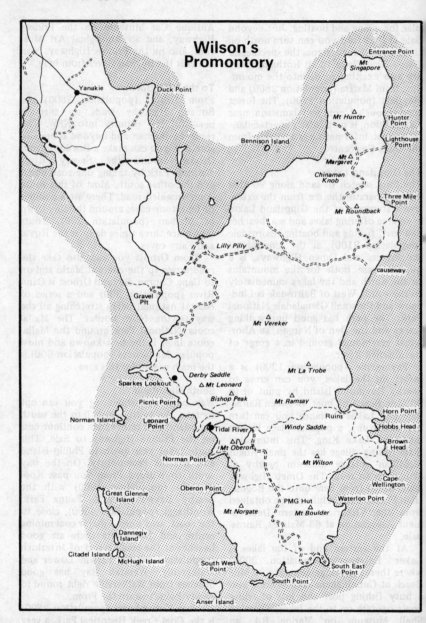

Wilson's Promontory

Entrance Point

Mt Singapore

Yanakie

Duck Point

Mt Hunter

Hunter Point

Bennison Island

Mt Margaret

Lighthouse Point

Chinaman Knob

Three Mile Point

Mt Roundback

Lilly Pilly

causeway

Gravel Pit

Mt Vereker

Derby Saddle

Mt La Trobe

Mt Leonard

Sparkes Lookout

Bishop Peak

Mt Ramsay

Picnic Point

Horn Point

Norman Island

Leonard Point

Tidal River

Ruins

Hobbs Head

Windy Saddle

Brown Head

Mt Oberon

Norman Point

Mt Wilson

Cape Wellington

Great Glennie Island

Oberon Point

PMG Hut

Waterloo Point

Mt Norgate

Mt Boulder

Dannegiv Island

Citadel Island

McHugh Island

South West Point

South East Point

South Point

Anser Island

popular re-creation of a coal mining town of the 19th century. Coal was first discovered here in 1872 and the Coal Creek mine operated from the 1890s right up to 1958. A little to the south is Leongatha (population 3600) with some beautiful countryside around it. The turn-off to the Prom is at Meeniyan or at Foster (population 1000).

Welshpool (population 400) is a dairying town which also engages in fishing at nearby Port Welshpool while the Bass Strait oil rigs are supplied from nearby Barry Beach. There's a Maritime Museum in Port Welshpool while the Agnes Falls, just north of the highway, are the highest in Victoria. Further along the coast Port Albert (population 200) was the first port in the state and an entry point for Chinese miners in the Gippsland gold rush days. Until a railway was constructed between Melbourne and Sale most of the region's trade was carried on through this port. The tiny town has a number of historic buildings along the main street while the Port Albert Hotel near the waterfront, first licensed in 1842, might be the oldest pub in the state.

Yarram (population 2100) is an access point to the western end of 90 Mile Beach. Woodside and Seaspray are two particularly popular patrolled beaches. North of the town is beautiful hill country with dense woods, fern glades and plenty of rosellas and lyrebirds. Here you will find the Tarra Valley and Bulga National Parks, on the scenic Grand Ridge Road. At Hiawatha, north-west of Yarram, are the Minnie Ha Ha Falls.

Wilsons Promontory

'The Prom' is one of the largest and most popular national parks in Australia, it covers the peninsula that forms the southernmost part of mainland Australia. It's a long day's walk from the car park to the tip of the Prom and if you want to see the lighthouse at the end you must phone ahead and arrange it. Tidal River is the main settlement in the park with an extensive camping area, a general store and a park office and information centre.

The Prom offers superb variety including a wonderful selection of beaches and more than 80 km of walking tracks. The tracks will take you through everchanging scenery — there are swamps, forests, marshes, valleys of tree ferns and long, sand-duned beaches. The variety of the beaches is equally an attraction — whether you want surfing, safe swimming or a secluded beach all to yourself you can find it on the Prom.

Finally there's the wildlife which, despite the park's popularity, abounds. There is a wide variety of birdlife, emus, kangaroos and, at night, plenty of wombats. The wildlife around Tidal River is very tame. It's probably walkers who get the best value from the Prom though, you don't have to get very far from the car parks to really get away from it all.

The park office at Tidal River has free leaflets on 'Short Walks' and 'Long Walks' and you can also get detailed maps of the park here. At peak holiday times the Tidal River camp site can be very crowded and booking is necessary. A permit is required if you wish to camp elsewhere in the park, this is easily obtainable from the park office at Tidal River.

UP THE HUME

The Hume Highway is the direct route between Melbourne and Sydney. It's far from Australia's most exciting road, in fact it's downright dull in stretches, and the heavy (by Australian standards) traffic can make life a little tedious. En route to the NSW border you pass through the 'Kelly Country' area, around which Australia's most famous outlaw, Ned Kelly, played out some of his most exciting brushes with the law. Not far to the east of the Hume are the Victorian Alps and in winter you'll catch glimpses of the snow-capped peaks from the highway.

Places to Stay

Although there are no youth hostels along the Hume there are plenty of other forms of accommodation. Beechworth, with its beautiful location in the alpine foothills, has an equally attractive hostel, not far off the Hume.

Getting There

As the main artery between Australia's two biggest cities it's hardly surprising that there's plenty of transport possibilities. You can fly to Albury-Wodonga with East-West from Melbourne or Sydney or with Kendell who have up to five flights a day. Or there are buses and trains, apart from the Melbourne-Sydney trains there are a variety of trains running just Melbourne-Albury or Sydney-Albury. From Melbourne fares (1st in brackets) include Seymour $5.40

($7.30), Benalla $10.50 ($14.20), Wangaratta $12.40 ($16.80), Wodonga $16 ($21.60).

Ansett Pioneer and Greyhound run along the Hume of course. Fares include Benalla $18.10, Wangaratta $18.80, Wodonga $19.50. Bus services fan out from Wangaratta and Wodonga to Beechworth, Bright, Corryong and other towns in the foothills as well as to the snow resorts.

Melbourne to Benalla

The new Hume Freeway bypasses Kilmore and Broadford (population 1600) near Mt Disappointment and the Murchison Falls. Seymour (population 6200) is close to several interesting vineyards including the very old Chateau Tahbilk and the very modern Mitchelton winery, see the Goulburn Valley section for more details. You can turn off the Hume here and take the alternate Newell Highway route to Sydney or Brisbane.

From Euroa (population 2700) you can take a scenic drive to Gooram Falls, near where Kelly performed one of his more amazing robberies at Faithfull Station. It's re-enacted every December.

Benalla (population 8300)

The Kelly gang's exploits finally came to an end in a bloody shoot out in nearby Glenrowan in 1880. Kelly was captured alive and eventually hung in Melbourne. There's everything from a statue of Ned with his armoured helmet

Victoria·

a. A traditional green and cream Melbourne tram on the tree-shaded 'Paris end' of Collins St.

b. Melbourne skyscrapers reflected in the calm waters of the Yarra River.

c. The tall pointy spire tops the Melbourne Cultural Centre Complex.

to a small museum of Kelly memorabilia in Glenrowan. Benalla also has a Pioneer Museum with Kelly exhibits. There are picnic areas along the Broken River through town and an excellent art gallery by the waterside. Benalla is a good place from which to visit the various northern Victorian wineries or the mountains. The town is also a very popular gliding centre. The ruins of the Kelly family homestead can be seen just off the highway at Greta.

Wangaratta (population 16,200)
Wang is the turn-off point to Mt Buffalo and the north of the Victorian alps along the Ovens Highway. The town has some pleasant parks and bushranger Mad Dog Morgan is buried here. On the Boorhaman Rd, eight km from town, Botharambo is a restored historic homestead, open on school and public holidays. There's lots of interest in the area around Wang — old gold towns, the alps, wineries.

The North-East Victoria Regional Tourist Authority has an office at 29 Ryley St.

Wodonga (population 13,600)
The Victorian half of the Albury-Wodonga growth centre is on the Murray River, the border between Victoria and NSW. Just south of the city, off the Hume Highway on Coyles Rd, there's the interesting Drage's biplane museum, open daily from 10 am to 5 pm.

THE VICTORIAN ALPS
As with the NSW Snowy Mountains the Victorian Alps are popular summer and winter. They're best known for their winter skiing but in summer they offer excellent bushwalking. The mountains actually begin immediately to the east of Melbourne (the Dandenongs are a Spur of the Great Dividing Range) and run north and north-east all the way to the NSW border. Only a few roads, none of them surfaced all the way, run right across the Great Dividing Range from north to south. In the north of the state the mountains slope down through delightful foothills into rolling country that includes some of Victoria's best winegrowing country. The Alpine Walking Track runs all the way from Mt Kosciusko to Walhalla, a superb long distance walk.

Places to Stay
Apart from all the usual accommodation possibilities there are also youth hostels at Beechworth and Mt Buller. In winter costs in the ski resorts tend to get pretty hair raising and many skiing visitors prefer to stay in the lower level towns, often only a short drive from the snow.

Victoria

A a. A jumble of rocks rise from the surrounding countryside at Hanging Rock.

B b. Near Port Campbell the Twelve Apostles are pounded by the seas of the Bass Strait.

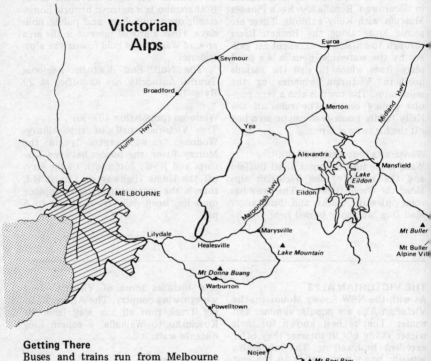

Victorian Alps

Getting There

Buses and trains run from Melbourne to Albury-Wodonga — see the Hume Highway section for more details. You can also fly to Albury-Wodonga. Buses run from Wangaratta and Wodonga to many points in the northern part of the region. There are also buses from Melbourne to Mt Buller in the south while you can reach Omeo by bus from Bairnsdale in the Gippsland region.

Victorian Wineries

There's no Barossa or Hunter Valley in Victoria so the state's wine producing activities are less well known than those of NSW or South Australia but in actual fact some of Australia's best wines are made here. Grape growing and wine producing started with the gold rush of the 1850s and before the turn of

the century Victorian wines had established a fine reputation in Europe. Then phylloxera, a disease of grapevines, devastated the Victorian vineyards and changing tastes in alcohol completed the destruction. Only recently has the Victorian wine industry started to recapture its former glory.

The oldest established wine producing area is in the north-east, particularly around Rutherglen but also across to Glenrowan and beyond. Other fine wine growing areas include the Goulburn Valley river flats south of Shepparton, Great Western between Stawell and Ararat on the Adelaide highway, around the Geelong area and in the Yarra Valley near Melbourne. In the far north-west the irrigation areas

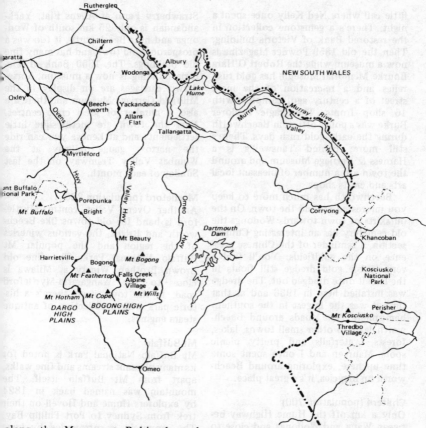

along the Murray at Robinvale and Mildura also produce wine.

Beechworth (population 3200)

This small town in the alpine foothills is both beautifully situated and plain beautiful. Beechworth is just 35 km from Wangaratta on the Hume Highway and it's only a few extra km to detour through Beechworth if you're travelling between Wangaratta and Wodonga. The difference is far more than distance for while Wang and Wodonga are on the flat plains, Beechworth is up in the hills. Even that's not all there is to the town for in the 1850s this was the centre of

the Ovens gold mining region and it became not just a rich but an extremely rich little metropolis. Signs of that gold wealth are still abundant, more than 30 buildings in this pretty little hill town are classified by the National Trust. Even the youth hostel, once the old Star Hotel, is of architectural significance.

Amongst the most interesting buildings are Tanswell's Hotel, a magnificent old laceworked hotel which also does very good counter meals. The post office has a superb clocktower and across the road the old jail has a dark little cell where Ned Kelly once spent a night. There's a gemstone collection in the restored Bank of Victoria building. Then the old 1859 Powder Magazine is now a museum while the Robert O'Hara Bourke Memorial Museum has gold rush relics and a re-creation of the main street of a century ago, complete with 16 shop fronts. The tragic explorer Burke was a police officer in Beechworth during the early gold rush days. There's still more; behind Tanswell's is a Harness & Carriage Museum and around the town are a number of pleasant local arts and crafts shops.

Beechworth has much more to keep you interested around the town. On the outskirts of town towards Wodonga the old cemetery has an interesting Chinese section, a reminder of the Chinese presence on the goldfields. You'll find a very visible gold dredge still floats in the lake it once dredged out. The dredge was installed here in 1936 and at that time it was the largest in the southern hemisphere. The roads around Beechworth lead to other small towns, lakes, forests, waterfalls and pretty picnic spots. Maureen and I once spent some time up here, exploring around Beechworth on bicycles, it's a great place.

Chiltern (population 700)
Only a km off the Hume Highway between Wang and Wodonga and close to Beechworth, this is another gold town with many reminders of its boom era. Author Henry Handel Richardson's home Lake View is preserved by the National Trust. In the old Grape Vine Hotel a courtyard is sheltered by the largest grape vine in Australia.

Yackandandah (population 500)
The pretty little 'strawberry capital' has been classified by the National Trust; not just the odd building but the entire town. Around here they have so many strawberries they even make them into strawberry wine — visit Schmidt's Strawberry Farm at Allens Flat. Yackandandah is only 25 km south of Wodonga and near Beechworth, it too was a prosperous gold town and has many fine old buildings. The 1850 Bank of Victoria building is now a museum, horse-drawn carriages are on display in the Millfield Carriage Museum and there are also a number of local craft centres. Near the town are picturesque little settlements and at Leneva you can ride the narrow gauge railway at the Wombat Valley Tramway on the last Sunday of each month.

Myrtleford (population 2800)
Another Ovens Valley centre, Myrtleford is hand for old towns like Beechworth and Bright, the various wineries of the region and the popular Mt Buffalo National Park. The fine old Brown Brothers Winery at Milawa is close to the Wangaratta-Myrtleford road. In the town itself there's a historic park with a collection of antique steam engines.

Mt Buffalo
Mt Buffalo National Park is noted for its many pleasant streams and fine walks, apart from Mt Buffalo itself. The mountain was named back in 1824 by explorers Hume and Hovell on their trek from Sydney to Port Phillip Bay. The mountain is surrounded by huge granite tors, great blocks of granite broken off from the massif by the expansion and contraction of ice in winter and other weathering effects. There is much plant life and wildlife around the park as well as over 140 km of walking tracks. Walk leaflets are available for the Gorge Nature Walk and the Dicksons Falls Nature Walk. You can stay in the park at the camp site by Lake Catani (open over the summer months) or at the Tatra Inn or The Chalet. A road leads up almost to the summit of 1720 metre Mt Buffalo.

Bright (population 1200)

Deep in the Ovens Valley, Bright today is a centre for the winter sports region, a summer bushwalking centre and in autumn it's renowned for its beautiful golden shades as the leaves change colour. In 1857 this was the centre for the notorious Buckland Valley riots when the diligent Chinese goldminers were forced off their claims with much less than a fair go. Bright is an easy drive from the snowfields at Mt Hotham, Mt Buffalo and Falls Creek.

Bright has a historic museum in the railway station while around the town are a number of excellent walking trails. You'll also enjoy excellent views if driving from Bright along the Alpine Way. Places of interest in the vicinity include the Stony Creek Trout Farm, the Pioneer Park open air museum and the pretty little town of Harrietville. A gold dredge continued operating in Harrietville right up to 1956 when it was sold and shipped off to Malaysia. The town is at the foot of 1979 metre Mt Feathertop and a regular bus runs to Mt Hotham. You continue through Harrietville to Mt Hotham and the Dargo High Plains, in spring the wildflowers here are very beautiful. Mt Bogong, to the east of Bright, is the highest mountain in Victoria at 1985 metres.

Rutherglen (population 1300)

Close to the alpine foothills and the Murray River, Rutherglen is the centre of Victoria's major wine growing area. Amongst the wineries in the area is All Saints with a National Trust classified winery building. Just 11 km from Rutherglen, on the Murray, Wahgunyah was once a busy port for the Ovens Valley gold towns. Its customs house is a relic of that era.

Omeo (population 300)

On the high plains on the southern side of the alpine region this small town is on the Omeo Highway, the southern access route to the snow country. In summer it's popular as a jumping off point for the Bogong High Plains. The road from here to Corryong, near the NSW border, is scenic but rough. Omeo still has a handful of interesting old buildings despite two earthquakes and a disastrous bushfire since 1885. The town has also had its own little gold-rush. The Bogong Plains Road from Omeo to Mt Beauty passes close by Mt Bogong, 1985 metres, Victoria's highest mountain.

Mansfield (population 1900)

Close to Lake Eildon and on the road up to Mt Buller there's a monument here recalling one of Ned Kelly's notorious clashes with the law. The graves of three police officers he shot at nearby Tolmie in 1878 are in the Mansfiled cemetery.

Skiing

The Victorian resorts are closer to Melbourne than the Snowy resorts are to Sydney so they're even more popular on weekends. See the NSW Snowy section for general information on skiing. The Victorian resorts are particularly good for ski-touring. Some of the main resorts, with distances from Melbourne are:

Mt Buller (241 km) You can get there by rail to Mansfield and connecting bus. Its proximity to Melbourne makes it, not surprisingly, the most crowded, especially at weekends when parking can be a problem. There are some excellent runs but the lifts are run by two opposing companies — you need two lift passes!

Mt Baw Baw (185 km) A smaller centre with runs more suited to the less expert amongst us. Baw Baw is a popular weekender but the lift capacity is generally quite adequate although the snow cover is not always the best.

Mt Buffalo (332 km) Since it is a

national park there are no private lodges in Victoria's oldest ski resort. Mt Buffalo is actually two virtually separate parts, several km apart — Dingle Dell and Tatra Inn. The skiing here is not the best in Australia but it's very picturesque and also fairly reasonably priced.

Falls Creek (379 km) When the snow's good the skiing is probably the best in Victoria and careful integration of the lifts around the natural bowl cuts out all that unpleasant ski-booted walking. Plenty of lift capacity and you can get here by bus from Albury.

Mt Hotham (403 km) A good-bad combination; Hotham is the furthest from Melbourne but enjoys the most consistent snow coverage, has some of the best ski-touring areas but terrible interconnection of the lifts necessitates lots of walking. The village is strung out along the road making a car a virtual necessity. There's very good cross-country skiing around Hotham which can be reached from the north or from the south via Bairnsdale and Omeo.

Others Mt Donna Buang, just 95 km from Melbourne via Warburton, and Lake Mountain, 109 km out via Healesville, are both very low-key resorts, good just for beginners and for the opportunity to say you've seen the snow.

THE SOUTH-WEST

The south-western corner of Victoria is really three separate areas. There's the spectacular Great Ocean Road stretch from south of Geelong to Warrnambool, one of the most magnificent and scenic coastlines in Australia. From there the south-west coastal region runs to the South Australian border. North of these coastal areas is the Western District, rich farmland dubbed 'Australia Felix' by the early explorer Thomas Mitchell and later to become one of the wealthiest farming regions in the country.

Places to Stay

There are countless camp sites and other holiday accommodation possibilities along the coastal stretches plus youth hostels at Camperdown and Port Fairy and hostel alternate accommodation at Apollo Bay.

Getting There

VicRail operate Melbourne-Geelong-Colac-Warrnambool with connecting buses on to Port Fairy and Portland. Economy fares (1st class in brackets) are Colac $8.50 ($11.50), Warrnambool $14.20 ($19.50), Port Fairy $15.20 ($20) and Portland $19 ($23.90). Ansett Pioneer buses operate from Melbourne to Hamilton ($11.20) and Mt Gambier ($12.30). You can also reach Hamilton by train to Ararat and connecting bus to Hamilton — $16 in economy, $20 in 1st. Hamilton is quite a centre for local bus routes — you can travel from here to Mt Gambier, Port land, Horsham, Warrnambool or Ballarat.

Hamilton is also connected to Melbourne by air on the Melbourne-Hamilton-Mt Gambier-Adelaide route.

THE GREAT OCEAN ROAD

For over 300 km from Torquay, a short distance south of Geelong, almost to Warrnambool, where the road rejoins the Princes Highway, the Great Ocean Road provides some of the most spectacular coastal scenery in Australia. For most of the distance the road hugs the coastline, passing some excellent surfing beaches, fine skin diving centres and even some hills from which hang-gliding enthusiasts launch themselves to catch

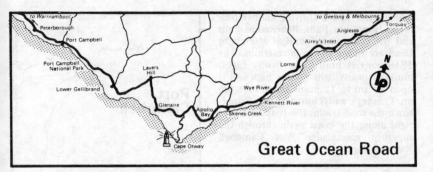

Great Ocean Road

the strong uplifts coming in from the sea in the evening.

The coast is well equipped with camp sites and other accommodation possibilities and if the seaside activities pall you can always turn inland to the bushwalks, wildlife, scenery, waterfalls and lookouts of the Otway Ranges which back the coast. The Great Ocean Road was only completed in 1932 as a depression works project and stretches of the country through which it runs are still relatively untouched.

Torquay (population 2600)

This popular resort town marks the eastern end of the Great Ocean Road, it's just 22 km south of Geelong. Some of the most popular surfing beaches are near here including Jan Juc and Bell's Beach. Bell's is the site for the Easter Australian surfing championships which each year attracts surfing enthusiasts from all over the world.

Anglesea (population 1400)

Another popular rseaside resort, Anglesea is 44 km from Geelong and apart from beach activities it also offers the nearby Angahook Forest Park with many bushwalking trails, Iron Bark Grove, Treefern Grove, Melaleuca Swamp and the Currawong Falls. The golf course at Anglesea is well known for the frequent visits by kangaroos which can be seen grazing the fairways.

Another 10 km along the Great Ocean Road is Airey's Inlet, a pleasant, smaller resort.

Lorne (population 900)

The small town of Lorne, 73 km from Geelong, was a popular seaside resort even before the Great Ocean Road was built. The mountains behind the town not only provide a spectacular backdrop but also gives the town a mild, sheltered climate year round. Lorne has good beaches, surfing and bushwalks in the vicinity. Climb up to Teddy's Lookout, behind the town, for the fine views over Loutit Bay. The beautiful Erskine Falls are also close behind Lorne.

Apollo Bay & Cape Otway

At Apollo Bay (population 1000), 118 km from Geelong, the road temporarily leaves the coast to climb up and over Cape Otaway. The coast is particularly beautiful and rugged on this stretch and there have been many shipwrecks here. Cape Otway is covered in rainforest, much of it still relatively untouched, and although many of the roads through the cape are unsealed and very winding they're no problem for the average car.

There are a number of scenic lookouts and nature reserves on this stretch of road but Melba Gully is probably the best with the beautiful ferns for which the cape is noted. Just beyond this small park is Lavers Hill, a tiny township which once had a thriving timber business. Hopetoun Falls, Beachamps Falls and the gemstones found at Moonlight Head are other Otway attractions. The 1848 convict built Cape Otway Lighthouse is nearly 100 metres high and is open 10 am to 12 noon and 2 to 4 pm on Tuesdays and Thursdays. At Princetown the road rejoins the coast and runs right along the coast again through the superbly spectacular Port Campbell National Park.

Port Campbell

If the Great Ocean Road offers some of the dramatic coastal scenery in Australia then the stretch through Port Campbell is its most exciting part. The views along here are fantastic with beautiful scenes like the rock formations known as the Twelve Apostles where 12 huge stone pillars soar out of the pounding surf. Or there's London Bridge, a bridge-like promontory arching across a furious sea.

Loch Ard Gorge has a sadder tale to tell. In 1878 the iron-hulled clipper *Loch Ard* was driven on rocks off shore at this point. Of the 50 or so board only two were to survive, an apprentice officer and an immigrant girl, both aged 18. They were swept into the narrow gorge now named after their ship. Although the papers of the time tried to inspire a romance between the two survivors the girl, a sole survivor of her family of eight, soon headed back to Ireland's safer climes. This was the last immigrant sailing ship to founder en route to Australia.

A little further along the coast is Port Campbell itself, the main centre in the park and again sited on a spectacular gorge with some fine walks in the hills behind the town. Soon after Port Campbell the Great Ocean Road leaves the coast at Peterborough and joins the Princes Highway just before Warrnambool.

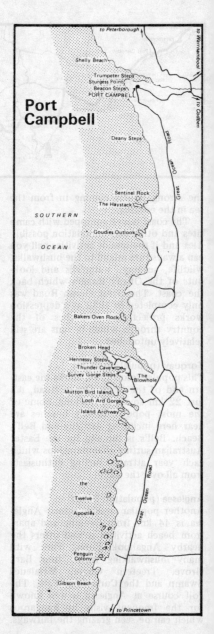

Port Campbell

THE SOUTH-WEST COAST

At Warrnambool the Great Ocean Road ends and you're on the final south-west coast stretch to South Australia on the Princes Highway. This stretch includes some of the earliest settlements in the state.

Warrnambool (population 20,200)

Warrnambool is 264 km from Melbourne and has some good beaches. Gun emplacements intended to repel the Russian invasion Australia feared in the 1880s can be seen near the lighthouse. This is now the site of the Warrnambool Maritime Village with a museum, restored sailing ships and port buildings of the era. It's open daily 9.30 am to 4.30 pm and admission is $2.50. Warrnambool also has a reptile park, a zoo and an antique vehicles museum while 12 km west of the town is Tower Hill with its huge crater lake and a game reserve with many emus.

Port Fairy (population 2400)

This small fishing port was one of the earliest settlements in the state, dating back to 1835 although temporary visitors had stayed here right back in 1826. These first arrivals were whalers and sealers, seeking shelter along the coast, but Port Fairy is still the home port for one of Victoria's largest fishing fleets. The fishing boats are one of the town's scenic attractions, the other is the many fine old buildings dating back to the town's early days. No less than 50 buildings in Port Fairy are classified by the National Trust, one of the finest is the bluestone home originally built for Captain Mills, a whaling boat skipper. Mott's Cottage, the early ANZ Bank, the Old Caledonian Inn and Seacombe House are other interesting buildings. Built in 1844 the Caledonian is the oldest licensed pub in Victoria.

Port Fairy also has an historical centre on Banks St, the old fort and signal station at the mouth of the river and Griffiths Island which is reached by a causeway from the town and has a lighthouse and a mutton bird rookery. Port Fairy was originally known as Belfast and although the name was later changed there's still a Northern Irish flavour about the place and a Belfast Bakery on the main street. Port Fairy is 27 km west of Warrnambool and has several camp sites and a number of motels.

Portland (population 8300)

Continuing west from Port Fairy you reach Portland, 72 km and just 75 km from the South Australian border. This is the oldest settlement in Victoria. Established in 1834 it predates Port Fairy by one year. It's an indication of the piecemeal development of Victoria that the first 'official' visitor, Major Thomas Mitchell, turned up here on an overland expedition from Sydney in 1836 and was very surprised to find it had been settled two years earlier. Whalers knew this stretch of coast long before the first permanent settlement and there were even earlier short term visitors.

Portland has numerous classified buildings including the old Steam Packet Hotel and Mac's Hotel plus the Customs House and Court House on Cliff St. The lighthouse at the tip of Cape Nelson, south of Portland, is also classified by the National Trust.

From Cape Bridgewater you can make pleasant walks to Cape Duquesne and Discovery Bay. From Portland the Princes Highway turns inland through Heywood and Dartmoor before crossing the border to Mt Gambier in South Australia but there is also a smaller road which runs closer to the coast, fringed by the Discovery Bay Coastal Park. It actually meets the coast just before the border at the delightful little town (village even) of Nelson, a popular resort for Mt Gambier. This is also a good access point to the Lower Glenelg National Park with its deep gorges and brilliant wildflowers.

THE WESTERN DISTRICT

The south-west of the state, inland from the coast and stretching to the South Australian border, is particularly affluent sheep raising and pastoral country. Malcolm Fraser is just one of the wealthy Australian prime ministers to come from the Western District.

Melbourne to Hamilton

You can reach Hamilton, the 'capital' of the Western District, via Ballarat along the Glenelg Highway or via Geelong along the Hamilton Highway. On the Glenelg Highway the small town of Lake Bolac (population 200) is beside a large freshwater lake, popular for watersports. Inverleigh (population 300) is an attractive little town along the Hamilton Highway. The Princes Highway runs further south, actually reaching the coast at Warrnambool. Winchelsea (population 900) is on the Princes Highway and has a museum in the 1842 Barwon Hotel and the National Trust operated Barwon Park Homestead, a fine old bluestone mansion which is open daily. The stone Barwon Bridge dates from 1867. You can reach the Grampians on a scenic route from Dunkeld on the Glenelg Highway.

Colac (population 10,400)

On the eastern edge of the Western District there are many volcanic lakes in the vicinity of the town. Alvie and Red Rock Lookouts give good views over the area. Colac has a botanic garden on the shore of Lake Colac. Provan's Mechanical Museum has vintage cars and motorcycles. South of the town are the Otways, scenic routes run through the ranges to the Great Ocean Road.

Camperdown (population 3600)

There are many volcanic crater lakes around this pleasant town, you can see nearly 40 of them from the lookout on top of Mt Leura, itself an extinct volcano. Lake Gnotuk and Lake Bullen Merri, two crater lakes close to the town, are notable because although they are very close together their water levels differ by about 50 metres! Also close to Camperdown is Victoria's largest lake, the salt Lake Corangamite. From Camperdown roads lead south through Cobden to Port Campbell and the Great Ocean Road.

Hamilton (population 9500)

The major town of the area, Hamilton is particularly noted for its superb art gallery on Brown St, it's one of the best in any Australian country town. Lake Hamilton is right in the centre of town and there's a zoo in the botanic gardens. Wannon Falls (15 km) and Nigretta Falls (seven km) are two local attractions, Mt Eccles National Park is 33 km out and has the crater Lake Surprise, there are two other extinct volcano craters close to town. These reminders of a volcanic history are evident all through the south-west region. There are great views from the summit of Mt Napier. Beyond Hamilton is Casterton (population 2200) with an historical museum in the old railway building and the very fine National Trust classified homestead Warrock, open daily. Coleraine (population 1300), another very early Victorian settlement, is between Hamilton and Casterton.

The South-West Regional Authority tourist office is on Lonsdale St.

CENTRAL WEST & THE WIMMERA

Several roads run west from the Victorian gold country to the South Australian border. The main road is the Western Highway which is also the busiest route between Melbourne and Adelaide. From Ballarat the road runs north of the Little Desert while to the north and south is the Wimmera, the seemingly endless Victorian wheatfields. From Horsham the Wimmera Highway splits off the Western Highway and runs through this area which also extends north-east to Warracknabeal and Donald. In the south of the region is one of the major attractions of the region, indeed one of the most spectacularly scenic areas of Victoria, the mountains of the Grampians.

Places to Stay

There's a *youth hostel* in Halls Gap, in the heart of the Grampians, and an associate hostel in Stawell.

Getting There

The Western Highway through the Central West is the main route between Melbourne and Adelaide and the Melbourne-Adelaide railway line takes the same route so there is no shortage of transport along this way. The nightly Overland runs right through to Adelaide while Monday to Saturday VicRail also have a morning train as far as Serviceton and a night train as far as Dimboola. Fares from Melbourne include Ararat $11.50 economy ($15.50 1st), Horsham $16.90 ($22.80), Stawell $13.30 ($17.90), Dimboola $19 ($25.60), Nhill $19 ($25.60), Kaniva $20.10 ($27.10).

Ansett Pioneer and Greyhound use the same route with fares Ararat $20.30, Stawell $21.90, Horsham $25.90, Dimboola $27.30, Nhill $28.20, Kaniva $32. Bus services connect north from Horsham to Ouyen and Mildura or south to Hamilton in the Western District.

Ballarat to Ararat

After leaving Ballarat by its long, tree-lined memorial drive you reach Beaufort (population 1200) about halfway to Ararat. For a brief period in its gold rush heyday this small town had an enormous population chasing the elusive metal at Fiery Creek. Today it's a quiet farming centre with good bush-walking areas in the Mt Cole State Forest, 16 km north-west.

Ararat (population 8300)

After a brief flirtation with gold in 1857, Ararat settled down as a farming centre. Ararat has a folk museum with an Aboriginal collection, an art gallery and some fine old bluestone buildings.

Only 16 km north-west of Ararat on the Western Highway, Great Western is one of Australia's best known champagne regions. Seppelt's Great Western vineyards were established in 1865. The unique Sisters Rocks are between here and Stawell. There are walks and barbecue sites in the Langi Ghiran State Forest, 14 km east. On the Melbourne side of Ararat there are some historic buildings in Buangor. Old gold towns in the area include Cathcart and Mafeking, which once had a population of 10,000.

Stawell (population 6200)

A centre for visits to the Grampians and another early Victorian gold town, Big Hill was the site of the town's first gold discovery. Stawell's Mini-World is a local attraction. The attractive little town has a number of National Trust classified buildings, an illuminated fountain, an animated clock in the town hall and a whole collection of war and other memorials. Bunjil's Cave, with Aboriginal rock paintings, is 11 km south and other local attractions include Sisters Rock by the Western Highway to the south-east, Roses Gap Wildlife Reserve, 17 km south, and the National

Trust Tottington Woolshed, 55 km north-east.

The Grampians

Named after the mountains of the same name in Scotland the Grampians are the south-west tail end of the Great Dividing Range. The area is a state forest, not a national park, but it's renowned for fine bushwalks, superb mountain lookouts, excellent rock climbing opportunities, prolific birdlife and, in the spring, countless wildflowers. The Grampians are at their best from August to November when the flowers also put on their most colourful display. Mt Arapiles, 16 km west of Horsham near Natimuk, is a particular favourite of rock climbers. There are also many Aboriginal rock paintings in the Grampians.

The Grampians lie immediately west of Ararat and south of the Western Highway between Stawell and Horsham. The tiny town of Hall's Gap (population 300) is the centre for the Grampians, indeed it's right in the middle of the region and has camping and motel facilities and a youth hostel. Hall's Gap is about 250 km from Melbourne.

Horsham (population 11,700)

A highway junction town and the main centre for the Wimmera, Horsham is also a good base for the Little Desert National Park and the Grampians. The town has an art gallery and 'Olde Horsham' with historic displays and a tea room in an old tram. There are a number of picnic and recreation areas on the Wimmera River and the various lakes in the vicinity. North-east of Horsham towards St Arnaud on the Wimmera Highway is Murtoa (population 1000) in the heart of the wheat-belt and dominated by a gigantic wheat storage silo and a water tower for the railway.

Little Desert

Just south of the Western Highway, reached from Dimboola or Nhill, the Little Desert is noted for its brilliant display of wildflowers in the spring. The name is a bit of a misnomer because it isn't really a desert at all nor is it that little! Part of the 'desert' is a national park but it actually extends well beyond the park boundaries. If you really intend to explore the bushland of the park you'll need four-wheel drive. The desert is at its finest in the spring when it is carpeted with wildflowers. A little beyond Dimboola the Kiata Lowan Sanctuary is an easily accessible area in the north of the park with walks and a resident ranger. The Big Desert is further north of the Western Highway.

Dimboola (population 1700) is a quiet, typical Australian country town on the Wimmera River. The name is a Sinhalese word meaning 'land of the figs'. The Pink Lake, just south of the highway, is a little beyond Dimboola. Beside the Wimmera River near here you can see Aboriginal canoe trees where canoes have been cut out in one piece from the bark. The Ebenezer Mission Station was established in Antwerp, north of Dimboola, to tend to local Aboriginals in 1859.

Nhill (population 2100) is the mid-point between Melbourne and Adelaide and is another Wimmera wheat farming centre although it also acts as a centre for the Mallee region to the north. The 1881 post office is classified by the National Trust and in the town centre is a memorial to the Clydesdale horses which were used extensively in the development of the Wimmera.

Kaniva (population 800), further west and just before the South Australian border, is also on the edge of the Little Desert. There's an interesting three km walking track, the Billy-Ho Bush Walk, about 10 km from the town with numbered examples of desert flora. Kaniva has a historical museum

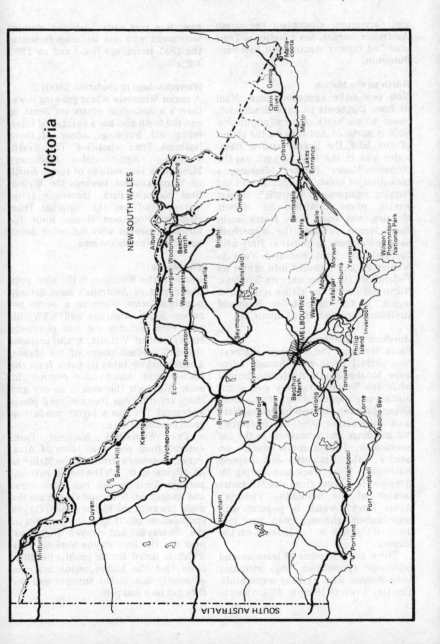

and Serviceton, almost on the South Australian border, has a National Trust classified railway station with basement dungeons.

North to the Mallee
You can make excursions from Nhill or from Dimboola to Lake Hindmarsh, about 40 km north. Jeparit (population 500) is north of Antwerp on the shores of the lake, the largest natural freshwater lake in the state. Jeparit has the Wimmera/Mallee Pioneer Museum, a collection of colonial buildings and old farming equipment. Australia's longest serving prime minister, Sir Robert Menzies, was born here. North again from Jeparit towards the Wyperfield park is Rainbow (population 700) with the National Trust classified Yuranga homestead and a tourist info centre on Federal St. It's open only on Sundays. North and west of the Mallee agricultural region is the dry Mallee bushland stretching for hundreds of square km.

Horsham to Edenhope
From Horsham the Wimmera Highway runs slightly south-west through Edenhope to the South Australian border while the Western Highway goes slight north-west, sandwiching the Little Desert between the two highways. Natimuk (population 500) has interesting old buildings and a museum in the old courthouse. There's much birdlife on nearby Lake Natimuk. Just beyond Natimuk is Mitre Rock and soaring Mt Arapiles; fine views from the 213 metre summit of the monolith, 'Victoria's Ayers Rock', which is popular with rockclimbers although you can also drive all the way to the lookout on the summit.

There are a number of lakes around Edenhope (population 900) including Lake Wallace with its many water birds. The tiny town of Harrow, 32 km south-

east, is a very early Victorian country settlement with old buildings including the 1851 Hermitage Hotel and an 1862 log jail.

Warracknabeal (population 2800)
A major Wimmera wheat growing town, there's a historical centre on Scott St and the town also has a number of interesting old buildings, some of them National Trust classified. The North-Western Agricultural Machinery Museum is just outside of town. North of Warracknabeal towards the Wyperfield National Park, Hopetoun (population 900) has the National Trust classified Hopetoun House, built for Edward Lascelles who did much development of the Mallee area.

The Mallee
North of the Wimmera is the least populated part of Australia's most densely populated state. Forming a wedge between South Australia and NSW this area even includes the one genuinely empty part of Victoria. It also includes the dull, endless plains of the Mallee, a region which takes its name from the Mallee scrub which once covered the area. Although this area is so dry and there are still large tracts of sand plains and scrub it's also a highly productive grain producing area.

The Wyperfield National Park, entered from the small town of Albacutya, preserves a stretch of the Mallee in its original state. It's the largest national park in Victoria and has many emus and kangaroos. Nhill and Ouyen are the main towns of the Mallee region. Ouyen (population 1600) is at the junction of the Sunraysia and Ouyen Highways, near the Hattah-Kulkyne National Park which is noted for its prolific birdlife. Note that the Mallee region becomes extremely hot in the summer and the flies can be a real pest.

GOULBURN VALLEY

The Goulburn Valley region runs in a wide band from Lake Eildon north-west across the Hume Highway and up to the NSW border. The Goulburn River joins the Murray upstream from Echuca. You'll also find Goulburn Valley centres in the Around Melbourne, Hume Highway and Murray River sections but the stretch from Seymour on the Hume Highway up to the Murray River is covered below.

Getting There

Trains run between Melbourne and Shepparton and sometimes on to Numurkah. From Shepparton or Numurkah connecting buses operate to Cobram and across the Murray to Tocumwal, from where you can connect on to Sydney. Fares are Shepparton $10 ($13.50 1st), Numurkah $11.50 ($15.50) and Cobram $13.30 ($17.30). Ansett Pioneer Melbourne-Brisbane bus services via Toowoomba operate up the Goulburn Valley with fares to Shepparton of $9.50 and to Echuca $10.20.

Nagambie (population 1100)

On the shores of Lake Nagambie which was created by the construction of the Goulburn Weir, Nagambie has some interesting old buildings, a historical society display and two of the best known wineries in Victoria are close by. Chateau Tahbilk's winery is a beautiful old building with notable cellars while just a few km away the Mitchelton Winery is modern as tomorrow with a strange 'control tower' looming unexpectedly over the sur-

rounding countryside. Mitchelton's winery is part of a whole complex including barbecue facilities and a swimming pool. Boat tours operate from Nagambie on the lake and up the river to the winery, which is built on the river banks.

Shepparton (population 25,800)

In a prosperous irrigated fruit and vegetable growing area Shepparton and its adjoining centre of Mooropna (population 2000) have a number of points of interest. Shepparton's modern Civic Centre has an art gallery and other fascilities, there's an International Village, a Historical Museum open on Sunday afternoons and a pottery a few km out of town. You can tour the Shepparton Preserving Company cannery, largest in the southern hemisphere, at 10 am or 2 pm on weekdays.

Other Towns

Rushworth (population 1000) is about 20 km west of the Goulburn Highway and was once a mining centre in the gold days. You can visit the local history museum on weekends or the Cheong Homestead a few km south of town at Whroo. Lake Waranga is popular for water sports. North of Shepparton and not far from the Murray River, Numurkah (population 2700) is another irrigation area town. It has a steam and vintage machinery display. Kyabram (population 5100) is a little south of Echuca and has a fauna and waterfowl park at the southern end of the town. It's the centre for a prosperous fruit growing district.

THE MURRAY RIVER

Although NSW and Victoria share the Murray from soon after its source all

the way to South Australia, most of the places of interest are on the Victorian side of the river. The Murray actually

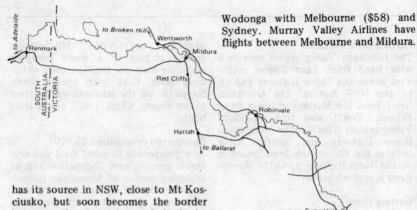

Wodonga with Melbourne ($58) and Sydney. Murray Valley Airlines have flights between Melbourne and Mildura.

The Goulburn Valley region runs in a wide band from Lake Eildon north-west across the Hume Highway and up to the NSW border. The Goulburn Meanders on the lake and up to the river joins the Murray.

Echuca. You'll also find the Goulburn Valley centres to the ...

Hume Highway ... Murray ... sections but the stretch from Seymour on the Hume Highway up to the Murray River is covered by the ...

Getting There
Trains run ... Melbourne and Shepparton ... sometimes run ... around ... in Shepparton, or ... connecting there operate and across the Murray ... from where you can connect ... there are Shepparton $10 ($12.60), ... Numurkah $11.50 ($13.50), and Cobram $12.80 ($15.50). Ansett Pioneer Melbourne-Brisbane bus

has its source in NSW, close to Mt Kosciusko, but soon becomes the border between the two states. Indeed the NSW-Victoria border is a straight, geometrical affair until it falls in with the twists and turns of Australia's greatest river.

The Murray is Australia's most important river for more than one reason. In terms of length it's the longest and economically it is of great importance. Irrigation schemes using Murray water have made huge areas of previously barren land agriculturally viable. It's also a river with a history, it was travelled up and down by some of Australia's earliest explorers and later became a great trade artery into the interior. Long before roads and railways crossed the land the Murray was an antipodean Mississippi with paddle steamers cruising up and down its winding waterways. Many of the river towns have museums, old buildings from the riverboat era or well-preserved old paddle steamers to recall that colourful era.

Places to Stay
Apart from motels, hotels and campsites — of which there are plenty because the Murray is a popular holiday area — there are also associate youth hostels at Echuca and Mildura.

Getting There
Air East-West Airlines connect Albury/

Bus Ansett Pioneer connect Mildura with Sydney ($63), Melbourne ($29) and Adelaide ($27). The Melbourne-Mildura service operates through Swan Hill ($20) and Robinvale ($26) while there is also a Melbourne-Deniliquin service that goes through Echuca ($10). Greyhound have similar services and also connect Mildura with Broken Hill on their Melbourne-Broken Hill service. Mildura-Broken Hill is $17. Albury/Wodonga is on the regular Melbourne-Sydney Hume Highway route for both bus operators. Wodonga is $42 from Sydney, $20 from Melbourne.

Rail VicRail have services to Albury/Wodonga, Swan Hill and Mildura. Albury/Wodonga is on the regular Melbourne-Sydney route. The regular fare to Wodonga is $16 in economy, $22 in 1st. Swan Hill services operate via Bendigo but there is usually only one service daily all the way to Swan Hill. The fare is $16 economy, $21 1st. Mildura services are on the daily Vinelander via Ballarat. The trip takes about 10½ hours and the fares are $23 in economy, $32 in 1st.

Corryong (population 1400)
The Murray is still an alpine stream at this point. Corryong is the Victorian gateway to the NSW Snowy Mountains and also the last resting place of Jack Riley, *The Man from Snowy River*. His grave is in the town cemetery and there's also a 'Man from Snowy River' museum in the town.

Tallangatta (population 900)
With the construction of the Hume Weir at Albury-Wodonga, Tallangatta

and at Cobram (population 3400), a town noted for its fine beaches, there are many sandy beaches along the river. Downstream Barmah is by a large loop in the river, it's the only town in Victoria north of the Murray.

Echuca (population 7900)
In the riverboat days this was the busiest riverport in Australia. It's strategically situated where the Goulburn and Campaspe Rivers join the Murray. Those pioneering days are conjured up in the old Port of Echuca area and the restored paddle-steamers *Pevensey* and *Adelaide*. The Star Hotel and the Bridge Hotel also date back to the riverboat era. Echuca has a Port of Echuca Museum, the Murray Museum and the Alambee Auto & Folk Museum. You can make riverboat cruises on the modern paddle-steamer *Canberra*.

was submerged by the rising waters of Lake Hume. The town was relocated on the shoreline of the new lake. Today it's popular as a watersports centre and also as an access point to the alpine region.

Wodonga to Echuca
See the Hume Highway section for details on Wodonga, the sister town to Albury on the NSW side of the Murray. By Wodonga the Murray has already become a larger, steady river and the Hume Highway crosses the border over the Hume Weir. Further downstream at Yarrawonga another weir created Lake Mulwala back in 1939. The river is particularly pleasant at this stretch and Yarrawonga (population 3300) is a popular stopping point. You can make short river cruises from the Mulwala foreshore every afternoon. Here

There's a Tourist Information Centre on Heygarth St in Echuca. The smaller NSW sister town of Moama is right across the river.

Echuca to Swan Hill
Cohuna (population 2100) is close to Gunbower Island, a long 'island' enclosed by the Murray and Gunbower Creek and with abundant animal and birdlife. Kow Swamp, to the south of Cohuna, is

also a wildlife sanctuary.

Kerang (population 4000) is 30 km south of the Murray and between here and the river are a sprawling group of lakes and marshes particularly noted for their population of ibis. The lakes here are also popular for sailing. In the town itself there is much birdlife in Korina Park while Strathclyde Cottage is a local arts and crafts centre. North of the town Murrabit, a small town on the Murray, has a local market on the first Saturday of each month. From Kerang the Murray Valley Highway runs by the series of lakes all the way to Swan Hill. Just 16 km before reaching there, Lake Boga has pleasant sandy beaches.

Swan Hill (population 7900)

One of the most interesting and touristically popular towns of the entire length of the Murray, Swan Hill was named by the early explorer Thomas Mitchell who spent a sleepless night here, due to a large contingent of noisy black swans. The town's major attraction today is the extensive riverside Swan Hill Pioneer Settlement. This working recreation of a river town in the paddle-steamer era even has the largest paddle boat on the Murray, the *Gem*, as one of its exhibits. The settlement has everything from an old locomotive to a working blacksmith and horse drawn vehicles act as transport around the old buildings. There's also an old newspaper office and the most amazing collection of old bits and pieces. Definitely worth a visit, admission is $4 and it's open daily. You can make short paddle steamer trips from here in the *Pyap* for $3.

Swan Hill also has a regional art gallery at Horseshoe Bend and a military museum. Continuing beyond Swan Hill it's worth a pause to visit the old Tyntynder Homestead, 17 km along the Murray Valley Highway. It's a beautifully restored old homestead from the earliest days of European settlement along the Murray. The homestead also has a small museum of pioneering and Aboriginal relics and many reminders of the hardships of early homestead life, like the wine cellar! Admission is $2.

Swan Hill is 340 km from Melbourne and has a Tourist Information Centre on Campbell St.

Swan Hill to Mildura

From Swan Hill the Murray Valley Highway runs close to the river to near Robinvale, from where the most direct route to Mildura is to cross the river and continue on the Sturt Highway on the NSW side. The Murray Valley Highway takes a longer route around a great loop of the river, running beside and through the Hattah-Kulkyne National Park. This park is one of the few fragments of the old Mallee scrub still remaining in the region. It's a valuable reminder that in this part of country the Murray is really running through a desert and only the great irrigation projects have made the desert bloom. North of the Murray is very empty country, stretching across the great expanse of NSW outback to Broken Hill.

On the river, though a little off the Murray Valley Highway, Robinvale (population 1700) is almost ringed in by a loop of the Murray. It's a centre for grape and citrus growing and has a busy wine industry with local wineries open for visits and tastings. A little downstream of the town is a weir and one of the largest windmills in Australia.

The Hattah-Kulkyne Park has good walking trails and much birdlife. It's a stretch of the Mallee bush preserved in its near original state.

Mildura (population 14,400)

On the banks of the Murray and nearly 550 km from Melbourne this was the site for the first development of irrigation from the Murray. The Canadian Chaffey brothers came out to Australia to develop irrigation projects late last century, they were persuaded to come out here by Alfred Deakin, a great believer in the possibilities of irrigation and later to become prime minister. His vision proved to be correct and the extensive irrigated land from here and down through South Australia all stems from the Chaffey brothers early work.

W B Chaffey settled in Australia and later became the first mayor of Mildura. You can see his statue on Deakin Avenue. His original home, Rio Vista, is now a museum and part of the Mildura Arts Centre. Mildura also has an Aboriginal Arts Centre at 77 Orange Avenue and an interesting little aviation museum by the airport (open weekends) with a collection of old aircraft mostly in bits. The Mildura Workingman's Club (visitors welcome) boasts one of the longest bars in the world, it stretches nearly 100 metres!

Lest you forget that this is riverboat country you can take paddle steamer trips from the Mildura Wharf. On weekday afternoons and Sundays the *PS Melbourne* does a two-hour round trip. It's also wine country with a number of popular wineries around the town. Leaving Mildura you don't have to travel very far before you realise just how desolate the country around here can be. Continuing west, now on the Sturt Highway, the road runs arrow straight and deadly dull to South Australia, about 130 km away. Crossing into NSW you follow the Murray another 32 km to Wentworth, one of the oldest river towns, then strike off north for 266 km along the Silver City Highway to remote Broken Hill. A popular excursion from Mildura is to Mungo Station in NSW to see the strange natural formation known as the Wall of China.

Mildura, which is noted for its exceptional amount of sunshine, has a Victorian Government Tourist Bureau on Deakin Avenue.

Western Australia

Area   2,526,000 square km
Population   1,200,000

Don't miss: Beautiful Perth with its 'ideal' climate, the rugged gorge country of the Pilbara and the Kimberleys to the north and the interesting old gold rush region around Kalgoorlie.

Western Australia is the largest, most lightly populated and most isolated state. Since the completion of surfacing the Eyre Highway across the Nullarbor in 1976 it is now considerably more accessible from the east coast and even if you travel between Darwin and Perth there are now only a few hundred km of unsealed road in the Kimberleys.

In the haphazard, fits and starts, manner in which most of Australia was established the first settlers arrived in Perth in 1929, three years after Britain had formally claimed it. They were there basically to beat any other Europeans to the area. Situated so far from the main Australian development it was not surprising that growth was painfully slow. Not until the gold rushes of the 1890s did WA really get off the ground. Today a larger and far more technologically advanced mineral rush forms the basis for the state's current prosperity.

The comparative newness of Perth accounts for its clean cut look. It is a shiny, modern city, pleasantly sited astride the Swan River with the port of Fremantle a few km downstream. Despite its late settlement WA has some of the oldest relics of European contact with Australia. A number of Dutch East Indiamen fell afoul of the WA coast while on their way to Batavia (Jakarta in Indonesia today) long before Captain Cook sailed up the east coast.

Away from the capital there are the goldfield ghost towns in the east of the state, the rugged coast and giant karri forests of the south plus the wine producing Swan Valley area closer to the capital. Heading north there is the harshly beautiful Pilbara gorge country, site of the state's immense mineral wealth, plus the old pearling town of Broome, now enjoying a tourist boom all of its own. The wild Kimberley area forms the top corner of the state and one of Australia's last frontiers.

Wildflowers

Western Australia is famed for its wildflowers and some people go all the way to WA just to see them. They spring into life in the late winter and early spring from August through October and can be seen all over the state. Even some of the driest deserts will put on a technicolour display with just a little rainfall as prompting. The variety of flowers is enormous — the south-west alone has over 3000 different species. Because of WA's isolation from the rest of Australia many of the flowers to be seen here are unique to the state. They're known as everlastings because the flower petals stay attached even after the flower has died. The speed with which the flowers appear is quite amazing — they seem to spring up almost overnight and transform vast areas within days. In some places the wildflowers form a virtual carpet of colour stretching as far as the eye can see with as many as one thousand million flowers per square km!

You don't even have to leave Perth to see WA's wildflowers, there's a section of King's Park where they are cultivated. Elsewhere in the state you can find them almost everywhere but the national parks and the south-west are prime areas. In the south-west the jarrah forests are particularly rich in wildflowers and WA's many coastal parks also put on brilliant displays. Near to Perth the Yanchep National Park and the John Forrest National Park in the Darling Range are both excellent prospects.

GEOGRAPHY

Western Australia's geography is somewhat like a reverse of the eastern side of Australia — but with much less green and much more desert. The equivalent of the long fertile coastal strip on the east coast is the small south-west corner of the state, here too a range of hills rise up behind the coast, but much smaller in scale than the Great Dividing Range on

1 South-West
2 Gold Country
3 Nullarbor Plains
4 North Coast
5 Pilbara
6 North-West
7 Kimberleys

the east coast. Further north it's dry and relatively barren and along the north-west coast the Great Sandy Desert runs right to the sea. This is a very inhospitable region.

There are, however, a couple of very interesting variations from the barren inland region of WA. The extreme north of the state is the Kimberleys, a wild and rugged area with a convoluted coast and spectacular gorges inland. This area gets very adequate annual rainfall — but all in one brief period each year. Taming the Kimberleys has been a long running dream which is still only partially fulfilled. Meanwhile it's a spectacular area well worth a visit. Further south in the Pilbara region is more magnificent gorge country which is also the treasure house from which the state derives its vast mineral wealth. In area, however, most of WA is simply a vast empty stretch of outback, the Nullarbor in the south, the Great Sandy Desert in the north.

GETTING AROUND

Buses of Ansett Pioneer and Greyhound run from Perth up the coast (or through the interior to the Pilbara with Greyhound) to the Northern Territory. Other bus companies also connect Perth to the eastern states. Western Australia's internal rail network, on the other hand, is very small. The state's internal air services, to the north-west in particular, are excellent. Airlines of Western Australia have a comprehensive network of flights connecting the northern towns with Perth with a frequency of flights which seems positively alarming when you look at the population up there. The reason why is quite simple. Much of that northern population is involved in the mining and oil drilling projects and for the companies it's often easier to fly people back and forth from Perth rather than have them living up there. The chart details the main WA routes and flight costs.

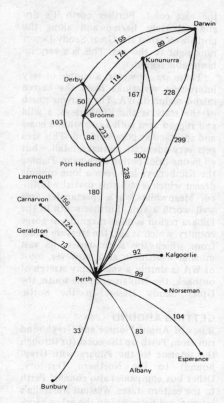

you'll probably get through quite a few dollars of tacky fast food while you hang around roadhouses waiting for a lift. By bus is probably a good contender — say $100 for a Sydney-Perth ticket with one of the cheaper bus lines. Driving yourself is probably cheapest of all. Ignoring the other operating costs (you have to register and insure your car whether you drive it to Perth or not) you'll probably get coast to coast for around $200 worth of fuel. Between four passengers that's just $50 a head.

ACTIVITIES

Bushwalking There are a number of bushwalking clubs in Perth. Popular areas include the Stirling Range National Park and Porongurup National Park, both near Albany. There are also a number of coastal parks in the south and south-west with good bushwalking tracks. There are good walks in the hills around Perth at places like Piesse Brook, Mundaring Weir, the Serpentine, Kalamunda and Bickley. They're particularly pleasant during the August-September spring wildflower season. If you're a really enthusiastic walker there is 640 km of marked walking track all the way from Perth to Albany — using old forest tracks.

Swimming & Surfing Perth sometimes claims, and with some justification, to have the best beaches and surf of any Australian city. Particularly popular surfing areas elsewhere in the state include Denmark (near Albany), Bunbury (south of Perth) and Geraldton (to the north).

Skin Diving Good diving can be found around a very large part of the WA coast from Esperance to Geraldton and then between Carnarvon and Exmouth. You can get to islands and reefs off the coast with small boats. Good areas include Esperance, Bremer Bay, Albany, Denmark, Windy Harbour, Margaret

Crossing Australia

The problem with Western Australia is that it's a long way from the rest of Australia. There's absolutely no way of covering all those km (Sydney-Perth is 3284 km as the airbus flies, more like 4000 km by road) cheaply. But what is the least costly way? Well it's certainly not by rail at $331 for a one-way economy ticket. Nor is it flying — even stand-by from Sydney to Perth costs $242. Hitching? Well possibly, but thumbing a lift across the Nullarbor is a task verging on the impossible and

River, Bunbury, Rottnest Island, Lancelin, Abrolhos Island (from Geraldton), Carnarvon and all around the North West Cape (Exmouth, Coral Bay).

PERTH (population 900,000)

On the banks of the Swan River, Perth is a clean, modern, attractive looking city, claimed to be the sunniest state capital in Australia. It was founded in 1829 as the Swan River Settlement but it grew very slowly until the reluctant decision was taken to bring in convicts in 1850. Even then it still lagged behind the eastern cities until the discovery of gold in the 1880s sparked interest in the region.

Information

The Western Australian Government Travel Centre (tel 321 2471) is at 772 Hay St, just down from the Hay St Mall. The centre is open 8.30 am to 5 pm Monday to Friday, 9 to 11.45 am on Saturday. They can supply brochures and information and make bookings for tours and transport in WA. Useful brochures to pick up are the excellent series of town brochures, each with a good map, and the *In & Around Perth* brochure with a good colour map of the city centre and the metropolitan area plus lots of information.

The Royal Autombile Club of WA (tel 325 0551) lives at 228 Adelaide Terrace. Their bookshop has an excellent travel section. Other good city bookshops are Angus & Robertsons at 196 Murray St and Down to Earth Books, downstairs at 874-876 Hay St. In Fremantle the Market St Book Arcade at 50 Market St is good. The Youth Hostel Association has their office (not the hostel!) at 257 St Georges Terrace. The GPO is in Forrest Place.

Perth's daily newspaper is the *West Australian*. There are plenty of cinemas around the city but the Kimberley Cinema on Central Barrack St in the city is good for quality films. Also the New Oxford Twin on the corner of Vincent and Oxford Sts. At 242 St Georges Terrace, right up at the King's Park end of town, Aboriginal Arts has an excellent collection of Aboriginal arts and crafts for sale. It's well worth a visit, although it's not the friendliest place.

Orientation

The city centre is a fairly compact area situated at a sweep of the Swan River. Murray St and parallel Hay St are the main shopping sts. The centre section of Hay St is a mall. The railway line forms a boundary to the central city area on the north side and immediately across the line, in North Perth there's a restaurant enclave and a number of popular hostels and cheap accommodation centres are also in this area. The west end of the city climbs into the pleasant Kings Park which overlooks the city and the Swan River. The Swan River serves as a spine from the city to Fremantle, the port for Perth, but it's suburbs all the way and also all the way out to Perth's superb Indian Ocean beaches.

King's Park

The 400 hectare park overlooks the city and the river, there are superb views across Perth from the lookout tower. The park includes a 12 hectare botanical garden, a section of natural bushland and in the spring you can see a cultivated display of WA's famed wildflowers. From the top of King's Park the steep steps of Jacob's Ladder will take you down to Mounts Bay Rd by the river. In the park look for the huge karri

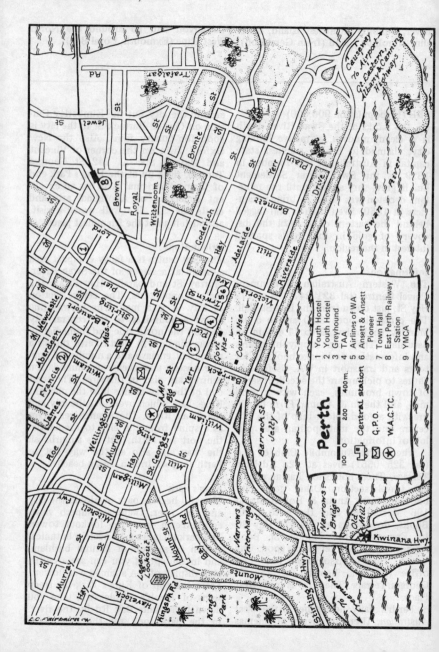

Perth

1 Youth Hostel
2 Youth Hostel
3 Greyhound
4 TAA
5 Airlines of WA
6 Ansett & Ansett
  Pioneer
7 Town Hall
8 East Perth Railway
  Station
9 YMCA

100 0 200 400 m.

🏨 Central Station
✉ Q.P.O.
✴ W.A.G.T.C.

L.C. Fairbairn

trunk on display and the crosscut section of California redwood, showing just how old a tree can be and how short human history in comparison. Beside the park is the Legacy Lookout on top of Dumas House on King's Park Rd. It's open Monday to Friday from 9.30 am to 4.30 pm. You can get to the park on a bus 106 or 107 from St Georges Terrace or buses 25, 27 and 28 drive through the park. Or you can simply walk up Mount St to the park from the city centre.

Around the City

At the corner of William St and St Georges Terrace the AMP Building has a good lookout from the top. There are guided tours lasting 20 minutes at 11 am and 2 pm from Monday to Friday but since they're often booked out it's wise to get your (free) ticket ahead of time. Between Hay St and St Georges Terrace in the centre is the narrow London Court — this photographer's delight looks very Tudor English but in fact dates from just 1937. At one end of the court St George and his dragon appear above the clock each quarter of an hour while at the other ends knights joust on horseback. The Hay St Mall clock face is a miniature replica of Big Ben. Perth has a modern Concert Hall on St Georges Terrace and an even more modern Entertainment Centre on Wellington St just down from the bus depot. The latter is probably the best rock concert venue in Australia.

City Buildings

Down towards the park end of St Georges Terrace The Cloisters dates from 1858 and is noted for its beautiful brickwork. It was originally a school and has now been integrated into a modern office block development. At the corner of St Georges Terrace and Pier St the Deanery was built in 1850 and is one of the few houses in WA surviving from that period. Close by on

St George's Terrace is Government House, a nostalgic Gothic looking fantasy built between 1859 and 1864. Behind the modern Council House in Stirling Gardens the Old Courthouse is one of the oldest buildings in Perth. It was built in Georgian style in 1836. Other old Perth buildings include the Town Hall on the corner of Hay and Barrack Sts (built 1867-70), the Treasury Building on Barrack St and St Georges Terrace (commenced 1874), the Old Perth Boys' School on St Georges Terrace opposite King St (built in 1854 and now used by the National Trust) and the recently restored His Majesty's Theatre on the corner of King and Hay Sts.

There's a memorial plaque set in the pavement near the Old Town Hall on the corner of Hay and Barrack Sts. It marks the founding announcement of Perth in 1829. The town hall was one of the early convict built buildings. On Mounts Bay Rd at the foot of Mt Eliza, Governor Kennedy's Fountain utilises a spring which was Perth's first public water supply. There are tours of the modern Council House at 27 St Georges Terrace four times daily.

Other Buildings

You can tour the Parliament buildings at 11.15 am and 3.15 pm Monday to Friday when parliament is not in session. When it is there are still brief tours Monday to Friday. Take a 2, 3, 4 or 6 Subiaco bus to the Parliament House on Harvest Terrace. In front of the building is the old Barracks Archway, the remains of an 1860 Barracks building. On the corner of Pier and Murray the Post & Telecom Museum is a fine example of early colonial architecture and its exhibits tell of communications developments in WA. It's open 10 am to 3 pm Monday to Friday.

The WA Museum

On Francis St, across the railway lines

from the city centre, the museum includes a gallery of Aboriginal art, a 25-metre whale skeleton and a good collection of meteorites, the largest of them weighs 11 tonnes. The Australian outback is a particularly good area for finding meteorites since they are unlikely to be disturbed there and only weathered. The museum complex also includes Perth's original prison, built in 1856 and used until 1888. Admission to the museum is free and it is open from 10.30 am to 5 pm from Monday to Thursday and from 1 to 5 pm on Friday, Saturday, Sunday.

Perth Zoo

Perth's popular zoo is across the river from the city at 20 Labouchere Rd, South Perth. It has an interesting collection including a nocturnal house which is open from 12 noon to 3 pm daily. The zoo is open from 10 am to 5 pm daily and admission is $2.20. You can reach the zoo by taking a bus 36 or 38 from St Georges Terrace or by taking the ferry across the river and then just strolling up the road from the Mends St Jetty.

Art Galleries

On Jones St through to Roe St, behind the railway station, the Western Australian Art Gallery is housed in a modern building and has a very fine permanent exhibit covering European, Australian and Asian-Pacific art. Visiting exhibits are also shown here. The gallery is open from 10 am to 5 pm daily.

Other Parks

Between the city and the river the Alan Green Conservatory on the Esplanade houses a controlled environment display which is open Monday to Saturday from 10 am to 5 pm and on Sundays from 2 to 6 pm. Also close to the city the Supreme Court Gardens are a popular place to eat your lunchtime sandwiches and in the summer there are often out-door concerts in the Perth Music Shell in the park. Queen's Gardens, at the eastern end of Hay St, is a pleasant little park with lakes — get there on a red clipper bus. Go up Williams St to Hyde Park in Highgate where the lake is a popular attraction for waterbirds, Lake Monger in Wembley is another hang out for local feathered friends, particularly Perth's famous black swans. Get there on a 90 or 91 bus from the central bus stand.

Beaches

Perth's claim to have the best beaches and surf of any Australian city really does have some justification. There are calm bay beaches on the Swan River at Crawley, Peppermint Grove and Como. Or you can try a whole string of patrolled surf beaches on the Indian Ocean coast including Perth's very popular nude beach at Swanbourne. Other good beaches are Cottesloe, Port, City, Scarborough and Trigg Island and most of them can be reached by public transport. Plus there's Rottnest Island, just off the coast from Fremantle.

Old Mill

Just across the Narrows Bridge stands one of Perth's landmarks, the finely restored flour mill which was originally built in 1835. It's open Sunday, Monday, Wednesday and Thursday from 1 to 5 pm and on Saturday from 1 to 4 pm. Inside the mill there are exhibits of pioneering era relics. You can get to the mill on a bus 34 from St Georges Terrace or you can walk there along the riverside from the Mends St ferry terminal.

Perth Suburbs

There is a wide variety of old buildings, wildlife parks, pleasant picnic spots, tourist attractions and other places to visit around the city area. In particular Armadale to the south-east of the city, along the Swan River to the north-east and the places in the Darling Range (see Around Perth) are popular spots.

Armadale Pioneer Village is Armadale's major attraction — a working village of a century ago with shops, public buildings, goldfield operations and craftsmen working at now extinct skills. It's open 10 am to 5 pm Monday to Friday, 1 to 9.30 pm on Saturday and 10 am to 6 pm on Sunday. You can get to Armadale by a 219 bus or a local train.

Just beyond Armadale is Elizabethan Village where, having left colonial WA behind, you move back to Shakespeare's England. It's open 10 am to 6 pm daily. At Kelmscott, just before Armadale, the Museum of WA has its Historical Shanty Town which is open 10 am to 5 pm on weekends and is full of colonial era relics. Transport details are the same as for Armadale.

The Cohunu Wildlife Park has a miniature railway running through the wildlife in a natural setting. It's open 10 am to 5 pm Wednesday to Sunday, daily during the school holidays. Boulder Rock is a pleasant picnic spot off the Brookton Highway near Armadale. Armadale is 27 km south-east of the city centre.

Up the Swan River There are a number of attractions in places up the Swan River from the centre of Perth, particularly in Guildford. Marylands Peninsula is enclosed by a loop of the Swan River, here you will find the beautifully restored old Tranby House of 1839. It's open daily except Thursday from 2 to 5 pm, on Sunday from 11 am to 1 pm and 2 to 5 pm.

On Railway Parade, Bassendean the Rail Transport Museum has all sorts of railway memorabilia. It's open from 1 to 5 pm on Sundays and public holidays. The Hall Collection at 105 Swan St, Guildford has an enormous collection of Australiana and other items,

housed in a building behind the 1840 Rose & Crown Hotel. It's open from 10 am to 4.30 pm daily except Monday. Get there on a 306 bus.

Nearby on Meadow St, Mechanics Hall is now a small folk museum, open 2 to 4.30 pm from March to mid-December. Woodbridge is a restored and furnished colonial mansion overlooking the river. It's open Monday to Saturday from 1 to 4 pm and on Sunday from 11 am to 1 pm and 2 to 5 pm but closed all day on Wednesday. This is one of the few pioneer homes in Perth which you can visit; get there on a 306 bus. In West Swan the Caversham Wildlife Park has a collection of Australian animals and birds. It's open daily except Friday from 10 am to 5.30 pm.

The Swan Valley vineyards are dotted along the river from around Guildford right up to Upper Swan. Many of them are open for tastings except on Sundays. The river cuts a narrow gorge through the Darling Range at Walyunga National Park in Upper Swan, off the Great Northern Highway. There are walking tracks along the river and it's a popular picnic spot.

Other Suburbs In Subiaco there's a Museum of Childhood at 160 Hamersley Rd. Across the Canning River towards Jandakot Airport is the excellent Aviation Museum on Benningfield Rd, Bullcreek. It's open from 1 to 5 pm on Tuesdays, Thursdays and weekends. Just off the Canning Highway to Fremantle is Wireless Hill Park and Telecommunications Museum in Melville. It has exhibits from early pedal operated radio equipment used in the outback to modern NASA communications equipment. It's open weekends from 2 to 5 pm. The Claremont Museum is in the Freshwater Bay School, 66 Victoria Avenue, Claremont and is open Wednesday, Saturday and Sunday from 2 to 5 pm.

On the road to Armadale in Cannington is Woodloes, a restored colonial home of 1874. It's open Sundays from 2 to 4.30 pm. The Liddelow Homestead in Kenwick is another restored little homestead. It's open Thursday from 10 am to 2 pm and Sunday from 11 am to 3 pm. Yet another early home is the mud brick and single Stirk's Cottage in Kalamunda. Built in 1881 it's open from March through November on Sundays from 2 to 4.30 pm.

Places to Stay

Perth is really very well equipped for places to stay in almost any category you care to name. It's got no less than four youth hostels of various types (two official, two unofficial) plus guest houses and lodges, some old fashioned central city hotels, some reasonably priced and reasonably central motel type accommodation, in fact quite a variety and much of it conveniently central. If you have trouble finding a place try ringing the Westralian Accommodation Centre (tel 277 9199) who claim to find you just what you're after and at no cost to you. They also have a desk at the airport.

Hostels Perth is particularly well endowed in the hostel line and they're also all reasonably conveniently central, particularly the two youth hostels. The main *YHA hostel* (tel 328 1135) at 60-62 Newcastle St was at one time the busiest youth hostel in Australia. It still gets quite a throughput although other hostels have overtaken it. It's also a really international place since Perth is such an important arrival point to Australia for people coming from Europe and west Asia. The hostel is about 15 minutes walk (a km) from the city centre, just go straight up Barrack or William St, across the railway line, until you hit Newcastle St then turn right. The hostel has all the usual hostel facilities and is a great meeting place, info centre. Cost is $4.50. The second *YHA*

Hostel (tel 328 7794) at 46 Francis St serves to some extent as an overflow place but you can also go directly there if you wish. It's not listed in the hostel booklet though.

At 196 Aberdeen St (same instructions as for getting to Newcastle St, just turn left when you hit Aberdeen) the *Top Deck Hostel* (tel 325 4830) was originally established to cater for Top Deck's trans-Australia bus passengers. It's not at all a bad place with dorm beds at $4.50 or a bed in a share-room at $5.50. All the rooms are air-con.

Finally there's the long running *Travel Mates* (tel 328 6685) at 496 Newcastle St — turn left at Newcastle St and it's then quite a distance. Take a bus along Newcastle St from the Williams St junction. Dorm beds cost $4.50 ($5 for just one night), extra charges if you want linen as well. They've also got a 'late arrivals room' where you can let yourself in, stretch your sleeping bag out and not disturb anybody, should you arrive in Perth at an unrealistic hour. Travel Mates have a number of share houses around Perth too, they cost $23 per person per week. Motor vehicles are not popular at Travel Mates, it's intended for backpackers although motorcycles and bikes are OK.

YMCAs & Guest Houses Perth has a couple of very central and excellent value YMCAs plus a couple of modern 'lodges' only a few km from the city centre. The *YMCAs* both take men or women and the main one (tel 325 2744) is at 119 Murray St, right in the city centre. There's an older wing at the back and a newer wing at the front with prices of $10 (old wing), $12 (new) for singles or $9, $10 or $18 per person in doubles and twins. The most expensive doubles have their own bathrooms but all others are share facilities. There's also a dorm at $7 and weekly rates are available — $60-70 for singles, $55, $60, $105 for doubles per person. YMCA and YWCA members get a 10% discount. The YMCA is central, convenient and has a TV lounge and laundry facilities. The rooms, particularly those in the new wing, are fine. There's no restaurant but you can get vouchers for a continental or full breakfast ($3) at *Tiffin*, a snack bar in the YMCA's arcade.

Only a couple of blocks further along Murray St is the *YMCA Jewell House* (tel 325 2744) at 180 Goderich St (as Murray St becomes after Victoria Square). This is an ex-nurses' quarters building and offers comfortable, fairly modern rooms at $12/20 for singles/doubles plus larger family rooms at $30. There's a dining room (with sometimes abominably slow service) and even a heated swimming pool. Again weekly rates are also available.

Beatty Lodge (tel 328 1288) at 235 Vincent St, West Perth has rooms at $11/20 for singles/doubles or $9 each in larger family rooms. Breakfast is available for $1.90 to $3.50, dinner for $3.30 to $4.50. Again the rooms are modern and comfortable although without private facilities or even washbasins in the rooms but there are laundry facilities and a swimming pool. Beatty Lodge is about three km from the city centre, on a street that runs more or less parallel to Newcastle St.

Ladybird Lodge (tel 444 7359) is at 193 Oxford St, Leederville, just a little further out from the centre. If you continue along Vincent St turn right when you cross Oxford St. The facilities here are remarkably similar and rooms cost $12.50/32 for singles/doubles. Take a 15 bus from the Barrack St terminal in the city.

Downtown Lodge (tel 325 6973) at 63 Hill St is, by contrast, an old fashioned sort of place. But it's very central, you can use the kitchen facilities and at $7 a person it's certainly not bad value.

Hotels There are quite a number of old fashioned hotels around the centre of Perth. Right across from the railway station there are a couple of them including the *Imperial Hotel* (tel 325 8877) at 413 Wellington St, a hotel of the 'old fashioned but majestic' school. The singles tend to be a bit minute but they've got wash basins and you can make tea or coffee down at the end of the corridor. Nightly costs are $14/20-24 for singles/doubles and it's fairly good value. Breakfast in the Imperial's rather imperial looking dining room will set you back from $3 for an equally old fashioned (ie substantial) breakfast.

The *Grand Central* (tel 325 5638) at 379 Wellington St is rather more basic (no sinks in the room) but again quite OK. Rooms are $9/15 for singles/doubles and it's succinctly described by the manager as 'basic accommodation, mate'.

Other hotels include the *Brittania* (tel 328 6121) across the railway lines at 253 William St. Here singles costs $10 to $12.50 (the more expensive rooms are on the verandah at the back, the cheaper ones are lit by a skylight) or doubles cost $20-26. Not bad but I'd prefer to spend a dollar or two more at the Imperial.

Motels & Units *City Waters Lodge* (tel 325 5020) at 118 Terrace Rd down by the river is conveniently central and good value. All the rooms have cooking facilities as well as the usual motel goodies — attached bathroom, colour TV and so on. There's also a laundrette in the block. Daily costs are $23/28 for singles/doubles and larger triples and family rooms are also available. Because they're so reasonably priced and so central they tend to be heavily booked so it's worth booking ahead with one night's deposit.

In East Perth the *Terminal Motor Lodge* (tel 325 3788) at 150 Bennett St has rooms at $18/27. There are a

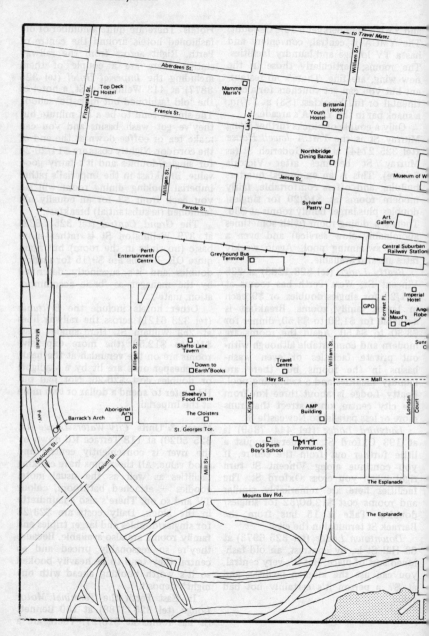

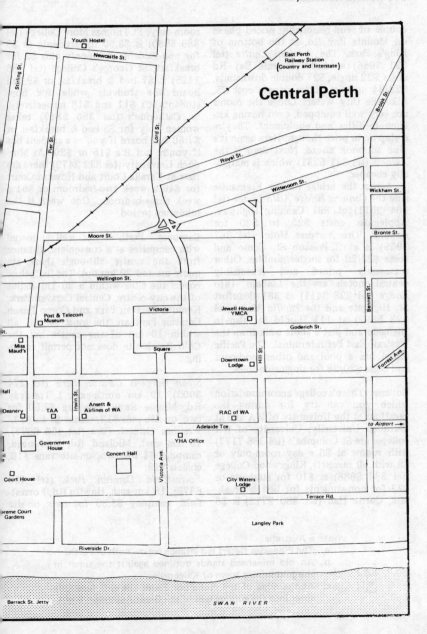

Central Perth

Youth Hostel

Newcastle St.

Stirling St.

Pier St.

Lord St.

East Perth
Railway Station
(Country and Interstate)

Brook St.

Royal St.

Wittenoom St.

Wickham St.

Moore St.

Bronte St.

Wellington St.

Post & Telecom
Museum

Victoria

Jewell House
YMCA

Bennett St.

Goderich St.

Miss
Maud's

Square

Downtown
Lodge

Hill St.

Hall

Irwin St.

Deanery

TAA

Ansett &
Airlines of WA

RAC of WA

Forrest Ave.

Adelaide Tce.

to Airport

Government
House

YHA Office

Concert Hall

Court House

Victoria Ave.

City Waters
Lodge

Terrace Rd.

reme Court
Gardens

Langley Park

Riverside Dr.

Barrack St. Jetty

SWAN RIVER

couple of semi-reasonably priced places on Mounts Bay Rd, at the bottom of King's Park. The *Adelphi Centre* (tel 321 7966) at 130A Mounts Bay Rd costs $22 single, $27 double downstairs, $29/34 upstairs. Extra people cost $5. Like the City Waters Lodge the rooms are very well equipped, even having kitchen facilities and equipment. They're a step up in price though. Here again it's wise to book ahead. Next door is the *Astoria* (tel 321 5231) which is marginally cheaper.

Across the bridge on the Fremantle side the *Canning Bridge Auto Lodge* (tel 364 2511) at 891 Canning Highway, Applecross costs $25 to $30 for doubles. The *Narrows Motel* (tel 367 7955) is at 2 Preston St, Como and costs $23/28 for singles/doubles. Other reasonably priced and reasonably central motels are the *Lincoln Auto Lodge* (tel 328 3411) at 381 Beaufort St, Highgate and the *Pacific Motel* (tel 328 5599) at 111 Harold St, also in Highgate and just a short walk from the Westrail East Perth terminal. The Pacific Motel has a pool and other mod-cons and costs $20/28 for singles/doubles.

Colleges There's college accommodation which you can try for during the vacations at the University of WA and at Murdoch University. University of WA colleges are St Columba's (tel 386 7177) with rooms at $6 a day room-only or $8 with all meals(!), Kingswood College (tel 386 8688) at $10 for students or $22 for non-students for bed & breakfast, Currie Hall (tel 380 2772) is $6

room-only, St Thomas More College (tel 386 5080) is $3.50 for students or $9 for non-students room-only plus $2 for breakfast, St George's College (tel 386 1425) is $7 bed & breakfast or $9 full board for students while for non-students it's $11 and $18 respectively, St Catherine's (tel 386 5847) takes women only for $5 bed & breakfast or $7.50 full board if you're a student but if you're not it's $15 or $20. At Murdoch University (tel 332 2472) there are flats at Yaralla Court and Howard Court for $46 a week two-bedroom or $51 a week three-bedroom. One week is the minimum period.

Camping Perth is not well endowed with campsites at a convenient distance from the centre although there are many around 20 km out. The list below covers the sites within a 20 km radius of the city centre. Central Caravan Park, Kenlorn Caravan Park and Como Beach Caravan Park are the most central, all within 10 km of the centre but the Colo Beach site does not permit camping.

Swan Gardens Caravan Park (tel 274 3002), 19 km north-east, 1 Toodyay Rd, Middle Swan, camping $3.50 for two, on-site vans $12, cabins $7 to $13. *Wesnova Caravan Park* (tel 453 6677), 19 km east, Midland Rd, Bushmead, camping $4 for two, on-site vans $16, chalets $18. *Forrestfield Caravan Park* (tel 453 6378), 18 km east, Hawtin Rd, Forrestfield, camping $3.50 for two, on-site

Western Australia

a. The Pinnacles Desert is a strange region noth of Perth.
b. An old minehead stands outlined against the sunet in the gold-mining town of Kalgoorlie.
c. At the edge of the Nullarbor Plains the cliff face falls sheer into the surging seas of the Great Australian Bight.

vans $11.

Perth Tourist Caravan Park (tel 453 6677), 15 km east, 319 Hale Rd, Forrestfield, camping $3.50 for two, on-site vans $10 for two.

Orange Grove Caravan Park (tel 453 6226), 19 km south-east Kelvin Rd, Orange Grove, camping $4 for two, on-site vans $16.

Guildford Caravan Park (tel 274 2828), 19 km north-east, 372 Swan Rd, Guildford, camping $4.50 for two, on-site vans $12.

Central Caravan Park (tel 277 5696), 7 km east, 34 Central Avenue, Redcliffe, camping $5 for two, on-site vans $50 per week.

Kenlorn Caravan Park (tel 458 2604), 9 km south-east, 229 Welshpool Rd, Queens Park, camping $6.50 for two, on-site vans $60 per week.

Como Beach Caravan Park (tel 367 1286), 6 km south, 4 Ednah St, Como, camping not permitted, on-site vans $70 to $100 per week.

Cherokee Village Tourist Park (tel 409 8511), 17 km north, Wanneroo & Hocking Rds, Wanneroo, camping $5 for two, on-site vans $10 to $16.

Watermans Bay Caravan Park (tel 447 1109), 16 km north-west, 37 West Coast Highway, Waterman, camping $3.50 for two, on-site vans.

Careniup Caravan Park (tel 447 6665), 14 km north, 467 Beach Rd, Gwelup, camping $4 for two, on-site vans $12 to $14.

Starhaven Caravan Park (tel 341 1770), 14 km north-west, 14-18 Pearl Parade, Scarborough, camping $3.50 for two,

on-site vans $50 to $75 per week.

Kingsway Caravan Park (tel 409 9267), 15 km north, Wanneroo Rd, Greenwood, camping $4.50 for two, on-site vans.

Caversham Caravan Park (tel 279 6700), 12 km north-east, Benara Rd, Caversham, camping $5 for two, on-site vans $35 per week.

Carine Gardens Caravan Park (tel 447 5046), 14 km north, Balcatta Rd, Carine, camping $5 per day, no on-site vans.

Springvale Caravan Park (tel 454 6829). Maida Vale Rd, Maida Vale, camping $4 for two, on-site vans $12.

Places to Eat

As with accommodation Perth has a wide variety of places to eat. Look for the excellent food centres where you can find all sorts of different international cuisines all at very reasonable prices. Or head across the railway tracks from the centre to William St, the restaurant centre of Perth.

Lunch & Snacks *Miss Maud's* on the corner of Murray and Pier Sts in the city used to do a very reasonably priced smorgasbord — it may well still be very good but it's also very expensive. However, right next door *Miss Maud's Sandwich Centre* does really excellent sandwiches at very reasonable prices. Even better there's a second sandwich centre a little further down at 198 Murray St, next door to Angus & Robertson's bookshop. Here they have a small sit-down area so you can eat your sandwiches in comfort.

Western Australia

a. Wolf Creek Meteorite Crater in the north of WA is one of the largest in the world.

b. Wave Rock, a unique natural rock formation near Hyden.

c. A few old pearling luggers can still be seen at Broome in the far north-west of the state.

At 138 Lower Barrack St, *Magic Apple* is very popular. It's a health food place with all sorts of salads, fruit salads, smoothies and the like. Some complaints about the Scientologist bent of the management though! Health food again (quiches, hunza pie, etc) at *Tastes Galore*, 840 Hay St. Prices from around $1.50. For a flashier lunchtime place you could try the Dutch *Tutt's Broodjeswinkel* behind the AMP building on the corner of William St and St Georges Terrace. They have filling and fancy sandwiches, rolls, cakes and pastries.

Sylvana Pastry is a string of very popular Lebanese coffee bars scattered around Perth. They're bright and clean and have a quite amazing selection of those sticky-sweet Lebanese pastries which usually look and taste delicious. At their 197 William St outlet they had a choice of Turkish delight, baklava, harisa, ladies fingers, ladies palms, manoul dates, bookaj, bogasha, barazi, mamoul walnut, boorma cashews, kool shkodr, canary's nests and a few others I couldn't read the signs for!

Food Centres The best recent food development in Perth, in fact one of the most heartening in Australia, is the rapid growth and high popularity of 'food centres'. Anyone who thinks, like me, that Singapore is a fantastic place to eat has to hand some of the credit to food centres. Essentially they're a group of 'kitchens' which share a communal dining area of tables and chairs. Thus you can eat from one place, your partner from another, have drinks from a third and dessert from a fourth. It's like eating out at a whole collection of restaurants all at once. This terrific Singaporean idea has really taken hold in Perth and nightly crowds prove that it's a very popular alternative to junk food.

The *Sunmarket Centre* is down an alley off the corner of Murray and Barrack St and here you can try a variety of Chinese, Burmese, Indian, pancakes, fruit juices and fruit salads. It's very good and very popular with meals generally in the $3 to $3.50 bracket.

Other food centres include *Sheehey's* at 895-897 Hay St. At the *Singapore Chinese Food Kitchen* $3 buys you really more food than you can manage — she looked as if she was worried I wasn't eating enough! A drink to go with it, followed by a slice of nice cheesecake from *De Maria* and a cup of tea from yet another stall left me with change from $5 and an appetite worked up by a day's hard biking on Rotto totally shot. De Maria's collects recommendations for its Italian food and you can also get Indian and Filipino food here.

At 217 William St, just across the tracks, the *Northbridge Dining Bazaar* has Malay, Vietnamese, health food, Italian, Singaporean and Chinese food, plus gelatis. They're all highly recommended and I sincerely hope they spread to other states.

Counter Meals Perth has the usual selection of counter meal places in the city centre area. At 196 Murray St counter meals in the basement *Albert Tavern* are around $4 — 'see through' barmaids too, something Perth seems to have an amazing enthusiasm for. Cheap counter meals (steak, salad & chips for $3.50) at the *Bohemia*, 290 Murray St. They run from 5.30 to 7 pm in the evenings. The *Railway Hotel* at 134 Barrack St has cheap meals from around $1.30 for a burger to more expensive meals around the $6 mark.

Sassella's Tavern, City Arcade off Hay St, does reasonably priced bistro meals and has entertainment too.

City There are plenty of places to eat around the city, particularly down at the King's Park end of Hay St where there is a real string of restaurants to try.

Like *Fast Eddy* on the corner of Hay and Milligan Sts. It's a big fast food and ice cream place, open 24 hours with a take-away and bar stool section in the front and much the same food (at higher prices) in a restaurant section behind. Pretty reasonable burgers. A bit further down is *Chico's* at 959 Hay St where they do a nightly $7.95 Mexican smorgasbord — closed Tuesday. *Himalaya* at 963 Hay is Indian but a bit pricey.

Mexican food has quite a following in Perth, back towards the centre at 905 Hay St is *Pancho's*, a very popular Mexican restaurant with main courses in the $5 to $7 range. Right by the YMCA at 117 Murray St is a pleasant and very reasonably priced little Japanese restaurant called *Jun & Tommy's*. Main courses are $4.50 to $5.50.

William St Perth really has a restaurant quarter — bounded by William St on the east side there is a multitude of restaurants on James St, Aberdeen St and Francis St. They include Chinese, Greek, Lebanese, Mexican, Indian, Italian, seafood places, Vietnamese, Dutch-Indonesian, even hamburger joints. They come in all price ranges too, from the very bottom to the very top.

Along William St itself some places to try include *Kim Anh* at 178 and the *Old Saigon* at 187, both Vietnamese. *Romany's* at 188 William St is, believe it or not, Italian. It's one of Perth's really long running Italian places and still low priced and popular. Further down you come to *Taco Bill's* at 276, with meals in the $4 to $6 range. Across the road the ever popular *Uncle Domenic's* at 287 has good Italian food in very large quantities. At 311 there's the *Bohemia* where the usual charcoal grilled specialities can be found as at the cheaper/ more spartan *Balkan Bar-B-Q* next door at 313.

Off William St *Mamma Maria's* at 105 Aberdeen on the corner of Lake St is a very popular Italian restaurant although most main courses are now $8 or more. Nice atmosphere and a reputation for some of the best Italian food in Perth.

Entertainment
Perth has a busy selection of pubs, clubs, discos and night clubs in the evenings. In the centre *Sassella's Tavern*, upstairs in the City Arcade off the Hay St Mall, has music and no cover charge. There's a disco downstairs in the *Brass Rail Tavern* in the National Mutual Arcade, also off Hay St Mall. Further down at 395 Murray St, that's on the corner of Shafto Lane, the *Shafto Lane Tavern* is usually crowded and noisy later on with bands or a disco, no cover charge.

Next door is *Pinocchio's* and across the road at 418 Murray St is *Beethoven's* — both with cover charges in the $5 to $10 bracket depending on who is on and what night it is. In the centre the *Melbourne Hotel* on the corner of Milligan and Hay Sts has a whole collection of bars — everything from a jungle bar to a piano bar.

Away from the centre there's the usual rock pub circuit with varying cover charges depending on the night of the week and who is playing. Popular venues include the *Leederville Stockade*, Vincent St, Leederville; the *Subiaco Hotel*, Hay & Rokeby Sts, Subiaco; *Hotel Cottesloe* (The Cott), John St, Cottesloe; the *Boomerang Hotel*, 1120 Albany Highway, Bentley; the *Broadway Tavern*, Broadway shopping centre, Nedlands near the university.

Other places to try include the *Nedlands Park Hotel*, better known as 'Steve's', which is the uni pub, near the university. Out at Fremantle the *Newcastle Club Hotel* is popular. On Fridays the *Daily News* has a fairly comprehensive Nightlife Guide.

Getting There

Air From the east coast there are TAA and Ansett flights from Sydney, Melbourne, Brisbane and Adelaide. Some Sydney and Melbourne flights go direct, some via Adelaide or, in the case of Sydney, via Melbourne. Brisbane flights all go via one or more of the other centres. Fares (standby in brackets) to Perth are Adelaide $249 ($186), Melbourne $288 ($216), Sydney $322 ($242), Brisbane $347.

The two airlines have two flights a week between North Queensland and Alice Springs to Perth and vice versa. Fares are $238 from Alice Springs, $285 from Mt Isa, $331 from Townsville. Darwin-Perth flights go via Alice Springs or Porth Hedland — TAA have just a handful of flights a week Airlines of Western Australia flies Darwin-Perth along the coast routes daily. Darwin-Perth is $299. See the introductory Getting Around section for details of Airlines of Western Australia fares.

Rail Along with the ghan to Alice Springs the long Indian-Pacific run is one of Australia's great railway journeys, a 65 hour trip between the Indian Ocean on one side of the continent and the Pacific Ocean on the other. It's a trip to talk about but it's certainly not the cheapest way across Australia — in fact it's even cheaper to fly. Even despite the fares the service still loses money but people who can find the cash certainly don't regret it. You see Australia at ground level and at the end of the journey you really appreciate the immensity of this country. From its starting point in Sydney you cross New South Wales in the late afternoon and overnight, arriving in Broken Hill around breakfast time. Then it's on to Port Pirie in South Australia and across the Nullarbor. From Port Pirie to Kalgoorlie the endless crossing of the virtually uninhabited centre takes nearly 30 hours including the 'long straight' on

the Nullarbor — 478 km long this is the longest straight stretch of railway line in the world. Unlike the trans-Nullarbor road which runs south of the Nullarbor, along the coast of the Great Australian Bight, the railway line actually crosses the Nullarbor Plain. From Kalgoorlie it's a straightforward run into Perth.

To or from Perth fares are Adelaide $281 1st, $216 economy; Melbourne $360 1st, $331 economy. Melbourne and Adelaide passengers connect to the Indian-Pacific at Port Pirie. Cars can be transported between Port Pirie and Perth for $180. The full distance from Sydney to Perth is 3961 km. You can break your journey at any stop along the way and continue later so long as you complete the trip within two months, six months on return trips. Westbound departures are made on Monday, Wednesday, Thursday and Saturday (arriving Perth on Thursday, Saturday, Sunday and Tuesday respectively). Eastbound the train departs on Sunday, Tuesday, Thursday and Saturday (arriving Sydney on Wednesday, Friday, Sunday and Tuesday).

In either 1st class or economy your fare includes a sleeping compartment. The main difference is that 1st class compartments are available as singles or twins, economy as twins only. 1st class twins have showers and toilets, 1st class singles toilets only — showers at the end of the compartment. Economy compartments have no facilities — the showers and toilets are at the end of the compartment. Meals are included in the fare and 1st class passengers also have use of a lounge compartment — complete with piano!

Between Adelaide and Perth you can also travel on the three times weekly Trans-Australian. This service originates at Port Pirie so you have to take the connecting train there from Adelaide. Fares are as for the Indian Pacific for 1st and economy including meals and sleeping berth but on some Trans-Australian services there are also economy seats available at a cost of $95 not including any meals. The Adelaide-Perth trip takes about 42 hours.

The only rail services within WA are the Prospector to Kalgoorlie and the Australind to Bunbury — see the relevant sections for details. The trains from the east coast and the WA services all run to and from the Perth terminal in East Perth as does the Westrail bus services. Ring 326 2811 for Westrail bookings or you can book through the WA Government Travel Centre on Hay St.

Bus Both Ansett Pioneer and Greyhound have daily bus services from Adelaide to Perth. Fares are $79 with Greyhound, $95 with Ansett Pioneer and the trip takes 35 to 37 hours. There are also a number of cheaper trans-Nullarbor bus services from Sydney, Melbourne and Adelaide. These don't offer the same frequency as the big two nor do they have the stopover options but in the last few years they've really proliferated so there was obviously a demand for a no-frills alternative. Of course Ansett Pioneer and Greyhound have pushed their fares down to compete. Typical of the alternative companies is Sandgroper Express which charges $95 from Sydney, $85 from Melbourne or Adelaide.

Ansett Pioneer (tel 325 8855) operate from the Ansett terminal at 26 St Georges Terrace. Greyhound (tel 478 1122) operate from the Central Bus Station on Wellington St. Both companies operate buses up the coast to Port Hedland, Broome and through the Kimberleys to Darwin. See the relevant sections for details. Perth-Darwin is a 60-hour journey costing $195 all the way. Greyhound also operate to Port Hedland via the more direct inland route through Newman.

Westrail operate bus services to a number of Western Australian centres including Bunbury-Collie, Hyden (Wave Rock) twice weekly, Esperance twice weekly, Geraldton almost daily, Mullewa twice weekly and on from Mullewa to Meekatharra once weekly.

Hitching & Rides Travel Mates (see hostels) operate a share-ride register for people heading for Darwin or the east coast states. It costs $6 for a driver to be hooked up to passengers, $10 for passengers to a driver. They do not recommend that solo women pasengers use this means of getting across. Usual per passenger cost is about $50 for fuel.

If you're hitching out of Perth to the north or east take a train to Midland. Travelling south take a train to Armadale. Some sexist noted in the youth hostel logbook that you should not try 'hitching across the Nullarbor' unless you've got big tits and nice legs'. Trans-Nullarbor hitching is not easy and the fierce competition between bus companies has certainly made bus travel much more attractive.

Getting Around

Perth has a central public transportation organisation, the Metropolitan Passenger Transport Trust or MTT. There are MTT information offices at 125 St Georges Terrace (open seven days a week) and at the Perth Central Bus Station, Wellington St (open Monday to Saturday). The MTT operate buses, trains and ferries. They can give you on the spot information and advice about getting around Perth and supply route maps and timetables. Phone 325 8511 for information.

Bus Around the central city area there are a number of free City Clipper services which operate from Monday to Saturday. They include a Red Clipper which make a loop up and down St Georges Terrace/Adelaide Terrace and Wellington St; a Yellow Clipper around the very central area of the city and a Cultural Clipper looping from the Barrack Square jetty area up past the WA Museum past Newcastle St (use this one for the youth hostel) and back down William St.

A short ride up to two sections long costs 45c but anything longer is a zone ticket entitling you to unlimited travel within the zone for two hours from the time of issue of the ticket. The ticket indicates on it when it expires and it can be used on MTT bus, rail and ferry tickets. Costs are one zone 80c, two zones 90c, three zones $1.30 and so on. Or you can get an all day ticket for the three inner zones for $4. Zone one extends as far out as Fremantle, 20 km from the centre, so you have quite a radius of action. You could, for example, use your two hour ticket to go down to the jetty in Perth, take the ferry across to the zoo and an hour or so later ferry then bus back, all for 80c. The ticket also covers all suburban train services. See Tours for the Sunday MTT bus tour.

Some useful bus services include the 101, 103, 106 and 107 to Fremantle. Routes 3 and 6 operate to Subiaco. Take a 70 or 72 for the university.

Rail Suburban trains all go from the City Station in Wellington St. Your rail ticket can also be used on buses within the ticket's time validity.

Ferries See Rottnest Island for details on the ferries from Perth to Fremantle and Rottnest. Ferries all depart from the Barrack St Jetty in Perth. There are services across the river from there to Mends St in South Perth every half hour at a cost of 45c. Take this ferry to get to Perth Zoo.

The MTT also have a number of river cruises. The *MV Countess II* goes up-

river at 2 pm daily (except Saturday) from September to May. Downriver trips are made on Saturday at 2 pm year round and on Tuesday, Thursday and Sunday at 1.45 pm from June to September. The trips take nearly three hours and cost $6. The old-fashioned double decker *SS Perth* goes downriver every Sunday at 2 pm on a 2½ hour cruise for $4. There are also special school holiday trips and other more expensive river cruises, which are covered under tours.

Car Rental The major rental organisations — Hertz, Budget, Avis and Thrifty — are all represented in Perth plus a string of local organisations. Renta Rocket (tel 328 7188) at 90 Newcastle St and Rent-an-Oldie (tel 322 1887) at 789 Wellington St have cars from $10 a day with unlimited km. Other companies have cars from around $6 a day (for a Moke) plus from around 10c a km. You could try Econo-Car Rentals (tel 328 6888) at 133-135 Pier St, Sydney Andersons (tel 328 1477) at 216 Stirling St, Handi Car Hire (tel 322 4376) at 579 Murray St, or Bayswater Hire Cars (tel 271 7722) at 381 Guildford Rd, Bayswater and also in Subiaco and Fremantle.

Airport Perth's airport is busy night and day, unlike so many Australian airports which shut down at night. It has to operate at night since Perth's isolation from the east coast plus its function as an international arrival point means flights have to arrive at all hours.

A taxi to the airport is around $6. Alternatively the Skybus costs $3 and runs between the airport terminals and the major city hotels, the Qantas, TAA and Ansett city terminals and the WA Travel Centre on Hay St. Weekdays it operates every 40 minutes to one hour from 6 am to 11 pm then meets all flights from midnight to 5 am. On weekends, Sunday in particular, the schedule is not so good but it still meets all the middle of the night flights.

Alternatively you can get into the city for just 80c on a 338 MTT bus to William St. They depart from the northern end of the terminal every 30 minutes from 5.30 am to 10.57 pm on weekdays and for nearly as long on Saturdays. Sunday services are less frequent.

The airport terminal handles domestic and international flights so there are money changing facilities there. Budget, Thrifty and Hertz have rent-a-car desks at the airport. There's also a desk for Westralian Accommodation Centre who claim to be able to book accommodation at any price level for you and at no cost to you.

Tours You can take a $10 city tour or for a similar price there are tours up the Swan Valley. Out of town tours to places like Yanchep, El Caballo Blanco and other attractions in the Perth vicinity range from $20 to $26. There

are a variety of tours up the Swan River. A three hour Swan River cruise costs $6 with the MTT, $7 on the Captain Cook Cruise. For $20 a vineyard tour takes you to wineries up the river — including lunch and wine. 'Good value' wrote some travelling wine tasters.

Another favourite of imbibers is the free tour of the Swan brewery. The tour takes two hours (followed by a beer tasting) and they take place at 10 am and 2.30 pm daily. Ring 350 0650 to make reservations. The brewery is at 25 Baile Rd, Canning Vale.

The MTT operate city bus tours on Sunday morning and afternoon at 10.30 am and 2.15 pm. The tours take about 2½ hours start from the MTT office at 125 St Georges Terrace and cost $5. They start from the city, loop around the narrows interchange, go out to Lake Monger to see the swans, back around by the Old Mill and Zoo south of the river then visit King's Park before completing the tour with a circuit of North Perth and East Perth.

FREMANTLE
Fremantle, Freo to enthusiastic name shorteners, is the port for Perth, at the mouth of the Swan River. Over the years Perth has sprawled out to eventually engulf Fremantle which is now more a suburb of the city than a separate town in its own right. But Fremantle has a wholly different atmosphere than gleaming, skyscrapered Perth. It's a place with a very real feeling of history and a very pleasant atmosphere. It's hardly surprising so many visitors to Perth discover Fremantle to be one of their favourite places or that it's such a popular weekend excursion for Perth residents.

Like Perth, Fremantle was founded in 1829 but, also like Perth, the settlement made little progress until it was reluctantly decided to take in convicts and with this cheap and hard worked labour most of the town's earliest buildings, some of them amongst the oldest in WA, were constructed. As a harbour Fremantle was an abysmal failure until the brilliant engineer C Y O'Connor (see the WA Goldfields section for more on his tragic story) built an artificial harbour in the 1890s. The town has numerous interesting old buildings, and a couple of really excellent museums. The National Trust produces two walking tour leaflets on Fremantle.

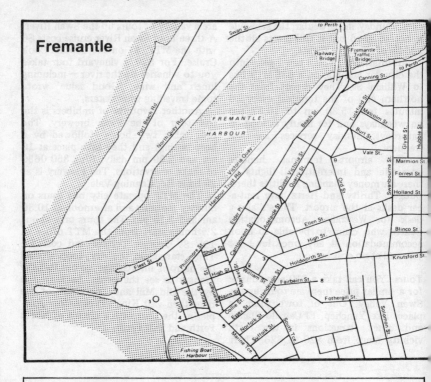

Fremantle

1 Round House
2 Town Hall
3 St John's Church
4 Maritime Museum
5 The Esplanade
6 Fremantle Market
7 Warders' Quarters
8 Gaol & Museum
9 WA Museum
10 Port Authority Building

Fremantle Museum & Arts Centre

Originally constructed by convict labourers as a lunatic asylum in the 1860s, the museum is on Finnerty St. It houses an intriguing collection including exhibits on Fremantle's early history, the colonisation of WA and the early whaling industry plus the intriguing story of the Dutch East Indiamen who first discovered the western coast of Australia and in several instances managed to wreck their ships on this inhospitable coastline. The arts centre occupies one wing of the museum and

it's a living centre where various crafts are carried on. The museum is open Monday to Thursday from 10.30 am to 5 pm and on Friday, Saturday, Sunday from 1 to 5 pm. Admission is free.

The Maritime Museum

On Cliff St near the waterfront the Maritime Museum occupies a building constructed in 1852 as a commissariat. Recently opened the museum has an intriguing display on WA's maritime history with particular emphasis on the famous wreck of the *Batavia*. One gallery is used as a working centre where you can see work on preservation of timbers from the *Batavia* actually being carried out. At one end of this gallery is the huge stone facade intended for an entrance to Batavia Castle in modern day Jakarta, Indonesia. It was being carried by the *Batavia* as ballast when she went down. The museum is open from 1 to 5 pm on Fridays, Saturdays and Sundays. Admission is free and like the Fremantle Museum it's a 'not to be missed'.

The Round House

On Arthur Head, near the Maritime Museum, the Round House was built in 1831 and is the oldest public building in WA. It actually has 12 sides and was built as a local prison (in the days before convicts were brought into WA). Here the colony's first hangings took place and it was later used to hold Aboriginals before they were taken across to Rottnest. Since the building later proved to be inconveniently sited smack between the jetty at Bather's Bay and High St, Fremantle, a tunnel was cut through the hill, underneath the Round House, in 1837. Admission is free, and it's open from 1.30 to 4 pm on Saturdays, 11 am to 4 pm on Sundays.

Convict Era Buildings

Other buildings date from the period after 1850, when convict labour was introduced. They include Fremantle Gaol, the unlucky convict's first building task. It's still used as a prison today. The entrance to the prison on Fairbairn St is particularly picturesque. Beside the prison gates at 16 The Terrace is a small museum on the convict era in WA. It's open from 1 to 4 pm on Saturdays, 10 am to 4 pm on Sundays, admission is free. Warders from the jail still live in the 1850s stone cottages on Henderson St.

Later Landmarks

Fremantle went through a boom period during the WA goldrush and many buildings were constructed during or shortly before this period. They include the fine St John's Church of 1882, the elegant Town Hall of 1887, the former German consulate building at 5 Mouat St, built in 1902, and the Fremantle Railway Station of 1907. The water trough in the park in front of the station is a memorial to two men who died of thirst on an outback expedition.

Around Town

Fremantle is well endowed with parks including the popular Esplanade Reserve beside the picturesque fishing boat harbour off Marine Terrace. St John's Reserve stands beside the church of the same name. Fremantle has an excellent Art Gallery in Pioneer Reserve between Phillimore and Short Sts. It's open from Wednesday to Sunday from 12 noon to 5 pm. The city is a popular centre for craft workers of all kinds and one of the best places to find them is at the imaginative Bannister St Workshops where a variety of craft workers can be seen in action and their work purchased. It's open 10 am to 4.30 pm weekdays, 10 am to 2 pm Saturdays, 1 to 5 pm Sundays. There's a potter's workshop beside the Round House.

From the viewing platform on top of the Port Authority Building you can enjoy a panoramic view of Fremantle harbour. A statue of C Y O'Connor stands in front of the building. A prime attraction is the Fremantle Markets on South Terrace at the corner of Henderson St. Originally opened in 1892 the new market was re-opened in 1975 and attracts crowds looking for anything from craft work to vegetables, jewellery to antiques. It's open 9 am to 9 pm on Fridays, 9 am to 1 pm on Saturdays.

Places to Eat

There are plenty of places to drop in

for a meal or a snack while exploring Fremantle. Or you could sip a beer in one of the town's picturesque old pubs. There is a string of places to try along South Terrace — like the popular *Papa Luigis* for coffee and gelati at number 17. It's packed on Sunday afternoons. Next door is the *Mexican Cantina* and across the road is *Pizza Bella Roma*.

Across from the Bannister St Workshops in the small shopping centre you could try a tasty panzerotto in *Vince's Panzerotto & Pizzas*. At 31 Market St, behind the GPO, the *Princess Coffee Lounge* is excellent value. Fish & chips on the Esplanade by the fishing boat harbour is something of a Fremantle tradition. Good, cheap counter food at the *Newcastle Club Tavern* on Market St.

ROTTNEST

Rotto, to the locals, is a sandy island about 19 km offshore from Fremantle. It's 11 km long by five km wide and is very popular as a day's outing or longer term escape for Perth residents. Which is hardly surprising because it's a quite delightful place. The island was discovered by Dutch explorer Vlaming in 1696. He named it 'Rat's Nest' because of the numerous king size rats he saw there. Actually they weren't big rats at all but quokkas, a miniature kangaroo. The quokkas are even more prolific today.

What do you do on Rotto? Well you bicycle around, you laze on the many superb beaches (the Basin is the most popular, Parakeet Bay is the place for skinny dipping), you climb the low hills, go fishing or boating, ride a glass-bottom boat (Rotto has some of the furthest southerly coral in the world and also a number of ship wrecks to be seen), you swim in the crystal clear water or you

Getting There

The passenger railway service between Perth and Fremantle has been stopped and although you could travel from Perth to Fremantle on the Rottnest ferry most people will go by bus. Buses 101 and 103 go from St Georges Terrace (north side) near King St to Fremantle via the Canning Highway. Or take the 105 which is a longer route but also south of the river. Buses 106 and 107 also depart from St Georges Terrace but go to Fremantle via the north side of the river. Bus 106 travels around the edge of King's Park. Fremantle is 19 km from Perth.

can even go quokka spotting (they're most active early in the morning).

The Rottnest settlement was originally established in 1838 as a prison for Aboriginals from the mainland — the early colonists had lots of trouble imposing their ideas of private ownership on the free ranging Aboriginals. The prison was abandoned in 1903 and the island soon became a popular escape for Perth society. It's only in the last 20 years, however, that it has really developed as a day-trip city getaway. The original prison settlement is of great interest as the buildings here are the oldest in WA apart from a couple in Perth and Fremantle.

Information

The Rottnest Island Board has an information centre just to the left of the wharf. Here and at the museum you can get a number of useful publications about the island. Two of particular interest are the pamphlets on a walk-

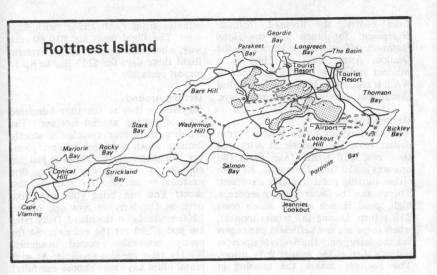

ing tour of the old settlement buildings and a description of the various shipwrecks around the island. Rottnest is very popular in the summer when the ferries and the accommodation are both heavily booked — plan ahead.

Things to See & Do

There's an excellent little museum (40c admission) with exhibits on the island, its history, wildlife and shipwrecks. You can pick up the walking tour leaflet here and wander around the interesting old convict-built buildings including the octagonal 1864 'Quad' where the prison cells are now hotel rooms. The island has a number of low-lying salt lakes and it's around them that you are most likely to spot quokkas although the bus tours have regular quokka feeding points where the small marsupials are programmed to appear on demand. Most of Rottnest's shipwrecks are accessible to snorkellers although most of them require a boat to get out to them. There are marker plaques around the island telling their sad tales.

Places to Stay & Eat

Most Rotto visitors day-trip but it's equally interesting to stay there and there is a wide variety of accommodation possibilities. You can camp for $1.85 per person or $6.80 for two in hire tents. *Tent-Land* (tel 292 5033) also has safari-cabins for $78 weekly. Book hired tents and cabins in advance but if you bring your own tent you can usually just turn up.

The Rottnest Island Board (tel 292 5044) has a whole collection of cabins, bungalows, flats, cottages and houses with weekly costs from as low as $24 (for an off-season four-person cabin which goes up to $71 at the height of the season). *Hotel Rottnest* (tel 292 5011) is fairly expensive at $25/35 for the cheapest singles/doubles with shared facilities but that does include dinner as well as breakfast. The *Quad* (tel 292 5026) has share facility rooms at $18/32 with breakfast.

The island has a general store and a bakery which is famed for its fresh bread and pies. There's also a fast food centre, the licensed *Rottnest Restaurant* for lunch and the *Hotel Rottnest*, affectionately known as the Quokka Arms. Built in 1864 as a summer residence for the governor of WA it is reputed to have an astronomical throughput of beer on hot summer days.

Getting There

You can ferry or fly to Rotto. Ferries depart from the Barrack St Jetty and they cost $13 return from Perth ($8 one-way), $10 from Fremantle, $8 from either starting point if you're a student. There's also the faster *Seaflyte* service, a high speed launch service which costs $18 return. During the winter months, when there are not sufficient passengers for the ferry, only the *Seaflyte* operates but it's then at the regular ferry prices. The *Seaflyte* makes the crossing in about one hour, the ferry is a bit slower. You can also get across by air in just 11 minutes from Perth airport with Skywest. The flight costs just $10.80 each way, where else can you take an overseas flight these days for $11? Bus to Rotto airport costs 50c.

Getting Around

Bicycles — they're the time honoured way of getting around Rottnest. The number of motor vehicles is strictly limited, which makes biking a real pleasure. Furthermore the island is just big enough to make a day's biking fine exercise — not too far and not too short! You can bring your own bike over on the ferry or rent one of the 1200 available on the island. Daily rates are just $2.20 for the old nails, $4 for pretty reasonable geared machines. Weekly rates are also available. As with rental bikes anywhere choose carefully! If you really can't hack biking there's a two-hour bus tour for $3.

AROUND PERTH

There are a great number of places of interest in day-trip distance from Perth. They include resorts and parks along the coast to the north and south of the capital and inland along the Avon River. The Darling Range runs parallel to the coast close to Perth and there are many places in the ranges for walks, picnics and barbecues. Many places in the range can be reached on MTT city buses.

North Coast

The coast north of Perth has often spectacular scenery with long sandy dunes. It quickly becomes the inhospitable looking land that deterred early visitors.

Yanchep The Yanchep National Park is 51 km north of Perth — there's bush, caves (including the limestone crystal and Yondemp Caves), Loch McNess, bushwalking trails and a wildlife sanctuary. Yanchep Sun City is a major marina and has been the base for several unsuccessful Australian challenges for the America's Cup yacht races. Yanchep also has a seals-dolphin-shark Marine park admission $5. Near Yanchep is Wanneroo (population 4300) an outer suburb of Perth and a popular wine producing area. Wanneroo has a lion park and on weekends the Wanneroo Markets are a good outing from Perth. North of Yanchep is Guilderton, a popular holiday resort. Near here the *Vergulde Draek* (Gilt Dragon, a Dutch East Indiaman), went aground in 1656. The coast road ends at Lancelin, a small fishing port, 130 km north of Perth but coastal tracks continue north and may be usable with four-wheel drive.

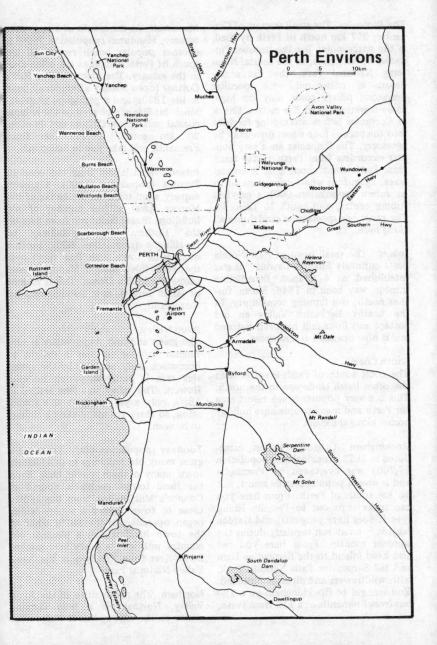

Perth Environs

0   5   10km

The Pinnacles The small seaport of Cervantes, 257 km north of Perth by road, is the entry point for the unusual Pinnacles Desert. Here, in the coastal Nambung National Park, the flat sandy desert is punctured with peculiar limestone pillars, some only cm high, some towering up to five metres. Check in Cervantes before attempting to drive into the park — four-wheel drive may be necessary. The Pinnacles are a very popular excursion from Perth — day tours from Perth coast about $35. A coastal track, again four-wheel drive, runs north to Jurien (population 600), a crayfish fishing centre, and south to Lancelin. The coast has spectacular sand dunes all along here.

Inland The small town of New Norcia has a curiously Spanish flavour — it was established as a Spanish Benedictine mission way back in 1846. Morra, further north, is a farming community. In the nearby Berkshire Valley an old cottage and flour mill has been restored and is now operated as a museum.

South Coast
The coast south of Perth is softer than the often harsh landscape to the north. This is a very popular beach resort area for Perth and many people have holiday homes along the coast.

Rockingham Originally a port, established in 1872, Rockingham (population 17,700) was overtaken by Fremantle and is now a popular seaside resort, just 45 km south of Perth. From here you can make trips out to Penguin Island (yes it does have penguins) and Garden Islands — boats run regularly during the summer months. From here you can also head inland to the Serpentine Dam and the Serpentine Falls National Park, with wildflowers and pleasant bushland. You can get to Rockhingham on a 120 bus from Fremantle or a 116 from Perth.

Mandurah At the mouth of a huge river estuary, Mandurah (population 7500) is another popular beach resort, 80 km south of Perth. Dolphins are often seen in the estuary. The town also has Hall's Cottage (open Sunday afternoons); built in the 1830s, and a geological museum. Much birdlife can be seen on the narrow coastal salt Lakes Clifton and Preston, 20 km south. A 117 bus from Fremantle will take you to Mandurah.

Inland Head inland from the coast to Pinjarra (population 1200), a picturesquely sited town on the banks of the Murray River with a number of old buildings. Steam trains run from here on the Hotham Valley Railway to Dwellingup (population 500), another quiet little town with fine views over the Peel Inlet behind Mandurah and across the Indian Ocean. This is an area of jarrah forests, as is Boddington, further inland.

Avon Valley
The green and lush Avon Valley is very English looking, it was a delight to homestick early settlers. In the spring this area is particularly rich in wildflowers. The valley was first settled in 1830, only a year after Perth's foundation, so there are many early buildings to be seen.

Toodyay (population 600) There are a great many old buildings in this historic town, many of them convict built. Even the local tourist centre is housed in Connor's Mill, dating from the 1850s. Close to town there's a winery which began operating in the 1870s while in the town itself there's a pleasant old country pub with a shady beer garden. Down-river from Toodyay is the Avon Valley National Park.

Northam The major town of the Avon Valley, Northam is a busy farming centre on the railway line to Kalgoorlie.

At one time the line from Perth ended abruptly here and miners had to make the rest of the weary trek to the goldfields by road. On the Avon River here you can see white swans as well as the more familiar black ones — a gift from Northam, England. At Wooroloo, about midway between Northam and Midlands, is El Caballo Blanco. This is a major Perth tourist attraction with its performing Andalusian horses. Performances are at 2.15 pm Tuesday to Sunday.

York The oldest inland town in Western Australia, York (population 1100) was first settled in 1830. There are many old buildings right along the main street of town and a stroll down this street is a real step back in time. The excellent Residency Museum from the 1840s, the old town hall, Castle Hotel dating from the coaching days, Faversham House, the old railway station and Settler's Hall are all of interest. Near York is the Balladong Farm Museum — a working farm of the pioneering era.

Beverley South of York, Beverley (population 800) is noted for its fine aeronautical museum. Its exhibits include a locally constructed biplane, built between 1928 and 1930. Further upriver is Brookton (population 600) and Pingelly (population 1000) in an area well known for its wildflowers.

The Darling Range
The hills that run parallel to the coast, fencing Perth in against the coast, are popular for picnics, barbecues and bush-walks. There are also some excellent viewpoints from where you can see across Perth down to the coast. Araluen with its waterfalls, the fire lookout at Mt Dale and Churchman's Brook are all off the Brookton Highway. Other places include the Zig Zag at Gooseberry Hill and Lake Leschenaultia. Kalamunda gives fine views over Perth, get there on a bus 297, 300 or 302 via Maida Vale Forrestfield or a 299 or 305 via Wattle Grove and Lesmurdie. Taking one route out and the other back you can make an interesting circular tour of the hill suburbs. There's a good walking track at Sullivan Rock, 69 km south-east on the Albany Highway.

Mundaring Weir Only 40 km from Perth in the ranges Mundaring (population 700) is the site of the Mundaring Weir — the dam built at the turn of the century to supply water to the goldfields, over 500 km to the east. The reservoir has an attractive bus setting and it is a popular excursion and picnic spot from Perth. The C Y O'Connor Museum has models and exhibits about the goldfields water pipeline, in its time one of the most amazing engineering feats in the world. It's open Monday, Friday and Saturday from 2 to 4 pm, Wednesday from 10 am to 12 noon, Sunday from 1 to 4 pm.

Near Mundaring is the Old Mahogany Inn, orginally built in 1837 as an outpost to protect travellers from unfriendly Aboriginals it now houses a museum and tearoom. It's open Wednesday to Sunday from 11 am to 6 pm. The John Forrest National Park in the Darling Range is also near Mundaring.

THE NULLARBOR
It's a little over 2700 km between Perth in Western Australia and Adelaide in South Australia, not much less than the distance from London to Moscow.

Driving on the long, lonely Eyre Highway from one side of Australia to another is still quite an adventure as you cross the vast Nullarbor Plains — bad Latin for 'no trees' — an accurate

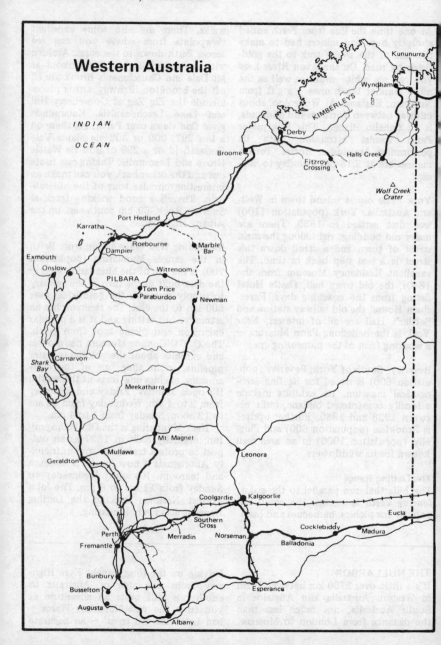

Western Australia

description of this flat, treeless waste-land.

The road across the Nullarbor takes its name from John Eyre, the explorer who made the first east-west crossing in 1841. It was a superhuman effort taking five months of nightmare hardship and resulting in the death of Eyre's companion John Baxter. In 1877 a telegraph line was laid across the Nullarbor, roughly delineating the route the first road would take. Later in the century gold miners en route to the goldfields of WA followed the same telegraph line route across the empty plains. In 1896 the first bicycle crossing was made and in 1912 the first car was driven across but in the next 12 years only three more cars managed to traverse the continent. In 1941 the war inspired the creation of a trans-continental highway, just as it had done for the Alice Springs-Darwin route. It was a rough and ready track when completed and in the '50s only a few vehicles a day would make the crossing. In the '60s the traffic flow increased to over 30 vehicles a day and in 1969 the WA government surfaced the road as far as the South Australian border. Finally in 1976 the final stretch from the South Australian border was sealed and now the Nullarbor crossing is a much easier drive, but still a hell of a long one.

There are actually three routes across the Nullarbor now. The new sealed road runs close to the coastline on the South Australian side. The Nullarbor plains end dramatically on the coast of the Great Australian Bight, falling sheer into the roaring sea. It's easy to see why this was a seafarer's nightmare for a ship driven on to the coast would quickly be pounded to pieces against the cliffs and climbing them would be a near impossibility. On the South Australian side the old Eyre Highway is a little distance north of the coast while the third route, the Indian-Pacific Railway, is about 150 km north of the coast

and actually on the Nullarbor Plains — unlike the road which only runs on the fringes of the great plain. For one 500 km long stretch the railway runs dead straight — the longest straight piece of railway line in the world.

Along the Eyre Highway

Ceduna is really the end of the line on the South Australian side of the Eyre Highway. You might travel this far west to see places in South Australia but if you were heading any further west it would be for only one reason — to leave South Australia and go to West Australia. At Ceduna it's still 520 km to Eucla, at the South Australia/Western Australia border and from there another 729 km to Norseman where the Eyre Highway ends, so you can see it's a very long way.

Ceduna's name comes from an Aboriginal word meaning 'a place to sit down and rest' — perhaps it's aptly named. From Ceduna there are several places with petrol and other facilities along the road. Penong is the end of all traces of cultivation and the start of the real treeless plain. You can make a short detour south of the town to see the Pink Lake and Point Sinclair. Nundroo is the real edge of the Nullarbor. Colona is the start of the last section of the Eyre to be sealed. The road passes through the Yalata Aboriginal Reserve and you'll often see Aboriginals by the roadside offering boomerangs and other artefacts for sale. For most of the way across the highway does not actually run on the Nullarbor Plain but at the tiny settlement of Nullarbor you'll see the plain. Most of the way the highway runs a little south of the Nullarbor, on the sloping stretch between the Nullarbor and the coast. From Nullarbor to the WA border, a distance of 187 km, the road has been rebuilt right along the coast with superb views over the Great Australian Bight. The old road is some distance to the north.

At the border there's a sign telling you to put your watch back by 45 minutes. From here to Caiguna you're in an intermediate time zone, halfway between South Australian and Western Australian time. There's a Travellers' Village at the border with camping facilities, a motel, cabins, service station, restaurant and so on. Just across the border is Eucla with the picturesque ruins of an old telegraph station, first opened in 1877. The line now runs along the railway line, about 160 km to the north, and the station is gradually subsiding into the sand dunes. The dunes make a spectacular view as you leave Eucla and drop down into the Eucla Pass.

After Eucla the next sign of life is the tiny settlement of Mundrabilla with a bird sanctuary behind the motel. Next up is Madura, close to the hills of the Hampton Tablelands. At one time horses were bred here for the Indian army. You get good views over the plains from near the town as the road climbs up. Cocklebiddy has the stone ruins of an Aboriginal mission and the area has a number of interesting caves, for real caving enthusiasts. At Caiguna watches go back another 45 minutes to Western Australian time. It's one of the longest and loneliest stretches of the Nullarbor from here to Balladonia, including a straight stretch of road 145 km long! Shortly before Balladonia, three km north of the road, are a number of natural rock waterholes known as Afghan Rocks. They often

hold water far into the summer. After Balladonia you may see the remains of old stone fences built to enclose stock. Clay saltpans are visible in the area. Finally the mine shafts and mullock heaps around Norseman announce the end of the Eyre Highway and the decision point where you either turn north to the Goldfields of WA or south to the coastal area.

Crossing the Nullarbor

See the Perth Getting There section for details of air, rail, bus and hitching information across the Nullarbor. Although the Nullarbor is no longer a torture trail where cars get shaken to bits by potholes and corrugations or where you're going to die of thirst waiting for another vehicle if you break down, it's still wise to avoid difficulties. The longest distance between petrol stops is about 200 km so if you're so foolish as to run out of petrol midway you'll have a nice long round trip to get more. Getting help for a mechanical breakdown could be equally time consuming and very expensive. So make sure your vehicle is in good shape and that you've got plenty of fuel, good tyres and at least a basic kit of simple spare parts. Carry some drinking water, just in case you do have to sit it out by the roadside on a hot summer day. Take it easy across the Nullarbor — plenty of people try to set speed records, plenty more have made a real mess of their cars when they run into big roos.

GOLD COUNTRY

Fifty years after its establishment in 1829 the WA colony was still going nowhere slowly. So the government in Perth was delighted when gold was discovered at Southern Cross in 1887. That first strike petered out pretty

quickly but more discoveries followed and WA went through a gold boom for the rest of the century. It was gold that put WA on the map and finally gave it the population to make it viable in its own right, rather than just a distant offshoot of the east coast colonies. The gold boom was, however, comparatively short lived. The major strikes were made in 1892 in Coolgardie and nearby Kalgoorlie but in the whole goldfields area Kalgoorlie is the only town still of considerable size. Coolgardie's period of prosperity lasted only until 1905 and many other gold towns went from nothing to populations of as much as 10,000 then back to nothing in just 10 years.

Their rise to prosperity was meteoric, however, as the many magnificent public buildings in the old towns grandly tell. Life in the goldfields in the early days was terribly hard. This area of WA is extremely dry — rainfall is erratic and never great. Even the little rain there is quickly disappears into the porous soil. Many early gold-seekers, propelled more by enthusiasm than common-sense, died of thirst while seeking the elusive metal or, later, of disease in the insanitary shanty towns. The completion of a 557-km long water pipeline in 1903 solved that serious problem but couldn't ensure the gold supply. Today Kalgoorlie is the main centre for the area and some gold-mining still continues there. Elsewhere there is a string of fascinating ghost and near ghost towns plus the modern nickel mines that have recently revived some areas of the gold country.

Water

Development of the Western Australian goldfields faced an enormous problem right from the start: water — there wasn't any. Early miners faced terrible hardships due to this lack and more than a few died from thirst out in the bush or from the outbreaks of disease in the unhygienic shanty towns. It soon became clear to the government that gold was WA's most important industry and yet development of the goldfields was likely to come to a grinding halt without a reliable water supply. Stop gap measures like huge condensation plants to produce distilled water from salt lakes or brackish bore water provided temporary relief and in 1898 engineer C Y O'Connor proposed a stunning solution. He would build a reservoir near Perth and construct a pipeline 557 km long to Kalgoorlie.

This was long before the current era of long oil pipelines and his idea was looked upon by some as a crazy impossibility. Especially when you add the fact that the water had to go uphill all the way, eventually reaching 400 metres greater altitude at Kalgoorlie! Nevertheless the project was approved and the pipeline laid at breakneck speed. In 1903 the water started to pour into Kalgoorlie's newly constructed reservoir and with various modifications the system works successfully to this day.

The story has an unhappy ending though. O'Connor was persecuted by those of lesser vision and in 1902, less than a year before his scheme was proved to work so well, O'Connor's tormentors proved too much for him and he committed suicide.

KALGOORLIE (population 23,000)

Kalgoorlie, the longest lasting and most successful of the WA gold towns, rose to prominence later than Coolgardie. In 1893 Paddy Hannan, a prospector from way back, set out from Coolgardie en route to another gold strike but stopped at the site of Kalgoorlie and found, just lying around on the surface, enough gold to spark another rush. As in so many places the surface gold soon petered out but at Kalgoorlie the miners went deeper and more and more gold was found. It wasn't the storybook chunky nuggets of solid gold; Kalgoorlie's gold had to be extracted from the rocks by costly and complex processes of grinding, roasting and chemical action but there was plenty of it.

Kalgoorlie quickly reached fabled heights of prosperity and the enormous and magnificent public buildings of the turn of the century speak clearly of just what a fabulously wealthy place this was. After WW I, however, increasing production costs combined with static gold values to push Kalgoorlie

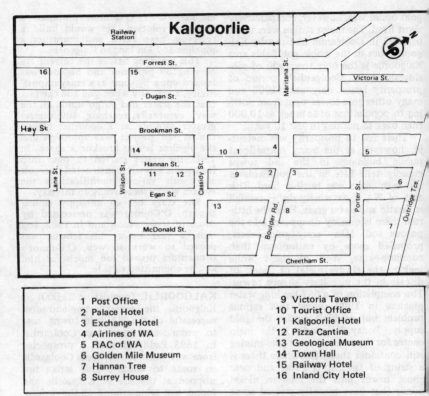

Kalgoorlie

1 Post Office
2 Palace Hotel
3 Exchange Hotel
4 Airlines of WA
5 RAC of WA
6 Golden Mile Museum
7 Hannan Tree
8 Surrey House
9 Victoria Tavern
10 Tourist Office
11 Kalgoorlie Hotel
12 Pizza Cantina
13 Geological Museum
14 Town Hall
15 Railway Hotel
16 Inland City Hotel

into a slow, but steady, decline. Today the famous 'golden mile' of Kalgoorlie's heyday is a shadow of its once hectic self and the only major operation is the huge Mt Charlotte mine, close to Paddy Hannan's original find. The mining that is still carried on, Kalgoorlie's importance as an outback centre, the busy tourist trade, plus the new nickel mines in the area combine to ensure the town's continued prosperity.

Information

There's an informative tourist bureau on Hannan St where you can get a good map of Kalgoorlie and make a 50c investment in the excellent and information packed *Gold Rush Country* map.

The office is open 8.30 am to 5 pm Monday to Friday, 9 to 11 am Saturdays. There's another tourist office on Burt St in Boulder. For an excellent book on the fascinating Kalgoorlie story read *The Glittering Years* by Arthur Bennet (St George Books, Perth, 1981). There's a daily paper in Kal (as it's known to its friends), the *Kalgoorlie Miner*. Kal can get very hot in December-January and overall the cool winter months are the best time to visit. From late-August through September, however, the town is packed out and accommodation of any type can be difficult to find.

Orientation

Although Kalgoorlie sprang up close to Paddy Hannan's original find the mining emphasis soon shifted a few km away to the 'golden mile', a square mile which area for area was probably the wealthiest gold mining area in the world. The satellite town of Boulder developed to service this town. There's a direct road between these two towns plus a longer route that runs by the airport.

Kalgoorlie itself is a grid of broad tree-lined streets. The main street, Hannan St, is flanked by imposing public buildings and is, of course, wide enough to turn a camel train in — a popular outback measuring stick! You'll find most of the hotels, restaurants and offices on or close to Hannan St.

Hainault Tourist Mine

Kalgoorlie's number one tourist attraction and it's not-to-be-missed feature is this mine, right in the golden mile near Boulder. Opened in 1898 the mine finally ceased operation in the 1960s. Today you can take the lift cage 61 metres down into the bowels of the earth and make an enthralling tour around the 'drives' and 'crosscuts' of the old mine — guided by an ex-miner. There's also a tour of the surface workings and an audio-visual show on mining and Kalgoorlie. The underground tour costs $4 or $4.60 including a surface tour as well. You can wander around the surface workings yourself for free. Underground tours are made at 10.30 am, 1, 2.30 and 3.45 pm daily. Near the mine the Lion's Lookout provides a good view over the golden mile, Boulder and Kalgoorlie. You can make an interesting loop drive around the golden mile, past the old mining works and the huge mountains of 'slime', the cast-offs from the mining process.

Other Attractions

Just off the end of Hannan St you can climb the road (ignore the private sign) to Mt Charlotte where the town's reservoir is situated. The view over the town is good but there's little to see of the reservoir which is covered over to limit evaporation. The School of Mines Museum on the corner of Egan and Cassidy Sts has a geology display including replicas of big nuggets. It's open Monday to Friday from 2 pm to 4 pm.

Along Hannan St you'll find the imposing town hall and even more imposing post office. In 1979 the largest chunk of debris from the fallen Skylab space vehicle crashed to earth in WA and was put on display in the town hall. There's an art gallery upstairs while sitting outside is a statue of Paddy Hannan himself, holding a water-bag drinking fountain. In 1982 he was removed to repair the effects of 50 years vandalism and plain old age but he should be back in place in 1983.

A block back from Hannan St is Hay St and one of Kalgoorlie's most famous 'attractions' although it's quietly ignored in the tourist brochures. Kalgoorlie has a block long strip of brothels where the red-lit ladies of the night beckon passing men to their true-blue Aussie galvanised iron doorways. Nelson's eye has been turned to this activity for so long that it has become an accepted and historical part of the town. Usually Kalgoorlie's famous (and illegal) two-up schools are also ignored but in late '82 a Perth gaming squad raid caused local outrage from the mayor on down.

On Outridge Terrace the tiny British Arms Hotel (narrowest hotel in Australia) now houses the interesting Golden Mile Museum with many relics from Kalgoorlie's pioneering days. It's open 10.30 am to 12.30 pm and 2.30 pm to 4.30 pm daily, admission is 50c. A little further along Outridge Terrace is Paddy Hannan's tree, marking the spot where the first gold strike was made. The Eastern Goldfields Historical

**GOLDEN MILE MUSEUM
KALGOORLIE, W.A.**

"BRITISH ARMS"   **1899**

Society also has a display at the June O'Brien Memorial Centre (daily except Thursday). The Royal Flying Doctor Base can be visited Monday to Friday at 2.30 pm. Hammond Park (40c) is a small fauna reserve with a miniature German castle.

Boulder

There is another fine old town hall in Boulder which also has the Goldfields War Museum (40c) by the Tourist Bureau on Burt St. At the Golden Mile the rip-roaring hotels of the Boulder Block never shut and thirsty miners off the shifts poured into them night and day. There's nothing much to be seen there today.

Places to Stay

There is a string of pleasantly old fashioned hotels right around the centre of Kalgoorlie. The *Exchange Hotel* (tel 21 2833) is the picture postcard place right in the centre of town by the traffic lights on Hannan St (the only traffic lights for 500 km). Rooms cost $15/26 without facilities, $22/34 if you must have your own bathroom. A few doors down at 9 Boulder Rd is *Surrey House* (tel 21 1340) where rooms cost $12 per person, $15 with breakfast. It's a popular place in the budget category.

Other cheap hotels include the *Inland City* (tel 21 2401) at 93 Forrest St, the *Kalgoorlie* (tel 21 3046) at 319 Hannan St, the *Railway* (tel 21 3047) at the corner of Wilson and Forrest Sts and the *Criterion* (tel 21 2271) at 123 Hannan St. The very basic *Nullabor Guest House* (yes that's how it's spelt) (tel 21 2176) is at 300 Hannan St and has rooms for just $9/14 for singles/doubles.

Motels aren't cheap in Kalgoorlie but the *Auto* on Hannan St (tel 21 1433) has singles for around $25, doubles $32. There are a number of campsites in Kalgoorlie.

Places to Eat

There are plenty of counter meal pubs and cafes in Kalgoorlie, particularly along Hannan St. The *Victoria Tavern* does good counter food lunch times and in the evenings in the $6 to $7 bracket. The *Exchange Hotel*, on the corner of Hannan and Boulder, has the Winter Lounge, also with main courses around $6. In the front bar there are also cheaper meals in the $2.50 to $5 range. The *Hotel York* also does counter meals, enter to the 'Steak Bar' where prices are generally around $5. Or there's the *Kalgoorlie Cafe* at 275 with burgers, souvlaki and other similar fast foods. At 211 Hannan St the *Pizza Cantina* does pretty good pizzas. Try the *Victory Cafe* at 246 Hannan St for an early breakfast. Over in Boulder you can get counter meals at *Tattersalls*. Kalgoorlie brews its own beer Hannan's.

Getting There

Air You can fly, rail or bus to Kalgoorlie. Airlines of WA fly there once or twice daily from Perth. The flight takes just under an hour and costs $92. The Airlines of WA office (tel 21 2277) is on Maritana St.

Rail The daily Prospector railcar service from Perth costs $36.30 or $21.25 with student discount. It's claimed to be the fastest railway service in Australia and takes about eight hours for the 600 km journey. It's modern, comfortable and provides good views of the generally monotonous scenery. The fare includes a meal en route. From Perth you can

Your Ticket on THE 'PROSPECTOR' Australia's Fastest Train

WESTERN AUSTRALIAN GOVERNMENT RAILWAYS

book seats at the WAGTB office in Hay St or the Westrail Terminal (tel 326 2811). It's wise to book ahead as this service is fairly popular, particularly in the tourist season. The Indian Pacific also goes through Kalgoorlie.

Bus Ansett Pioneer and Greyhound buses operate through Kalgoorlie on their Adelaide-Perth services. Fares are $95 from Adelaide, $25 from Perth but note that the buses pull into Kalgoorlie at an ungodly hour of the night when everything is closed up and finding a place to stay can be difficult. Unfortun-

ately most days of the week the Prospector also arrives in Kalgoorlie at an uncomfortably late hour. There's a three times weekly bus to Esperance from Kalgoorlie — once via Kambalda and Norseman, twice via Coolgardie and Norseman, the trip takes 5½ hours. By road it's 597 km between Perth and Kalgoorlie.

Getting Around
You can rent cars from Hertz, Budget, Letz (at the airport) or Avis in Kalgoorie and if you want to explore very far you'll either have to have wheels, hitch or take a tour since public transport is limited. There's an airport bus meeting flights for $1.50 or a taxi will be $3 to $4. Make sure they use the meter around town! You can hire bicycles from Johnston Cycles (tel 21 1157) at 76 Boulder St.

Between Kal and Boulder there's a regular bus service (timetable from the tourist office) costing 50c. You'll have to walk from the Boulder junction about two km to the Hainault mine. Hitching shouldn't be too difficult. For about $2 you can take the morning school bus to Coolgardie, comes back in the afternoon.

Goldrush Tours are the main tour operators in Kalgoorlie. Book through the tourist office or direct to their office on Boulder St. They have town tours ($7.50 not including admission charges) and tours to Coolgardie ($10), Kambalda ($10), ghost towns ($14) and for avid fossickers a gold detector tour ($10).

AROUND THE GOLD COUNTRY
Kalgoorlie is the metropolis of the gold-fields but there are many other towns, most of them mere ghost towns today, of great interest. Coolgardie, only 40 km from Kalgoorlie, is the best known while others vary from odd heaps of rubbles to tiny outposts with superb town halls and equally magnificent old country hotels, kept alive today

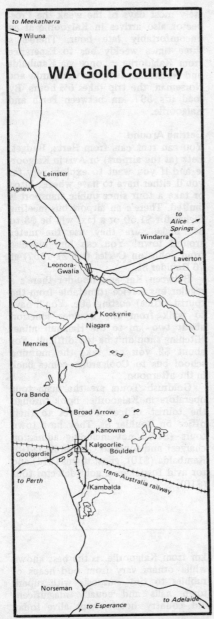

WA Gold Country

to Meekatharra
Wiluna
Leinster
Agnew
to Alice Springs
Windarra
Leonora-Gwalia
Laverton
Kookynie
Niagara
Menzies
Ora Banda
Broad Arrow
Kanowna
Kalgoorlie-Boulder
Coolgardie
to Perth
trans-Australia railway
Kambalda
Norseman
to Esperance
to Adelaide

only by the tourist traffic. Before setting out to explore this area get a copy of the excellent and highly informative *Gold Rush Country* map. Remember that this is remote, sparsely populated, rugged and very dry country — carry plenty of water and be prepared if you intend to wander off the beaten track. There is still quite a bit of local private mining going on in the old goldfields, the lure continues!

Coolgardie (population 700)

A popular pause for people crossing the Nullarbor and also the turn-off point for Kalgoorlie, Coolgardie really is a ghost of its former self. You only have to glance at the huge town hall and post office building to appreciate the size of town Coolgardie once was. Gold was discovered here in 1892 and by the turn of the century the population had boomed · to 15,000. Then the gold petered out and the town withered away just as quickly. There's plenty of interest for the visitor though.

For a start there are 150 informative historical markers scattered in and around the town. They tell you what was once there or what the buildings were formerly used for. The Goldfields Museum is open 9.30 am to 4.30 pm every day of the week and has a fascinating display of goldfields memorabilia. You can even find out about American President Herbert Hoover's days on the WA goldfields. It's the largest museum in the goldfields and worth the $1.50 admission, which includes a film, shown a few doors up the road at the Coolgardie Tourist Bureau. The railway station is also operated as a museum and here you can discover the incredible story of the miner trapped 300 metres underground by floodwater in 1907 and his rescue, 10 days later, by divers!

Just out of town on the Perth side the town-cemetery includes many early graves including that of pioneer explorer Edward Giles. At Coolgardie's unhealthiest time it's said that 'one half of the population buried the other half'. Coolgardie's most amazing sight, however, is Prior's Museum. Right by the road a large empty lot is cluttered with every kind of antique junk you could imagine — from old mining equipment to half a dozen rusting old cars, it's all here. Open 24 hours a day, 365 days a year, admission is free!

Places to Stay & Eat Coolgardie has a fine old *youth hostel* (tel 26 6051) at 56-60 Gnarlbine Rd. It costs $4 per night, has plenty of room and a noted graffiti wall! You can get bed & breakfast for $10 in the *Railway Lodge* on the main street or for $14 in the *Denver City Hotel* (tel 26 6031) also on Bayley St. The Denver City is one of Coolgardie's original hotels and it's a fine old building with long, shady verandahs. At the *Safari Village Holiday Centre* (tel 26 6037) at 2 Renou St bed & breakfast costs $14/ 22. There's also a campsite. The *Denver Hotel* does counter lunches and teas.

Norseman (population 2000)

To most people Norseman is just a crossroads where you turn east for the trans-Nullarbor Eyre Highway, south to Esperance or north to Coolgardie and Perth. The town also has gold mines still in operation today, many old workings and a museum.

Kambalda (population 5000)

Kambalda died as a gold town in 1906 but nickel was dicovered here in 1966 and today this is the major mining centre in the goldfields region. There are tours of the mining operation from Monday to Friday from the tourist office. The town is on the shores of salt Lake LeFroy and land-yachting is a popular local activity.

North of Kalgoorlie

The road is sealed from Kalgoorlie all the way to Leonora-Gwalia, 240 km north, and on from there to Laverton (130 km north-east) and Leinster (100 km north). Off the main road, however, traffic is virtually non-existent and rain can quickly cut the dirt roads.

Towns of interest include Kanowna, just 22 km north-east of Kal but along a dirt road. In 1905 this town had a population of 12,000, 16 hotels, many churches and an hourly train service to Kalgoorlie. Today, apart from the station platform and the odd pile of rubble, absolutely nothing remains!

Broad Arrow now has a population of 20, versus 2400 at the turn of the century, but one of the town's original eight hotels still operates in virtually unchanged condition. Ora Banda has gone from 2000 to less than 50. Menzies, 130 km north of Kal, has about 90 people today versus 5000 in 1900. Many early buildings still remain including the railway station with its 120-metre long platform and the town hall with its clockless clocktower. The ship bringing the clock from England sank en route.

With a population of 500 Leonora is still a reasonably sized little town. It serves as the railhead for the nickel from Windarra and Leinster. In adjoining Gwalia, the Sons of Gwalia Goldmine, closed in 1964, was the largest in WA outside of Kalgoorlie. At one time the mine was managed by Herbert Hoover, later to become President of the USA. The Gwalia Historical Gallery is housed in the 1898 mine office — it's a fascinating local museum open daily. Off the main road Kookynie is an interesting little place with a population of just 10, in 1905 it was 1500. Nearby Niagara is a total ghost town.

From Leonora you can turn northwest to Laverton, where the sealed road ends. The population here declined precipitously from 1000 in 1910 to 200 in 1970 when the Poseidon nickel discovery (beloved of stockmarket speculators in the late '60s and early '70s) revived mining operations at nearby Windarra. The town now has a population of 1500. From here it is just 1710 km north-west to Alice Springs but you'll need four-wheel drive for the rough track, permission to enter the Aboriginal reserves along the way, enough fuel capacity for at the very least 650 km and don't consider it from November to March when the route is closed for safety reasons.

North of Leonora the road is now sealed to Leinster, another modern nickel town. Nearby Agnew is another old gold town which has now all but completely disappeared. It's another 170 km north to Wiluna from where it's another 170 km to Meekatharra on the sealed Great Northern Highway to Port Hedland. Wiluna mined arsenic through the '30s when it had a population of 8000 and was a modern, prosperous town. Then the ore ran out in 1948 and the town quickly declined. Today the minute population is mainly Aboriginal.

THE SOUTH & SOUTH-WEST

Many travellers on the road between the east and west coasts take the direct route through WA — across the Nullarbor then from Norseman north to Coolgardie and then directly west to Perth. It's certainly worth getting up into the goldfields around Coolgardie and Kalgoorlie but turning south from Norseman to Esperance and then travelling along the Leeuwin Way, around the south-west corner of Australia, is an equally interesting trip. This is a very varied area with some real contrasts to the dry and barren country found in so many other parts of the state.

The southern stretch, 'The Great Southern', has some magnificent coastline pounded by huge seas but there is also beautiful country inland as well as Albany, the oldest settlement in Western Australia. Inland are the spectacular and rugged Stirling Range and Porongurups. The south-west corner is one of the lushest, greenest and most fertile areas of WA. Here you will find the great karri and jarrah forests, plus prosperous farming land and more of the state's beautiful wildflowers.

Places to Stay

The towns in the south-west and south coast regions are popular holiday resorts so there are plenty of hotels, motels, holiday flats and campsites. There is also a string of youth hostels right around the coastal region including the popular Esperance hostel, Albany, Denmark, Tingledale, Pemberton, Augusta, Bridgetown, Noggerup, Bunbury and Quindalup. Enough hostels, in fact, to make a really interesting hostelling circuit of the region.

Getting There

Air Skywest (phone TAA — 323 3333 in Perth) have a fairly comprehensive network of flights to towns in the south and south-west. They include Bunbury ($32), Albany ($83), Esperance ($104) and Norseman ($99).

Bus & Rail Westrail have a number of bus and rail services into the region including a three times weekly bus service from Kalgoorlie to Esperance. From Perth the Westrail Road Service bus to Esperance runs via Jerramangup on Mondays, via Lake Grace on Fridays. The trip takes about 11 hours and costs $33.80, $16.90 with student discount. Via Kalgoorlie the Westrail fare to Esperance is $48.60 ($27.30 with student discount). A complete loop costs $82.40 ($44.20). There are also Westrail bus services to Albany and Hyden, while to Bunbury there is a bus service and the Australind train service. Greyhound buses have a once weekly service between Norseman and Albany ($34) and Eaglepass holders can use Westrail services between Perth and Albany.

Esperance is 750 km from Perth via Lake Grace, 950 km Coolgardie or 894 km via Albany. To do a complete road loop from Perth out to Kalgoorlie, down to Esperance and back round by the coast would involve something over 2000 km.

Esperance (population 5500)

On the coast 200 km south of Norseman, Esperance has become a popular coastal resort for the region. Although the first settlers came to the area in 1863 it was during the goldrush in the 1890s that the town really became established as a port. When the gold fever subsided and then petered out Esperance went into suspended animation until after WW II. In the 1950s it was discovered that adding missing trace elements to the soil around Esperance would restore it to fertility and since then the town has grown rapidly as an agricultural centre.

Esperance has some excellent beaches and the seas offshore are studded with the many, many islands of the Archipelago of the Recherche. The town's Municipal Museum has the usual pioneering exhibits but also a major Skylab display. When Skylab crashed to earth it made it's fiery re-entry right over Esperance. The museum is on the corner of James and Dempster Sts and is open daily from 1.30 pm to 4.30 pm. George's Oceanarium has a sealife display and you can also see the town's original homestead on Dempster St, although it is not open to the public.

Only three km from the town the Pink Lake, with its prolific birdlife, really is pink; salt is dredged from the lake, as much as half a million tonnes a year. Twilight Bay and Picnic Cove are popular local swimming spots while you can look out over the bay and islands from nearby Observatory Point or from the Rotary Lookout on Wireless Hill. There are about 100 small islands in the Recherche Archipelago with colonies of seals, penguins and a wide variety of waterbirds. Woody Island is being developed as a wildlife sanctuary. There are cruises out to the islands during the peak season of January-February.

Cape Le Grand National Park is a coastal park extending from about 20 to 60 km east of Esperance. The park has spectacular coastal scenery, some good beaches and excellent walking tracks. Frenchman's Peak, at the western end of the park, gives fine views. Further east is the coastal Cape Arid National Park, at the start of the Great Australian Bight and on the fringes of the Nullarbor Plain.

Esperance to Albany (476 km)

From Esperance the road runs inland before turning back to the coast at Albany. The tiny town of Ravensthorpe (population 300) was once in a gold mining area and later copper mining also took place here. Today wheat and sheep are the local industries. The fine beaches and bays around Hopetoun are immediately south. The coastal Fitzgerald River National Park can be reached from here or from Jerramangup, further west.

Albany (population 13,700)

The commercial centre of the southwest region, the pretty town of Albany is also the oldest settlement in the state, established in 1826, shortly before Perth. Its excellent harbour on King George Sound led to Albany becoming a thriving whaling port. Later, when steamships came into operation between the UK and Australia, Albany was a coaling station for ships bound for the east coast.

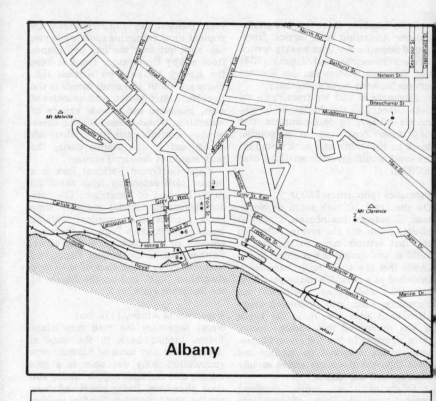

Albany

1 Strawberry Hill Farm
2 Desert Mounted Corps Memorial
3 Post Office
4 Tourist Office
5 Post Office

6 Patrick Taylor Cottage
7 Old Gaol & Museum
8 Residency Museum
9 Old Post Office
10 Railway Station

With this long history it's not surprising that Albany has some fine old colonial buildings and Main St, leading down to the sea, is particularly noted for its Victorian shopfronts. The Old Gaol & Museum dates from 1851, it's now a folk museum. There's also a full scale replica of the *Amity*, the brig which brought Albany's founding party to the settlement. Historical exhibits can also be seen at the Albany Residency Museum. Patrick Taylor Cottage dates

from 1832, it has been restored with period furniture. On top of Mt Clarence is the Desert Mounted Corps Memorial, originally erected in Port Said as a memorial to the events of Gallipoli. When the Suez crisis in 1956 made colonial reminders less than popular in Egypt it was brought here. The old farm at Strawberry Hill, near to Albany, is the oldest in the state.

There are fine views over the coast and inland from the Twin Peaks, overlooking the town. Near Albany there are good beaches at Jimmy Newhill's Harbour, Emu Point, Oyster Harbour and in town at the long sweep of sand at Middleton Beach. At Frenchman's Bay, 21 km from town, the Cheyne's Beach Whaling Station only ceased operations in 1978. Impressive rock formations and blowholes along the coast include The Gap and Natural Bridge, 16 km out, and the Blowhole and Gorge.

Albany has a travel centre at 171 York St.

Mt Barker (population 1600)

Directly north of Albany, Mt Barker is south of the Stirling Ranges and west of the Porongurups. The town is overlooked by the enormous TV tower on top of Mt Barker. The town has been settled since the 1830s and the old police station and jail of 1868 is preserved as a museum. Today the area is developing a reputation for wine producing. Kendenup, 16 km north of Mt Barker, was the actual site of WA's first gold discovery, though considerably overshadowed by the later and much larger finds in the Kalgoorlie area. North of Mt Barker, Cranbrook (population 400) is an access point to the Stirling Range National Park. Mt Barker has a tourist office at 47 Lowood Rd.

The Stirling Range & Porongurups

The beautiful Prongurup range provides panoramic views, beautiful scenery and excellent bushwalks. Castle Rock (570 metres) and Nancy's Peak (652 metres) are easy climbs. The Devil's Slide (670 metres) is another popular Porongurup walk. In the Stirling Range Toolorunup (for views), Bluff Knoll (for the height — at 1037 metres it's the highest peak in the range) and Toll Peak (for the wildflowers) are popular half day walks. The 96-km long range is noted for its spectacular colour changes through blues, reds and purples. The mountains rise abruptly from the surrounding flat and sandy plains.

Denmark (population 800)

Situated 55 km west of Albany, Denmark has fine beaches (William Bay for swimming, Ocean Beach for surfing) and is a good base for trips into the karri forests. The town is picturesquely sited on the Denmark River and first became established supplying timber for goldfield developments. In the town Winniston Park is a modern house packed with fine English antiques, it's open daily. Copenhagen House, opposite the tourist office on Strickland St, shows local crafts. You can get fine views from Mt Shadforth Lookout.

Nornalup-Walpole

The road continues close to the coast to Nornalup, a small town on the banks of the tranquil Frankland River. The heavily forested Nornalup National Park stretches between Nornalup and Walpole. The Frankland River is popular for canoeing. Only 13 km east of Walpole is the 'Valley of the Giants', a series of giant karri and tingle trees including one which soars 46 metres high. Pleasant shady and ferny paths lead through the forest. From Walpole the road bends away from the coast to Manjimup.

Manjimup (population 3700)

The commercial centre of the southwest this is a major agricultural centre, particularly for apple growing and timber getting. The town has a Timber Museum and from here you can make short excursions to the Warren National Park, One Tree Bridge and the four superb karri trees at Four Acres, just along the riverbank. Manjimup has a tourist office on Giblett St.

Pemberton (population 800) & Northcliffe (population 200)

These two towns are both in superb karri forests. The nice little town of

Pemberton has a very good local museum, an art gallery and a trout hatchery. The Brockman Sawpit is a restoration showing timber cutting activities of the 1860s. If you're feeling fit you can make the scary 60 metre climb to the top of the Gloucester Tree, highest fire lookout in Australia. It's just outside Pemberton. Northcliffe has a pioneer museum and the popular and picturesque Lane Poole Falls. The beaches of Windy Harbour and cliffs of Point D'Entrecasteaux are directly to the south. There's a tourist bureau on Brockman St, Pemberton.

Bridgetown (population 1100) & Nannup (population 500)

A quiet country town in an area of karri forests and farmland, Bridgetown has some old buildings including the National Trust restored Blechynden House of 1862. Continuing west you reach Nannup with the largest jarrah sawmill in WA and the fine old Colonial House, dating from 1895. Boyup Brook (population 600) has a number of points of interest including a fauna reserve and a large butterfly and beetle collection. Nearby is Norlup Pool with glacial rock fountains and Wilga with an old timber mill and vintage engines.

Augusta (population 500) & Margaret River (population 700)

A popular holiday resort, Augusta is only a little north of Cape Leeuwin with its lighthouse and waterwheel from 1895. Between here and Margaret River to the north there are a number of limestone caves — they include the Jewel Cave, Lake Cave and Mammoth Cave. Fossilised skeletons of Tasmanian tigers have been found in the Mammoth Cave. In all 120 caves have been discovered between Cape Leeuwin and Cape Naturaliste but only these three and Yallingup Cave, near Busselton, are open to visitors.

There are some fine beaches and good surfing spots between Augusta and Margaret River, which is prettily situated on a riverside. The Augusta-Margaret River Tourist Bureau is on the corner of Bussel Highway and Wallcliffe. The direct Augusta-Margaret River-Busselton runs slightly inland but there is also an old coastal road right along the coast which is worth considering as an alternative route. The coast here has real variety — rock cliff faces, long beaches pounded by rolling surf, calm sheltered bays.

Busselton (population 5600)

On the shores of Geographe Bay you can see relics of the founding Bussell family of the 1830s in Prospect Villa, now a small museum in the centre of town. Like Bunbury, further north, Busselton is a popular holiday resort. The town also has a cinema museum, the National Trust Wonnerup House of 1859 and, until it was shortened by a cyclone in 1978, Australia's longest timber jetty. Yallingup, to the south-west, is a Mecca for surfing enthusiasts. Near here is Yallingup Cave and some fine coastal viewpoints such as Cape Naturaliste. Dunsborough (population 300) is a pleasant little town with fine beaches like Meelup, Eagle and Bunker Bays, just to the west of Busselton. The Bannamah Wild Life Park is two km from the town. Busselton has a tourist bureau in the Civic Centre.

Bunbury (population 20,000)

Port, industrial town and holiday resort, Bunbury is a centre for the gourmet blue manna crabs. The town's old buildings include King's Cottage which now houses a museum. There's also a shell museum on Mangles St and two old steam trains from the 1890s, the Leschenault Lady and the Koombana Queen, make trips from the town. Bunbury has a tourist information centre in the Old Government School Buildings on Arthur St; the town is 193 km south of Perth.

Australind (population 800)

There's a pleasant 11 km drive from Bunbury to Australind, another holiday resort. The town takes its name from an 1840s plan to make it a port for trade with India. The plan never worked but the strange name (Australia-India) remains. Australind has a tiny church just four by seven metres, said to be the smallest in Australia. There's also a motorcycle museum and a gemstone museum in the town plus the Wellesley Wildlife Park nearby.

Inland

Inland from the south-west coast interesting centres include Harvey (population 2400) in a popular bushwalking area of rolling green hills to the north of Bunbury. There are dam systems and some beautiful waterfalls near here and the Yalgorup National Park is north of town. There's a tourist office on Young St.

Further south Donnybrook (population 1000) is in the centre of an apple-growing area. Collie (population 6800) is WA's only coal town and has a historical museum and a steam locomotive museum. There is some pleasant bushwalking country around the town and plenty of wildflowers in season.

WHEATLANDS

Stretching north from the Albany coastal region to north of the Perth-Coolgardie road (the Great Eastern Highway) is the WA wheatfields region. The area is noted for its unusual rock formation, best known of which is Wave Rock near Hyden, and for its many Aboriginal rock carvings.

Cunderdin (population 800) & Meckering

Meckering was badly damaged by an earthquake in 1968 and the Agricultural Museum in Cunderdin has exhibits about that quake. The museum is housed in an old pumping station used on the goldfields water pipeline. Further east Kellerberrin (population 1200) has a historical museum in the old courthouse of 1897 and is overlooked by a hill named Killabin by Aboriginals.

Merredin (population 3700)

On the Perth-Kalgoorlie railway line and the Great Eastern Highway, Merredin has a National Trust restored homestead and the old town railway station is also preserved as a museum. North of Merredin there are some interesting rock formations around Koorda.

Southern Cross (population 900)

Although the gold quickly gave out Southern Cross was the first goldrush town in the WA goldfields. The big rush soon moved further east to Coolgardie and then Kalgoorlie. Like the name of the town itself Southern Cross's streets are also named after stars and constellations. Situated 378 km east of Perth, this is really the end of the wheatlands area and the start of the desert, travelling by train the change is fairly dramatic. In the spring the sandy plains around Southern Cross are carpeted with wildflowers.

Hyden & Wave Rock

Just three km from the tiny town of Hyden is the unusual rock formation known as Wave Rock. It's a real surfer's delight, the perfect wave, 15 metres high and frozen in solid rock. Wave Rock is 350 km from Perth and is one of WA's major tourist attractions. The curling rock is marked with different colour bands. Other interesting rock formations in the area bear names like Hippo's Yawn and The Humps; Bates Caves have Aboriginal rock paintings. There's a wildlife sanctuary by Wave Rock.

Other Towns

There is a fine rock formation known

as Kokerbin, an Aboriginal word for high place, near Bruce Rock. Corrigin (population 900) has a folk museum and there's an observation tower west of the town. Narembeen has a small church museum. Jilakin Rock is 18 km from Kulin (population 400) while further south-east Lake Grace (population 600) is near the lake of the same

name. Narrogin (population 4800) is an agricultural centre, with the Courthouse Museum in the town and a couple of unusual rock formations near the town. Dumbleyung (population 300) also has a historical museum. Wagin (population 1700) has an art gallery and some fine old buildings plus there is good bushwalking around Mt Latham, six km west.

THE GREAT NORTHERN HIGHWAY

Although most people heading north to the north-west region of Western Australia and the Kimberleys will travel up the coast there is also the more direct route via the Great Northern Highway. This takes a more or less straight line from Perth to Newman and then skirts around the eastern edge of the Pilbara to Port Hedland via Marble Bar. Total distance is 1670 metres and the last 480 km from Newman, the mining town, to Port Hedland are not sealed.

This is not exactly the most interesting road in Australia. In fact for most of the way it passes through country which is flat, dull and dreary in the extreme. Once you've passed through the old gold towns from the Murchison River goldfields — Mt Magnet, Cue and Meekatharra — there's really nothing for another 400 km until you reach Newman.

Getting There

Greyhound have three buses a week up to Newman ($62) via Meekatharra ($28). The trip takes about 15 hours to Newman and once a week the bus continues on to Port Hedland. Westrail also

have one bus a week to Meekatharra, via Mullewa. Skywest fly to Meekatharra from Perth for $160.

Mount Magnet (population 400)

An old gold mining town which is today a popular stopping point on the long drive north.

Cue (population 300)

Like Mount Magnet this was once an important centre in the Murchison goldfields. There are still some interesting old buildings of solid stone in the town. Mining ghost towns in the area include Day Dawn and Big Bell.

Meekatharra (population 800)

Meekatharra is still a mining centre today. At one time it was a railhead for cattle brought down from the Northern Territory and the east Kimberleys. There are various old gold towns in the area and from Meekatharra you can approach the WA goldfields area around Kalgoorlie from the north. It's a bit over 700 km to Kalgoorlie, more than half of it on unsealed roads.

UP THE COAST

The road up the west coast is now sealed all the way to the Kimberleys and even the final stretch between Fitzroy Crossing and Halls Creek is due for seal-

ing by 1986. It's still a hell of a long way but it's no longer a rough road endurance test. There's a fair bit to see along the way so you can easily spread the distance out over a few days even if you travel straight through. But don't underestimate it — Perth-Port Hedland is 1950 km by the coast and in summer they can be very hot km.

Getting There
Airlines of Western Australia fly from Perth to Geraldton ($73), Carnarvon ($124) and Learmonth (for Exmouth) ($156) plus other centres further up the west coast in the north-west and Kimberley region.

Westrail have bus services to Geraldton every day of the week except Saturday, there are several services on Friday. Greyhound have three buses a week up the coast to Port Hedland and beyond, Ansett Pioneer have four. From Perth fares are Geraldton $39, Carnarvon $52, Minilya (turn-off for Exmouth) $63 and Nanutarra (turn-off for Wittenoom) $63 with Greyhound. Ansett Pioneer fares vary slightly.

Perth to Geraldton (424 km)
From Perth you follow the Brand Highway past the turn off to the Pinnacles Desert and Jurien, eventually coming down to the coast at Dongara (population 300) — a pleasant little port with fine beaches and lots of rock lobsters! Russ Cottage, open Sundays and public holidays from 2 to 5 pm, is a local attraction. Nearby is the similar small port of Port Denison (population 500).

Further north, only about 20 km south of Geraldton, Greenough was once a busy little mining town but today it's just a quiet farming centre. The Pioneer museum (open daily, 10 am to 4 pm) dates from 1860. A few km east is the Station Museum in the old 1887 railway station at Walkway. It's open Saturday, Sunday and Wednesday from 2 to 4 pm.

Inland
The area inland from Dongara and Geraldton is noted for its spring wild-flowers. Mingenew (population 400), Morawa (population 800) and Mullewa (population 900) all have brilliant wild-flower displays in the spring. Tallering Peak and Gorges, 58 km north of Mullewa, is particularly splendid. Mingenew has a small museum while Carnamah (population 400) is near the Yarra Yarra Lake, noted for its birdlife. This area is also a gateway to the Murchison goldfields and there are old gold mining centres and ghost towns around Perenjori (population 300). Yalgoo is a tiny outback settlement, way out in the middle of nowhere, about halfway between Geraldton and Mt Magnet.

Geraldton (population 18,800)
The major town in the mid-west region, Geraldton is situated on a spectacular stretch of coast and has a fine climate, particularly in the winter. Geraldton was probably one of the first European 'settlements' in Australia. In 1629 the Dutch East Indiaman *Batavia* was wrecked on the Abrolhos Islands, about 60 km off the coast. Before the survivors could be rescued from the inhospitable island a bloody mutiny took place and the Dutch commander hanged some of the mutineers and dumped two of them off on the mainland, never to be seen again. In the following century at least two more Dutch ships were wrecked here. The Maritime Museum tells the story of these early wrecks and has assorted relics from the Dutch ships. The museum is open daily but for rather varied hours.

Geraldton also has a shell museum at 240 Chapman St (also daily) and a Gem & Mineral Museum on the corner of Mark and Pope Sts (daily again). Geraldton's St Francis Xavier Cathedral is just one of a number of buildings in the Geraldton and WA mid-west designed by Monsignor John Hawes, a strange priest-architect who later left WA in 1939 and spent the rest of his life (he died in 1965) a hermit on an island in the Caribbean. You can look out over Geraldton from the Waverley Heights Lookout on Brede St; view the rock lobster boats at Fisherman's Wharf on the end of Marine Terrace or go to the Point Moore Lighthouse, in operation since 1878.

The Geraldton Tourist Bureau is in the Civic Centre on Cathedral Avenue and is open 9 am to 5 pm Monday to Friday, 9 am to 12 noon on Saturday.

Dutch Shipwrecks

During the 17th century ships of the Dutch East India Company, sailing out to Batavia in Java from Europe, would head due east from the horn of Africa then beat up the Western Australian coast to Indonesia. It only took a small miscalculation for a ship to run aground on the coast and a number did just that with usually disastrous results. The west coast of Australia is often decidedly inhospitable and the chances of rescue at that time were remote.

Four wrecks of Dutch East Indiamen have been located including the earliest and in many ways most interesting, the *Batavia*. In 1629 the *Batavia* went aground in the Abrolhos Islands near Geraldton and the survivors set up camp, sent off a rescue party to Batavia in the ship's boat and waited. It took three months before a rescue party arrived and in that time a mutiny took place and more than 120 of the surviving passengers had been murdered. The two ringleaders of the mutineers were unceremoniously dumped on the coast.

In 1656 the *Vergulde Draeck* (Gilt Dragon) struck a reef about 100 km north of Perth and although a party made their way to Batavia, apart from some scattered coins no trace was ever found of the other survivors who struggled to shore. The *Zuytdorp* ran aground beneath the towering cliffs near the mouth of the Murchison River in 1712. Wine bottles and the remains of fires were later found on the cliff top but again no trace of the survivors.

In 1727 the *Zeewyk* followed the ill-fated *Batavia* to destruction in the Abrolhos Islands. Again a small party of survivors made their way to Batavia but many of the sailors encamped awaiting rescue died before it came. Many relics of these shipwrecks can be seen today in the museums in Fremantle and Geraldton — particularly relics of the *Batavia*.

Geraldton to Carnarvon (482 km)

Northampton (population 700) is the jumping-off point for the Hutt River Province where a local farmer decided that tourism must be an easier game than farming, appointed himself 'Prince Leonard of Hutt' and seceded from Australia. Today 60,000 people annually visit his 'independent principality' although it's actually nothing much more than a bare outback station. The turn-off is north of Northampton, towards Kalbarri.

The area inland from Northampton is noted for its wildflowers in the spring. The town was founded to exploit lead and copper discovered in 1848 and lead is still produced here. An early mine manager's house, Cliverton House, is now a fine Municipal Museum. The local-stone building was constructed between 1868 and 1875. Horrock's Beach, 21 km away, is a popular holiday resort. The nearby Gwalia Church cemetery also tells its tales of the early days.

Lynton, near Port Gregory, has the ruins of a convict hiring station. Kalbarri (population 700) is a pleasant coastal holiday resort in the Kalbarri National Park. There are many spectacular gorges on the Murchison River in the park. From Kalbarri it's only a 35 km drive to the Loop and Z-Bend, two particularly impressive gorges.

Continuing north towards Carnarvon it's a long, dull, boring and often very hot run. Shark Bay attracts fish and fishermen in large numbers — yes there are plenty of sharks there. On the bay Denham (population 350) is the most westerly town in Australia and was once a pearling port. Today prawns are the local money maker. In 1616 Dutch explorer Dirk Hartog landed on the island in Shark Bay which now bears his name.

Carnarvon (population 5400)

At the mouth of the Gascoyne River, Carnarvon is noted for its tropical fruit production, particularly bananas. Subsurface water, which flows even when the river is dry is tapped to irrigate the riverside plantations. Solar salt is also produced near Carnarvon. On the nearby Brown's Range the 'big dish' is a huge 26.5 metre reflector of the Overseas Telecommunications Commission earthstation. This was once a NASA station and there's a museum beside the tourist office relating its role in NASA space shots. The main street of Carnarvon is 40 metres wide, a reminder of the days when camel trains used to pass through here.

Pelican Point, only five km from town, is a good swimming and picnic spot but you'll need four-wheel drive to get to Bush Bay (turn-off 20 km) or New Beach (40 km). Other attractions in the vicinity are the spectacular blowholes 70 km north; there's a fine beach about a km south of the blowhole. Cape Cuvier, where salt is loaded for Japan, is 100 km north. Rock Pool is a superb swimming hole, 55 km inland along the Gascoyne River. Remote Gascoyne Junction is 61 km inland from Carnarvon in the gemstone rich Kennedy Range.

The Carnarvon District Tourist Bureau is in the Civic Centre on Robinson St.

Exmouth

The road to Exmouth forks off the main coast road and runs up to the US Navy Base at the top of the North-West Cape. Here a very hush-hush communications base is marked by 13 very low frequency transmitter station towers. Twelve of them are higher than the Eiffel Tower but they're all there simply to support the 13th which is 396 metres high, the tallest structure in the southern hemisphere. The base cost getting on towards $100 million to build.

Otherwise Exmouth is chiefly noted for its excellent fishing although there are also some fine beaches on the Exmouth Gulf. Coral Bay, near WA's only coral reef, is 150 km south of Exmouth on the north-west cape. It's very popular for fishing. This is also a productive prawning area. Maureen and I have a soft spot for Exmouth because it was here where we first set foot in Australia; we had hitched a ride on a yacht from Bali and made our Australian landfall at Exmouth. The town of Exmouth is all brand new, built to service the US navy base. The road up the cape to Exmouth is 221 km from the Minilya roadhouse turn-off.

Carnarvon to Port Hedland (855 km)

After the Exmouth turn-off the road runs inland from the coast for some distance before rejoining it almost at Dampier. Onslow (population 200), on the coast, is 82 km off the road. This was an early pearling port but now exists mainly to service the oilfield operations on Barrow Island. The town was actually shifted to its present location from its original site when cyclones seemed to arrive simply too often. The climate is OK in the April to September period but in the wet this is still 'cyclone city'.

Karratha (population 4300) is a dormitory town for the Dampier area further north, Dampier being the main working centre. Situated on King Bay, Dampier (population 4300) faces the islands of the Dampier Archipelago. They were named after the English pirate-explorer William Dampier who visited the area in 1699 and immortalised himself as not only one of Australia's first knockers but also its first whinging pom — he thought it was a pretty miserable place. Dampier is the port for the Tom Price and Paraburdoo ore deposits and the huge port facilities can handle ships up to 230,000 tonnes. There are also ore treatment works here and solar salt is also loaded for export. Permits are needed to inspect the port facilites. Off shore on the north-west shelf huge natural gas fields are in the process of being developed.

Roebourne, only 32 km further along the road, is the oldest active town of the north-west. It had an early history of gold and copper mining and there are still some fine old buildings to be seen. The town was once connected to Cossack, 13 km away on the coast, by a tramway but Cossack is now a ghost town. It's a solid ghost though, the buildings were sturdily constructed of local stone to withstand cyclones. The sole inhabitant of Cossack today tends the local museum. The modern port here is Wickham (population 2300) on Cape Lambert with its three km long jetty. All along this coast it's wise to keep well clear of the sea. It may look inviting but the water is full of nasties and swimming is definitely not recommended.

PORT HEDLAND (population 11,500)

At one time WA's fastest growing city, this is the port from where the Pilbara's iron ore production is shipped off to Japan — to return a few months later as shiny new Toyotas. The town is built on an island surrounded by tidal-flats and connected to the mainland by causeways. The main highway into Port Hedland enters over a causeway three km long. The port handles the largest annual tonnage of any Australian port. Like other towns along the coast it's also a centre for salt production, huge 'dunes' of salt can be seen six km from the town.

Port Hedland had an early history with grazing in the area from 1864, then a fleet of 150 pearling luggers in the 1870s before the Marble Bar gold rush put the town even more firmly on the map. But in 1946 the population had dwindled away to a mere 150. The port is on a mangrove-fringed inlet — there's good fishing, crabs, oysters and lots of bird life to be seen. As Port Hedland has grown satellite towns have sprung up, both to handle the mining output of the area and also for accommodation for the area's workforce.

You can visit the wharf area to see the huge ore carriers loaded without any prior arrangement. There's a tour of the Mt Newman Mining Company's operations at Nelson's Point every weekday at 1.30 pm. The bus leaves from the main gate at Wilson St. Next to the gate is a limestone ridge with Aboriginal carvings — if the site is locked you can borrow the key from the tourist office. The Drysdales Seashells International collection (plus gemstones and other items) is also worth inspecting.

Don't swim in the sea here — there's everything from sea snakes and stonefish to blue-ringed octopus and sharks. There's an Olympic swimming pool by the Civic Centre and Pretty Pool is a safe tidal pool. October to March is the cyclone season in Port Hedland. The Aboriginal Progress Association sells Aboriginal artefacts opposite the tourist office.

Information & Orientation

Port Hedland is in two parts — Port Hedland proper occupies a long (very long) and narrow strip of land along the coast. About 20 km away, separated by salt pans and mangrove flats, is South Hedland. Port Hedland is the old town, South Hedland a dormitory town established when space ran out in Port Hedland. The airport is midway

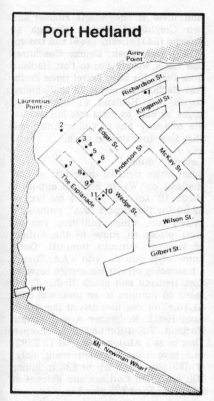

Port Hedland

Airey Point

Richardson St.

Kingsmill St.

Laurentius Point

Edgar St.

Anderson St.

McKay St.

The Esplanade

Wedge St.

Wilson St.

Gilbert St.

jetty

Mt. Newman Wharf

1	Hostel
2	Greyhound Buses
3	North-West Guest House
4	TAA
5	Picture Gardens
6	Tourist Bureau
7	Pier Hotel
8	Post Office
9	Airlines of WA & Ansett Pioneer
10	Bruno's Pizza
11	Esplanade Hotel

between the two. At one end of Port Hedland is Cooke Point with the campsite and Pretty Pool. At the other end is the town 'centre' with most places of importance on or close to Wedge St, the main street in the centre. There's a useful little tourist bureau with a good map of the town and other information at 13 Wedge St. It's open daily and, in the tourist season, on Saturday mornings. TAA, Airlines of WA, Greyhound and the post office are all within a stone's throw.

Places to Stay

Head down Wedge St to the corner where *North-West House* at number 1 is

run by Geoff Schafer. It's sort of YH connected (sort of because it's not really approved of) and costs $5 a night dorm-style. NW House is really men-only but there's another hostel (check at 1 Wedge St first) back at 3A Kingsmill St — it's the nissen hut. They're both quite rough and ready places but friendly and quite OK for any traveller who has knocked about a bit. On waking up there on the first morning I heard somebody saying, 'jeez mate, how'd you get pissed so fast?', to which came the reply 'groan . . . . double bourbons!' Sort of sums up Port Hedland.

Otherwise there's the *Pier Hotel* (tel 73 1488) on the Esplanade with a travellers' special (share room) at $9 a night or motel rooms at $25/38 for singles/doubles. Just down at the corner with Anderson St the *Esplanade Hotel* (tel 73 1798) is $26/36 expensive like everything else in Hedland. There are a couple of motels in town and one out by the airport but they're even more expensive.

You can camp in South Hedland, by the airport or, most conveniently, at the *Cooke Point Caravan Park*, three km from the centre. Camping there costs $2.50 per person but there are no on-site vans, as there are at the other two sites. The Cooke Point park, incidentally, sells the cheapest petrol in Hedland.

Places to Eat

The two hotels do counter meals and bar snacks at lunch time. There are also a number of coffee bars and other places you can get a pie or pasty. In the evening there's *Bruno's Pizza Bar*, next to the Esplanade Hotel, where the pizzas start from around $3.50 (small) and run to around $8 (large). Not cheap. Just down the road is the new *Oriental Gallery* with Chinese food, again not cheap. The *Hedland Hotel* does excellent value counter lunches at $4 to $6. The air-con is really popular here in the summer. Counter teas are available on Friday and Saturday nights only, until 8 pm. Plenty of supermarket supplies are available in Hedland if you want to fix your own food.

Getting There

You can fly to Port Hedland from Darwin ($228) or Perth ($180) with Airlines of Western Australia but it's rather cheaper with TAA. Airlines of WA also connect Port Hedland with other towns in the north-west. Phone numbers are Airlines of WA 73 1777 or TAA 73 2222.

Ansett Pioneer and Greyhound both have bus services from Perth to Port Hedland. Fares are $75 on Ansett Pioneer, $69 on Greyhound. Some of the Greyhound services take the inland route via Newman and Marble Bar rather than up the coast. North of Hed-

land there is one Ansett Pioneer and two Greyhound services through to Broome ($41), Derby ($56) and Darwin ($143) each week. Deluxe Coachlines also run a weekly bus to Port Hedland from Perth for $68. Travel times Perth-Port Hedland are about 23 to 25 hours, Darwin-Port Hedland 41 hours. You might be able to get a free bus ride on the company bus to Goldsworthy and Shay Gap, four times a week.

Getting Around

Buses arrive right in the centre of Port Hedland on Wedge St. The airport is about 10 km out — $14 by taxi or $2.50 for the airport 'bus', probably a shared taxi, which will drop you off most places en route to the Airlines of Western Australia terminal. Don't know what you do with TAA. There's a reasonably regular bus service between Port Hedland and South Hedland — it takes 40 minutes to an hour and costs $1.10. You can hire cars at the airport from Hertz, Budget or Avis. In South Hedland Y-Not-Rent-a-Car is cheaper. They're at 1 Abalone Way (tel 72 2292) and have Lasers (sealed roads only) at $18 plus 12c a km or $33 including 200 km. Also Cortinas and Falcons at $20 plus 13c or $22 plus 14c.

THE PILBARA

The Pilbara is the iron ore producing area which accounts for much of WA's prosperity — from some of the hottest country on earth. Gigantic machines are used to tear the dusty red ranges apart. It's isolated, harsh and fabulously wealthy. The Pilbara towns are almost all company town creations — they're either mining centres where the ore is wrenched from the earth or ports from where it's shipped abroad. Exceptions are the beautiful gorges of

the Wittenoom area and earlier, historic mining centres like Marble Bar.

Places to Stay

There are campsites and motels in the various Pilbara towns. Wittenoom also has an unofficial youth hostel at 67 Fifth Avenue. It's organised by Geoff Schafer from Port Hedland. Nightly cost is $5, ask at the shire office.

Getting There

Greyhound have three buses a week

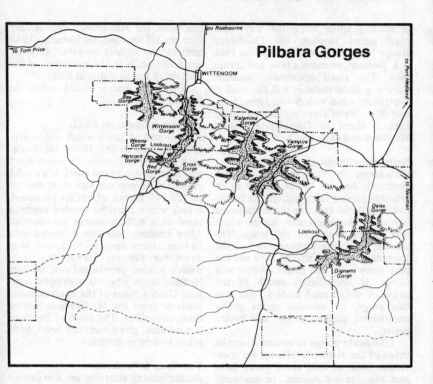

Pilbara Gorges

to Roebourne

to Tom Price

WITTENOOM

to Port Hedland

Bee Gorge

Wittenoom Gorge

Weona Gorge

Lookout

Hancock Gorge

Red Gorge

Knox Gorge

Kalamina Gorge

Vampire Gorge

to Newman

Dales Gorge

Lookout

Dignams Gorge

from Perth to Newman — 15 hours, $62. One of them continues through to Port Hedland. Services are the same in the opposite direction — Port Hedland-Newman takes eight hours and costs $28. Airlines of Western Australia fly to the main Pilbara towns. Fares from Perth are Paraburdoo $144, Tom Price $149, Wittenoom $184, Newman $147. From Port Hedland it costs $72 to Newman. Skywest have flights between Port Hedland and Newman via Marble Bar and Fortescue Air Charter also fly into Wittenoom. There is no bus service to Wittenoom although it is sometimes possible to get on a tour bus from Port Hedland. Otherwise you really need your own transport. If you ask nicely you may be able to get to Goldsworthy

and Shay Gap from Port Hedland on the company bus, for free.

Most of the roads in the Pilbara are unsealed. The Great Northern Highway is sealed as far as Newman but the rest of the way north through Marble Bar is all dirt. Ditto for all the roads into Wittenoom which you can approach from Port Hedland (295 km), from Newman via Roy Hill (268 km), Roebourne via Millstream (289 km) or from Nanutarra on the North-West Coastal Highway about midway between Carnarvon and Roebourne (377 km).

Inland to Wittenoom

A little beyond Roebourne a road turns inland to Wittenoom, it's 264 km from the turn-off and there are a number of interesting spots along the way. The road passes through the Chichester Range National Park where Python Pool is a pleasant swimming hole and picnic spot. The small Millstream National Park is a little distance off the road — a pleasant oasis with pools, trees, ferns and lilies. Water from the natural spring here is piped to Dampier, Karratha, Wickham and Cape Lambert.

Wittenoom (population 1000)

Wittenoom is the Pilbara's tourist centre. It had an earlier history as an asbestos mining town but mining finally halted in 1966 and it is the magnificent gorges of the Hamersley Range which now draws people to the town. Wittenoom is at the northern end of the Hamersley Range National Park and the best known of the gorges, Wittenoom Gorge, is immediately south of the town. A sealed road leads 13 km into this gorge, by asbestos mines and a number of smaller gorges and pretty pools.

Like other gorges in central Australia those of the Hamersley Range are spectacular both in their sheer rocky faces and their varied colours. In the early spring the park is often carpeted in colourful wilflowers. Travel down the Newman road 24 km and there's a turn-off into the Yampire Gorge where blue veins of asbestos can be seen in the rock. Fig Tree Well, in the gorge, was once used by Afghan camel drivers as a watering point. The road continues through Yampire Gorge to Dales Gorge, only the first couple of km of its 45 km length can be reached. On this same route you can get to Circular Pool and a nearby lookout and, by a footpath, to the bottom of the Fortescue Falls. The Joffre Falls road will take you to Oxer's Lookout at the junction of the Red, Weano and Hancock Gorges. Following the main road to Tom Price you pass through the small Rio Tinto Gorge, 43 km from Wittenoom, and just beyond

this point the Hamersley Gorge is only four km off the road. Mt Meharry (1245 metres), the highest mountain in Western Australia, is in the south-east of the Hamersley Range National Park.

Wittenoom has a tourist centre on Second Avenue.

Newman (population 5500)

At Newman, a town which only came into existence in the 1970s, Mt Whaleback is being systematically taken apart and railed down to the coast. It's a solid mountain of iron ore and every day up to 120,000 tonnes of ore are produced, a task which required moving nearly a third of a million tonnes of material. After crushing, the ore is loaded into 144-car trains two-km long, and sent down the 426 km railway line, Australia's longest private railway, to Port Hedland from where it is shipped overseas. Guided tours of the operations are available from the Mt Newman Mining Company office. The town of Newman is a modern, green company town, built solely to service the mine.

Tom Price & Paraburdoo

Similar mining activities are also carried on in these towns. The ore is railed down to the coast at Dampier. Check with the Hamersley Iron office about inspecting the mine works.

Goldsworthy & Shay Gap

Godsworthy (population 1000) was the first Pilbara iron town and, like Newman, its production is shipped out from Port Hedland. At one time Mt Goldsworthy was 132 metres high but it's now a big hole in the ground. When it has been totally emptied the emphasis will shift to Shay Gap (population 900), 69 km further east, another town built solely to exploit the iron ore reserves. Shay Gap, like Goldsworthy, was devastated by Cyclone Enid in 1980.

Marble Bar (population 300)

Reputed to be the hottest place in Aus Australia, Marble Bar had a stretch in the 1920s when for 160 consecutive days the temperature topped 100°F! On one occasion in 1905 the mercury soared to 49.1^{O}C. From October to March days over 40°C are commonplace. It's uncomfortable. The town is 193 km south-east of Port Hedland and takes its name from a bar of red jasper across the Coongan River, five km from the town. The town came into existence when gold was found here in 1891. At its peak the population was 5000 and gold, as well as other minerals, are still mined here today. In the town the old Government Buildings of 1895 are still in use. In late winter, as the spring flowers begin to bloom, Marble Bar can actually be quite a pretty place.

BROOME (population 2900)

Broome is a town having a boom — completion of sealing the road from Port Hedland has sparked off a tourist rush to this delightful old pearling port. Amazingly the town has also become something of a travellers' centre. From Port Hedland it's 624 generally rather dull km to Broome, the road crosses the coastal fringes of the Great Sandy Desert, the driest desert in Australia.

Broome's colourful early history was based on pearling, established here in the 1880s. At its peak in the early 1900s Broome had 400 pearling luggers worked by 3000 men and it supplied 80% of the world's mother-of-pearl. Today only a dozen or so pearlers still operate, gathering oysters for use in pearl farms. Pearl diving was a very unsafe occupation, as Broome's Japanese cemetery attests. The divers were from a number of Asian countries and they've left a real Oriental flavour to the town, Broome even has a tiny Chinatown with a string of Chinese restaurants. In August or September each year the Shinju Matsumi, or 'Festival of the Pearl', remembers those early pearling days.

Information

The shiny new Broome tourist office is right across the road from the old DC-3 which used to operate as an information centre.

Chinatown

Broome's a pleasant, if dusty, old town. Chinatown occupies just a block or so and is probably over-rated, but worth seeing all the same. Sun Pictures, the old open-air cinema in this area, is now derelict but the Roebuck Bay Hotel still rocks along despite its squeaky clean new motel section. A noisy night at the Roebuck Bay is like one of those cartoons where the walls of the bar continuously quake in and out and bodies come flying through the swing doors with reasonable regularity. Great fun, just stand clear of the occasional fights!

Pearling

You'll often see pearling luggers drawn up by Streeter's Jetty in the mangroves at the end of Short St. Beside Carnarvon St there's a preserved lugger on display with statues of the men who founded the modern pearl farming business in the region. The Broome Historical Society Museum on Saville St has interesting exhibits on both Broome and its history and on the pearling industry and its dangers. It's housed in the old customs house and is closed on Thursdays and Sundays.

The cemetery, on the outskirts of town, just off the Cable Beach road, also amply exhibits the dangers of pearl diving when equipment was so primitive and knowledge of diving techniques so limited. In 1914 alone 33 divers died of

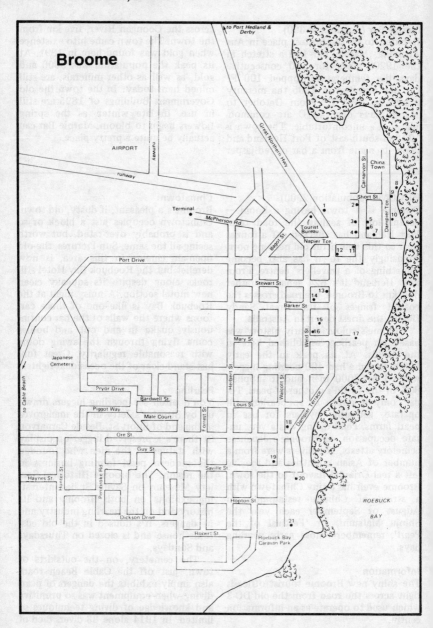

Broome

AIRPORT

runway

RUNWAY

to Port Hedland & Derby

Great Northern Hwy

China Town

Terminal

McPherson Rd

Tourist Bureau

Napier Tce

Bagot St

Port Drive

Stewart St

Barker St

Mary St

Herbert St

Weld St

Wacott St

Dampier Terrace

Carnarvon St

Short St

Dampier Tce

Japanese Cemetery

to Cable Beach

Pryor Drive

Bardwell St

Piggot Way

Male Court

Ore St

Guy St

Saville St

Hopton St

Forrest St

Louis St

Pembroke Rd

Hunter St

Haynes St

Dickson Drive

Robert St

Roebuck Bay Caravan Park

ROEBUCK BAY

1
2
3
4
5
6
7
8
9
10
11
12
13
14
15
16
17
18
19
20
21

1 DC-3 Museum	12 Mango Jack's
2 Sun Pictures	13 Post Office
3 Tang's Cafe	14 Airlines of WA
4 Pearl Lugger	15 Library & Civic Centre
5 Kool Spot	16 Wackett Aircraft
6 Rabbit's Restaurant	17 Mangrove Motel
7 Roebuck Bay Hotel	18 Continental Hotel
8 Streeter's Jetty (luggers)	19 Tropicana Motel
9 MacWade's (bike hire)	20 Museum
10 Pearl & Shell Shops	21 Pioneer Cemetery
11 Boab Bazaar	

the bends and in 1908 a cyclone killed 150 seamen caught out at sea. The Japanese section of the cemetery is one of the largest and most interesting and so many of those buried there died very young. You can be certain few Japanese hung around in Broome to die of old age.

Other Attractions

Across Napier Terrace from Chinatown is the Boab Bazaar, a small Asian crafts shop, with a magnificent boab tree beside it. There's another boab tree behind, outside what used to be the old police lock-up, with a rather sad little tale on a plaque at its base. It was planted by a police officer when his son was born in 1898 but the son was killed in France in WW I and the father died, in Broome, of sunstroke in 1920. The boab tree is doing fine.

The old DC-3 opposite the tourist office was a Garuda aircraft which crashed at Broome while on a charter operation. It was patched together and used as a unique tourist office for some years and is now a rather poor excuse for an aviation museum, admission is $1. On Weld St, by the library and civic centre, there's a Wackett aircraft on display which used to belong to Horrie Miller, founder of MacRobertson Miller Airlines, now Airlines of Western Australia. He's buried in Broome cemetery.

There's an old pioneer cemetery by the old jetty site at the end of Robinson St and a small museum at the police

station. The old 1888 court house used to house the transmitting equipment for the old cable station here. Shell enthusiasts can have a field day in Broome — there are a number of shell and pearl displays at outlets on Dampier Terrace by Chinatown and in other places.

Out of Town

In Roebuck Bay, at the entrance to Dampier Creek, there's a landmark to explorer William Dampier and his ship *Roebuck*. He is said to have careened it here in 1699. Broome has enormous tides, up to 11 metres in the spring. Six km from town, Cable Beach is the most popular swimming beach, the telegraph cable used to cross to Java in Indonesia from here. One side of the beach is now a popular nude bathing beach. There are other good beaches along Roebuck Bay to Gantheaume Point, seven km south of Broome. The cliffs there have been eroded into curious shapes and at low tide you may be able to find 130 million year old dinosaur tracks. There are casts of the tracks on the cliff tops.

Places to Stay

Bring a tent with you if you want any kind of cheap accommodation in Broome. The Broome boom caught the town completely unawares and now there's a major accommodation shortage and it's worst at the bottom end. There's quite a bit of construction going on but it's almost all for motel units which in Broome can cost over $60 a night and

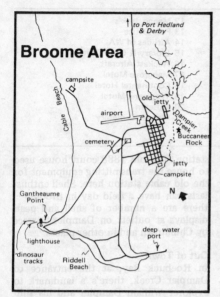

Broome Area

to Port Hedland
& Derby

campsite

Cable Beach

old jetty

airport

Dampier Creek

cemetery

Buccaneer
Rock

jetty

campsite

N

Gantheaume
Point

deep water
port

lighthouse

dinosaur
tracks

Riddell
Beach

are still likely to be booked out. Cheapest are the *Hotel Continental* (tel 92 1002) on Weld St with rooms at $40/47 or the *Hotel Roebuck Bay* (tel 92 1221) at $42/47. The Roebuck Bay, with it's rough and ready old bars, also has a handful of older hotel rooms at $29/37.

The Broome campsites are equally likely to be booked out, in part due to hidebound local health officers who decided to play things hard by the rules. There's the *Bali Hai* out at Cable Beach where it costs $3 to camp and there are on-site vans at $30 for two, chalets (also fully equipped) at $46 for two. In town there's the *Roebuck Bay* campsite where camping costs $6.50 per night (no on-site vans). There's a recently opened site a few km out of town on the Derby road.

Since there's such a shortage of space in the tourist season a blind eye is turned to people camping in unofficial places. There are a host of quiet little turn-offs to the sand dunes along Cable Beach. Or just ask at the tourist office.

They have a list of people who will let you camp in their backyards and use their facilities and they may also be able to suggest some other accommodation possibilities.

Places to Eat

A place to stay in Broome may be a hassle but eating out is no sweat at all. *Kool Spot* is a sure sign of Broome's trendification — food like they provide (breakfast and lunchtime) would have been pretty odd in Broome not so long ago. Rolls, sandwiches, various fancy foods, exotic cakes, fruit juices, smoothies. Not cheap but not too expensive either and very nice. A bit further along Carnarvon St, *Rabbit's Restaurant* is another indicator of Broome's changes — vegetarian, jaffles, salads, quiches and the like; all at around the $2 mark. Plus nice desserts (fruit salads, carrot cake, etc), fancy teas, the inevitable smoothies. Very laid back, easy going and pleasant; the sort of place where people pass around guitars and sing songs.

Broome also has its traditional dining possibilities of course — counter lunches at the *Roebuck Bay Hotel* and the *Continental Hotel* (around $5 to $6). The usual fast foods at *Mango Jacks* or *Chipmonks* and there's the *Pizza Bar*. Good sandwiches and rolls in the bakery at the corner of Carnarvon and Short St but they tend to run out early. Plus Broome's noted Chinese restaurants — there are several scattered around the Chinatown area. *Tang's Cafe* on Carnarvon St is very straightforward (even basic) with most dishes $4 to $6. *Tong's* on Napier Terrace, *Wing's* on Dampier Terrace and *Chin's* on Hamersley St are others.

Getting There

Airlines of Western Australia fly to Broome regularly on their Perth through to Darwin operations. See the introductory Getting Around section for air fares details. The AWA office (tel 92 1101) is on the corner of Barker and Weld Sts. Ansett Pioneer pick up from there, Greyhound from opposite the tourist office, which is also their agent in Broome. Ansett Pioneer come through Broome once weekly, Greyhound twice. Fares include Derby $17, Darwin $120, Port Hedland $41, Perth $91. Broome is the southern gateway to the Kimberleys.

Getting Around
There is no public transport in Broome but you can hire bikes from MacWades on Dampier Terrace for $7 a day. It's no problem riding out to Cable Beach (six km), Gantheaume Point (seven km) or the port (eight km). Hertz, Budget and Letz have rent-a-car desks at the airport. You can hire Mokes ($20 a day plus 18c a km) from Broome Hire Cars (tel 92 1369) or Ricci's Moke Hire (tel 92 1557). Airport transport is $1, if they bother charging you. The airport is so close you could easily walk it.

THE KIMBERLEYS
The rough and rugged Kimberleys at the northern end of WA is one of Australia's last frontiers. Despite staggering advances in the last decades this is still a little travelled and very remote area of great rivers and magnificent scenery. The Kimberleys suffer from climatic extremes — heavy rains in the wet followed by searing heat in the dry but irrigation projects have made great changes to the region. Nevertheless rivers like the Fitzroy can be storming torrents in the December to March wet but just a series of waterholes in the dry. April to November, when the daytime temperatures are around 30°C, is the best time for a Kimberley visit. Kimberley attractions include the old pearling port of Broome, the spectacular gorges on the Fitzroy River, the huge Wolf Creek meteorite crater and the Ord River irrigation projects.

DERBY (population 2400)
Only 216 km from Broome, Derby is a major centre for the Kimberleys — an administrative centre, a shipping port for the cattle production of the region and a jumping-off point for the spectacular gorges in the region. The town is on King Sound, north of the mouth of the Fitzroy, the mighty river that drains the West Kimberley region. The river mouth is enormously wide, flat and muddy and Derby itself is surrounded by vast expanses of usually-dry tidal flats. The occasional 'king tides' bring the water level up to the town. Derby is a pretty dull town, there's no real reason to stop here.

In Derby itself there's a small 'museum' in the cultural centre but the town's main attraction would have to be the open-air picture house. Video is going to kill these places so if you're ever in Derby and the movies are on drop in, sit back in a tattered 'deck chair' and experience a bit of cinematic history. Seven km out of town, just before the airport, is the prison boab tree. Found only in the Kimberleys and Northern Territory, though closely related to the boababs of Africa and Sri Lanka, the boab is an unusual tree with a fat trunk topped by small branches sprouting out of the top. They're seen all over the region and the prison boab is an enormous one, 14 metres around and hollow. It is said to have been used as a primitive lock-up. Also by the road is Myall's bore, a huge cattle trough, 120 metres long.

Places to Stay & Eat
There's a campsite in the centre of town where camping sites cost $4.50 and on-site vans are available for $19 to $22.

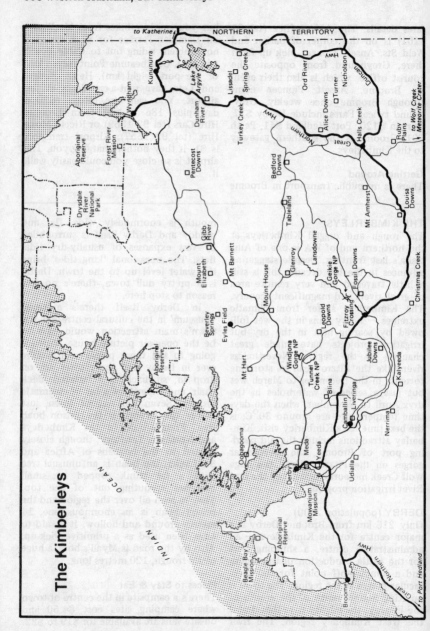

The Kimberleys

Otherwise there's the central *Spinifex Hotel* (tel 91 1233) right in the centre on Clarendon St with singles at $25 to $37 (cheaper rooms don't have attached bathrooms) or doubles at $44. Also in the centre is the *YWCA* (tel 91 1522) on Loch St with rooms at $18/28 for singles/doubles. The *Boab Inn* (tel 91 1044) is more expensive.

At the bottom of Loch St the *Chinese Restaurant* has meals from $6, the *Spinifex* does terrible counter meals (mostly around $6) and there are the usual fast food places.

Getting There

By air it's $50 from Broome, $235 from Perth. Ansett Pioneer and Greyhound buses run through Derby. Fares include Broome $17, Darwin $74, Port Hedland $49, Perth $100. The airport bus costs $1.90.

The Gorges

The roads into the Kimberleys from Derby have been much improved of late. You can make an interesting loop from Derby to visit the spectacular gorge country — or you can pick them up between Fitzroy Crossing and Derby. The Windjana Gorge National Park on the Lennard River and Tunnel Creek National Park on Tunnel Creek are only about a hundred km from Derby. It only adds about 40 km to the trip to Fitzroy Crossing, although the road is mostly not sealed, if you want to visit these gorges.

The walls at the Windjana Gorge soar 90 metres above the Lennard River which rushes through here in the wet but in the dry becomes just a series of pools. Three km from the river are the ruins of Lillimilura, an early homestead. Tunnel Creek is a 750 metre long tunnel, cut by the creek right through a spur of the Oscar Range. The tunnel is generally from three to 12 metres high and 15 metres wide and you can walk right through it. You'll need a

good light and don't attempt it during the wet when the creek may suddenly flash flood. Half-way through a collapse has produced a shaft right to the top of the range. Flying foxes (bats) also inhabit the tunnel for part of the year.

If you've not got your own transport Kimberley Safaris in Derby (book (through the Derby Tourist Bureau on Clarendon St) do a day trip ($50) and also two, four and six day safaris at prices from $140 to $420 per person.

Gibb River Road

This is the 'back road' from Derby to Wyndham. It's more direct by several hundred km than the Fitzroy Crossing-Hall's Creek route but it's almost all unsealed. You can reach many of the Kimberley gorges along this road — like the Barnett Gorge, Galvan's Gorge, Adcock Gorge, Manning Gorge — without four-wheel drive. Fuel is available at Mt Barnett station, near Manning Gorge.

Fitzroy Crossing (population 300)

A tiny settlement where the road crosses the Fitzroy River, this is another jumping-off point for the gorges and waterholes of the area. The Geikie Gorge is just 19 km from the town. The gorge on the Fitzroy River flows through a small national park, only eight km by three km. During the wet season the river rises nearly 17 metres, and the campsite by the river is seven metres below the waterline! In the dry the river completely stops flowing although a series of waterholes remain. The ranges the gorge cut through are actually a fossil coral reef some 350 million years old. The vegetation around the beautiful gorge is dense and there is also much wildlife to be seen including the harmless Johnston crocodile. Sawfish and stingrays, usually only found in or close to the sea, can also be seen in the river. A variety of kangaroos and wallabies also live around the gorge which is a sanctuary area. Visitors are not permitted to go anywhere except along the prescribed part of the west bank. There is an excellent walk along that bank and you can also swim with the crocodiles in the gorge. Twice a day there's a national park boat trip lasting two hours and covering 16 km of the gorge, it costs $2.50. The campsite at the gorge costs $3 per night per vehicle. The camp site and the gorge trips are usually in operation only during the April to November dry season.

Halls Creek (population 800)
In the centre of the Kimberleys and on the edge of the Great Sandy Desert this was the site of a gold rush back in 1885, the first in WA. The gold soon petered out and today the town is a cattle centre, 14 km from the original site where some crumbling remains can still be seen. Six km north of Halls Creek there's another China Wall. Australia seems to have a few of them! The major attraction in the area is the 135 km trip to the 835 metre wide and 50 metre deep Wolf Creek Meterorite Crater, the second largest in the world. The road to the crater is fairly good and you can camp and get supplies at the Carranya Station homestead nearby. Halls Creek is nearly 3000 km from Perth.

Ord River Area
The Ord River has the greatest annual waterflow of any Australian river but,

like other Kimberley rivers, it was a boom or bust situation — too much in the wet, not enough in the dry. The emormous Ord River irrigation project is changing all that and Lake Argyle, created by the Ord River Dam, is now the biggest storage reservoir in Australia. In the centre of the Ord River irrigation scheme Kununurra (population 1500) is the main town. It was only founded in the 1960s and from Kelly's Knob Lookout you can get a good view over the irrigated fields. From here you can cruise on Lake Kununurra or visit Lake Argyle, 72 km to the south.

At Lake Argyle there's a pioneer museum in the old Argyle Homestead which was moved here when its original site was flooded. The lake tourist centre has a camp site and other facilities. From Kununurra it's a picturesque 108 km drive north to Wyndham (population 1400), the port for the Ord region. Wyndham gets very hot and humid in the summer but there's lots of birdlife in the lagoons near the town. Only a short distance from town, the Grotto is a pleasant waterhole.

Getting There Airlines of Western Australia connect Kununurra with Darwin ($89) and other Western Australian towns like Broome ($114). Port Hedland ($167) or Perth ($300). Ansett Pioneer come through Kununurra once a week, Greyhound buses twice a week. Darwin-Kununurra is $51, it takes over 20 hours.

Index

564 Index

STOP PRESS

page 25 — credit cards
Mastercard is about to re-enter the Australian market with major bank affiliation so it's possible that it may once again become readily usable.

page 25 — overseas banks
With a couple of minor exceptions only Australian banks have been allowed to operate in Australia but that may be about to change. Depending on the outcome of the 1983 election there may soon be up to 10 overseas banks operating alongside the Australian ones.

page 30 — opening hours
Bank opening hours have been extended. Normal Monday to Thursday hours are now 9.30 am to 4 pm, on Fridays 9.30 am to 5 pm. Some banks are open 8 am to 6 pm, Monday to Friday. Some are open to 9 pm on Fridays.

page 48 — air fare increases
Make that three increases for the year. In other words Australian domestic air fares continue to increase far more rapidly than inflation.

page 56 — bus fares
In early '83 competition between the major bus companies and their numerous independent competitors had become cut throat and there were lots of special deals on offer. Possibly this may drive some of the smaller operators to the wall and permit the big boys to push fares up?

page 490 — prime ministers
With luck that might be 'ex-PM Malcolm Fraser' as Big Mal may well have lost the March '83 election before this book emerges.

page 535 — fastest train
The Prospector may have lost that title to the new XPT trains now operating in NSW.

LONELY PLANET NEWSLETTER
We collect an enormous amount of information here at Lonely Planet. Apart from our research we also get a steady stream of letters from people out on the road — some of them are just one line on a postcard, others go on for pages. Plus we always have an ear to the ground for the latest on cheap airfares, new visa regulations, borders opening and closing. A lot of this information goes into our new editions or 'update supplements' in reprints. But we want to make better use of this information so, we also produce a quarterly newsletter packed full of the latest news from out on the road. It appears in January, April, July and October of each year. If you'd like an airmailed copy of the most recent newsletter just send us A$1.50 (A$1 within Australia) or A$5 (A$4 in Australia) for a year's subscription.

OTHER LONELY PLANET PRODUCTS
We have Lonely Planet T-shirts (A$5, state size and colour preference) and self-adhesive LP stickers (A$1 for two).

Sweden: Esselte Kartcentrum AB, Vasagatan 16, S-111 20 Stockholm
Thailand: Chalermnit, 1-2 Erawan Arcade, Bangkok
UK: Roger Lascelles, 16 Holland Park Gardens, London W14 8DY
USA (west): Bookpeople, 2940 Seventh St, Berkeley, CA 94710
USA (east): Hunter Publishing Inc, 171 Madison Ave, New York, NY 10016
West Germany: Buchvertrieb Gerda Schettler, Postfach 64...

576 Notes

Lonely Planet travel guides
Africa on the Cheap
Australia — a travel survival kit
Alaska — a travel survival kit
Burma — a travel survival kit
Bushwalking in Papua New Guinea
Canada — a travel survival kit
Hong Kong, Macau & Canton
India — a travel survival kit
Israel & the Occupied Territories
Japan — a travel survival kit
Kashmir, Ladakh & Zanskar
Kathmandu & the Kingdom of Nepal
Korea & Taiwan — a travel survival kit
*Malaysia, Singapore & Brunei — a travel
    survival kit*
Mexico — a travel survival kit
New Zealand — a travel survival kit
North-East Asia on a Shoestring
Pakistan — a travel survival kit
Papua New Guinea — a travel survival kit
The Philippines — a travel survival kit
South America on a Shoestring
South-East Asia on a Shoestring
Sri Lanka — a travel survival kit
Tramping in New Zealand
Trekking in the Himalayas
Thailand — a travel survival kit
Turkey — a travel survival kit
USA West
*West Asia on a Shoestring (formerly Across
    Asia on the Cheap)*

Lonely Planet travel guides are available around the world. If you can't find them, ask you bookshop to order them from one of the distributors listed below. For countries not listed if you would like a free copy of our latest booklist write to Lonely Planet in Australia.

Australia Lonely Planet Publications, PO Box 88, South Yarra, Victoria 3141.
Canada Milestone Publications, Box 2248, Sidney British Columbia, V8L 3S8.
Denmark Scanvik Books aps, Store Kongensgade 59 A, DK-1264 Copenhagen K.
Hong Kong The Book Society, GPO Box 7804, Hong Kong.
India UBS Distributors, 5 Ansari Rd, New Delhi.
Israel Geographical Tours Ltd, 8 Tverya St, Tel Aviv 63144.
Japan Intercontinental Marketing Corp, IPO Box 5056, Tokyo 100-31.
Malaysia MPH Distributors, 13, Jalan 13/6, Petaling Jaya, Selangor.
Nepal see India
Netherlands Nilsson & Lamm bv, Postbus 195, Pampuslaan 212, 1380 AD Weesp.
New Zealand Caveman Press, PO Box 1458, Dunedin.
Papua New Guinea Gordon & Gotch (PNG), PO Box 3395, Port Moresby.
Singapore MPH Distributors, 116-D JTC Factory Building, Lorong 3, Geylang Square,
    Singapore, 1438.
Sweden Esselte Kartcentrum AB, Vasagatan 16, S-111 20 Stockholm.
Thailand Chalermnit, 1-2 Erawan Arcade, Bangkok.
UK Roger Lascelles, 16 Holland Park Gardens, London W14 8DY.
USA (West) Bookpeople, 2940 Seventh St, Berkeley, CA 94710.
USA (East) Hippocrene Books, 171 Madison Ave, New York, NY 10016.
West Germany Buchvertrieb Gerda Schettler, Postfach 64, D3415 Hattorf a H.